COMPLETE

Technology in Action

8th Edition

Alan Evans • Kendall Martin
Mary Anne Poatsy

20X131

Prentice Hall

Boston   Columbus   Indianapolis   New York   San Francisco   Upper Saddle River

Amsterdam   Cape Town   Dubai   London   Madrid   Milan   Munich   Paris   Montréal   Toronto

Delhi   Mexico City   São Paulo   Sydney   Hong Kong   Seoul   Singapore   Taipei   Tokyo

Editor in Chief: Michael Payne
Product Development Manager:
  Eileen Bien Calabro
Development Editor: Jennifer Lynn
Editorial Project Manager: Laura Burgess
AVP/Executive Acquisitions Editor: Stephanie Wall
Editorial Assistant: Nicole Sam
Director of Marketing: Kate Valentine
Marketing Manager: Tori Olson Alves
Marketing Coordinator: Susan Osterlitz
Marketing Assistant: Darshika Vyas
Senior Managing Editor: Cynthia Zonneveld
Managing Editor: Camille Trentacoste
Production Project Manager: Mike Lackey
Operations Director: Nick Sklitsis
Operations Specialist: Natacha Moore
Art Director: Jonathan Boylan
Cover Design: Anthony Gemmellaro

Cover Art: © Dieter Matthes
Manager, Visual Research: Karen Sanatar
Photo Researcher: David Tietz
Manager, Rights and Permissions: Zina Arabia
Permissions Project Manager: Hessa Albader
Text Permission Researcher: Michele Pridmore
Director of Digital Development: Zara Wanlass
Editor, Digital Learning & Assessment: Paul Gentile
Product Development Manager, Media: Cathi Profitko
Media Project Manager, Editorial: Alana Coles
Media Project Manager, Production: John Cassar
Full-Service Project Management:
  MPS Content Services
Composition: MPS Limited, a Macmillan Company
Printer/Binder: Quebecor World Color/Versailles
Cover Printer: Lehigh/Phoenix
Text Font: 10/12 Palatino

Credits and acknowledgments borrowed from other sources and reproduced, with permission, in this textbook appear in the Rear Matter of this book.

Microsoft® and Windows® are registered trademarks of the Microsoft Corporation in the U.S.A. and other countries. Screen shots and icons reprinted with permission from the Microsoft Corporation. This book is not sponsored or endorsed by or affiliated with the Microsoft Corporation.

Many of the designations by manufacturers and seller to distinguish their products are claimed as trademarks. Where those designations appear in this book, and the publisher was aware of a trademark claim, the designations have been printed in initial caps or all caps.

Library of Congress Cataloging-in-Publication Data

Evans, Alan (Alan D.)
  Complete technology in action / Alan Evans, Kendall Martin, Mary Anne
Poatsy. -- 8th ed.
       p. cm.
  Includes bibliographical references and index.
  ISBN 0-13-139157-7 (alk. paper)
  1. Microcomputers.   I. Martin, Kendall. II. Poatsy, Mary Anne. III. Title.
QA76.5.E9195 2011b
004.16--dc22

                                    2010046480

Prentice Hall
is an imprint of

www.pearsonhighered.com

10 9 8 7 6 5 4 3 2 1

ISBN 10: 0-13-139157-7
ISBN 13: 978-0-13-139157-4

Contents at a Glance

eighth EDITION
8

Contents

Chapter 3

Using the Internet:
Making the Most of the Web's Resources 92

TECHNOLOGY IN FOCUS
Information Technology Ethics

Chapter 4

Application Software:
Programs That Let You Work and Play

Chapter 5

Using System Software: The Operating System, Utility Programs, and File Management

Chapter 6

Understanding and Assessing Hardware: Evaluating Your System

Chapter 7

Networking: Connecting Computing Devices

TECHNOLOGY IN FOCUS

Careers in IT

Chapter 10

Behind the Scenes:
Building Applications

Chapter 11

Behind the Scenes: Databases and Information Systems

Chapter 12

Behind the Scenes: Networking and Security in the Business World

Chapter 13

Behind the Scenes: How the Internet Works 606

Dedication

For my wife Patricia, whose patience, understanding, and support continue to make this work possible … especially when I stay up past midnight writing! And to my parents, Jackie and Dean, who taught me the best way to achieve your goals is to constantly strive to improve yourself through education.

Alan Evans

For all the teachers, mentors, and gurus who have popped in and out of my life.

Kendall Martin

For my husband Ted, who unselfishly continues to take on more than his fair share to support me throughout this process; and for my children, Laura, Carolyn, and Teddy, whose encouragement and love have been inspiring.

Mary Anne Poatsy

What's New
Technology in Action, Eighth Edition

Thank you for your continued use of *Technology in Action*. To ease your transition, here are highlights of changes for the 8th edition.

The following list includes comprehensive changes for the 8th edition:

- **New Multiple-Choice Questions**
  All chapters have all-new, multiple-choice questions. In addition, multiple-choice questions have been added to all Technology in Focus features.

- **New Ethics Projects**
  Each chapter now concludes with a special team-oriented ethics project that discusses new and interesting developments in technology that relate directly to the real world.

- **New and Updated End-of-Chapter Projects**
  More than 80% of all of the end-of-chapter projects for Making the Transition to . . . Next Semester, Making the Transition to . . . the Workplace, Critical Thinking Questions, and Team Time are all new or have been updated.

- **New and Updated "Active Helpdesks"**

- **Completely revised for the 8th edition**

- **New look and feel**

- **Updated Windows 7 and Office 2010 content**

The following list includes changes specific to each chapter for the 8th edition:

Chapter 1: Why Computers Matter to You: Becoming Computer Literate
- Updates to computer system statistics
- New section on military careers that use computers

Chapter 2: Looking at Computers: Understanding the Parts
- New coverage of Apple's Mac Mouse
- Updates to how to select a printer and statistics on media storage
- New coverage of USB 3.0 technology

Chapter 3: Using the Internet: Making the Most of the Web's Resources
- New "How Cool Is This?" topic: WolframAlpha
- New coverage of wireless in-flight service
- Updates to Internet connection speeds

Chapter 4: Application Software: Programs That Let You Work and Play
- New coverage of free software, Software as a Service (SaaS), and Web-based software
- Updated coverage of note-taking software
- New coverage of open source software licensing and reinstalling software
- New Bits and Bytes: "Working with Different File Formats," "Making a Winning Presentation," and "Getting Rid of Bloat"

Chapter 5: Using System Software: The Operating System, Utility Programs, and File Management
- Updated coverage of operating systems for cell phones, Microsoft Windows editions, and RAM requirements
- New sections on operating systems and platforms, running multiple operating systems on a single computer, and using Linux

- New coverage of system repair discs and Windows' Problem Steps Recorder

Chapter 6: Understanding and Assessing Hardware: Evaluating Your System
- Updates to the "Ideal Computer System" worksheet
- Updated coverage of all hardware statistics, including processors
- New Bits and Bytes: "3D Explosions" and "Taking Your System Out of the Box"
- New coverage of SuperFetch and RAID technology

Chapter 7: Networking: Connecting Computing Devices
- Chapter revised to refocus content on setting up and working with a home Ethernet network
- New section on troubleshooting wireless networks

Chapter 8: Digital Lifestyle: Managing Digital Data and Devices
- Updated coverage of smartphone connection speeds and operating systems, digital cameras, and printers
- New coverage on syncing computers with mobile devices, MiFi access, and Bluetooth tethering
- New Trends in IT: "World Changing: Impact of Mobile Technology" and "Ecosystem of New Tools: Augmented Reality"

Chapter 9: Securing Your Systems: Protecting Your Digital Data and Devices
- Updated coverage of cybercrimes and Facebook privacy
- New and updated coverage of data backups, including online backups
- New Bits and Bytes: "CAPTCHA: Keeping Web Sites Safe From Bots"

Chapter 10: Behind the Scenes: Building Applications
- Updated "How Cool Is This?" topic: XNA Game Studio
- New coverage of Objective C

Chapter 11: Behind the Scenes: Databases and Information Systems
- New "How Cool Is This?" topic: JustTweetIt.com
- New section on Facebook as a database
- Updated coverage on Microsoft Access
- New Bits & Bytes: "Music Database Helps You Find Music," "iTunes Smart Playlists—They're Just Queries!" and "CRM Tools Go Online"
- New Trends in IT: "User-Populated Databases"

Chapter 12: Behind the Scenes: Networking and Security in the Business World
- New coverage of using wired connections in business networks
- Updated network cabling statistics
- New Bits and Bytes: "Print Documents Anywhere . . . From Your Phone!" and "PAN Clothing—Organization and Power for Portable Gear"
- Updated Ethics in IT: "Network Technicians' Access to Networks—Who Is Watching the Watchers?"

Chapter 13: Behind the Scenes: The Internet: How It Works
- New Ethics in IT: "Web Browsing—Not as Private As You May Think"
- New sections on crowdsourcing and email encryption

About the Authors

Alan Evans, MS, CPA

aevans@mc3.edu

Alan is currently a faculty member at Moore College of Art and Design and Montgomery County Community College teaching a variety of computer science and business courses. He holds a B.S. in accounting from Rider University and an M.S. in information systems from Drexel University, and he is a certified public accountant. After a successful career in business, Alan finally realized his true calling was education. He has been teaching at the college level since 2000. Alan enjoys giving presentations at technical conferences and meets regularly with computer science faculty and administrators from other colleges to discuss curriculum development and new methods of engaging students.

Kendall Martin, PhD

kmartin@mc3.edu

Kendall has been teaching since 1988 at a number of institutions, including Villanova University, DeSales University, Arcadia University, Ursinus College, County College of Morris, and Montgomery County Community College, at both the undergraduate and graduate level.

Kendall's education includes a B.S. in electrical engineering from the University of Rochester and an M.S. and a Ph.D. in engineering from the University of Pennsylvania. She has industrial experience in research and development environments (AT&T Bell Laboratories) as well as experience with several start-up technology firms.

At Ursinus College, Kendall developed a successful faculty training program for distance education instructors. She makes conference presentations throughout the year.

Mary Anne Poatsy, MBA

mpoatsy@mc3.edu

Mary Anne is a faculty member at Gwynedd-Mercy College and a senior faculty member at Montgomery County Community College, teaching various computer application and concepts courses in face-to-face and online environments. She enjoys speaking at various professional conferences about innovative classroom strategies. She holds a B.A. in psychology and education from Mount Holyoke College and an MBA in finance from Northwestern University's Kellogg Graduate School of Management.

Mary Anne has been in teaching since 1997, ranging from elementary and secondary education to Montgomery County Community College, Gwynedd-Mercy College, Muhlenberg College, and Bucks County Community College, as well as training in the professional environment. Before teaching, she was a vice president at Shearson Lehman Hutton in the Municipal Bond Investment Banking Department.

Acknowledgments

First, we would like to thank our students. We constantly learn from them while teaching, and they are a continual source of inspiration and new ideas.

We could not have written this book without the loving support of our families. Our spouses and children made sacrifices (mostly in time not spent with us) to permit us to make this dream into a reality.

Although working with the entire team at Prentice Hall has been a truly enjoyable experience, a few individuals deserve special mention. The constant support and encouragement we receive from Stephanie Wall, Associate Vice President/Executive Editor, and Michael Payne, Editor in Chief, continually makes this book grow and change. Our heartfelt thanks go to Jennifer Lynn, our developmental editor. Jennifer continues to have a positive impact on the book, and we have benefited greatly from her creative ideas and efficient time management skills. In addition, Laura Burgess, our project manager, has done a fantastic job of coordinating all details of the project and always keeping the entire project on track. As Media Development Manager, Alana Coles works tirelessly to ensure that the media accompanying the text is produced professionally and is delivered in a timely fashion. Despite the inevitable problems that crop up when producing multimedia, she handles all challenges with a smile. We also would like to extend our appreciation to Mike Lackey, our Production Project Manager, who works tirelessly to ensure that our book is published on time and looks fabulous. The timelines are always short, the art is complex, and there are many people with whom he has to coordinate tasks.

There are many people whom we do not meet in person at Prentice Hall and elsewhere who make significant contributions by designing the book, illustrating, composing the pages, producing multimedia, and securing permissions. We thank them all. We would also like to thank the supplement authors for this edition: Lisa Beach, Sharon Behrens, Michael Callahan, Kevin Cleary, Barbara Edington, Stefanie Emrich, Stacy Everly, Wanda Gibson, Mary Carole Hollingsworth, Terri Holly, Ruth Neal, Tonya Pierce, and Linda Stoudemayer.

And finally, we would like to thank the reviewers and the many others who contribute their time, ideas, and talents to this project. We appreciate their time and energy, as their comments help us turn out a better product each edition.

Reviewers

Prentice Hall and the authors would like to thank the following people for their help and time in making this book what it is. We couldn't publish this book without their contributions.

Nazih Abdallah	University of Central Florida
Allen Alexander	Delaware Technical & Community College
Joan Alexander	Valencia Community College—West
Beverly Amer	Northern Arizona University
Wilma Andrews	Virginia Commonwealth University
Gregg W. Asher, Ph.D.	Minnesota State University—Mankato
LaDonna Bachand	Santa Rosa Junior College
Wendy Barron	Lehigh Carbon Community College
LeeAnn Bates	
Elise J. Bell, MA, Educ.	City College of San Francisco
Linda Belton	Springfield Technical Community College
David Billings	Guilford Technical Community College
Kim Binstead, Ph.D	University of Hawaii at Manoa
Susan Birtwell	Kwantlen University College
Henry Bojack	Farmingdale State University of New York
Julie Boyles	
Brenda K. Britt	Fayetteville Technical Community College
Cathy J. Brotherton	Riverside Community College
Gerald U. Brown Jr.	Tarrant County College
Jeff Burton	Daytona Beach Community College
Kristen Callahan	Mercer County Community College
Judy Cameron	Spokane Community College
Jill Canine	Ivy Tech Community College of Indiana
Heather Cannon	Blinn College
Judy Cestaro	California State University—San Bernardino
Deborah Chapman	University of Southern Alabama
Gerianne Chapman	Johnson & Wales University
John P. Cicero, Ph.D	Shasta College—Redding, CA
Dan Combellick	Scottsdale Community College
Joann Cook	College of DuPage
Mark Connell	SUNY Cortland
Gail Cope	Sinclair Community College
Françoise Corey	California State University, Long Beach
John Coverdale	Riverside Community College
Thad Crews	Western Kentucky University
Doug Cross	Clackamas Community College
Geoffrey Crosslin	Kalamazoo Valley Community College
Becky Cunningham	Arkansas Tech University
John Cusaac	Fullerton College
James Bac Dang	Tarrant County College
Marvin Daugherty	Ivy Tech
Ronald G. Deardorff	Shasta Community College
Joseph DeLibero	Arizona State University
K. Kay Delk	Seminole Community College
Charles DeSassure	Tarrant County College
Gretchen V. Douglas	State University of New York at Cortland
Susan N. Dozier	Tidewater Community College
Annette Duvall	Albuquerque Technical Vocational Institute

Laurie Eakins	East Carolina University
Roland Eichelberger	Baylor University
James Fabrey	West Chester University
Catherine L. Ferguson	University of Oklahoma
Marj Feroe	Delaware County Community College
Judy Firmin	Tarrant County College
Beverly Fite	Amarillo College
Howard Flomberg	The Metropolitan State College of Denver
Richard A. Flores	Citrus College
Alicen Flosi	Lamar University
Linda Foster-Turpen	Central New Mexico Community College
Susan Fry	Boise State University
Yvonne Galusha	University of Iowa
Barbara A. Garrell	Delaware County Community College
Ernest Gines	Tarrant County College
Tim Gottleber	North Lake College
Sherry Green	Purdue University—Calumet Campus
Debra Gross	The Ohio State University
Vivian Haddad	Nova Southeastern University
Don A. Halcomb	Bluegrass Community and Technical College
Lewis Hall	Riverside City College
Rachelle Hall	Glendale Community College
Eric Hamilton	Community College of Denver
Bill Hammerschlag	Brookhaven College
Terry Hanks	San Jacinto College—South Campus
Susan Hanson	Albuquerque Technical Vocational Institute
Marie Hartlein	Montgomery County Community College
Ronda D. Hayes	North Lake College
Susan E. Hoggard	Tulsa Community College
Jim Hendricks	Pierce College
Catherine Hines	Albuquerque Technical Vocational Institute
Norm Hollingsworth	Georgia Perimeter College
Bill Holmes	Chandler-Gilbert Community College
Mary Carole Hollingsworth	Georgia Perimeter College
Sherry Hopkins	Anne Arundel Community College
Christie Jahn Hovey	Lincoln Land Community College
Jeffrey Howard	Finger Lakes Community College
John L. Howard	East Carolina University
Judy Irvine	Seneca College
Glen Johansson	Spokane Community College
Kay Johnson	Community College of Rhode Island
Stephanie Jones	South Plains College
Steve St. John	Tulsa Community College
Kathy Johnson	DeVry Chicago
Richard B. Kalman	Atlantic Cape Community College
Dr. K. Kamel	TSU
Darrel Karbginsky	Chemkeketa Community College
Linda Kavanaugh	Robert Morris University
Robert R. Kendi	Lehigh University
Annette Kerwin	College of DuPage
David Kight	Brewton-Parker College
Kai S. Koong	University of Texas Pan American
Frank Kuehn	Pikes Peak Community College

Jackie Lamoureux	Albuquerque Technical Vocational Institute
David K. Lange	Grand Valley State University
Joanne Lazirko	University of Wisconsin—Milwaukee
Michael R. Lehrfeld	Brevard Community College
Yvonne Leonard	Coastal Carolina University
Judith Limkilde	Seneca College—King Campus
Richard Linge	Arizona Western College
Christy Lopez	East Carolina University
Joelene Mack	Golden West College
Lisa Macon	Valencia Community College
Donna Madsen	Kirkwood Community College
Daniela Marghitu	Auburn University
Norma Marler	Catawba Valley Community College
Carol Prewitt Martin	Louisiana State University at Alexandria
Toni Marucco	Lincoln Land Community College
Evelynn McCain	Boise State University
Dana McCann	Central Michigan University
Lee McClain	West Washington University
Sandra M. McCormack	Monroe Community College
Sue McCrory	Missouri State University
Phil McCue	Lone Star College—Montgomery
Helen McFadyen	Mass Bay Community College—Framingham
Charles J. McNerney Ph.D.	Bergen Community College
Dr. Dori McPherson	Schoolcraft College
Laura Melella	Fullerton College
Josephine Mendoza	California State University, San Bernardino
Mike Michaelson	Palomar College
Gina Bowers Miller	Harrisburg Area Community College
Johnette Moody	Arkansas Tech University
Dona Mularkey	Southern Methodist University
Rebecca A. Mundy	University of Southern California
Linda Mushet	Golden West College
Lisa Nademlynsky	Johnson & Wales University
Maguerite Nedreberg	Youngstown State University
Brad Nicolajsen	Carteret Community College
Omar Nooraldeen	Cape Fear Community College
Judy Ogden	Johnson County Community College
Connie O'Neill	Sinclair Community College
Claudia Orr	Northern Michigan University
James R. Orr	East Carolina University
Sung Park	Pasadena City College
Brenda Parker	Middle Tennessee State University
Patricia Partyka	Schoolcraft College
Woody Pekoske	North Carolina State University
Judy Perhamus Perry	Riverside Community College—Norco Campus
Carolyn Poe	Lone Star College—Montgomery
Mike Puopolo	Bunker Hill Community College
Paul Quan	Albuquerque Technical Vocational Institute
Ram Raghuraman	Joliet Junior College
Patricia Rahmlow	Montgomery County Community College
Shirley Reid	Indian Hills Community College
Ruth Robbins	University of Houston—Downtown
Teresa Roberts	Wilson Community College

Catherine J. Rogers	Laramie County Community College
Russell Sabadosa	Manchester Community College
Peg Saragina	Santa Rosa Junior College
Judith Scheeren	Westmoreland County Community College
Samuel Scott	Pierce College
Vicky Seehusen	The Metropolitan State College of Denver
Ralph Shafer	Truckee Meadows Community College—Reno
Mirella Shannon	Columbia College
Laurie Evin Shteir	Temple University
Sheila Smart Sicilia	Onondaga Community College
Greg A. Simpson	Phoenix College—Phoenix, AZ
Robert G. Sindt	Johnson County Community College
Gary R. Smith	Paradise Valley Community College
Steven Singer	Kapi'olani Community College
Robert Smolenski	Delaware County Community College
Diane Stark	Phoenix College
James Stark	Milwaukee Area Technical College
Suzanne Mello Stark	Community College of Rhode Island
Kriss Stauber	El Camino College
Neal Stenlund	Northern Virginia Community College
Linda Stoudemayer	Lamar Institute of Technology
Catherine Stoughton	Laramie County Community College
Lynne Stuhr	Trident Technical College
Song Su	East Los Angeles College
John Taylor	Hillsborough Community College—Brandon Campus
Dennie Templeton	Radford University
Joyce Thompson	Lehigh Carbon Community College
Lou Thompson	University of Texas at Dallas
Janine Tiffany	Reading Area Community College
Janet Towle	New Hampshire Community Technical College—Nashua
Goran Trajkovski	Towson University
Deborah Tyler	Tarrant County College
Pamella M. Uhlenkamp	Iowa Central Community College—Fort Dodge, Iowa
Erhan Uskup	Houston Community College—Northwest
Emily Vandalovsky	Bergen Community College
Bill VanderClock	Bentley Business University
Glenna Vanderhoof	Missouri State University
Michelle Vlaich-Lee	Greenville Technical College
Karen Weil-Yates	Hagerstown Community College
Catherine Werst	Cuesta College
Janice L. Williams	Seward County Community College
Melanie Williamson	Bluegrass Community and Technical College
Steven H. White	Anne Arundel Community College
Barbara Yancy	Community College of Baltimore County—Essex Camp
Thomas Yip	Passaic County Community College
Mary Zajac	Montgomery County Community College
Mary T. Zegarski	Northampton Community College
Mary Ann Zlotow	College of DuPage

Letter from the Authors

Why We Wrote This Book

Our combined 43 years of teaching computer concepts have coincided with sweeping innovations in computing technology that have affected every facet of society. From iPads to Web 2.0, computers are more than ever a fixture of our daily lives—and the lives of our students. But although today's students have a greater comfort level with their digital environment than previous generations, their knowledge of the machines they use every day is still limited.

We wrote *Technology in Action* to focus on what matters most to today's student. Instead of a history lesson on the microchip, we focus on what tasks students can accomplish with their computing devices and what skills they can apply immediately in the workplace, the classroom, and at home. We strive to be as current as the publishing timelines will allow us, constantly looking for the next technology trend or gadget. The result is a book that sparks student interest by focusing on the material they want to learn (such as how to integrate computing devices into a home network) while teaching the material they need to learn (such as how networks work). The sequence of topics is carefully set up to mirror the typical student learning experience.

As they read through this text, your students will progress through stages of increasing difficulty:

1. Examining why it's important to be computer fluent and how computers impact our society
2. Examining the basic components of the computer
3. Connecting to and exploring the Internet
4. Exploring software
5. Learning the operating system and personalizing the computer
6. Evaluating and upgrading computing devices
7. Exploring home networking and keeping the computer safe from hackers
8. Going mobile with smartphones, netbooks, iPads and laptops
9. Going behind the scenes, looking at technology in more detail

We have written the book in a "spiraling" manner, intentionally introducing on a basic level in the earlier chapters those concepts that students have trouble with and then later expanding on those concepts in more detail when students have become more comfortable with them. Thus, the focus of the early chapters is on practical uses for the computer, with real-world examples to help the students place computing in a familiar context. For example, we introduce basic hardware components in Chapter 2, and then we go into increasingly greater detail on some hardware components in Chapter 6 and in the "Under the Hood" Technology in Focus feature.

The Behind the Scenes chapters venture deeper into the realm of computing through in-depth explanations of how programming, networks, the Internet, and databases work. They are specifically designed to keep more experienced students engaged and to challenge them with interesting research assignments.

We have also developed a comprehensive multimedia program to reinforce the material taught in the text and to support both classroom lectures and distance learning. The Helpdesk training content, created specifically for *Technology in Action*, enables students to take on the role of a helpdesk operator and work through common questions asked by computer users. Exciting Sound Byte multimedia—fully integrated with the text—expands student mastery of complex topics.

Now that the computer has become a ubiquitous tool in our lives, a new approach to computer concepts is warranted. This book is designed to reach the students of the twenty-first century and prepare them for the challenges they will face in the new global economy.

Visual Walk-Through

TOPIC SEQUENCE

Concepts are covered in a spiraling manner between chapters to mirror the typical student learning experience.

CHAPTER 2

CHAPTER 6

CHAPTER 6

Hardware First Introduced
Chapter 2 is the first time students read about introductory hardware. It is covered at the beginning level because this is their experience level at this point of the book.

Hardware Taught in More Depth in Additional Chapters
In later chapters, students are taught hardware in greater depth because they are more experienced and comfortable working with their computer.

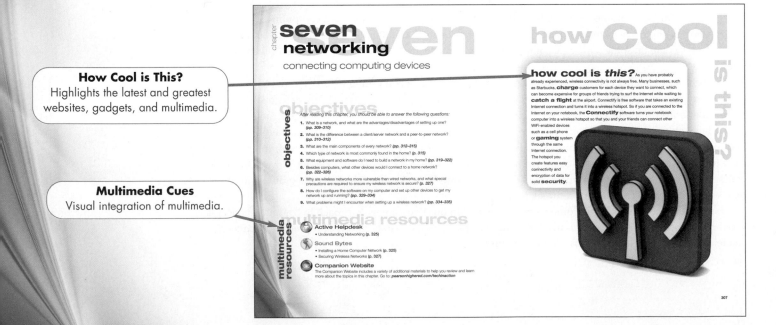

How Cool is This?
Highlights the latest and greatest websites, gadgets, and multimedia.

Multimedia Cues
Visual integration of multimedia.

Student Textbook

eighth EDITION
8

Ethics in IT boxes examine the ethical dilemmas caused by technology.

Trends in IT boxes explore newer topics involved in computing.

Dig Deeper boxes cover technical topics in depth to challenge advanced students.

Bits and Bytes teach good habits for safe computing.

Question/Answer Format
Written in an engaging and easy-to-read format.

NEW

Multiple Choice and True/False

Technology in Focus
Five special features that teach key uses of technology today.

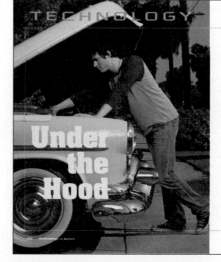

The Multimedia

Student CD
The launch pad to the multimedia.

Companion Website
Includes an interactive study guide,
online end-of-chapter material,
additional Internet exercises,
and much more.

www.prenhall.com/techinaction

Active Helpdesk
Interactive training that puts the student in the role of a helpdesk staffer fielding questions from callers.

Completely Revised
Features textbook page references within each call and assessment at the end of each call.

Supervisor available to assist students.

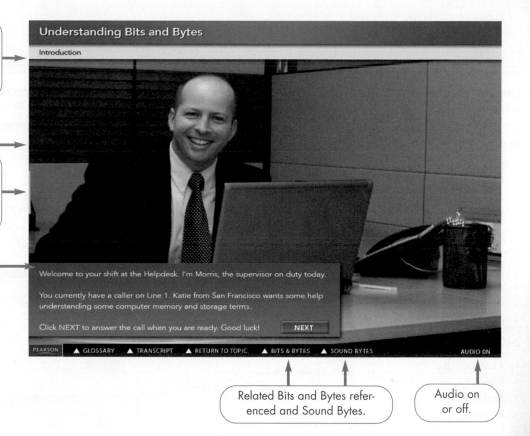

Understanding Bits and Bytes
Introduction

Welcome to your shift at the Helpdesk. I'm Morris, the supervisor on duty today.

You currently have a caller on Line 1. Katie from San Francisco wants some help understanding some computer memory and storage terms.

Click NEXT to answer the call when you are ready. Good luck!   NEXT

PEARSON   ▲ GLOSSARY   ▲ TRANSCRIPT   ▲ RETURN TO TOPIC   ▲ BITS & BYTES   ▲ SOUND BYTES   AUDIO ON

Related Bits and Bytes referenced and Sound Bytes.

Audio on or off.

Transcript button used to turn transcript on or off.

Sound Bytes
Multimedia lessons with video, audio, or animation and corresponding labs featuring multiple-choice quizzing.

NEW Also available as podcasts.

Technology In Action
Welcome to the Web

1 Introduction
2 What We Will Cover
3 The New York Times Learning Network
4 Microsoft at Home
5 How Stuff Works
6 Webopedia
7 Wrapping Up
8 Web Links

Transcription ON

WELCOME TO THE WEB

Navigational tool.

Audio leads students through.

Video or animation teaches key concepts.

Annotated Instructor Edition

Provided with each chapter are two divider pages like the ones outlined below.

FRONT OF CHAPTER TAB

On the front side of each chapter tab, you will find the following categories:

IN THE CLASSROOM: Activities you can use in a classroom or in online classes, including:

- PowerPoint Presentations
- Discussion Exercises
- Active Helpdesk Calls
- Sound Bytes

HOMEWORK: Activities used out of class for assessment or preparation for the next chapter, including:

- Web Resource Projects
- Active Helpdesk Calls
- Sound Byte Labs
- Online Study Guides

ASSESSMENT:

- Blackboard
- WebCT
- TestGen
- myitlab

The back side of each chapter tab includes the relevant Sound Bytes for that chapter.

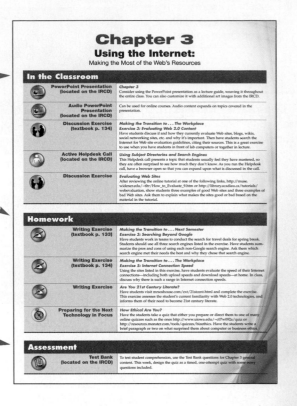

FRONT OF ETHICS TAB

On the front of the Ethics tab, you will find the following:

OPPOSING VIEWPOINTS TABLE: Outlines debatable ethics topics that you can use in the classroom.

KEYWORDS: Provides you with additional words to search the Internet for more information related to the ethics topic.

For a list of the resources available for every chapter and where they are located, see the back of this tab.

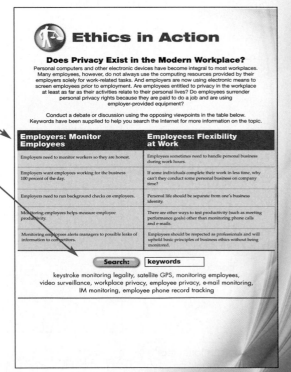

Instructor Resource CD

GREATLY ENHANCED

Instructor Resource CD

- **NEW! Interactive Course Builder** to help you integrate all the instructor resources.
- **NEW! Recommended chapter lectures** written by the authors that you can customize.
- All resources included with the *Technology in Action* Instructional System.

TIA 8E

Technology in Action 8E - Complete - Instructor Resource CD - Disk 2

Technology in Action

View Active Helpdesks   Download Instructor Resources   Exit

© 2012 by Pearson Education, Inc., Upper Saddle River, NJ 07458

Contact your local Prentice Hall sales rep to learn more about the
Technology in Action instructional system.

Technology in Action

8th Edition

Alan Evans • Kendall Martin
Mary Anne Poatsy

Prentice Hall

Boston   Columbus   Indianapolis   New York   San Francisco   Upper Saddle River
Amsterdam   Cape Town   Dubai   London   Madrid   Milan   Munich   Paris   Montréal   Toronto
Delhi   Mexico City   São Paulo   Sydney   Hong Kong   Seoul   Singapore   Taipei   Tokyo

chapter

one
why computers matter to you:
becoming computer literate

multimedia resources

Active Helpdesk

This chapter has no Active Helpdesks.

Sound Bytes

- Questions to Ask Before You Buy a Computer **(p. 6)**
- The History of the Personal Computer **(p. 21)**

Companion Website

The Companion Website includes a variety of additional materials to help you review and learn more about the topics in this chapter. Go to ***pearsonhighered.com/techinaction***

how cool is *this?*

Whether you want a handmade piece of jewelry, a **vintage handbag**, or a handblown glass vase, **Etsy** is the site for you. This person-to-person e-commerce site is beautifully designed and allows artists and craftspeople to take full advantage of technology and connect with customers around the globe.

If you are thinking of opening a storefront for your own handmade goods, Etsy provides an extremely easy entry into e-commerce. It costs just **20 cents** to list an item, and Etsy provides workshops, marketing support, and forums for store owners to exchange ideas.

In the full **spirit** of the modern Web, Etsy enthusiasts have created a variety of ways to connect and collaborate. These include blogs about Etsy and a wiki with info for Etsy buyers and sellers. You'll also find mentions of Etsy on **Flickr** photography sites, and a YouTube video in which Etsy's founder, Rob Kalin, talks about creating "a **handmade** market-place." Facebook gets in on the act with a My Etsy tab whereby Etsy sellers can create a special tab on their profile page to share Etsy shops and favorite items.

Now the **artistic** among us can easily use technology to expand our world.

Why Should You Become Computer Literate?

It's safe to say that computers are nearly everywhere in our society. You find them in schools, cars, airports, shopping centers, toys, phones, medical devices, and homes, and in many people's pockets. You interact with computers almost every day, sometimes without even knowing it. Whenever you buy something with a credit card, you interact with a computer. And, of course, most of us can't imagine our lives without e-mail. Even if you don't yet have a computer and don't feel comfortable using one, you still feel the impact of technology: Countless ads for computers, cell phones, digital cameras, and an assortment of Web sites surround us each day. We're constantly reminded of the ways in which computers, the Internet, and technology are integral parts of our lives.

So, just by being a member of our society, you already know quite a bit about computers. But why is it important to learn more about computers, becoming what is called *computer literate?* Being **computer literate** means being familiar enough with computers that you understand their capabilities and limitations (see Figure 1.1), and you know how to use them. Being computer literate means more than just knowing about the parts of your computer. The following are some other benefits:

- As a computer literate individual, you can use your computer more

wisely and be a more knowledgeable consumer.
- Computer-literate employees are sought after in almost every vocation.
- Becoming computer literate will help you better understand and take advantage of future technologies.

In addition, understanding computers and their ethical, legal, and societal implications will make you a more active and aware participant in society.

Anyone can become computer literate—no matter what your degree of technical expertise. Being computer literate doesn't mean you need to know enough to program a computer or build one yourself. With a car, for example, you should know enough about it to take care of it and use it effectively, but that doesn't mean you have to know how to build one. You should try to achieve the same familiarity with computers.

Becoming a Savvy Computer User and Consumer

One of the benefits of becoming computer literate is being a savvy computer user and consumer. What does this mean? The following are just a few examples of what it may mean to you:

- **Avoiding hackers and viruses.** Do you know what hackers and viruses are? Both can threaten a computer's security.

Figure 1.1

Do you know what all the words in a computer ad mean? Can you tell whether the ad includes all the information necessary to make a purchasing decision?

Processor:	Intel i7-965 Extreme, Factory O'Cd to 3.73 GHz
RAM:	12 GB Tri Channel Corsair DDR3 (1066 MHz)
Video:	ATI Radeon HD 5870 X2 with 1 GB DDR5
Audio:	Creative Labs X-Fi Elite Pro; HDA 7.1 surround channel sound
Network:	Native Gigabit Ethernet
Optical Drive:	Blu-ray burner
Storage Drive:	1 TB Serial ATA hard drive with support for up to 5 additional drives with RAID options
Ports:	8 USB and 2 USB 3.0 2 DVI and 1 S-Video 2 IEEE 1394 1 S/PDIF out
Physics Accelerator:	Ageia PhysX Card
Cooling:	Two-stage liquid cooling system
Portable Storage:	Bluetooth wireless 19-in-1 media hub with VoIP stereo headset
Operating System:	Windows 7 Ultimate 64-bit

NEW!

Being aware of how hackers and viruses operate and knowing the damage they can do to your computer can help you avoid falling prey to them.

- **Protecting your privacy.** You've probably heard of identity theft—you see and hear news stories all the time about people whose "identities" are stolen and whose credit ratings are ruined by "identity thieves." But do you know how to protect yourself from identity theft when you're online?

- **Understanding the real risks.** Part of being computer literate means being able to separate the real privacy and security risks from things you don't have to worry about. For example, do you know what a *cookie* is? Do you know whether it poses a privacy risk for you when you're on the Internet? What about a *firewall?* Do you know what one is? Do you really need one to protect your computer?

- **Using the Internet and the Web wisely.** Anyone who has ever searched the Web can attest that finding information and finding good information are two different things. People who are computer literate make the Internet a powerful tool and know how to find the information they want effectively. How familiar with the Web are you, and how effective are your searches?

- **Avoiding online annoyances.** If you have an e-mail account, chances are you've received electronic junk mail, or **spam** (see Figure 1.2). How can you avoid being overwhelmed by spam? What about *adware* and *spyware*—do you know what they are? Do you know the difference between those and viruses, worms, and Trojan horses? Do you know what **software** programs (or the instructions that tell the computer what

to do) you should install on your computer to avoid online annoyances?

- **Being able to maintain, upgrade, and troubleshoot your computer.** Learning how to care for and maintain your computer and knowing how to diagnose and fix certain problems can save you a lot of time and hassle. Do you know how to upgrade your computer if you want more memory, for example? Do you know which software and computer settings can help you keep your computer in top shape?

www.CartoonStock.com

"Wow! I've got one from someone I know!"

Figure 1.2

Understanding how to use e-mail effectively is just one example of what it means to be computer literate.

Everywhere you go, you see ads like the one in Figure 1.1 for computers and other devices: notebooks (laptops), printers, monitors, cell phones, digital cameras, and GPS (global positioning system) devices. Do you know what all the words in the ads mean? What is *RAM?* What is a *CPU?* What are *MB, GB, GHz,* and *cache?* How fast do you need your computer to be, and how much memory should it have? Understanding computer terminology and keeping current with technology will help you better determine which computers and devices match your needs.

Finally, becoming computer literate means knowing which technologies are on the horizon and how to integrate them into your home setup when possible (see Figure 1.3). Can you connect your notebook to a wireless network? What is Bluetooth, and does your computer "have" it? Can a USB 3.0 flash drive be plugged into an old USB 1.0 port? (For that matter, what is a USB port?) How much memory should your cell phone have? Knowing the answers to these and other questions will help you make better purchasing decisions.

The benefits of being computer literate will help you in your career and in running your personal life. You'll be able to save money, time, and endless frustration by having a strong background in the basics of how computers and computer systems operate.

Figure 1.3

Can you identify all of these devices? Do you know how to get them all to work well together?

the workplace, see the Technology in Focus section, "Careers in IT."

Becoming truly computer literate—understanding the capabilities and limitations of computers and what you can do with them—will undoubtedly help you perform your job more effectively. It also will make you more desirable as an employee and more likely to earn more and advance your career. So, let's begin with a look at how computer systems are used in a wide range of careers. Whether you become an employee in one of these industries or a user of its services, you will have a great advantage if you understand computer systems.

Computers in Today's Careers

We all are used to seeing computers at the checkout counter in stores, at the check-in area at an airport, and so on, but there are many ways that computers are being used that you probably aren't aware of. Before we begin looking at a computer's parts and how it operates, let's take a look at a whole range of industries and examine how computers are a part of getting work done. Whether you plan on a career in one of these fields or will just be a user of their products and services, your life will be affected by the use of computers in areas including retail, arts, law enforcement, the military, agriculture, and more.

Being Prepared for Your Career

Computer careers are on the rise. Regardless of which profession you pursue, if computers are not already in use in that career, they most likely will be soon. **Information technology (IT)** is a field of study focused on managing and processing information and the automatic retrieval of information. Information technology includes computers, telecommunications, and software deployment. IT careers are on the rise, and the seven fastest-growing occupations are computer related. New technology in the workplace is creating a demand for new skill levels from employees. A study from the National Research Council concludes that by the year 2030 computers will displace humans in 60 percent of the current occupations. It will be more critical than ever for employees to have advanced skills. For more information about computers and

Retail: Working in a Data Mine

Businesses accumulate a lot of data, but how do they manage to make sense of all of it? How do they separate the anomalies from the trends? They use a technique known as **data mining**, the process of searching huge amounts of data with the hope of finding a pattern (see Figure 1.4). For example, large retailers often study the data gathered from register terminals to determine which products are selling on a given day and in a specific location. In addition to inventory control systems helping managers figure out how much merchandise they need to order to replace stock that is sold, data mining opens the door to more detail. Managers can use mined data to determine that if a certain product is to sell well, they must lower its price—especially if they cut the price at one store and see sales increase, for example. Data mining thus allows retailers to respond to consumer buying patterns.

Did you ever wonder how Amazon or Netflix can suggest items that fit your taste? Or how such Web sites automatically display lists of items people bought after they ordered the camera you just picked out? Data mining can keep track of the purchases customers are making, along with their geographic data, past buying history, and lists of items they examined but did not purchase. This can be translated into extremely specific marketing that is immediate and customized to your shopping experience. This is the motivation behind all of the discount cards that grocery stores and drugstores offer. In exchange for tracking your personal buying habits, they offer you some kind of special pricing. How much is your private information worth?

Business: Data on the Go

Did you know that United Parcel Service (UPS) handles more than 3.9 billion packages and letters a year? Just how does the "brown" company ensure that all its

customers' packages get from points A to B without ending up forever at point C? The company uses a sophisticated database and a highly efficient package tracking system that follows the packages as they move around the world.

For UPS, package tracking starts when the sender drops off a package and the company creates a "smart label" for the package (see Figure 1.5a). In addition to the standard postal bar code and a bar code showing UPS

Figure 1.4

Data mining is the art of combining huge volumes of raw data into views that provide insight.

Figure 1.5

(a) Package tracking starts when the package is sent with the generation of a smart label, which includes the UPS MaxiCode. (b) Portable handheld devices allow UPS personnel to scan packages for accurate transfer of information. (c) Devices with built-in GPS are used to find directions to customers, capture customer signatures, and transfer information.

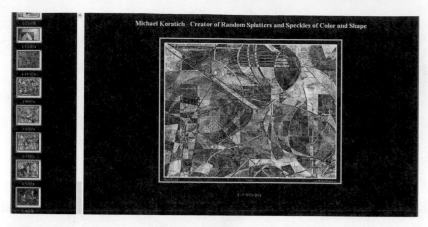

Figure 1.6

Artists such as Michael Koratich display and sell their creations by using custom Web galleries such as this one (**michaelkoratich.com**).

customer numbers, this smart label contains something called a *MaxiCode*. The MaxiCode is a specially designed, scannable sticker that resembles an inkblot and contains all the important information about the package (class of service, destination, etc.). When the package is handled in processing centers, UPS workers scan the MaxiCode using portable handheld devices (see Figure 1.5b). These devices use **Bluetooth technology** (a type of wireless communication) to transmit the scanned data through radio waves to a terminal. This terminal then sends the data across a wireless network, where it is recorded in the UPS database.

To track package delivery, UPS carriers use delivery acquisition devices (see Figure 1.5c) that feature wireless networking capability, GPS positioning, infrared scanners (to scan the smart labels and transmit the information back to the UPS database), and an electronic pad to capture customer signatures. By capturing all of this data and making it available on its Internet database, UPS enables its customers to track their packages. UPS is also able to make informed decisions about staffing and deploying equipment (trucks, airplanes, etc.) based on the volume and type of packages in the system at any given time.

Arts: Ink, Paints, and a Notebook?

Some art students think that because they're studying art, there is no reason for them to study computers. However, unless you plan

to be a "starving artist," you'll probably want to sell your work. To do so, you'll need to advertise to the public and contact art galleries to convince them to purchase or display your work. Wouldn't it be helpful if you knew how to create a Web site like the one shown in Figure 1.6?

Using computers in the arts and entertainment fields goes far beyond using the Internet. Dance and music programs like the ones at the Atlanta Ballet and the Juilliard School of Music use computers to create new performances for audiences. As shown in Figure 1.7, a live dancer can be wired with sensors that are connected to a computer that captures the dancer's movements. Based on the data it collects, the computer generates a virtual dancer on a screen. The computer operator can easily manipulate this virtual dancer, as well as change the dancer's costume, with the click of a mouse. This allows artists to create new experiences for the audience.

Of course, not all artwork is created using traditional materials such as paint and canvas. Many artists today work exclusively with computers. Mastery of software programs such as Adobe Illustrator, Adobe Photoshop, and Corel Painter is essential to creating digital art.

Figure 1.7

A dancer is wired with light electronic sensors so that her movements can be digitized for computer analysis.

Other artists are pushing the envelope of creating art with computers even further. For example, MacArthur Fellow and artist Camille Utterback uses a computer to create works of art that react to the presence—and the absence—of movement of the viewers in the gallery (see Figure 1.8). When no one is near the art piece, the image paints a small series of dots. However, as onlookers in the gallery move closer to the work, a camera mounted on the ceiling of the art gallery captures the onlookers' movements and dimensions. A computer with specialized software then uses this captured data to create smears of color and patterns of lines that reflect their movements. Because the image itself is created from the current and past movements and sizes of the gallery patrons, the work looks different each time it is viewed. You can learn more about Utterback's digital art at **macfound.org**.

Video Game Design: A Long Way from Pac-Man

Revenues from video game sales in the United States are now larger than the movie industry's box office. Computer gaming topped $21 billion in 2008 and is projected to continue its rapid growth over the next decade. The field is competitive, and games must be creative to grab their audience. Large-scale games are impossible to create on your own—you must be part of a team. The good news is that because computer games are best developed for a local market by people native to that market, game development will most likely stay in the United States instead of being **offshored** (sent to other countries), as many other types of programming jobs have been.

You'll need an in-depth knowledge of computers to pursue a career in game programming or as a gaming artist. Mastering software animation tools, such as 3ds Max, will enable you to create compelling new worlds and new characters like those in the story-driven role-playing game Final Fantasy XIII (see Figure 1.9).

Education: Teaching and Learning

Today's teachers need to be at least as computer savvy as their students. Computers are part of most schools, even preschools. In fact, at many colleges, students are required to have their own computers. Courses are designed around course management software such as Blackboard or Moodle so that students can communicate outside of class, take quizzes online, and find their class materials easily. Teachers must therefore

have a working knowledge of computers to integrate computer technology into the classroom effectively.

The Internet has obvious advantages in the classroom as a research tool for students, and effective use of the Internet allows teachers to expose students to places students otherwise could not access. There are simulations and instructional software programs on the Web that are incredible learning tools. Teachers can employ these products to give students a taste of running a global business (see Figure 1.10) or provide the experience of the Interactive Body (**bbc.co.uk/science/ humanbody**).

Many muscums have virtual tours on their Web sites that allow students to examine objects in the museum collections. Often, these virtual tours include three-dimensional photos that can be viewed from all angles. So, even if you teach in Topeka, Kansas, you can take your students on a virtual tour of the Smithsonian Institution in Washington, D.C.

But what about when you want to take your students to visit museums in person?

Figure 1.8

Computers even figure directly into the development of artwork. Artist Camille Utterback develops interactive art that changes with the presence and movement of viewers in the gallery.

Figure 1.9

Using powerful software, game developers can create complex worlds and characters to satisfy even the most demanding gamer.

Figure 1.10

Internet applications have become sophisticated learning resources. **IndustryMasters.com** allows students to compete online for domination of a global market while giving instructors the chance to introduce many business concepts.

Today, technology is often used to enhance visitors' experiences at museums. New York's Museum of Modern Art (MoMA), for example, offers a full range of options for tech-savvy visitors: old-fashioned museum audio guides, podcasts you can listen to with your smartphone, and multimedia tours that you can download through MoMA WiFi (**moma.org**) to your own MP3 device such as a Zune or an iTouch. These multimedia guides let you listen to music that the artist listened to when he or she was creating a particular work or look at other works that reflect similar techniques or themes to those of the one you're viewing (see Figure 1.11). While looking at works by more modern artists, you can watch interviews with the artist explaining his or her motivation for the work. You can even connect quickly to other members of your

group and direct them to specific works you want them to see. Being literate with technology may help make your museum tour even more memorable.

Computers in the classroom will become more prevalent as prices continue to fall and parents demand that their children be taught the computer skills they will need to be successful in the workplace. Therefore, as an educator, being computer literate will

Figure 1.11

Multimedia tours using mobile devices and wireless technology are commonplace in museums and galleries.

help you integrate computers constructively into lesson plans for your students and use technology to interact with them.

Law Enforcement: Put Down That Mouse—You're Under Arrest!

Today, wearing out shoe leather to solve crimes is far from the only method available to investigators trying to catch criminals. Computers are being used in police cars and crime labs to solve an increasing number of crimes. For example, facial reconstruction systems like the one shown in Figure 1.12 can turn a skull into a finished digital image of a face, allowing investigators to proceed far more quickly with identification.

Figure 1.12

(a) The FastScan wand lets forensics teams quickly grab three-dimensional images of skulls. (b) Tissue-rendering programs then add layers of muscles, fat, and skin to create faces that can be used to identify victims.

One technique used by modern detectives to solve crimes uses computers to search the vast number of databases on the Internet. Proprietary law enforcement databases such as the National Center for the Analysis of Violent Crime database enable detectives to analyze a wealth of information about similarities between crimes, trying to detect patterns that may reveal serial crimes. Where the law permits, detectives can also use their knowledge of wireless networking to intercept and read a criminal suspect's e-mail messages and chat sessions when he or she is online, all from the comfort of a car parked outside the suspect's home.

As detective work goes more high tech, so, too, does crime. To fight modern crime, a law enforcement specialty called **computer forensics** is growing. This specialty analyzes computer systems with specific techniques to gather potential legal evidence. For example, in 2009 Steven Zirko was convicted for two Chicago-area murders based on computer forensics work. FBI-trained computer forensics examiners scoured Zirko's computer and located searches for terms like "hire a hitman" and "GHB," the date rape drug. Zirko also had used his computer to find the daily schedule for his victim's two school-aged children and to get directions to her home. This case is one of many solved by the use of computer forensics techniques. In many cases, files, videos, and conversations conducted using a computer can be recovered by forensics specialists and used as evidence of criminal activity.

Computers are also used in training law enforcement officers to be more effective. For example, the Federal Bureau of Investigation (FBI) and the Transportation Security Administration (TSA) use computer-based training to teach officers to recognize lies and evasive behavior. Dr. Paul Ekman has spent a career studying *microexpressions*, brief (1/25th of a second) flashes of emotion. When a person is being deceptive, microexpressions, which cannot be controlled, reveal true emotions in his or her body language. The Microexpression Training Tool software system (**paulekman.com**), a program developed by Ekman's company, trains users to recognize emotions such as fear, disgust, contempt, and anger in these flashes of microexpressions (see Figure 1.13). You can try the online demo to see if you are a "natural," one of the rare people who can recognize and read emotion without training.

Figure 1.13

The Microexpression Training Tool software trains law enforcement officials to distinguish true emotion from deception.

You're probably already using your computer in many different ways to fit your lifestyle. Perhaps you're ripping your CD collection to MP3 files and downloading movies so that you can transfer them from your computer to your iPod or Zune. Maybe you're burning a CD of all your favorite songs for a party you're having. But wouldn't it be great if you could manage the music for your party straight from your computer? And what about that video of your friend's birthday party you shot last week? You've already imported it to your computer, edited it, and added a music track. But when your friends come over for the party this weekend, wouldn't it be fun to be able to show them the video on the TV in the living room instead of having them crowd around your computer monitor?

Or use the notebook computer upstairs to play a dance song through the big speakers in the basement audio system?

When in the future will you be able to do all this? Right now if you set up a digital home. Setting up a **digital home** means having an appropriate computer and digital devices that are all connected to a home network. Let's discuss the key components you need to get started with a digital living room, some of which are shown in Figure 1.14.

1. **A media computer:** A computer is the nerve center of any digital home, allowing you to interface with all the different digital devices you have connected to the network. For a Windows-based computer (see Figure 1.15), you should opt for a computer running

Media center computer system

LED Internet-ready TV

Universal remote control

Wireless keyboard with built-in trackpad

Figure 1.14

You can create a digital living room with only a few devices.

Military Careers: Drive That Drone

Developing and using cutting-edge technology has always been an important component of a military career, and advanced technology is especially important in modern times. The need for electronic communications in the field means that many soldiers are trained computer specialists in areas such as satellite transmissions, radio controllers, and computer networking. Whether the job is in electronics, aviation support, art and media production, or logistics and supply, many of the most

desirable military positions require knowledge of computer software and hardware.

Right from the start, planning a career in the military is easier for those who are computer literate. The ASVAB (Armed Services Vocational Aptitude Battery) exam is a requirement for entry into the U.S. armed services, and the scores on various sections of this exam determine if you are eligible to enlist, indicate which branch or branches of the military will consider you, and identify which military careers are appropriate. Studying for this timed multiple-choice exam can involve using tools such as an iTouch

Figure 1.15

Media Center in Microsoft Windows 7 allows you to manage all your media entertainment from your computer.

the current version of Microsoft Windows 7 or Windows Vista as its operating system. (We'll discuss operating systems in more detail in Chapter 5.)

A typical media PC will be equipped with the software to customize it to the tasks of a digital entertainment center. Windows 7 already incorporates versions of much of the software you might want to add. Windows Media Center is part of Windows 7 and functions as a digital video recorder (DVR), a video player, and a music player. You can use Media Center to view and organize the digital audio and video files on your computer. The DVR software allows you to turn your computer into a DVR similar to TiVo. Digital video recorders record TV programs like analog VCRs used to do, but they use the computer's hard drive to store the video.

There are some other hardware components most users want to add to their media computer:

a. **A TV tuner:** A TV tuner allows your computer to receive television channels from a cable connection and display them on your computer monitor. In fact, you can install more than one TV tuner on your computer, allowing you to receive multiple television channels at the same time.

b. **Blu-ray, DVD, and CD players and recorders:** To make it easy to transfer your audio or video files from one device to another, Blu-ray and DVD/CD players and recorders allow you to play all kinds of optical media. You can also record files onto high-definition media (such as Blu-ray discs) or onto DVDs and CDs instead of your hard drive.

c. **A network adapter:** A network adapter is a device that is installed in your computer and allows it to communicate with other devices on a network. (You'll learn more about network adapters in Chapter 7.) For digital devices to communicate with each other, they need to be connected to a network.

2. **A network:** Unless you're going to view digital and audio files only on your computer, you will need a network to transfer files easily to other devices (such as televisions) in your home. A wireless network has an advantage over a wired network because it is easier to relocate devices on a wireless network. (You'll learn all about wired and wireless networks in Chapter 7.)

3. **An Internet-ready digital television:** Newer plasma and organic light-emitting diode (OLED) televisions (see Figure 1.14) or high-definition TVs (HDTVs) are an important part of any digital home because they are the best way to show off all your digital media. Internet-ready televisions are featured in most companies' product lines now. These have network adapters built in and include software that allows you to access a limited number of Internet sites. Often YouTube is available, for example, as well as support for streaming videos using video-on-demand services from Netflix and Amazon.

4. **A universal remote:** A universal remote is a single remote control that works with any infrared-controlled device (such as your computer, amplifiers, receivers, and game consoles) and allows you to access media such as MP3 files no matter where in the house it is stored. Universal remotes such as the Pronto from Philips (see Figure 1.14) come with software that allows you to program your own custom interface for the remote. You can even program macros that perform multiple commands with the press of a button.

With these devices installed, you can get the maximum benefit from your computer and all your digital entertainment devices. When you're in your living room, you can play digital music files stored on your computer (in the den) for the party you're throwing. You can also display the video of your friend's birthday party (downloaded to your computer) on the TV for your friends to see. And when you're in your room, you can watch the latest episode of *CSI*, which you recorded on your computer's hard drive, while your sister is listening to MP3 files stored on your computer on the TV in the living room.

Web app or an online tutorial. Many public libraries have access to databases that store sample ASVAB questions and provide learning modules to guide you in your preparation for the exam. Knowing how to use all these tools will give you an advantage.

The U.S. military branches have some of the most highly technological projects ever developed. For example, the Air Force employs unmanned aerial vehicles, called *UAVs* or *drones*, to perform surveillance operations and to deliver missiles (see Figure 1.16).

Modern drones use complex video and guidance systems to do their work, all while the driver is in a remote location thousands of miles away. Recent software innovations such as the Gorgon Stare software package feeds 12 video screens of information—covering an area of 1.5 square miles—back to the "pilot" in Virginia. The pilot can decide to deliver Hellfire missiles and bombs to any section of that area. Models of drones that can take off and land on aircraft carriers are expected to be on the scene in the next few years. Maintaining and operating highly technological tools is part of military life for many soldiers.

Figure 1.16

Unmanned drones can be controlled remotely, even at distances of thousands of miles, by modern avionics systems.

Agriculture: High-Tech Down on the Farm

You might think that ranching and farming are low-tech operations that have little use for computers and software. The growing season can't be changed by any computer program! Even so, new technologies are changing life on farms and ranches in many ways.

Ranchers face many challenges in modern meat production. For example, they must watch for and prevent outbreaks of diseases such as hoof and mouth, mad cow, and *E. coli*. The meat you purchase can be introduced to these dangers at many different places in the processing chain from the ranch to the supermarket.

Fortunately, outbreaks can be managed and minimized with the use of **radio frequency identification tags (RFID tags)**. These RFID tags are small versions of the roadway electronic toll systems used in many states to collect tolls automatically as drivers pass through toll stations. Each tag looks like a tiny button and is attached to a cow's ear. It contains a microchip that holds a unique sequence of numbers used to identify that animal. When the cow walks past a panel reader, its location is automatically recorded and tracked in a database.

If a cow is identified as having a disease, all of its recorded movements can be checked in the database that stores the RFID information. It is then simple to identify the exact food lots where that and other animals ate. Using RFID tags, potential crises can be averted or at least better controlled.

In cranberry bogs, computer technology is being used in some interesting ways. For example, cranberry crops easily can be destroyed by frost. In the past, growers had to race to protect the bogs of berries on cold nights by turning on water pumps to surround the berries with water and keep them from freezing. Today, growers use a Web-based system that can automatically control the pumps. It analyzes information about the time, the temperature measured near the berries, watering schedules, rainfall, and wind conditions and then automatically turns the pumps around the bog fields on and off as needed.

Automotive Technology: Sensors and CPUs

An automotive technician is required to have knowledge of a range of tools—impact hammers, wrenches, pneumatic tools, lathes, and welding and flame cutting equipment. Individuals considering a career in automotive repair today require a sophisticated level of computer literacy as well (see Figure 1.17). Environmental trends and governmental regulation are driving auto manufacturers to develop vehicles that produce lower emissions as the push for more efficient cars and higher gas mileage continues.

These changes have increased the number of sensors and computer CPU (central processing unit) systems needed in a typical vehicle. The fuel injection and engine management systems possible today go far beyond what a simple carburetor can do. Several sensors measure everything from air pressure to air temperature, engine temperature, and throttle position, for example. The data from these sensors is then used to compute the precise amount of fuel to spray into the cylinders, resulting in less fuel waste and reduced pollution. The braking, transmission, and steering systems also are primarily controlled by computers and electronic components.

In 2010, Toyota issued a recall for more than 6 million cars as a response to consumer complaints of sudden acceleration. One suspect in the investigation was a malfunction of the ETCS-I, the electronic throttle control system module. The National Highway Traffic Safety Association (NHTSA) performed tests on the recalled cars but used a safety protocol for accelerators that was from 1973, before electronic throttles were introduced. The incident began a debate over how much electronics are controlling modern cars and what limits should be set in giving control of vehicles to electronic computer systems.

At the same time, consumers expect digital music systems, airbags, voice-controlled phones, and GPS navigation screens in their cars, so the number of computer subsystems may continue to grow. In addition to these driver-friendly features, the computers in today's cars even alert drivers when it's time to take the cars in for maintenance or repair.

As a result, automotive technicians must be able to update documentation through the Internet, use computer databases to learn about common problems and solutions, and use computer systems to interface with and run diagnostics on all the different automotive computer systems. The days of working on a car in the driveway with some screwdrivers and a socket wrench are fading quickly.

Medicine: Technologies of Today and Tomorrow

In some movies set in the distant future, humans interface with computers just by thinking and looking at a screen or monitor. Until recently, such scenes took place only in movies. But since 2006, companies such as BrainGate have been working to understand the human neural interface system. Using the BrainGate Neural Interface, a patient suffering from amyotrophic lateral sclerosis (ALS, which is also known as Lou Gehrig's disease), who no longer had any control of muscle movement, was able to control the movement of a robotic arm.

The BrainGate software translates his thoughts into commands to the robotic limb. The patient has had a tiny array of microelectrodes implanted in his brain (see Figure 1.18a). The computer equipment receiving data from his neural activity (see Figure 1.18b) identifies the impulses that the

brain associates with physical movement (of his arm, for example) and then translates the instructions into commands to the robot. Patient Stephen Heywood explained, "After being paralyzed for so long, it is almost impossible to describe the magical feeling of imagining a motion and having it occur."

In addition to being an integral part of many medical research projects, computers are helping doctors and nurses learn their trades. Training for physicians and nurses can be difficult even in the best of times. Often, the best way for medical students to learn is to experience a real emergency situation. The problem is that students are then confined to watching as the emergency unfolds and trained personnel care for patients. Students rarely get to train in real-life situations; when they do, a certain level of risk is involved.

Medical students now have access to better training opportunities thanks to a

Figure 1.17
These automotive technicians for BMW Sauber gather around their car before the start of the Malaysian Grand Prix. They need computer skills to run all of the electronic checks of automotive subsystems.

BITS AND BYTES
NASA Wants You ... to Learn

As you read this chapter, hundreds of satellites are orbiting the globe and taking wonderfully detailed pictures of Earth. Until recently, these photos weren't available to the general public. However, thanks to NASA (and U.S. taxpayer dollars) and some savvy software developers, an application called World Wind is now making some 10 trillion bytes of imagery available to you. Do you need a picture of Mount Fuji for your science project or an aerial picture of your house for your PowerPoint presentation? Just download the software from **learn.arc.nasa.gov**, and you're ready to go. You'll find several terrific learning applications here as well. *Virtual Lab* lets you pretend you have your own scanning electron microscope, and *Moonbase Alpha* is a game built off of the Unreal engine and is complete with 3D graphics, team play, and the ability to do in-play chatting. With a few clicks, you can have interactive learning resources that open the world to you.

Figure 1.18

(a) The BrainGate Neural Interface is implanted in the patient's brain. (b) A signal converter recognizes patterns and then translates them into commands to a robotic arm.

Figure 1.19

Patient simulators allow health care students to practice medical procedures without risk of injury or death to real patients.

computer technology called a **patient simulator** (see Figure 1.19). Patient simulators are life-sized, computer-controlled mannequins that can speak, breathe, and blink (their eyes respond to external stimuli). They have a pulse and a heartbeat, and they respond just like humans to procedures such as the administration of intravenous drugs.

Medical students can train on patient simulators and experience firsthand how a human would react to their treatments. The best thing about these "patients" is that if they "die," students can restart the computer simulation and try again. Even the U.S. military is using patient simulators to train medics to respond to terrorist attacks that involve chemical and biological agents.

Even more exciting than patient simulators is the work being done on modeling complete human biological systems. The Physiome Project began as the brainchild of

the Bioengineering Institute in Auckland, New Zealand. It now is a global **public domain** effort (not covered by copyright) in which bioengineers are creating realistic computer simulations of all systems and features of the human anatomy.

Although the Physiome Project's current system models a theoretical human's lungs, researchers hope to one day use computers to simulate a specific person's anatomical systems. With such a system, imaging scans (CTs, MRIs, etc.) of your body and a sample of your DNA would be fed into a computer, which would create an exact computer model of your body. This would allow doctors to experiment with different therapies to see how you would react to specific treatments. A great deal of work is still to be done before this refinement becomes a reality, and computer-literate medical professionals will be needed to make it happen.

In the operating room, computer literacy is now a must. Surgeons are even using computer-guided robots to perform surgery. Humans are limited by their manual dexterity and can have trouble making small, precise incisions. Robots can help. Robotic surgery devices can exercise much finer control than a human when making delicate incisions with a scalpel. To use the robots, doctors look into a surgery control device where they manipulate controls that move robotic devices hovering over the patient (see Figure 1.20). One robot control arm contains a slender imaging rod that allows the doctor to see inside the patient when the rod is inserted into the patient. Doctors can now perform a coronary bypass by making two small incisions in the patient and inserting the imaging rod in one incision and another robotic device with a scalpel into the other. The ability to make small incisions instead of the large ones required by conventional surgery means less trauma and blood loss for the patient. Theoretically, surgeons do not even have to be in the same room as the patient. They could be thousands of miles away, controlling the movements of the robotic devices from a control station.

Medicine: The Chip Within

When you mention implanting technology into the human body, some people conjure up images of the Terminator, a futuristic cybernetic life form from the movie *The Terminator*. But the more realistic goals of modern biomedical chip research are to provide technological solutions to physical problems and to provide a means for positively identifying individuals.

We are at a stage when biology and technology are fusing. Figure 1.21 shows a nerve cell grown on a silicon chip. The cell was cultured on the chip until it formed a network with nearby cells. The chip contains a transistor that stimulates the cell above it, which in turn passes the signal to neighboring neurons.

Figure 1.21

Researchers are experimenting with implantable chips such as this one to repair nerve damage and restore movement or sensation to parts of the body.

Figure 1.20

(a) A doctor manipulates controls that move the robotic instrument tips inside the patient. (b) This shows what surgeons might see as they operate on the patient.

Figure 1.22

The MIT eyeball chip is a retinal implant that may restore at least partial vision to certain groups of legally blind patients.

One potential application of biomedical chip implants is to provide sight to the blind. Macular degeneration and retinitis pigmentosa are two diseases that account for the majority of blindness in developing nations. Both diseases result in damage to photoreceptors in the retina. (Photoreceptors convert light energy into electrical energy that is transmitted to the brain, allowing us to see.) Researchers at the Massachusetts Institute of Technology (MIT) are experimenting with a microchip that would attach to the outside of the eye (see Figure 1.22), with human trials expected to begin in 2010. The chip would take over processing from damaged photoreceptors and transmit electrical images to the brain. Biomedical chips such as these exemplify the types of medical devices you may "see" in the future.

One type of chip is already being implanted in humans as a means of verifying a person's identity. Produced by Positive ID and called the *VeriChip*, this "personal ID chip" is about the size of a grain of rice and is implanted under the skin. When exposed to radio waves from a scanning device, the chip emits a signal that transmits its unique serial number to the scanner. The scanner then connects to a database that contains the name, address, and medical conditions of the person in whom the chip has been implanted.

The creators of the VeriChip envision it helping keep Alzheimer's patients safe and

Figure 1.23

No bigger than the period at the end of this sentence, the Hitachi μ-chip can hold digital information, which can then be read when it passes a detector.

being used with other devices (such as electronic ID cards) to provide tamperproof security measures. If someone stole your credit card, that person couldn't use it if a salesclerk had to verify your identity by scanning a chip in your arm before authorizing a transaction.

Currently, nonimplant versions of identity chips are used in hospitals. When chips are attached with bands to newborn infants, the hospital staff can monitor the location of any baby instantly. Elevators and doors are designed to allow only certain people to enter with a specific baby, even if the hospital power is interrupted. Although the use of these tags is becoming more commonplace, it remains to be seen whether people generally will decide that the advantages of having personal identity and medical data quickly available justifies having chips implanted into their bodies.

Hitachi has a similar device, called the μ-chip ("mu chip"), which is smaller than the period at the end of this sentence (see Figure 1.23). Those concerned with privacy issues worry because the μ-chip could be easily attached to, or ingested by, a person without his or her knowledge. On the other hand, researchers are excited by the possibility of using the μ-chip to monitor the safety of the food supply chain and how it might be mixed into paints to monitor heat and moisture conditions and be embedded in paper and plastics.

Science: Simulating Reality

Thanks to a partnership between the National Severe Storms Lab and the National Center for Supercomputing Applications, tornado forecasting may be getting more accurate (see Figure 1.24). Scientists have been able to create a model so detailed that it takes nine days for a supercomputer to generate it, even though the computer is executing 4 trillion operations each second. Simulations also can model the

Figure 1.24

Software that combines radar information in new ways increases the accuracy of tornado predictions and allows for earlier warning of threatened towns.

structure of solar magnetic flares, which can interfere with broadcasts on Earth. By studying the data produced by these simulations, forecasters hope to improve their predictions about weather phenomena.

Other technological applications in the sciences are being used on some of the oldest sites on Earth. The ancient site of Pompeii has been under the intense scrutiny of tourists and archaeologists for decades. Sadly, decades of foot traffic and hundreds of years of exposure to the elements have eroded portions of the ruins. Today, scientists are using three-dimensional scanners and imaging software to capture a detailed record of the current condition of the ruins (see Figure 1.25). The virtual re-creation of the ruins is so lifelike that archaeologists can study the ruins on screen instead of at the actual site. Using the scans as well as satellite imagery, aerial photography, and other data, scientists will eventually be able to re-create missing portions of the ruins in a virtual model. And scientists won't stop at Pompeii. This method will soon be used to make records of other decaying sites.

Sports Science: Compute Your Way to a Better Game

Want to be a world-class swimmer or baseball player? Getting an Olympic-caliber coach and training for hours every day are no longer enough. To get that competitive edge, you really need to use a computer.

That's right, computers are often used to help athletes analyze their performance and improve their game. How does this work? First, video recordings are made of the athlete in action. The video is then transferred into special motion-analysis software on a computer. This software measures the exact angles of the athlete's body parts as they progress through ranges of motion, such as the angle of a baseball player's left arm relative to his body as he swings the bat. Minor adjustments can be made on the computer regarding positioning of body parts and the force used in performing various movements. This helps baseball players, for example, enhance their performance by determining what adjustments they should make to hit the ball harder and farther.

The U.S. Olympic Training Center in Colorado uses computers extensively in training athletes such as swimmers. The major objective in training swimmers to swim faster is to reduce drag from the water and minimize turbulence, which also slows down a swimmer. Software has been developed that simulates the way water flows around the parts of a swimmer's body when in motion. Coaches can use the software to experiment with small changes in the position of a swimmer's arms or legs and determine whether turbulence and drag are reduced. The coaches can then train the swimmers to use the new techniques to improve their strokes and speed.

Aren't planning on competing in the next Olympics or playing in the major leagues? How about improving your weekend golf game? Employees in golf shops are now using sophisticated motion-capture equipment to improve golfers' swings. To have your golf swing analyzed, shop personnel hook you up

Figure 1.25

A digital re-creation of the ruins of Pompeii allows archaeologists to study the ruins without even being there, as well as re-create Pompeii as it looked before the devastation.

into shoulder, leg, and hip harnesses containing motion sensors. As you swing away at a variety of shots (drives, chips, and so on), computers capture information about the motion of your swing, comparing it to a database of the ideal positions of pro golfers (see Figure 1.26). Trainers then suggest adjustments you can make so that your swing more closely emulates that of successful golfers. Even weekend warriors can benefit from high-tech analysis.

Nanotechnology: Careers Yet to Come

Developments in computing based on the principles of nanoscience are being touted as the next big wave in computing. Ironically, this realm of science focuses on incredibly small objects. **Nanoscience** involves the study of molecules and structures (called *nanostructures*) that range in size from 1 to 100 nanometers. It will provide numerous career paths and high-tech positions over the next several decades.

The prefix *nano* stands for one billionth. Therefore, a nanometer is one billionth of a meter. To put this in perspective, a human hair is approximately 50,000 nanometers wide. Put side by side, 10 hydrogen atoms (the simplest atom) would measure approximately one nanometer. Anything smaller than a nanometer is just a stray atom or particle floating around in space. Therefore, nanostructures represent the smallest human-made structures that can be built.

Nanotechnology is the science of using nanostructures to build devices on an extremely small scale. Right now, nanoscience is limited to improving existing products, such as enhancing fibers used in clothing with coatings so that they repel stains, resist odors, or stop wrinkles. However, someday scientists hope to use nanostructures to build computing devices that will be too small to be seen by the naked eye. Nanowires (see Figure 1.27), which are extremely small conductors, could be used to create extremely small pathways in computer chips. Developments such as this could lead to computers the size of a pencil eraser that will be far more powerful than today's desktop computers.

Ever since the movie *Fantastic Voyage*, people have dreamt of *nanoprobes*, tiny machines that can be injected into the bloodstream. Nanotechnology researchers are now using carbon nanotubes to create devices that deliver medicine and information. We are still a long way from developing nanoscale machines. However,

Figure 1.26

(a) High Definition Golf does a complete analysis on your swing and projects the flight path the ball would have taken. (b) It can also simulate many popular golf courses, such as Pebble Beach.

Figure 1.27
Nanowires hold promise for use in constructing even smaller computing devices.

researchers are investigating the use of nanostructures to deliver precise doses of drugs on a molecule-by-molecule basis within the human bloodstream. Universities and government laboratories are investing billions of dollars in nanotechnology research every year. If you have the background and interest in computing technology and science, this is the time to pursue an education in nanoscience.

Psychology: You Should Smile . . . Now

Science fiction shows and movies such as *Transformers* have always been populated with robots that emulate humans, seemingly effortlessly. So, when will we have Bumblebee, C-3PO, or the Terminator laughing at our jokes or bringing us our favorite snack when they recognize we're sad? It is a question that pushes us to explore the nature of being human and the nature of machines.

Psychologists and computer scientists are jointly conducting research to develop computer systems that respond to human affect and emotional expression, as well as enable computer systems to develop social and emotional skills. **Affective computing** is computing that relates to emotion or deliberately tries to influence emotion. Most computers you are familiar with can perform calculations and do the tasks they are programmed for much faster than humans can, but they fail miserably in telling a good joke or modifying their behavior based on your frustration. This

wide gap in the computing abilities of computers versus their emotional abilities is the target of research in affective computing.

One project to emerge is the emotional-social prosthesis (ESP) device developed by a group at the MIT Media Lab. The ESP system is targeted at helping people who have autism. Autistic individuals can have extremely high intelligence but do not easily sense nonverbal cues such as facial expressions and tone of voice. ESP is a wearable system that isolates the movements and facial expressions of people, interprets what their mood and intention probably are, and communicates this information back to the user.

Another project at the Media Lab will help people who have difficulty maintaining focus on a specific task. This project centers on the creation of computer systems that can analyze a person's movements, watch how the person uses the mouse, and interpret the pressure patterns on the chair in which the person is seated. That data is used to determine the individual's level of attention. The computer could then interrupt an individual who is beginning to lose concentration and refocus him or her on a certain task.

While engineers work to create computers that can understand us emotionally, psychologists and computer scientists are also working to evolve systems toward a more human appearance (see Figure 1.28). Teams at the University of Michigan, Ohio State University, and the French Institute of Computer Science

Figure 1.28
Robots with articulated joints that mimic human limbs can balance, stand, walk, and even hug.

SOUND BYTE

The History of the Personal Computer

In this Sound Byte, you will explore the history of the personal computer, including the events that led to the development of today's computers and the people who made them possible.

What would your life be like if you had never touched a computer because you simply couldn't afford one? What if there were no computers in your town? By 2009, almost 75% of the United States had Internet access. But for those not served, and for many around the world, access to the opportunities and knowledge computers and the Internet offer is impossible. The discrepancy between the haves and have-nots with regard to computer technology is commonly referred to as the **digital divide**.

This discrepancy is a growing problem. People with access to computers and the Internet (that is, those who can afford them) are poised to take advantage of the many new developments technology offers, whereas poorer individuals, communities, and school systems that can't afford computer systems and Internet access are being left behind.

For example, in the United States, more teachers are using the Internet to communicate with parents than ever before. E-mail updates on student progress, Web sites with homework postings that allow parents to track assignments, and even online parent–teacher conferences are becoming popular. Unwired parents and students are left out of the loop. In the United States, children who do not have access to the Internet and computers won't be prepared for future employment, contributing to the continuing cycle of poverty.

But the digital divide isn't always caused by low income. Terrain can be a factor that inhibits connectivity (see Figure 1.29). In Nepal's mountainous terrain, for example, even though a village might only be a few miles away "as the crow flies," it might take two days to hike there because of the lack of roads.

Figure 1.29

Terrain such as this glacial lake and mountainous region in Nepal show that there can be barriers beyond income to conquering the digital divide.

Volunteers, funded by a generous donor, have installed 12 outdoor access points complete with directional antennas to connect a series of villages to the Internet via a wireless network. The last access point in the connectivity chain connects to an Internet service provider 22 miles away. The villagers are now able to hold meetings, attend school classes, and access the Internet without trekking across miles of mountainous terrain. Unfortunately, this solution isn't available throughout all of Nepal . . . or even throughout some areas of the United States.

What is being done to bridge the digital divide? Organizations worldwide are working to raise awareness and to increase government involvement. Groups are sponsoring referendums that increase Internet capacity in schools, for example, and are urging state legislatures to provide additional funding for technology to struggling school systems. Community organizations are rising to the challenge as libraries and recreation centers work to provide free Internet access to the public.

You can help directly by donating used computer equipment to nonprofit groups that refurbish computers. These organizations repair and upgrade retired systems before distributing the systems to needy families at low cost. The Web site Techsoup (**techsoup.org**) maintains national resource lists that can help you find such organizations in your area. Some technology companies have programs in place to help with these efforts. The Microsoft Authorized Refurbisher (MAR) program, for example, supports refurbishers by allowing certain Microsoft operating systems and Office software to be installed for free on refurbished systems.

Research are working on robots that move in a more human fashion. Their biped (two-legged) robot named Rabbit is able to walk, run, and climb stairs. It may lead to industrial robots that can tackle new tasks for us.

Understanding the Challenges Facing a Digital Society

Part of becoming computer literate is being able to understand and form knowledgeable opinions on the challenges that face a digital society. Although computers offer us a world of opportunities, they also pose ethical, legal, and moral challenges and questions. For example, how do you feel about the following?

- Since the tragic events of September 11, 2001, various nationwide surveillance programs have been proposed. Some programs include installing surveillance cameras in public places that could be considered attractive areas in which to stage terrorist activities. These cameras would be monitored via the Internet, possibly by volunteers. Should the government be allowed to monitor your activities in public places, à la George Orwell's famous book *1984,* to help keep the country secure?

- Advances in surveillance device technology (see Figure 1.30) are allowing these devices to become smaller and less noticeable. In certain jurisdictions, courts have upheld the rights of employers to install surveillance devices in the workplace (sometimes without needing to notify employees) to cut down on theft and prevent industrial espionage. And in 2009 a school district in suburban Philadelphia met with a lawsuit for possible wiretapping. School officials are alleged to have recorded images through student notebook webcams (the notebooks were provided by the school district) and used those images as evidence of illegal behavior by students in their own bedrooms. Do you know if someone is watching you?

- Many employees don't know that employers have the right to monitor e-mail and network traffic on the systems they use at work because those systems are provided at the employer's expense for the sole purpose of allowing employees to do their jobs. Have you visited Web sites that you don't want your employer to know about (such as employment sites as part of a new job search)? Have you sent personal e-mail through your company e-mail system? Does your employer know about these activities? Should employers have the right to know?

These are just a few examples of the kinds of questions active participants in today's digital society need to be able to think about, discuss, and, at times, take action on. Being computer literate enables you to form educated opinions on these issues and to take stands based on accurate information rather than media hype and misinformation. Here are a few other questions that you, as a member of our digital society, may be expected to think about and discuss:

- What privacy risks do biomedical chips such as the VeriChip pose? Do the privacy risks of

such chips outweigh the potential benefits?

- Should companies be allowed to collect personal data from visitors to their Web sites without their permission?

- Should school officials be allowed to use webcams to watch students while on school grounds or attending school events? What about when students are at home?

- Should spam be illegal? If so, what penalties should be levied on people who send spam?

- Is it ethical to download music off the Web without paying for it (see Figure 1.31)? How about downloading a newly released movie using a torrent? What about copying a friend's software onto your computer?

- What are the risks involved in humans attempting to create computers that can learn and become more human?

- Should we rely solely on computers to provide security for sensitive areas such as nuclear power plants?

As a computer user, you must consider these and other questions to define the boundaries of the digital society in which you live.

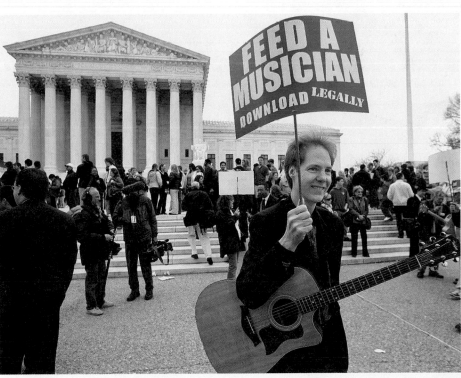

Figure 1.30

Should the government be allowed to install microcameras without your knowledge?

Figure 1.31

Does downloading music without paying for it hurt anyone? Or is it merely a cost absorbed by huge record companies? How will your choices create the music market you will experience in the future?

one summary

1. What does it mean to be "computer literate"?

Computer literacy goes beyond knowing how to use a mouse and send e-mail. If you are computer literate, you understand the capabilities and limitations of computers and know how to use them wisely. Being computer literate also enables you to make informed purchasing decisions, use computers in your career, and understand the many ethical, legal, and societal implications of technology today. Anyone can become computer literate.

2. How does being computer literate make you a savvy computer user and consumer?

By understanding how a computer is constructed and how its various parts function, you'll be able to get the most out of your computer. Among other things, you'll be able to avoid hackers, viruses, and Internet headaches; protect your privacy; and separate the real risks of privacy and security from those you don't have to worry about. You'll also be better able to maintain, upgrade, and troubleshoot your computer; make good purchasing decisions; and incorporate the latest technologies into your existing equipment.

3. How can becoming computer literate help you in a career?

As computers become more a part of our daily lives, it is difficult to imagine any career that does not use computers in some fashion. Understanding how to use computers effectively will help you be a more productive and valuable employee, no matter which profession you choose.

4. How can becoming computer literate help you understand and take advantage of newly emerging careers?

In today's world, many changes are a result of new computer technologies. Understanding how today's computers function should help you utilize technology effectively now. And by understanding computers and how they work today, you can contribute to the technologies of tomorrow such as nanoscience and new medical technologies.

5. How does becoming computer literate help you deal with the challenges associated with technology?

Although computers offer us great opportunities, they also pose ethical, legal, and moral challenges and questions. Being computer literate enables you to form educated opinions on these issues and to take stands based on accurate information rather than media hype and misinformation.

one key terms

key terms

buzzwords

Word Bank

- affective computing
- Bluetooth technology
- computer forensics
- computer literate
- data mining
- digital divide

- digital home
- information technology (IT)
- nanoscience
- nanotechnology
- offshoring

- patient simulator
- public domain
- radio frequency identification tags (RFID tags)
- software
- spam

Instructions: Fill in the blanks using the words from the Word Bank above.

Becoming computer literate is necessary in modern life and helps with just about any career path you can imagine. (1) _____, the study of incredibly small computing devices built at the molecular level, is one field that is expanding and offers great potential but requires computer literacy. (2) _____ uses an understanding of computer systems to take criminologists beyond what they could accomplish with conventional investigation techniques. And as the science of (3) _____ advances, computers will perform more and more like human beings in emotion and social cueing.

There are many advantages to becoming (4) _____, that is, understanding more about the capabilities and limitations of computers. Doing so can help you manage computer annoyances like unwanted e-mails, which are called (5) _____. You will also know how to upgrade your system to the latest standards such as wireless (6) _____.

More and more aspects of how our homes are run are being coordinated through computers, giving rise to the term (7) _____. You may even find you enjoy computers so much you want to explore careers in (8) _____.

Be forewarned—people who fail to keep up with the knowledge of how to use and maintain computer systems will fall to one side of the gap known as the (9) _____. When an entire country begins to fall behind in computer expertise, jobs are relocated to other, more tech-savvy countries. This shift of work is known as (10) _____.

becoming computer literate

Using the key terms and ideas you learned in this chapter, write a one- or two-paragraph summary for your school adviser so that he or she can use it to explain to students the importance of being computer literate in today's job market. Using the Internet, find additional examples of careers most people would not expect to require computer knowledge and show how computer literacy is still critical to success in those careers. Add these examples to your document to support your position.

Instructions: Answer the multiple-choice and true–false questions below for more practice with key terms and concepts from this chapter.

Multiple Choice

1. Which is *not* a current use of computers in the military?
   a. Using RFID tags to avert potential crises like *E. coli* epidemics
   b. Studying for the standardized exam for enlisting
   c. Navigating unmanned aerial vehicles remotely
   d. Coordinating communications across wired and wireless networks

2. Artists interface with technology often, but cannot yet
   a. use computers to generate images that respond to the environment.
   b. use computers to create a virtual storefront.
   c. use software to suggest plot endings.
   d. use software to create and enhance virtual performances.

3. People who do not read emotion easily in others hope for new progress in the field of
   a. affective computing.
   b. nanotechnology.
   c. patient simulators.
   d. forensic science.

4. A necessary ingredient for a digital home is a
   a. network.
   b. videocassette recorder.
   c. radio tuner.
   d. smartboard.

5. Automotive technology requires an understanding of computers to
   a. properly bill customers.
   b. control computerized pneumatic tools.
   c. keep carburetor settings at optimal positions.

   d. run sensors and CPU diagnostics for a vehicle's many computerized subsystems.

6. A device that tracks movement is
   a. a PSS.
   b. an RFID tag.
   c. an MP3 device.
   d. a patient simulator.

7. Computer forensics uses computer systems and technology to
   a. simulate a person's anatomical system.
   b. train law enforcement officers to be more effective.
   c. improve fuel injection and engine management systems.
   d. gather potential legal evidence.

8. IT is the abbreviation for
   a. information training.
   b. Internet training.
   c. Internet technology.
   d. information technology.

9. Which allows retailers to respond to consumer buying patterns?
   a. RFID tags
   b. Data mining
   c. Smart labels
   d. Bluetooth technology

10. Robotic surgery devices help physicians because
    a. they make incisions that are more accurate.
    b. the doctor does not have to be involved in the surgery.
    c. they monitor and make suggestions to the surgeon during the procedure.
    d. if the operation runs into complications, they can suggest creative alternatives.

True–false

_____ 1. Researchers believe that microchips may one day restore sight to the blind.

_____ 2. Anyone can become computer literate—no matter what their degree of technical expertise.

_____ 3. Supercomputers can accurately forecast tornadoes within minutes.

_____ 4. Criminal investigators may find evidence on a computer, but that evidence cannot be used in court.

_____ 5. Many modern museums offer WiFi networks and multimedia downloads to their patrons to enrich their experience.

1. **Computer Literacy**

   In your college career, you'll be spending time understanding the requirements of the degree program you choose. At many schools, computer literacy requirements exist either as incoming requirements (skills students must have before they are admitted) or outgoing requirements (skills students must prove they have before graduating). Does your program require specific computer skills? Which skills are these? Should they be required? How can students efficiently prove that they have these skills? How often does the set of skills need to be reviewed and updated?

2. **Does Size Matter?**

   Think about your typical school schedule. What type of computing solution would best support your needs—a desktop computer, a notebook, or a netbook? Think about the level of computing power required by your courses. Will any course require you to use a specialty software product such as a nutrition monitoring program or a statistics training application? Or do you just need word processing capabilities and Internet connectivity? How much does portability matter, and do you need a larger-than-usual screen? How many years do you expect to be able to use the computer you purchase today?

3. **Old Technologies Holding On**

   What courses and careers have not felt the impact of computer technology? Think of three courses that are taught effectively with no use of technology. Think of three careers that do not use computers in a significant way. Research and find the average salary and the rate of growth in these careers.

4. **Digital Dorm**

   What features of a digital home would make living in your dorm room more productive? Do you already have access to high-speed Internet? Do you have wireless access? Do you have a way to time-shift television and audio programming using a digital media recorder? Do you have remote control of your lights and dorm room fridge? What about being able to monitor the status of your laundry in the basement washer and dryer using your cell phone? Identify three additional tools that could be added to dorm life that would be popular and useful for you or your fellow students.

5. **Military Computing**

   In this chapter, we discussed the use of high-level technology in the U.S. military. Review the computer science programs at the U.S. Air Force Academy, the U.S. Military Academy at West Point, and the U.S. Naval Academy. What specific courses or paths of study do these institutions have that are specific to military settings? What information do the department Web sites provide on why an understanding of computers matters to the military? How would this training support a transition from a military career to the civilian workplace?

making the transition to... the workplace

making the transition to ... the workplace

1. **The Productivity Paradox**

   In this chapter, we highlighted several careers that require computer skills. With all of the advancements in computing technology, you might expect to see a great rise in workforce productivity, yet statistics since 2004 report a decline in productivity. How is this possible? Do you think it applies in the profession you are in or plan to enter? Can you think of reasons in which the increased use of computers would decrease productivity? How has the shift toward more technology in your personal life impacted you? Are you more or less productive there? How do computers affect creativity?

2. **Patients and Medical Computing**

   There are some major changes in the flow of medical information that impact patients every day. As more hospitals and doctor's offices begin to use electronic medical records (EMRs), the flow of information among the different doctors and care facilities a patient uses could become much more reliable. In their training and work, doctors and nurses rely on computers. What about patients? Examine Google Health at **health.google.com** for an example of an electronic medical history. How does this migration from a traditional paper records system impact the skills required for medical office workers? New ethical questions also often arise when technology changes. How would a medical facility now protect and verify its data records? What risks are there with a product like Google Health?

3. **Computer Literacy at Work**

   Computer literacy is a requirement in most professions today. Based on your course of study, identify two potential jobs (using resources such as **Monster.com**) that you would consider applying for after graduation. Research these professions and determine what the computer literacy requirements are for these types of jobs. How would you go about proving to a potential employer that you possess the requisite skill set?

4. **Using Video in Your Business**

   With the widespread use of video on the Web, many companies find it essential to have an online video presence to generate interest in their products. Review a few of the "Will It Blend?" videos produced by Blendtec (**blendtec.com/willitblend**). These simple videos became cult hits on YouTube and remarkably increased Blendtec's sales of its high-end blenders. Assume you are working for a company that makes graphic T-shirts. What types of videos could you deploy that would increase awareness of your shirts? If you worked for a local restaurant and bar, what types of videos would draw customers to your business?

5. **Social Media Careers**

   With the explosion of users on social media sites, businesses need to establish their presence on social media sites. Just search for "Vans" or "Subway" on Facebook for examples of company sites. To manage their interaction with customers (and fans), companies need to hire social media managers. Using a job site such as **Monster.com**, search on social media manager and review the job postings. What are the educational requirements for social media managers? What technical skills do these jobs require? Given your major, what companies would you do well for as a social media manager? What steps should you take while in school to prepare yourself for a career as a social media manager?

6. **Portfolio of Electronic Skills**

   Job seekers want to highlight their skills for prospective employers—show employers both what they can do right now to contribute and provide evidence that they can learn quickly and grow into new technologies and new responsibilities. What skills could you place in a portfolio to demonstrate your current mastery of computer concepts and computer applications? How would you document for your employer your ability to learn, quickly adapt to changes in technology, and acquire new skills?

Instructions: Albert Einstein used *Gedankenexperiments*, or critical thinking questions, to develop his theory of relativity. Some ideas are best understood by experimenting with them in our own minds. The following critical thinking questions are designed to demand your full attention but require only a comfortable chair—no technology.

1. Your Own IT Department

This chapter lists many ways in which knowing about computers (or becoming computer literate) is beneficial. Imagine that you are self-employed—you've started a business out of your home. What areas of computing would be most important for you to understand? How would you decide when to pay for support and when you could handle the problem yourself? How would an understanding of computer hardware and software help in establishing and marketing your new business?

2. Interactive Art

This chapter briefly discusses the integration of computer technology and art. Pieces like Flight Time at the Museum of Modern Art use the vast amounts of data around us to create images and interactive exhibits that are visually exciting. What kind of design can you envision that brings the data around us into an interactive, visual experience of beauty? What computer skills would you need to acquire to make that a reality?

3. Perception of Truth

As you learned in the chapter, computer simulations are incredibly sophisticated tools. Given that the public knows that images and videos can be easily edited digitally, what role do you think simulations will play in the legal system? What impact would a simulation, a video, or an image have on a jury in deciding "truth" when the public knows that these items can be manipulated digitally? Perception plays a role in the integration of computers to other arenas as well. How do you think public perception of computers impacts a patient's decision to use a digital "surgeon" like the da Vinci robotic surgery system?

4. . . . and Bandwidth for All

In 2010, Google announced it would select a group of communities in the United States to create an experimental fiber-optic network providing Internet connection speeds of 1 Gb/s, about 300 times the average broadband service. How would that kind of access change the way you live? How would it change the community in which you live? What new applications would be possible? Are there disadvantages you can identify?

5. Affective Computing

Affective computing is the science that attempts to produce machines that understand and can respond to human emotions and social mores. Do you think humans will ever create a machine that cannot be distinguished from a human being? In your opinion, what are the ethical and moral implications associated with that development?

6. The World Stage

How might access to (or denial of) electronic information improve the education of a country's citizens? Could that affect who the world's next technology power will be? Could it eliminate third world status? Examine the ideas behind the Next Einstein from Africa project at **nexteinstein.org** to explore this further. What consequence might developments in Africa have on you, your family, and your experiences?

team time

Promoting Future Technologies

Problem

People are often overwhelmed by how quickly technology changes and by how frustrating it can be not to know how to use it easily. In response, some people react by using only the minimum technology they need. In this Team Time, we consider how that reaction might limit the options available in a career path and what strategies might assist someone in becoming more comfortable with the pace of technological change.

Task

Talk to the members of your group and find out what each person is most passionate about—a hobby, a field of study, or some other personal interest. Your mission is to investigate technological tools that would be useful in developing that area of passion and interest into a career.

Process

Divide the class into three or more teams.

1. With the other members of your team, use the Internet to research up-and-coming technologies that would support your interests. Do people use social media tools to connect into groups to exchange ideas? What computer hardware would let you turn your hobby into a marketable product? What software programs would you need to pursue turning your interest into a professional career? Prepare a list of skills, tools, and experiences that would prepare you with the technological training to succeed.
2. Present your group's findings to the class for debate and discussion. How many of these skills do you have under your belt already? What access do you need to learn the rest? What new tools will appear in the next four years that you may need to know after graduation?
3. Write a strategy paper that details how you plan to make sure you have the computer skills and exposure to put you in a strong position to start your career. Note any barriers you may have to overcome—for example, finding access to the software programs, getting enough time on specialized equipment, or finding the right training.

Conclusion

The future of technology is unknown, but we do know that the career options available in four years will include many job paths that don't even exist today. To be prepared to take advantage of the opportunities that technology will bring, no matter what area you are interested in pursuing, will take good planning and attention. Begin now—learn how to stay on top of technology.

In this exercise, you will research and then role-play a complicated ethical situation. The role you play might or might not match your own personal beliefs; regardless, your research and use of logic will enable you to represent the view assigned. An arbitrator will watch and comment on both sides of the arguments, and together team members will agree on an ethical solution.

Topic: Digital Rights Management

Digital entertainment downloads are here to stay: iTunes alone has surpassed 1 billion downloads. Books, movies, and television shows are all delivered electronically to consumers. But these industries and consumers still wrestle with the ethical conduct they can expect of each other. Some recording companies support their artists in releasing free song downloads to publicize an album; others refuse. Some consumers feel they serve the recording company by spreading a start-up band's music, but sometimes companies push for criminal and civil charges against such action.

Digital rights management (DRM) policies are in place now to try to clarify what conduct is and is not criminal. DRM varies from product to product and item to item. For example, you might pay one price for a song on iTunes and get the rights to put the song on only five computers—or you might pay another price and be able to put the song anywhere. And while negotiating all of these rights policies, the consumer still has access to many ways to illegally obtain unrestricted use of the same materials.

Research Areas to Consider

- Electronic Arts' DRM policy for the Will Wright video game *Spore*
- Legal and illegal torrents
- Electronic Frontier Foundation
- Amazon Kindle and text-to-speech feature

Process

Divide the class into teams.

1. Research the areas cited above and devise a scenario in which someone has violated DRM rules.
2. Team members should write a summary that provides background information for their character—for example: artist/creator, consumer, or arbiter—and details their character's behaviors to set the stage for the role-playing event. Then team members should create an outline to use during the role-playing event.
3. Team members should arrange a mutually convenient time to meet for the exchange, using either the chat room feature of MyITLab or the discussion board feature of Blackboard or by meeting in person.
4. Team members should present their case to the class or submit a PowerPoint presentation for review by the rest of the class, along with the summary and resolution they developed.

Conclusion

As technology becomes ever more prevalent and integrated into our lives, more and more ethical dilemmas will present themselves. Being able to understand and evaluate both sides of the argument, while responding in a personally or socially ethical manner, will be an important skill.

The History of the PC

Do you ever wonder how big the first personal computer was, or how much the first portable computer weighed? Computers are such an integral part of our lives that we don't often stop to think about how far they've come or where they got their start. In just 35 years, computers have evolved from expensive, huge machines that only corporations owned to small, powerful devices found in millions of homes. In this Technology in Focus feature, we look at the history of the computer. Along the way, we will discuss some developments that helped make the computer powerful and portable, as well as some people who contributed to its development. However, we will start with the story of the personal computer and how it grew to be as integral to our lives as the automobile is.

The First Personal Computer: The Altair

Our journey through the history of the personal computer starts in 1975. At that time, most people were unfamiliar with the mainframes and supercomputers that large corporations and the government owned. With price tags exceeding the cost of buildings, and with few if any practical home uses, these monster machines were not appealing or attainable to the vast majority of Americans. That began to change when the January 1975 cover of *Popular Electronics* announced the debut of the **Altair 8800**, touted as the first personal computer (see Figure 1). For just $395 for a do-it-yourself kit or $498 for a fully assembled unit (about $2,000 in today's dollars), the price was reasonable enough that computer fanatics could finally own their own computers.

The Altair was a very primitive computer, with just 256 bytes (not *kilo* bytes, just bytes) of memory. It didn't come with a keyboard, nor did it include a monitor or printer. Switches on the front of the machine were used to enter data in machine code (strings of 1s and 0s). Flashing lights on the front indicated the results of a program. User-friendly it was not—at least by today's standards.

Despite its limitations, computer "hackers" (as computer enthusiasts were called then) flocked to the machine. Many people who bought the Altair had been taught to program, but until that point, they had access only to big, clumsy computers. These people were often hired by corporations to program routine financial, statistical, or engineering programs in a workplace environment. The Altair offered these enthusiasts the opportunity to create their own programs. Within three months, Micro Instrumentation and Telemetry Systems (MITS), the company behind the Altair, received more than 4,000 orders for the machine.

The release of the Altair marked the start of the personal computer (PC) boom. In fact, two men who would play large roles in the development of the PC were among the first Altair owners. Recent high school graduates Bill Gates and Paul Allen were so enamored by this "minicomputer," as these personal computers were called at the time, that they wrote a compiling program

Why Was It Called the "Altair"?

For lack of a better name, the Altair's developers originally called the computer the PE-8, short for Popular Electronics 8-bit. However, Les Soloman, the *Popular Electronics* writer who introduced the Altair, wanted the machine to have a catchier name. The author's daughter, who was watching *Star Trek* at the time, suggested the name Altair. (That's where the *Star Trek* crew was traveling that week.) The first star of the PC industry was born.

Figure 1

In 1975, the Altair was touted as the "world's first minicomputer" in the January issue of Popular Electronics.

(a program that translates user commands into commands that the computer can understand) for the Altair. The two friends later convinced the Altair's developer, Ed Roberts, to buy their program. This marked the start of a small company called Microsoft. We'll get to that story later. First, let's see what their future archrivals were up to.

The Apple I and II

Around the time the Altair was released, **Steve Wozniak**, an employee at Hewlett-Packard, was becoming fascinated with the burgeoning personal computer industry and was dabbling with his own computer design. He would bring his computer prototypes to meetings of the Homebrew Computing Club, a group of young

Figure 2 *Steve Jobs (a) and Steve Wozniak (b) were two computer hobbyists who worked together to form the Apple Computer Company.*

Figure 3 *The first Apple computer, the Apple I, looked like a typewriter in a box. It was one of the first computers to incorporate a keyboard.*

computer fans in Palo Alto, California who met to discuss computer ideas. **Steve Jobs**, who was working for computer game manufacturer Atari at the time, liked Wozniak's prototypes and made a few suggestions. Together, the two built a personal computer, later known as the **Apple I**, in Wozniak's garage (see Figures 2 and 3). In that same year, on April 1, 1976, Jobs and Wozniak officially formed the **Apple Computer Company**.

No sooner had the Apple I hit the market than Wozniak began working to improve it. A year later, in 1977, the **Apple II** was born (see Figure 4). The Apple II included a color monitor, sound, and game paddles. Priced around $1,300 (almost $4,700 in today's dollars), it included 4 kilobytes (KB) of random access memory (RAM) as well as an optional floppy disk drive that enabled users to run additional programs. Most of these programs were games. However, for many users, there was a special appeal to the Apple II: The program that made the computer function when the power was first turned on (the operating system) was stored in read-only memory (ROM).

Figure 4 *The Apple II came with a monitor and an external floppy disk drive.*

Previously, the operating system had to be rewritten every time the computer was turned on The friendly features of the operating system on the Apple II, such as automatic loading, encouraged less technically oriented computer enthusiasts to try writing their own software programs.

An instant success, the Apple II would be the most successful product in the company's early line, outshining even its successor, the **Apple III**, which was released in 1980. Eventually, the Apple II would include a spreadsheet program, a word processor, and desktop publishing software. These programs gave personal computers like the Apple functions beyond gaming and special programming, and led to their increased popularity. We will talk more about these advances later. For now, we will look at which other players were entering the market.

Enter the Competition

Around the time that Apple was experiencing success with its computers, a number of competitors entered the market. The largest among them were Commodore, RadioShack, and IBM. As Figure 5 shows, just a few years after the introduction of the Altair, the market was filled with personal computers from a variety of manufacturers.

The Commodore PET and TRS-80

Among Apple's strongest competitors were the **Commodore PET 2001**, shown in Figure 6, and Tandy RadioShack's **TRS-80**, shown in Figure 7. Commodore introduced the PET in January 1977. It was featured on the cover of *Popular Science* in October 1977 as the "new $595 home computer." Tandy RadioShack's home computer also garnered immediate popularity. Just one month after its release in 1977, the TRS-80 Model 1 had sold approximately 10,000 units. Priced at $594.95, the easy-to-use machine included a monochrome display and 4 KB of memory. Many other manufacturers followed suit over the next decade, launching new desktop computers, but none were as successful as the TRS-80 and the Commodore.

The Osborne

The Osborne Company introduced the industry's first portable computer, the **Osborne**, in April 1981 (see Figure 8). Although portable, the computer weighed 24.5 pounds, and its screen was just five inches wide. In addition to its hefty weight, it came with a hefty price tag of $1,795. Still, the Osborne included 64 KB of memory, two floppy disk drives, and preinstalled programs such as word processing and spreadsheet software. The Osborne was an overnight success, and its sales quickly reached 10,000 units per month. Despite the Osborne's popularity, the

Why Is It Called "Apple"?

Steve Jobs wanted Apple Computer to be the "perfect" computer company. Having recently worked at an apple orchard, Jobs thought of the apple as the "perfect" fruit because it was high in nutrients, came in a nice package, and was not easily damaged. Thus, he and Wozniak decided to name their new computer company Apple.

Figure 5
Personal Computer Development

YEAR	APPLE	IBM	OTHER
1975			MITS Altair
1976	Apple I		
1977	Apple II		Tandy RadioShack's TRS-80 Commodore PET
1980	Apple III		
1981		IBM PC	Osborne
1983	Lisa		
1984	Macintosh	286-AT	IBM PC clones

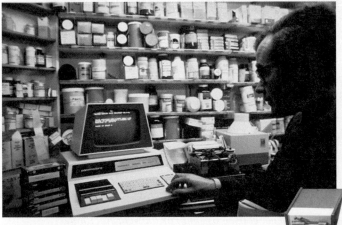

Figure 6 *The Commodore PET was well received because of its all-in-one design.*

Figure 7 *The TRS-80 hid its circuitry under the keyboard. The computer was nicknamed "trash-80," which was more a play on its initials than a reflection of its capabilities.*

Photo Courtesy of The Computer History Museum

release of a successor machine, called the **Executive**, reduced sales of the Osborne significantly, and the Osborne Company eventually closed. Compaq bought the Osborne design and in 1983 produced its first portable computer.

IBM PCs

By 1980, IBM recognized that it needed to get its feet wet in the personal computer market. Up until that point, the company had been a player in the computer industry, but primarily made mainframe computers, which it sold only to large corporations. It had not taken the smaller personal computer seriously. In August 1981, however, IBM released its first personal computer, appropriately named the **IBM PC**. Because many companies were already familiar with IBM mainframes, they readily adopted the IBM PC. The term *PC* soon became

Photo Courtesy of The Computer History Museum

Figure 8 *The Osborne was introduced as the first portable personal computer. It weighed a whopping 24.5 pounds and contained just 64 KB of memory.*

the term used to describe all personal computers.

The IBM PC came with 64 KB of memory, expandable to 256 KB, and prices started at $1,565. IBM marketed its PC through retail outlets such as Sears and Computerland in order to reach the home market, and it quickly dominated the playing field. In January 1983, *Time* magazine, playing on its annual "man of the year" issue, named the computer "1982 machine of the year" (see Figure 9).

Other Important Advancements

It was not just the **hardware** of the personal computer that was developing during the 1970s and 1980s. At the same time, advances in programming languages and operating systems and the influx of application software were leading to more useful and powerful machines.

Figure 9 *The IBM PC was the first (and only) nonhuman object chosen as "man of the year" (actually, "machine of the year") by* Time *magazine. This designation, in Time's January 1983 issue, indicated the impact the PC was having on the general public.*

The Importance of BASIC

The software industry began in the 1950s with the development of programming languages such as FORTRAN, ALGOL, and COBOL. These languages were used mainly by businesses to create financial, statistical, and engineering programs for corporate enterprises. However, the 1964 introduction of **Beginners All-Purpose Symbolic Instruction Code (BASIC)** revolutionized the software industry. BASIC was a programming language that the beginning programming student could easily learn. It thus became enormously popular—and the key language of the PC. In fact, **Bill Gates** and **Paul Allen** (see Figure 10) used BASIC to write their program for the Altair. As we noted earlier, this program led to the creation of **Microsoft**, a company that produced software for the microcomputer.

Figure 10 *Bill Gates and Paul Allen are the founders of Microsoft.*

The Advent of Operating Systems

Because data on the earliest personal computers was stored on audiocassettes (not floppy disks), many programs were not saved or reused. Rather, programs were rewritten as needed. Eventually Steve Wozniak designed a smaller 5.25-inch-floppy disk drive subsystem, called the **Disk II**, which was introduced in July 1978. With the introduction of the floppy drive, programs could be saved with more efficiency, and operating systems (OSs) developed.

Operating systems were (and still are) written to coordinate with the specific processor chip that controlled the computer. Apples ran exclusively on a Motorola chip, while PCs (IBMs and so on) ran exclusively on an Intel chip. **Disk Operating System (DOS)**, developed by Wozniak and introduced in December 1977, was the OS that controlled the first Apple computers. The **Control Program for Microcomputers (CP/M)**, developed by Gary Kildall, was the first OS designed for the Intel 8080 chip (the processor for PCs). Intel hired Kildall to write a compiling program for the 8080 chip, but Kildall quickly saw the need for a program that could store computer operating instructions on a floppy disk rather than on a cassette. Intel wasn't interested in buying the CP/M program, but Kildall saw a future for the program and thus founded his own company, Digital Research.

In 1980, when IBM was considering entering the personal computer market, it approached Bill Gates at Microsoft to write an OS program for the IBM PC. Although Gates had written versions of BASIC for different computer systems, he had never written an OS. He therefore recommended that IBM investigate the CP/M OS, but they could not arrange a meeting with the founder, Gary Kildall. Microsoft reconsidered the opportunity and developed **MS-DOS** for IBM computers. (This was one meeting that Digital Research certainly regretted not arranging.)

MS-DOS was based on an OS called **Quick and Dirty Operating System (QDOS)** that was developed by Seattle Computer Products. Microsoft bought the nonexclusive rights to QDOS and distributed it to IBM. Eventually, virtually all personal computers running on the Intel chip used MS-DOS as their OS. Microsoft's reign as one of the dominant players in the PC landscape had begun. Meanwhile, many other programs were being developed, taking personal computers to the next level of user acceptance.

The Software Application Explosion: VisiCalc and Beyond

Inclusion of floppy disk drives in personal computers not only facilitated the storage of operating systems, but also set off an application software explosion, because the floppy disk was a convenient way to distribute software. Around that same time, in 1978, Harvard Business School student Dan Bricklin recognized the potential for a spreadsheet program that could be used on PCs. He and his friend Bob Frankston (see Figure 11) created the program **VisiCalc**. VisiCalc not only became an instant success, but was also one of the main reasons for the rapid increase in PC sales. Finally, ordinary home users could see how owning a personal computer could benefit their lives. More than 100,000 copies of VisiCalc were sold in its first year.

Figure 11 *Bob Frankston and Dan Bricklin created VisiCalc, the first business application developed for the personal computer.*

After VisiCalc, other electronic spreadsheet programs entered the market. **Lotus 1-2-3** came on the market in January 1983, and **Microsoft Excel** entered the scene in 1985. These two products became so popular that they eventually put VisiCalc out of business.

Meanwhile, word processing software was gaining a foothold in the PC industry. Up to this point, there were separate, dedicated word processing machines, and the thought hadn't occurred to anyone to enable the personal computer to do word processing. Personal computers, it was believed, were for computation and data management. However, once **WordStar**, the first word processing application, came out in disk form in 1979 and became available for personal computers, word processing became another important use for the PC. In fact, word processing is now one of the most common PC applications. Competitors such as **Word for MS-DOS** (the precursor to Microsoft Word) and **WordPerfect** soon entered the market. Figure 12 lists some of the important dates in application software development.

The Graphical User Interface

Another important advancement in personal computers was the introduction of the **graphical user interface (GUI)**, which allowed users to interact with the computer more easily. Until that time, users had to use complicated command- or menu-driven interfaces to interact with the computer. Apple was the first company to take full commercial advantage of the GUI, but competitors were fast on its heels, and soon the GUI became synonymous with personal computers. Who developed the idea of the GUI?

You'll probably be surprised to learn that a company known for its photocopiers was the real innovator.

Xerox

In 1972, a few years before Apple launched its first PC, photocopier manufacturer **Xerox** was hard at work in its Palo Alto Research Center (PARC) designing a personal computer of its own. Named the **Alto** (shown in Figure 13), the computer included a word processor, based on the What You See Is What You Get (WYSIWYG) principle, that incorporated a file management system with directories and folders. It also had a mouse and could connect to a network. None of the other personal computers of the time had any of these features. For a variety of reasons, Xerox never sold the Alto commercially. Several years later, it developed the Star Office System, which was based on the Alto. Despite its convenient features, the Star never became popular, because no one was willing to pay the $17,000 asking price.

The Lisa and the Macintosh

Xerox's ideas were ahead of its time, but many of the ideas of the Alto and Star would soon catch on. In 1983, Apple introduced the **Lisa**,

Figure 12	*Application Software Development*
YEAR	**APPLICATION**
1978	**VisiCalc:** First electronic spreadsheet application. **WordStar:** First word processing application.
1980	**WordPerfect:** Thought even now to be the best word processing software for the PC, WordPerfect was eventually sold to Novell, and was later acquired by Corel.
1983	**Lotus 1-2-3:** Added integrated charting, plotting, and database capabilities to spreadsheet software. **Word for MS-DOS:** Introduced in the pages of *PC World* magazine on the first magazine-inserted demo disk.
1985	**Excel:** One of the first spreadsheets to use a graphical user interface. **PageMaker:** The first desktop publishing software.

Figure 13 *The Alto was the first computer to use a graphical user interface, and it provided the basis for the GUI that Apple used. However, because of marketing problems, the Alto never was sold.*

Photo Courtesy of The Computer History Museum

Figure 14 *The Lisa was the first computer to introduce a GUI to the market. Priced too high, it never gained the popularity it deserved.*

shown in Figure 14. Named after Apple founder Steve Jobs's daughter, the Lisa was the first successful PC brought to market that used a GUI. Legend has it that Jobs had seen the Alto during a visit to PARC in 1979 and was influenced by its GUI. He therefore incorporated a similar user interface into the Lisa, providing features such as windows, drop-down menus, icons, a hierarchical file system with folders and files, and a point-and-click device called a mouse. The only problem with the Lisa was its price. At $9,995 ($21,530 in today's dollars), few buyers were willing to take the plunge.

A year later, in 1984, Apple introduced the **Macintosh**, shown in Figure 15. The Macintosh was everything the Lisa was and then some, and at about a third of the cost. The Macintosh was also the first personal computer to utilize 3.5-inch floppy disks with a hard cover, which were smaller and sturdier than the previous 5.25-inch floppies.

The Internet Boom

The GUI made it easier for users to work on the computer. The Internet provided another reason for consumers to buy computers. Now they could conduct research and communicate with each other in a new and convenient way. In 1993, the Web browser **Mosaic** was introduced. This browser allowed

users to view multimedia on the Web, causing Internet traffic to increase by nearly 350 percent.

Meanwhile, companies discovered the Internet as a means to do business, and computer sales took off. IBM-compatible PCs became the personal computer system of choice when, in 1995, Microsoft (the predominant software provider to PCs) introduced Internet Explorer, a Web browser that integrated Web functionality into Microsoft Office applications, and **Windows 95**, the first Microsoft OS designed to be principally a GUI OS, although it still was based on DOS.

About a year earlier, in mid-1994, Jim Clark, founder of the computer company Silicon Graphics Inc., Marc Andreessen, and others from the Mosaic development team developed

Figure 15 *The Macintosh became one of Apple's best-selling computers, incorporating a graphical user interface along with other innovations such as the 3.5-inch floppy disk drive.*

the Netscape commercial Web browser. Netscape's popularity grew quickly, and it soon became a predominant player in browser software. However, pressures from Microsoft became too strong. In the beginning of 1998, Netscape announced it was moving to the open source market, would no longer charge for the product, and would make the code available to the public.

Making the PC Possible: Early Computers

Since the first Altair was introduced in the 1970s, more than a billion personal computers have been distributed around the globe. Because of the declining prices of computers and the growth of the Internet, it's estimated that a billion more computers will be sold within the next decade. What made all of this possible? The computer is a compilation of parts, each of which is the result of individual inventions. From the earliest days of humankind, we have been looking for a more systematic way to count and calculate. Thus, the evolution of counting machines led to the development of the computer we know today.

Figure 16 *The Jacquard loom used holes punched in stiff cards to make complex designs. This technique would later be used in punch cards that controlled the input and output of data in computers.*

The Pascalene Calculator and the Jacquard Loom

The **Pascalene** was the first accurate mechanical calculator. This machine, created by the French mathematician **Blaise Pascal** in 1642, used revolutions of gears, like odometers in cars do, to count by tens. The Pascalene could be used to add, subtract, multiply, and divide. The basic design of the Pascalene was so sound that it lived on in mechanical calculators for more than 300 years.

Nearly 200 years later, **Joseph Jacquard** revolutionized the fabric industry by creating a machine that automated the weaving of complex patterns. Although not a counting or calculating machine, the **Jacquard loom** (shown in Figure 16) was significant because it relied on stiff cards with punched holes to automate the weaving process. Much later, this punch-card process would be adopted as a means for computers to record and read data.

Babbage's Engines

Decades later, in 1834, **Charles Babbage** designed the first automatic calculator, called the **Analytical Engine** (see Figure 17). The machine was actually based on another machine called the **Difference Engine**, which was a huge steam-powered mechanical calculator that Babbage designed to print astronomical tables. Babbage stopped working on the Difference Engine to build the Analytical Engine. Although it was never developed, Babbage's detailed drawings and descriptions of the Analytical Engine include components similar to those found in today's computers, including the store (akin to RAM) and the mill (a central processing unit), as well as input and output devices. This invention gave Charles Babbage the title of "father of computing."

Meanwhile, Ada Lovelace, who was the daughter of poet Lord Byron and was a student of mathematics (which was unusual for women of that time), was fascinated with Babbage's Engines. She translated an Italian paper on Babbage's machine, and at the request of Babbage added her own extensive notes. Her efforts are thought to be the best description of Babbage's Engines.

The Hollerith Tabulating Machine

In 1890, **Herman Hollerith**, while working for the U.S. Census Bureau, was the first to take Jacquard's punch-card concept and apply it to computing. Hollerith developed a machine called the **Hollerith Tabulating Machine** that used punch cards to tabulate census data. Up until that time, census data had been tabulated manually in a long, laborious process. Hollerith's tabulating machine automatically read data that had been punched onto small punch cards, speeding up the tabulation process. Hollerith's machine became so successful that he left the Census Bureau in 1896 to start the Tabulating Machine Company. His company later changed its name to International Business Machines, or IBM.

Figure 17 *The Analytical Engine, designed by Charles Babbage, was never fully developed, but included components similar to those found in today's computers.*

The Z1 and the Atanasoff–Berry Computer

German inventor **Konrad Zuse** is credited with a number of computing inventions. His first, in 1936, was a mechanical calculator called the **Z1**. The Z1 is thought to be the first computer to include certain features that are integral to today's systems, such as a control unit and separate memory functions. These were important breakthroughs for future computer design.

In late 1939, John Atanasoff, a professor at Iowa State University, and his student Clifford Berry built the first electrically powered digital computer, called the **Atanasoff–Berry Computer (ABC)**, shown in Figure 18. The computer was the first to use vacuum tubes, instead of the mechanical switches used in older computers, to store data. Although revolutionary at its time, the machine weighed 700 pounds, contained a mile of wire, and took about 15 seconds for each calculation. (In comparison, today's personal computers can perform billions and billions of calculations in 15 seconds.) Most importantly, the ABC was the first computer to use the binary system. It was also the first computer to have memory that repowered itself upon booting. The design of the ABC would end up being central to that of future computers.

The Harvard Mark I

From the late 1930s to the early 1950s, **Howard Aiken** and **Grace Hopper** designed the Mark series of computers at Harvard University. The U.S. Navy used these computers for ballistic and gunnery calculations. Aiken, an electrical engineer and physicist, designed the computer, while Hopper did the programming. The **Harvard Mark I**, finished in 1944, could perform all four arithmetic operations (addition, subtraction, multiplication, and division).

However, many believe Hopper's greatest contribution to computing was the invention of the **compiler**, a program that translates English-language instructions into computer language. The team was also responsible for a common computer-related expression. Hopper was the first to "debug" a computer when she removed a moth that had flown into the Harvard Mark I and caused the computer to break down (see Figure 19). After that, problems that caused a computer not to run were called "bugs."

Figure 18 *The Atanasoff–Berry Computer laid the design groundwork for many computers to come.*

9/9

0800 ondam started

1000   " stopped - ondam ✓

13"uc (032) MP - MC

(033)   PRO 2   2.130476415

conct   2.130676415

Relays 6-2 in 033 failed special speed test

1m relay   " 10.000 test .

Relays changed

1100 Started Cosine Tape (Sine check)

1525 Started Mult+ Adder Test.

1545 Relay #70 Panel F (moth) in relay.

Actual moth pasted into notebook

First actual case of bug being found.

1630 andant started.

Figure 19 *Grace Hopper coined the term* computer bug *when a moth flew into the Harvard Mark I, causing it to break down.*

The Turing Machine

Meanwhile, in 1936, the British mathematician **Alan Turing** created an abstract computer model that could perform logical operations. The **Turing Machine** was not a real machine, but rather was a hypothetical model that mathematically defined a mechanical procedure (or algorithm). Additionally, Turing's concept described a process by which the machine could read, write, or erase symbols written on squares of an infinite paper tape. This concept of an infinite tape that could be read, written to, and erased was the precursor to today's RAM.

The ENIAC

The **Electronic Numerical Integrator and Computer (ENIAC)**, shown in Figure 20, was another U.S. government-sponsored machine developed to calculate the settings used for weapons. Created by **John W. Mauchly** and **J. Presper Eckert** at the University of Pennsylvania, it was placed in operation in June 1944. Although the ENIAC is generally thought of as the first successful high-speed electronic digital computer, it was big and clumsy. The ENIAC used nearly 18,000 vacuum tubes and filled approximately 1,800 square feet of floor space. Although inconvenient, the ENIAC served its purpose and remained in use until 1955.

The UNIVAC

The **Universal Automatic Computer**, or **UNIVAC**, was the first commercially successful electronic digital computer. Completed in June 1951 and manufactured by the company Remington Rand, the UNIVAC operated on magnetic tape. This set it apart from its competitors, which ran on punch cards. The UNIVAC gained notoriety when, in a 1951 publicity stunt, it was used to predict the outcome of the Stevenson–Eisenhower presidential race. After analyzing only 5 percent of the popular vote, the UNIVAC correctly identified Dwight D. Eisenhower as the victor. After that, UNIVAC soon became a household word. The UNIVAC and computers like it were considered **first-generation computers** and were the last to use vacuum tubes to store data.

Transistors and Beyond

Only a year after the ENIAC was completed, scientists at the Bell Telephone Laboratories in New Jersey invented the **transistor**, which was another means to store data. The transistor replaced the bulky vacuum tubes of earlier computers and was smaller and more powerful than tubes were. It was used in almost everything, from radios to phones. Computers that used transistors were referred to as **second-generation computers**. Still, transistors were limited as to how small they could be made.

A few years later, in 1958, **Jack Kilby**, while working at Texas Instruments, invented the world's first **integrated circuit**, a small chip capable of containing thousands of transistors. This consolidation in design enabled computers to become smaller and lighter. The computers in this early integrated-circuit generation were considered **third-generation computers**.

Other innovations in the computer industry further refined the computer's speed, accuracy, and efficiency. However, none were as significant as the 1971 introduction by the Intel Corporation of the **microprocessor chip**, a small chip containing millions of transistors. The microprocessor functions as the central processing unit (CPU), or brains, of the computer. Computers that used a microprocessor chip were called **fourth-generation computers**. Over time, Intel and Motorola became the leading manufacturers of microprocessors. Today, the Intel Core i7 is one of Intel's most powerful processors.

As you can see, personal computers have come a long way since the Altair, and have a number of inventions and people to thank for their amazing popularity. What will the future bring? If current trends continue, computers will be smaller, lighter, and more powerful. The advancement of wireless technology will also play a big role in the development of the personal computer.

Figure 20 *The ENIAC took up an entire room and required several people to manipulate it.*

Multiple Choice

Instructions: Answer the multiple-choice questions below for more practice with key terms and concepts from this Technology in Focus feature.

1. What was the name of the first Web browser?
   a. Mosaic
   b. Internet Explorer
   c. Netscape
   d. Firefox

2. Which programming language revolutionized the software industry?
   a. ALGOL
   b. BASIC
   c. COBOL
   d. FORTRAN

3. Why was the invention of the integrated circuit important?
   a. It enabled computers to store more data.
   b. It enabled monitors to display a better image.
   c. It enabled more processing memory.
   d. It enabled computers to become smaller and lighter.

4. Which computer is touted as the first personal computer?
   a. Altair
   b. Commodore PET
   c. Lisa
   d. Osborne

5. What was the importance of the Turing machine to today's computers?
   a. It described a system that was a precursor to today's notebook computer.
   b. It was the first electronic calculator and a precursor to the computer.
   c. It was the first computer to have a monitor.
   d. It described a process to read, write, and erase symbols on a tape and was the precursor to today's RAM.

6. Which computer first stored its operating system in ROM?
   a. Apple I
   b. Apple II
   c. Lisa
   d. Macintosh

7. What was the first word processing application?
   a. Lotus 1-2-3
   b. Word for MS-DOS
   c. WordPerfect
   d. WordStar

8. Which components are characteristic of second-generation computers?
   a. Transistors
   b. Vacuum tubes
   c. Integrated circuits
   d. Microprocessor chips

9. For what is the Atanasoff-Berry Computer best known?
   a. It was the first computer used to tabulate U.S. census data.
   b. It was the first computer to use the binary system.
   c. It was the first computer to incorporate the punch-card system.
   d. It was the first computer used as a mechanical calculator.

10. Who are the founders of Microsoft?
    a. Paul Allen and Bill Gates
    b. Bill Gates and Steve Wozniak
    c. Steve Jobs and Bill Gates
    d. Bill Gates and Gary Kildall

two
looking at computers
understanding the parts

objectives

After reading this chapter, you should be able to answer the following questions:

1. What exactly is a computer, and what are its four main functions? *(p. 48)*

2. What is the difference between data and information? *(p. 48)*

3. What are bits and bytes, and how are they measured? *(pp. 48–49)*

4. What devices do I use to get data into the computer? *(pp. 51–60)*

5. What devices do I use to get information out of the computer? *(pp. 60–66)*

6. What's on the motherboard? *(pp. 67–68)*

7. Where are information and programs stored? *(pp. 69–71)*

8. How are devices connected to the computer? *(pp. 71–75)*

9. How do I set up my computer to avoid strain and injury? *(pp. 77–79)*

multimedia resources

Active Helpdesk
- Understanding Bits and Bytes **(p. 49)**
- Using Input Devices **(p. 58)**
- Using Output Devices **(p. 62)**
- Exploring Storage Devices and Ports **(p. 72)**

Sound Bytes
- Binary Numbers Interactive **(p. 48)**
- Tablet and Notebook Tour **(p. 56)**
- Virtual Computer Tour **(p. 68)**
- Port Tour: How Do I Hook It Up? **(p. 72)**
- Healthy Computing **(p. 77)**

Companion Website
The Companion Website includes a variety of additional materials to help you review and learn more about the topics in this chapter. Go to: *pearsonhighered.com/techinaction*

how cool

how cool is *this?*

If you have ever thought about **customizing** the layout of your **keyboard**, this Luxeed Dynamic Pixel LED Keyboard is the one for you. If you're a gamer, you can program specific keys to control your game and to **glow** with different colors that indicate each key **action**. If you're not a gamer but just would like to add a bit of fun to your otherwise dull keyboard, you can **animate** colored scenarios to "play" on the keys, or create an **illuminated** pattern or design. With 430 LEDs, the Luxeed is capable of individually lighting each key in your choice of color.

The keyboard comes in either black or white. The keys of the white keyboard light up more brightly and have a semitransparent look. The keys of the black keyboard can be set so just the letters light up.

47

Understanding Your Computer

After reading Chapter 1, you can see why becoming computer literate is so important. But where do you start? You've no doubt gleaned some knowledge about computers just from being a member of society. However, although you have undoubtedly used a computer before, do you really understand how it works, what all its parts are, and what these parts do? In this section, we discuss what a computer does and how its functions make it such a useful machine.

Computers Are Data Processing Devices

Strictly defined, a **computer** is a data processing device that performs four major functions:

1. It *gathers* data, or allows users to input data.
2. It *processes* that data into information.
3. It *outputs* data and information.
4. It *stores* data and information.

What is the difference between data and information? People often use the terms *data* and *information* interchangeably. Although they may mean the same thing in a simple conversation, the actual distinction between data and information is an important one.

In computer terms, **data** is a representation of a fact, a figure, or an idea. Data can be a number, a word, a picture, or even a recording of sound. For example, the number 7135553297 and the names Zoe and Richardson are pieces of data. Alone, these pieces of data probably mean little to you. **Information** is data that has been organized

or presented in a meaningful fashion. When your computer provides you with a contact listing that indicates Zoe Richardson can be reached by phone at (713) 555-3297, then the previous data suddenly becomes useful—that is, it becomes information.

How do computers interact with data and information? Computers are excellent at **processing** (manipulating, calculating, or organizing) data into information. When you first arrived on campus, you probably were directed to a place where you could get an ID card. You most likely provided a clerk with personal data (such as your name and address) that was entered into a computer. The clerk then took your picture with a digital camera (collecting more data). This information was then processed appropriately so that it could be printed on your ID card (see Figure 2.1). This organized output of data on your ID card is useful information. Finally, the information was probably stored as digital data on the computer for later use.

Bits and Bytes: The Language of Computers

How do computers process data into information? Unlike humans, computers work exclusively with numbers (not words). To process data into information, computers need to work in a language they understand.

SOUND BYTE   Binary Numbers Interactive

This Sound Byte helps remove the mystery surrounding binary numbers. You'll learn about base conversion between decimal, binary, and hexadecimal numbers interactively using colors, sounds, and images.

Figure 2.1

Computers process data into information.

This language, called **binary language**, consists of just two digits: 0 and 1. Everything a computer does, such as processing data or printing a report, is broken down into a series of 0s and 1s. Each 0 and 1 is a **binary digit**, or **bit** for short. Eight binary digits (or bits) combine to create one **byte**. In computers, each letter of the alphabet, each number, and each special character (such as the @ sign) consists of a unique combination of eight bits, or a string of eight 0s and 1s. So, for example, in binary (computer) language, the letter K is represented as 01001011. This equals eight bits, or one byte. (We discuss binary language in more detail in the Technology in Focus section "Under the Hood.")

What else can bits and bytes be used for? You've probably heard the terms *kilobyte (KB)*, *megabyte (MB)*, and *gigabyte (GB)*. Bits and bytes not only are used as the language that tells the computer what to do but also are what the computer uses to represent the data and information that it inputs and outputs. Word processing files, digital pictures, and even software are represented inside a computer as a series of bits and bytes. These files and applications can be quite large, containing thousands or millions of bytes.

To make it easier to measure the size of these files, we need units of measure larger

than a byte. Kilobytes, megabytes, and gigabytes are therefore simply amounts of bytes. As shown in Figure 2.2, a **kilobyte (KB)** is approximately 1,000 bytes, a **megabyte (MB)** is about 1 million bytes, a **gigabyte (GB)** is around 1 billion bytes, and a **terabyte (TB)** is around 1 trillion bytes. As our information-processing needs have grown, so too have our storage needs. Today, personal computers store terabytes of data, and many business computers can store up to a petabyte of data. The Google search engine processes more than 1 petabyte of user-generated data per *hour*—that's a lot of bytes!

How does your computer process bits and bytes? Your computer uses a combination of hardware and software to process data into information and enables you to complete tasks such as writing a letter or playing a game. An anonymous

Figure 2.2 | HOW MUCH IS A BYTE?

Name	Abbreviation	Number of Bytes	Relative Size
Byte	B	1 byte	Can hold one character of data.
Kilobyte	KB	1,024 bytes (2^{10})	Can hold 1,024 characters or about half of a double-spaced typewritten page.
Megabyte	MB	1,048,576 bytes (2^{20} bytes)	Can hold approximately 768 pages of typed text.
Gigabyte	GB	1,073,741,824 bytes (2^{30} bytes)	Approximately 786,432 pages of text; 500 sheets of paper is approximately 2 inches, so this represents a stack of paper 262 feet high.
Terabyte	TB	1,099,511,627,776 bytes (2^{40} bytes)	This represents a stack of typewritten pages almost 51 miles high.
Petabyte	PB	1,125,899,906,842,62 bytes (2^{50} bytes)	The stack of pages is now 52,000 miles high, or approximately one-fourth the distance from the Earth to the moon.
Exabyte	EB	1,152,921,504,606,846,976 bytes (2^{60} bytes)	The stack of pages is now 52 million miles high, or just about twice the distance between the Earth and Venus.
Zettabyte	ZB	1,180,591,620,717,411,303,424 bytes (2^{70} bytes)	The stack of pages is now 52 billion miles high. That's some 20 times the distance between the Earth and Pluto.

person once said that hardware is any part of a computer that you can kick when it doesn't work properly. A more formal definition of **hardware** is "any part of the computer you can physically touch." However, a computer needs more than just hardware to work: It also needs some form of software (computer programs). Think of a book without words or a CD without music. Without words or music, these two common items are just shells that hold nothing.

Similarly, a computer without software is a shell full of hardware components that can't do anything. Software is the set of computer programs that enables the hardware to perform different tasks. There are two broad categories of software: application software and system software.

When you think of software, you are most likely thinking of application software. **Application software** is the set of programs you use on a computer to help you carry out tasks such as writing a research paper. If you've ever typed a document, created a spreadsheet, or edited a digital photo, for example, then you've used a form of application software.

System software is the set of programs that enables your computer's hardware devices and application software to work together. The most common type of system software is the **operating system (OS)**—the program that controls the way in which your computer system functions. It manages the hardware of the computer system, such as the monitor and the printer. The operating system also provides a means by which users can interact with the computer. We'll cover software in greater depth in Chapters 4 and 5. For the rest of this chapter, we'll explore hardware.

Your Computer's Hardware

Are all computers the same?

Considering the amount of amazing things computers can do, they are really quite simple machines. You learned in the previous section that a basic computer system is made up of software and hardware. There are two basic designs of computers: portable and stationary. A **notebook computer** (or laptop computer) is a portable computer that is powered by batteries (or a handy electrical outlet) and has a keyboard, a monitor, and other devices integrated into a single compact case. A **netbook** is a small, lightweight notebook computer that is generally 7 to 10 inches wide and has a longer battery life than a notebook computer. A **tablet PC** is similar to a notebook but features a touch-sensitive screen that can swivel and fold flat (see Figure 2.14 later in this chapter). Users input data and commands on a tablet PC via a special pen called a *stylus* or with their fingers. A **desktop computer** is intended for use at a single location, and therefore, is stationary. Desktop computers consist of a separate case that houses the main components of the computer plus peripheral devices. A **peripheral device** is a component, such as a monitor or keyboard, that is connected to the computer. An **all-in-one computer** such as the Apple iMac (see Figure 2.3), the Dell Studio One 19", or the Gateway One houses not just the computer's processor and memory but also its monitor.

Figure 2.3

The Apple iMac is an example of an all-in-one computer.

Are there other types of computers besides desktop and notebook computers? Desktop and notebook computers are the computers that you will most likely encounter. Although you may never come into direct contact with the following types of computers, they are still important to our society:

• A **mainframe** is a large, expensive computer that supports hundreds of users simultaneously. Mainframes are often used in insurance companies, for example, where many people are working on similar operations (such as claims processing) all at once. Your college also may use mainframe computers to handle the multitude of processing needs throughout the campus. Mainframes excel at executing many

Figure 2.4

Each part of the computer serves a special function.

different computer programs at the same time.

- A **supercomputer** is a specially designed computer that can perform complex calculations extremely rapidly. Supercomputers are used in situations in which complex models requiring intensive mathematical calculations are needed (such as weather forecasting or atomic energy research). The main difference between a supercomputer and a mainframe is that supercomputers are designed to execute a few programs as quickly as possible, whereas mainframes are designed to handle many programs running at the same time but at a slower pace.

- An **embedded computer** is a specially designed computer chip that resides in another device, such as your car or the electronic thermostat in your home. Embedded computers are self-contained computer devices that have their own programming and typically do not receive input from you or interact with other systems.

In the following sections, we look more closely at your computer's hardware. Each part has a specific purpose that coordinates with one of the functions of the computer—input, processing, output, or storage (see Figure 2.4).

Additional devices, such as modems and routers, help a computer communicate with the Internet and other computers to facilitate the shar-

ing of documents and other resources. We begin our exploration of hardware by looking at your computer's input devices.

Input Devices

An **input device** enables you to enter data (text, images, and sounds) and instructions (user responses and commands) into the computer. The most common input devices are the keyboard and the mouse. A **keyboard** is used to enter typed data and commands, and a **mouse** is used to enter user responses and commands.

There are other input devices as well. Microphones input sounds, and scanners and digital cameras input nondigital text and digital images, respectively. A **stylus** is an input device that looks like a skinny pen but has no ink. You use it like a mouse or pen to tap commands or draw on a screen. Electronic pens are also becoming quite popular and are often used in conjunction with graphics tablets that can translate a user's handwriting into digital input (see Figure 2.5).

Figure 2.5

An electronic pen is a type of input device that is used with graphics tablets.

Figure 2.6

QWERTY keyboard layout.

Keyboards

Aren't all keyboards the same?
Most desktop and notebook computers come with a standard **QWERTY keyboard** (see Figure 2.6). This keyboard layout gets its name from the first six letters in the top-left row of alphabetic keys on the keyboard and is the standard English-language keyboard layout. Over the years, there has been some debate over what is the best keyboard layout. The QWERTY layout was originally designed for typewriters and was meant to slow typists down and prevent typewriter keys from jamming. Although the QWERTY layout is considered inefficient because it slows typing speeds, efforts to change to more efficient layouts, such as that of the Dvorak keyboard, have not been met with much public interest. The Dvorak keyboard is an alternative keyboard layout that puts the most commonly used letters in the English language on "home keys," which are the keys in the middle row of the keyboard. The Dvorak keyboard's design reduces the distance your fingers travel for most keystrokes, increasing typing speed.

Figure 2.7

On many notebooks, certain letter keys can function as number keys.

How do notebook keyboards differ?
To save space and weight, some of the smaller notebook keyboards (14" and under) are more compact than standard desktop keyboards and, therefore, have fewer keys. To retain the same functionality as a standard keyboard, many of the notebook keys have alternate functions. For example, many notebook keyboards do not have a separate numeric keypad. Instead, some letter keys function as number keys when they are pressed in combination with another key such as the function (Fn) key. The keys you use as numeric keys on notebooks have number notations on them so you can tell which keys to use (see Figure 2.7).

What if the standard keyboard doesn't work for me?
Because recent development efforts have focused on reducing the size and weight of notebook computers, the keyboards have had to shrink accordingly. Flexible keyboards are a terrific alternative if you want a full-sized keyboard for your notebook. You can roll one up, fit it in your backpack, and plug it into the USB port when you need to use it. The virtual laser keyboard (see Figure 2.8a) is about the size of a cellular phone. It projects the image of a keyboard on any surface, and sensors detect the motion of your fingers as you "type" on a desk or other flat surface. Data is transmitted via **Bluetooth** technology, which is a wireless transmission standard that facilitates the connection of electronic computing devices such as cell phones, smartphones, and computers to peripheral devices such as keyboards and headsets. We'll discuss Bluetooth in further detail in Chapter 8.

Gamers love keyboards such as the DX1 from Ergodex (see Figure 2.8b). These keyboards allow placement of the keys in any position on the keyboard pad. The keys can be programmed to execute individual keystrokes or macros (a series of tasks) to perform specific tasks. This makes it easy for gamers to configure a keyboard in the most desirable way for each game they play.

How can I use my keyboard most efficiently?
All keyboards have the standard set of alphabetic and numeric keys that you regularly use when typing. As shown in Figure 2.9, many keyboards for notebook and desktop computers have additional keys that perform special functions.

a

b

Figure 2.8

(a) The virtual laser keyboard projects the image of a QWERTY keyboard on any surface. Sensors detect typing motions, and data is transmitted to a computing device via Bluetooth technology. (b) The Ergodex DX1 allows keys to be relocated anywhere on the pad and reprogrammed easily, making the keyboard popular with gamers.

because they start with the letter F followed by a number. Each software application has its own set of tasks assigned to various function keys. For example, the F2 key moves text or graphics in Microsoft Word but allows editing of the active cell in Microsoft Excel. Many keys are universal: the F1 key is the Help key in most applications.

- The Control (Ctrl) key is used in combination with other keys to perform shortcuts and special tasks. For example, holding down the Control (Ctrl) key while pressing the B key adds bold formatting to selected text. The Alt key works with other keys to execute additional shortcuts and special tasks. (On Macs, the Control function is the Apple key or Command key, and the Alt function is the Option key.)

Knowing how to use these special keys will help you improve your efficiency:

- The numeric keypad allows you to enter numbers quickly.
- Function keys act as shortcut keys you press to perform special tasks. They are sometimes referred to as the "F" keys

Figure 2.9

Keyboards have a variety of keys that help you work more efficiently.

Function keys · Multimedia controls · Internet controls · Toggle and other keys · Numeric keypad · Control (Ctrl) key · Windows key · Alt key · Windows key · Cursor control keys

- The Windows key is specific to the Windows operating system. Used alone, it opens the Start menu, although you use it most often in combination with other keys to perform shortcuts. For example, in Windows 7 and Vista, pressing the Windows key plus the M key minimizes all windows, and the Windows key plus the L key locks a computer (a good habit to get into when you use a computer in a group setting such as a business office).

What are some other features on keyboards? Some keyboards (such as the one shown in Figure 2.9) also include multimedia and Internet keys or buttons that enable you to open a Web browser, view e-mail, access Help features, or control your CD/DVD player. These buttons are not always in the same position on every keyboard, but the symbols on top of the buttons generally help you determine their function. Some desktop keyboards include USB ports

to facilitate attaching other devices, such as a mouse or a keyboard.

Another set of controls on standard keyboards are the cursor control keys that move your *cursor* (the flashing I symbol on the monitor that indicates where the next character will be inserted). A **cursor control key** is also known as an *arrow key* because each one is represented by an arrow on standard keyboards. The arrow keys move the cursor one space at a time in a document: up, down, left, or right.

Above the arrow keys, you'll usually find Page Up (PGUP) and Page Down (PGDN) keys that move the cursor up or down one full page or even to the document's beginning (Home), or to the end of a line of text or document (End). The Delete (Del) key allows you to delete characters, and the Insert key allows you to insert or overwrite characters within a document. The Insert key is a *toggle key* because its function changes between one of two options each time you press it: When toggled on, the Insert key inserts new text within a line of existing text. When toggled off, the Insert key replaces (or overwrites) existing characters with new characters as you type. Other toggle keys that switch between an on state and an off state include the Num Lock key and the Caps Lock key.

Are all conventional keyboards connected to the computer via wires? Although most desktop PCs ship with wired keyboards, wireless keyboards are available. Wireless keyboards are powered by batteries. They send data to the computer using a form of wireless technology that uses radio frequency (RF). A radio transmitter in the keyboard sends out radio wave signals that are received either through a small receiving device that is plugged into a USB port or a Bluetooth receiving device that is contained in the system unit. RF keyboards used on home computers can be placed as far as 6 feet to 30 feet from the computer, depending on their quality. RF keyboards that are used in business conference rooms or auditoriums can be placed as far as 100 feet away from the computer, but they are far more expensive than traditional wired keyboards.

Mice and Other Pointing Devices

What kinds of mice are there? The mouse type you're probably most familiar with is the **optical mouse** (see Figure 2.10a).

BITS AND BYTES

Keystroke Shortcuts

Did you know that you can combine certain keystrokes to take shortcuts within an application, such as Microsoft Word, or within the operating system itself? The following are a few of the most helpful Windows shortcuts. Use them to make more efficient use of your time. For more shortcuts for Windows-based PCs, visit **support. microsoft.com**. For a list of shortcuts for Macs, see **apple.com/support**.

Text Formatting	File Management	Cut/Copy/ Paste	Windows Controls
CTRL+B Applies (or removes) **bold** formatting to selected text	**CTRL+O** Opens the Open dialog box	**CTRL+X** Cuts (removes) selected text from document and stores in Clipboard	**Alt+F4** Closes the current window
CTRL+I Applies (or removes) *italic* formatting to selected text	**CTRL+N** Opens a new document	**CTRL+C** Copies selected text to Clipboard	**Windows Key+ Tab** Cycles through open programs using Flip 3-D
CTRL+U Applies (or removes) underlining to selected text	**CTRL+S** Saves a document	**CTRL+V** Pastes selected text (previously cut or copied) from Clipboard	**Windows Key+L** Locks the computer
	CTRL+P Opens the Print dialog box		**Windows Key+F** Opens the Search (Find Files) dialog box

---

An optical mouse uses an internal sensor or laser to detect the mouse's movement. The sensor sends signals to the computer, telling it where to move the pointer on the screen. Optical mice are often preferable to other types of mice because they have fewer moving parts, which lessens the chances that dirt will interfere with the mechanisms or that parts will break down. Optical mice also do not require a mouse pad, though you can still use one to protect your work surface from being scratched. You may still find a mouse at home or in school that has a rollerball on the bottom, which moves when you drag the mouse across a mouse pad. The movement of the rollerball controls the movement of the cursor that appears on the screen.

A **trackball mouse** (see Figure 2.10b) has the rollerball on top or on the side of the mouse, and you move the ball with your fingers, allowing the mouse to remain stationary. A trackball mouse doesn't demand much wrist motion, so it's considered better for the wrist than an optical mouse. Mice also have two or three buttons that enable you to execute commands and open shortcut menus. (Mice for Macs sometimes have only one button.) Many mice have additional programmable buttons and wheels that let you quickly scroll through documents or Web pages.

Do notebook computers include a mouse? Most notebooks do not have a mouse. Instead, they have an integrated pointing

device such as a **touch pad**, a small, touch-sensitive area at the base of the keyboard (see Figure 2.11). To use the touch pad, you simply move your finger across the pad. Some touch pads are sensitive to taps, interpreting them as mouse clicks, while others have buttons beneath the pads to record mouse clicks. Other notebooks incorporate a **trackpoint device**, a small, joystick-like nub that allows you to move the cursor with the tip of your finger.

Are there wireless mice? Just as there are wireless keyboards, there are wireless mice, both optical and trackball. Wireless mice are similar to wireless keyboards in that they use batteries and send data to the computer by radio frequency or Bluetooth technologies. If you have an RF wireless keyboard, then your RF wireless mouse and keyboard usually can share the same RF receiver. Wireless mice for notebooks have their own receivers that often clip into the

Optical laser (sensor)

Wheel

Trackball

Figure 2.10

(a) An optical mouse has an optical laser (or sensor) on the bottom that detects its movement. (b) A trackball mouse turns the traditional mouse on its back, allowing you to control the rollerball with your fingers.

Figure 2.11

Touch pads and trackpoint devices take the place of a mouse on notebook computers.

Trackpoint

Touch pad

bottom of the mouse for easy storage when not in use.

Apple has developed Magic Mouse, the first multitouch wireless mouse (see Figure 2.12a). The top surface of the mouse, which is virtually the mouse itself, is the button. Use your finger to scroll in any direction, swipe your finger across the mouse to move through Web pages and photos, and tap on the mouse to click and double-click.

Small, compact devices like the MoGo Mouse (see Figure 2.12b) are designed for portability. The MoGo Mouse fits into a peripheral slot on the side of a notebook; this slot serves to store the mouse, protect it, and charge its batteries all at the same time. The MoGo Mouse is wireless and uses Bluetooth technology to transmit data to the notebook.

What else can I do with my mouse? Manufacturers of mice are constantly releasing new models that allow you to perform useful tasks with a few clicks of the mouse. On some mouse models, Microsoft and Logitech now provide features such as the following:

- **Magnifier:** Pulls up a magnification box that you can drag around the screen to enhance viewing of hard-to-read images (see Figure 2.13). This feature is often used by people with visual disabilities.
- **Customizable buttons:** Provide extra buttons on the mouse that you can program to perform the functions that you use most often to help you speed through tasks.

Figure 2.12

(a) The Magic Mouse by Apple has multitouch technology. (b) The MoGo Mouse is a portable mouse that stores and charges in a PC Card slot.

Figure 2.13

The magnifier is a mouse feature that provides instant magnification of images or text.

- **Web search:** Allows you to quickly highlight a word or phrase and then press the search button on the mouse to start a Web search.
- **File storage:** Includes a wireless USB receiver that contains flash memory to store or back up your files (for example, a USB drive).

What other input devices are used with games? Game controllers such as joysticks, game pads, and steering wheels are also considered input devices because they send data to the computer. Game controllers, which are similar to the devices used on gaming consoles, such as the Xbox 360 and the PlayStation, are also available for use with computers. They have buttons and miniature pointing devices that provide input to the computer. Force-feedback joysticks and steering wheels deliver data in both directions. They translate your movements to the computer and translate its responses into forces on your hands, creating a richer simulated experience. Most game controllers, such as those for Rock Band and the Wii system, are wireless to provide extra mobility.

Touch Screens

How else can I input data and commands? You've seen and used touch-sensitive screens in fast food restaurants, airport check-in kiosks, and ATM machines for quite some time. A **touch screen** is a display screen that responds to commands initiated by a touch with a finger or a stylus. Touch screens are becoming increasingly popular on many computing devices, including desktops, notebooks, smartphones, and portable media players (PMPs). Tablet PCs were one of the first devices with touch-screen capabilities (see Figure 2.14). Although all tablet PCs have built-in keyboards that allow you to type text just as you would with a normal keyboard, the touch-screen functionality often makes it a better choice when inputting with a keyboard is impracti-

Window provides magnified view

SOUND BYTE

Tablet and Notebook Tour

In this Sound Byte, you'll take a tour of a Tablet PC and a notebook computer, learning about the unique features and ports available on each.

Figure 2.14

Tablet PCs use the finger or a stylus to input data and commands on a touch-screen display that twists and folds flat.

cal or unwieldy. The Apple iPod Touch, iPad, and iPhone all have touch capability, as do portable gaming devices such as the Nintendo DS. Dell and Hewlett Packard have released all-in-one desktop PCs with touch-screen displays.

Tablet PCs, which were developed primarily because many people find it easier to write than to type input into a computer, are expensive compared to conventional notebooks. An alternative is a digital pen like the Dane-Elec Digital Pen (see Figure 2.15). This pen works in conjunction with a flash drive

Figure 2.15

The Dane-Elec Digital Pen captures writing and stores it in a flash drive for later transfer to a computer. No typing is required!

(a portable electronic storage device that connects to a USB port on a computer). You can write with the pen on any conventional paper. The pen captures your writing and then wirelessly transmits and stores it in the flash drive. When the flash drive is connected to a computer, you can use software to translate your writing into digital text.

Image Input

How can I input digital images into my computer? Digital cameras, camcorders, and cell phones are common devices for capturing pictures and video, and all of them are considered input devices. Digital cameras and camcorders are usually used in remote settings (away from a computer) to capture images and video for later downloading to the computer. These devices either connect to a computer with a data cable or transmit data wirelessly. Windows automatically recognizes these devices when they are connected to a computer and makes the input of the digital data to the computer simple and easy. Scanners can also input images. They work similar to a photocopy machine, but instead of generating the image on paper, they create a digital image, which can then be printed, saved in storage, or e-mailed.

How do I capture live video from my computer? A **webcam** (see Figure 2.16) is a small camera that sits on top of a

Figure 2.16

A webcam is either built into a notebook monitor or placed on top of a monitor.

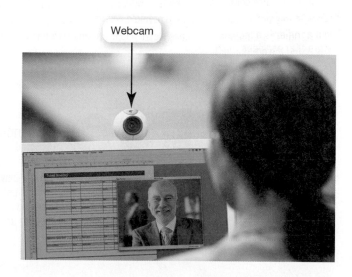

What Is Ethical Computing?

If you were asked to cite an example of unethical behavior while using a computer, you could easily provide an answer. You've probably heard news stories about people using computers to commit such crimes as unleashing viruses or committing identity theft. You may also have read about students who were prosecuted for illegally sharing copyrighted material such as videos. Or perhaps you heard about the case where the school district was monitoring students through notebook computer webcams without the students' knowledge. All of these are examples of unethical behavior while using a computer. However, if you were asked what constitutes *ethical* behavior while using a computer, could you provide an answer just as quickly?

Loosely defined, *ethics* is a system of moral principles, rules, and accepted standards of conduct. So what are the accepted standards of conduct when using computers (see Figure 2.17)? The Computer Ethics Institute developed the Ten Commandments of Computer Ethics, which is widely cited as a benchmark for companies that are developing computer usage and compliance policies for employees. These guidelines are applicable for schools and students as well. The ethical computing guidelines listed below are based on the Computer Ethics Institute's work.

Ethical Computing Guidelines

1. Avoid causing harm to others when using computers.
2. Do not interfere with other people's efforts at accomplishing work with computers.
3. Resist the temptation to snoop in other people's computer files.
4. Do not use computers to commit theft.
5. Agree not to use computers to promote lies.
6. Do not use software (or make illegal copies for others) without paying the creator for it.

7. Avoid using other people's computer resources without appropriate authorization or proper compensation.
8. Do not claim other people's intellectual output as your own.
9. Consider the social consequences of the products of your computer labor.
10. Only use computers in ways that show consideration and respect for others.

Figure 2.17

Make sure the work you claim as your intellectual output is the product of your intellect alone.

The United States has enacted laws that support some of these guidelines, such as Guideline 6, the breaking of which would violate copyright laws, and Guideline 4, which is enforceable under numerous federal and state larceny laws. Other guidelines, however, require more subtle interpretation as to what behavior is unethical because there are no laws designed to enforce them.

Consider Guideline 7, which covers unauthorized use of resources. The college you attend probably provides computer resources for you to use for coursework. But if the college gives you access to computers and the Internet, is it ethical for you to use those resources to run a business on eBay in between classes or on the weekends? Although it might not be technically illegal, you are tying up computer resources that could be used by other students for their intended purpose: learning and completing coursework. (This behavior also violates Guidelines 2 and 10.)

Throughout the chapters in this book, we touch on many topics related to these guidelines. So keep them in mind as you study, and think about how they relate to the actions you take as you use computers in your life.

Using Input Devices

ACTIVE HELP-DESK

In this Active Helpdesk call, you'll play the role of a helpdesk staffer, fielding calls about different input devices, such as the different mice and keyboards on the market, what wireless input options are available, and how to best use these devices.

computer monitor (connected to the computer by a cable) or is built into a notebook computer. Although some webcams are able to capture still images, they are used mostly for transferring live video directly to a computer. Webcams make it possible to transmit live video over the Web. They are often used to facilitate videoconferencing or calls made with video phones. Videoconferencing technology allows a person sitting at a computer equipped with a web-cam and a microphone to transmit video and audio across the Internet.

Sound Input

Why would I want to input sound to my computer? Equipping your computer to accept sound input opens up a variety of possibilities. You can conduct audio conferences with work colleagues, chat with friends or family over the Internet instead of using a phone, record podcasts, and more. Inputting sound to your computer requires equipping it with a **microphone** or **mic**, a device that allows you to capture sound waves (such as your voice) and transfer them to digital format on your computer. Many notebook computers come with built-in microphones, and some desktop computers come with inexpensive microphones. If you don't have a microphone or you aren't getting the quality you need from your existing microphone, then you probably need to shop for one.

What types of microphones are available? There are several different types of microphones available for a variety of needs. Desktop microphones, which have an attached base that allows them to sit on a flat surface (see Figure 2.18), are convenient for recording podcasts or in other situations in which you might need your hands to be free. Unidirectional microphones pick up sound from only one direction. These are best used for recording podcasts with a single voice or making phone calls over the Internet with only one person on the sender's end of the call. Omnidirectional microphones pick up sounds from all directions at once. These mics are best for recording more than one

Figure 2.18

Professional-quality microphones such as the Snowball are essential for producing quality podcasts.

Figure 2.19

For people who have physical disabilities, devices such as this keyboard adapt to accommodate special needs. This keyboard is shaped and designed for individuals who can only use one hand.

voice, such as during a conference call when you need to pick up the voices of multiple speakers.

Clip-on microphones (also called *lavalier microphones*) are useful in environments such as presentations, where you need to keep your hands free for other activities (such as writing on a white board) or move around the room. Many of these microphones are wireless.

Close-talk microphones, which are usually attached to a headset, facilitate using speech-recognition software, videoconferencing, or making telephone calls. With a microphone attached to a headset, your hands are free to perform other tasks while you speak (such as making notes or referring to paper documents), and the headset allows you to listen as well (such as when making Internet phone calls or playing games online).

What input devices are available for people with disabilities? Many people who have physical challenges use computers often, but they sometimes need special input devices to access them. For visually impaired users, voice recognition is an obvious option. For those users whose visual limitations are less severe, keyboards with larger keys are available. Keyboards that display on a touch screen can make input easier for some individuals. These keyboards are displayed as graphics on the computer monitor. The user presses the keys with a pointing device or simply presses on the touch-screen monitor. There are also keyboards designed for individuals who can only use one hand such as the Maltron keyboard (see Figure 2.19).

People with motor control issues may have difficulty with pointing devices. To aid such users, special trackballs are available that can easily be manipulated with one finger and can be attached to almost any surface, including a wheelchair. When arm motion is severely restrained, head-mounted pointing devices can be used. Generally, these involve a camera mounted on the computer monitor and a device attached to the head (often installed in a hat). When the user moves his or her head, the camera detects the movement, which controls the cursor on the screen. In this case, mouse clicks are controlled by a switch that can be manipulated by the user's hands or feet or even by using an instrument that fits into the mouth and senses the user blowing into it.

Output Devices

An **output device** enables you to send processed data out of your computer in the form of text, pictures (graphics), sounds (audio), or video. One common output device is a **monitor** (sometimes referred to as a **display screen**), which displays text, graphics, and video as soft copies (copies you can see only on screen). Another common output device is the **printer**, which creates hard copies (copies you can touch) of text and graphics. Speakers and earphones (or earbuds) are the output devices for sound.

Figure 2.20

LCDs (flat-panel monitors) save precious desktop space and weigh considerably less than older CRT monitors.

Monitors

What are the different types of monitors? The most common type of monitor is a **liquid crystal display (LCD)** (see Figure 2.20). An LCD monitor, also called a **flat-panel monitor**, is light and energy efficient. Some newer LCD monitors use light-emitting diode (LED) technology, which is even more energy efficient, and may have better color accuracy and thinner panels than traditional LCD monitors. LCD monitors have replaced the cathode ray tube (CRT) monitor. CRT monitors are difficult to find or buy because they have become **legacy technology**, or computing devices or peripherals that use techniques, parts, and methods from an earlier time that are no longer popular. Although legacy technology may still be functional, it is quickly being replaced by newer technological advances. This doesn't mean that if you have a CRT monitor that is functioning well you should replace it with an LCD monitor. However, when your CRT monitor fails, you will most likely only be able to replace it with an LCD monitor.

How do monitors work? Monitor screens are grids made up of millions of tiny dots, each of which is called a **pixel**. Illuminated pixels create the images you see on your monitor. Each pixel is actually comprised of three subpixels of red, blue, and green, and some newer TVs on the market have added a fourth color: yellow. LCD monitors are made of two or more sheets of material filled with a liquid crystal solution (see Figure 2.21). A fluorescent panel at the back of the LCD monitor generates light waves. When electric current passes through the liquid crystal solution, the crystals move around and either block the fluorescent light or let the light shine through. This blocking or passing of light by the crystals causes images to form on the screen. The various combinations of red, blue, and green make up the components of color we see on our monitors.

Figure 2.21

A magnification of a single pixel in an LCD monitor.

Rear glass

Colored light

Polarizer

Front glass

Unpolarized white light from backlight

Polarizer

Liquid crystals

Color filters

What factors affect the quality of an LCD monitor?   When choosing an LCD monitor, there are several factors to consider, such as aspect ratio and resolution. The **aspect ratio** is the width-to-height proportion of a monitor. Traditionally, aspect ratios have been 4:3, but newer monitors are available with an aspect ratio of 16:9 or 16:10. The screen **resolution**, or the clearness or sharpness of the image, reflects the number of pixels on the screen. An LCD monitor may have a native (or maximum) resolution of $1,600 \times 1,200$, meaning it contains 1,600 vertical columns with 1,200 pixels in each column. The higher the resolution, the sharper and clearer the image will be, but generally the resolution of an LCD monitor is dictated by the screen size and aspect ratio. Although you can change the resolution of an LCD monitor beyond its native resolution, the images will become distorted. Generally, you should select a monitor with the highest resolution available for the screen size (measured in inches).

Other factors to consider when judging the quality of an LCD monitor include the following:

- **Contrast ratio**: This is a measure of the difference in light intensity between the brightest white and the darkest black that the monitor can produce. If the contrast ratio is too low, colors tend to fade when you adjust the brightness to a high or low setting. A contrast ratio between 400:1 and 1,000:1 is preferable. Some monitors may sport a dynamic contrast ratio that may be 10,000:1 or 50,000:1. This measurement is taken when the backlight is turned off completely; normal contrast ratio measurements have the backlight dimmed to its lowest setting but not completely off. Unfortunately, in normal use, the backlight is not turned off, so the dynamic contrast ratio is not a relevant measure, unless you are using an LED monitor.
- **Viewing angle**: An LCD's viewing angle, which is measured in degrees, tells how far you can move to the side of (or above or below) the monitor before the image quality degrades to unacceptable levels. For monitors that measure 17 inches or more, a viewing angle of at least 150 degrees is usually recommended.

- **Brightness**: Measured as candelas per square meter (cd/m^2) or *nits*, brightness is a measure of the greatest amount of light showing when the monitor is displaying pure white. A brightness level of $300cd/m^2$ or greater is recommended.
- **Response time**: This is the measurement (in milliseconds) of the time it takes for a pixel to change color. A lower response time value means faster transitions; therefore, moving images will appear less jerky on the monitor.

Is a bigger screen size always better?   The bigger the monitor, the more you can display, and depending on what you want to display, size may matter. In general, the larger the panel, the larger number of pixels it can display. For example, a 21-inch monitor will typically be able to display 1680×1050 pixels, while a 19-inch monitor may only be able to display 1440×900 or 1280×1024. If you watch many high-definition movies on your monitor, you will need a monitor with at least the 1920×1080 resolution required to display HD-DVDs and Blu-ray movies. Larger screens can also allow you to view multiple documents or Web pages at the same time, creating the effect of using two separate monitors side by side. Again, be mindful of cost. Buying two smaller monitors might be cheaper than buying one large monitor. For either option—a big screen or two screens—you should check that your computer has a special adapter card to support these video display devices.

  BITS AND BYTES   Cleaning Your Monitor

Have you ever noticed how quickly your monitor attracts dust? It's important to keep your monitor clean because dust buildup can act like insulation, keeping heat in and causing the electronic components to wear out much faster. To clean your LCD monitor, follow these steps:

1. Turn off the monitor (or your notebook computer) and make sure it is unplugged from the electrical power outlet.
2. Use a 50/50 solution of rubbing alcohol and water on a soft cloth and wipe the screen surface gently. Never spray anything directly onto the monitor. (Check your monitor's user manual to see if there are cleaning products you should avoid using.)
3. In addition to wiping the screen, wipe away the dust from around the case.

Also, don't place anything on top of the monitor or pack anything closely around it. This may block air from cooling it. Finally, avoid placing magnets (including your speaker system's subwoofer) anywhere near the monitor because they can interfere with the mechanisms inside the monitor.

What other features should I look for in an LCD monitor? Some monitors, especially those on notebook computers, come with convenient built-in features such as speakers, webcams, and microphones. A built-in multiformat card reader is convenient to display images directly on the monitor or to download pictures quickly from a camera memory card to the PC. Another nice feature to look for in a desktop LCD monitor is a built-in USB port. This will enable you to connect extra peripherals easily without reaching around the back of the PC.

If these features are important to you, then look for a monitor that has them, but be careful that the price of buying a monitor with these additional features isn't more than what it would cost you to buy the monitor and extra peripherals separately.

How do I show output to a large group of people? Crowding large groups of people around your computer isn't practical. However, it is possible to use a **projector**, a device that can project images from your computer onto a wall or viewing screen (see Figure 2.22). Projectors are commonly used in business and education settings such as conference rooms and classrooms. These projectors are small and lightweight, and some, like the 3M MPro 150, are small enough to fit into the palm of your hand! These portable projectors are ideal for businesspeople that have to make presentations at client locations. *Entertainment projectors*, such as the Wonderwall, include stereo speakers and an array of multimedia connectors, making them a good option for use in the home to display TV programs, DVDs, digital images, or video games in a large format.

Printers

What are the different types of printers? There are two primary categories of printers: inkjet and laser, both of which are considered nonimpact printers. A **nonimpact printer** sprays ink or uses laser

beams to transfer marks onto the paper. Today, nonimpact printers have replaced impact printers almost entirely. An **impact printer** has tiny hammerlike keys that strike the paper through an inked ribbon, making marks on the paper. The most common impact printer is the dot-matrix printer. The only place you may see a dot-matrix printer is at a company that still uses them to print multipart forms. For most users, dot-matrix printers are truly legacy technology.

What are the advantages of inkjet printers? An **inkjet printer** (see Figure 2.23) is the standard type of printer found in most homes. Inkjet printers are popular because they are affordable and produce high-quality color printouts quickly and quietly. Inkjet printers work by spraying tiny drops of ink onto paper and are great for printing black-and-white text as well as color images. In fact, when loaded with the right paper, higher-end inkjet printers can print images that look like professional-quality photos. One thing to consider when buying an inkjet printer is the type and cost of the ink cartridges the printer needs. Some printers use two cartridges: black and color. Other printers use four or more cartridges, typically black, magenta, cyan, and yellow. Often the cost of buying replacement cartridges is more than that of a brand-new printer! Depending on how frequently you

Figure 2.22

Inexpensive projectors are showing up more frequently in business and the home to provide large images for movie viewing and gaming.

print, you might want to consider a laser printer.

Why would I want a laser printer? Laser printers (see Figure 2.24) are most often used in office or classroom settings because they have a faster printing speed than inkjet printers and produce higher-quality printouts. A **laser printer** uses laser beams and static electricity to deliver toner (similar to ink) onto the correct areas of the page. Heat is used to fuse the toner to the page, making the image permanent. In the past, laser printers generally were not found in the home because of their high purchase price and because they did not produce great color images. Recently, however, the quality has improved and the price of color laser printers has fallen dramatically, making them highly price competitive with high-end inkjet printers. When you include the price of ink or toner in the overall cost, laser printers can be more economical than inkjets.

What kind of printer can I take with me? Although some inkjet printers are small enough to carry with you, you may want to consider a printer designed for portability for added mobility and flexibility (see Figure 2.25). Portable printers are often compact enough to fit in a briefcase, are

Figure 2.23

Inkjet printers are popular among home users, especially with the rise of digital photography. Many inkjet printers are optimized for printing photos from digital cameras.

lightweight, and sometimes run on battery power instead of AC power.

Are there wireless printers? One reason you may have bought a notebook was to be able to use a computer without the restriction of wires. Wireless printing offers you the same freedom. In addition, wireless printers allow several people to print to the same printer from different places. There are two different types of wireless printers: WiFi and Bluetooth. Both WiFi and Bluetooth printers have a range of up to approximately 300 feet. WiFi, however, sends data more quickly than Bluetooth. If your printer is not Bluetooth enabled, you can add Bluetooth by plugging a Bluetooth adapter into a USB port. This lets you take advantage of a great printing solution for photos stored on your cell phone or any other Bluetooth-enabled portable device.

Are there any other types of specialty printers? An **all-in-one printer** is a device that combines the functions of a printer, scanner, copier, and fax into one machine. Popular for their space-saving convenience, all-in-one printers can use either inkjet or laser technology. A **plotter** is another type of printer. Plotters produce oversize pictures that require the drawing of

Figure 2.25

Modern portable printers feature Bluetooth connectivity, allowing them to be used with mobile devices.

Figure 2.24

Laser printers print quickly and offer high-quality printouts.

Figure 2.26

Plotters are large printers used to print oversize images, maps, and architectural plans.

Figure 2.27

Thermal printers are used in many restaurants to print receipts.

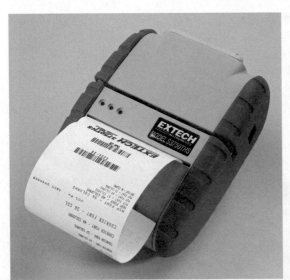

precise and continuous lines, such as maps, detailed images (see Figure 2.26), and architectural plans. Plotters use a computer-controlled pen that provides a greater level of precision than the series of dots that laser or inkjet printers are capable of making.

A **thermal printer**, such as the one shown in Figure 2.27, is another kind of specialty printer. These printers work either by melting wax-based ink onto ordinary paper (a process called *thermal wax transfer printing*), or by burning dots onto specially coated paper (a process called *direct thermal printing*). They are used in stores to print receipts and in airports for electronic ticketing, among other places. Thermal printers are also emerging as a popular technology for mobile and portable printing in conjunction with smartphones and similar devices. Many models, such as the printers that car rental agencies use to give you an instant receipt when you drop off your rental car, feature wireless infrared technology for complete portability.

How do I select the best printer? There is a printer for every printing need. First, you need to decide what your primary printing need is. If you will use your printer mostly to print digital images, then you will want to select a photo printer. If not, then a general-purpose printer will be a better choice. General-purpose printers have a finer, faster text output, whereas photo printers have a more distinctive color output. It's also important to determine whether you want just a printer or a device that prints and scans, copies, or faxes (an all-in-one). In addition, you should decide whether you want an inkjet or laser printer, and whether or not you want to print wirelessly. Once you have narrowed down the type of printer you want, the following criteria will help you determine the best model to meet your needs.

- **Speed:** A printer's speed determines how many pages it can print per minute. Print speed is expressed as *pages per minute* or *ppm*. The speed of inkjet printers has improved over the years, and many inkjet printers now print as fast as laser printers. Printing speeds vary by model and range from 8 ppm to 38 ppm for both laser and inkjet printers. Text documents printed in black and white print faster than documents printed in color.

- **Resolution:** A printer's resolution (printed image clarity) is measured in dots per inch (dpi), which is the number of dots of ink in a one-inch line. The higher the dpi, the greater the level of detail and quality of the image. You'll sometimes see dpi represented as a horizontal number multiplied by a vertical number, such as 600×600, but you may also see the same resolution simply stated as 600 dpi. For general-purpose printing, 1,200 dpi is sufficient. For printing photos, 4,800 dpi is better. The dpi for professional photo-quality printers is twice that.

- **Color output:** If you're using an inkjet printer to print color images, buy a four-color printer (cyan, magenta, yellow, and black) or a six-color one (four-color plus light cyan and light magenta) for the highest-quality output. Although some printers come with a single ink cartridge for all colors and others have two ink cartridges (one for black and one for color), the best setup is to have an individual ink cartridge for each color so you can replace only the specific color cartridge that is empty. Color

How Inkjet and Laser Printers Work

Ever wonder how a printer knows what to print and how it puts ink in just the right places? Most inkjet printers use drop-on-demand technology in which the ink is "demanded" and then "dropped" onto the paper. Two different processes use drop-on-demand technology: Thermal bubble is used by Hewlett-Packard and Canon, and piezoelectric is used by Epson. The difference between the two processes is how the ink is heated within the print cartridge reservoir (the chamber inside the printer that holds the ink).

In the thermal bubble process, the ink is heated in such a way that it expands (like a bubble) and leaves the cartridge reservoir through a small nozzle. Figure 2.28 shows the general process for thermal bubble.

In the piezoelectric process, each ink nozzle contains a crystal at the back of the ink reservoir that receives an electrical charge, causing the ink to vibrate and drop out of the nozzle.

Laser printers use a completely different process. Inside a laser printer is a big metal cylinder (also called a *drum*) that is charged with static electricity. When asked to print something, the printer sends signals to the laser in the laser printer, telling it to "uncharge" selected spots on the charged cylinder. These spots correspond to characters and images in the document you wish to print. Toner, a fine powder that is used in place of liquid ink, is only attracted to those areas on the drum that are not charged (the areas where the desired characters and images are to be printed). The toner is transferred to the paper as it feeds through the printer. Finally, the toner is melted onto the paper. All unused toner is swept back to the toner hopper before the next job starts the process all over again.

Inkjet Printer

Print head

Nozzles

Print cartridges

Inverted print cartridge

The print cartridge is positioned inside your inkjet printer so that the print head faces down toward the paper. The print head has 50 to several hundred nozzles, or small holes, through which ink droplets fall. These nozzles are narrower than a human hair. Inside the print head of color inkjet printers, there are three ink reservoirs that hold magenta (red), cyan (blue), and yellow ink. Depending on your printer, a fourth ink reservoir may be required to hold black ink, as well. (In non-color inkjet printers, there is only one ink reservoir for the black ink.)

(1) Ink, Resistor, Firing chamber, Nozzle

(2) Bubble forming, Ink forced out of the nozzle

(3) Ink drop

(4) Ink dot

STEP 1: Once the printer receives the command to print, electrical pulses flow through thin resistors in the print head to heat the ink.

STEP 2: The heated ink forms a bubble. The bubble continues to expand until it is forced out of the nozzle.

STEP 3: The ink drops onto the paper.

STEP 4: As the ink leaves the cartridge, the chamber begins to cool and contract, creating a vacuum to draw in the ink for the process to begin again.

Figure 2.28

How a thermal bubble inkjet printer works.

Does It Matter What Paper I Print On?

The quality of your printer is only part of what controls the quality of a printed image. The paper you use and the printer settings that control the amount of ink used are equally important. If you're printing text-only documents for personal use, then using low-cost paper is fine. You also may want to consider selecting draft mode in your printer settings to conserve ink. However, if you're printing more formal documents such as résumés, you may want to choose a higher-quality paper (determined by the paper's weight, whiteness, and brightness) and adjust your print setting to "normal" or "best."

The weight of paper is measured in pounds, with 20 pounds being standard. A heavier paper may be best for projects such as brochures, but be sure to check that your printer can handle the added thickness. The degree of paper whiteness is a matter of personal preference. Generally, the whiter the paper, the brighter the printed color. However, for more formal documents, such as résumés, you may want to use a creamier color. The brightness of paper usually varies from 85 to 94. The higher the number, the brighter the paper, and the easier it is to read printed text. Opacity is especially important if you're printing on both sides of the paper because it determines the amount of ink that shows through from the opposite side of the paper.

If you're printing photos, then paper quality can have a big impact on the results. Photo paper is more expensive than regular paper and comes in a variety of textures ranging from matte to high gloss. For a photo-lab look, high-gloss paper is the best choice. Semigloss (often referred to as *satin*) is good for portraits, while a matte surface is often used for black-and-white printing.

laser printers have four separate toner cartridges (black, cyan, magenta, and yellow), and the toner is blended in various quantities to produce the entire color spectrum.

- **Use and cost of the printer:** If you will be printing mostly black-and-white, text-based documents or will be sharing your printer with others, then a black-and-white laser printer is best because of its printing speed and overall economy for volume printing. If you're planning to print color photos and graphics, then an inkjet printer or color laser printer is a must, even though the cost per page will be higher. Keep in mind a printer's reported duty cycle. A duty cycle is a manufacturer's figure that refers to how long a machine can keep operating before it needs a rest, or what percentage of the time it's designed to be in use. For a printer, the duty cycle generally refers to the number of printed pages the printer can reliably produce on a monthly basis. If you buy a printer with a duty cycle of 1,000 copies per month, and you

generally only print 100 copies a month, then you will have overpurchased. Alternatively, exceeding the duty cycle estimates might lead to printer malfunctions.

- **Cost of consumables:** You should carefully investigate the cost of consumables (such as printer cartridges and paper) for any printer you are considering purchasing because the cost of inkjet cartridges often can exceed the cost of the actual printer when purchased on sale. Reviews in consumer magazines such as *PC World* and *Consumer Reports* can help you evaluate the overall cost of producing documents with a particular printer.

Sound Output

What are the output devices for sound?
Most computers include inexpensive speakers. A **speaker** is an output device for sound. These speakers are sufficient to play the standard audio clips you find on the Web and usually enable you to participate in videoconferencing or phone calls made over the Internet. However, if you plan to digitally edit audio files or are particular about how your music sounds, then you may want to upgrade to a more sophisticated speaker system, such as one that includes subwoofers (special speakers that produce only low bass sounds) and surround-sound speakers. A **surround-sound speaker** is a system of speakers and audio processing that envelops the listener in a full 360-degree field of sound. Wireless speaker systems are available now to help you avoid cluttering up your rooms with speaker wire. We discuss surround sound in more detail in Chapter 6.

If you work in close proximity to other employees or travel with a notebook, then you may need to use headphones or earbuds for your sound output to avoid distracting other people. Both devices will plug into the same jack on the computer that speakers connect to, so using them with a computer is easy. Studies of users of portable media players have shown that hearing might be damaged by excessive volume, especially when using earbuds, because they fit into the ear canals. Exercise caution when using these devices.

Processing and Memory on the Motherboard

We just looked at the components of your computer that you use to input and output data. But where does the processing take place, and where is the data stored? The **motherboard** is the main circuit board that contains the central electronic components of the computer, including the computer's processor (its brain), its memory, and the many circuit boards that help the computer function. On a desktop, the motherboard is located inside the **system unit**, the metal or plastic case that also houses the power source and all the storage devices (CD/DVD drive and hard drive). With a notebook computer, the system unit is combined with the monitor and the keyboard into a single package.

What's on the motherboard? Recall that the motherboard is the main circuit board that contains the set of chips that powers the system, including the central processing unit (CPU). The motherboard also houses ROM, RAM, and cache, the chips that provide the short-term memory for the computer. The motherboard also includes slots for **expansion cards** (or **adapter cards**), which are circuit boards that provide additional functionality (see Figure 2.29). Typical expansion cards found in the system unit are the sound and video cards. A **sound card** provides a connection for the speakers and microphone, whereas a **video card** provides a connection for the monitor. Many low-end computer models have video and sound capabilities integrated into their motherboards. High-end models use expansion cards to provide video and sound capabilities. Other expansion cards provide a means for network and Internet connections. These include the **modem card**, which provides the computer with a connection to the Internet via a traditional phone line, and a **network interface card (NIC)**, which enables your computer to connect with other computers or to a cable modem to facilitate a high-speed Internet connection. Lastly, some expansion cards provide additional USB and FireWire ports.

Memory

What exactly is RAM? **Random access memory (RAM)** is the place in a computer where the programs and data the computer is currently using are stored. RAM is much faster to read from and write to than the hard drive and other forms of storage. The processor can request the RAM's contents, which can be located, opened, and delivered to the CPU for processing in a few nanoseconds (billionths of a second). If you look at a motherboard, you'll see RAM as a series of small cards (called *memory cards* or *memory modules*) plugged into slots on the motherboard.

Because the entire contents of RAM are erased when you turn off the computer, RAM is a temporary or **volatile storage** location. To save data permanently, you need to save it to the hard drive or to another permanent storage device such as a CD or flash drive. You can think of RAM as

Figure 2.29

A motherboard contains the CPU, the memory (RAM) modules, and slots for expansion cards.

Expansion slot

Memory modules (RAM)

CPU

Expansion cards

the computer's temporary memory and the hard drive as permanent memory.

Does the motherboard contain any other kinds of memory besides RAM? In addition to RAM, the motherboard also contains a form of memory called **read-only memory (ROM)**. ROM holds all the instructions the computer needs to start up when the computer is powered on. Unlike data stored in RAM, which is volatile storage, the instructions stored in ROM are permanent, making ROM a nonvolatile storage location, which means the data is not erased when the power is turned off.

Processing

Figure 2.30

Two are faster than one! With their dual core processors, Intel CPUs can work in parallel, processing two separate programs at the same time instead of switching back and forth between them.

What is the CPU? The **central processing unit** (**CPU**, or **processor**) is sometimes referred to as the "brains" of the computer because it controls all the functions performed by the computer's other components and processes all the commands issued to it by software instructions. Modern CPUs can perform as many as 45 billion tasks per

second without error, making them extremely powerful components.

How is processor speed measured? Processor speed is measured in units of hertz (Hz). Hertz means "machine cycles per second." A machine cycle is the process of the CPU getting the data or instructions from RAM and decoding the instructions into something the computer can understand. Once the CPU has decoded the instructions, it executes them and stores the result back into system memory. Older machines ran at speeds measured in **megahertz (MHz)**, or millions of machine cycles per second, whereas current systems run at speeds measured in **gigahertz (GHz)**, or billions of machine cycles per second. Therefore, a 3.8 GHz processor performs work at a rate of 3.8 billion machine cycles per second. It's important to realize, however, that CPU clock speed alone doesn't determine the performance of the CPU.

What else determines processor performance? Although speed is an important consideration when determining processor performance, CPU performance also is affected by other factors. One factor is the number of *cores*, or processing paths, a processor has. Until just a few years ago, processors only could handle one instruction at a time. Now, processors have been designed so that they can have two, four, and even eight different paths, allowing them to process more than one instruction at a time (see Figure 2.30). Applications such as virus protection software and the operating system, which are always running behind the scenes, can have their own processors, freeing up the other processor to run other applications such as a Web browser, Word, or iTunes more efficiently.

Besides the number of cores, are there other factors that determine processing power? In addition to the number of cores in a processor, you should consider other factors such as cache memory

Single path vs. dual path processors for data

Single core processor   Dual core processor

and front side bus (FSB). (FSB determines how fast data is exchanged between the CPU and RAM.) These factors will be discussed in greater detail in Chapter 6. The "best" processor will depend on your particular needs and is not always the processor with the highest GHz and the greatest number of cores. Intel, one of the leading manufacturers of computer processor chips, has created a pictorial rating system for CPU chips. Intel uses one to five stars to illustrate the relative computing power of each type of CPU within the Intel line of processors. It also provides an overall ranking of "smart," "smarter," and "genius" and an overview of each processor's key benefits.

Storing Data and Information

Earlier we characterized RAM as temporary or volatile memory because the entire contents of RAM are erased when you turn off the computer. Thus, if you permanently want to save the files you're working on, as well as your music, digital images, and any software applications you use, you need to store them in a different location than RAM. To save data permanently, you need to save it to the hard drive or to another permanent storage device such as a CD, DVD, or flash drive. Each of these permanent storage devices is located in your desktop or notebook computer in a space called a **drive bay** (see Figure 2.31). There are two kinds of drive bays—internal and external—as described below:

- Internal drive bays cannot be seen or accessed from outside the system unit. Generally, internal drive bays are reserved for internal hard drives. An **internal hard drive** usually holds all permanently stored programs and data.

CD/DVD drive

Empty drive bay

Hard drive

Figure 2.31

Storage devices in desktop and notebook computers.

- External drive bays can be seen and accessed from outside the system unit. External drive bays house CD and DVD drives, for example. On desktop computers, sometimes there are empty external drive bays that can be used to install additional drives. These extra spaces are covered by a faceplate on the front panel. Notebook computers generally do not give you the ability to add additional drives. Such expansion is done by attaching an external drive to the computer through a USB port.

You may occasionally see a PC that still has a bay for a *floppy disk drive*, which reads and writes to easily transportable floppy disks that hold a limited amount of data (1.44 MB). Some computers also feature what's called a *Zip disk drive*, which resembles a floppy disk drive but has a slightly wider opening. Zip disks work just like standard floppy disks but can carry much more data (up to 750 MB). These storage devices are legacy technologies and are not found on new computers.

Hard Drives

Which storage device holds the most data? The **hard drive** (see Figure 2.32a) is your computer's primary device for permanent storage of software and documents. The hard drive is a **nonvolatile storage** device, meaning it holds the data and instructions your computer needs permanently, even after the computer is turned off. Today's internal hard drives, with capacities

Figure 2.32

(a) Internal hard drives hold the data and instructions that the computer needs and are inaccessible from outside the system unit. (b) High-capacity external hard drives are often used to back up data on internal hard drives. (c) Smaller external hard drives enable you to take a significant amount of data and programs on the road with you.

Figure 2.33

Flash drives are a convenient means of portable storage, and come in many different shapes and sizes.

of as much as 3.5 terabyte (TB), can hold more data than would fit in the books in a school's library.

Are all hard drives located inside the system? Because the hard drive stores all of the computer's data and programs, special measures are taken to protect the hard drive from any possible damage. Unlike other storage devices on the computer, the hard drive is enclosed in a case and is not accessible from the outside of the system unit. If you need a more portable solution, external hard drives are readily available. An **external hard drive** (see Figures 2.32b and 2.32c) is essentially like an internal hard drive. However, it has been made portable by making it small and lightweight and enclosing it in a protective case. Some external hard drives, which are small enough to fit into your pocket, have storage capacities of 1 or 2 TB (or larger). An external hard drive is often used to back up (make a copy of) data that is contained on

an internal hard drive in case a problem develops with the internal hard drive and data needs to be recovered.

Optical Storage

What other kinds of storage devices are available? Internal hard drives are used to store your data, files, and installed software programs. Hard drives store their data on magnetized platters. Also included on most desktop and notebook computers is at least one **optical drive** that can read from and maybe even write to CDs, DVDs, or Blu-ray discs. Data is saved to a **compact disc (CD)**, **digital video** (or **versatile**) **disc (DVD)**, or **Blu-ray disc (BD)** as tiny pits that are burned into the disc by a high-speed laser. CDs were initially created to store audio files. DVDs are the same size and shape as CDs but can hold more data. DVDs that store data on just one side and in one layer can store about seven times more data. If you're looking for more storage capacity, a double-sided/single-layer DVD is the next step. These discs have up to 8.5 GB of storage, and a double-sided/double-layer DVD can store nearly 16 GB of data. What if you want even more storage capacity? Blu-ray is the latest incarnation of optical storage to hit the market. Blu-ray discs, which are similar in size and shape to CDs and DVDs, can hold as much as 50 GB of data— enough to hold approximately 4.5 hours of movies in the high-definition (HD) digital format that has become so popular. Many systems are now available with BD-ROM drives and even Blu-ray burners. External BD drives are another inexpensive way to add HD storage capacity to your system.

Flash Storage

A **flash drive**, sometimes referred to as a **jump drive**, **USB drive**, or **thumb drive**, is a way of storing portable data. Flash drives plug into USB ports. These devices originally were more or less the size of a thumb, but now they vary in size and are often combined with other devices such as pens or pocketknives (see Figure 2.33). Despite their diminutive size, flash drives have significant storage capacity—currently as much as 256 GB.

Several manufacturers now also include slots on the front of the system unit in which you can insert a portable **flash memory card** such as a Memory Stick or CompactFlash card. Many notebooks also include slots for flash memory cards in the sides. Flash memory cards let you transfer digital data between your computer and devices such as digital cameras, PDAs, smartphones, video cameras, and printers. Although incredibly small—some are just the size of a postage stamp—these memory cards have capacities that exceed the capacity of a DVD. We discuss flash memory in more detail in Chapter 8.

Some hard drives are also based on flash memory. A **solid state drive (SSD)** does not have any spinning platters or motors, so they are more efficient, run with no noise, emit very little heat, and require very little power.

Figure 2.34 shows the storage capacities of the various portable storage media used in your computer's drive bays.

Connecting Peripherals to the Computer

Throughout this chapter, we have discussed peripheral devices that input, store, and output data and information. A **port** is a place through which a peripheral device attaches to the computer so that data can be exchanged between it and the operating system. Many ports are located on the back

Figure 2.34 | STORAGE MEDIA CAPACITIES

Medium	Image	Capacity
Mechanical hard drive		As much as 3.5 TB
Solid state drive (SSD)		5 TB or more
External portable hard drive		4 TB or more
Flash drive		256 GB or more
Blu-ray (dual layer)		50 GB
Flash memory card		Up to 128 GB
Blu-ray (BD)		25 GB
DVD DL (dual layer)		88.5 GB
DVD		4.7 GB
CD		700 MB

Memory card slots

USB ports

Figure 2.35

Many of the same ports appear on both (a) notebook and (b) desktop computers.

Audio/video ports

Ethernet port

S-video

FireWire ports

of a notebook computer and the system unit of a desktop computer. However, some commonly used ports are placed on the front and sides of many desktop and notebook computers (see Figure 2.35) for easier access when connecting devices such as flash drives or digital and video cameras.

High-Speed and Data Transfer Ports

What is the most common way to connect devices to a computer? A **universal serial bus (USB) port** is now the most common port type used to connect input and output devices to the computer. This is mainly because of a USB port's ability to transfer data quickly. USB 2.0 ports (see Figure 2.36) are the current standard and transfer data at 480 megabits per second (Mbps), approximately 40 times faster than the original USB ports. USB ports can connect a wide variety of peripherals to the computer, including keyboards, printers, mice, smartphones, external hard drives, flash drives, and digital cameras. The new USB 3.0 standard provides transfer speeds of 4.8 Gbps, which is 10 times the

ACTIVE HELP-DESK

Exploring Storage Devices and Ports

In this Active Helpdesk call, you'll play the role of a helpdesk staffer, fielding calls about the computer's main storage devices and how to connect various peripheral devices to the computer.

SOUND BYTE

Port Tour: How Do I Hook It Up?

In this Sound Byte, you'll take a tour of both a desktop system and a notebook system to compare the number and variety of available ports. You'll also learn about the different types of ports and compare their speed and expandability.

speed of USB 2.0. USB 3.0 should quickly become the port of choice.

A traditional serial port sends data one bit (piece of data) at a time. Serial ports were often used to connect modems (devices used to transmit data over telecommunications lines) to the computer. Sending data one bit at a time was a slow way to communicate. A parallel port could send data between devices in groups of bits at speeds of 500 Kbps and was much faster than traditional serial ports. Parallel ports were often used to connect printers to computers. The speed advantage offered by USB ports has made serial and parallel ports legacy technology.

What are other types of ports? You may also see other ports, such as **FireWire 400** and **FireWire 800**. The FireWire 400 interface moves data at 400 Mbps, while the FireWire 800 doubles the rate to 800 Mbps. Devices such as external hard drives, digital video cameras, portable music players, and digital media

Figure 2.36
A USB port and a USB connector.

players all benefit from the speedy data transfer capabilities of FireWire. The FireWire 3200 standard, with data transfer rates of 3.2 Gbps, has been ratified but has yet to reach the market. FireWire 400 ports and connectors have two different configurations, as shown in Figure 2.37. FireWire 400 ports on computers generally have six pins, while FireWire ports on digital cameras have four pins.

6-pin 4-pin

Figure 2.37
FireWire ports come in different configurations, some of which are illustrated here.

To transfer data between the two devices, a special cable that has an appropriate connector at each end is needed. The faster FireWire 800 requires a nine-pin connection and is found on storage devices such as external and portable hard drives.

Connectivity and Multimedia Ports

Which ports help me connect with other computers and the Internet? Another set of ports on your computer helps you - communicate with other computers. A **connectivity port** can give you access to networks and the Internet or enable your computer to function as a fax machine. To find a connectivity port, look for a port that resembles a standard phone jack but is slightly larger. This port is called an **Ethernet port** (see Figure 2.38). Ethernet ports transfer data at speeds up to 1,000 Mbps. You can use an Ethernet port to connect your computer to a digital subscriber line (DSL) or cable modem, or a network. Many computers still feature a second connectivity port that will accept a standard phone line connector. This jack is the **modem port**. It uses a traditional telephone signal to connect to the Internet over a phone line.

How do I connect monitors and multimedia devices? Other ports on the back of the computer include the audio and video ports (see Figure 2.39). Video ports are necessary to hook up monitors. Whether you are attaching a monitor to a desktop computer, or adding a second, larger display to a notebook computer, you will use video ports. The **video graphics array (VGA)** port is the port to which CRT monitors connect.

Figure 2.38
An Ethernet port and an Ethernet connector.

S-video port for connecting your PC to your TV

DVI port for digital LCDs

VGA port for CRTs and analog LCDs

Speakers

Microphone

Headphones

Figure 2.39

DVI, VGA, and S-video ports connect your monitors and multimedia devices to the computer.

Many older LCD monitors also connect with a VGA port. The newer LCD monitors, as well as other multimedia devices such as televisions, DVD players, and projectors, connect to **digital video interface (DVI)** and **S-video (super video)** ports. Audio ports are where you connect headphones, microphones, and speakers to the computer.

How can I connect my computer to TVs and gaming consoles? The latest digital connector designed for use in high-definition home theater environments is **high-definition multimedia interface (HDMI)**, a compact audio–video interface that carries both high-definition video and uncompressed digital audio on one cable. (DVI can only carry video signals.) Because HDMI can transmit uncompressed audio and video, there is no need to convert the signal, which could ultimately reduce the quality of the sound or picture. Most

Figure 2.40

HDMI is the latest digital connector type for HD home theater equipment.

devices such as DVD players, TVs, and game consoles have at least one HDMI port (see Figure 2.40).

Adding Ports: Expansion Cards and Hubs

What if I don't have all the ports I need? Because almost everything connects to your computer using USB ports, your desktop computer should have at least six USB ports, and a notebook computer should have at least three USB ports. Therefore, if you are looking to add the newest ports to an older computer or to expand the number of ports on your computer, you can use special expansion cards. For example, your computer may have only USB 2.0 ports, but you would like to upgrade to the new USB 3.0 ports. You can install expansion cards in your system unit to provide additional ports (such as USB 3.0 and FireWire). Like other expansion cards, these cards clip into an open expansion slot on the motherboard. Figure 2.41 shows an example of such an expansion card.

What if there are no open slots on the motherboard where I can insert an expansion card? If there are no open slots on the motherboard and you

Figure 2.41

This expansion card provides your computer with additional ports.

USB

FireWire

Figure 2.42
If you don't have enough USB ports to support your USB devices, consider getting an expansion hub, which can add four or more USB ports to your system.

still need extra ports, you can add an expansion hub (shown in Figure 2.42). An expansion hub is a device that connects to one port, such as a USB port, to provide additional new ports. It works like the multiplug extension cords used with electrical appliances.

You also can add ports to an empty drive bay, giving you easy-to-reach new ports. The Koutech 10-in-1, shown in Figure 2.43, fits into a regular drive bay and adds front-panel access to two USB 2.0 ports, two FireWire ports, three audio jacks, and a six-in-one digital media card reader.

Power Controls

What's the best way to turn my computer on and off? The **power supply**, which is housed inside the system unit, transforms the wall voltage to the voltages required by computer chips. A desktop system typically has a power-on button on the front panel of the system unit, though you may also find power-on buttons on some keyboards. On notebooks, the power-on button is generally located near the top of the keyboard. Powering on your computer from a completely turned off state, such as when you start your computer in the morning, is called a **cold boot**.

How do I power down a computer properly? Powering off your computer

properly helps to save energy, keeps your computer more secure, and ensures that your data is saved. You can turn your computer off by pressing the computer's power button or using the Shut Down button on the Start menu.

Should I turn off my computer every time I'm done using it? Some people say you should leave your computer on at all times. They argue that turning your computer on and off throughout the day subjects its components to stress because the heating and cooling process forces the components to expand and contract repeatedly. Other people say you should shut down your computer when you're not using it. They claim that it's not as environmentally friendly, and you'll end up wasting money on electricity to keep the computer running all the time. Modern operating systems include power-management settings that allow the most power-hungry components of the system (the hard drive and monitor) to shut down after a short idle period. With the power-management options of Windows 7, for example, you really need to shut down your computer completely only when you need to repair or install hardware in the system unit or move the system unit to another location. However, if you use your computer only for a little while each day, it would be best to power it off completely after each daily use.

Figure 2.43
You can use an empty drive bay to add additional ports and even a flash card reader to the front panel of the system unit.

Figure 2.44

The Sleep and Hibernate settings are good for the environment and for your wallet.

>To open the Power Options dialog box, click the **Start** button, click **Control Panel**, and then click **Power Options**.

Can I "rest" my computer without turning it off completely? As mentioned earlier, your computer has power-management settings that help it conserve energy. In Windows 7, the two main methods of power management are Sleep and Hibernate. When your computer enters **Sleep mode**, all of the documents, applications, and data you were using remain in RAM (memory), where they are quickly accessible when you restart your computer. (In Windows XP, this mode is called Standby.)

Hibernate is another power-saving mode that stores your data in memory and saves it to your computer's hard drive. In either Sleep or Hibernate mode, the computer enters a state of greatly reduced power consumption, which saves energy. The big advantage to using Hibernate is that if there is a power failure while your computer is conserving power, your information is protected from loss, because it is saved on the hard drive. To put your computer into Sleep or Hibernate, open the Start menu and select the appropriate Sleep or Hibernate option. To wake up your computer, tap a key on the keyboard or move the mouse. In a few seconds, the computer will resume with exactly

the same programs running and documents displayed as when you put it to sleep.

In Windows 7, you can change what happens when you press the power button on the Start menu. By accessing the Power Options screen (see Figure 2.44), you can decide if you want your computer to Sleep or Hibernate when you click the power button.

What's the restart option in Windows for? If you're using Windows 7, you have the option to restart the computer when you click the right arrow button next to the Shut Down button on the Start menu (see Figure 2.45). Restarting the system while it's powered on is called a **warm boot**. You might need to perform a warm boot if the operating system or other software

Right arrow button

Figure 2.45

The Start menu in Windows 7 presents several power options. For a warm boot, choose **Restart**. To power down the computer completely, choose **Shut Down**. To put your computer into a lower power mode, select **Sleep** or **Hibernate**.

>To select a particular power option, click the **Start** menu button in the taskbar and then click the right arrow button.

application stops responding or if you have installed new programs. It takes less time to perform a warm boot than to power down completely and then restart all of your hardware.

Setting It All Up

It's important that you understand not only your computer's components and how they work together but also how to set up these components safely. *Merriam-Webster's Dictionary* defines **ergonomics** as "an applied science concerned with designing and arranging things people use so that the people and things interact most efficiently and safely." In terms of computing, ergonomics refers to how you set up your computer and other equipment to minimize your risk of injury or discomfort.

Why is ergonomics important? You don't have to have a desk job to run the risk of becoming injured by working improperly on a computer. Studies suggest that teenagers, on average, spend 31 hours online each week. When you factor in other computer uses such as typing school reports and playing video games, there is great potential for injury. The repetitive nature of long-term computer activities can place too much stress on joints and pull at the tendons and muscles, causing repetitive stress injuries such as carpal tunnel syndrome and tendonitis. These injuries can take months or years to develop to a point where they becomes painful, and by the time you notice the symptoms, the damage has already taken place. If you take precautionary care now, you may prevent years of unnecessary pain later on.

How can I avoid injuries when I'm working at my computer? As Figure 2.46 illustrates, it is important to

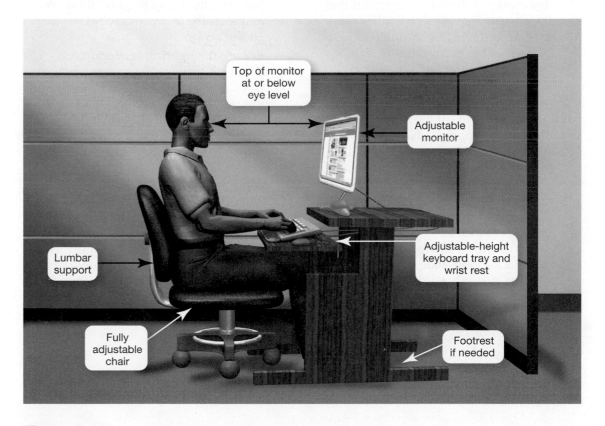

Figure 2.46

Using proper equipment that is adjusted correctly helps prevent repetitive strain injuries while working at a computer.

Figure 2.47
Ergonomic keyboards that curve and contain built-in wrist rests help maintain proper hand position and minimize wrist strain.

arrange your monitor, chair, body, and keyboard in ways that will help you avoid injury, discomfort, and eyestrain as you work on your computer. The following additional guidelines can help keep you comfortable and productive:

- **Position your monitor correctly.** Studies suggest it's best to place your monitor at least 25 inches from your eyes. You may need to decrease the screen resolution to make text and images more readable at that distance. Experts recommend that the monitor be positioned either at eye level or so that it is at an angle 15 to 20 degrees below your line of sight.

- **Purchase an adjustable chair.** Adjust the height of your chair so that your feet touch the floor. (You may need to use a footrest to get the right position.) The back support needs to be adjustable so that you can position it to support your lumbar (lower back) region. You should also be able to move the seat or adjust the back so that you can sit without exerting pressure on your knees. If your chair doesn't adjust, placing a pillow behind your back can provide the same support.

- **Assume a proper position while typing.** A repetitive strain injury (RSI) is a painful condition caused by repetitive or awkward movements of a part of the body. Improperly positioned keyboards are one of the leading causes of RSIs in computer users. Your wrists should be flat (not bent) with respect to the keyboard, and your forearms should be parallel to the floor. Additionally, your wrists should not be resting on the keyboard while typing. You can either adjust the height of your chair or install a height-adjustable keyboard tray to ensure a proper position. Specially designed ergonomic keyboards such as the one shown in Figure 2.47 can help you achieve the proper wrist position.

- **Take breaks from computer tasks.** Remaining in the same position for long periods of time increases stress on your body. Shift your position in your chair and stretch your hands and fingers periodically. Likewise, staring at the screen for long periods of time can lead to eyestrain, so rest your eyes by periodically taking them off the screen and focusing them on an object at least 20 feet away.

- **Ensure the lighting is adequate.** Ensuring that you have proper lighting in your work area is a good way to minimize eyestrain. To do so, eliminate any sources of direct glare (light shining directly into your eyes) or reflected glare (light shining off the computer screen) and ensure there is enough light to read comfortably. If you still can't eliminate glare from your computer screen, you can purchase an antiglare screen to place over your monitor. Look for ones that are polarized or have a purplish optical coating. These will provide the greatest relief.

Is ergonomics important when using mobile devices? Working with mobile computing devices presents interesting challenges when it comes to injury prevention. For example, many users work with notebooks resting on their laps, placing the monitor outside of the optimal line of sight and thereby increasing neck strain. The table in Figure 2.48 provides guidelines on preventing injuries when computing on the go.

So whether you're computing at your desk or on the road, consider the ergonomics of your work environment. Doing so will help you avoid injury and discomfort.

Figure 2.48 | PREVENTING INJURIES WHILE ON THE GO

	PDA/Smartphone RSIs	PMP Hearing Damage	Small-Screen Vision Issues	Lap Injuries	Back, Neck, and Shoulder Injuries
Malady	Repetitive strain injuries (such as DeQuervain's tendonitis) from constant typing of instant messages.	Hearing loss from high decibel sound levels in earbuds or headphones.	Blurriness and dryness caused by squinting to view tiny screens on mobile devices.	Burns on legs from heat generated by notebook.	Pain caused from carrying notebook (messenger) bag hung over your shoulder.
Preventative measures	Restrict length and frequency of messages, take breaks often, and perform other motions with your thumbs and fingers during breaks to relieve tension.	Turn down volume (you should be able to hear external noises such as people talking), use software programs that limit sound levels (not over 60 decibels), and use external, over-ear style headphones instead of earbuds.	Blink frequently or use eye drops to maintain moisture level in eyes, after 10 minutes take a break and focus your eyes on something at least 8 feet away for 5 minutes, use an adequate amount of light, increase the size of fonts.	Place a book, magazine, or notebook cooling pad between your legs and your notebook.	Use a conventional backpack with two shoulder straps, lighten the load by only carrying essential equipment, and consider buying a lightweight notebook.

Today, LCD monitors dominate the desktop PC and notebook markets. Lighter and less bulky than previous monitors, they can be easily moved and take up less space on a desk. LCD technology has improved significantly over the past several years, and now monitors are sporting increased viewing angles, higher resolutions, and faster pixel response time, which makes full-motion video (critical for gamers) appear extremely smooth.

LCD technology has also infiltrated the television market and, along with plasma technology, has made the boxy TV as obsolete as the CRT monitor. However, as good as LCD technology is, some technology that is beginning to hit the market is even better.

OLED Displays

Organic light-emitting diode (OLED) displays use organic compounds that produce light when exposed to an electric current. Unlike LCDs, OLEDs do not require a backlight to function and therefore draw less power and have a much thinner display, sometimes as thin as 3 mm. They are also brighter, cheaper to manufacture, and more environmentally friendly than plasma displays or LCDs. Because of their lower power needs, OLED displays run longer on a single battery charge than do LEDs, which is why OLED technology is currently being used in small screens of mobile devices such as cell phones, portable media players, and digital cameras.

More recently, OLED technology has been incorporated in some high-end televisions. The benefits of OLED technology may make LCD flat-panel displays quickly obsolete (see Figure 2.49). The pixels in OLED screens illuminate quickly, like lightbulbs, and produce brighter images than does LCD technology. Because of the quick on/off illumination capacity of OLED pixels, the faster refresh rate enables these screens to display full-motion videos with lifelike motion. Sony and Toshiba have already produced OLED televisions. Eventually, you might not even need a separate display device; it could very well be built into the walls of your house!

Figure 2.49

Because they do not need a backlight, OLED displays are much thinner than LEDs, making LCD screens seem bulky!

Flexible Screens

An offshoot of OLED technology is the flexible OLED (FOLED). Unlike LCDs, which use rigid surfaces such as glass, FOLED screens use lightweight, inexpensive, flexible material such as transparent plastics or metal foils. As shown in Figure 2.50, these flexible screens can play a full-motion video while being completely bent.

Figure 2.50

This 2.5-inch screen is playing a full-motion video while being bent into a semicircle.

Figure 2.51

Personal media viewers allow you to have a big-screen experience with your mobile devices. The display is projected in front of your eyes, giving you an "in the action" experience.

FOLEDs would allow advertising to progress to a new dimension. Screens could be hung where posters hang now (such as on billboards). Wireless transmission of data to these screens would allow advertisers to display easily updatable full-motion images. Combining transparency and flexibility, these displays can be mounted on windshields and eyeglasses.

Wearable Screens

Who needs a computer screen when you can just wear one? With the rise of the iPod and other portable devices that play digital video, users are demanding larger viewing areas. Although a larger screen is often incompatible with the main design features of portable devices (light weight and long battery life), wearable virtual displays offer a solution. Personal media viewer displays such as the *myvu*, shown in Figure 2.51, are available now (**myvu.com**). Eventually, when the technology advances sufficiently, you might be able to purchase conventional eyeglasses with displays built right in. Wearable displays might eventually replace heavier screens on notebooks, desktops, and even PDAs.

"Bistable" Screens

Your computer screen constantly changes its images when you are surfing the Internet or playing a game. Because PDA and cell phone screens don't necessarily change that often, something called a "bistable" display, which is currently used in retail stores for pricing signs and in Amazon's Kindle (a wireless reading device), may one day be used in these devices. A bistable display has the ability to retain its image even when the power is turned off. In addition, bistable displays are lighter than LCD displays and reduce overall power consumption, resulting in longer battery life— perhaps as much as 600 times longer, according to Motorola. Because the market for portable devices such as smartphones continues to explode, you can expect to see bistable technologies emerging in mobile computer screens.

two summary

summary

1. What exactly is a computer, and what are its four main functions?

Computers are devices that process data. They help organize, sort, and categorize data to turn it into information. The computer's four major functions are to (1) gather data (or allow users to input data), (2) process (manipulate, calculate, or organize) that data, (3) output data or information (display information in a form suitable for the user), and (4) store data and information for later use.

2. What is the difference between data and information?

Data is a representation of a fact or idea. The number 3 and the words *televisions* and *Sony* are pieces of data. Information is data that has been organized or presented in a meaningful fashion. An inventory list that indicates that "three Sony televisions" are in stock is processed information. It allows a retail clerk to answer a customer query about the availability of merchandise. Information is more powerful than raw data.

3. What are bits and bytes, and how are they measured?

To process data into information, computers need to work in a language they understand. This language, called *binary language*, consists of two numbers: 0 and 1. Each 0 and each 1 is a binary digit, or bit. Eight bits create one byte. In computers, each letter of the alphabet, each number, and each special character consists of a unique combination of eight bits (one byte)—a string of eight 0s and 1s. For describing large amounts of storage capacity, the terms *megabyte* (approximately 1 million bytes), *gigabyte* (approximately 1 billion bytes), and *terabyte* (approximately 1 trillion bytes) are used.

4. What devices do I use to get data into the computer?

An input device enables you to enter data (text, images, and sounds) and instructions (user responses and commands) into a computer. You use keyboards to enter typed data and commands, whereas you use the mouse to enter user responses and commands.

Keyboards and mice come in both wired and wireless versions, as well as other special layouts and designs to fit almost every need.

Touch screens are display screens that respond to commands initiated by a touch with a finger or a stylus. Images are input into the computer with scanners, digital cameras, camcorders, and cell phones. Live video is captured with webcams and digital video recorders. Microphones capture sounds. There are many different types of microphones, including desktop, headset, and clip-on models.

5. What devices do I use to get information out of the computer?

Output devices enable you to send processed data out of your computer. It can take the form of text, pictures, sounds, or video. Monitors display soft copies of text, graphics, and video, while printers create hard copies of text and graphics. LCDs are the most popular type of monitor.

There are two primary categories of printers used today: inkjet and laser. Specialty printers are also available. These include all-in-one printers, plotters, and thermal printers. When choosing a printer, you should be aware of factors such as speed, resolution, color output, and cost.

Speakers are the output devices for sound. Most computers include speakers, with more sophisticated systems including subwoofers and surround sound.

6. What's on the motherboard?

The motherboard, the main circuit board of the system, contains a computer's central processing unit (CPU), which coordinates the functions of all other devices on the computer. The performance of a CPU is affected by the speed of the processor (measured in gigahertz), the amount of cache memory, the speed of the front side bus (FSB), and the number of processing cores. RAM, the computer's volatile memory, is also located on the motherboard. RAM is where all the data and instructions are held while the computer is running. ROM, a permanent type of memory, is responsible for housing instructions to help start up a computer. The motherboard also houses a set of slots for expansion cards, which have specific functions that augment the computer's basic functions. Typical expansion cards found in the system unit are the sound and video cards.

7. Where are information and programs stored?

To save programs and information permanently, you need to save them to the hard drive or to another permanent storage device such as a CD, DVD, or flash drive. The hard drive is your computer's primary device for permanent storage of software and files. The hard drive is a nonvolatile storage device, meaning it holds the data and instructions your computer needs permanently, even after the computer is turned off. Mechanical hard drives have spinning platters on which data is saved, whereas newer solid state hard drives (SSD) use solid state memory, similar to that used with flash drives. External hard drives are essentially internal hard drives that have been made portable by enclosing them in a protective case and making them small and lightweight. Optical drives that can read from and maybe even write to CD, DVD, or Blu-ray discs are another means of permanent, portable storage. Data is saved to compact discs (CDs), digital video discs (DVDs), and Blu-ray discs (BDs) as tiny pits that are burned into the disc by a high-speed laser. Flash drives are another portable means of storing data. Flash drives plug into USB ports. Flash memory cards let you transfer digital data between your computer and devices such as digital cameras, smartphones, video cameras, and printers.

8. How are devices connected to the computer?

There are a wide variety of ports that allow you to hook up peripheral devices (such as your monitor and keyboard) to your system.

The most common type of port used to connect devices to a computer is the USB port. USB technology has replaced serial ports and parallel ports, which are now considered legacy technology. USB 2.0 is the current standard but will be quickly replaced by the newer, faster, USB 3.0 standard. FireWire ports provide additional options for data transfer.

Connectivity ports give you access to networks and the Internet and enable your computer to function as a fax machine. Connectivity ports include Ethernet ports and modem ports. Multimedia ports include VGA, DVI, and S-video ports. They connect the computer to monitors and other multimedia devices. Audio ports are where you connect headphones, microphones, and speakers to the computer. HDMI ports are used as a connection between monitors, TVs and gaming consoles and work with both audio and video content.

9. How do I set up my computer to avoid strain and injury?

Ergonomics refers to how you arrange your computer and equipment to minimize your risk of injury or discomfort. This includes positioning your monitor correctly, buying an adjustable chair that ensures you have good posture while using the computer, assuming a proper position while typing, making sure the lighting is adequate, and not looking at the screen for long periods of time. Other good practices include taking frequent breaks and using other specially designed equipment such as ergonomic keyboards. Ergonomics is also important to consider when using mobile devices.

key terms

Word Bank

- CPU
- DVI
- ergonomics
- external hard drive
- FireWire
- inkjet printer
- laser printer

- LCD
- microphone
- monitor
- mouse
- notebook
- optical mouse
- QWERTY

- RAM
- ROM
- speakers
- SSD
- system unit
- USB
- webcam

Instructions: Fill in the blanks using the words from the Word Bank above.

Austin had been getting a sore back and stiff arms when he sat at his desk, so he redesigned the (1) _____ of his notebook setup. He placed the notebook in a stand so the (2) _____ was elevated to eye level and was 25 inches from his eyes. He decided to improve his equipment in other ways. His (3) _____ was old, so he replaced it with a(n) (4) _____ that didn't need a mouse pad. To plug in the mouse, he used a(n) (5) _____ port on the side of his (6) _____. He considered buying a larger (7) _____ keyboard with a number pad because it's not convenient to input numeric data with his current keyboard. Because he often printed flyers for his band, Austin decided to buy a printer that could print text-based pages quickly. Although he decided to keep his (8) _____ to print photos, he decided to buy a new (9) _____ to print his flyers faster. While looking at printers, Austin also noticed widescreen (10) _____ monitors that would provide a larger display than that on his notebook, so he bought one on sale. He hooked up the monitor to the (11) _____ port on the back of the notebook. He also bought a(n) (12) _____ that was attached to a headset and a(n) (13) _____ so he could talk to his friends over the Internet. Austin also knew he had to buy a(n) (14) _____ to back up all his files. Finally, knowing his system could use more memory, Austin checked out prices for additional (15) _____.

becoming computer literate

Your grandparents live a day's drive from your school and have just called asking you for help in purchasing a new computer, but they don't know what type of computer to get.

Instructions: Because you can't help them in person, write a letter to your grandparents detailing the differences between desktop, notebook, tablet PC, and netbook computers. Include the pros and cons of each device, and explain why or why not each device may suit your grandparents. Because your grandparents are not as familiar about these devices as you are, you should also incorporate images for each device in the letter. You may use the Internet for information, device pictures, and illustrations, but remember to credit all sources.

Instructions: Answer the multiple-choice and true–false questions below for more practice with key terms and concepts from this chapter.

Multiple Choice

1. What controls the way in which your computer system functions?
   a. System software
   b. Operating system
   c. Application software
   d. Hardware

2. Which is the most common type of monitor?
   a. LCD monitor c. LED monitor
   b. CRT monitor d. HD monitor

3. What enables your computer to connect with other computers?
   a. Expansion card
   b. Adapter card
   c. Video card
   d. Network interface card

4. Which is NOT another name for a flash drive?
   a. Zip   c. Jump
   b. USB   d. Thumb

5. To add additional ports to your computer, what do you need?
   a. A digital media card reader
   b. An external hard drive
   c. An expansion card
   d. A flash memory card

6. Which holds the instructions the computer needs to start up?
   a. CPU   c. USB
   b. RAM   d. ROM

7. Which is TRUE about mainframe computers?
   a. They perform complex calculations rapidly.
   b. They support hundreds of users simultaneously.
   c. They execute many programs at a fast pace.
   d. They excel at running a few programs quickly.

8. Which is NOT important to consider when buying a printer?
   a. Paper
   b. Duty cycle
   c. Cost of consumables
   d. Resolution

9. Which is NOT a storage device?
   a. External hard drive
   b. DVD
   c. Flash memory card
   d. Touch screen

10. What lets you transfer digital data between your computer and devices such as digital cameras?
    a. Flash memory card
    b. Optical drive
    c. Connectivity port
    d. HDMI port

True–False

_____ 1. The CPU clock speed determines the performance of the CPU.

_____ 2. The hard drive is an example of a nonvolatile storage device.

_____ 3. Ergonomics is important only with desktop computers, not mobile devices.

_____ 4. For printing photos, printing at 1,200 dpi is sufficient.

_____ 5. Some mice include wireless USB receivers that contain flash memory to store your files.

making the
transition to...
next semester

two chapter

making the
transition to...
next semester

1. Choosing the Best Keyboard and Mouse

Once you become more familiar with software products such as Microsoft Office, you may want to migrate to customized keyboard and mouse designs. Although most keyboards and mice have similar setups, there are some devices that provide special features to support different users and their specific needs. For example, some keyboards are designed specifically for multimedia use, Internet use, or gaming use. Some mice have buttons for certain tasks. Which ones are best for you?

a. Examine the various keyboard setups at the Microsoft Web site (**microsoft.com/hardware/mouseandkeyboard/default.mspx**). Which keyboard would best suit your needs and why? What features would be most useful to you?

b. Look at the new cool mice at **laptopshop.co.uk/news/2009/05/coolest-computer-mice**. Would any of these mice or the multitouch Magic Mouse by Apple mentioned earlier in this chapter work for you? Why or why not?

2. Watching Device Demos

YouTube is a great resource for product demonstrations. Open your browser, navigate to the YouTube Web site (**youtube.com**), and search on any type of computer peripheral discussed in this chapter to see if you can find a demonstration of a cool product.

How helpful are these demonstrations? Make a demonstration of a computing device you have and upload it to YouTube.

3. Communicating with the Computer

You want to start using Voice over Internet Protocol (VoIP) to chat over the Internet with your family and friends who live far away. On the Web, investigate the following:

a. List the devices you need to start using VoIP.

b. Research the prices and features of each required device and create a shopping list of the specific devices you would purchase.

4. Turn Your Monitor into a TV

You've heard how easy it is to convert an LCD monitor into a TV. Your parents just bought a new computer and are giving you their old PC monitor. You need a new TV for your dorm room, so you decide to give it a try.

a. What does your monitor need to retrofit it into a TV? What other devices do you need?

b. How much will it cost?

c. How much do new LCD TVs cost? Is this something you would consider doing? Why or why not?

d. What would you do if your parents gave you their old LCD TV? Could you turn it into a monitor? If so, what would you need to do that?

5. Green Computing

Reducing energy consumption and promoting the recycling of computer components are key aspects of many businesses' "green" (environmentally friendly) initiatives. Using the Web, research the following:

a. What are the key attributes of the Energy Star and EPEAT Gold green PC certifications? Does your PC have these certifications?

b. What toxic components are contained in computers and monitors? Where can you recycle computers and monitors in your area?

c. Check out **goodcleantech.com** and find out which companies are currently working toward better green technology. If your school had to replace computers in a lab, which environmentally friendly company would you recommend? Why?

two making the transition to... the workplace

making the transition to... the workplace

1. Backing up your Work

You have embarked on a position as a freelance editor. You will be using your own computer. Until now you have not worried too much about backing up your data. Now, however, it's extremely important that you back up all your work frequently.

Research the various backup options that are available including online backup, external hard drives, and portable flash storage. What are the size limitations of each? What are the initial and ongoing costs of each? How frequently do the various options allow you to perform backups? Which would be the option you would choose, and why?

2. What Hardware Will You Use?

When you arrive at a new position for a company, your employer will most likely provide you with a computer. Based on the career you are in now or are planning to pursue, answer the following questions:

a. What kind of computer system would the company mostly likely provide to you—desktop, notebook, tablet PC, or something else? How does that compare with the type of system you would prefer to work with?

b. If you were required to use a type of computer you had never used before (such as a Mac instead of a PC), how would you go about learning to use the new computer?

c. What other devices might your employer provide? Consider such items as smartphones or printers. How important is it in for these devices to conform to the latest trends?

d. Should you be able to use employer-provided equipment, such as a smartphone, for personal benefit? Does your answer differ if you have to pay for part or all of the device?

3. Exploring Monitors

You have been asked to help edit video for a friend. You have a great notebook computer, which is powerful enough to handle this type of task, but you need to buy a separate LCD monitor to hook up to your computer and are not exactly sure what to buy. You know it should be larger than 15", capable of displaying HD, and can't cost more than $200.

a. Research five different monitors that would fit your needs. Create a table that lists each monitor and its specifications, including display type, screen size, aspect ratio, native resolution, and response time. Also list the types of ports and connectors the monitor has.

b. Note whether each monitor has HDMI. Why or why not would HDMI capability be important?

c. Research two LED monitors. Would an LED monitor be a viable option? Explain.

Explain which of the five monitors would best suit your needs and why.

4. What's the Coolest Mouse?

The Luxeed Dynamic Pixel LED Keyboard is a very cool keyboard that was described in the "How Cool Is *This?*" feature at the beginning of the chapter. There are some equally cool and innovative mice on the market. For example, some mice have vertical orientations, are washable, and can be used without touching a surface. Investigate some of these new mice and come up with your list of the top five coolest ones. Which one would be your choice to be "The Coolest Mouse"?

5. Choosing the Best Laser Printer

You are looking to replace your inkjet printer with a laser printer. You haven't decided whether a color laser printer is necessary.

a. What are the cost considerations between getting a laser printer and a color laser printer (i.e., initial costs, costs of cartridges, and so on)?

b. Investigate wireless and Bluetooth options. What are the considerations involved with regard to these features?

c. Investigate all-in-one laser printers that have printer, scanner, and fax capabilities. How much more expensive are they than laser printers? Are there any drawbacks to these multipurpose machines? Do they perform each function as well as their stand-alone counterparts do? Can you print in color on these machines?

Based on your research, which printer would be your choice, and why?

Instructions: Albert Einstein used *Gedankenexperiments*, or critical thinking questions, to develop his theory of relativity. Some ideas are best understood by experimenting with them in our own minds. The following critical thinking questions are designed to demand your full attention but require only a comfortable chair—no technology.

1. Computer of the Future

Think about how mobile our computing devices have become and the convergence of different devices such as cameras, phones, computers, etc. What do you think the computer of the future will be like? What capabilities will it have that computers currently don't have? Do you see desktop computers becoming obsolete in the near future?

2. Table Monitors and Surface Monitors

Table monitors and surface monitors are tabletop devices that are designed to "grab" and manipulate objects on the display. Like an iPod touch or iPhone, the display is multitouch and can accept simultaneous input from multiple users, so the table monitor can be helpful with games or other products that require interactivity. Microsoft launched a product called "Surface" in 2007, and although it never really took off, you see similar devices featured on some TV crime-fighting shows as detectives manipulate crime evidence and photos. Why do you think this device never really captured the interest of the public? Would this be a useful object to have in your home, classroom, or office? Why or why not?

3. Storage on the Web

There are many options available to store your files in the "cloud" (i.e., on the Web). What do you think are the advantages of this type of storage versus storing your files on a physical device such as a hard drive or flash drive? What are the disadvantages?

4. Computers and Productivity

How have computers increased your productivity as a student? How have computers decreased your productivity? Would your answers be any different if you were working in an office? Why or why not? Would your parents answer any differently if you asked them how computers have increased or decreased their productivity levels?

5. "Smart" Cars

Cars are becoming more technically advanced every day. They are now able to parallel park by themselves, avoid collisions, alert you if you are falling asleep at the wheel, provide emergency response, and sense if you are going to back up over something inadvertently. What other technical advances do you see cars incorporating? Do you think that any of these current or potential advancements could result in unexpected negative consequences? If so, what?

6. iPad

The Apple iPad has been enthusiastically accepted because of its multitouch screen, useful applications, and small, light frame. But it is without certain features that might make it even better. If Steven Jobs, the CEO of Apple, were to ask you for your advice as to what to include in the next version of the iPad, what would you suggest?

two team time

Notebook Versus Desktop: Which Is Best?

Problem

You have joined a small business that is beginning to evaluate its technology setup. Because of the addition of several new sales representatives and other administrative employees, many new computers need to be purchased. You are trying to decide which would be better to purchase: notebook computers, tablet PCs, or desktops or a combination.

Task

Split your class into small groups, divide each group into three teams, and assign the following tasks:

Member A explores the benefits and downfalls of desktop computers.
Member B explores the benefits and downfalls of notebook computers.
Member C explores the benefits and downfalls of tablet PCs.

Process

1. Form the teams. Think about what the technology goals are for the company and what information and resources you need to tackle this project.
2. Research and then discuss the components of each system you are recommending. Are any components better suited for the particular needs of the various employees (sales representatives versus administrative staff)? Consider all the input, output, processing, and storage devices. Are any special devices or peripherals required?
3. Consider the different types of employees in the company. Would a combination of devices be better than a single solution? If so, what kinds of employees would get which type of computer?
4. As a team, write a summary position paper. Support your system recommendation for the company. Each team member should include why his or her type of computer will be part of the solution or not.

Conclusion

Desktop, notebook, and tablet PC computers have their own merits as computing systems. Beyond portability, there are other things to think about. Being aware of the options in the marketplace, knowing how to analyze the trade-offs of different designs, and recognizing the different needs each type fulfills allows you to become a better consumer as well as a better computer user.

ethics
project
two
chapter

ethics
project

Ethical conduct is a stream of decisions you make all day long. In this exercise, you will research and then role-play a complicated ethical situation. The role you play may or may not match your own personal beliefs but your research and use of logic will enable you to represent whichever view is assigned. An arbitrator will watch and comment on both sides of the arguments, and together the team will agree on an ethical solution.

Topic: Green Computing

Green computing—conducting computing needs with the least possible amount of power—is on everyone's minds. Although it's hard to argue with an environmentally conscious agenda, the pinch to our pocketbooks and the loss of some comforts sometimes makes green computing difficult. Businesses, including colleges, need to consider a variety of issues and concerns before jumping into a complete green overhaul.

Research Areas to Consider

- End-of-life management: E-waste and recycling
- Energy-efficient devices
- Costs of green computing
- Government funding and incentives

Process

Divide the class into teams.

1. Research the areas cited above and devise a scenario in which your college is considering modifying its current technology setup to a more green IT strategy.
2. Team members should write a summary that provides background information for their character—for example, environmentalist, college IT administrator, or arbitrator—and details their character's behaviors to set the stage for the role-playing event. Then, team members should create an outline to use during the role-playing event.
3. Team members should arrange a mutually convenient time to meet for the exchange, using the chat room feature of MyITLab, the discussion board feature of Blackboard, or meeting in person.
4. Team members should present their case to the class or submit a PowerPoint presentation for review by the rest of the class, along with the summary and resolution they developed.

Conclusion

As technology becomes ever more prevalent and integrated into our lives, more and more ethical dilemmas will present themselves. Being able to understand and evaluate both sides of the argument, while responding in a personally or socially ethical manner, will be an important skill.

three
using the Internet:
making the most of the Web's resources

objectives

After reading this chapter, you should be able to answer the following questions:

1. What is the origin of the Internet? *(pp. 94–95)*
2. How can I communicate through the Internet? *(pp. 95–99)*
3. How can I communicate and collaborate using Web 2.0 technologies? *(pp. 99–105)*
4. What are the various kinds of multimedia files found on the Web, and what software do I need to use them? *(pp. 106–108)*
5. What is e-commerce, and what e-commerce safeguards protect me when I'm online? *(pp. 108–110)*
6. What is a Web browser, and what is a URL and what are its parts? *(pp. 110–111)*
7. How can I use hyperlinks and other tools to get around the Web? *(pp. 112–115)*
8. How do I search the Internet effectively, and how can I evaluate Web sites? *(pp. 115–118)*
9. How does data travel on the Internet? *(pp. 118–121)*
10. What are my options for connecting to the Internet? *(pp. 121–126)*

multimedia resources

 Active Helpdesk

- Doing Business Online **(p. 110)**
- Getting Around the Web **(p. 117)**
- Using Subject Directories and Search Engines **(p. 118)**
- Connecting to the Internet **(p. 122)**

 Sound Bytes

- Creating a Web-Based E-mail Account **(p. 97)**
- Blogging **(p. 60)**
- Welcome to the Web **(p. 114)**
- Finding Information on the Web **(p. 118)**
- Connecting to the Internet **(p. 121)**

 Companion Website

The Companion Website includes a variety of additional materials to help you review and learn more about the topics in this chapter. Go to: ***pearsonhighered.com/techinaction***

how cool is *this?*

how cool is *this?* Looking for answers on the Web? Check out WolframAlpha.com, a **new way to search** for information on the Web!

Where do you go when you need to find something online? Google? Dogpile? Although these and other common Internet tools **help** you find information, they generally lead you to where you can find an answer, but don't always provide the answer—or an answer that you trust. Enter WolframAlpha.com (**wolframalpha.com**), a "**computational knowledge engine**" that computes the answers to a wide range of questions that have factual answers.

For example, if you ask, "What is the monthly payment for a $20,000, five-year loan at 5% interest?" you'll get not only the payment but also the total interest paid and the effective interest rate. A search for "pear" results in average nutrition facts, taxonomy information, and the digital representation of the color "pear." WolframAlpha **understands questions** and computes answers, unlike traditional Internet search tools that simply retrieve Web files that might contain an answer.

The foundation of this unique tool is a set of models from a variety of fields of knowledge, combined with **massive** amounts of data and algorithms that represent **real-world knowledge**. It knows about technology, geography, cooking, business, travel, music, and more. The information it delivers uses more than 5,000 different **visual representations** such as table styles and graphs.

Ask WolframAlpha.com a question today to see how cool it really is.

93

The Internet

It's hard to imagine life without the **Internet**, the largest computer network in the world. It's actually a network of networks that connects billions of computer users globally. We use it to shop, to communicate, to research, to find places and get directions, and to entertain ourselves (see Figure 3.1). It's accessible from our computers, smartphones, and portable music players (PMPs), and we can get to it while at home, at work, at school—even at Starbucks or in the car. But what exactly is the Internet, and how did it begin?

Why was the Internet created? The concept of the Internet was developed while the United States was in the midst of the Cold War with the Soviet Union. At that time, the U.S. armed forces were becoming increasingly dependent on computers to

Figure 3.1

From buying sneakers on eBay to getting directions on your cell phone to checking messages or finding out about the latest amusement park features, the Internet makes it all possible.

early 1960s, there was no reliable way to connect computers from different manufacturers because they used different proprietary designs and methods of communication. What was lacking was a common communications method that all computers could use. The Internet was created to respond to these two concerns: establishing a secure form of military communications and creating a means by which all computers could communicate.

Who invented the Internet? The modern Internet evolved from an early U.S. government–funded "internetworking" project called the Advanced Research Projects Agency Network (ARPANET). ARPANET began as a four-node network involving UCLA, Stanford Research Institute, the University of California at Santa Barbara, and the University of Utah in Salt Lake City. The first real communication occurred in late 1969 between the computer at Stanford and the computer at UCLA. Although the system crashed after the third letter was transmitted, it was the beginning

coordinate and plan their activities. They needed a computer system that would operate efficiently and that was located in various parts of the country so that it could not be disrupted easily in the event of an attack.

At the same time, researchers hoped the Internet would address the problems involved with getting different computers to communicate with each other. Although computers had been networked since the

of a revolution. Many people participated in the creation of the ARPANET, but two men who worked on the project, Vinton Cerf and Robert Kahn, are generally acknowledged as the "fathers" of the Internet. They earned this honor because in the 1970s they were primarily responsible for developing the communications protocols (standards) that are still in use on the Internet today.

So are the Web and the Internet the same thing? Because the **World Wide Web** (**WWW** or the **Web**) is what we use the most, we sometimes think of the

Internet and the Web as being interchangeable. However, the Web is only one component of the Internet, the means we use to access information over the Internet (hence the *www* at the beginning of Web addresses). Other components of the Internet include FTP, Gopher, Telnet, and BitTorrent, which will be discussed later in this chapter. What distinguishes the Web from the rest of the Internet is its use of

- common communication protocols that enable different computers to talk to each other and display information in compatible formats, and
- special links that enable users to navigate from one place to another on the Web.

Did the same people who invented the Internet invent the Web? The Web was invented many years after the original Internet. In 1989, Tim Berners-Lee, a physicist at the European Organization for Nuclear Research (CERN), wanted a method for linking his research documents so that other researchers could access them. In conjunction with Robert Cailliau, Berners-Lee developed the basic architecture of the Web and created the first **Web browser** (or **browser**), software that enables a user to display and interact with text and other media on the Web. The original browser could handle only text and was usable only on computers running the NeXT operating system, a commercially unsuccessful operating system (OS), which limited its usage. So Berners-Lee put out a call to the Internet community to assist with development of browsers for other platforms.

In 1993, the National Center for Supercomputing Applications released its Mosaic browser for use on the Macintosh and Windows operating systems. Mosaic could display graphics as well as text. The once-popular Netscape Navigator browser evolved from Mosaic and heralded the beginning of the Web's monumental growth.

How much has the Internet grown? The Internet experienced explosive growth in the early to mid-1990s. By 1997, Internet access was global.

Because of such global Internet availability and access, as well as the increasing capabilities of hardware and software, the number of **Web sites**—locations on the Internet—grew exponentially, as shown in

Internet domain survey host count

Figure 3.2. The growth of the Web is by no means complete. In January 2010, more than 732 million Web sites were online.

Figure 3.2

The growth of the number of Web sites on the Internet has been explosive since the first Web site was hosted in 1990.

Source: www.isc.org/solutions/survey.

Communicating Through the Internet: E-Mail and Other Technologies

Think of all the different ways you communicate with your friends, family, professors, and business associates over the Internet. You can use instant messaging, group communications, social networking, web logs and video logs, wikis, podcasts, and webcasts to communicate via the Internet. (You can even talk over the phone through the Internet, which will be discussed in Chapter 8.) Like any other means of communication, you need to know how to use these tools efficiently to get the most out of them.

E-Mail

Why did e-mail catch on so quickly? **E-mail** (short for **electronic mail**) is a written message that is sent and received over the Internet. The messages can be formatted and enhanced with graphics and may also include other files as attachments. E-mail became the primary method of electronic communication worldwide because it's fast and convenient. Initially, another attraction to e-mail was that it reduced the costs of postage and long-distance phone calls. Currently, e-mail is predominately the main means of communication in the business community. For social exchanges, e-mail often offers a more "private" conversation away from the very public exchanges on social networks. Lastly, e-mail accounts are necessary to join and then receive updates of activity on other Web sites. Because of these and other reasons, a September 2009 study reports that approximately 89 percent of adult Americans who access the Internet send and receive e-mail.

Is e-mail private? E-mails are not private. In fact, the information in e-mail is no more private than a postcard. E-mails can be easily viewed by others, either by being printed out or forwarded, so you never know who eventually could read your e-mail. Also, most e-mail is not encrypted, so you should never use e-mail to send personal or sensitive information such as bank account numbers or Social Security numbers. Doing so could lead to identity theft. Employers have access to e-mail sent from the workplace, so use caution when putting negative or controversial content in an e-mail. It could come back to haunt you. Finally, remember that even after you've deleted a message, it doesn't really vanish. Many Internet service providers and companies archive e-mail, which can then be accessed or subpoenaed in the event of a lawsuit or investigation.

How do I write a good e-mail? E-mail between friends does not have to follow any specific guidelines and can be as casual as your IM or texting exchanges. But when you send e-mail for professional reasons, like at your job, then you should be aware of proper e-mail etiquette. Following good e-mail etiquette maintains professionalism, increases efficiency, and might even help protect a company from costly lawsuits.

Common guidelines include being concise and to the point, using spell-check, avoiding texting abbreviations such as *u*, *r*, *LOL*, *BRB*, and others. Also, make sure you include a meaningful subject line. This helps recipients prioritize, organize, and categorize e-mails, and identify contents later on after the e-mail has been read. One problem with e-mail is that the meaning within the message often can be misinterpreted. Therefore, some means of conveying emotion (when necessary) can be helpful. Often smilies—simple strings of characters that reflect facial expressions—can help reflect the writer's emotions. Use them sparingly to retain their effectiveness. Finally, include a signature line with your basic contact or corporate information.

What do I need to send and receive e-mail? All you need to send and receive e-mail is a computer, an Internet connection, and an e-mail account. Each component, however, entails additional considerations, which will be addressed later in the chapter. Although it's most common to send and receive e-mail from your computer, today many e-mail messages are exchanged wirelessly among smartphones and other portable devices.

Are there different types of e-mail accounts? Many people have more than one e-mail account. You may have a personal account, a work account, and an account you use when filling out forms on the Internet. To

Figure 3.3

You can organize your e-mail and assign messages to topic-specific folders.

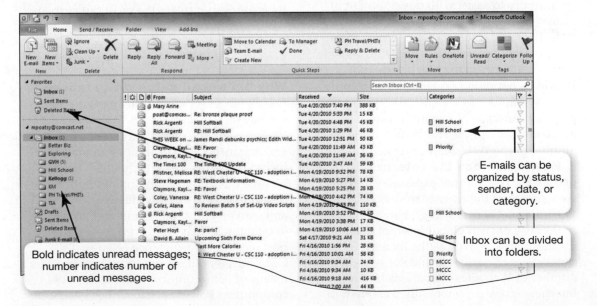

Bold indicates unread messages; number indicates number of unread messages.

E-mails can be organized by status, sender, date, or category.

Inbox can be divided into folders.

read, send, and organize your e-mail, you can use an e-mail client. **E-mail clients** such as Microsoft Outlook are software programs running on your computer that access your Internet service provider (ISP), which acts like an electronic post office. However, with these e-mail clients, you are able to view your e-mail only from a computer on which the e-mail client program is installed, which can be less than convenient if you travel or want to view your e-mail when you're away from that computer.

Today, most high-speed providers and ISPs offer the services of a Web-based e-mail client so that users can look at their e-mail directly from the Web. Web-based e-mail uses the Internet as the e-mail client. Free e-mail accounts such as Yahoo! Mail, Hotmail, or Gmail are Web-based e-mail clients. Some e-mail providers—AOL, for example—offer both client-based and Web-based access to e-mail.

What are the advantages of a Web-based e-mail account? Unlike client-based e-mail, which is accessible only from a computer on which the e-mail client is installed, Web-based e-mail accounts make your e-mail accessible from any computer as long as you can access the Internet. No special e-mail client software is necessary. Even if you use a client-based account, having a secondary Web-based e-mail account, such as Yahoo! or Gmail, also provides you with a more consistent e-mail address. Your other e-mail accounts and addresses may change when you switch ISPs or change employers, so having a consistent e-mail address is important.

Why would I need a client-based e-mail program? One of the benefits of using a client-based e-mail program such as Microsoft Outlook is that you can download your e-mail from many different e-mail accounts so that it all can be accessed in one location. In addition, client e-mail programs offer several features to help you manage and organize your e-mail and coordinate e-mail with your calendar, tasks, and contact lists. As you can see in Figure 3.3, you can organize your e-mail by task, sender, or priority, or you can file your messages to designated folders within your inbox. Some Web-based e-mail systems such as Yahoo! feature many of the same organizational tools, but client-based programs are generally more fully featured.

Instant Messaging

What is instant messaging? Instant messaging (IM) services are programs that enable you to communicate in real time with others who are online (see Figure 3.4). Although IM is most often used for casual

Figure 3.4

Instant messaging services such as Facebook Chat enable you to have real-time online conversations.

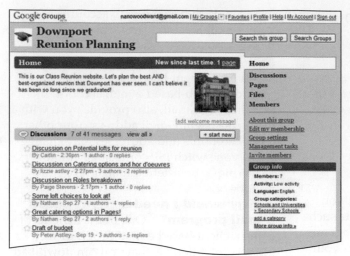

Figure 3.5
Google Groups is a convenient means to join a group or to create your own.

conversations between friends, many businesses use IM as a means of quick and instant communication between co-workers.

AOL's AIM has been one of the most popular instant messaging services. Facebook Chat, ICQ, Yahoo!, Google, and Windows Live Messenger also host popular instant-messaging services. Most of these services are proprietary, meaning you can chat only with those who share the same IM service. But there are universal chat services such as Trillian, Pidgin, and Digsby that allow users of all the popular IMs to chat with each other regardless of the service they use. Meebo is a new Web-based universal chat service that lets you communicate with users on a variety of IM services from any computer anywhere. No software download is required because it's Web-based.

How do I keep track of my IM contacts? When you use IM, you set up a list of contacts, often called a *buddy list*. To communicate (or chat) with someone from your buddy list, that person must be online at the same time as you are. When someone wants to chat with you, a window pops open with his or her message. If it's not convenient to chat at that time, you can close or ignore the message. Some programs such as Yahoo! and AOL's AIM offer stealth settings so that you can appear offline to certain buddies.

If you want to chat with more than one person, you can hold simultaneous individual conversations, or if you all want to chat together, you can create custom IM chat groups. Many IM services offer chat services so you can speak with your buddies if you have a microphone and speakers. A webcam allows you to see them as you chat.

Group Communication

What kinds of online group communication exist? E-mail and IM allow you to chat with one or a few people that you know personally. Sites such as Facebook, which are certainly the most common form of group communication on the Internet, further connect you to your circle of friends and family. Sometimes, however, you might want to connect with others who share your interests but who you might not know personally. You can communicate and interact online with people who share similar interests through chat rooms, newsgroups, and Internet Relay Chat (IRC).

A **chat room**, such as those found at **icq.com/icqchat**, is a form of synchronous communication in which online conversations occur in real time and are visible to everyone in the chat room. Usually, chat rooms are organized around a specific theme or topic. Wireclub (**wireclub.com**) has a variety of chat rooms to suit every interest. A **newsgroup** is similar to a discussion group or forum in which people create threads (conversations). In a thread, a newsgroup member posts messages and reads and replies to messages from other members of the newsgroup. Google Groups is a great source for various newsgroups. Google Groups (see Figure 3.5) allows you to join a group or create your own. **Internet Relay Chat (IRC)** is primarily a means of synchronous group communication used in discussion forums. Trillion, Pidgin, and XChat are popular IRC clients, and ChatZilla is a Firefox add-on; Mibbit is a Web-based client.

Social networking is another popular means of communicating with many people, which we will discuss in the Web 2.0 section next.

Are there rules for group communications? General rules of etiquette, often referred to as **netiquette**, exist across chat rooms and other online forums, including obvious standards of behavior such as introducing yourself when you enter the room and specifically addressing the person to whom you are talking. Chat room users also are expected to refrain from swearing, name-calling, and using explicit or prejudiced language, and they are not allowed to harass other participants. In addition, chat room users cannot post the same text repeatedly with the intent to disrupt the chat, a behavior called *flooding*. Similarly, users shouldn't type in all capital letters, because this is interpreted as shouting.

Web 2.0 Technologies: Collaborating and Communicating Through the Internet

Over time, our use of the Internet has evolved from passively using Web content created for us to actively creating, sharing, and collaborating on our own Web content. **Web 2.0** describes an evolved type of Web interactions between people, software, and data. It can be classified as the *social Web*, in which the user is also a participant. Additionally, Web 2.0 describes a trend of new applications to combine the functionality of multiple applications. Hundreds of companies now exist to help us share, recommend, collaborate, create, and socialize (see Figure 3.6). The following discussions focus more on the social, collaborative,

and communicative nature of Web 2.0 applications. Other Web-based productivity applications will be discussed in Chapter 4.

Social Networking

What is social networking? **Social networking** is a means by which people use the Internet to communicate and share information among their immediate friends, and meet and connect with others through common interests, experiences, and friends (see Figure 3.7). Social networking services such as Facebook (**facebook.com**) and MySpace (**myspace.com**) have become amazingly popular because they provide ways for members to communicate with their friends in a variety of means such as by voice, chat, instant message, and videoconference so that members don't need separate communication accounts. These services were first accepted broadly among the younger, nonprofessional population, but now many adults create their own social networking profiles on Facebook and MySpace. In fact, the largest increase of Facebook users in 2009 was adults aged 55 and over, with a growth rate of nearly 925%! Ning (**ning.com**) is a social networking site that allows you to create your own network around your own common topic or join a social networking group that has already been formed.

Is social networking just for fun? Networking has long been a means

www.futureexploration.net

Figure 3.6

Hundreds of companies and Web sites make up the Web 2.0 landscape, which helps us share, recommend, collaborate, create, and socialize.

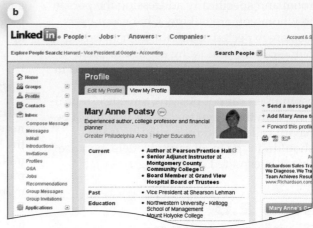

Figure 3.7

Social networking sites are popular places for people to keep up with friends and learn more about the people they meet.

of creating links between you and your friends—and their friends and acquaintances. Traditionally, networking has been helpful in the business community for the purposes of finding and filling open job positions as well as finding clients. The Internet, with its speedy connections and instantaneous means of communicating, facilitates such business networking as well as promoting more socially based networks. The professional, business-oriented online networks such as LinkedIn® (**linkedin.com**) are helpful for members seeking to find potential clients, business opportunities, jobs, or job candidates. Like a true business network, LinkedIn® helps you meet other professionals through the people you know.

Are there precautions I should take with my social networking content? When social networking sites first became popular, there was huge concern over privacy issues, especially for young teenagers who put personal information on their pages without considering the possibility of that information being misused by a stalker or identity thief. Although those concerns still exist, many of the most popular social networking sites have improved their privacy policies, thereby reducing, but not eliminating, such concerns. Still, users must be cautious about the type of content they post on these sites. For example, think before you add information like "your mother's maiden name" or "your first pet's name" because these are often security questions that are used to verify your identity.

Social networking sites are a great way to exchange photos, but again, use caution when posting images. Although privacy settings may offer some comfort, some images may be available for view through search engines and may not require site registration to be viewed. Online images may become public property and subject to reproduction,

and there might be some images that you don't want distributed. Additionally, many employers use social networks as another means of gaining information about a potential job candidate before granting an interview or extending a job offer. The responsibility for your content rests with you. Make sure your profile, images, and site content project an image that accurately represents you.

Weblogs (Blogs) and Video Logs (Vlogs)

What is a blog? A **weblog**, or **blog**, is a personal log or journal posted on the Web. The beauty of blogs is that they are simple to create, manage, and read. Anyone can create a blog, and there are millions of blogs available to read, follow, and comment on.

Several key characteristics define a blog. Blogs are generally written by a single author and are arranged as a listing of entries on a single page, with the most recent blog (entry) appearing at the top of the list. In addition, blogs are public. Blogs have searchable and organized content, making them user friendly. They are accessible from anywhere using a Web browser.

The traditional form of a blog is primarily text-based but may also include images and audio. A **video log** (**vlog** or **video blog**) is a

SOUND BYTE — Blogging

In this Sound Byte, you'll see why blogs are one of today's most popular publishing mediums. You'll also learn how to create and publish your own blog.

personal journal that uses video as the primary content. It can also contain text, images, and audio. Vlogs quickly are becoming a highly popular means of personal expression, and many can be found by searching the most popular video-sharing site today, YouTube (**youtube.com**). Software such as Vlog It! makes adding video content to your blog easy, although you can easily upload unedited video straight from your computer, video camera, or cell phone. Blinkx (**blinkx.com**) is a video search engine that helps you sift through all the video posted on the Web (see Figure 3.8).

Why would I want to create a blog? Many people use blogs as a sort of personal scrapbook. Whenever the urge strikes, they just write a stream-of-consciousness flow of thoughts or a report of their daily activities. Many blogs, however, focus on a particular topic. For example, **themovieblog.com** contains reviews and opinions about movies, and **engadget.com** (see Figure 3.9) is a blog that devotes itself to discussing techno-gadgets. Many corporations, such as WalMart and Best Buy, have blogs written by employees. Blogcatalog (**blogcatalog.com**) and Bloghub (**bloghub.com**) are two of many blog directories that can help you find blogs that best fit your interests.

How do I create a blog? It is easy to write and maintain a blog, and many Web sites provide the necessary tools for you to create your own. Two sites that offer free blog hosting are **blogger.com** and

wordpress.com. You can add other features to your blog such as pictures or subpages. Another alternative is to host your blog yourself. Hosting your own blog requires that you have your own Web site and a URL so that people can access it.

Are there problems with blogs? The popularity of blogs has brought about a new problem: spam blogs (splogs), which are artificially created blog sites filled with fake articles or stolen text (a tactic known as *blog scraping*). Splogs, which contain links to other sites associated with the splog's creator, have the intention of either increasing traffic to, or increasing search engine rankings for, these usually disreputable or useless Web sites. Although not terribly bad, splogs are another unwanted form of

Figure 3.8

Video logs use video in addition to text, images, and audio. Blinkx is a video search engine that helps you sift through the increasing number of vlogs.

Figure 3.9

(a) Some blogs, like this one from **engadget.com**, are set up as online reviews organized by category. (b) Alternatively, they can appear as personal journals that record a blogger's thoughts, viewpoints, and feelings in reverse chronological order.

content that continues to grow like weeds on the Web.

Wikis

What are wikis? Unlike traditional Web content, which the viewer of the site cannot change, a **wiki** is a type of Web site that allows users to change its content by adding, removing, or editing the content (see Figure 3.10). Wikis add the extra benefit of tracking revisions so that past versions can be easily accessed at any time by any reader. Like blogs, wikis can be used to express thoughts and opinions about certain topics. Unlike blogs, wikis can be edited and therefore can present an emergent "common" opinion rather than the individual opinion of the initial writer.

The popular collaborative online encyclopedia Wikipedia (**wikipedia.org**) uses wiki technology so that the content can be updated continually. Some Web-based document products, such as Google Docs (**docs.google.com**), have wiki-like features to promote online collaboration.

What are wikis used for? Wikis provide an excellent source for collaborative writing, both in and out of the classroom. Wiki technology is currently incorporated in course management systems such as Blackboard, to encourage collaborative learning in online courses. Wikis are also becoming popular tools for business collaboration. Rather than passing documents back and forth via e-mail and losing track of which updated version is the most recent, wikis allow all who have access to the wiki page to post their ideas and modify the content of just one document. A history of all changes is kept so users can revert to earlier versions if desired.

These same collaborative efforts extend to user manuals. One site, wikiHow (**wikihow. org**), is an online project that uses both wikis and the collaborative process to build a large, online how-to manual. Blender (**blender.org**), an open source software application for 3D modeling, uses MediaWiki, a more feature-rich wiki implementation product, to provide users with documentation, help with game development and 3D modeling, and tutorials for Blender software.

How accurate is Web content that anyone can change? The idea behind content that is managed and edited by many users, such as that found in large public wikis such as Wikipedia, is that the group will keep the content valid. Those challenging the validity of publicly editable wikis argue that the content cannot be trusted because wikis are easily tampered with, whereas supporters argue that the community of users can quickly catch erroneous content and correct it.

In late 2005, Wikipedia content was measured for accuracy in its scientific content and was found to be as accurate as the *Encyclopedia Britannica*. Nonetheless, free and easy access to edit pages also can lead to improper manipulation, which results in tighter access controls. To thwart malicious editing of the wiki content, for example, users who want editing privileges are required to register. Citizendium (**citizendium.org**), another open wiki encyclopedia, requires contributors to provide real names and sign an ethics pledge, and all postings are monitored.

Podcasts and Webcasts

What is a podcast? A **podcast** is a clip of audio or video content that is broadcast over the Internet using compressed audio and video files such as MP3s and MP4s. This content might include radio shows, audiobooks, magazines, and even educational programs. The word *podcast* is a combination of *broadcasting* and *iPod*—not because

Figure 3.10
Rather than collaborating by exchanging e-mails and attachments—and potentially losing track of the most recent version of a document—different users can collaborate on a wiki page.

Elijah provides initial text (in black)

Project Home
Week 7: *Publicity Law*
9/17/12 – 9/23/12

9/18/12
Mackenzie-Jordan Law Associates has a significant number of celebrity clients. One of the most important aspects of our legal counsel to these individuals is to help protect the use of their images and likenesses.
Sometimes this is referred to as the right of publicity. This right is a valuable asset because there are endless licensing opportunities that can be quite lucrative.
Some states have a publicity law that protects a celebrity's image and likeness for 100 years, but as yet that law has not been enacted in the state of Texas.

9/19/12
The merchandising of celebrity images has become a huge source of income for many celebrities as well as others. In recent years, legal disputes have resulted from artists and illustrators manipulating celebrity images.
In the past, courts have typically protected the First Amendment rights of artists in these cases. But recently there have been a few cases where celebrities have been allowed to sue creators of fictional works for the violation of the right of publicity.
~~The right of publicity is intended to prevent others from capitalizing on a celebrity's fame.~~ Many people in the entertainment industry are fearful that unauthorized biographies, docudramas, and celebrity spoofs and satires will no longer be protected. Many entertainment lawyers say a celebrity's right to publicity is intended solely for ads and merchandise, not for literary works.

Jordan includes additional text (shaded yellow)

Stephanie removes text (shaded with green and shown with strikethrough)

you have to use an iPod but because iPods are the most popular form of portable media player (PMP) and because people download audio files to listen to on their iPods. However, you don't have to listen to podcasts on a portable media player. You can listen to podcasts on your computer or even on a smartphone as long as the device can play the content. To listen to a podcast on your computer, you'll need a media player such as iTunes or Windows Media Player. If you want to enjoy a video podcast on your PMP, you need to make sure your mobile device can play video as well as audio files.

So what makes podcasting different from just listening to an audio file on the computer or a PMP? The difference is that podcasts are files that come to you through syndication so you do not have to search for them. Perhaps you are used to getting your news from a certain Web site, but the only way you can determine that new content has been added is to go to the site and look for the newly added information. In contrast, if you subscribe to podcasts, when the content changes, it is brought to you. Some podcasts provide the opportunities for listeners to submit questions or even take listener's calls live. What's more, if you have several favorite Web sites, rather than individually checking the content, you can collect all the site updates in one place. Podcasts are possible because of RSS technology, which makes it more efficient for you to gather updates to your favorite content.

What is RSS? Really Simple Syndication (RSS) is an XML-based format that facilitates the delivery of frequent content updates on Web pages. Using RSS, Web content can be formatted in such a way that **aggregators** can find it and download only the new content to your computer. Aggregators are software

programs that go out and grab the latest updates of Web material according to your specifications. They are available for all major operating systems as well as some mobile devices such as smartphones.

Where can I find podcasts? Podcasts can be found all over the Web. Most newspapers, TV news organizations, and radio sites offer podcasts of their programs. Although many podcasts are news related, many podcasts offer more entertaining and informative content. The television network ABC, for example, offers podcasts of some of its most popular TV shows, such as *Grey's Anatomy* and *Lost*. Sites such as Yoga Today offer extensive yoga classes. Many schools are beginning to recognize this format as a way to supply students with course content updates, and instructors create podcasts of their lectures.

iTunes (**itunes.com**), Podcast Alley (**podcastalley.com**), and Podcast.com (**podcast.com**) are aggregators as well as great directories of podcasts, organized by genre, to help you easily locate podcasts of most interest to you (see Figure 3.11). If there is a particular topic for which you'd like to hear a podcast,

Figure 3.11

Podcasts are available in a wide variety of topics and content. Web sites such as **podcast.com** allow you to add your own podcast to their directories.

You, as well as many of your classmates, wear flip-flops year round—even in winter—and you think that flip-flops in school colors would be an extremely popular product. Your school's bookstore carries everything else with the school's colors and logo, just not flip-flops. You have asked your friends and several classmates, and most of them indicated they would buy flip-flops in the school's colors. So what do you do next? How do you move from product concept to actually selling your physical product?

Before the advent of the Internet and e-commerce, it would have been much more difficult and expensive to get your product produced and distributed. First, you would have needed to find someone with industrial design experience to design your flip-flops. Then, to make the flip-flops, you would have had to find a manufacturer, which likely required a high minimum order (maybe tens of thousands of pairs of flip-flops). You also would have needed a package design, marketing brochures, company logo (and other branding devices), a storage facility, and more. Finally, the largest hurdle would have been convincing a brick-and-mortar retailer, such as your campus bookstore, to carry your product.

Fortunately, the Internet brings the power of the global economy right to your door. For product design and manufacturing, you can visit a site like **Alibaba.com** (see Figure 3.12), which helps entrepreneurs locate

manufacturers of all sorts of products located in many different countries. And many manufacturers are happy to work with you to custom design your product. So if you find a flip-flop style you like, you probably can get it customized with your school colors.

But what happens if the bookstore doesn't want to sell your flip-flops? You can always set up a Web site to sell them yourself. But you'll probably need help with Web site design, company logo design, and Web programming to construct the site if you don't already have these skills. Fortunately, you can tap the global marketplace for skilled professionals by using sites such as **guru.com** or **elance.com** (see Figure 3.13). These

Figure 3.12

A search for men's flip-flops on Alibaba.com reveals almost 2,500 suppliers with minimum order quantities as low as 1,000 units.

Podscope (**podscope.com**) is a podcast-specific search engine that searches podcasts for specific words or phrases and then displays the results with audio clips. YouTube is also becoming a popular source of RSS feeds for video content.

Can I create my own podcast?
It is simple to create audio content that can be delivered to the Web and then listened to by people all over the world. In fact, you could become a radio broadcaster overnight. Although high-end equipment always will produce a more sophisticated output, you really need only the most basic equipment to make your own podcast.

To record the content, at the minimum you need a computer with a microphone.

If you want to make a video podcast, you also need a Web camera (webcam) or video camera. Additional software may be needed to edit the digital audio and video content. After the podcast content has been recorded and edited, it needs to be exported to MP3 format. Sound-editing software, such as the freeware program Audacity, can be used to record and edit audio files and then export them to MP3 format. The last steps involve creating an RSS feed and then uploading the content to the Web.

What's a webcast?
A **webcast** is the broadcast of audio or video content over the Internet. Unlike podcasts that are prerecorded and made available for download, most webcasts are live or one-time events.

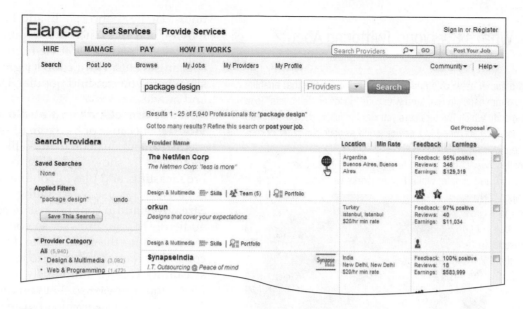

Figure 3.13

Need to design a package? Many freelancers at Elance.com are ready to help!

sites help you locate freelance professionals to work on projects for you. You can create a description of the job you need done (say, logo design for a flip-flop company), post it on the site, and invite freelancers to bid on your job. You can contact freelancers that look promising, review samples of their work, and decide on someone who can help you—and at a competitive price. After your Web site is designed and up and running, you can place your business on social networking sites, such as Facebook, to help potential customers discover your product and spread the word about your great flip-flops. You probably already have lots of friends on Facebook who attend your school and would be good potential customers.

If you aren't selling your flip-flops in a physical store, where will you store them, and who will package and ship them when customers buy them? If your parent's basement isn't large enough, you can outsource warehousing and order fulfillment to **Amazon.com**. Fulfillment by Amazon is a service in which Amazon (for a fee) will warehouse your inventory and then package and ship it when customer orders are received. Orders do not have to come through Amazon's site (although that is an option); you can just provide ordering information to Amazon that is collected on your site, and Amazon will take care of all the tedious work.

Although there is always a cost to starting up a business, up-front costs are much lower when you take advantage of the global marketplace and Internet tools. So take that brilliant idea you have and turn it into a business today!

Webcasts are not updated automatically, but some, such as Microsoft's On-Demand Webcasts, are RSS feeds. Webcasts use a special kind of media technology that continuously feeds the audio and video content, which facilitates the viewing and downloading process of large audio and video files. Webcasts can include noninteractive content such as simulcasts of radio or TV broadcasts. More recent webcasts invite interactive responses from the viewing or listening audience. For example, **ORLive.com** provides surgical webcasts that demonstrate the latest surgical innovations and techniques (see Figure 3.14). Webcasts also are used in the corporate world to broadcast annual meetings and in the educational arena to transmit seminars.

Figure 3.14

ORLive provides webcasts that demonstrate the latest surgical techniques.

What's Everyone Twittering About?

Twitter (**twitter.com**) is a social networking and microblogging service that enables you to exchange short text messages in real time with your friends or "followers" (see Figure 3.15). It lets you specify which Twitter users you want to follow so you can read their messages in one place. All you need is a device (such as your computer or mobile device) connected to the Internet.

Twitter messages, called *tweets*, are limited to 140 characters, so comments exchanged in Twitter are short and simple. While Twitter works well among close-knit groups for messages such as "Joe and I are going to Murphy's Café. See you there," it can also be used to gain a sense of the "pulse" of what the general public is talking about within a broader community. Businesses are using Twitter to respond to customer queries or to broadcast new services or products. Your Twitter account tracks the number of "followers," or people who are paying attention to your tweets, and the number of "friends," or people you are following. So, "tweet" away to stay connected.

Figure 3.15

Twitter is a social networking and microblogging service for staying connected to "followers" in real time.

Web Entertainment: Multimedia and Beyond

Internet radio, music files such as MP3 and advanced audio coding (AAC), streaming video, and interactive gaming are all part of a growing entertainment world available over the Internet. What makes the Web appealing to many people is its rich **multimedia** content. Multimedia is anything that involves one or more forms of media in addition to text.

Many types of multimedia are used on the Web. Graphics (drawings, charts, and photos) are the most basic form of multimedia. Audio files are what give sound to the Web—the clips of music you hear when you visit certain Web sites, MP3 files that you download, or live broadcasts you can listen to through Internet radio. Video files on the Web range from the simple (such as short video clips) to the complex (such as

hour-long live concerts). In addition to movies, you can watch live or prerecorded television broadcasts, movie trailers, and sporting events. **Hulu.com** is a great Web site where you can find popular TV shows and movies.

What are streaming audio and video? Because of the large file sizes of media content, watching video files such as movies or TV shows, listening to live audio broadcasting, and playing online games is possible because of streaming media. **Streaming audio** continuously feeds an audio file to your browser so you avoid having to wait for the entire file to download completely before listening to it. Likewise, **streaming video** continuously feeds a video file to your browser so that you can watch large files as they download instead of first having to download the files completely.

What kinds of games are played on the Web? Streaming audio and video helped to bring popularity to online user interactivity and online gaming. Many game Web sites, such as Addicting Games (**addictinggames.com**), offer thousands of free online games in arcade, puzzle, sports, shooting, word, and strategy categories. Simple multiplayer games such as backgammon, chess, and checkers became popular and offered users the chance to play the game with others from around the world.

In addition, there are many **multiplayer online games** in which play occurs among hundreds or thousands of other players over the Internet in a persistent (or always-on) game environment. In these games, you can interact with other players around the world in a meaningful context by trading, chatting, or playing cooperative or combative minigames. There are several types of **massive multiplayer online role-playing games (MMORPGs)** in which participants assume the role of a fictitious character in a virtual game world. World of Warcraft (**worldofwarcraft.com**), shown in Figure 3.16, and Guild Wars (**guildwars.com**) are among the most popular MMORPGs. Other types of multiplayer online games include first-person shooter games such as **battlegroundeurope.com**, sports games such as **footballsuperstars.com**, and racing games such as **needforspeed.com**. Second Life (**secondlife.com**) can also be considered an MMORPG, but with its own well-established, in-world virtual economy, it has transcended into a much bigger concept and function.

Do I need anything besides a browser to view or hear multimedia on the Web? Without any additional software, most graphics on the Web will appear in your browser. However, to view and hear some multimedia files—for example, podcasts, videos on YouTube, and audio files—you might need a special software program called a **plug-in** (or **player**). Figure 3.17 lists the most popular plug-ins.

If you purchased your computer within the past several years, many plug-ins probably came preinstalled on your computer. If a Web site requires a plug-in you don't have, then it usually displays a message on the screen that includes links to a site where you can download the plug-in free of charge. For example, to use streaming video on a Web site, your browser might send you to **adobe.com**, where you can download Flash Player.

Do I need to update players and plug-ins? As with most technological resources, improvements and upgrades are available for players and plug-ins, and most will alert you to check for and download upgrades when they are available. It is best to keep the players and plug-ins as current as possible so that you get the full effects of the multimedia running with these players.

Are there any risks with using plug-ins? When a browser requires a plug-in to display particular Web content, it usually automatically accesses the plug-in.

Depending on your settings, this access happens without asking you for consent to start the plug-in. Such automatic access can present security risks. To minimize such risks, update your plug-ins and browser software frequently so that you will have the most up-to-date remedies against identified security flaws.

Is there any way to get multimedia Web content to load faster? When you're on the Internet, your browser keeps track of the Web sites you've visited so that it can load them faster the next time you

Figure 3.16

World of Warcraft is a popular massive multiplayer online role-playing game.

Figure 3.17 | POPULAR PLUG-INS AND PLAYERS AND THEIR USES

	Plug-In or Player Name	Where You Can Get It	What It Does
	Adobe Reader	**adobe.com**	Views and prints portable document format (PDF) files.
	Flash Player	**adobe.com**	Plays animation and movies through Web browsers.
	QuickTime Player	**apple.com**	Plays MP3 animation, music, musical instrument digital interface (MIDI), audio, and video files.
	Shockwave Player	**adobe.com**	Plays interactive games, multimedia, graphics, and streaming audio and video on the Web.
	Silverlight	**microsoft.com**	Similar to Flash. Plays Web-based animations and videos.
	Windows Media Player	**microsoft.com**	Plays MP3 and WAV files, music files and live audio, and views movies and live video broadcasts on the Web.

visit them. This *cache* (temporary storage place) of the text pages, images, and video files from recently visited Web sites can make your Internet surfing more efficient, but it also can congest your hard drive. Additionally, if you don't have your cache settings to check for updates to the Web page, your browser may not load the most recent content. To keep your system running efficiently, delete your temporary Internet cache periodically. To ensure the most recent Web site content is displayed, click Refresh or

press the F5 key if you revisit a site in the same browsing session. All popular Web browsers have an option to clear the Internet cache manually, and most have a setting to allow you to clear the cache automatically every time you exit the browser.

Conducting Business over the Internet: E-Commerce

E-commerce, or **electronic commerce**, is the process of conducting business online, such as through advertising and selling products. A good example of an e-commerce business (also called an *e-business*) is Amazon.com. The company's online presence offers customers a convenient way to shop for almost anything. Its success is the result of creative marketing, an expanding product line, and reliable customer service and product delivery—all hallmarks of traditional businesses as well.

Are there different types of e-commerce businesses?   Traditional stores, those stores with a physical building to shop in, which also have an online presence, are referred to as *click-and-brick* businesses. These stores, such as Best Buy (**bestbuy.com**), and Target (**target.com**), provide a variety of services on their Web sites. Customers can visit their sites to check the availability of items or to get store locations and directions. Some click-and-bricks allow online purchases and in-store pickup and returns.

A significant portion of e-commerce consists of **business-to-consumer (B2C)** transactions—exchanges that take place between businesses and consumers—such as the purchases that consumers make at online stores. There is also a **business-to-business (B2B)** portion of e-commerce; this consists of businesses buying and selling goods and services to other businesses. An example is Omaha Paper Company (**omahapaper.com**), which distributes paper products to other companies. Finally, the **consumer-to-consumer (C2C)** portion of e-commerce consists of consumers selling to each other through online auction and exchange sites such as eBay (**ebay.com**) and Craigslist (**craigslist.org**).

What are the most popular e-commerce activities?   Approximately $100 billion each year is spent on goods purchased over the Internet, accounting for approximately 25 percent of all retail sales. So what is everyone buying online? Consumers now buy books, music and videos, movie and event tickets, and toys and games more often online than in retail stores. Travel items such as plane tickets, hotel reservations, and rental car reservations, and even automobile purchases are also frequently made online. With the advent of more lenient return policies, online retail sales of clothing and shoes also have increased. Sites such as eBay and Craigslist, together with payment exchange services such as PayPal and Google Checkout, are becoming the online equivalent of the weekend yard sale and have dramatically increased in popularity.

"Just how safe are online transactions?"

But e-commerce encompasses more than just shopping opportunities. Today, anything you can do inside your bank you can do online, and more than 50 percent of U.S. households do some form of online banking. Many people use online services to check their account balances, pay bills online, as well as check stock and mutual fund performances. Credit card companies allow you to view, schedule, and pay your credit card bill; brokerage houses allow you to conduct investment activities online.

credentials unsecured. To certify that their online transactions are secure, businesses hire security companies such as VeriSign. But just seeing the VeriSign seal is not always a guarantee that the site is secure because the seal can be copied and pasted onto virtually any site. Therefore, be sure to check that the beginning of the URL changes from "http://" to "https://"—with the "s" standing for *secure socket layer*. Another indication that a Web site is secure is the appearance of a small icon of a closed padlock (in both Microsoft Internet Explorer and Mozilla Firefox), as shown in Figure 3.19. Still, despite these indications, you also need to consider the validity of the site and place everything in context.

How else can I shop safely online? To ensure that your online shopping experience is a safe one, follow these guidelines:

• **Shop at well-known, reputable sites.** If you aren't familiar with a site, then investigate it with the Better Business Bureau (**bbb.org**) or at **bizrate.com**. When you place an order, print a copy of the order and make sure you receive a confirmation number. Make sure the

Figure 3.19

A closed padlock icon, "https" in the URL, and the VeriSign seal are indications that the site is secure.

E-Commerce Safeguards

Just how safe are online transactions? When you buy something online, you most likely use a credit card; therefore, the exchange of money is done directly between you and a bank. Because online shopping eliminates a salesclerk or other human intermediary from the transaction, it can actually be safer than traditional retail shopping. Still, because users are told to be wary of online transactions and because the integrity of online transactions is the backbone of e-commerce, businesses must have some form of security certification to give their customers a level of comfort.

Some sites have created secure logins that you can change to before signing in, which is safer than sending your login

ACTIVE HELPDESK

Doing Business Online

In this Active Helpdesk call, you'll learn about e-commerce and what e-commerce safeguards protect you when you're doing business online.

company has a phone number and street address in addition to a Web site.

- **Avoid making online transactions when using public computers.** Public computers might have programs that track and log your keystrokes, so you do not want to use public computers when typing sensitive information such as credit card numbers or bank account numbers. Public computers might also have other types spyware installed to retrieve private information. Similarly, unless you have specific protection on your own notebook computer, avoid making wireless transactions in public hotspots.

- **Pay by credit card, not debit card.** Federal consumer credit laws protect credit card users, but debit card users do not have the same level of protection. If possible, reserve one credit card for Internet purchases only; even better, use a prepaid credit card that has a small credit limit. For an extra layer of security, find out if your credit card company has a service that confirms your identity with an extra password or code that only you know to use when making an online transaction or offers a one-time use credit card number. Also, consider using a third-party payment

processor such as PayPal or Google Checkout. PayPal also offers a security key that provides additional security to your PayPal account.

- **Check the return policy.** Print a copy and save it. If the site disappears overnight, this information may help you in filing a dispute or reporting a problem to a site such as the Better Business Bureau.

Whether you're doing business, playing games, or communicating with friends or colleagues, the Internet makes all of these activities more accessible. The Internet can potentially make these experiences and activities more enriched as well, although you must take cautions for the safest of experiences.

Accessing the Web: Web Browsers

None of the activities for which we use the Web could happen without an important software application: a Web browser. Recall that a **Web browser**, or **browser**, is software installed on your computer system that allows you to locate, view, and navigate the Web. Most browsers in use today are *graphical* browsers, meaning they can display pictures (graphics) in addition to text and other forms of multimedia such as sound and video.

What are some common Web browsers? Internet Explorer (IE) is the browser from Microsoft and is included in the Windows operating system. It has been the most widely used browser since 1999, and still enjoys predominant market share, although its popularity has slipped over the years. Other browsers, discussed below, have become popular alternatives to Internet Explorer.

- **Firefox** is a popular open source browser from Mozilla (**mozilla.org**). Firefox's popularity continues to increase, capturing approximately 21.5 percent of the U.S. browser market. Add-ons are available to customize and increase the functionality of Firefox. Examples include Video Download Helper that converts Web videos, like those found on YouTube, to files you can save, as well as a Facebook toolbar that integrates Facebook functionality into your browser. Other handy features

BITS AND BYTES

Why Should You Run the Latest Version of Browser Software?

When new file formats are developed for the Web, browsers need new plug-ins to display content properly. Constantly downloading and installing plug-ins can be a tedious process. Although many Web sites provide links to sites that enable you to download plug-ins, not all do, resulting in frustration when you can't display the content you want. When new versions of browsers are released, they normally include the latest versions of popular plug-ins. Corrections of security breaches are typically included in these versions of browser software as well. Therefore, upgrading to the latest version of your browser software provides for safer, more convenient Web surfing. Fortunately, most updates are free, and you can set most of the popular Web browsers to notify you when updates are available or to download the updates automatically.

found in Firefox are spell-checking for e-mail, blogs, and other Web postings, as well as Session Restore, which brings back all your active Web pages if the browser or system shuts down unexpectedly.

- **Safari** is a browser developed by Apple (**apple.com**). Although it was created as the default browser for Macintosh computers and is included with the Mac OS, a Windows-based version is also available. Safari has quickly gained public acceptance, and it now has approximately an 8 percent share of the U.S. browser market.

- **Google Chrome** is the newest browser on the market, distributed by Google (**google.com**) (see Figure 3.20). The unique features offered by Chrome include thumbnail access to your most recently visited sites from Chrome's main page and shortcuts to Google applications.

What features do browsers offer?

Most browsers' toolbars provide tabbed browsing and Quick Tabs for convenient navigation and Web page management tools (see Figure 3.21). Quick Tabs, in Internet Explorer 7 and higher, shows thumbnail images of all open Web pages in open tabs, and Google Chrome offers thumbnail images of most recently visited sites on its main page. Firefox offers a bookmark toolbar for quick access to the most frequently used bookmarked sites. Most of the popular Web browsers have tabbed browsing in which Web pages are loaded in "tabs"

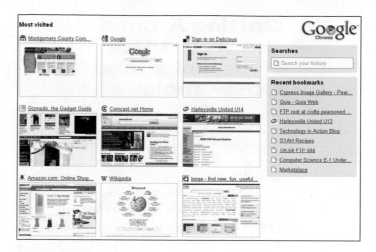

Figure 3.20

Google Chrome includes thumbnails of the most recently visited Web sites for easy access.

within the same browser window. Rather than having to switch among Web pages in several open windows, you can flip between the tabs in one window. You can even open several of your favorite Web sites from one folder and choose to display them as tabs. You may also save a group of tabs as a Favorites group, if there are several tabs you often open at the same time.

Most browsers also include a built-in search box in which you can designate your preferred default search engine and tools for printing, page formatting, and security settings. For extra browsing privacy, most browsers also offer a feature, such as InPrivate Browsing in Microsoft Internet Explorer, that allows users to surf without leaving a trace.

Figure 3.21

Internet Explorer (IE) includes tabbed browsing and Quick Tabs. IE has also reduced the display of navigation tools to a simple toolbar and built a Google search engine right into the browser.

Getting Around the Web: URLs, Hyperlinks, and Other Tools

You gain initial access to a particular **Web site**, which is a collection of Web pages, by typing its unique address, or **Uniform Resource Locator** (**URL**, pronounced "you-are-ell"), in your browser. For example, the URL of the Web site for *Popular Science* magazine is http://www.popsci.com. By typing this URL for *Popular Science* magazine, you connect to the **home page**, or main page, of the Web site. Once you are at the home page, you can move all around the site by clicking specially formatted pieces of text called *hyperlinks*. Let's look at these and other navigation tools in more detail.

Figure 3.22
The parts of a URL.

URLs

What do all the parts of the URL mean?

As noted earlier, a URL is a Web site's address. A Web site is comprised of many different Web pages, each of which is a separate document with its own unique URL. Like a regular street address, a URL is comprised of several parts that help identify the Web document for which it stands (see Figure 3.22). The first part of the URL indicates the *protocol* (set of rules) used to retrieve the specified document. The protocol is generally followed by a colon, two forward slashes, *www* (indicating *World Wide Web*), and the **domain name**. (Sometimes the domain name is also thought to include the *www*.) The domain name is also referred to as the *host name*. Individual pages within a Web site are further identified after the domain name, following another forward slash. These are referred to as the *path*. It should be noted that most current browsers no longer require you to enter the protocol and the www. Some, like Firefox, don't even require the domain if it's a .com. But even though these parts of the URL are not physically entered, they are still part of each Web site's URL.

What's the protocol? Most URLs begin with *http*, which is short for **hypertext transfer protocol (HTTP)**. HTTP is the protocol that allows files to be transferred from a **Web server**—a computer that hosts the Web site you are requesting—so that you can see the Web site on your computer by using a browser.

Another common protocol used to transfer files over the Internet is **file transfer protocol (FTP)**. It is used to upload and download files from your computer to a Web server. FTP files use an FTP file server, whereas HTTP files use a Web server. To connect to most FTP servers, you need a user ID and a password. FTP addresses, like e-mail addresses or URLs, identify one location on the Internet. To upload and download files from FTP sites, you can use a Web browser or file transfer software such as WS_FTP, Fetch, Filezilla, or WinSCP.

What's in a domain name? The domain name identifies the site's **host**, the location that maintains the computers that store the Web site files. For example, **berkeley.edu** is the domain name for the University of California at Berkeley.

The suffix in the domain name after the dot (such as .com or .edu) is called the **top-level domain**. This suffix indicates the kind of organization to which the host belongs.

Figure 3.23

Domain Name	Who Can Use It
.biz	Businesses
.com	Originally for commercial sites, but now can be used by anyone
.edu	Degree-granting institutions
.gov	Local, state, and United States government
.info	Information service providers
.mil	United States military
.name	Individuals
.net	Originally for networking organizations but no longer restricted
.org	Organizations (often not-for-profits)

COMMON TOP-LEVEL DOMAINS AND THEIR AUTHORIZED USERS

Figure 3.24

Country Code	Country
.au	Australia
.ca	Canada
.jp	Japan
.uk	United Kingdom

Note: For a full listing of country codes, refer to **norid.no/domenenavnbaser/domreg.html.**

Figure 3.23 lists the most frequently used top-level domains.

Each country has its own top-level domain. These are two-letter designations such as .za for South Africa and .us for the United States. A sampling of country codes is shown in Figure 3.24. Within a country-specific domain, further subdivisions can be made for regions or states. For instance, the .us domain contains subdomains for each state, using the two-letter abbreviation of the state. For example, the URL for Pennsylvania's Web site is **state.pa.us**.

What's the information after the domain name that I sometimes see?   When the URL is only the domain name (such as **nytimes.com**), you are requesting a site's home page. However, sometimes a forward slash and additional text follow the domain name, such as in **nytimes.com/pages/cartoons**. The information after the slash indicates a particular file or **path** (or **subdirectory**) within the Web site. The path or subdirectory is what identifies each different page within a particular Web site; it follows the top-level domain and is preceded by a slash. In Figure 3.22, you would connect to the cartoon pages on the *New York Times* site.

Hyperlinks and Beyond

What's the best way to get around in a Web site?   Unlike text in a book or a Microsoft Word document, which is linear (meaning you read it from top to bottom, left to right, one page after another), the Web is anything but linear. As its name implies, the Web is a series of connected paths, or links, that connect you to different Web sites. You can jump from one Web page (the document indicated by the path in the URL), to another Web page within the same Web site or navigate to another Web site altogether by clicking on a specially coded element called a **hyperlink**, as shown in Figure 3.25. Generally, text that operates as a hyperlink appears in a different color (often blue) and is underlined. Sometimes images also act as hyperlinks. When you pass your cursor over a hyperlinked image, for example, a cursor may change to a hand with a finger pointing upward. To access the hyperlink, you simply click the image.

How do I return to a Web page I've already visited?   To retrace your steps, some sites also provide a **breadcrumb trail**—a list of pages within a Web site you've visited. It usually appears at the top of a page. Figure 3.25 shows an example of a breadcrumb trail. "Breadcrumbs" get their name from the fairy tale "Hansel and Gretel," in which the characters drop breadcrumbs on the trail to find their way out of a forest. By clicking on earlier links in a breadcrumb trail, you can retrace your steps back to the page on which you started.

To get back to your original location or visit a Web page you viewed previously, you use the browser's Back and Forward buttons (see Figure 3.25). To back up more than one

Figure 3.25

When you click on a hyperlink, you jump from one location in a Web site to another. When you click on the links in a breadcrumb trail, you can navigate your way back through a Web site.

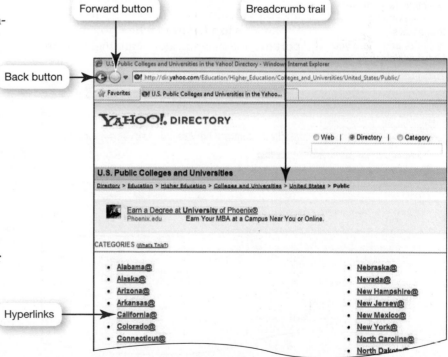

page, click the down arrow next to the Forward button to access a list of most recently visited Web sites. By selecting any one of these sites in the list, you can return directly to that page without having to navigate through other Web sites and Web pages you've visited.

The History list (see Figure 3.25) on your browser's toolbar is also a handy feature. The History list shows all the Web sites and pages that you've visited over a certain period of time. These Web sites are organized according to date and can go back as far as three weeks. To access the history list in Internet Explorer, click the down arrow next to the navigation arrows. On the Firefox toolbar, the history button is the alarm clock icon.

Favorites, Live Bookmarks, and Tagging

What's the best way to mark a site so I can return to it later? If you want an easy way to return to a specific Web page without having to remember to type in the address, you can use your browser's **Favorites** or **Bookmarks** feature. Internet Explorer and Safari call this feature Favorites; Firefox and Google Chrome call the same feature a Bookmark. This feature places a marker of the site's URL in an easily retrievable list in your browser's toolbar. To organize the sites into categories, most browsers offer tools to create folders. Most browsers also provide features to export the list of bookmarks to a file from which you can import to another computer or another browser.

Favorites and Bookmarks are great for quickly locating those sites you use the most, but they are accessible to you only when you are on your own computer. One way to access your Bookmarks and Favorites from any computer is to use MyBookmarks (**mybookmarks.com**), a free Internet service that stores your Bookmarks and Favorites online.

What are live bookmarks? The **live bookmark** feature of the Firefox browser adds the technology of RSS feeds to bookmarking. Because the Web is constantly changing, the site you bookmarked last week may subsequently change and add new content. Traditionally, you would notice the change only the next time you visited the site. With live bookmarks, the content comes to you. Instead of constantly checking your favorite Web pages for new content, a live bookmark delivers updates to you as soon as they become available. Live bookmarks are useful if you are interested in the most up-to-date news stories, sports scores, or stock prices.

What is social bookmarking? **Social bookmarking**, also known as **tagging**, lets you store, organize, and manage bookmarks (or tags) of Web pages. A social bookmark or tag is a keyword or term that is assigned to a piece of information such as a Web page, digital image, or video. A tag describes the item so that it can be found again by browsing or searching. Tags were popularized by Web 2.0 Web sites such as YouTube and Flickr.

The social bookmarking Web site Delicious (**delicious.com**) gives you the ability to add tags as bookmarks to your favorite Web sites (see Figure 3.26). The tag can

Figure 3.26

Delicious is a social bookmarking Web site that allows you to organize and share your favorite Web sites.

Installed Toolbar buttons for easy tagging

Number of people who also tagged article

Tags created to identify article

List of all tags

Figure 3.27

Icons of some popular social bookmarking Web sites.

be something meaningful to you, or you can select one from a list of suggested tags. Later, you can go back to Delicious, conduct a search using your tag, and find bookmarks tagged with the same word from everyone in your network. You can also see how many other Web users tagged the same site. Delicious offers convenient toolbars for your browsers, and many Web sites incorporate bookmarking icons for ease of use.

Figure 3.27 lists several popular social bookmarking tag tools. Diigo (**diigo.com**) allows you not only to tag and bookmark Web sites but also to annotate the pages with highlights and sticky notes. Through Diigo, the Web pages can be archived, so they are always available. Digg (**digg.com**) and Newsvine (**newsvine.com**) offer similar systems for organizing news content. StumbleUpon (**stumbleupon.com**) is like a personalized search engine and recommends Web sites based on your personal interests and preferences, as well as the recommendations of people you know or the general surfing public.

Searching the Web Effectively

With its billions of Web pages, the Web offers visitors access to masses of information on virtually any topic. To narrow down the quantity of Web information to something more useful, use a search engine and a keyword query. A **search engine** is a set of programs that searches the Web for **keywords**—specific words you wish to look for (*query*)—and then returns a list of the Web sites on which those keywords are found. Popular search engines include Google, Yahoo!, Bing, and Ask.com.

For some searches, you also can search the Web using a **subject directory**, which is a structured outline of Web sites organized by topics and subtopics. Librarians' Internet Index (**ipl.org**) is a subject directory, and some popular search engines such as Yahoo! also feature directories. If you can't decide which search engine is best, then you may want to try a **metasearch engine**. Metasearch engines, such as Dogpile (**dogpile.com**), search other search engines rather than individual Web sites. Figure 3.28 lists search engines and subject directories that are alternatives to Google, Yahoo!, Bing, and Ask.com.

Search Engines

How do search engines work? Search engines have three parts. The first part is a program called a **spider**. The spider constantly collects data on the Web, following links in Web sites and reading Web pages. Spiders get their name because they crawl over the Web using multiple "legs" to visit many sites simultaneously. As the spider collects data, the second part of the search engine, an indexer program, organizes the data into a large database. When you use a search engine, you interact with the third part: the search engine software. This software searches the indexed data, pulling out relevant information according to your search. The resulting list appears in your Web browser as a list of hits (sites that match your search).

Why don't I get the same results from all search engines? Each search engine uses a unique formula, or *algorithm*, to formulate the search and create the resulting index of related sites. In addition, search engines differ in how they rank the search results. Most search engines rank their results based on the frequency of the appearance of your queried keywords in Web sites as well as the location of those words in the sites. Thus, sites that include the keywords in their URL or site name most likely appear

Figure 3.28 | POPULAR SEARCH ENGINES AND SUBJECT DIRECTORIES

Search Tools on the Internet		
AltaVista	**altavista.com**	Keyword search engine
Clusty	**clusty.com**	Keyword search engine that groups similar results into clusters
ChaCha	**chacha.com**	This site lets you chat with a real live professional guide who helps you search, and it's free of charge. Also available by texting your questions to 242242.
CompletePlanet	**completeplanet.com**	Deep Web directory that searches databases not normally searched by typical search engines
Dogpile	**dogpile.com**	Metasearch engine that searches Google, Yahoo!, Bing, and Ask
Excite	**excite.com**	Portal with keyword search capabilities
InfoMine	**infomine.com**	Subject directory of academic resources with keyword search engine capabilities
Rollyo	**rollyo.com**	Short for "Roll Your Own Search Engine." This site lets you create your own search engine (searchroll) that searches just the sites you want it to search.
Open Directory Project	**dmoz.org**	Subject directory with keyword search capabilities
Stumbleupon	**stumbleupon.com**	Lets you rate pages "thumbs up" or "thumbs down." As it learns your preferences, your search results improve.
Technorati	**technorati.com**	A great search engine for blog content.

Note: For a complete list of search engines, go to **searchengineguide.com**.

at the top of the hit list. After that, results vary because of differences in each engine's proprietary formula.

BITS AND BYTES

Searching to Do Good

There are many volunteer and charitable organizations to participate in, but for most of us it's hard to incorporate such activities into our daily lives, and it's equally difficult to contribute financially to them all. Now there is an easy way to "do good" while doing something we all do daily—use a search engine. GoodSearch (**goodsearch. com**) is a Yahoo-powered search engine that donates half of its revenues to approved U.S. charities and schools that users designate. The money GoodSearch donates comes from the site's advertisers and amounts to approximately a penny per search.

If you're a big fan of the SPCA, a local hospital, or the neighborhood public elementary school, check to see if that particular organization has been approved. If so, you can add it as your designated charity and start searching. You can easily track how much GoodSearch has raised for your organization. More than 86,000 charitable organizations are being helped by GoodSearch, but if the organization you are interested in is not on the list, as long as it is a registered U.S. not-for-profit organization, you can apply to have it added.

You can also contribute to your favorite charity by shopping online through GoodShop. Instead of going directly to your favorite Web shop, go to **Goodshop.com** first, find and click through to the store of your choice, and start shopping. Participating stores donate up to 30 percent of the purchased amount. So, search and shop away—and do some good!

In addition, search engines differ as to which sites they search. For instance, Google and Ask.com search nearly the entire Web, whereas specialty search engines search only sites that are relevant to a particular subject. Specialty search engines exist for almost every industry or interest. For example, **dailystocks.com** is a search engine used primarily by investors that searches for corporate information to help them make educated decisions. Search Engine Watch (**searchenginewatch.com**) has a list of many specialty search engines organized by industry.

Can I use a search engine to search for images and videos? With the increasing popularity of multimedia, search engines such as Google, Ask.com, and Yahoo! have capabilities to search the Web for digital images and audio and video files. YouTube (**youtube.com**) is one of many sites that has gained recent popularity because of its wealth of video content. In addition to the amusing videos that are captured in popular news, YouTube contains instructional and informational videos.

How can I refine my searches for better results? When you conduct a

Web search, you may receive a list of hits that includes thousands—even millions—of Web pages that have no relevance to the topic you're trying to search. Initially, Boolean operators were needed to help refine a search. **Boolean operators** are words such as *AND*, *NOT*, and *OR* that describe the relationships between keywords in a search.

Today, most search engines offer an advanced search page that provides the same types of strategies in a well-organized form (see Figure 3.29). Using the advanced search form can make your Internet research a lot more efficient. With the simple addition of a few words or constraints, you can narrow your search results to a more manageable and more meaningful list.

Are there other helpful search strategies? Instead of using the advanced search form, you can use other strategies to help refine your searches when entering your search phrases:

- **Search for a phrase.** To search for an exact phrase, place quotation marks around your keywords. The search engine will look for only those Web sites that contain the words in that exact order. For example, if you want information on the movie *Lord of the Rings* and you type these words without quotation marks, your search results will contain pages that include either of the words *Lord* and *Rings*, although not necessarily in that order. Typing "Lord of the Rings" in quotes guarantees that search results will include this exact phrase.

- **Search within a specific Web site.** To search just a specific Web site, you can use the search keyword, then *site:* followed by the Web site's URL. For example, searching with *processor site:wired.com* returns

results about processors from the Wired.com Web site. The same method works for entire classes of sites in a given top-level domain or country code.

- **Use a wild card.** The asterisk "*" is a wild card, or placeholder, feature that is helpful when you need to search with unknown terms. For example, searching with *Congress voted *on the* bill* returns sites that mention how Congress voted on various bills.

How else can I customize my searches? A lot of other specialty search strategies and services are available. Clicking on the "more" hyperlink in the Google search engine, for example, takes you to all the various search products Google offers. Google Scholar searches scholarly literature such as peer-reviewed papers, theses, and publications from academic organizations. Each search result contains bibliographic information as well. Google Custom Search enables you to create a customized search engine to search only a selected set of sites tailored to your specific needs. This specialized search engine can be added to a Web site or blog, or designed for a specific organization. Google Book Search enables you to search through the full-text content of millions of books. Google News searches through thousands of news stories from around the world. Google News can be further customized to search stories within specific categories such as Business or Entertainment, and a News Archives Timeline shows selected results from relevant time periods (see Figure 3.30).

Figure 3.29

Most search engines have an advanced search form to help you refine your searches.

Advanced search tips for additional search strategies

Google Advanced Search   Advanced Search Tips | Abo...

Use the form below and your advanced search will appear here

Find web pages that have...
all these words:
this exact wording or phrase:
one or more of these words: OR   OR

But don't show pages that have...
any of these unwanted words:

Need more tools?
Results per page: 10 results
Language: any language
File type: any format
Search within a site or domain:
                          (e.g. youtube.com, .edu)

Date, usage rights, numeric range, and more

                                    Advanced Search

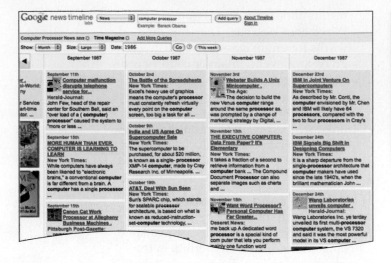

Figure 3.30

The Google News Archives Timeline enables you to zero in on search results from a specific period.

Evaluating Web Sites

How can I make sure a Web site is appropriate to use for research?

When you're using the Internet for research, you shouldn't assume that everything you find is accurate and appropriate to use. Before you use an Internet resource, consider the following.

1. **Authority:** Who is the author of the article or the sponsor of the site? If the author is well known or the site is published by a reputable news source (such as the *New York Times*), then you can feel more confident using it as a source than if you are unable to locate such information. *Note:* Some sites include a page with information about the author or the site's sponsor.

2. **Bias:** Is the site biased? The purpose of many Web sites is to sell products or services or to persuade rather than inform. These sites, though useful in some situations, present a biased point of view. Look for sites that offer several sets of facts, or consider opinions from several sources.

3. **Relevance:** Is the information in the site current? Material can last a long time on the Web. Some research projects (such as historical accounts) depend on older records. However, if you're writing about cutting-edge technologies, you need to look for the most recent sources. Therefore, look for a date on information to make sure it is current.

4. **Audience:** For what audience is the site intended? Ensure that the content, tone, and style of the site match your needs. You probably wouldn't want to use information from a site geared toward teens if you were writing for adults, nor would you use a site that has a casual style and tone for serious research.

5. **Links:** Are the links available and appropriate? Check out the links provided on the site to determine whether they are still working and appropriate for your needs. Don't assume that the links provided are the only additional sources of information. Investigate other sites on your topic as well. You should also be able to find the same information on at least three different Web sites to help verify the information is accurate.

The answers to these questions will help you decide whether you should consider a Web site to be a good source of information.

The Internet and How It Works

The Internet is such an integral part of our lives that it's hard to imagine life without it. Looking forward, our ability to use and

Plagiarism and Copyright Violation—
What Can You Borrow from the Internet?

You've no doubt heard of plagiarism—claiming another person's words as your own. And you've probably heard the term *copyright violation*, especially if you've been following the music industry's battle to keep "free" music off the Web. But what constitutes plagiarism, and what constitutes copyright violation? And what can you borrow from the Web? Consider these scenarios:

1. You find a political cartoon that would be terrific in a PowerPoint presentation you're creating for your civics class. You copy it into your presentation.

2. Your hobby is cooking. You design a Web site that includes videos of you preparing recipes, as well as the recipes themselves. Some of these recipes you take from your favorite cookbooks; others you get from friends. You don't cite your sources, nor do you obtain permission from the originators of the recipes you post to your Web site.

3. You're pressed for time and need to do research for a paper due tomorrow. You find information on an obscure Web site and copy it into your paper without documenting the source.

4. You download a song from the Internet and incorporate it into a PowerPoint presentation for a school project. Because you figure everyone knows the song, you don't credit it in your sources.

Which of the preceding scenarios represent copyright violations? Which represent plagiarism? The distinctions between these scenarios are narrow in some cases, but it's important to understand the differences.

As noted earlier, plagiarism occurs when you use someone else's ideas or words and represent them as your own. In today's computer society, it's easy to copy information from the Internet and paste it into a Word document, change a few words, and call it your own. To avoid plagiarism, use quotation marks around all words you borrow directly, and credit your sources for any ideas you paraphrase or borrow. Avoiding plagiarism means properly crediting all information you obtain from the Internet, including words, ideas, graphics, data, and audio and video clips.

Web sites such as **turnitin.com** (for teachers and institutions) and **WriteCheck.com** (specifically for students), as shown in Figure 3.31, help check for plagiarism violations. WriteCheck.com compares your document to a database of magazines, newspapers, journals, and books, as well as Web content and previously submitted student papers. Although some common phrasing may be truly coincidental, real and purposeful plagiarism is reasonably easy to identify. Students can use WriteCheck.com before submitting an assignment to ensure their papers will not be confused with plagiarized work. In most schools, plagiarism is a serious offense, often resulting in a 0 for an assignment, or an F for the class. It's best to

ensure your paper doesn't even have unintended instances of plagiarized work.

Copyright violation is more serious because it, unlike plagiarism, is punishable by law. Copyright law assumes that *all* original work—including text, graphics, software, multimedia, audio and video clips, and other intellectual property—is copyrighted even if the work does not display the copyright symbol (©). Copyright violation occurs when you use another person's material for your own personal economic benefit, or when you take away from the economic benefit of the originator. Don't assume that by citing a source you're abiding by copyright laws. In most cases, you need to seek and receive written permission from the copyright holder.

There are exceptions to this rule. For example, there is no copyright on government documents, so you can download and reproduce material from NASA, for example, without violating copyright laws. The British Broadcasting Corporation (BBC) is also beginning to digitize and make available its archives of material to the public without copyright restrictions.

Teachers and students receive special consideration regarding copyright violations. This special consideration falls under a provision called *academic fair use*. As long as the material is being used for educational purposes only, *limited* copying and distribution is allowed. One standard applied to academic fair use is the effect the use has on the potential market. For example, an instructor could make copies of a book chapter and distribute it to her class one time but could not do it on a regular basis or over different semesters because that might affect the potential market or sales of the book. Similarly, a student can include a cartoon in a PowerPoint presentation without seeking permission from the artist. However, to avoid plagiarism in these situations, you still must credit your sources of information.

So, do you now know which of the four scenarios above are plagiarism or copyright violations? Let's review them.

1. You are not in violation because the use of the cartoon is for educational purposes and falls under the academic fair use provision. You must still credit the source, however.

2. If you maintain your Web site for your economic benefit, you would be in violation of copyright laws because no credit was given for the recipes, and you are presenting them as your own.

3. You are guilty of plagiarism because you copied content from another source and implied it was your own work.

4. Again, because your copying is for a school project, you are not in violation because of the academic fair use provision. However, it's always important to document your sources.

Figure 3.31

By using **WriteCheck.com**, students can compare their work to a database of publications to check for unintended plagiarism.

interact with the Internet and the World Wide Web will converge even more with our daily lives. Therefore, it's important to understand how the Internet works and the choices available for connecting to it.

How does the Internet work?
Computers connected to the Internet communicate with (or "talk" to) each other in turns, just as we do when we ask a question and get an answer. Thus, a computer connected to the Internet acts in one of two ways: it is either a **client**, a computer that asks for data, or it is a **server**, a computer that receives the request and returns the data to the client. Because the Internet uses clients and servers, it is referred to as a **client/server network**. (We'll discuss such networks in more detail in Chapter 7.)

How do computers talk to each other? Suppose you want to access the Web to check out snow conditions at your favorite ski area. As Figure 3.32 illustrates, the following events take place:

1. When you type the Web site address of the ski area in your Web browser, your computer acts as a client computer because you are asking for data from the ski area's Web site.

2. Your browser's request for this data travels along several pathways that can be likened to interstate highways. The largest and fastest pathways are the main arteries of the Internet, called **Internet backbones**. All intermediary pathways connect to these backbones.

3. Your data flows along the backbone and then on to smaller pathways until it reaches its destination, which is the server computer for the ski area's Web site.

4. The server computer returns the requested data to your computer using the most expedient pathway system (which may be different from the pathway the request took).

Figure 3.32

How the Internet's client/server network works.

STEP 3:
Server at skislope.com receives request

National access
(Internet Backbone)

Regional access

STEP 2:
Request travels to server through Internet access companies

STEP 1:
Client computer requests access to skislope.com through browser

STEP 4:
Request travels back to client computer through Internet access companies

5. Your Web browser interprets the data and displays it on your monitor.

How does the data get sent to the correct computer? Each time you connect to the Internet, your computer is assigned a unique identification number. This number, called an **Internet Protocol address** (or **IP address**), is a set of four numbers separated by periods and commonly referred to as a *dotted quad* or *dotted decimal* such as 123.45.245.91. IP addresses are the means by which all computers connected to the Internet identify each other. Similarly, each Web site is assigned an IP address that uniquely identifies it. However, because the long strings of numbers that make up IP addresses are difficult for people to remember, Web sites are given text versions of their IP addresses. So the ski area's Web site mentioned earlier may have an IP address of 66.117.154.119 and a text name of **skislope.com**. When you type "skislope.com" into your browser window, your computer (with its own unique IP address) looks for the ski area's IP address (66.117.154.119). Data is exchanged between the ski area's server computer and your computer using these unique IP addresses.

Connecting to the Internet

To take advantage of the resources the Internet offers, you need a means to connect your computer to it. Home users nowadays have several connection options available. Originally, the only means to connect to the Internet was with a **dial-up connection**. With dial-up connections, you connect to the Internet using a standard telephone line. However, dial-up connections are becoming legacy technology because other, faster connection options exist. In many parts of the world, these faster connections are quickly becoming the preferred method of connecting to the Internet.

Broadband Connections

What is broadband? **Broadband**, often referred to as "high-speed Internet," refers to a type of connection that offers a faster means to connect to the Internet. Broadband usually has a data transmission rate of 256 Kbps (kilobits per second) or greater. This high rate of access is in contrast to dial-up Internet access, which has a maximum transmission speed of 56 Kbps.

What types of broadband are available? The standard broadband technologies in most areas are **digital subscriber line (DSL)**, which uses a standard phone line to connect your computer to the Internet, and **cable**, which uses your television's cable service provider to connect to the Internet. **Fiber-optic service**, which uses plastic or glass cables to transfer data at the speed of light, has in the past few years become available as a broadband service to the home. Satellite broadband is mostly used in rural or mountain areas that cannot get DSL, cable, or fiber-optic service.

How does cable work? A cable Internet connection uses the same coaxial cable used by cable TV; however, cable TV and cable Internet are separate services. Cable TV is a one-way service in which the cable company feeds programming signals to your television. To bring two-way Internet connections to homes, cable companies must upgrade their networks with two-way data transmission capabilities.

How does DSL work? Similar to a dial-up connection, DSL uses telephone lines to connect to the Internet. However, unlike dial-up, DSL allows phone and data transmission to share the same line, thus eliminating the need for an additional phone line. Phone lines are made of pairs of twisted copper wires known as *twisted-pair wiring*. The bandwidth of the copper wires is split into three sections, similar to a three-lane highway on which only one lane is used to carry voice data. DSL uses the remaining two lanes to send and receive data separately at much higher frequencies. Thus, although it uses a standard phone line, a DSL connection is much faster than a dial-up connection.

Can anyone with a phone line have DSL? Having a traditional phone line in your house doesn't mean that you have access to DSL service. Your local phone company must have special DSL technology to offer you the service. Although more phone companies are acquiring DSL

technology, many areas in the United States, especially rural ones, still do not have DSL service available.

What are the limitations to DSL and cable? Although cable and DSL speeds are about the same, each has its own particular limitations. DSL signals are sensitive to distance. There is a maximum distance of about 3 miles between where the signal originates, called the *central office*, and the customer's location. The further the connection is from the central office, the weaker the signal is. Although cable is not limited by distance like DSL, cable services are shared between users, so in peak usage times, cable connection speeds can slow down.

How does fiber-optic service work? Fiber-optic service uses fiber-optic lines, which are strands of optically pure glass or plastic that are as thin as a human hair. They are arranged in bundles called *optical cables* and transmit data via light signals over long distances. Because light travels so quickly, this technology can bring an enormous amount of data to your home at superfast speeds. When the data reaches your house, it's converted to electrical pulses that transmit digital signals your computer can "read."

> **"Fiber-optic service transfers data at the speed of light."**

What special equipment do I need to hook up to broadband? A broadband Internet connection requires a **modem**. Depending on the type of broadband service you have, you will have either a cable modem or DSL modem. The modem works to translate the broadband signal into digital data and back again. With both cable and DSL services, the modem allows the data to travel on the unused capacity of the transmission medium.

For example, a DSL modem (see Figure 3.33) separates voice signals from data signals so that they can travel in the right "lane" on the twisted-pair wiring. Voice data travels at a slower speed than digital data, which can travel at rates ranging from 500 Kbps to 6,000 Kbps [6 megabits per second (Mbps)]. Sometimes a DSL filter is required in DSL installations. Filters are necessary to reduce interference caused when the DSL equipment shares the same lines as the standard phone line. If a filter is

ACTIVE HELP-DESK Connecting to the Internet

In this Active Helpdesk call, you'll play the role of a helpdesk staffer. You will field calls about various options for connecting to the Internet and how to choose an Internet service provider.

required, the phone line fits into the filter, and the filter plugs into the phone's wall jack.

Generally, the modem is located somewhere near your computer and is connected to an expansion (or adapter) card called a **network interface card (NIC)**, which is located inside your computer. If you want to share your Internet connection with more than one computer, you will also need a router.

What options exist when cable and DSL are not available? Satellite Internet is another way to connect to the Internet. Most people choose satellite Internet when other high-speed options are unavailable. To take advantage of satellite Internet, you need a satellite dish, which is placed outside your home and connected to your computer with coaxial cable, the same type of cable used for cable TV. Data from your computer is transmitted between your personal satellite dish and the satellite company's receiving satellite dish by a satellite that sits in a geosynchronous orbit thousands of miles above the Earth.

Wireless

Why is wireless Internet access necessary? In our ever-more-mobile lifestyles, accessing the Internet wirelessly can make our lives more productive, and perhaps a bit more flexible, allowing us to work away from our desks. Students can use their notebook computers or smartphones to send instant messages to each other across campus, and business travelers can quickly grab their e-mail between flights. At home, wireless networks allow us to share an Internet connection and print from our notebooks from any room without having to attach and detach wires.

In some communities, organizations are now installing wireless or WiFi networks; and in some cities and towns, local governments are installing municipal WiFi

Cable runs to network interface card

Figure 3.33
You need a special DSL modem to connect to the Internet using DSL.

networks. The newest wireless access technology to be deployed for mobile and stationary broadband access is WiMAX. WiMAX is designed to extend local WiFi networks across greater distances, such as across a campus. Mobile WiMAX is an alternative to cellular transmission of voice and high-speed data. Even wireless in-flight Internet service is available! Gogo (**gogoinflight. com**) is a wireless broadband network that provides coverage on participating airlines across the continental United States, so when you are cleared to use your portable electronic devices, you can comfortably access wireless Internet from 35,000 feet.

How does one access the Internet wirelessly? To access the Internet wirelessly, you need to be in a wireless fidelity (WiFi) hot spot and have the right equipment on your mobile device. Most notebooks, smartphones, game systems, and PMPs sold in the past several years come equipped with wireless capability built in, but if not, several wireless adapters are available.

For your own personal WiFi, it's simple to set up a wireless network at home (see Chapter 7 for details), and many businesses and schools, as well as public places such as airports, libraries, bookstores, and restaurants, offer WiFi. Some public places offer free WiFi access, but many others require you to buy wireless access through a wireless access service plan. For example, McDonald's provides WiFi access through AT&T, Barnes & Noble provides WiFi through T-Mobile, and Starbucks uses Boingo for its WiFi access. To access these WiFi services, you can pay for a single session or a monthly membership, or you can sign up for a longer-term subscription in which you receive monthly bills. WiFi Free Spot (**wififreespot.com**) and **WiFiHotSpotList.com** will help you locate a free hot spot wherever you are planning to go.

If you need to access the Internet wirelessly and do not want the hassle of looking for a WiFi hot spot, you can

Discovering the Semantic Web

How do we find information on the Web? Generally, we access Google or another search engine, type in the keyword or search phrase, and click the search button. As a result, millions of links to Web pages display. At best, we click on the first several links that seem reasonably relevant to our search. Rarely, if ever, do we explore all of the links that are found in the search results.

Similarly, think about all the other types of data on the Web that we access manually, such as contact information, appointment times, transportation schedules, entertainment schedules, medical treatments, and store types, locations, and hours. It would seem that computers would be helpful in plugging through all of this Web data, but oddly, that is not the case. Web pages are designed for people to read, not for computers to manipulate. Although computers can determine the parts and functionality of Web pages (headers, hyperlinks, etc.), as yet no reliable way exists for computers to process the meaning of the data so that they can use the information to see relationships or make decisions.

The Semantic Web is an evolving extension of the World Wide Web in which information is defined in such a way to make it more easily readable by computers. Tim Berners-Lee, the inventor of the World Wide Web, and the implementation of HTTP and HTML, thought up the Semantic Web.

Right now, search engines function by recognizing keywords such as *appointment*, *dentist*, and *root canal*, but they cannot determine in which office and on what days Dr. Smith works and what his available appointment times are. The Semantic Web would enable computers to find and manage that type of information and coordinate it with your other schedules and preferences.

Similarly, think about the convenience and efficiency that online shopping has brought to our lives. Then think about all the time we actually spend researching and comparing products, brands, stores, prices, and shipping options. Ultimately, after all that effort, we make the final buying decision and place the order. With the Semantic Web in place, you could enter your preferences into a computerized software agent, which would then search the Web for you, find the best option based on your criteria, and place the order. Additionally, the agent would be able to record the financial transaction into your personal bookkeeping software and arrange for a technician to help install your purchase, if needed.

The Semantic Web would use software agents that roam from page to page, completing sophisticated tasks. These agents would not read words, look at pictures, and process information as humans do, but rather would search through metadata. Metadata is machine-readable data that describes other data in such a way that the agents can identify and define what they need to know. Like Web page coding, which is now done in HTML, XML, and other formats, metadata would be invisible to humans reading pages on the Web but would be clearly visible to computers, in essence turning the Web into a giant database.

The introduction of eXtensible Markup Language (XML) has helped make the user of the Web more of a participant. Web 2.0 technologies such as blogs, wikis, and social networking sites, as well as Web-based applications, are in part possible because of XML's tagging functionalities. RSS feeds also use technologies that are an underlying component of the Semantic Web.

The Semantic Web would build on this type of capability so that each Web site would have text and pictures (for people to read) and metadata (for computers to read) describing the information on the Web (see Figure 3.35). The metadata would contain all the attributes of the information, such as condition, price, or schedule availability, in a machine-readable format. Businesses, services, and software would all use the same categorization structures so that similar information would share the same attributes, ensuring consistency of metadata throughout the Web. Then, with Web data properly identified and categorized, computerized agents could read the metadata found on different sites, compare the information, and process the information based on user-defined criteria.

Figure 3.34

Aircards like the ones pictured here fit into the USB port or PC card slot on your netbook or notebook to allow you to surf the Internet wirelessly when you don't have access to a WiFi hot spot.

purchase an **aircard** such as the ones shown in Figure 3.34. Aircards, sometimes referred to as *cellular modems*, are devices that fit either into a USB port or a special slot on the side of a notebook called an **Express card slot** (also known as a *PC card slot*). The aircard enables users to have wireless Internet access with notebooks and netbooks. They require a service plan, similar to a cell phone plan. When considering purchasing an aircard and service plan, be sure to check the coverage and costs before deciding, because they vary among providers.

What are concerns with wireless? Most public hot spots are unsecured, so use caution when accessing the Internet from public locations. Although

Figure 3.35

Web 2.0 technologies enable us to become creators and users of Internet content. The Semantic Web enables the computer to add context to Web content, providing meaning to information from different sources.

Although some of the Semantic Web functionalities are beginning to emerge in Web 2.0 technologies, the majority of the functionality and implementation of the Semantic Web is still in development. The World Wide Web Consortium (W3C), led by Tim Berners-Lee, is the primary organization leading the charge. The greatest challenge is recoding all the information currently available on the Web into the type of metadata that computers could recognize. The very grandeur of that task means that we will not see a fully functional Semantic Web until sometime in the distant future. In the meantime, we can continue to benefit from each small step toward that goal.

casually surfing the Internet is fine, it's best not to use your credit card, for example, to purchase items online from a public hot spot because your credit card information can be captured by a lurking identity thief. See additional information on wireless security in Chapter 7.

Dial-Up Connections

How does a dial-up connection work?   A dial-up connection needs only a standard phone line and a modem. The word *modem* is short for *modulate/demodulate*. A **dial-up modem** is a device that converts (modulates) the digital signals the computer understands into analog signals that can travel over phone lines. The computer on the other end also must have a modem to translate (demodulate) the received analog signal back to a digital signal that the receiving computer can understand. Modern computers generally come with internal modems built into the system unit.

What are the advantages and disadvantages of dial-up?   A dial-up connection is the least costly way to connect to the Internet. Although slower than broadband connections, dial-up connections are often fine for casual Internet users who do not need a fast connection. The major downside to dial-up is speed. Dial-up modems transfer data at a much slower rate than that of a basic broadband connection. Although

Figure 3.36 COMPARING CABLE, DSL, AND FIBER-OPTIC INTERNET CONNECTION OPTIONS

	DSL	Cable	Fiber-Optic
Maximum download speeds	Average speeds of 1.5 Mbps, with a maximum of 7 Mbps	Average speeds of 5 Mbps, with a maximum of 30 Mbps	Average speeds of 20 Mbps, with a maximum speed of 50 Mbps.
Pros	Lets you surf the Net and talk on the same phone line simultaneously.	Speeds are not dependent on distance from central office.	Increased speeds. Service is not shared or dependent on distance from central office.
Cons	Speed drops as you get farther from phone company's central office. Not every phone line will work.	Line is shared with others in neighborhood; speeds may vary due to peak and nonpeak usage. May require professional installation if cable not already present.	Cost, although this is a diminishing concern as the technology continues to be deployed and accepted. Not available in all areas.

Note: The data transfer rates listed in this table are approximations. As technologies improve, so do data transfer rates.

many Web pages can be sent without graphics as plain text, it still can take a long time to load a Web page, especially if it contains multimedia, which is the norm for most Web pages today. Similarly, if you visit many Web sites at the same time or receive or send large files through e-mail, you'll find that a dial-up connection is especially slow. Another disadvantage of dial-up is that when you're on the Internet, you tie up your phone line if you don't have a separate line.

Choosing the Right Internet Connection Option

How do I choose which Internet connection option is best for me? According to a Federal Communications Commission report released in early 2010, more than 75 percent of adults in the United States use the Internet, and 65 percent of adults have home broadband access. Depending on the area in which you live, you might not have a choice as to the type of broadband connection that is available. Check with your local cable TV provider, phone company, and satellite TV provider(s) to determine what broadband options are available where you live and what the transfer rates are in your area. It might also be good to check with your neighbors to see what kind of broadband connections they use. Speeds vary by neighborhood, sometimes exceeding advertised rates, so it's always good to check actual experiences.

One factor to consider in choosing the right Internet connection is speed. **Data transfer rate** is the measurement of how fast data travels between computers. It is also informally referred to as *connection speed*. For example, dial-up connections have a maximum data transfer rate of 56 Kbps (56K) while broadband connections can achieve data-transfer rates of 10 to 1000 megabits per second (Mbps). Comparatively, satellite Internet is slower than DSL and cable, and fiber-optic provides the fastest transmission.

Finally, you may also need to consider which other services you want bundled into your payment, such as phone or TV. The table in Figure 3.36 compares several features of cable, DSL, and fiber-optic service to help you with your decision.

The Future of the Internet

The Internet of the future will have more bandwidth and offer increased services. Because of the prevalence of wireless technologies, the Internet will be more accessible, and we will become more dependent on it.

However, because commerce and communication activities are increasingly dominating the Internet, the concern is that there will be no bandwidth left for one of the Internet's original purposes: exchange of scientific and academic research. Two major projects currently under way in the United States to develop advanced technologies for the Internet are the large scale networking (LSN) program and Internet2.

What are the large scale networking and Internet2 programs? Out of a project titled the Next Generation Internet (which ended in 2002), the U.S. government created the **large scale networking (LSN)** program. Large scale networking's aim is to fund the research and development of cutting-edge networking and wireless technologies and to increase the speed of networks.

The Internet2 is a research and development consortium of more than three hundred universities (supported by government and industry partners) that seeks to expand the possibilities of the Internet by developing new Internet technologies and disseminating them as rapidly as possible to the rest of the Internet community. Many of the current technologies of the commercial Internet are possible because of the research done by the Internet2 consortium. The Internet2 backbone supports extremely high-speed communications—up to 8.8 gigabits per second (Gbps)—and provides an excellent testing area for new data transmission technologies.

How else will the Internet become a more integral part of our lives? As this chapter explained, the Internet is already an integral part of our lives. It is the way we communicate, shop, research, entertain, and express ourselves. Many of the tools on the Web that have been described in this chapter—social networking sites, wikis, podcasts, and user content databases such as YouTube (for videos) and Flickr (for photos)—are part of a wave of Web-based services that emphasizes online collaboration and sharing among users. The future Internet will continue to evolve with more Web-based applications driven by user input, interaction, and content.

In the future, you can expect to use the Internet to assist you with many day-to-day tasks that you now do manually. No longer will PCs and mobile devices be our primary access to the Internet. We can already see the convergence of the Internet with telephony, television, and gaming devices.

BITS AND BYTES   National Broadband Plan

If the Federal Communications Commission (FCC) has its way, by 2020 nearly 100 million, or 90%, of U.S. homes, as well as schools, hospitals, and government offices, will have access to more affordable broadband access of at least 100 Mbps. This $15.5-billion National Broadband Plan proposes that such universal broadband access would pave the way for "economic growth, job creation, global competitiveness, and a better way of life." Universal Internet access can change how education, health care, energy, and public safety are delivered and managed.

In addition to ensuring that virtually every American has access to broadband Internet, the plan proposes to ensure that other aspects of Internet usage such as networks, devices, content, and applications are strong and functional. The plan also proposes to help encourage greater competition in the broadband market, which can lead to competitive pricing and more innovative products and services among providers. Although the National Broadband Plan is just that—a plan—and is yet to be implemented, the prospects of such as plan, and the resulting innovations, is intriguing and may make the U.S. a leader in mobile innovation.

As other less obvious Internet-enabled devices become popular and more accessible to the common consumer, our lives will become more Internet dependent. For example, Internet-enabled appliances and household systems are now available that allow your home virtually to run itself. Today, there are refrigerators that can monitor their contents and go online to order more diet soda when they detect that the supply is getting low. Meanwhile, Internet heating and cooling systems can monitor weather forecasts and order fuel deliveries when supplies run low or bad weather is expected. These appliances will become more widespread as the price of equipment drops.

The uses of the Internet are limited only by our imaginations and the current constraints of technology. At some point, the Internet will no longer be a place we "go" to but an integral part of our lives.

1. What is the origin of the Internet?

The Internet is the largest computer network in the world, connecting millions of computers. Government and military officials developed the early Internet as a reliable way to communicate in the event of war. Eventually, scientists and educators used the Internet to exchange research. Today, we use the Internet and the Web (which is a part of the Internet) to shop, research, communicate, and entertain ourselves.

2. How can I communicate through the Internet?

Communication was one of the reasons the Internet was developed and is one of the primary uses of the Internet today. E-mail allows users to communicate electronically without the parties involved being available at the same time, whereas instant-messaging services are programs that enable you to communicate in real time with others who are online at the same time. Other forms of group communication include social networking sites, chat rooms, newsgroups, and IRC.

3. How can I communicate and collaborate using Web 2.0 technologies?

Web 2.0 is a trend of Web interactions among people, software, and data. Examples of these technologies include blogs, wikis, and more. Blogs are journal entries posted to the Web that are generally organized by a topic or area of interest and are publicly available. Generally, one person writes the blog, and others can comment on the journal entries. Video logs are personal journals that use video as the primary content in addition to text, images, and audio. Wikis are a type of Web site that allows users to change content by adding, removing, or editing it. A wiki is designed to allow many users to collaborate on the content. Podcasts are audio or video content that is broadcast over the Internet. Users subscribe to receive updates to podcasts. Social networking sites enable users to communicate and share information with existing friends as well as to meet and connect with others through common interests, experiences, or friends.

4. What are the various kinds of multimedia files found on the Web, and what software do I need to use them?

The Web is appealing because of its enriched multimedia content. Multimedia is anything that involves one or more forms of media in addition to text, such as graphics, audio, and video clips. Sometimes you need a special software program called a *plug-in* (or *player*) to view and hear multimedia files. Plug-ins are often installed in new computers or are offered free of charge at manufacturers' Web sites.

5. What is e-commerce, and what e-commerce safeguards protect me when I'm online?

E-commerce is the business of conducting business online. E-commerce includes transactions between businesses (B2B), between consumers (C2C), and between businesses and consumers (B2C). Because more business than ever before is conducted online, numerous safeguards have been put in place to ensure that transactions are protected.

6. What is a Web browser, and what is a URL and what are its parts?

Once you're connected to the Internet, in order to locate, navigate to, and view Web pages, you need to install special software called a Web browser on your system. The most common Web browsers are Internet Explorer, Firefox, Google Chrome, and Safari. You gain access to a Web site by typing in its address, called a Uniform Resource Locator (URL). A URL is composed of several parts, including the protocol, the domain, the top-level domain, and paths (or subdirectories).

7. How can I use hyperlinks and other tools to get around the Web?

One unique aspect of the Web is that you can jump from place to place by clicking on specially formatted pieces of text or images called *hyperlinks*. You can also use the Back and Forward buttons, History lists, breadcrumb trails, and Favorites or Bookmarks to navigate the Web. Favorites, live bookmarks, and social bookmarking help you return to specific Web pages without having to type in the URL and help you organize the Web content that is most important to you.

8. How do I search the Internet effectively, and how can I evaluate Web sites?

A search engine is a set of programs that searches the Web using specific keywords you wish to query and then returns a list of the Web sites on which those keywords are found. Search engines can be used to search for images, podcasts, and videos in addition to traditional text-based Web content. A subject directory is a structured outline of Web sites organized by topic and subtopic. Metasearch engines search other search engines.

Not all Web sites are equal, and some are better sources for research than others. To evaluate whether it is appropriate to use a Web site as a resource, determine whether the author of the site is reputable and whether the site is intended for your particular needs. In addition, make sure that the site content is not biased, the information in the site is current, and all the links on the site are available and appropriate. If multiple sites offer the same content, then it is another indication that the information is accurate.

9. How does data travel on the Internet?

A computer connected to the Internet acts as either a client (a computer that asks for information) or a server (a computer that receives the request and returns the information to the client). Data travels between clients and servers along a system of communication lines or pathways. The largest and fastest of these pathways is the Internet backbone. To ensure that data is sent to the correct computer along the pathways, IP addresses (unique ID numbers) are assigned to all computers connected to the Internet.

10. What are my options for connecting to the Internet?

Home users have many options for connecting to the Internet. A dial-up connection, in which you connect to the Internet using a standard phone line, was at one time the standard way to connect to the Internet. Today's broadband connections are faster and have made dial-up a legacy connection technology. Broadband connections include cable, DSL, and fiber-optic. Satellite is a connection option for those who do not have access to faster broadband technologies. WiFi allows users to connect to the Internet wirelessly, but are not as fast as wired connections.

three key terms

key terms

Word Bank

- blogs (weblogs)
- Bookmarks
- broadband
- DSL
- fiber-optic service (FiOS)
- hyperlink

- instant messaging (IM)
- keyword
- podcast
- search engine
- social bookmarking
- social networking
- tag

- Uniform Resource Locators (URLs)
- Web 2.0
- Web browser
- WiFi
- wiki

Instructions: Fill in the blanks using the words from the Word Bank above.

Juan rests his new notebook on his lap and powers it up while waiting for his next class to begin. Using the (1) _____ access provided by his college, Juan is able to connect to the Internet wirelessly. Although the school's wireless access to the Internet is fast, it's not as fast as the (2) _____ connection at home, because his parents just switched to (3) _____, which transfers data at the speed of light.

Knowing he has only a few minutes before class, Juan launches Internet Explorer, the (4) _____ software from Microsoft that allows him to connect to the Internet. He quickly goes to Facebook, the (5) _____ site, to catch up on the activities of his friends. He also reads a few of the updates to the online journal Engadget.com, one of his favorite (6) _____. He's glad that the new (7) _____ technologies make such collaboration possible. Just before class begins, Juan's friend Marie, who is using her (8) _____ service, sees that Juan is available on her buddy list. She sends him a quick, real-time note to let him know she'll catch up with him after class.

At home, Juan types in a (9) _____ in Google, the (10) _____, to find Web sites for a research paper. One of the first sites listed is Wikipedia, the online encyclopedia that takes advantage of the collaborative nature of (11) _____ technology. Because anyone can add, change, or edit content on Wikipedia, Juan knows that he can't rely completely on this information but finds that it is usually a pretty good starting point for his research. Juan clicks on a (12) _____, the specially coded text at the bottom of the Wikipedia article, which links him to another Web site. He adds a (13) _____ with a meaningful keyword in the (14) _____ site Delicious so he can return to it later. Finally, before going to bed, Juan listens to a (15) _____ of one of his favorite radio shows that he subscribed to recently.

becoming computer literate

Using key terms from the chapter, write a letter to the owners of your local coffee shop explaining why they should make it a WiFi hot spot. Include in your letter the advantages WiFi would bring to the customers and identify some security considerations that customers need to be aware of.

Instructions: Answer the multiple-choice and true–false questions below for more practice with key terms and concepts from this chapter.

Multiple Choice

1. Which is NOT true about the Internet?
a. It is the largest computer network in the world.
b. It was created to establish a secure form of military communications.
c. It was developed as a method for linking research documents.
d. It was invented as a way for all computers to communicate.

2. What do you need to read, send, and organize e-mail from any computer?
a. An e-mail client program
b. An e-mail server
c. An Internet service provider
d. A Web-based e-mail account

3. Which is NOT an example of social networking?
a. E-mail
b. Instant messaging
c. Blogging
d. Listserv

4. In which way is a blog different from a wiki?
a. Blogs are used to express opinions.
b. Blogs are written by a single author.
c. Blogs include images and audio.
d. Blogs are arranged as a listing of entries.

5. Which is true about plug-ins?
a. Plugs-ins rarely require updating.
b. Plug-ins track the Web sites you've visited.
c. Plug-ins are necessary for viewing most Web graphics.
d. Plug-ins can present security risks.

6. What feature is a list of pages you've visited within a Web site?
a. Favorites
b. Breadcrumb trail
c. Bookmarks
d. History

7. Which is NOT part of a search engine?
a. Spider
b. Indexer program
c. Subject directory
d. Search engine software

8. When using the Internet for research, you
a. can assume that everything you find is accurate and appropriate.
b. should evaluate sites for bias and relevance.
c. should use the most current sources.
d. can assume that the links provided on the site are the only additional sources of information.

9. Which connection type provides the fastest data transmission?
a. DSL
b. Cable
c. Fiber-optic
d. Satellite

10. What current program funds the research and development of cutting-edge networking and wireless technologies?
a. Large scale networking
b. Internet2
c. Web 2.0
d. ARPANET

True–False

_____ 1. The information in e-mail is no more private than a postcard.
_____ 2. Consumers buy books, movie tickets, and games more often online than in retail stores.
_____ 3. The VeriSign seal on a Web site guarantees that the Web site is secure.
_____ 4. Each time you connect to the Internet, your computer is assigned the same IP address.
_____ 5. Internet connection speeds vary by neighborhood, sometimes exceeding advertised rates.

making the transition to... next semester

1. Online Support Facilities

Your school most likely has many online support facilities. Do you know what they are? Go to your school's Web site and search for online support.

   a. Is online tutoring available?
   b. Can you reserve a book from the library online?
   c. Can you register for classes online?
   d. Can you take classes online?
   e. Can you buy books online?

2. Plagiarism Policies

Does your school have a plagiarism policy?

   a. Search your school's Web site to find the school's plagiarism policy. What does it say?
   b. How well do you paraphrase? Find some Web sites that help test or evaluate your paraphrasing skills.
   c. Create an account at **Turnitin.com**. This Web site checks your written work against content on the Web and produces an originality report. Submit at least three different drafts of your work to Turnitin.com to check for any intended or unintended cases of plagiarism before submitting your final work for a grade. What were the results?

3. Searching Beyond Google

While Google is probably your first choice among search engines, there are many other very good search engines that are good to know about. Conduct searches for inexpensive travel deals for spring break by using the following search engines. Record your results and a summary of the differences among search engines. Would you choose to use any of these search engines again? Why or why not?

   a. Clusty.com
   b. Dogpile.com
   c. Rollyo.com

4. Free Speech Online

Leila was suspended from school for several days because her posts on MySpace about her teacher and a few of her classmates were "vulgar" and "derogatory." Daniel was expelled from his school because the picture he posted of himself was in violation of his school's code of conduct. Similarly, Bill, a local employer, changed his mind about a job offer to a recent graduate after seeing questionable content on the candidate's Facebook page.

   a. Should a person be penalized for his or her content on any Web site?
   b. Is the issue denial of free speech or prudent reactions to improper behavior?
   c. The Federal Bureau of Investigation (FBI) is working undercover in social networking sites to gather information. What are the benefits and drawbacks of this?

5. Using Web 2.0 in Education

Social networking sites, blogs, and wikis are commonly referred to as Web 2.0 technologies. Sites that use Web 2.0 offer opportunities for collaboration, creativity, and enterprise. Describe how Web 2.0 sites such as Wikipedia, YouTube, Delicious, and Digg might change how you learn and manage information.

three

making the transition to... the workplace

making the transition to... the workplace

1. Online Résumé Resources

Using a search engine, locate several Web resources that offer assistance in writing a résumé. For example, the University of Minnesota (**umn.edu/ohr/careerdev/resources/resume**) has a résumé tutor that guides you as you write your résumé.

a. What other Web sites can you find that help you write a résumé?
b. Do these sites all offer the same services and have the same features?

2. Online Job Search

After you've created a resume, you need to know how to get it to the right people and manage the job search process. A wealth of online job search resources is available to help you with these details. Research the following Web sites and write a brief description of each that outlines the benefits and role in a job search:

a. LinkedIn.com
b. JibberJobber.com
c. VisualCV.com
d. Monster.com

3. Evaluating Web 2.0 Content

You are aware of the guidelines you should use to evaluate the quality of content on a Web site, but you find yourself using other kinds of Web content such as blogs, wikis, social networking sites, and social bookmarks. Visit **http://library.albany.edu/usered/eval/evalweb** and review the new guidelines for evaluating Web content in the 2.0 environment. After reviewing the guidelines, describe the guidelines for evaluating Web content in the following:

a. Blogs and wikis
b. Google Scholar (**scholar.google.com**)
c. California Digital Library (**cdlib.org**)
d. Twitter (**twitter.com**)
e. Delicious (**delicious.com**)
f. Connotea (**connotea.org**)

4. Internet Connection Option

Now that you've graduated, you are planning to move into your first apartment and leave behind the comforts of broadband access at the residence halls. Evaluate the Internet options available in your area.

a. Create a table that includes information on broadband services in your area. The table should include the name of the provider, the cost of the service, information on bundled services (TV, Internet, phone), and the cost of bundled services.
b. Based on the table you create, write a brief paragraph describing which service you would choose, and why.

5. Internet Connection Speed

You would like to know how fast your Internet connection speed is. Your co-worker in the information technology (IT) department recommended that you check out broadband.gov.

a. Test your connection speed. How is the test conducted? What is used to measure the connection speed?
b. List reasons why you would be interested in measuring your Internet connection speed.

6. Facebook Privacy and Security

Your aunt contacted you last night. Your cousin, who is 14, wants a Facebook account. Your aunt has heard lots of stories of how difficult it is to protect your privacy on Facebook, and she wants your advice. Research the privacy and security settings on Facebook and create a "Users Guide" for your aunt to work through with your cousin. Make sure you include information on how to remove your cousin from Facebook search results, make contact information private, keep friendships private, adjust Wall posting visibility, set up photo album privacy, customize photo tagging, and explain what personal information should and should not be included on your cousin's profile.

Instructions: Albert Einstein used *Gedankenexperiments*, or critical thinking questions, to develop his theory of relativity. Some ideas are best understood by experimenting with them in our own minds. The following critical thinking questions are designed to demand your full attention but require only a comfortable chair—no technology.

1. Social Networking and Society

Social networking seems to have taken over our lives! Almost everyone is on Facebook and Twitter. But is this a good thing?

a. What advantages and disadvantages does social networking bring to your life?
b. What positive and negative effects has social networking had on society as a whole?
c. How are businesses using social networking?
d. How might you see social networking evolving in the next two or three years?

2. File Swapping Ethics

Downloading free music, movies, and other electronic media from the Internet, although illegal, still occurs on sites such as BitTorrent.

a. Do you think you should have the ability to download free music files of your choice? Do you think the musicians who oppose online music sharing have made valid points?
b. Discuss the differences you see between sharing music files online and sharing CDs with your friends.
c. The current price to buy a song online is about $1. Is this a fair price? If not, what price would you consider to be fair?

3. The Power of Google

Google is the largest and most popular search engine on the Internet today. Because of its size and popularity, some people claim that Google has enormous power to influence a Web user's search experience solely by its Web site ranking processes. What do you think about this potential power? How could it be used in negative or harmful ways?

a. Some Web sites pay search engines to list them near the top of the results pages. These sponsors therefore get priority placement. What do you think of this policy?
b. What effect (if any) do you think that Google has on Web site development? For example, do you think Web site developers intentionally include frequently searched words in their pages so that they will appear in more hits lists?
c. When you google someone, you type their name in the Google search box to see what comes up. What privacy concerns do you think such googling could present? Have you ever googled yourself or your friends?

4. Internet and Politics

What role has the Internet played in political campaigns? What role will it play in the future? Do you see the day when voting will happen through the Internet? Why or why not?

Comparing Internet Search Methods

Problem

With millions of sites on the Internet, finding useful information can be a daunting—and, at times, impossible—task. However, there are methods to make searching easier, some of which have been discussed in this chapter. In this Team Time, each team will search for specific items or pieces of information on the Internet and compare search methodologies.

Process

Split your group into three or more teams, depending on class size. Each group will create a team wiki using free wiki software such as that found at **pbworks.com**. To appreciate the benefits of wiki collaboration fully, each team should have at least five or six members.

1. Each team should come up with a theme for its wiki. Suggestions include the following:
   • Best computer technology Web sites
   • Coolest new technology gadgets
   • All-time greatest rock 'n' rollers
   • All-time greatest athletes
   • Best places to visit in the United States
   • Best beaches in the United States
   • Best skiing areas in the United States

2. Each student should pick one example to research and then must design a wiki page highlighting that subject. For example, if the team chose all-time greatest rock 'n' rollers, one student could select Bruce Springsteen and create a wiki page on Bruce Springsteen. The wiki page should contain links to other Web sites and, if possible, images and videos.

3. After the team wikis are created, teams should make their wikis available to the other teams for comments.

Conclusion

After all the team wikis have been completed and shared, discuss the following with your class. What is the benefit of using wiki technology to create team pages? How did wikis help or hinder the team process? What other conclusions can the class draw about using wiki technology?

In this exercise, you will research and then role-play a complicated ethical situation. The role you play may or may not match your own personal beliefs, but your research and use of logic will enable you to represent whichever view is assigned. An arbitrator will watch and comment on both sides of the arguments, and together the team will agree on an ethical solution.

Topic: Plagiarism

Plagiarism, or portraying another's work as your own, has been around for a long while and extends well beyond the classroom. For example, Nick Simmons, the son of Gene Simmons (KISS) and a member of A&E's *Family Jewels* reality series, created a comic book series "Incarnate." Radical Publishing picked up the series but quickly stopped publication when Internet messages accused the author of copying from other similar series. Similarly, the Australian band Men at Work was cited for copying a melody from "Kookaburra Sits in the Old Gum Tree" for its 1980s hit "Down Under" and owes the owner years of royalties.

Research Areas to Consider

- Plagiarism violations

- Comic book series "Incarnate"

- Australian band Men at Work

- Plagiarism consequences

Process

Divide the class into teams.

1. Research the areas cited above and devise a scenario in which someone has violated plagiarism rules.

2. Team members should write a summary that provides background information for their character—for example: author, publisher, or arbitrator—and details their character's behaviors to set the stage for the role-playing event. Then team members should create an outline to use during the role-playing event.

3. Team members should arrange a mutually convenient time to meet for the exchange, using the chat room feature of MyITLab, the discussion board feature of Blackboard, or meeting in person.

4. Team members should present their case to the class, or submit a PowerPoint presentation for review by the rest of the class, along with the summary and resolution they developed.

Conclusion

As technology becomes ever more prevalent and integrated into our lives, more and more ethical dilemmas will present themselves. Being able to understand and evaluate both sides of an argument, while responding in a personally or socially ethical manner, will be an important skill.

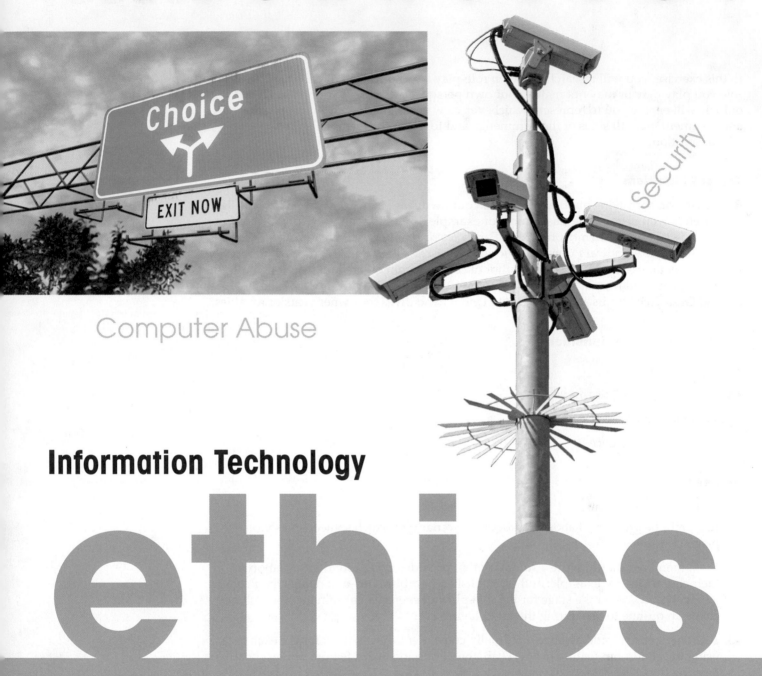

TECHNOLOGY

Choice

EXIT NOW

Security

Computer Abuse

Information Technology

ethics

In this Technology in Focus section, we explore what ethics is, how your personal ethics develop, and how your personal ethics fit into the world around you. We'll also examine how technology and ethics affect each other and how technology can be used to support ethical conduct. Finally, we'll examine several key issues in technology ethics today, including the areas of social justice, intellectual property rights, privacy, e-commerce, free speech, and computer abuse.

IN FOCUS

Intellectual Property

Censorship

People speak of ethics—and the lack of ethics—casually all the time, but the ethical choices that individuals make are an extremely serious matter and can have a far-reaching impact. It is important to have a clear idea of what ethics are, what your personal ethics are, and how personal ethics fit into the world at large.

ETHICS IN COMPUTING

You just bought a new notebook computer. You know you can go to BitTorrent or LimeWire to download the latest summer blockbuster movie and its soundtrack. You also probably know this is unethical. Although pirating music and videos is a valid example of unethical behavior, it has been overused as an illustration of the ethical challenges of technology. There is a vast range of ethical issues surrounding technology (as shown in Figure 1), several of which we will discuss in this section. Many other issues are discussed in the Ethics in IT sections of each chapter throughout the book.

WHAT IS ETHICS?

Ethics is the study of the general nature of morals and of the specific moral choices made by individuals. Morals involve conforming to established or accepted ideas of right and wrong (as generally dictated by society), and are usually viewed as black and white. Ethical issues often involve subtle distinctions, such as the difference between fairness and equity. Ethical values are the guidelines you use to make decisions each day. For example, the person in front of you at the coffee shop drops a dollar on the floor and doesn't notice it. Do you tell him or her about it, or do you pick up the dollar and use it to pay for your coffee?

Doesn't everyone have the same basic ethics?   There are many systems of ethical conduct. **Relativism** is a theory that holds that there is no universal moral truth and that instead there are only beliefs, perspectives, and values. Everyone has his or her own ideas of right and wrong, and so who are we to judge

anyone else? Another ethical philosophy is **situational ethics**, which states that decision making should be based on the circumstances of a particular situation and not on fixed laws.

Many other ethical systems have been proposed over time, some of which are defined by religious traditions. For example, the expression "Judeo-Christian ethics" refers to the common set of basic values shared across the Jewish and Christian religious traditions. These include behaviors such as respecting property and relationships, honoring one's parents, and being kind to others.

Are laws established to guide people's ethical actions?   Laws are formal, written standards designed to apply to everyone. Laws are enforced by government agencies (such as the police, the Federal Bureau of Investigation, the Food and Drug Administration, and so on) and interpreted by the courts. It is not possible to pass laws that cover every possible behavior that human beings can engage in. Therefore, **societal ethics** provides a general set of unwritten guidelines for people to follow.

Rule utilitarianism is an ethical theory that espouses establishing moral guidelines through specific rules. The idea behind this system is that if everyone adheres to the same moral code, society as a whole will improve and people will be happier. Many societies follow this system in general terms, including the United States. For instance, laws against nudity in public places (except for a few nude beaches) in the United States help define public nudity as immoral.

Don't some people behave unethically?   Although many valid systems of ethical conduct exist, sometimes people act in a manner that violates the beliefs they hold or the beliefs of the ethical system they say they follow. **Unethical behavior** can be defined as not conforming to a set of approved standards of social or professional behavior. For instance, using your phone to text message a test answer to your friend during an exam is prohibited by many colleges' rules of student conduct. This behavior is different from **amoral behavior**, in which a person has no sense of right and wrong and no interest in the moral consequences of his or her actions.

Is unethical behavior a euphemism for illegal activity?   Unethical behavior does not have to be illegal. An example of an unethical but not illegal practice is supermarket

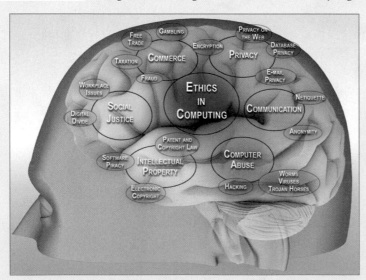

slotting fees. These are fees that some supermarkets charge to produce companies and product manufacturers for the privilege of having their products placed on store shelves. This is considered unethical by many people because it puts smaller companies, which often don't have the financial resources to pay these fees, at a disadvantage.

Not all illegal behavior is unethical. Civil disobedience, which is manifested by intentionally refusing to obey certain laws, is used as a form of protest to effect change in extreme situations. Gandhi's nonviolent resistance to the British rule of India, which led to India's establishment as an independent country, is an example of civil disobedience. Although the British were ruling India, is it ever ethical for one country to control another country's people?

Which system of ethics works best?
There is no universal agreement on which is the best system of ethics. Most societies use a blend of different systems. Regardless of the ethical system of the society in which you live, all ethical decisions are greatly influenced by personal ethics.

PERSONAL ETHICS

What are personal ethics?
Every day you say certain things and take specific actions, and at each point you are making decisions based on some criterion. It may be that you are trying to care for the people around you, or are trying to eliminate a source of pain or anger in your life. Your words and actions may also be driven by a combination of criteria. As you choose your words and actions, you are following a set of personal ethics—a checklist of personal decisions you have compiled to organize your life. Some people have a clear, well-defined set of principles they follow. Others' ethics are inconsistent or are applied differently in similar situations.

It can be challenging to adhere to your own ethical system if the consequences of your decisions today might lead to an unhappy result for you in the short term. For instance, to get the job of your dreams, should you exaggerate a bit on your résumé and say you've already finished your college degree, even though you are still one credit short? Is this lying? Is

such behavior justified in this setting? After all, you do intend to finish that last credit, and you would work really hard for this company if you were hired. If you tell the truth and state that you haven't finished college yet, then you might be passed over for the position. Making this choice is an ethical decision (see Figure 2).

How do a person's ethics develop?
Many elements contribute to your ethical development (see Figure 3). Naturally, your family has a major role in establishing the values you cherish in your own life, and these might include a cultural bias toward certain moral positions. Your religious affiliation is another major influence in your ethical life, because most religions have established specific codes of ethical conduct. How these sets of ethics interact with the values of the larger culture is often challenging. Issues such as abortion, the death penalty, and war force confrontations between personal ethical systems and the larger society's established legal-ethical system.

FIGURE 2

It would be nice if there were signposts to ethical conduct, but the issues are complex.

FIGURE 3

Many different forces shape your ethical worldview.

Family
Don't litter.

Religion
Don't tell lies.

Your ethical behavior

Experience
Don't speed or you'll get a ticket.

Teachers
Don't cheat on tests or you'll fail.

As you mature, your life experiences also affect your personal ethics. Does the behavior you see around you make sense within the ethical principles that your family, your church, or your first-grade teacher taught you? Has your experience led you to abandon some ethical rules and adopt others? Have you modified how and when you apply these laws of conduct, depending on what is at stake?

What if I'm not sure what my personal ethics are? When you have a clear and firm idea of what values are most important to you, it may be easier to handle situations in your professional and your personal life that demand ethical action. Follow these steps to help define your personal ethics:

1. **Describe yourself.** Write down words that describe who you are, based on how others view you. Would a friend describe you as honest, or helpful, or kind?

2. **List your beliefs.** Make a list of all the beliefs that influence your decision making. For example, would you be comfortable working as a research assistant in a lab that infected animals with diseases and used them for medical research? How important is it to you that you never tell a lie? Consider whether your answers to each of these questions are "flexible." Are there situations in which your answers might change (say, if a friend were ill or in danger)?

3. **Identify external influences.** Consider the places where you work and live and how you relate to the people you see during the day. Are there things that you would like to change about these

relationships that would merit listing them in a code of ethics?

4. **Consider "why."** After writing down your beliefs, think about why you believe them. Have you accepted them without investigation? Do they stand up in the context of your real-world experiences? For which of these values would you make short-term sacrifices in order to uphold your beliefs?

5. **Prepare a statement of values.** It can be useful to distill what you have written into a short list. By having a well-defined statement of the values you hold most important in your own life, which you can refer to in times of challenge, it will be easier for you to make ethical decisions.

Are there tangible benefits to ethical living? Society has established its own set of rules of conduct in the form of laws. Ignoring or being inconsistent in following these principles can surely have an immediate impact. Whether it is complying with a law that affects the way your business is run, or with a law that affects your personal life (don't exceed the speed limit or you'll receive a fine), decision-making principles that work with society's legal boundaries can make your life much simpler.

More and more research is showing the health benefits of ethical living. When your day-to-day decisions are in conflict with the values you consider most important as a human being, you often develop stress and anger. Constant conflict between what you value and what actions you are forced to take can lead to a variety of types of mental and physical damage.

Perhaps even happiness itself is a result of living ethically (see Figure 4). **Positive psychology** is a new focus in the field of psychology. Pioneered by Dr. Martin Seligman of the University of Pennsylvania, this field works to discover the causes of happiness instead of addressing the treatment of mental dysfunctions. Dr. Seligman's research has shown that, by identifying your personal strengths and values, and then aligning your life so that

FIGURE 4

The field of positive psychology shows that living and working ethically affects your happiness.

Cheating
Stealing
Selfish
Lying

Generosity
Honesty
Trust

you can apply them every day, you can experience an increase in happiness (and a decrease in depression) equivalent to the effects of antidepressant medication and therapy. Thus, finding a way to identify and then apply your ethics and values to your daily life can have an impact on your health and happiness.

PERSONAL ETHICS AND YOUR WORLDVIEW

How do my personal ethics fit into the world at large?
All of your actions, words, and even thoughts are controlled by your personal ideas of right and wrong. But do your ethics shift when you go to work? Your employer expects you to follow the ethics and rules of conduct that the owner has established for the business. Although each person at your workplace may be trying to follow corporate ethical guidelines, each person will follow them differently based on his or her personal ethics. Person A may feel it is acceptable to tell white lies to get more funding for his project, whereas Person B might believe that telling the truth at all times is the best and only way that she can foster the teamwork and cooperation necessary to complete a project.

This doesn't mean that individuals need to blindly follow practices they feel are unethical or detrimental to society at large. Most **whistle-blowers** are people that report businesses to regulatory agencies for committing illegal acts. Other whistle blowers expose unethical (but still legal) acts by their employers by publicizing unethical behavior through various media outlets.

In summary, when you are working in a business environment, your ethics are guided by the ethical principles that are defined by the business owner or management, but you are still ultimately guided by your personal ethics.

How do employers affect personal ethics?
Should your employer have control (or even input) about your conduct outside of the office? Do behavior, integrity, and honesty off the job relate to job performance? They might. But even if they don't, your actions could reflect poorly on your employer from your employer's perspective. Consider Ellen Simonetti, who was fired by Delta Airlines for blogging. Even though Ms. Simonetti never mentioned Delta Airlines by name on her blog ("Queen of the Sky: Diary of a Dysfunctional Flight Attendant"), Delta

Airlines objected to photos that she posted of herself and fellow flight attendants in their Delta uniforms. Delta Airlines felt that the photos were inappropriate and portrayed negative images of Delta Airlines employees. Another example is Jillian Tomlinson, the Australian surgeon who was suspended by her employer for discussing medical procedures, her work environment, and fellow employees, and for posting CAT scans of patients on her blog (although patient names were not revealed). Therefore, although your ethics might dictate one mode of behavior, you need to consider how your employer might view your actions (see Figure 5).

How does making ethical choices in a business setting differ from making personal ethical choices?
Most personal ethical decisions involve few people, unless the decision results in a significant impact on society. When making ethical choices in the business world, give careful consideration to the stakeholders of the business. **Stakeholders** are those people or entities who are affected by the operations of a business. Before making an ethical choice for a business, you need to consider the effect that choice will have on all of the stakeholders. Typical stakeholders for most businesses are customers, suppliers, employees, investors (shareholders), financial lenders, and society.

For instance, suppose you decide to cut costs in your restaurant by hiring undocumented workers. While this might boost profits in the short term, the long-term impact on stakeholders can be severe. Potential employees who are eligible to work in the United

FIGURE 5

Is your boss watching you? Does that make you more or less inclined to behave ethically?

"The new hidden cameras will allow us to see if anyone is violating our privacy policy by reading someone else's email."

States will be denied jobs. If you are caught using undocumented workers, fines will be levied against the business, which will cause investors to lose money and may affect the company's ability to repay lenders. The negative publicity from being caught may cause a downturn in business, which, in turn, might force layoffs of employees or even closure of the business. Your simple decision on cutting costs isn't as simple as it may seem!

TECHNOLOGY AND ETHICS: HOW ONE AFFECTS THE OTHER

In both good and bad ways, technology affects our community life, family life, work environment, education, and medical research, to name only a few areas of our lives. Because technology moves faster than rules can be formulated to govern it, how technology is used is often left up to the individual and the guidance of his or her personal ethics.

Technology constantly challenges our ethics as individuals and as a society. In the rest of this Technology in Focus feature, we will explore some issues involving the relationship between technology and ethics. Specifically, we will examine situations in which ethics and technology touch each other: social justice (whistle-blowing), intellectual property (international piracy), privacy (personal privacy and technology), e-commerce (geolocation), electronic communication issues (free speech), and computer abuse (cyberbullying).

Ethical considerations are never black and white. They are complex, and reasonable people can have different yet equally valid views. We present alternative viewpoints in each setting for you to consider and discuss. Figure 6 summarizes these issues.

USING COMPUTERS TO SUPPORT ETHICAL CONDUCT

Although there are many opportunities to use computers and the Internet unethically, many more ways are available to use technology to support ethical conduct.

Many charitable organizations use the Internet for fund-raising. When a major earthquake struck Haiti in 2010, organizations such as the Salvation Army (see Figure 7) and other charities supporting relief efforts used their Web pages to help donors quickly, easily, and securely make contributions to aid earthquake victims. Using technology to garner contributions enables charities to raise billions of dollars quickly for relief efforts.

When you spot unethical behavior at your company, you need a fast, secure way to report it to the appropriate members of management. The Sarbanes–Oxley Act requires companies to provide mechanisms for employees and third parties to report complaints, including ethics violations. These mechanisms are required to provide the employees with anonymity. In addition, many businesses are using their Web sites to allow whistle-blowers to report

FIGURE 6

Ethics in Computing

TOPIC	ETHICAL DISCUSSION	DEBATE ISSUE
Social justice	Are there limits to whistle-blowing?	Does technology provide too easy an access for whistle-blowing?
Intellectual property	Do entire countries support software piracy?	Can we impose our values and intellectual property laws on the world?
Privacy	Is personal privacy a casualty of the modern age?	Should personal privacy be protected?
E-commerce	Do geolocation devices and applications threaten privacy?	Do the benefits of geolocation devices and applications outweigh the risks?
Electronic communication	When does big business limit free speech?	Should companies allow the Chinese government to dictate when to curtail free speech?
Computer abuse	Whose responsibility is it to monitor cyberbullying?	Should parents bear all the responsibility of monitoring cyberbullying, or should it be in the hands of public officials?

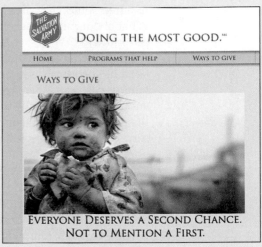

FIGURE 7

Most major charities facilitate donations through the Internet.

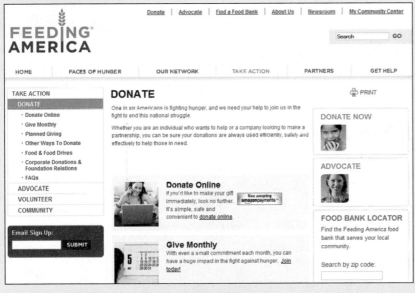

company intranet ensures that employees have access to information whenever they need it. By using e-mail, a company can communicate new policies, or changes to existing policies, to employees quickly and efficiently.

Throughout your life, you will encounter many ethical challenges relating to information technology. Your personal ethics—combined with the ethical guidelines your company provides and the general ethical environment of society—will guide your decisions.

For further information on ethics, check out the following Web sites:

- **ethics.csc.ncsu.edu**
- **ethicscenter.net**
- **business-ethics.com**
- **business-ethics.org**

wrongdoing anonymously, replacing previous e-mail and telephone hotline systems, which did not shield employees from being identified. With an electronic system, it is easier for a company to sort and classify complaints and designate them for appropriate action.

Electronic systems such as intranets and e-mail are also excellent mechanisms for informing employees about ethics policies. Storing ethics guidelines electronically on a

Social Justice

Whistle-Blowing with Web 2.0

SUMMARY OF THE ISSUE

In a free democracy, are there still things the public does not have a right to see? What about military secrets? What about ongoing negotiations with foreign governments? What access should corporate whistle-blowers have to distributing the documents and materials they have that allege abuses? Historically, there have been tight controls over access to the media, and exceptions have been rare. One famous case is the Pentagon Papers, a 7,000-page U.S. government report on policy and planning for the Vietnam War. State department official Daniel Ellsberg leaked the document in 1971, and it was published by *The New York Times*. A complicated series of lawsuits was then filed against *The New York Times* for making the document public.

With the tools of Web 2.0, the entire model for the distribution of information has shifted, and now everyone has the ability to create content for the Web. WikiLeaks (**wikileaks.org**) is using that ability to make private and public documents available for viewing. Wikileaks describes itself as "a public service designed to protect whistle-blowers, journalists, and activists who have sensitive materials to communicate to the public." *Time* magazine said of WikiLeaks, "[I]t could become as important a journalistic tool as the Freedom of Information Act."

Does society have a responsibility to use technology to help achieve social justice? Where are the boundaries of that responsibility? One controversial WikiLeaks case was the leak of a video showing a U.S. Army helicopter strike from 2007 in Baghdad that claimed the lives of several civilians including two children (see Figure 8). An Army intelligence analyst delivered the classified combat video to WikiLeaks in 2010. Another video leaked showed a May 2009 air strike near the Afghanistan village of Garani that killed nearly 100 civilians, mostly children. The Pentagon had released a report on that event but refused to show video of the attack to reporters.

QUESTIONS TO THINK ABOUT AND RESEARCH

1. Is the staff of WikiLeaks responsible for the accuracy and quality of the information it releases?

2. If information leaked through WikiLeaks leads to the death of an undercover officer, who is responsible for the consequences of the publication of information?

3. Does providing the public with official Pentagon updates of military missions mean that video of these events also must be released?

4. How does the meaning of "free speech" change as technology makes distribution of information universal and immediate? Do protections need to be modified?

POINT

Technology Provides Access to Information

The advocates of WikiLeaks argue that it allows an unprecedented means for those without power to hold those with power accountable for their actions.

1. If information can only be leaked if you happen to find an interested journalist, is society really protected?

2. Technology is not responsible for the actions or the consequences of the actions of people.

3. Technology has provided new tools that expose cover-ups, corruption, and abuses of power.

COUNTERPOINT

Technology Should Only Allow Controlled Access to Information

Critics maintain that the anonymity that WikiLeaks provides makes if difficult to check the accuracy of anything reported on the Web site.

1. The small staff of WikiLeaks cannot verify the accuracy of each document to the level of professional journalists.

2. If technology is used irresponsibly, it can cause panics because the information is available to so many people so quickly.

3. If each person in an organization can easily leak confidential information, the integrity of national security or of corporate security is at risk.

FIGURE 8

What boundaries should there be on the availability of sensitive information?

International Pirates

SUMMARY OF THE ISSUE

Intellectual property (such as music, writing, and software) is protected by copyright law. But there have been challenges in enforcing these standards in other countries. What happens to "fair trade" if some countries refuse to enforce copyright laws? How should the trade partners of these countries respond?

The Business Software Alliance (BSA) estimated that in 2009, 79 percent of China's computers ran on pirated software (see Figure 9). For comparison, the BSA estimated piracy in Denmark and Sweden at levels of 25 percent. This discrepancy means that businesses in China do not have to budget for software for operating systems or for productivity software, and that gives Chinese businesses an immediate advantage in the international marketplace. Although some companies, like Microsoft, continue to do business in China despite the piracy, smaller companies cannot survive. Tom Adams, the chief executive of Rosetta Stone, pulled his company and its language training software products out of China. "What the Chinese government requires you to do is allow them to host it on their servers," said Adams. "We cannot make it in China because they will steal the software." He described China as a "kleptocratic society."

The chief executives of twelve major software companies—Microsoft, Adobe, Autodesk, Symantec, and others—have pressured the U.S. administration and lawmakers to put more pressure on China to crack down on illegal copying. With a potential market of more than 1 billion people, and an increasing number of technologically hungry purchasers, companies dread the idea of missing out on the Chinese market, but if China continues to have such disinterest in following international copyright laws, there may be a migration of foreign business to other Asian countries. "Intellectual property protection in China is not just lower than other places, it's very low, very, very low," said Steve Ballmer, CEO of Microsoft. "We see better opportunities in countries like India and Indonesia than China because the intellectual property protection is quite a bit better."

It is not just China that has weakly enforced copyright laws. U.S. lawmakers recently singled out five countries that are not doing enough to prevent piracy of music, movies, and software: Canada, China, Mexico, Russia, and Spain. "We are losing billions and billions of dollars because of the lack of intellectual property protections," said Senator Orrin Hatch of Utah. "These five countries have been robbing Americans." The BSA estimated the loss at more than $51 billion per year, although there is debate around the exact value.

Most people have had the opportunity to participate in the piracy of copyrighted materials through illegal peer-to-peer sharing and the use of torrents. Now that behavior is multiplied to the level of nations, and the consequences are still being explored.

QUESTIONS TO THINK ABOUT AND RESEARCH

1. Should a government be penalized for failing to actively enforce the laws they have within their own country? If so, what should the penalties be, and how should they be enforced?
2. Does each government have the right to make its own decision on a stand against piracy?
3. How can other countries respond to international piracy?
4. Does individual piracy have any connection to the enforcement of copyright laws on an international level?

POINT

International Copyright Protections Need to Be Vigorously Enforced

Artists and software developers depend on the integrity of the protection of intellectual property, both within the United States and internationally, to make a fair profit on their work.

1. If other countries do not fight piracy, artists and developers have an unfair advantage in the marketplace.

2. By allowing massive piracy, these other countries are stealing from the United States.

3. Every country needs to have a common understanding and enforcement of intellectual property laws for trade to be fair and beneficial to everyone.

COUNTERPOINT

Global Business Demands Understanding Other Cultures

Most countries have laws on their books regarding intellectual property. It is not the job of the United States to tell a foreign government how to conduct internal affairs.

1. The existing laws on intellectual property have worked to serve the interests of these countries. If U.S. companies do not want to sell to the billion-person market of China, that is their choice.

2. Piracy exists within the United States, so it is hypocritical to be chastising foreign governments for software piracy.

3. Companies can pursue restitution for piracy through the foreign court systems.

FIGURE 9

The issues of intellectual property play an important role in international trade.

Privacy

Does Social Media Erode Personal Privacy?

SUMMARY OF THE ISSUE

Like respect and dignity, privacy is a basic human right. What, exactly, is privacy? Simply stated, privacy is the right to be left alone to do as one pleases. The idea of privacy is often associated with hiding something (a behavior, a relationship, or a secret). However, privacy really means not being required to explain your behavior to others. But social media sites such as Facebook are inherently about sharing information with others. Does this mean there is no such thing as personal privacy (see Figure 10) on social media sites?

Facebook and other social media sites earn revenue by sharing information about their users with advertisers. This helps businesses target advertisements to individuals who might be more interested in their products and services. But social media sites have recently been criticized for making their privacy policies and controls too obscure. Champions of personal privacy argue that sites that make information sharing the default option or "opt-out" (that is, users have to make a specific request or change a specific setting to stop their information from being shared) exposes users to misuse of their personal details. Also, social media sites often track and store user actions and preferences (such as "liking" something on Facebook). Personal privacy advocates are suspicious of how this information is used or to whom it is sold.

Web site owners argue that the entire premise of social media is built on sharing information, which makes it easy for others to find an individual. Social media administrators feel that information sharing improves the users' experience by tailoring advertisements and offers to their specific interests. And because most social media sites do not charge users for the service, the owners of the sites need ways to generate revenue and their most valuable asset is the information that users provide about themselves.

The large social media sites (such as Facebook) have been responding to concerns by modifying their privacy settings and making it easier for users to select which information is shared and with whom. But critics still argue that users do not have enough control over opting out of sharing information. The control and privacy of information will continue to be a fine balancing act for the foreseeable future with companies trying to make money while appeasing the concerns of privacy advocates. Leaving a trail of electronic breadcrumbs is to a certain extent inevitable. But cleaning up or hiding your "trail" is still important to many users, not because they are trying to hide something but because they just value their basic rights of privacy.

QUESTIONS TO THINK ABOUT AND RESEARCH

1. Should you be able to decide exactly what information on a social networking site you share with others? Would you be willing to pay for this privilege?
2. Do you know what your privacy settings are on the social media sites you use? Is there any information being shared publicly that you weren't aware was being shared?
3. Should social media sites be allowed to sell information collected on your surfing habits without your permission? Is this practice legal in the United States?
4. Is there any information on sites you use that you want to restrict people from seeing? Do these sites allow you to restrict the information you with to protect?

POINT

Social Media Sites Should Protect Personal Privacy

The advocates of protecting privacy in the United States argue that the right to privacy is a basic human right that should be afforded to everyone. Personal privacy concerns should outweigh the business needs of a corporation.

1. Social media sites have an inherent duty to protect the data of their users.

2. If site owners are collecting information by recording users' surfing habits, they might misuse or lose control of the data.

3. Default privacy settings should all be opt-out, allowing users the ultimate control over who views their data.

COUNTERPOINT

Social Media Sites Are Entitled to Freely Share Information

Advocates for unrestricted sharing of information feel that business concerns outweigh privacy concerns. Social media sites offered free of charge must make money to survive and therefore need to be able to provide information to third parties to generate revenue.

1. The "cost" of using the site is the agreement to share some of your personal information.

2. Users can make their own privacy decisions and choose (opt-out) not to post or share sensitive information.

3. In the digital age, loss of a certain amount of privacy is inevitable.

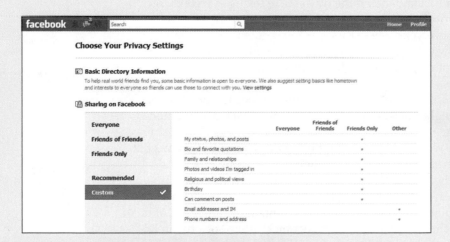

FIGURE 10

What information are you sharing on Facebook?

E-Commerce

Geolocation: Marketing Tool or Invasion of Privacy?

SUMMARY OF THE ISSUE

"Where are you?" is the burning social-networking question these days, and your smartphone probably has the answer. The technology is called *geolocation*, and most smartphones have a GPS (global positioning system) chip that uses satellite data or cell towers to calculate your exact position. Services such as Foursquare, Gowalla, Brightkite, and Loopt are all hoping that you will use them in the process, so you can use geolocation to find your friends or let your friends find you. Through the apps, you can receive recommendations of places to visit or things to do nearby. Some apps, such as Loopt (see Figure 11) and Gowalla, have created partnerships with local establishments that generate freebies, special offers, and travel trips. Businesses are using geolocation apps to promote their products and offer rewards for "check-ins" to help drive customers to their location.

But the question remains, when you leave your home and announce your constant whereabouts through tweets and check-ins, do you lose some of your privacy in exchange for "fun" and "convenience"? Although you can set certain levels of privacy in the apps, there is still the potential for someone with bad intentions (stalkers, robbers) to follow your updates. For example, the Web site PleaseRobMe.com was set up to illustrate how telling the world where you are at all times may not be such a great idea. After generating much discussion and awareness, the Web site is no longer active, but the message is clear:

> "The danger is publicly telling people where you are. This is because it leaves one place you're definitely not . . . home. So . . . on one end we're leaving lights on when we're going on a holiday, and on the other we're telling everybody on the Internet we're not home. It gets even worse if you have 'friends' who . . . enter your address, to tell everyone where they are. Your address . . . on the Internet . . . Now you know what to do when people reach for their phone as soon as they enter your home. That's right, slap them across the face."

In addition to opening yourself up to potential robbery, geolocation devices also can track the activities you might not want publicized, and that once documented can later be used against you.

It wasn't long ago that we were concerned about using our real names online, but now we are comfortable with sharing our exact location in a very public way. As Facebook CEO Mark Zuckerberg said, "People have really gotten comfortable not only sharing more information and different kinds, but more openly and with more people." But does such acceptance justify neglecting to maintain certain levels of privacy? Again, it seems that technology has moved more quickly than society can address the potential risks and dangers.

QUESTIONS TO THINK ABOUT AND RESEARCH

1. Do the benefits of geolocation outweigh the risks?
2. What other devices besides cell phones track and record our movements/locations as digital records?
3. How have social networks increased the risks of geolocation privacy?
4. What risks does geolocation pose for college students? How can users mitigate those risks?

POINT

Geolocation Devices Do Not Threaten Privacy

The advocates of using geolocation devices with minimal concern for threatened privacy are those who believe the social norm has shifted, and people have become comfortable with sharing more information.

1. Businesses are adopting geolocation apps as a part of their social media strategy in order to drive customers to their business. They would lose revenue if such activities ceased.

2. As the devices and apps become better and more precise, they may become useful as public safety and news-gathering devices.

3. Society may need to reevaluate its views about how much privacy is needed to maintain in people's digital lives, as well as assume greater responsibility for making sensible decisions about sharing information through the Internet.

COUNTERPOINT

Geolocation Devices Are a Threat to Privacy

The advocates for tighter privacy controls and awareness campaigns about the potential risks of using geolocation devices suggest that the threats are too big to ignore. Society has become too complacent with privacy issues.

1. Privacy settings on apps and GPS devices should be more restrictive to avoid broadcasting one's location and risking personal assault.

2. Laws and regulations will need to be created as to the use and distribution of digital location information.

3. Consumers need to be educated about geolocation and the ways it can impact them so that they are able to make informed choices.

FIGURE 11

Geolocation applications help you find cool places and businesses. But who do you want to find you with geolocation?

Electronic Communication

Does Free Speech Have a Price?

SUMMARY OF THE ISSUE

In early 2006 when Google launched its search engine services in China, it conceded to Beijing's demands that it self-censor its search engine, restricting search results for sensitive information such as the details of the Tiananmen Square protests and of human rights groups. This decision prompted much discussion, with some condemning Google's decision for putting business profits over basic human rights. Google justified its actions by stating that a company must operate within the rules of the market in which it operates and that the benefits of increased access to information for people in China "outweighed our discomfort in agreeing to censor some results." And, compared to search results from Baidu, the leading Chinese search engine, Google was not censoring all information. However, in 2010, Google announced that it was no longer willing to censor search results and moved the site to Hong Kong where it hopes there will be less censorship. The departure was a reaction to a sophisticated targeted cyberattack that Google believes was done to gather information on Chinese human rights activists. Google had about a 35 percent market share.

Microsoft, also in the Chinese market with its new search engine, Bing, announced in response to Google's departure, that it had no plans to leave. Microsoft has only a 1 percent share of the market, so the decision to stay has huge upside potential. The question remains as to how Microsoft will manage search information. When Microsoft started in China, searches on controversial topics weren't just blocked in China, they were blocked from everyone around the world (see Figure 12). Microsoft corrected that, but some current searches show that although they are not censoring as much as Baidu, they are still censoring less than Google was. Microsoft says it is trying to do the right thing. Before honoring any censor requests, Microsoft insists that Chinese authorities make legally binding requests in writing. Microsoft, along with Google and Yahoo!, joined Global Network Initiative (**globalnetworkinitiative.org**), a group that has established a code of conduct for free expression and privacy. The goal of GNI is to help companies do the right thing under difficult circumstances. However, it's too early to tell whether Microsoft will indeed take the high road or succumb to China's censorship requirements.

QUESTIONS TO THINK ABOUT AND RESEARCH

1. Will Google's move from Mainland China to Hong Kong have a major impact on China's censorship laws?

2. Will Microsoft's compliance with censorship laws further Beijing's cooperation on combating software piracy in China? Are Microsoft's financial incentives even deeper than just Internet market share?

3. Can the U.S. government compel technology companies to take a firmer stance on free speech in China and elsewhere by instituting criminal charges if U.S. companies do not take reasonable steps to protect human rights?

POINT

U.S. Companies Should Comply with Local Laws

Those who protest Microsoft's actions are individuals and groups that fight for human rights in many contexts. They feel that Microsoft's compliant behavior only condones China's censorship policies and continues to thwart the effort to promote human rights initiatives in China.

1. Microsoft is sacrificing free speech for business. This action violates human rights, international law, and corporate ethics.

2. Cooperating with China violates human rights.

3. If international businesses can't stand up to China, how will China ever have an incentive to change?

4. Most other rights hang on the community's ability to have open discussions. Preventing that from happening is a serious assault on human rights.

5. If the policy were to make children work or to kill women, would the companies choose not to comply? Are human rights and freedom of speech any different?

COUNTERPOINT

U.S Companies Should Put What Is Right Ahead of What Is Financially Expedient

Those who are in favor of Google's actions are believers that international corporations should begin to take a firm stance against governments that do not promote basic human rights.

1. China will never change unless there are financial interests to do so.

2. Google's withdrawal from China threatens the viability of many advertising resellers in China. Will this added pressure help or hinder human rights efforts?

3. Microsoft's presence, as muted as it is, continues to advance the slow progress the Chinese government is making toward democracy. U.S. companies can ethically stay in China if they make an effort to improve human rights there. U.S. companies operating in China should agree on guidelines that respect human rights.

FIGURE 12

Is free speech possible in countries (such as China) where information availability is restricted by law?

Computer Abuse

Cyberbullying—Who Should Protect Children from Each Other?

SUMMARY OF THE ISSUE

Cyberbullying is just like normal bullying, but it involves the use of digital technologies such as the Internet, cell phones, or video (see Figure 13). Instead of a bully chasing someone on the playground at recess, cyberbullying involves minors (children) harassing, threatening, humiliating, embarrassing, or tormenting other minors by means of technology. Cyberbullying is a child-on-child process that might result in criminal charges depending upon the type of incident.

There are many types of cyberbullying. The main types are as follows:

- Bombarding a victim with harassing instant messages or text messages
- Stealing a password and then using the victim's account to embarrass the victim by sending harassing, threatening, or lewd messages while pretending to be the victim
- Spreading rumors or lies on social networking sites
- Posting embarrassing photos or videos on the Web (such as candid nude shots taken in a locker room)
- Infecting the victim's computer with malware, usually to spy on the victim

The effects of cyberbullying can be devastating. For children, their standing in peer groups is a critical component of their self worth. Adults have freedom in their lives to change bad situations, such as changing jobs, when they feel their esteem is under attack. Children often feel powerless because they have such limited options. Children don't usually have the option of changing schools without uprooting the entire family. Aside from developing severe feelings of depression, rage, frustration, and powerlessness, children have committed suicide over cyberbullying incidents. Suicide can often be the unfortunate result, as in the case of student and soccer player Alexis Pilkington who at 17 committed suicide in 2010 after being repeatedly taunted on social networking sites.

Unfortunately, cyberbullying is often difficult for adults to detect because the bullying often takes place online and anonymously. Signs that a child is victim of cyberbullying are often the same signs related to various types of depression. A child may suddenly lose interest in normal activities, be reluctant to go to school, lose his or her appetite, have trouble sleeping, appear upset after using the Internet, or experience unusual mood swings (such as bursting into tears for no apparent reason). Signs that a child might be perpetrating cyberbullying include excessive Internet use, sending large volumes of text messages, clearing the computer screen when others enter a room, or conducting clandestine Internet activities (refusal to say what they are doing). Vigilance over children's online activities is obviously key to spotting both victims and perpetrators of cyberbullying.

But who is responsible for monitoring children? Parents obviously need to protect their children, but bullying usually doesn't happen until children are repeatedly exposed to other groups of children such as in daycare or school. So then, should teachers and caregivers shoulder the major responsibility for detecting, reporting, and mitigating cyberbullying? Children often spend more time in school during the day than they spend under the supervision of their parents. But cyberbullying activities don't just take place in school. Most children have access to the Internet at home and can carry on campaigns of terror from the privacy of their own bedroom (see Figure 14).

Children themselves could also be made part of the solution. Research shows that one of the best ways to prevent bullying is to make children aware of what behaviors constitute bullying and the consequences of their actions.

Although there is currently no federal law prohibiting cyberbullying, sixteen states have laws that address this issue. Anti-cyberbullying laws tend to place the burden of detection on the schools. A Massachusetts law passed in 2010 requires school employees to report bullying when they become aware of it to the school administration. The law also requires training for school employees in the detection and prevention of bullying. Most legislatures are reluctant to pass laws that instruct parents on how to raise their children because this tends to raise issues about personal freedom. Therefore, the focus so far has been primarily on teachers and caregivers detecting cyberbullying. But a coordinated effort between parents and teachers may be a better approach.

QUESTIONS TO THINK ABOUT AND RESEARCH

1. What should parents do to protect their children from cyberbullying? How can parents protect their children when the children are not under their direct supervision?

2. What level of responsibility should school employees have for protecting children from cyberbullying?

3. Should there be federal laws that make cyberbullying a crime? If so, how would these laws be enforced?

4. What types of education for children would be beneficial in preventing cyberbullying? When should these programs begin, and how often should children be required to participate?

FIGURE 13

Cyberbullying involves the use of digital technologies both to bully and disseminate acts of bullying.

Computer Abuse

POINT

Parents Must Protect Their Children from Cyberbullying

Proponents of parental responsibility for detecting and preventing cyberbullying feel that it is a personal behavior issue. Individuals are responsible for their own behavior as long as it doesn't harm others. Parents should be allowed to educate their children according to their own standards of behavior and preferences in terms of moral behavior (such as religion).

1. Parents are ultimately responsible for protecting their children.

2. Bullying is a personal behavior issue, and all decisions regarding personal freedom and behavior should be made by parents.

3. Because educating children about bullying is key to preventing it, decisions about the content of such training needs to be controlled by parents.

COUNTERPOINT

Schools Must Bear the Major Responsibility for Protecting Students from Cyberbullying

Cyberbullying affects society because it can severely damage an individual's self esteem. Cyberbullying is similar to other hate crimes and should enlist public officials (such as educators) in enforcement of the laws.

1. Parents do not supervise their children 24/7 and therefore require help from other responsible adults to protect their children.

2. Parents need to be assured that publicly funded institutions such as schools and libraries are "safe havens" where their children will not be exposed to malicious activities.

3. Educators have better skills than most parents for teaching children about the serious effects of cyberbullying.

FIGURE 14

Cyberbullying should be stopped, but by whom?

Multiple Choice

Instructions: Answer the multiple-choice questions below for more practice with key terms and concepts from this Technology in Focus feature.

1. Which theory states that there is no universal moral truth?
   a. Relativism
   b. Ethical behavior
   c. Amoral behavior
   d. Personal ethics

2. The ethical theory that describe that society as a whole will improve if everyone adheres to the same morale code is known as
   a. rule utilitarianism.
   b. societal ethics.
   c. moral prescription.
   d. personal ethics.

3. Which ethical philosophy states that decision making should be based on the circumstances surrounding a given situation, not fixed laws?
   a. Societal ethics
   b. Judeo-Christian ethics
   c. Relativism
   d. Situational ethics

4. Which of the following statement is *false*?
   a. Individuals who apply ethics inconsistently exhibit amoral behavior.
   b. All ethical decisions are greatly influenced by personal ethics.
   c. Unethical behavior is not always illegal.
   d. Life experience affects an individual's personal ethics.

5. Not conforming to a set of approved ethical standards is known as
   a. societal behavior.
   b. unethical behavior.
   c. amoral behavior.
   d. unprofessional behavior.

6. The field of psychology that theorizes that happiness results from ethical living is known as
   a. principled psychology.
   b. positive psychology.
   c. moral psychology.
   d. affirmative psychology.

7. Which system of ethics is most widely agreed upon to be the best system?
   a. Rule utilitarianism
   b. Relativism
   c. Situational ethics
   d. There is no universally agreed-upon best system.

8. Which is *not* a tangible benefit of ethical living?
   a. Improved health
   b. A simpler lifestyle
   c. Happiness
   d. Increased motivation

9. Using your neighbor's unsecured wireless connection is an ethical issue of
   a. intellectual property.
   b. privacy.
   c. electronic communication.
   d. None of the above.

10. Business ethics differs from personal ethics because
    a. ethical choices typically affect many stakeholders rather than a small group.
    b. human resources personnel require employees to sign a code of ethics.
    c. employees are bound by the ethics of the business.
    d. short-term gains can have long-term impacts.

four

application software:

programs that let you work and play

multimedia resources

Active Helpdesk

Sound Bytes

Companion Website

The Companion Website includes a variety of additional materials to help you review and learn more about the topics in this chapter. Go to: *pearsonhighered.com/techinaction*

how cool

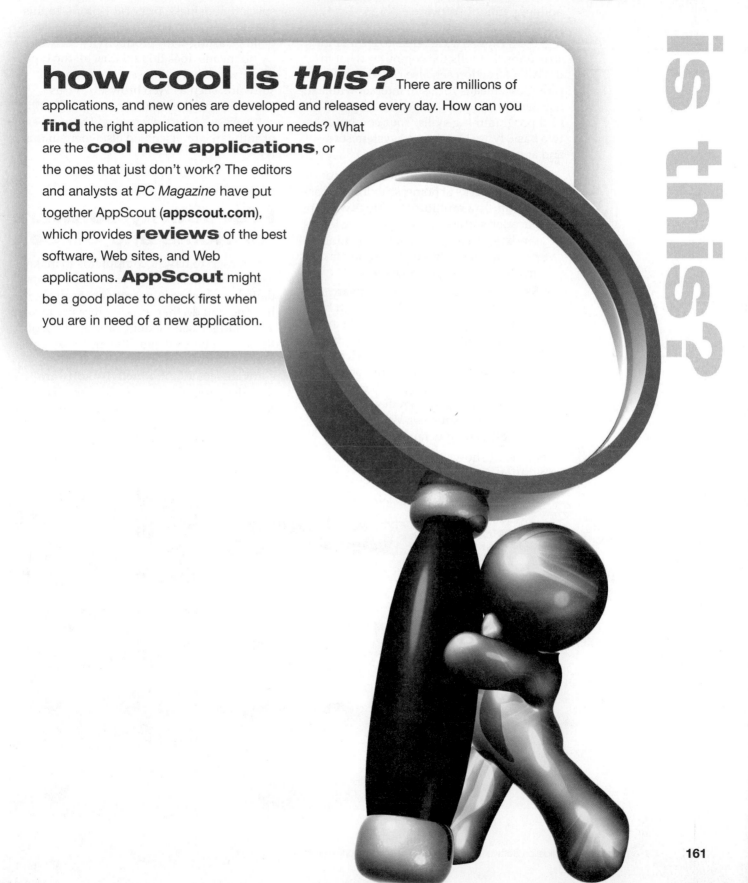

how cool is *this*? There are millions of applications, and new ones are developed and released every day. How can you **find** the right application to meet your needs? What are the **cool new applications**, or the ones that just don't work? The editors and analysts at *PC Magazine* have put together AppScout (**appscout.com**), which provides **reviews** of the best software, Web sites, and Web applications. **AppScout** might be a good place to check first when you are in need of a new application.

is this?

The Nuts and Bolts of Software

A computer without software is like a sandwich without filling. Although a computer's hardware is critical, a computer system does nothing without software.

What is software? Technically speaking, the term **software** refers to a set of instructions that tells the computer what to do. An instruction set, also called a **program**, provides a means for us to interact with and use the computer, even if we lack specialized programming skills. Your computer has two basic types of software: system software and application software.

- **Application software** is the software you use to do tasks at home, school, and work. You can do a multitude of things with application software, such as writing letters, sending e-mail, paying taxes, creating presentations, editing photos, and taking an online course, to name a few.
- **System software** includes software such as Windows and Mac OS X, which help run the computer and coordinate instructions between application software and the computer's hardware devices. System software includes the operating system and utility programs (programs in the operating system that help manage system resources). We discuss system software in detail in Chapter 5.

Figure 4.1 shows the various types of application software that you can use to be productive—at home and at work. In addition, applications are available to produce and edit media as well as for entertainment. Lastly, there are applications that are more applicable to business uses, whether it's for a home office, big business, specialty business, or not-for-profit. In this chapter, we look at each of these types in detail, starting with productivity software. By no means does this exhaust all the types of software that is in use. Other types of software, such as Web browsers, virus protection, backup and recovery, and utility software are in use every day. These types of software are discussed elsewhere in this book.

Productivity Software for Home and Office

One reason to have a computer is to make it easier to tackle the tasks you have in your daily life. Productivity software is all about helping you do that, making it easier to keep your budget, send letters, or keep track of the kids' school events. It's safe to say you regularly use some form of productivity software already. **Productivity software** includes programs that enable you to perform various tasks required at home, school, and business. This category includes word processing, spreadsheet, presentation, database, and personal information manager (PIM) programs.

Figure 4.1

Application software enables computer users to do a variety of tasks.

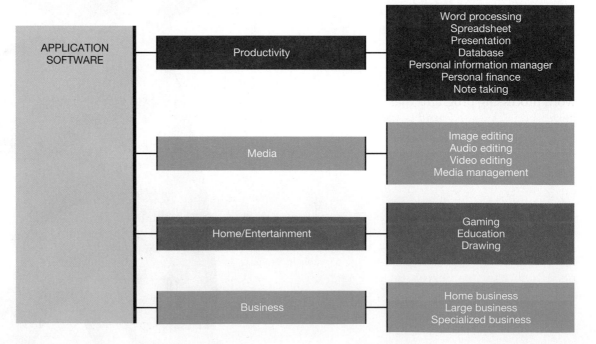

Word Processing Software

What is the best software to use to create general documents? Most students use **word processing software** to create and edit documents such as research papers, letters, and résumés. Because of its general usefulness, word processing software is the most widely used application. Word processing software has a key advantage over its ancestral counterpart, the typewriter: you can make revisions and corrections without having to retype an entire document. Instead, you can quickly and easily insert, delete, and move pieces of text, as well as move and insert text from one document into another seamlessly. Microsoft Word and Corel WordPerfect are examples of popular word processing programs.

Are there free or more affordable alternatives? If you're looking for a more affordable alternative to software such as Microsoft Word or other Microsoft Office products, you may want to consider downloading free open source software. **Open source software** is program code that is publicly available and has few restrictions. Unlike **proprietary software**, which is neither free nor open source, the code can be copied, distributed, or changed without the stringent copyright protections of software products you purchase.

Writer, a word processing program from the OpenOffice.org suite (**openoffice.org**), and AbiWord (**abiword.com**) are gaining in popularity because they are available as free downloads from the Internet. Both AbiWord and Writer have many of the same features as their higher-priced Word and WordPerfect competitors, making either a great choice for cost-conscious consumers.

Also gaining in popularity are several word processing programs that are Web-based, such as those found in Google Docs (**docs.google.com**) and Microsoft Office Web Apps. **Web-based applications**, which was discussed in greater detail in Chapter 3, can be accessed from any computer that has an Internet connection. Web-based applications are great for collaborating and coordinating input from a variety of users on a single document. Keep one thing in mind when you choose a free or Web-based software product: support. Unlike Microsoft Office and other applications, these applications offer little or no formal support. Instead, open source and Web-based applications are

supported from their community of users across Web sites and newsgroups. For more information on alternative software, see the Technology in Focus feature "Computing Alternatives" on page 252.

How do I control the way my documents look? An advantage of word processing software is that you can easily format, or change the appearance of, your document. As a result, you can produce professional-looking documents without having to hire a professional. With the extensive formatting options available, you can change fonts, font styles, and sizes; add colors to text; adjust margins; add borders to portions of text or entire pages; insert bulleted and numbered lists; and organize your text into

BITS AND BYTES — Working with Different File Formats

There are lots of great word processing software applications available now. Although each program has basic functional similarities, each program has a different file format that defines the way information is stored in the file, which in turn enables the program to open and save the file. Some of these formats are shown in the following table.

Microsoft Word 97-2003	.doc
Microsoft Word 2007, 2010	.docx
Microsoft Works	.wps
Corel WordPerfect	.wpd
Zoho	.sxw
AbiWord	.abw
Apple iWork Pages	.pages
OpenOffice.org Writer	.odt

So, how easy is it to share documents created in different applications with different file formats? It's not as difficult as you think. Most applications will open documents created in another application, and they can also save files in a different format so that they can be opened in another application. So, for example, say you have Microsoft Word 2010 installed on your computer, but your classmate has sent you an e-mail with a document he created in OpenOffice.org Writer. Microsoft Word will be able to open the file, and you will also be able to save it as a Word file. Conversely, if you send your classmate a file you create in Word, he will be able to open it in OpenOffice.org Writer and save it as a Writer document. The open source programs and Web-based applications are designed to work with a variety of file formats, so there should not be a problem. You can upload almost any type of word processing, spreadsheet, or presentation file into Google Docs and work with it. Using Google Docs may actually facilitate sharing files made in dissimilar programs, although you may lose some of the features, since Google Docs only has very basic capabilities.

Figure 4.2
Drop cap
Section headings
Two-column text
Formatted headers
Bullets and numbering
WordArt

Figure 4.2

Nearly every word processing application has formatting features to give your document a professional look.

columns. You also can insert pictures from your own files or from a gallery of images and graphics, such as clip art and SmartArt, which are included with the software. You also can enhance the look of your document by creating an interesting background or by adding a "theme" of coordinated colors and

Designs and other visual effects
Bibliography tool organizes sources

Figure 4.3

Writer, the word processing program in the OpenOffice.org suite, has many of the same features as Word and WordPerfect.

styles throughout your document. Figure 4.2 shows what a document can look like when formatting options found in many word processing applications are incorporated. Although many of the open source and Web-based applications have great formatting capabilities, many are not as fully featured as the proprietary applications, such as Microsoft Word.

What special tools do word processing programs have? You're probably familiar with the basic tools of word processing software. Most applications come with some form of spelling and grammar checker and a thesaurus, for example. Another popular tool is the search-and-replace tool that allows you to search for text in your document and automatically replace it with other text.

The average user is unaware of many interesting word processing software tools. For example, did you know that you could translate words or phrases into another language or automatically correct your spelling as you type? You also can automatically summarize key points in a text document, add bibliographical references, and include illustrations with different picture styles. Writer, the word processing program in the OpenOffice.org suite, has many of the same tools you're used to seeing in Microsoft Word and Corel WordPerfect (see Figure 4.3).

Spreadsheet Software

Why would I need to use spreadsheet software?
Spreadsheet software—such as Microsoft Excel and OpenOffice.org Calc—enables you to do calculations and numerical analyses easily. You can use spreadsheet software to track your expenses and create a simple budget. You also can use it to determine how much you should be paying on your student loans, car loan, or credit card bills each month. You know you should pay more than the minimum payment to spend less on interest, but how much more can you afford to pay, and for which loan? Spreadsheet software can help you evaluate different scenarios, such as planning the best payment strategy.

How do I use spreadsheet software?
The basic element in a spreadsheet program is the worksheet, which is a grid consisting of columns and rows. As shown in Figure 4.4, the columns and rows form individual boxes called *cells.* Each cell can be identified according to its column and row position. For example, a cell in column A, row 1 is referred to as "cell A1." You can enter several types of data into a cell:

- **Text:** Any combination of letters, numbers, symbols, and spaces. Text is often used as labels to identify the contents of a worksheet or chart.
- **Values:** Numerical data that represent a quantity or an amount and are often the basis for calculations.
- **Formulas:** Equations that you build yourself using addition, subtraction, multiplication, and division, as well as values and cell references. For example, in Figure 4.4, you would type the formula "=B8-B22" to calculate net income for September.
- **Functions:** Formulas that are preprogrammed into the spreadsheet software. Functions help you with calculations ranging from the simple (such as adding groups of numbers) to the complex (such as determining monthly loan payments), without you needing to know the exact formula. Therefore, in

Figure 4.4, to calculate your average earned income in September, you could use the built-in AVERAGE function, which would look like this: =AVERAGE(B4:B7).

The primary benefit of spreadsheet software is its ability to recalculate all functions and formulas in the spreadsheet automatically when values for some of the inputs change. For example, as shown on the spreadsheet on the right side of Figure 4.4, you can insert an additional row (Memberships), change a value (September clothing expense), and then recalculate the results for Total Expenses and Net Income without having to redo the worksheet from scratch.

Because automatic recalculation enables you to see immediately the effects that different options have on your spreadsheet, you can quickly test different assumptions

Formula · Values · Changed value

Cell · Labels

Function =SUM(B10:B21) · Formula (=B8-B22) · Inserted row · Results of recalculated formulas

Figure 4.4
Spreadsheet software enables you to calculate and manipulate numerical data easily with the use of built-in formulas.

SOUND BYTE

Creating Web Queries in Excel 2010

In this Sound Byte, you'll learn what Excel Web queries are, as well as how to use them effectively.

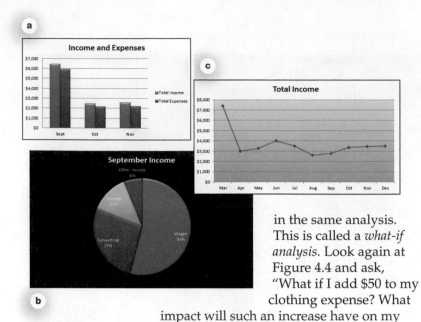

Figure 4.5

(a) Column charts show comparisons. (b) Pie charts show how parts contribute to the whole. (c) Line charts show trends over time.

Figure 4.6

Sparklines, a new feature for Excel 2010, are tiny graphs that fit into a single cell.

in the same analysis. This is called a *what-if analysis*. Look again at Figure 4.4 and ask, "What if I add $50 to my clothing expense? What impact will such an increase have on my total budget?"

What kinds of graphs and charts can I create with spreadsheet software? Sometimes it's easier to see the meaning of numerical information when it is shown in a graphical format such as a chart. As shown in Figure 4.5, most spreadsheet applications allow you to create a variety of charts, including basic column charts, pie charts, and line charts, with or without three-dimensional (3D) effects. In addition to these basic charts, you can use stock charts (for investment analysis) and scatter charts (for statistical analysis), or create custom charts. New in Excel 2010 are sparklines, which are small charts that fit into a single cell. Sparklines (see Figure 4.6) easily show data trends.

Are spreadsheets used for anything besides financial analysis? There are so many powerful mathematical functions built into spreadsheet programs that they can be used for serious numerical analyses or simulations. For example, an Excel spreadsheet could be designed to

compute the output voltage at a point in an electrical circuit or to simulate customer arrival and wait times. In these settings, spreadsheet programs can often solve problems that formerly required custom programming. Many spreadsheet applications also have database capabilities and can sort, filter, and group data.

Presentation Software

What software do I use to create presentations? You've probably sat through presentations during which the speaker's topic was displayed in slides projected on a screen. These presentations can be the most basic of outlines, containing only a few words and simple graphics, or elaborate multimedia presentations with animated text, graphic objects, and colorful backgrounds. You use **presentation software** such as Microsoft PowerPoint, OpenOffice.org Impress, or Zoho Show (shown in Figure 4.7) to create these types of dynamic slide shows. Because these applications are simple to use, you can produce high-quality presentations without a lot of training. With some of the new capabilities in PowerPoint 2010, you can embed online videos, as well as change the color, add effects, and even trim video clips without the need for a separate video editing program.

How do I create a presentation? Using the basic features included in presentation software, creating a slide show is simple. To arrange text and graphics on your slides, you can choose from a variety of slide layouts. These layouts give you the option of using a single or double column of bulleted text, various combinations of bulleted text, and other content such as clip art, graphs, photos, and even video clips.

You also can lend a theme to your presentation by choosing from different design templates. You can use animation effects to control how and when text and other objects enter and exit each slide. Slide transitions add different effects as you move from one slide to the next during the presentation.

Database Software

How can I use database software? **Database software** such as Oracle, MySQL, and Microsoft Access are powerful

Sparklines

applications that allow you to store and organize data. As mentioned earlier, spreadsheet applications include database features and are easy to use for simple database tasks such as sorting, filtering, and organizing data. However, you need to use a more robust, fully featured database application to manage larger and more complicated groups of data that contain more than one table; to group, sort, and retrieve data; and to generate reports.

Traditional databases are organized into fields, records, and tables, as shown in Figure 4.8. A field is a data category such as "First Name," "Last Name," or "Street Address." A record is a collection of related fields such as "Douglas Seaver, Printing Solutions, 7700 First Avenue, Topeka, KS, (888) 968-2678." A table groups related records such as "Sales Contacts."

How do you benefit when businesses use database software?
FedEx, UPS, and other shipping companies let customers search their online databases for tracking numbers, allowing customers to get instant information on the status of their packages. Other businesses use databases to keep track of clients,

invoices, and personnel information. Often that information is available to a home computer user. For example, at Amazon.com you can use the company's Web site to access the entire history of all the purchases you have made.

Note Taking Software

Is there software to help students with note taking? Programs are available to help students take notes during lectures and organize and

Figure 4.7

Several programs allow you to create presentation materials: (a) Microsoft Office PowerPoint 2010, (b) OpenOffice.org Impress, and (c) Zoho's Show.

Table

ID ▾	FirstName ▾	LastName ▾	Company ▾	Street ▾	City ▾	State ▾	ZipCode ▾	Business
1	Susan	Scantosi	eWidget Plus	363 Rogue Street	St. Louis	MO	63136	(612) 444
2	Thomas	Mazeman	BooksRUs	2165 Piscotti Avenue	Springfield	IL	62702	(888) 234
3	Douglas	Seaver	Printing Solutions	7700 First Avenue	Topeka	KS	66603	(888) 968
4	Amir	Raviv	TechStands	1436 Riverfront Road	St. Louis	MO	63136	(877) 867
5	Franklin	Scott	WorkSuite	8789 Ploughman Ave	Tulsa	OK	74101	(800) 864
6	Ronald	Komeika	Creekside Financial	1264 Pond Hill Road	Toledo	OH	43601	(343) 332
7	Barbara	Mitchell	Market Tenders	9823 Bridge Street	La Porte	IN	46350	(888) 283
*	(New)							

SalesContacts

Field

Record

Figure 4.8

In databases, information is organized into tables, fields, and records.

Make a Winning Presentation

We've all sat through bad presentations. Don't make your audience sit through another one! Here are some tips for designing good presentations:

1. **Color:** Avoid using clashing text and background colors. Instead, choose dark text on a light background or white text on dark background.

2. **Bullets:** Use bullets for key points. Limit the number to four to six bulleted points per slide.

3. **Text:** Limit the amount of text on a slide to about six words per bullet point. Avoid full sentences and paragraphs,

4. **Images:** Images can convey a thought or illustrate a point. Make sure any text over an image can be read easily. Consider using SmartArt diagrams for interesting text arrangements.

5. **Font size and style:** Keep the font size large enough to read from the back of the room. Avoid script or fancy font styles. Limit the number to one or two styles per presentation.

6. **Animation and background audio:** Keep to a minimum. They can be distracting.

lectures can be added. Students can search for a term across the full set of notebooks they have created during the semester, helping them to find connecting ideas among their courses. Because OneNote has co-authoring and version tracking capabilities, it's also perfect for organizing team and other collaborative projects. OneNote 2010 incorporates a new Wiki system, which allows individuals to quickly link to another page within OneNote or a document outside of OneNote.

Are there free or portable note taking applications? There are several free and online note taking options available to help you take full-blown notes or just jot down a quick reminder. Some are even available for your smartphone. Evernote (**evernote.com**), for example, allows you to take notes via the Web, your phone, or your computer and then sync your notes between the Web, your phone, and any computer. You can save text, audio, and images, as well as screen captures, Web pages, and photos. The beauty of Evernote is that everything is searchable. StickyNotes (**sticky-notes.net**) are digital equivalents to paper sticky notes. These notes can be customized, saved, and shared via e-mail, and they even have reminders.

Figure 4.9

The Outlook Today feature in Microsoft Outlook includes common PIM features such as a summary of appointments, a list of tasks, and the number of new e-mail messages.

maintain their lecture notes and the recordings they create from lectures. For example, Microsoft OneNote allows students who have Tablet PCs to write their notes directly onto the tablet, using it as an electronic notebook. Students can also use OneNote with a notebook or desktop computer, and type the information onto the sheets; then the pieces of text can be easily moved around the page. Notes can also be organized into tabbed sections that provide further help in organizing and reorganizing pages. With one click, Web links can be quickly integrated and audio or video recordings of

Personal Information Manager (PIM) Software

Which applications should I use to manage my time, contact lists, and tasks? Most productivity suites contain some form of **personal information manager (PIM) software** such as Microsoft Outlook or Lotus Organizer. Chandler (**chandlerproject.org**) is another PIM program that is open source and, therefore, free. These programs strive to replace the management tools found on a traditional desk—a calendar, address book, notepad, and to-do list, for example. Some PIMs contain e-mail management features so that you not only can receive and send e-mail messages but also organize them into various folders, prioritize them, and coordinate them with other activities in your calendar (see Figure 4.9).

E-mail inbox   Calendar items   Task reminder   Messages

If you share a network at home or at work and are using the same PIM software as others on the network, you can use a PIM program to check people's availability before scheduling meeting times. Whether coordinating a team project or a family event, you can create and electronically assign tasks to group members by using a PIM. You can even track each person's progress to ensure that the tasks are finished on time.

Are there Web-based PIM programs? Many Web-based e-mail clients such as Yahoo!, Google, and AOL have developed coordinating calendar and contacts programs similar to Microsoft Outlook. Yahoo! includes Notepad for jotting down notes and tasks. Google's calendar and contacts sync with Outlook so that you can access your Outlook calendar information by logging into Google, giving you access to your schedule anywhere you have access to a computer and an Internet connection. AOL's Instant Messenger, AIM, has coordinated e-mail, calendar, and contact functions.

Productivity Software Features

What tools can help me work more efficiently with productivity software? Whether you are working on a word processing document, spreadsheet, database, or slide presentation, you can make use of several tools to increase your efficiency:

- A **wizard** is a systematic guide that walks you through the steps necessary to complete a complicated task. At each step, the wizard asks you questions. Based on your responses, the wizard helps you complete that portion of the task. When you install software, you are often guided by a wizard.
- A **template** is a predesigned form. Templates are included in many productivity applications. They provide the basic structure for a particular kind of document, spreadsheet, or presentation. Templates can include specific page layout designs, formatting and styles relevant to that particular document, and automated tasks (macros). Typical templates allow you to lay out a professional-looking résumé, structure a home budget, or communicate the results of a project in a presentation.

- A **macro** is a small program that groups a series of commands so they will run as a single command. Macros are best used to automate a routine task or a complex series of commands that must be run frequently. For example, a teacher may write a macro to sort the grades in her grade book automatically in descending order and to highlight those grades that add up to less than a C average. Every time she adds the results of an assignment or test, she can set up the macro to run through that series of steps automatically.

Integrated Software Applications

What's an integrated software application? An **integrated software application** is a single software program that incorporates the most commonly used tools of many productivity software programs into a single integrated program. Note that integrated software applications are not substitutes for the full suite of applications they replace. Generally, because they don't include many of the more complex features of the individual productivity software applications, they can be thought of as "software lite." To have access to the full functionality of word processing and spreadsheet software, for example, you should get the individual applications or a suite that includes each of these applications.

Microsoft Works is an example of an integrated software application. This integrated software application includes word

Figure 4.10

Software suites provide users with a cheaper method of obtaining all of the software they want to buy in one bundle.

Software Suites

What's a software suite?   A **software suite** is a group of software programs that have been bundled as a package. You can buy software suites for many different categories of software, including productivity, graphics, and virus protection (see Figure 4.10). There are three primary developers of productivity software suites: Microsoft, Corel, and Apple. Microsoft Office 2010 is the leader's latest release, and Corel offers two separate suites. WordPerfect Office X5 has a traditional look and feel with classic toolbars, while Home Office sports the new tabbed arrangement of features that first came out with Microsoft Office 2007. Apple offers productivity software for the Macs in its iWork suite.

Which applications do productivity software suites contain?   Most productivity software suites contain similar basic components, such as word processing, spreadsheet, presentation, and PIM software. However, depending on the version and manufacturer, they may also include other types of applications, such as database programs and desktop publishing software. When you are shopping for software, it can be difficult to figure out which bundle is the right one for your needs. For example, Microsoft Office 2010 is bundled in five different ways; the three bundles that are available for individual purchase are described in Figure 4.11. Be sure to research carefully the bundling options for software you are buying.

What are the advantages of software suites?   Most people buy software suites because doing so is cheaper than buying each program individually. In

processing, spreadsheet, and database functionality as well as templates, a calendar, a dictionary, and map features.

Why would I use an integrated software application instead of individual stand-alone programs?   Integrated software applications are perfect if you don't need the more advanced features found in the individual full versions of each program. Like stand-alone applications, an integrated software program provides templates for frequently developed documents such as résumés and invoices. An integrated software program is also less expensive than its individual, fully featured alternatives. If you find your needs go beyond the limited capabilities of an integrated program, you might want to consider buying the individual programs that meet your particular requirements or a software suite.

Figure 4.11 | A SAMPLING OF MICROSOFT OFFICE 2010 SUITES

Application	Function	Home and Student 2010	Home and Business 2010	Professional 2010
Word	Word processing	X	X	X
Excel	Spreadsheet	X	X	X
PowerPoint	Presentation	X	X	X
Access	Database			X
Outlook	PIM		X	X
Publisher	Desktop publishing			X
OneNote	Note taking	X	X	X

addition, because the programs bundled in a software suite come from the same company, they work well together (that is, they provide for better integration) and share common features, toolbars, and menus. For example, when using applications in the Microsoft Office suite, you can seamlessly create a spreadsheet in Excel, import it into Access, and then link a query created in Access to a Word document. It would be much harder to do the same thing using different applications from a variety of software developers. Another example is Apple iWork, which includes word processing (Pages), presentation (Keynote), and spreadsheet (Numbers) applications. Each program can access and share certain common elements such as photographs.

Personal Financial Software

What software can I use to prepare my taxes? Everyone has to deal with taxes, and having the right computer software can make this burden much simpler and keep it completely under your control. **Tax preparation software** such as Intuit TurboTax and H&R Block At Home enable you to prepare your state and federal taxes on your own instead of hiring a professional. Both programs offer a complete set of tax forms and instructions, as well as videos that contain expert advice on how to complete each form. Each company also offers free Web-based versions for federal forms and instructions. In addition, error-checking features are built into the programs to catch mistakes. TurboTax also can run a check for audit alerts, file your return electronically, and offer financial planning guidance to help you effectively plan and manage your financial resources in the following year (see Figure 4.12). Remember, however, that the tax code changes annually, so you must obtain an updated version of the software each year.

Which software can I use to help keep track of my personal finances? **Financial planning software** helps you manage your daily finances. Intuit Quicken and Microsoft Money are popular examples. Financial planning programs include electronic checkbook registers and automatic bill payment tools. With these features, you can print checks from your computer or pay recurring monthly payments, such as rent or student loans, with automatically scheduled

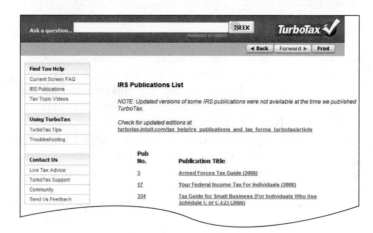

online payments. The software records all transactions, including online payments, in your checkbook register. In addition, you can assign categories to each transaction and then use these categories to analyze your spending patterns. You even can set up a budget and review your spending habits.

Web-based programs such as Mint (**mint.com**) and Yodlee MoneyCenter (**yodlee.com**) are rapidly gaining in popularity (see Figure 4.13). Both are great at analyzing your spending habits and offering advice on how to manage your spending better. Like some other full-featured applications such as Quicken or Mint (both by Intuit), you can track your investment portfolio as well. Because they are Web-based, you can monitor and update your finances from any computer in a private and secure setting. Each product also has versions of its applications to load on smartphones, so your information is conveniently accessible. Users also have access to a network of other users with whom to exchange tips and advice.

Figure 4.12

Tax preparation software, such as Intuit TurboTax, enables you to prepare and file your taxes using a guided, systematic process.

Figure 4.13

Mint.com is an online financial management tool. An extensive online community provides helpful tips and discussions with other people in similar situations.

Financial planning applications also coordinate with tax preparation software. Quicken, for example, integrates seamlessly with TurboTax, so you never have to go through your checkbook and bills to find tax deductions, tax-related income, or expenses. Many banks and credit card companies also offer online services that download a detailed monthly statement into Quicken. Quicken even offers a credit card. All of your purchases are organized into categories and are downloaded automatically to your Quicken file to streamline your financial planning and record keeping.

Media Software for Home

From movies and television to music and photography, the entertainment world is becoming digital. Your computer can help you create, organize, and modify digital images, songs, and movies, if you have the right software. **Multimedia software** includes image, video, and audio editing software; animation software; and other specialty software required to produce computer games,

Figure 4.14

There are many varieties of graphics and multimedia software.

animations, and movies. In this section, we look at several popular types of multimedia software, as shown in Figure 4.14.

Digital Image Editing Software

What can I do with a digital image that I can't do with a photograph? Once the image information is in a digital format (taken with a digital camera or scanned), you can use it easily with all your other software. For example, you can store a digital picture of each person in your Outlook contacts list or add a digital image you captured into a newsletter you are writing.

Products such as Microsoft Photo Story and Google Picasa, which are both free downloads, make it easy for you to use your collection of digital images in new ways. In Photo Story, you can add text, music, and camera movement to create a fully featured slide show with your images. Using Picasa, you can create a poster or several different styles of collages from your images.

What software can I use to edit my photos? As its name implies, **image editing software** (sometimes called **photo editing software**) enables you to edit photographs and other images. Image editing software includes tools for basic modifications to digital images such as removing red-eye; modifying contrast, sharpness, and color casts; or removing scratches or rips from scanned images of old photos. Many of these software packages now also include an extensive set of painting tools such as brushes, pens, and artistic media (such as paints, pastels, and oils) that allow you to create realistic-looking images. Often graphic designers use digital photos and images as a basis for their design and then modify these images within image editing software to create their final products.

Adobe Photoshop and Corel PaintShop Pro Photo are fully featured image editing applications. They each offer sophisticated tools for tasks like layering images (placing pictures on top of each other) and masking images (hiding parts of layers to create effects such as collages). As shown in Figure 4.15, these image editing applications offer sophisticated tools. Designers use these more sophisticated tools to create the enhanced digital images used commercially in logos, advertisements, and on book and CD covers.

Figure 4.15

With some image editing software, you can take two individual pictures and combine them into one picture.

of a professional athlete or other famous person.

If you want to use a program that offers more than basic features but is still easy to use, try Adobe Photoshop Elements (see Figure 4.16). With this program, you can improve the color balance of an image, touch up an image (by removing red-eye, for example), add creative effects to an image, or group images together to create montages. If you later decide to upgrade to the professional version of Adobe Photoshop, you will already be familiar with the user interface.

Figure 4.16

Image editing software such as Adobe Photoshop Elements makes it easy to create (a) calendars, (b) greeting cards and postcards, (c) slide shows.

Can a nonprofessional use image editing software? Image editing programs such as Adobe Photoshop Elements and Roxio PhotoSuite are geared toward the casual home user. Adobe also offers Adobe Photoshop Album Starter Edition, which is a free download. With these applications, you can perform the most common image editing tasks, such as taking out red-eye and cropping and resizing pictures. These programs enable you to add creative effects such as borders and frames. Some include templates so you can insert your favorite pictures into preformatted calendar pages or greeting cards. They may also have photo fantasy images that let you paste a face from your digital image onto the body

SOUND BYTE

Enhancing Photos with Image Editing Software

In this Sound Byte, you'll learn tips and tricks on how to best use image editing software. You'll learn how to remove the red-eye from photos and incorporate borders, frames, and other enhancements to produce professional effects.

Speech Recognition Software

Speech recognition software (or **voice recognition software**) translates your spoken words into typed text. With this software, you can dictate documents and e-mail messages, use voice commands to start and switch between applications, control the operating system, and even surf or fill out forms on the Web. Several programs are available for personal use, such as Dragon Naturally Speaking, and the technology is being used in automobiles, call centers, and even in military aircraft.

Microsoft has incorporated a speech recognition system into the Windows operating system. After starting speech recognition (from the Start menu, type "speech" in the search box and click on "Windows Speech Recognition"), the speech recognition toolbar appears and indicates whether or not the computer is "listening" for voice input. Just click the microphone icon to make the computer listen to or ignore voice input. Figure 4.17 shows how you can use the Windows' speech recognition functionality to run commands within an application.

Speech recognition software is complicated. As you speak, the software divides each second of your speech into 100 individual *samples* (sounds). It then compares these individual sounds with a database (called a *codebook*) that contains samples of every sound a human being can make. When it finds a match, it gives your voice sound a number that corresponds to the number of the similar sound in the database.

After your voice sounds are assigned values, these values are matched with another database containing phonemes for the language being spoken. A *phoneme* is the smallest phonetic unit that distinguishes one word from another. For example, "b" and "m" are both phonemes that distinguish the words *bad* and *mad* from each other in the English language. Many languages, including English, are made up of thousands of different phonemes. Moreover, because of differences in pronunciation, some phonemes may actually have several different corresponding matching sounds.

Once all the sounds are assigned to phonemes, word and phrase construction can begin. The phonemes are matched against a word list that contains transcriptions of all known words in a particular language. Because pronunciation can vary (for example, the word *the* can be pronounced so that it rhymes with either *duh* or *see*), the word list must contain alternative pronunciations for many words. Each phoneme is worked on separately; the phonemes are then chained together to form words that are contained in the word list. Because a variety of sounds can be put together to form many different words, the software analyzes all the possible values and picks the one value that it determines has the best probability of correctly matching your spoken word. The word is then displayed on the screen or is acted on by the computer as a command.

However, there are problems with speech recognition software. We don't always speak every word the same way, and accents and regional dialects produce great variation in pronunciations. Therefore, speech recognition is not perfect and requires training. Training entails getting the computer to recognize your particular way of speaking by reading prepared text into the computer so the phoneme database can be adjusted to your specific speech patterns.

Another approach to improve speech inconsistencies is to restrict the word list to a few keywords or phrases, and then have the computer guess the probability that a certain phrase is being said. This is how cell phones that respond to voice commands work. The phone doesn't really figure out that you said "call home" by breaking down the phonemes. It just determines how likely it is that you said "call home" as opposed to "call office." This reduces the processing power needed as well as the chance of mistakes. However, it also restricts the words you can use to achieve the desired results.

Though not perfect, speech recognition software programs can be invaluable to individuals who don't type well or who have physical limitations that prevent them from using a keyboard or mouse. For those whose careers require a lot of typing, using speech recognition software reduces their chances of incurring debilitating repetitive-strain injuries. In addition, because most people can speak faster than they can write or type, speech recognition software can help individuals work more efficiently. Doctors are incorporating speech recognition software into their practices to create a summary of the visit before the patient leaves the room. This eliminates the need for a dictated summary to be transcribed by a separate service, and it increases the physician's in-office efficiency.

Using Speech Recognition Software

In this Sound Byte, you'll see a demonstration of the speech recognition software included with Windows 7. You'll also learn how to access and train speech recognition software so that you can create and edit documents without typing.

Digital Audio Software

Why would I have digital audio files on my computer?
Best-selling novels, newspapers, and radio shows all can be purchased as audio files from sellers such as Audible, Inc. (**audible.com**). Huge numbers of free audio files are also available through the phenomenon of *podcasting*, the distribution of audio files such as radio shows and music videos over the Internet. Offered by subscription, these audio files are delivered to your machine free with the release of each episode. You may also choose to extract (*rip*) your CD collection to store on your computer. In addition, with programs such as MAGIX Music Maker or Apple GarageBand, you can compose your

Figure 4.17

Speech recognition software allows you to create documents using simple voice commands.

Speech recognition software also can help you to be productive during generally nonproductive times. For example, you can dictate into a digital recording device while doing other things, such as driving, then download the digital file to your computer and let the program type up your words for you. Recently, voice recognition technologies have been incorporated into in-car communication and entertainment systems, such as Ford SYNC, which allows drivers to control mobile phones and digital music players with voice commands.

Speech recognition should continue to be incorporated into our daily lives. Aside from the obvious benefits to persons with disabilities, it will provide continued efficiencies to many others as well.

own songs or soundtracks with virtual instruments, voice recorders, synthesizers, and special audio effects. You may quickly have several gigabytes of audio files on your hard drive before you even know it!

Why are MP3 files so popular?

MP3, short for MPEG-1 Audio Layer 3, is a type of audio compression format that reduces the file size of traditional digital audio files so that they will take up less storage capacity. It is also a standard of digital audio compression, which has made it possible to transfer and play back music on personal media players. For example, a typical CD stores between 10 and 15 songs in uncompressed format, but with files in MP3 format, the same CD can store between 100 and 180 songs. The smaller file size not only lets you store and play music in less space, but also allows quick and easy distribution over the Internet. You can find hundreds of digital audio applications that allow you to copy, play, edit, and organize MP3 files, and record and distribute your own music online. Ogg Vorbis (or just OGG) is a free, open source audio compression format alternative. Most digital audio software programs support one of the following functions.

Others, such as iTunes, incorporate many of these capabilities into one multifunctional program:

- **MP3 recording** allows you to record directly from streaming audio and other software or microphone sources to MP3 format.
- **CD ripping** allows you to copy or extract CDs and encode to the MP3 format.
- **CD burning** allows you to create your own CDs from your MP3 collection.
- **Encoding and decoding** is done by *encoders*, programs that convert files to MP3 format at varying levels of quality. Most ripping software has encoders built in to convert the files directly into MP3 format.
- **Format conversion** programs allow you to convert MP3 files to other digital audio formats such as WAV (short for Waveform audio format), WMA (Windows Media Audio), and AIFF (Audio Interchange File Format).

Can I edit audio files? Audio **editing software** includes tools that make editing your audio files as easy as editing your text files. Software such as the open source Audacity (**audacity. sourceforge.net**) and Sony Sound Forge Pro 10 (**sonycreativesoftware.com**) enables you to perform such basic editing tasks as cutting

dead air space from the beginning or end of the song or cutting a portion from the middle. You also can add special sound effects, such as echo or bass boost, and remove static or hiss from your MP3 files. Both of these applications support recording sound files from a microphone or any source you can connect through the input line of a sound card.

Digital Video Editing Software

What kind of software do I need to edit my digital videos? With the boom of digital camcorders and the improved graphics capabilities on home computers, many people are experimenting with **digital video editing software**. Several video editing applications are available at a wide range of prices and capabilities. Although the most expensive products (such as Adobe Premiere Pro and Final Cut Pro) offer the widest range of special effects and tools, some moderately priced video editing programs have enough features to keep the casual user happy. Microsoft Live Movie Maker and Apple iMovie have intuitive drag-and-drop features that make it simple to create professional-quality movies with little or no training (see Figure 4.18). Microsoft Live Movie Maker (**download.live.com/ moviemaker**) is a free download from Microsoft. Other software developers offer free trial versions so that you can decide whether their product meets your needs before purchasing it.

Figure 4.18

Video editing programs such as Apple iMovie make it easy to create and edit movies.

Video clips in clips pane

Window used to view or edit movie clips

Movie clips display in clip viewer

Trans icon controls transition effects between clips

Does video editing software support all kinds of video files?

Video files come in a number of formats such as flash video (FLV for YouTube), MPEG-1, MPEG-2, and MPEG-4, VCD, SVCD, DVD, AVI, WMV, MOV and even AVCHD. AVCHD (Advanced Video Coding High Definition) is a format for high-definition video. Many of the affordable video editing software packages support most types of video files.

For more information on video editing software, see the section "Digital Video" on page 386 of Chapter 8.

In what format are the videos I watch on my portable media player?

Videos that can be watched on portable media players, such as the fifth-generation iPod and iPod Touch, are in the MP4 (MPEG-4) video format. This format stores digital audio and digital video streams, as well as other items, such as text for subtitles and still images. Similar to the MP3 format, MP4 compresses the audio and video content into a more manageable file size. Most MP4 files have the file extension .mp4. However, Apple has created other MPEG-4 extensions to identify specific content such as .m4b, which is often used to identify audio book and podcast files, and .m4r, which is used to identify ringtone files for the iPhone.

Media Management Software

How do I manage the audio, video, and image files on my system?

Many people add hundreds or even thousands of files to their systems by purchasing music and downloading images and video. Your hard drive is a convenient place to store all your music and images, but only if you can find what you're looking for!

Software such as Windows Media Player, Winamp, and Apple iTunes allows you to organize audio and video files so that you can sort, filter, and search your music collection by artist, album, or category (see Figure 4.19). Using these programs, you can manage individual tracks, generate playlists,

and even export the files to a database or spreadsheet application for further manipulation. Then you can burn the songs to a CD, and the program will print liner notes that you can place inside the CD case.

Are there Web-based programs available to edit, share, and store my photos?

One great advantage of taking digital images is that you can easily share the images via the Internet. Initially, we had to send images as e-mail attachments—and our exuberance in sending several images at the same time often clogged someone's inbox. Several online photo sharing and photo storing sites, such as Snapfish (**snapfish.com**), Kodak (**kodak.com**), and Shutterfly (**shutterfly.com**), enable you to upload your digital images from your computer, create photo albums, and share them with friends and family. These sites offer printing and card-making services as well.

Flickr (**flickr.com**) is probably one of the best of these online photo management and photo sharing applications. It lets you organize your images and then share them publicly with millions of users, or just with your closest friends and family. Discussion boards are available so that groups can exchange comments about the images, just as you would if you were passing them around the dinner table. In addition, taking advantage of online mapping technologies, Flickr enables you to link your images to a map so

Album covers flow by in a smooth display

Smart playlists select song lists based on criteria you specify

Figure 4.19

Software programs such as iTunes help you manage all the music files on your computer. You can sort, filter, and search your collection by artist, album, or category, and you can create playlists.

that you can show exactly where you took the images or see where others took theirs.

Google Picasa (**picasa.google.com**) is another popular application in the online photo editing, storing, and sharing field. Picasa helps you send images to your friends, your mobile devices, or your blog by automatically resizing a huge 12-megapixel image to a more manageable size for electronic transmission. With Picasa, you can then attach the image to an outgoing e-mail message, or transfer the image directly to your blog or to a mobile device such as an iPod or smartphone.

Software Fun for Home

As the term implies, **entertainment software** is designed to provide users with thrills, chills, and all-out fun! Computer games make up the vast majority of entertainment software. These digital games began with Pong, Pac-Man, and Donkey Kong, and have evolved to include many different categories, including action, driving, puzzles, role-playing, card-playing, sports, strategy, and simulation games. Entertainment software also includes other types of computer applications, such as **virtual reality programs** that turn artificial environments into a realistic experience.

Gaming Software

Do I need special equipment to run entertainment software?   As with any software, you need to make sure your system has enough processing power, mem-

ory (RAM), and hard drive capacity to run the program. Because games often push the limit of sound and video quality, be sure your system has the appropriate sound cards, video cards, speakers, monitor, and CD or DVD drives.

Some gaming software may require a special controller. Some games, such as *Steel Battalion*, *Rock Band*, and many games in the Nintendo Wii system, are sold with their own specialized controllers (see Figure 4.20). These controllers also can be adapted to your computer. Complex programs can benefit from configurable wireless controllers such as the Cyborg Evo.

How do I tell what computer games are appropriate for a certain user?   The **Entertainment Software Rating Board (ESRB)** is a self-regulatory body established in 1994 by the Entertainment Software Association (**esrb.org**). The ESRB's rating system helps consumers choose the computer and video games that are right for their families by providing information about game content so they can make informed purchasing decisions. ESRB ratings have two parts: rating symbols that suggest age appropriateness, and content descriptors that indicate elements in a game that may have triggered a particular rating or be of interest or concern. It's important to check both the rating symbol (on the front of the game box) and the content descriptors (on the back of the game box). The rating symbols currently in use by the ESRB include E (Everyone), T (Teens), M (Mature), and AO (Adult Only).

Can I make video games?   Now that video games represent an industry with revenue of more than $20 billion each year, designing and creating video games is emerging as a desirable career opportunity. Professionally created video games involve artistic storytelling and design, as well as sophisticated programming. Major production houses such as Electronic Arts use applications that are not easily available to the casual home enthusiast. However, you can use the editors and game engines available for games such as *EverQuest*, *Oblivion*, and *Unreal Tournament* to create custom levels and characters or to extend the game.

If you want to try your hand at creating your own video games, multimedia applications such as Adobe Flash and RPG Maker VX provide the tools you need to explore game design and creation. The program

Figure 4.20

Computer controllers can be specialized. *Rock Band* controllers include a guitar, a drum set, and a microphone.

GameMaker (**yoyogames.com**) is a free product that allows you to build a game without any programming; key elements of the new game creation are dragged and dropped into place. Alice (**alice.org**) is another free environment to check out. It lets you easily create 3D animations and simple games and includes the actual Sims characters!

Educational Software

What kinds of educational applications are there? Although a multitude of educational software products are geared toward the younger set, software developers have by no means ignored adult markets. In addition to all the products relating to the younger audience, there are software products that teach users new skills such as typing, languages, cooking, and playing the guitar. Preparation software for students who will be taking the SAT, GMAT, LSAT, and MCAT exams is also popular. In addition, there are many computer and online brain training games and programs designed to improve the health and function of our brains. Lumosity (**lumosity.com**) is one such site that has a specific "workout" program. Brain Age[2] (**brainage.com**) has software for the Nintendo DS and is designed for players of all ages.

What types of programs are available to train you to use software or special machines? Many programs provide tutorials for popular computer applications. These programs use illustrated systematic instructions to guide users through unfamiliar skills. Some training programs, known as **simulation programs**, allow users to experience or control the software as if it were the actual software or an actual event. Such simulation programs include commercial and military flight training, surgical instrument training, and machine operation training. Often these simulators can be delivered locally on CD or DVD or over the Internet.

One benefit of these simulated training programs is that they safely allow users to experience potentially dangerous situations such as flying a helicopter during high winds. Consequently, users of these training programs are more likely to take risks and learn from their mistakes—something they could not afford to do in real life. Simulated training programs also help prevent costly errors. Should something go awry, the only cost of the error is restarting the simulation program.

Do I need special software to take courses online? As long as you have a compatible Web browser, online classes will be accessible to you. Depending on the content and course materials, however, you may need a password or special plug-ins to view certain videos or demos.

Taking classes over the Internet is rapidly becoming a popular method of learning because it offers greater schedule flexibility for busy students. Although some courses are run from an individually developed Web site, many online courses are run using **course management software** such as Blackboard, Moodle, and Angel. These programs provide traditional classroom tools such as calendars and grade books over the Internet (see Figure 4.21). Special areas are available for students and professors to exchange ideas and information through the use of chat rooms, discussion forums, and e-mail. Other areas are

Figure 4.21

Course management software such as Blackboard provides a method for doing traditional classroom tasks, such as participating in discussions and taking tests, in an online environment.

BITS AND BYTES — How to Open the Unknown

Normally, when you double-click a file icon on your desktop, the program that is associated with the selected file runs automatically. For example, when you double-click a *.doc or *.docx file, the file will open in Microsoft Word. However, if the file has no extension or Windows has no application currently associated with that file type, an "Open with" dialog box appears and asks what program you want to use to open the file. In other cases, a document may open with a program other than the one you wanted to use to open it. This is because many applications can open several file types and the program you expected the file to open in is not currently the program associated with that file type. To assign a program to a file type or to change the program to open a particular file type, follow these instructions:

1. Click the Windows Explorer icon, which is pinned to the Windows 7 taskbar by default.
2. Use the search and navigation tools in this folder to locate the file you want to change. (For example, you can search for all Word files by searching for *.doc or *.docx). Right-click on a file of the correct type, and then either click Open With or point to Open With, and click Choose Default Program.
3. A list of programs installed on your computer will appear. Click the program that you want to use to open this type of file. Although you can choose to open individual files with a certain program, normally you would select the "Always use the selected program to open this kind of file" check box, and then click OK.

When you double-click that type of file in the future, the file will open in the program you selected.

ACTIVE HELP-DESK — Choosing Software

In this Active Helpdesk call, you'll play the role of a helpdesk staffer, fielding calls about the different kinds of multimedia software, educational and reference software, and entertainment software.

available for posting assignments, lectures, and other pertinent class information.

Drawing Software

Figure 4.22

The drawing program Visio lets you create different types of diagrams easily with drag-and-drop options.

What kind of software should I use for simple illustrations? Drawing software (or illustration software) lets you create or edit two-dimensional, line-based drawings. You can use drawing software to create technical diagrams or original nonphotographic drawings, animations, and illustrations using standard drawing and painting tools such as pens, pencils, and paintbrushes. You also can drag geometric objects from a toolbar onto the canvas area to create images and use paint bucket, eyedropper, and spray can tools to add color and special effects to the drawings.

Are there different types of drawing software? Drawing software is used in both creative and technical drawings. Applications such as Adobe Illustrator include tools that let you create professional-quality creative and technical illustrations. Illustrator's tools help you create complex designs, such as muscle structures in the human body, and use special effects, such as charcoal sketches. Its warping tool allows you to bend, stretch, and twist portions of your image or text. Because of its many tools and features, Illustrator is one of the preferred drawing software programs of most graphic artists.

There are many software packages to help plan the layout of rooms, homes, and landscapes, such as those offered by Broderbund. Microsoft Visio is a program used to create technical drawings, maps, basic block diagrams, networking and engineering flowcharts, and project schedules, but it can also be used by the more casual designer. Visio uses project-related templates with special objects that you drag onto a canvas. For example, Visio allows you to quickly drag and drop objects to create diagrams like the one shown in Figure 4.22. Visio also provides mindmapping templates to help you organize your thoughts and ideas.

Business Software for Home and Office

With the amount of power available in a typical home computer, you have more opportunities than ever to run a business from your home. No matter what service or product you provide, there are common types of software you'll want to consider. Accounting software will help manage the flow of money, and desktop publishing and Web page creation tools will help you market and develop your new enterprise. A number of software packages are designed to organize and help with the daily operations of a typical business. If you ever plan to run a business from your own home, or even if you are just a user of large business products and services, it is helpful to know what functions business software can perform.

Home Business Software

Which programs are good for small-business owners?   If you have a small business or a hobby that produces income, then you know the importance of keeping good records and tracking your expenses and income. **Accounting software** helps small-business owners manage their finances more efficiently by providing tools for tracking accounts receivable and accounts payable. In addition, these applications offer inventory management, payroll, and billing tools. Examples of accounting applications are Intuit QuickBooks and Peachtree by Sage. Both programs include templates for invoices, statements, and financial reports so that small-business owners can create common forms and reports.

What software can I use to lay out and design newsletters and other publications?   **Desktop publishing (DTP) software** allows you to incorporate and arrange graphics and text in your documents in creative ways. Although many word processing applications allow you to use some of the features that are hallmarks of desktop publishing, specialized desktop publishing software such as QuarkXPress and Adobe InDesign allows professionals to design books and other publications that require complex layouts (see Figure 4.23).

What tools do desktop publishing programs include?   Desktop publishing programs offer a variety of tools with which you can format text and graphics. With text formatting tools, you easily can change the font, size, and style of your text and arrange text on the page in different columns,

> **Accounting software helps small-business owners manage their finances more efficiently.**

shapes, and patterns. You also can import files into your documents from other sources, including elements from other software programs (such as a chart from Excel or text from Word) and image files. You can readily manipulate graphics with tools that crop, flip, or rotate images or modify the image's color, shape, and size. Desktop publishing programs also include features that allow you to publish to the Web.

What software do I use to create a Web page?   **Web page authoring software** allows even the novice to design interesting and interactive Web pages, without knowing any HyperText Markup Language (HTML) code. Web page authoring applications often include wizards, templates, and reference materials to help you easily complete most Web page authoring tasks. More experienced users can take advantage of these applications' advanced features, such as features that enable you to add headlines and weather information, stock tickers, and maps to make your Web content current, interactive, and interesting. Microsoft Expression Web and Adobe Dreamweaver are two of the programs to which both professionals and casual page designers turn.

Are there other ways to create Web pages?   If you need to produce only the occasional Web page and do not need a separate page authoring program, you'll find that many applications include features that enable you to convert your document into a Web page. For example, in some Microsoft Office applications, if you choose to save a file as a Web page, the application will automatically convert the file to a Web-compatible format.

Large Business Software

There is an application for almost every aspect of business. There are specialized programs for marketing and sales, finance, point of sale, general productivity, project management, security, networking, data management, e-commerce, and human resources, to name just a few. In the following sections, we discuss some of these specialized programs from this seemingly endless list.

Tool palette

Style Sheets palette

Colors palette

Measurements palette

Page Layout palette

Figure 4.23

Major publishing houses use professional publishing programs such as QuarkXPress to lay out the pages of textbooks.

What software do businesses use for planning and management?

Planning is a big part of running a successful business. Software programs such as Palo Alto Software's Business Plan Pro and Marketing Plan Pro help users write strategic and development plans for general business and marketing needs. Another category of business planning software is **project management software**, such as Microsoft Project. This type of software helps project managers create and modify scheduling charts like the one shown in Figure 4.24, which help them plan and track specific tasks and coordinate personnel resources.

Customer relationship management (CRM) software stores sales and client

contact information in one central database. Sales professionals use CRM programs to get in touch with and follow up with their clients. These programs also include tools that enable businesses to assign quotas and create reports and charts that document and analyze actual and projected sales data. Customer relationship programs coordinate well with PIM software such as Outlook and can be set up to work with smartphones. GoldMine from FrontRange Solutions is one example of a CRM program.

An **enterprise resource planning (ERP) system** lets a business consolidate multiple systems into one and improve coordination of these business areas across multiple departments. ERP systems are used to control many "back office" operations and processing functions such as billing, production, inventory management, and human resources management. These systems are implemented by third-party vendors and matched directly to the specific needs of a company. Oracle and SAP are well-known companies that sell ERP software.

What software helps business travelers? Mapping programs such as DeLorme Street Atlas USA and Microsoft Streets & Trips are perfect for businesses that require employees to travel frequently. These programs provide street maps and written directions to locations nationwide, and users can customize maps to include landmarks and other handy traveling sites such as airports, hotels, and restaurants. More users now turn to an **online mapping service** such as Google Maps, MapQuest, Yahoo! Maps, or Google Earth than to a more traditional mapping software program because the online services are easily accessible with any Internet connection and are updated more frequently than offline ones. Mapping programs, which can work in conjunction with a global positioning system (GPS), are available in versions for smartphones and for cars. Such programs help you navigate unfamiliar territory and are essential for sales representatives or delivery-intensive businesses. They are useful for nonprofessionals traveling to unfamiliar locations.

Is mapping software just used to assist with travel? Travel is only one of several applications that uses mapping technologies to assist businesses in making complex decisions and managing complex systems. Many companies use a geographic information system (GIS) to assist with managing, analyzing, and displaying data, most often in spatial or map form (see Figure 4.25). These maps are used by power companies to manage electric grids, by water distribution companies to manage water distribution, by shipping and transportation companies to determine the most efficient routes, and even by school districts to manage the flow of students to the appropriate schools. Many of these systems are complex, proprietary ones such as those produced by ESRI. Google Earth and interactive maps like Google Maps are simple and free examples of basic forms of a GIS.

What software is used with e-commerce? It seems that every business has an online presence to display com-

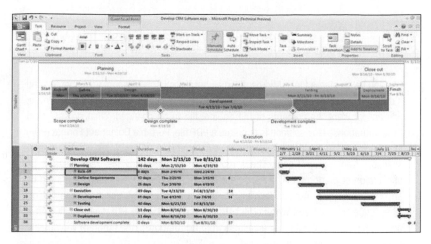

Figure 4.24

A Gantt chart in Microsoft Project gives project managers a visual tool for assigning personnel and scheduling and managing tasks.

pany information or products, handle online sales, or offer customer service and support. Depending on the size of the company and its specific needs, it may use products such as IBM's WebSphere, GoEmerchant, and ProStores Business from ProStores (an eBay company). These products offer bundled Web site creation and hosting services, shopping cart setup, and credit card processing services. For larger businesses, specialized software to handle each aspect of e-commerce is available; alternatively, a large business might develop

Figure 4.25

A geographic information system (GIS) applies geographic data to provide solutions to complex business situations.

Digital elevation

Streets

Land use and cover

Topographic map

Digital line graph of rivers

Real world

proprietary software tailored to its specific needs.

Specialized Business Software

Some applications are tailored to the needs of a particular company or industry. Software designed for a specific industry is called **vertical market software**. For example, the construction industry uses software such as Sage Master Builder, which features estimating tools to help construction companies bid on jobs. It also integrates project management functions and accounting systems that are unique to the construction industry.

Other examples of vertical market software include property management software for real estate professionals; ambulance scheduling and dispatching software for emergency assistance organizations; and library automation software that combines cataloging, circulation, inventory, online catalog searching, and custom report printing.

In addition to these specific business applications, which companies can buy off the shelf, programs often are custom developed to address a company's specific needs.

What software is used to make 3D models? Computer-aided design (CAD) programs are a form of 3D modeling that engineers use to create automated designs, technical drawings, and model visualizations. Specialized CAD software such as Autodesk's AutoCAD is used in areas such as architecture, the automotive industry, aerospace, and medical engineering.

With CAD software, architects can build virtual models of their plans and readily visualize all aspects of design before actual construction. Engineers use CAD software to design everything from factory components to bridges. The 3D nature of these programs allows engineers to rotate their models and make adjustments to their designs where necessary, thus eliminating costly building errors.

CAD software also is being used in conjunction with GPS devices for accurate placement of fiber-optic networks around the country. The medical engineering community uses CAD to create anatomically accurate solid models of the human anatomy, allowing them to develop medical implants quickly and accurately. The list of CAD applications keeps growing as more and more industries realize the benefits CAD can bring to their product development and manufacturing processes.

Many graphics, animation, video, and gaming systems use applications from Autodesk called Autodesk 3ds Max and Autodesk Maya to create 3D models with complex textures and lighting models. Autodesk 3ds Max and Autodesk Maya are complex and rich programs. A slightly simpler package is the open source program Blender (**blender.org**.), which is available free of charge. A simple, Web-based, and fairly full-featured free 3D modeling application is Google's SketchUp. SketchUp designs coordinate well with other Google applications so, for example, you could easily import a 3D image of a deck you created in SketchUp into a Google Earth image of your home.

Getting Help with Software

If you need help while you are working with software, you can access several different resources to find answers to your questions. For general help or information about a product, many manufacturers' Web sites offer answers to frequently asked questions (FAQs).

Where can I find help while I'm working in an application? Some programs offer online help and support. Online help may consist of documentation comparable to a user's manual. However, many applications' online help allows you to chat over the Internet with an online support team member. Some applications are context sensitive and offer task-specific help or

Software can take us beyond what is familiar to us and into alternate realities. Virtual reality uses software to allow people to interact in a simulated three-dimensional environment that users can manipulate and explore as if they were in that world. Beyond video games, the applications of virtual reality are almost endless. Three-dimensional environments created by computers are getting better and better at helping people experience new things or experience familiar things in new ways.

Virtual environments are used in military training programs, the space program, and, as discussed in Chapter 1, in the medical field. Studies show that soldiers who have gone through virtual reality (VR) training are just as effective as those who have trained in traditional combat situations. Flight simulators are used by airlines to prepare commercial pilots to fly in a wide range of flight conditions; the military and NASA also use them. The obvious benefit of simulators and VR is that there is little machine or human expense when a mistake is made in virtual conditions—but there would be in "live" conditions.

Engineers and designers are also using virtual reality technologies. Car manufacturers build virtual prototypes of new vehicles, test them, and make alterations in design before producing a single physical part. Architects create virtual models of building plans so that clients or potential buyers can "walk through" and get a more realistic idea of what the completed building will be like.

Second Life, a virtual world launched in 2003 by Linden Research, Inc., has gained worldwide popularity. Users create avatars, or virtual representations of themselves, with which they interact in the virtual world. *Second Life* has its own economy, where users have created "in-world" businesses and residents can legally trade in the world's own currency, called Linden dollars.

Second Life has also begun to permeate the outside world. "Outside world" businesses now assist and advise "in-world" businesses. For example, real-world programmers build complex in-world projects for clients such as Dartmouth College, Major League Baseball, and Lego. Real-world accountants offer services to advise "in-world" businesses on finance, strategic planning, or budget forecasting. There is fertile ground for innovative and entrepreneurial thinkers both inside and outside *Second Life*.

Finally, businesses and educational institutions also recognize the marketing potential in *Second Life*, and they use the virtual world to test new ideas. Educational institutions such as Harvard, Princeton, and Ohio University have built virtual campuses with the intention of offering "virtual tours" to prospective students. At these "campuses," current students can take courses (see Figure 4.26), participate in student organizations, or meet and collaborate online just as they would if they met in the real-world student center.

Virtual worlds such as *Second Life* are innovative ways to hold distance learning classes. Online classes held in a virtual world environment give students the online convenience of not having to travel to class, while providing a more enjoyable and perhaps even more effective experience. In a virtual world, students are able to convene in traditional classrooms, on sandy Malibu beaches, or in open-air venues—environments limited only by the imagination of the instructor and the students. Given such enjoyable choices, students might be more inclined to make time to attend classes, thus increasing their productivity and the interactivity of the online classroom.

Virtual classroom environments may add an additional layer of experience that students may be able to bring into their professional lives. Seton Hall University, for example, uses *Second Life* in an emergency preparedness course that allows students to work in simulated catastrophic situations, which would otherwise be difficult to experience in the real world.

Just as in the real world, the virtual world has its problems. However, it is likely that virtual reality and virtual environments will continue to find uses in entertainment, education, distance learning, design, and manufacturing.

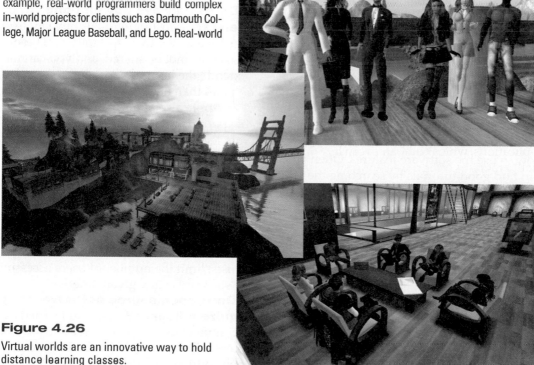

Figure 4.26

Virtual worlds are an innovative way to hold distance learning classes.

Figure 4.27
Microsoft Office gives you tips on tasks you're working on and answers specific questions you have about using online and offline resources.

screen tips to explain where your cursor is resting.

In Microsoft Office applications, you will see a question mark icon on the far top right of the program screen. This icon takes you to the main Help interface. **Integrated help** means that the documentation for the product is built directly into the software so you don't need to keep track of bulky manuals. You can type your question, search for a term, or browse the Help topics (see Figure 4.27). Like many software packages, Microsoft Office offers help documentation, which is installed locally on your machine, and online help resources, which are updated continually.

Finally, the Help menu, found on the menu bar of most applications, lets you choose to search an index or content outline to find out the nature of almost any Microsoft application feature.

Where do I go for tutorials and training on an application? If you need help learning how to use a product, the product's developer may offer online tutorials or program tours that show you how to use the software features. Often you can find good tutorials by searching the Internet. MalekTips (**malektips.com**), for example, includes a vast array of multimedia help files; you can find podcasts for applications such as Excel and Photoshop in iTunes; and even YouTube has some helpful videos.

Buying Software

These days, you no longer need to go to a computer supply store to buy software. You can find software in almost any retail

environment. In addition, you can purchase software online, through catalogs, and at auctions.

Software Licenses

Don't I own the software I buy? Most people don't understand that, unlike other items they purchase, the software they buy doesn't belong to them. The only thing they're actually purchasing is a license that gives them the right to use the software for their own purposes as the *only* user of that copy. The application is not theirs to lend or copy for installation on another computer, even if it's another one of their own machines.

What is a software license? A **software license** is an agreement between you, the user, and the software company. You accept this agreement before installing the software on your machine. It is a legal contract that outlines the acceptable uses of the program and any actions that violate the agreement. Generally, the agreement will state who the ultimate owner of the software is, under what circumstances copies of the software can be made, and whether the software can be installed on any other machine. Finally, the license agreement will state what, if any, warranty comes with the software.

Do you always buy just one license? Most individuals buy single licenses to cover their specific use. These licenses cannot be shared, and you cannot "extend" the license to install the software on more than one of your computers. However, Apple also offers a "family license" that permits a user to install some of its software legally on as many as five computers, and some versions of Microsoft Office come with three licenses. Businesses and educational institutions often buy multiuser licenses that allow more than one person to use the software. Some multiuser licenses are per-seat and limit the number of users overall, while others, called *concurrent licenses*, limit the number of users accessing the software at any given time.

Does open source software require a license? As you learned earlier, anyone using open source software has access to the program's code. Therefore, open source software programs can be tweaked by another user and redistributed.

A computer user who copies an application onto more than one computer is participating in **software piracy**, unless his or her license specifically provides for multiple distributions. What many software users do not realize, or do not think about, is that when they purchase software, they are actually purchasing a license to use it, rather than purchasing the actual software. That license is what tells you how many times you can install the software, so it is important to read it. If you make more copies of the software than the license permits, you are pirating. Historically, the most common way software has been pirated among computer users has been by supplementing each other's software library by borrowing installation CDs and installing the software on their own computers. Larger-scale illegal duplication and distribution by counterfeiters are quite common as well. In addition, the Internet provides various ways to copy and distribute pirated software illegally.

Is it really a big deal to copy a program or two? As reported by the Business Software Alliance, 40 percent of all software is pirated. Not only is pirating software unethical and illegal, but the practice has financial impacts on all software consumers. The dollars manufacturers lose when software is pirated decreases the amount of money available for further software research and development, while increasing the up-front costs to legitimate consumers.

To determine whether you have a pirated copy of software installed on your computer at work or at home, you can download a free copy of GASP (a suite of programs designed to help identify and track licensed and unlicensed software and other files) from the Business Software Alliance Web site (**bsa.org/usa**). A similar program is available at the Microsoft Web site (**microsoft.com/piracy**). These programs check the serial numbers of the software installed on your computer against software manufacturer databases of official licensed copies and known fraudulent copies. Any suspicious software installations are flagged for your attention.

As of yet, there's no such thing as an official software police force, but software piracy is so rampant that the U.S. government is taking steps to stop piracy worldwide. Efforts to stop groups that reproduce, modify, and distribute counterfeit software over the Internet are in full force. Software manufacturers also are becoming more aggressive in programming mechanisms into software to prevent repeated installations. For instance, with many Microsoft products, installation requires you to activate the serial number of your software with a database maintained at Microsoft. This is different from the traditional "registration" that enrolled you voluntarily and allowed you to be notified of product updates, for example. Activation is required, and failure to activate your serial number or attempting to activate a serial number that has been used previously results in the software going into a "reduced functionality mode" after the 50th time you use it. Therefore, without activation, you would not be able to save documents in Office—a strong motivator to let Microsoft watch how many times you install the software you purchased!

A free software license, the GNU General Public License, is required and grants the recipients the right to modify and redistribute the software. Without such license, the recipient would be in violation of copyright laws. This concept of redistributing modified open source software under the same terms as the original software is known as **copyleft**. Thus, all enhancements, additions, and other changes to copylefted software must also be distributed as free software.

Pre-Installed Software

What application software comes with my computer? Virtually every new computer comes with an operating system as well as some form of application software, although the particular applications depend on the hardware manufacturer and computer model. You usually can count on your computer having some form of productivity software preinstalled, such as Microsoft Works or Corel WordPerfect Office.

Multimedia-enriched computers also may offer graphics software or a productivity suite that includes page authoring software. Many new computers also include some software that is of interest to home users, such as image editing or financial planning software.

Are there any problems associated with pre-installed software? There is such generous space on system hard drives these days that leaving pre-installed applications on a system isn't problematic from a storage perspective. However, some manufacturers can include applications that they hope you will try, so as to build interest in their product. Some of these applications, especially virus protection software, are trial versions for which a user gets a short-term temporary software license. When the license expires, the software disables (but is still installed), and a permanent license must be purchased to reinstate the software. In addition, many types of pre-installed programs are available free from the Web, so the pre-installation is not an advantage. In fact, having so many pre-installed programs on your system can degrade the system performance by allocating memory away from active applications. For notebook computers, such software can also reduce battery life. If you don't use the software or don't renew the license, then the software just clogs up your system unnecessarily. For this reason, this pre-installed software is referred to as **bloatware**. The best thing to do is to delete the programs.

Can I get the manufacturer to uninstall or install software before shipping? Several years ago, Dell began to allow buyers of certain computers to decline unwanted bloatware. Dell also included an extra uninstall utility program on certain computers to make it easier to remove unwanted software. On the other hand, if you know you'll need a particular type of software not offered as standard on your new computer, you may want to see if the computer manufacturer has a special offer that will allow you to add that particular software at a reduced price. Sometimes, initially buying software through the hardware manufacturer is less expensive than buying software on the retail market. This is not always the case, so do some comparative pricing before you buy.

If my computer crashes, can I get the pre-installed software back? Most manufacturers no longer include a system restore disc. Instead, they use a separate partition on the hard drive that holds an image, or copy, of the pre-installed software. However, it's not always possible to reboot from the partitioned hard drive, especially when your computer crashes, so one of the first things you should do after you purchase a new computer is create a restore disc. Generally the manufacturer will have placed a utility on your system, or you can use the utility included in Windows 7, to create a restore disc. To create a restore disc with Windows 7, click the Start Menu, select Control Panel, and then select System & Security. From there, select Backup and Restore, and then click Create a system repair disc. Next, insert a blank DVD in your DVD drive and select the drive. Click "Create disc." Once the copy has been made, label the disc and put it away in a safe place.

Web-Based Applications

Does all application software require installation on my computer? Most application software you acquire, whether by purchasing a CD or DVD at a retail store or by downloading the software from a Web site, must be installed on your computer before use. There is a relatively new trend of on-demand software deployment, referred to as **Software as a Service (SaaS)**, that many software developers are taking advantage of. Instead of the traditional model that requires software to be purchased and installed on individual machines or network servers, with the SaaS delivery model, the application is hosted online by the vendor and made available to the customer over the Internet. These applications are also referred to as **Web-based applications**.

What kinds of Web-based applications are available? Along with its release of Office 2010, Microsoft made available Microsoft Office Web Apps. Office Web Apps are similar to the full-featured installable versions of Word, Excel, PowerPoint, and OneNote, but it comes with only the Home and Insert tabs, and it has fewer options (see Figure 4.28).

Google Docs (**docs.google.com**) is a Web-based suite of productivity software with word processing, spreadsheet, and presentation capabilities. Sites such as Zoho (**zoho.com**) as shown in Figure 4.29, and ThinkFree (**thinkfree.com**) offer Web-based applications that cover not only word processing, presentation, and spreadsheet needs, but also a wealth of other business applications such as project management, 3D drawing, and customer relationship management software. Some other examples of Web-based applications include Intuit's QuickBooks online, Salesforce.com, and Citrix Online.

What advantages do Web-based applications have? As long as you have a Web browser, you can access your files, which are stored securely online. Although these free applications are not as fully featured as their installable counterparts, most can read and export to many different file formats and can be used with other software packages. Besides being able to access your documents from any computer or smartphone that has Internet access, Web-based applications are great for collaborations. You can invite people to share your files and work together in real time, watching as others make changes to the document.

Is all Web-based software free? Web-based applications are run from software stored completely on a Web server instead of your hard drive. Web-based applications are a reflection of a movement toward a new software distribution model.

Although most Web-based software programs are free, some Web sites charge a fee for their online products. TurboTax Online (**turbotax.com**) is a version of the popular tax preparation software that you can access online to prepare your tax returns. While the standard version is free, you're charged for the more full-featured product. In addition to saving you the hassle of software installation, TurboTax Online stores your information in a secure location so that you can retrieve it anytime.

Discounted Software

Is it possible to buy software at a discount? Software manufacturers understand that students and educators often need to use software for short periods of time because of specific classes or projects.

Figure 4.28

Microsoft Web Apps are similar to the full-featured versions of Word, Excel, PowerPoint, and OneNote. Although the Word and Excel Web applications have fewer options available, the functionality and user interface are the same.

In addition, they want to encourage you to learn with their product, hoping you'll become a long-term user of their software. Therefore, if you're a student or an educator, you can purchase software that is no different from regularly priced software at prices that are sometimes substantially less than general consumer prices.

Campus computer stores and college bookstores sometimes offer discounted prices to students and faculty who possess a valid ID. Online software suppliers such as Journey Education Marketing (**journeyed.com**), CampusTech, Inc. (**campustech.com**), and Academic Superstore (**academicsuperstore.com**) also offer

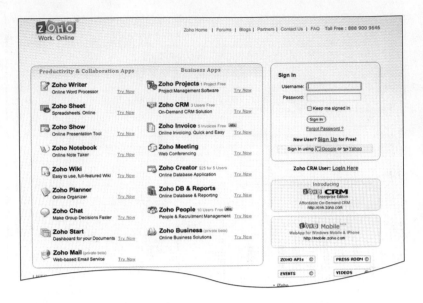

Figure 4.29

Zoho.com is one of the many emerging Web sites that offers free Web-based productivity software.

popular software to students at reduced prices.

Can I buy used software? Often you can buy software through online auction sites such as eBay. If you do so, be sure that you are buying licensed (legal) copies. Computer shows that display state-of-the-art computer equipment are generally good sources for software. However, here, too, you must exert a bit of caution to make sure you are buying licensed copies and not pirated versions.

Can I buy software directly from the Internet? As with many other retail products, you can buy and download software directly from many companies and

retail Web sites such as Microsoft.com and Amazon.com. You also can use the Internet to buy software that is custom developed for your specific needs. Companies such as Ascentix Corporation (**ascentix.com**) act as intermediaries between you (the software user) and a software developer, who tweaks open source software code to meet your particular needs.

When buying software from the Internet, you should also request that the software be sent to you on CD or DVD, if this is available. Without a physical copy of the software, it is much more difficult to reinstall the software if you change computers or if your hard drive crashes. If a physical copy is not available, make sure you create a backup and keep it in a safe place.

The Microsoft .NET program (**microsoft.com/net**) offers software over the Internet for all devices—not just computers—that have a connection to the Internet. Therefore, you can download software specifically for your smartphone by using .NET. In addition, if you have a Microsoft .NET account (available free of charge at the Microsoft Web site), you can connect to any other .NET-connected device.

Freeware and Shareware

Can I get software for free legally? **Freeware** is any copyrighted software that you can use for free. Plenty of freeware exists on the Web, ranging from games and screen savers to business, educational, graphics, home and hobby, and system utility software programs. To find free software, type "freeware" in your search engine. Good sources of a large variety of freeware programs are Butterscotch (**butterscotch.com**), shown in Figure 4.30, and Freeware Home (**freewarehome.com**).

Although they do not charge a fee, some developers release free software and request that you mail them a postcard or send them an e-mail message to thank them for their time in developing the software and to give them your opinion of it. Such programs are called *postcardware* and *e-mailware*, respectively.

Another option is to search for an open source program to fit your needs. Open source programs are free to use on the condition that any changes you make to improve the source code also must be

Applications on the Go—There Is an App for That

More and more of us carry some kind of mobile digital device that enables us to use software on the go. We can install productivity, entertainment, communication, and navigation software on our iPhones, Blackberries, iPods, iPads, and other mobile devices. Microsoft Office 2010 has modestly featured Web-based Word, Excel, Power-Point, and OneNote applications, so you'll have access to your productivity documents without having to worry about transferring files from one machine to another. Although mobile applications have been available for smartphones for a while, they have been limited in scope and content, in addition to being slightly pricey.

One of the features that makes the iPhone and iPod Touch so popular is their ability to run small apps. Many of these applications are fun and free (such as the flashlight and Sudoku applications), while others (such as the Tip Calculator, the Remember the Milk list, or a connection to your online banking files) help you be more productive. The full list of available applications for the iPhone and iPod Touch is available on the iTunes apps store Web site.

distributed for free. SourceForge.net (**sourceforge.net**) is an excellent site to begin your hunt for a group that may already have built a solution that will work for you!

While many legitimate freeware exists, some unscrupulous people use freeware to distribute viruses and malware. Be cautious when installing such programs, especially if you are unsure of the provider's legitimacy.

Can I try new software before it is really released? Some software developers offer beta versions of their software free of charge. A **beta version** is an application that is still under development. By distributing free beta versions, developers hope users will report errors, or bugs, they find in their programs. Many beta versions are available for a limited trial period, and are used to help the developers correct any errors before they launch the software on the market.

Is it still freeware if I'm asked to pay for the program after using it for a while? One model for distributing software is to run a version free of charge for only a limited time. These are fully functional packages, but they expire if not purchased within a certain timeframe. This is referred to as **shareware**. Shareware software is distributed free, but with certain conditions. Sometimes the software is released on a trial basis only and must be registered after a certain period of time; in other cases, no support is available unless the software is registered. In some cases, direct payment to the author is required. Shareware is not freeware. If you use the software after the initial trial period is over, then you are breaking the software license agreement.

Software developers put out shareware programs to get their products into users' hands without the added expense and hassle of marketing and advertising. Therefore, quite a few great programs are available as shareware, and they can compete handily with programs on retail shelves. For example, TechSmith Corporation (**techsmith.com**) offers screen capture and desktop recording applications as shareware, including SnagIt Screen Capture and Camtasia Studio, a screen recording and presentation application. You can try these products for free for a 30-day period, after which time you must purchase the software to continue using it. For a listing of other shareware programs, visit the CNET site Tucows (**tucows.com**), as shown in Figure 4.31.

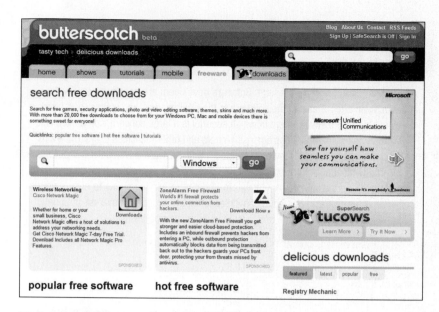

Figure 4.30

Butterscotch.com is a useful site for finding freeware applications and provides product reviews, tutorials, and related podcasts.

Can shareware programmers make me pay for their shareware once I have it? The whole concept of shareware assumes that users will behave ethically and abide by the license agreement. However, to protect themselves, many developers have incorporated code into the program to stop it from working completely or to alter the output slightly after the trial period expires.

Figure 4.31

Tucows.com is a useful site for finding shareware and freeware applications. The site provides product reviews, hardware requirements, and details about the limitations of free versions of software.

Are there risks associated with installing beta versions, freeware, and shareware or downloading them from the Internet? Not all files available as shareware and freeware will work on your computer. You easily can crash your system, and may even need to reinstall your operating system as a result of loading a freeware or shareware program that was not written for your computer's operating system.

Of course, by their very nature, beta products are unlikely to be bug free, so you always run the risk of something going awry with your system. Unless you're willing to deal with potential problems, it may be best to wait until the last beta version is released. By that time, most of the serious bugs will have been worked out.

As a matter of precaution, you should be comfortable with the reliability of the source before downloading a freeware, shareware, or beta version of software. If it's a reliable developer whose software you are already familiar with, you can be more certain that a serious bug or virus is not hiding in the software. However, downloading software from an unknown source could potentially put your system at risk of contracting a virus. (We discuss viruses in detail in Chapter 9.)

A good practice to establish before installing any software on your system is to use the Windows 7 operating system's Restore feature and create a *restore point*. That way, if anything goes wrong during installation, you can restore your system to the way it was before you started. (We discuss the System Restore utility in Chapter 5.)

Also, make sure that your virus protection software is up-to-date.

Software Versions and System Requirements

What do the numbers after software names indicate? Software companies change their programs to repair problems (or bugs) or add new or upgraded features. Generally, they keep the software program's name but add a number to it to indicate that it is a different version. Originally, developers used numbers only to indicate different software versions (major upgrades) and releases (minor upgrades). Today, however, they also use years (such as Microsoft Office 2010) and letters (such as WordPerfect Office X5) to represent version upgrades.

When is it worth buying a newer version? Although software developers suggest otherwise, there is no need to rush out and buy the latest version of a software program every time one is available. Depending on the software, some upgrades may not be sufficiently different from the previous version to make it cost-effective for you to buy the newest version. Unless the upgrade adds features that are important to you, you may be better off waiting to upgrade every other release. You also should consider whether you use the software frequently enough to justify an upgrade and whether your current system can handle the new system requirements of the upgraded version.

If I have an older version of software and someone sends me files from a newer version, can I still open them? Software vendors recognize that people work on different versions of the same software. Vendors, therefore, make new versions backward compatible, meaning that they can recognize (open) files created with older versions. However, some software programs are not forward compatible, so older versions cannot recognize files created on newer versions of the same software.

How do I know whether the software I buy will work on my computer? Every software program has a set of **system requirements** that specify the minimum recommended standards for the operating system, processor, primary memory (RAM), and hard drive capacity. Sometimes there are other specifications for the video card, monitor, CD drive, and other peripherals. These requirements generally are printed on the software packaging or are available at the manufacturer's Web site. Before installing software on your computer, ensure that your system setup meets the minimum requirements by having sufficient storage, memory capacity, and processing capabilities.

Installing, Uninstalling, and Starting Software

Before you use your software, you must permanently place it, or install it, on your system. The installation process will differ slightly depending on whether you've purchased the software from a retail outlet and have an installation CD or are downloading it from the Internet. Deleting or uninstalling software from your system requires that you take certain precautions to ensure you remove all associated programs as well.

How do I install software? When you purchase software, the program files may come on a CD or a DVD. For most programs created for installation on a PC, an installation wizard automatically opens when you insert the disc, as shown in Figure 4.32. By following the steps indicated by the wizard, you can install the application on your system. If the wizard doesn't open automatically for some reason, the best way to install the software is to go to the Programs and Features icon, located on the Control Panel on the Start menu. This feature locates and launches the installation wizard.

How is the installation process different for software I download from the Web? When you download software from the Web, you typically do not get an

installation disc. Instead, everything you need to install and run the downloaded program is contained in one file that has been compressed (or zipped) to make the downloading process quicker. For the most part, these downloaded files unzip or decompress themselves and automatically start or launch the setup program. During the installation and setup process, these programs select or create the folder on your computer's hard drive in which most of the program files will be saved. Usually, you can select a different location if you desire. Either way, note the name and location of the files, because you may need to access them later.

What do I do if the downloaded program doesn't install by itself? Some programs you download do not automatically install and run on your computer. Although the compressed files may unzip automatically as part of the download process, the setup program may not run without some help from you. In this case, you need to locate the files on the hard drive (this is why you must remember the location of the files) and find the program that is controlling the installation (usually named *setup.exe* or sometimes *install.exe*). Files ending with the .exe extension are executable files or applications. All the other files in the folder are support, help, and data files. Once the setup program begins, you will be prompted to take the actions necessary to complete the installation.

Figure 4.32

Part of the installation process in Windows is a security check to confirm that the software is from a reliable source.

What's the difference between a custom installation and a full installation? One of the first steps in the installation wizard asks you to decide between a full installation and a custom installation. A **full installation** will copy all the files and programs from the distribution disc to the computer's hard drive. By selecting **custom installation**, you can decide which features you want installed on the hard drive. Installing only the features you know you want allows you to save space on your hard drive.

Can I just delete a program to uninstall it? An application contains many different files—library files, help files, and other text files—in addition to the main file you use to run the program. By deleting only the main file, or only the icon on your desktop, you are not ridding your system of all the pieces of the program. In addition, some applications make changes to a variety of settings, and none of these will be restored if you just delete the desktop icon or remove the main file from your programs list.

Some programs place an Uninstall Program icon in the main program folder on the Start menu. Using this icon runs the proper cleanup routine to clear out all of the files associated with the application, and also restores any settings that have been changed. If you can't locate the uninstall program for a particular application, click the Start menu, click Control Panel, and then click Programs and Features. This will give you a list of applications installed on your system; from this list, you can choose which application you would like to uninstall.

Is there a best way to start an application? The simplest way to start an application is by clicking its icon in the All Programs list found on the Start menu. Every program that you install on your system is listed on the Start menu. However, in Windows 7, if you find you use only a few programs often, you can place a shortcut to those programs on the taskbar or on your desktop. To place a program on the taskbar, right-click the program icon on your desktop or right-click the program name on the Start menu. From the shortcut menu that is displayed, select Pin to Taskbar. Windows then places an icon for this program on the Taskbar (see Figure 4.33a). To uninstall a taskbar or Start menu icon, select remove or

Figure 4.33

For quick access to an application you use often, you can (a) create shortcuts on (b) the desktop or taskbar.

Desktop shortcuts can be created easily

Arrow indicates shortcut

Windows 7 taskbar

unpin this program from taskbar or from this list, respectively.

To create a shortcut on the desktop, right-click the icon of the desired program, click Send To, and select Desktop (see Figure 4.33b). This places the shortcut icon directly on the Desktop. You can identify a shortcut icon by the arrow in its lower left corner, as shown in Figure 4.31a.

There is virtually an application for almost anything you want or need to do on your computer, whether it's work related or just for entertainment purposes. And there are a variety of types of applications for almost every application such as proprietary, open source, Web-based, freeware, and shareware. Have fun exploring all the various possibilities!

1. What's the difference between application software and system software?

Application software is the software you use to do everyday tasks at home, school, and work. Application software includes productivity software, such as word processing and finance programs; media software, such as applications used for image and video editing; home and entertainment software, such as games or educational programs; and business software for small and large businesses. System software is the software that helps run the computer and coordinates instructions between application software and the computer's hardware devices. System software includes the operating system and utility programs.

2. What kinds of applications are included in productivity software?

Productivity software programs include word processing, spreadsheet, presentation, note taking, personal information manager (PIM), and database programs. You use word processing software to create and edit written documents. Spreadsheet software enables you to do calculations and numerical and what-if analyses easily. Presentation software enables you to create slide presentations. Note taking software provides a convenient means to take extensive notes or to just jot down a few thoughts. You can easily organize and search your notes. PIM software helps keep you organized by putting a calendar, address book, notepad, and to-do lists within your computer. Database programs are powerful applications that allow you to store and organize data. Individuals can also use software to help with business-like tasks such as preparing taxes and managing personal finances.

3. What are the different types of multimedia software?

Multimedia software includes digital image, video, and audio editing software; animation software; and other specialty software required to produce computer games. Many software programs are available for playing, copying, recording, editing, and organizing multimedia files. Because modern users have so many audio, video, and image files, many software solutions are available for organizing and distributing these types of files.

4. What are the different types of entertainment software?

Beyond the games that most of us are familiar with, entertainment software includes virtual reality programs that use special equipment to make users feel as though they are actually experiencing the program in a realistic 3D environment.

5. What are the different types of drawing software?

Drawing software includes a wide range of software programs that help you create and edit simple line-based drawings or create more complex designs for both imaginative and technical illustrations. Floor plans, animations, and mind maps are some of the types of images that can be created.

6. What kinds of software do small and large businesses use?

Many businesses, including home businesses, use software to help them with finance, accounting, strategic planning, marketing, and Web-based tasks common to most businesses. In addition, businesses may use specialized business software (or vertical market software) that is designed for their specific industry.

7. Where can I go for help when I have a problem with software?

Most software programs have a Help menu built into the program with which you can search through an index or subject directory to find answers. Some programs group the most commonly asked questions into a single "frequently asked questions" (FAQ) document. In addition, many free and fee-based help and training resources are available on the Internet and through booksellers.

8. How can I purchase software or get it for free?

Almost every new computer system comes with some form of software to help you accomplish basic tasks. You must purchase all other software unless it is freeware or open source code, which you can download from the Web for free. You can also find special software called shareware you can run free of charge for a test period. Although you can find software in many stores, as a student you can purchase the same software at a reduced price with an academic discount.

9. How do I install, uninstall, and start software?

When installing and uninstalling software, it's best to use the uninstall feature provided in the software, or if not included to use the Add or Remove Program feature that comes with the operating system. Most programs are installed using an installation wizard that walks you through the installation. Other software programs may require you to activate the setup program, which then will begin the installation wizard. Using the Add or Remove Programs feature when uninstalling a program will help you ensure that all additional program files are removed from your computer.

Word Bank

- application software
- beta version
- freeware
- illustration software
- image editing software
- integrated help
- integrated software
- productivity software
- shareware
- software piracy
- software suite
- spreadsheet
- system requirements
- system software
- templates
- Web-based applications
- wizards
- word processing

Instructions: Fill in the blanks using the words from the Word Bank above.

Roxanne is so pumped! Her aunt is upgrading to a newer computer and is giving Roxanne her old one. Roxanne has just enrolled in college and knows she's going to need at least (1) a(n) _____ program to help her write papers and (2) a(n) _____ program to help her keep track of expenses while she is at school. Because both of these applications are part of a larger group of applications called (3) _____, she knows she can buy them as a group. She's been told that it's cheaper to buy them as (4) a(n) _____ than to buy them individually. Because she knows she'll need the stable, tested versions of the software, she cannot get by using (5) a(n) _____ of the program. Roxanne is also aware of many interesting (6) _____ that are available from the Internet and that she can access anywhere she has an Internet connection.

As a graduation present, Roxanne received a new digital camera. She needs to install the (7) _____ that came with her camera to edit and manage her digital pictures. Although she's used the software a couple of times on her parents' computer, she is still glad for the (8) _____ feature to assist her with specific feature-related questions and the (9) _____ that provide systematic guides to help her do things.

Roxanne especially likes the decorative preformatted (10) _____ she can use to insert pictures and make them seem professional. She also knows of some (11) _____ games she can download without cost from the Internet and other (12) _____ programs that she could try but eventually pay for. She found some really useful utility programs under the category of (13) _____ programs, which she can download for no charge and would like to install and try out. It's tempting for her to borrow software from her friends, but she knows that it's considered (14) _____. She also knows that before installing any of the programs she must check the (15) _____ to determine if the software is compatible with her system as well as whether the system has enough resources to support the software.

becoming computer literate

Using key terms from this chapter, write a letter to a new business owner advising them of the types of software they should get to help them run their company. Make sure you identify the type of business in the letter, and think of all possible software that would fit that specific type of business in addition to general business software that most businesses would require.

Instructions: Answer the multiple-choice and true–false questions below for more practice with key terms and concepts from this chapter.

Multiple Choice

1. The minimum set of recommended standards for a program is known as the
   a. operating system.
   b. system requirements.
   c. setup guide.
   d. installation specs.

2. Software that is freely distributed but comes with conditions is
   a. proprietary software.
   b. system software.
   c. freeware.
   d. shareware.

3. What type of software enables you to easily perform calculations and numerical analyses?
   a. Word processing   c. Presentation
   b. Spreadsheet   d. Database

4. Which is NOT an advantage of using a software suite?
   a. The cost is cheaper than buying programs individually.
   b. The programs provide for better integration.
   c. The programs integrate easily with programs from other software suites.
   d. The programs share common features such as toolbars.

5. The two primary types of software used with a computer are
   a. system software and word processing software.
   b. e-mail software and word processing software.
   c. application software and system software.
   d. Web browser and application software.

6. What kind of software is responsible for back office operations such as billing and inventory?
   a. Enterprise resource planning
   b. Project management
   c. Business accounting
   d. Personal information

7. Which of the following is true about open source software?
   a. The program code is confidential.
   b. The program can be changed and freely distributed.
   c. The program can be freely distributed as long as the program code is not changed.
   d. The program code is subject to copyright protection.

8. An example of free image editing software is
   a. Picasa.
   b. Illustrator.
   c. Photoshop Elements.
   d. iMovie

9. Which program incorporates a Wiki system and is good for collaboration?
   a. Word
   b. EverNote
   c. OneNote
   d. iWork

10. What is another name for Software as a Service (SaaS)?
    a. Web-based application
    b. ERP software
    c. Apps
    d. Software suite

True–False

_____ 1. A macro is a small program that groups a series of commands so that they run as a single command.

_____ 2. When you need help with software, you should use the program's help features or manufacturer FAQs, not online help like podcasts or YouTube videos.

_____ 3. System software includes the operating system and utility programs.

_____ 4. An integrated software application is a group of programs bundled as a package.

_____ 5. To remove a program you no longer want, it's better to delete it than uninstall it.

four

making the
transition to...
the workplace

making the
transition to...
the workplace

1. Surveying the Competition

You are asked to develop a departmental report that analyzes the key competitors in your market. You will need to take the following steps:

a. Identify the major competitors in your market.
b. Gather information on their companies, their sales, and the features of their products.
c. Organize your data so it can be easily sorted and filtered.
d. Analyze the trends in the marketplace and predict future direction of growth.
e. Create a final report and presentation to deliver to the department heads.

Identify what software products you would use to complete each of these tasks. How would you use them, and how would they work together to support your efforts?

2. Sharing Calendars

Microsoft Outlook is a great personal information management tool to organize your e-mail, tasks, and appointments. But what happens when you try to schedule a meeting with several people and need to coordinate calendars? It can be a nightmare. Research how you can share calendars through Google calendars and other online calendar sharing programs. What are the benefits of these applications? What can be the areas for concern?

3. Tracking Your Personal Finances

You are finally out on your own—graduated from college and working your first job. It's time to track how much you spend versus what you are earning. You really don't want to live from paycheck to paycheck, and want to begin a savings plan to build a rainy-day fund. Investigate online financial planning sites such as mint.com and yodlee.com and then choose the one that seems best to you. If you can, download a version of the software for your smartphone. Track your expenses for a few weeks, and identify areas in which you can cut back on your spending. What are the features of the software that you like? Discuss how this may or may not help you in your goal to financial independence.

4. Going Beyond PowerPoint

Your boss is tired of looking at presentations with the same designs and features and has asked you to research different presentation software packages. In particular, she has suggested you look into Prezi (**prezi.com**) and Sliderocket (**sliderocket.com**). Using one of these software applications (both have free trials), create a presentation that compares these two products to Microsoft PowerPoint, Apple Keynote, and OpenOffice.org Impress.

Instructions: Albert Einstein used *Gedankenexperiments*, or critical thinking questions, to develop his theory of relativity. Some ideas are best understood by experimenting with them in our own minds. The following critical thinking questions are designed to demand your full attention but require only a comfortable chair—no technology.

1. Selling After Upgrading

Several years ago you purchased Adobe Acrobat so you could make PDFs and edit and mark up PDFs. You have since changed computers, and your version of Acrobat is not compatible with the operating system on your new computer. You are required to purchase an upgrade of Adobe Acrobat to run on the new machine. Your sister wants to install the old version of Adobe Acrobat on her computer since you're not using it anymore. Do you think this will be legal to do? Why or why not?

2. What's Your App?

Small applications are being developed every day for smartphones. If you have a smartphone, what applications are the most useful to you? If you do not, what kind of app do you think would be the most useful? Describe an app that is currently not available that would be your "killer app."

3. Media Management

Less than a decade ago, most home users had few media files on their computer systems. Today, many users have a library of music, a collection of digitized movies, personal photo collections, and even a large set of recorded television shows. Examine three different software packages on the market today for managing these materials. What features do they need to make the PC the primary entertainment device for a home? What would make users move their PC from the office into the living room?

4. Software and Microcredit

The 2006 Nobel Peace Prize was awarded to Muhammad Yunus, who created the Grameen Bank. This bank makes quite small loans to the poor of Bangladesh, without requiring collateral. Often these loans are smaller than $200, but they allow women to begin small businesses and climb out of poverty. How has software made the Grameen Bank productive and able to serve almost 7 million borrowers? What other ways could software make a difference to the struggling peoples of the world?

5. Software for the Disabled

Think of the various issues people with disabilities have with interacting with the computer, such as using the mouse, reading the screen, typing on a keyboard, and listening to audio output. You learned about how speech recognition software can assist those who cannot use a keyboard. Describe other types of software solutions that are currently on the market, or that may not be on the market, that you believe would be useful to those with disabilities. Consider a range of disabilities, including physical and cognitive disabilities.

four team time

Software for Startups

Problem

You and your friends have decided to start Recycle Technology, a not-for-profit organization that would recycle and donate used computer equipment. In the first planning session, the group recognized the need for certain software to help them with various parts of the business such as tracking inventory, designing notices, mapping addresses for pickup and delivery, and soliciting residents by phone or e-mail about recycling events, to name a few.

Task

Split your class into as many groups of four or five as possible. Make some groups responsible for just locating free or Web-based software solutions, and other groups responsible for finding proprietary solutions. Another group could be responsible for finding mobile app solutions. The groups will present and compare results with each other at the end of the project.

Process

1. Identify a team leader who will coordinate the project and record and present results.
2. Each team is to identify the various kinds of software that Recycle Technology needs. Consider software that will be needed for all the various tasks needed to run the organization such as communication, marketing, tracking, inventory management and financial.
3. Create a detailed and organized list of required software applications. Depending on your team, you will either specify proprietary software or open source software.

Conclusion

Most organizations require a variety of software to accomplish different tasks. Compare your results with those of other team members. Were there applications that you didn't think about, but that other members did? How expensive is it to ensure that even the smallest company has all the software required to carry out daily activities, or can the needs be met with free, open source products?

Ethical conduct is a stream of decisions you make all day long. In this exercise, you will research and then role-play a complicated ethical situation. The role you play might or might not match your own personal beliefs; in either case, your research and use of logic will enable you to represent the view assigned. An arbitrator will watch and comment on both sides of the arguments, and together the team will agree on an ethical solution.

Topic: Open Source Software

Proprietary software has set restrictions on use and can be very expensive; while open source software is freely available for users to use as is, or change, improve, and redistribute. Open source software has become acceptable as a cost-effective alternative to proprietary software, so much so that it is reported that the increased adoption of open source software has caused a drop in revenue to the proprietary software industry. But there is more than just reducing the IT budget that is involved in determining which software to use.

Research Areas to Consider

- Open source software (Linux, OpenOffice.org suite, and Mozilla.org)
- Proprietary software (Microsoft Windows and Office, Apple Mac OS and iWork)
- Copyright licensing
- Open source development

Process

Divide the class into teams.

1. Research the areas cited above and devise a scenario in which someone is a proponent for open source software but is being rebuffed by a someone who feels "you get what you pay for" and is a big proponent of using proprietary software.

2. Team members should write a summary that provides background information for their character—for example: open source proponent, proprietary developer, or arbitrator—and details their character's behaviors to set the stage for the role-playing event. Then, team members should create an outline to use during the role-playing event.

3. Team members should arrange a mutually convenient time to meet for the exchange, either using the collaboration features of MyITLab, the discussion board feature of Blackboard, or meeting in person.

4. Team members should present their case to the class, or submit a PowerPoint presentation for review by the rest of the class, along with the summary and resolution they developed.

Conclusion

As technology becomes ever more prevalent and integrated into our lives, more and more ethical dilemmas will present themselves. Being able to understand and evaluate both sides of the argument, while responding in a personally or socially ethical manner, will be an important skill.

chapter

five
using system software:

the operating system, utility programs, and file management

objectives

objectives

After reading this chapter, you should be able to answer the following questions:

1. What software is included in system software? *(pp. 208–209)*
2. What are the different kinds of operating systems? *(pp. 209–210)*
3. What are the most common operating systems? *(pp. 210–214)*
4. How does the operating system provide a means for users to interact with the computer? *(pp. 214–215)*
5. How does the operating system help manage resources such as the processor, memory, storage, hardware, and peripheral devices? *(pp. 215–219)*
6. How does the operating system interact with application software? *(pp. 220–221)*
7. How does the operating system help the computer start up? *(pp. 221–224)*
8. What are the main desktop and window features? *(pp. 224–227)*
9. How does the operating system help me keep my computer organized? *(pp. 227–232)*
10. What utility programs are included in system software, and what do they do? *(pp. 232–241)*

multimedia resources

multimedia resources

Active Helpdesk

- Managing Hardware and Peripheral Devices: The OS **(p. 221)**
- Starting the Computer: The Boot Process **(p. 223)**
- Organizing Your Computer: File Management **(p. 232)**
- Using Utility Programs **(p. 237)**

Sound Bytes

- Customizing Windows **(p. 212)**
- File Management **(p. 230)**
- File Compression **(p. 234)**
- Hard Disk Anatomy Interactive **(p. 239)**
- Letting Your Computer Clean Up After Itself **(p. 240)**

Companion Website

The Companion Website includes a variety of additional materials to help you review and learn more about the topics in this chapter. Go to: ***pearsonhighered.com/techinaction***

how cool is *this?* Have you ever wanted to capture what appears on your **monitor screen**? You can use the PrtScr (print screen) key on your keyboard, but that captures the entire screen, and only onto the clipboard. You then need to crop and save the file for that **screen capture** to be useful. There are also screen capture software programs that you can purchase. However, Windows 7 includes a **Snipping Tool** to capture an entire screen image or to take a freeform or rectangular "snip" of any window or object on the screen. Once snipped, you can **annotate**, save, or **share** the object. You can find the Snipping Tool by clicking the Start button, selecting All Programs, and then opening the Accessories folder. **Jing** (**jingproject.com**), a freeware tool from TechSmith, not only captures still screen shots, but also records video of on-screen action. You can share Jing files over the Web, via instant messaging, or e-mail.

System Software Basics

As you learned in the last chapter, there are two basic types of software on your computer: application software and system software. **Application software** is the software you use to do everyday tasks at home and at work. **System software** is the set of programs that helps run the computer and coordinates instructions between application software and the computer's hardware devices. From the moment you turn on your computer to the time you shut it down, you are interacting with system software. System software consists of two primary types of programs: the operating system and utility programs.

What does an operating system do? The **operating system (OS)** is a group of programs that controls how your computer system functions. The OS manages the computer's hardware, including the processor (also called the *central processing unit*, or *CPU*), memory, and storage devices, as well as peripheral devices such as the monitor and printer. The OS also provides a consistent means for software applications to work with the CPU, and it is responsible for the management, scheduling, and coordination of tasks as well as system maintenance. Your first interaction with the OS is the user interface—the features of the program such as the desktop, icons, and menus that allow the user to communicate with the computer system.

System software also includes utility programs. A **utility program** is a small program that performs many of the general housekeeping tasks for the computer, such as system maintenance and file compression.

Do all computers have operating systems? Every computer, from the smallest notebook to the largest supercomputer, has an operating system. Even cell phones, game consoles, automobiles, and some appliances have operating systems. The role of the OS is critical; the computer cannot operate without it. As explained more fully in the section of this chapter titled "What the Operating System Does," the operating system coordinates the flow of data and information through the computer system by coordinating the hardware, software, user interface, processor, and system memory.

"Every computer has an operating system."

Are all operating systems alike? Although most computer users can name only a few operating systems, many types exist. Some operating systems, such as those found in household appliances and car engines, don't require any user intervention at all. Some are proprietary systems developed specifically for the devices they manage. Some operating systems are available for personal and business use, and other operating systems coordinate resources for many users on a network. These operating systems were traditionally classified into categories, depending on the number of users they served (single user or multiple users) and the tasks they performed (single task or multitask). However, as devices begin to converge in their functionalities, and the operating systems continue to become more powerful, the distinction in the traditional categorization of operating systems begins to blur (see Figure 5.1).

For example, personal computers were at one time run by single-task, single-user operating systems such as the **Microsoft Disk Operating System (MS-DOS)**. MS-DOS (or DOS) was the first widely installed operating system in personal computers. Compared to the operating systems we are familiar with today, DOS was a highly user-unfriendly OS. To use it, you needed to type specific commands, and didn't have the option to click on **icons** (pictures that represent an object such as a software application or a file or folder) or choose from menus or lists.

Eventually, operating systems such as Apple's Mac OS and Microsoft's Windows replaced DOS because these systems allowed a single user to **multitask**, or to perform more than one process at a time. (The Mac and Windows operating systems are discussed in more detail later in this chapter.)

Then, networking capabilities were added to these personal computer operating systems to facilitate sharing peripheral devices and Internet access among multiple computers at home. These systems, while still traditionally used as single-user, multitask operating systems, technically became multiuser, multitask operating systems because of their networking capabilities. Similar transitions are happening with mobile devices, as cell phones and PDAs (personal digital assistants) converge to

Figure 5.1

Devices no longer fit neatly into categories of operating systems, which traditionally were defined by the number of users (single or multiple) and the number of simultaneous tasks the device was able to perform (single or multiple).

Multitask

Single-user ← → Multiuser

Personal computers

Notebooks and netbooks

Home servers

Mainframes

Tablets

Smartphones

Cameras, e-book readers personal media players

Game consoles

Single-task

smartphones and incorporate the functionalities of cameras and personal media players. Although smartphones were initially single-task devices, with combined functionalities, the newer devices are beginning to add multitasking capabilities.

In the next section, we will look at different types of operating systems that work with a variety of computers.

Types of Operating Systems

Operating systems can be categorized by the type of device in which they are installed, such as robots and specialized equipment, mainframes and network computers, mobile devices, and personal computers.

Real-Time Operating Systems

Why do machines with built-in computers need an operating system? Machinery that is required to perform a repetitive series of specific tasks in an exact amount of time requires a **real-time operating system (RTOS)**. Real-time operating systems, also referred to as *embedded systems*, require minimal user interaction. The programs are written specifically for the needs of the devices and their functions. Therefore, there are no commercially available standard RTOS software programs. This type of operating system is a program with a specific purpose, and it must guarantee certain response times for particular computing tasks; otherwise, the machine is useless. Devices that must perform regimented tasks or record precise results—such as measurement instruments found in the scientific, defense, and aerospace industries—require real-time operating systems. Examples include digital storage oscilloscopes and the Mars Reconnaissance Orbiter.

Where else are RTOSs in use today? You also encounter real-time operating systems in everyday life. They are in devices such as fuel-injection systems in car engines, inkjet printers, VoIP phones, and some medical devices (see Figure 5.2), as well as common appliances such as washing machines, dryers, and furnaces. Real-time operating systems are also found in many

Figure 5.2

Devices such as some cars, washing machines, VoIP phones, and printers use real-time operating systems.

types of robotic equipment. Television stations use robotic cameras with real-time operating systems that glide across a suspended cable system to record sports events from many angles.

What kind of operating system controls a simple cell phone? Simple cell phones are separate, single-function devices; they only require operating systems that perform one task at a time. Cell phones have their own proprietary embedded operating systems.

Operating Systems for Networks, Servers, and Mainframes

What kind of operating system do networks use? A **multiuser operating system** (also known as a **network operating system**) enables more than one user to access the computer system at one time by efficiently handling and prioritizing requests from multiple users. Networks (groups of computers connected to each other for the purposes of communicating and sharing resources) require a multiuser operating system because many users simultaneously access the **server**, which is the computer on a network that manages network resources such as printers.

The latest versions of Microsoft Windows and Mac OS X can be considered network operating systems; they enable users to set up networks in homes and small businesses. (A more complete discussion of Microsoft Windows and Mac OS can be found in the "Operating Systems for Personal Computers" section.) In larger networks, a network operating system is installed on the server and manages all user requests, ensuring they do not interfere with each other. For example, on a network where users share a printer, the printer can produce only one document at a time. The OS is therefore responsible for managing all the printer requests and making sure they are processed one at a time. Examples of network operating systems include Linux and UNIX.

What is UNIX? UNIX is a multiuser, multitask operating system used as a network operating system, primarily with mainframes, although it is also often found on PCs. Developed in 1969 by Ken Thompson and Dennis Ritchie of AT&T's Bell Labs, the UNIX code was initially not proprietary—in other words, no company owned it. Rather, any programmer was allowed to use the code and modify it to meet his or her needs. Later, AT&T licensed the UNIX program code to the Santa Cruz Operation Group. UNIX is a brand that belongs to the company The Open Group, but any vendor that meets testing requirements and pays a fee can use the UNIX name. Individual vendors then modify the UNIX code to run specifically on their hardware. HP/UX from Hewlett-Packard, Solaris from Sun, and AIX from IBM are some of the UNIX systems currently available in the marketplace.

What other kinds of computers require a multiuser operating system? Large corporations with hundreds or thousands of employees often use powerful computers known as *mainframes*. A **mainframe** is responsible for storing, managing, and simultaneously processing data from all users. Mainframe operating systems fall into the multiuser category. Examples include UNIX and IBM's IBM i and z/OS.

Supercomputers also use multiuser operating systems. Scientists and engineers use supercomputers to solve complex problems or to perform massive computations. Some supercomputers are single computers with multiple processors, whereas others consist of multiple computers that work together.

Operating Systems for Mobile Devices

What kind of operating system do smartphones use? A smartphone does more than let the user make and answer phone calls. It also has productivity features, in addition to features found on personal media players and cameras as well as the ability to connect to the Web. Examples of smartphones include BlackBerry devices, Apple's iPhone, Google Android, and Palm Pre. Initially, although multifunctional, smartphones were only capable of doing one task at a time. Now most modern smartphones have modest multitasking capabilities such as checking e-mail while on a phone call. The most common operating systems that can be found on smartphones include Symbian by Nokia, BlackBerry by RIM, Windows Mobile by Microsoft, iPhone OS X by Apple, Android by Google, and webOS by Palm. The newest versions of the iPhone's OS X and the Palm Pre's webOS enable the user to run more than one application concurrently.

Figure 5.3

Gaming devices such as the Nintendo Wii and PlayStation 3 have their own system software.

Do gaming consoles and personal media players require an operating system? Gaming systems, like Microsoft's Xbox 360, the Nintendo Wii, and the Sony PlayStation (see Figure 5.3), as well as personal media players like Microsoft's Zune, Apple's iPod, and SanDisk's Sansa, all require some form of customized system software that is developed specifically for the particular device. The system software includes system programs—also known as **firmware**—that control the device, as well as other programs that come with the personal media player or the gaming device. For example, the programs included with most portable media players allow users to manage music files on the player and to rip audio CDs. The operating systems on gaming consoles support Web browsing and file storage of media and photos as well as playing DVDs and games.

Operating Systems for Personal Computers

What is the Microsoft Windows operating system? Microsoft **Windows** began as an operating environment that worked with MS-DOS and incorporated a user-friendly interface like the one that was first introduced with Apple's operating system. In 1995, Microsoft released Windows 95, a comprehensive update that made changes to the user interface and incorporated multitasking capabilities. Windows XP was another major update; it provided networking capabilities in its consumer editions. The newest release of Microsoft's operating system, **Windows 7**, follows Windows Vista, and builds on the security and user interface upgrades that the Windows Vista release provided. It also gives users with touch-screen monitors the ability to use touch commands to scroll, resize windows, pan, and zoom. What was once only an operating system on which only one user could perform one task at a time, Windows is now a powerful operating system that can support simple networking tasks. Over time, Windows improvements have concentrated on increasing user functionality and friendliness, improving Internet capabilities, and enhancing file privacy and security.

What is the difference between the various editions of Windows 7 operating systems? With each new version of its operating system, Microsoft continues to make improvements. However, it's still not a one-size-fits-all operating system. Windows 7 comes in several editions to accommodate different users: home users (Starter, Home Basic, Home Premium), business users (Professional and Enterprise), and combination users (Ultimate). In addition, there are 32-bit and 64-bit versions of Windows. The 32-bit version is built for computers that have up to 4 GB of RAM. For those systems with more than 4 GB of

Figure 5.4 | WINDOWS 7 EDITIONS

Edition	Description
Windows 7 Starter	This edition is designed to run on small netbooks and is for those users who have basic computing requirements. There is no Aero interface, and only 32-bit versions are available.
Windows 7 Home Premium	This edition incorporates multimedia functions as core components. No extra software is needed to run DVDs and other audio and video files. Networking as well as file and peripheral sharing across PCs are included.
Windows 7 Professional	As its name implies, this edition is aimed at the business market but is also appropriate for the advanced home user. This edition builds on Windows 7 Home Premium and features advanced networking capabilities.
Windows 7 Ultimate	This is the "ultimate" operating system for high-end PC users, gamers, multimedia professionals, and PC enthusiasts.

RAM, a 64-bit version is required. Figure 5.4 outlines the features and benefits of each edition of Windows 7.

What is the Mac Operating System?   In 1984, **Mac OS** became the first commercially available operating system to incorporate a graphical user interface (GUI) with user-friendly point-and-click technology. For more information on Mac OS, see the Technology in Focus feature "Computing Alternatives" on page 252.

Does it matter what operating system is on my computer?   The type of processor in the computer determines which operating system a particular personal computer uses. The combination of operating system and processor is referred to as a computer's **platform**. For example, Microsoft Windows operating systems are designed to coordinate with a series of processors from Intel Corporation and Advanced Micro Devices (AMD), which share the same or similar sets of instructions. Until a few years ago, the Macintosh operating systems worked primarily with processors from the Motorola Corporation and IBM, which were designed specifically for Apple computers. Now Intel also makes processors for Apple computers.

Yet even if both computers have processors from the same manufacturer, the two operating systems (Windows and Mac OS) are not really interchangeable. Without using special software, if you attempted to load Microsoft Windows on a Mac, for example, the processor in the Mac would not understand the Windows OS and would not

function properly. A utility called Boot Camp, available with the newest version Mac OS X Snow Leopard, allows you to run Windows on a Mac while also running OS X. Most application software is also platform dependent. For example, there are special Mac versions of Microsoft Office, Adobe Photoshop Elements, Intuit Quicken, and other "traditional" PC software applications.

Despite their inability to run the same software applications, PCs and Macs can be networked so that both types of computers can easily share files and even peripherals, such as printers, scanners, and cameras.

Can I have more than one operating system on my computer?   If you are unsure whether you want to upgrade to the next edition of your current operating system, you might want to consider taking the newest edition for a test drive. Or perhaps you would like to have a Linux distribution to work with, in addition to your Windows operating system. Even some Mac users may want to also run Windows on their machines. Although it might seem impossible to run more than one operating system on a single computer, the generous size of the hard drives, in addition to some additional software capabilities, enable users to do just that: run multiple versions of operating systems on a single machine. In the case of running two versions of Windows, or a Windows–Linux setup, you just need to separate the hard drive into different sections (called *partitions*) and install the second operating system in the new partition.

What is Linux?   **Linux** is an open source operating system designed for use on personal computers and as a network operating system. Open source software is freely available for developers to use or modify as they wish. The Linux operating system is based on the central programming code of an operating system, and the rest of the code is from the GNU (pronounced "g-noo") Project and other sources. Linux began in

SOUND BYTE

Customizing Windows

In this Sound Byte, you'll find out how to customize your desktop. You'll learn how to configure the desktop, set up a screen saver, change pointer options, customize the Start menu, and manage user accounts.

Emerging Technologies: Open Source Software—
Why Isn't Everyone Using Linux?

Proprietary software such as Microsoft Windows and Mac OS is developed by corporations and sold for profit. This means that the **source code**, the actual lines of instructional code that make the program work, is not accessible to the general public. Without being able to access the source code, it's difficult for a user to modify the software or see exactly how the program author constructed various parts of the system.

Restricting access to the source code protects companies from having their programming ideas stolen, and it prevents customers from using modified versions of the software. However, in the late 1980s, computer specialists became concerned that large software companies (such as Microsoft) were controlling a large portion of market share and driving out competitors. They also felt that proprietary software was too expensive and contained too many bugs (errors).

These people felt that software should be developed without a profit motive and distributed with its source code free for all to see. The theory was that if many computer specialists examined, improved, and changed the source code, a more full-featured, bug-free product would result. Hence, the open source movement was born.

Open source software is freely distributed (no royalties accrue to the creators), contains the source code, and can in turn be redistributed freely to others. Most open source products are created by teams of programmers and are modified (updated) by hundreds of other programmers around the world. You can download open source products for free from the Internet. Linux is probably the most widely recognized name in open source software, but other products such as MySQL (a database program) and OpenOffice.org (a suite of productivity applications) are also gaining in popularity.

So, if an operating system such as Linux is free, why does Windows (which users must pay for) have such a huge market share (nearly 92 percent), and why does Linux have less than 1 percent of the desktop

market? One reason is that corporations and individuals have grown accustomed to one thing that proprietary software makers can provide: technical support. It is almost impossible to provide technical support for open source software because anyone can freely modify it; thus, there is no specific developer to take responsibility for technical support (see Figure 5.5). Similarly, corporations have been reluctant to install open source software extensively because of the cost of the internal staff of programmers that must support it.

Companies such as Red Hat have been combating this problem. Red Hat offers a free, open source operating system called Fedora. In addition, Red Hat has modified the original Linux source code and markets a version, Red Hat Enterprise Linux, as a proprietary program. Fedora is the testing ground for what eventually goes into this proprietary program.

Red Hat Enterprise Linux 6 is the current system on the market, and comes in versions for servers and desktops. Purchasers of Red Hat Enterprise Linux receive a warranty and technical support. Packaging open source software in this manner has made its use much more attractive to businesses. As a result, many Web servers are hosted on computers running Linux.

When will free versions of Linux (or another open source operating system) be the dominant OSs on home computers? The answer is, maybe never. Most casual computer users won't feel comfortable without technical support; therefore, any open source products for home use will need to be marketed the way Red Hat markets Enterprise Linux. In addition, many open source products are not easy to maintain.

Figure 5.5

Companies like Ubuntu and Xandros provide free (or low-cost) Linux software, but users must purchase technical support.

However, some companies are making easy-to-use visual interfaces, such as GNOME and KDE, which work with the Linux operating system. If one of these companies can develop an easy-to-use product and has the marketing power to challenge Microsoft, you may see more open source OSs deployed in the home computer market in the future.

1991 as a part-time project of Finnish university student Linus Torvalds, who wanted to create a free OS to run on his home computer. He posted his OS code to the Web for others to use and modify. It has since been tweaked by scores of programmers as part of the Free Software Foundation GNU Project (**gnu.org**).

Linux is gaining a reputation as a stable OS that is not subject to crashes or failures. Because the code is open and available to

anyone, Linux can be tweaked quickly to meet virtually any new operating system need. For example, only a few weeks were necessary to get the Linux OS ready for the Intel Xeon processor, a feat unheard of in proprietary OS development. Some Linux-based operating systems have been modified to run on iPods and gaming systems. Linux is also gaining popularity among computer manufacturers, which have begun to ship it with some of their latest PCs.

Where else is Linux used? Android, the new operating system developed by Google, is Linux-based. Because the overall size of Android is much smaller than that of Windows, many netbook users choose to use it in place of the factory-installed Windows operating system (see Figure 5.6). Another Linux-based newcomer to the OS market is MeeGo, a joint project between Nokia and Intel.

Where can I get Linux? You can download open source versions of Linux for free from the Internet. These free, open source Linux distributors include Mandriva, Ubuntu, Fedora, Suse, Debian GNU/Linux, and Gentoo Linux. However, several versions of Linux are more proprietary in

Figure 5.6

Developed by Google, the new Android operating system is based on Linux and runs easily on netbooks.

nature and must be purchased. These versions come with support and other features that are not generally associated with the open source Linux. Red Hat has been packaging and selling versions of Linux since 1994 and is probably the best-known Linux distributor. For a full listing and explanation of all Linux distributors, visit Distrowatch (**distrowatch.com**). For more information on Linux, see the Technology in Focus feature "Computing Alternatives" on page 252.

What the Operating System Does

As shown in Figure 5.7, the operating system is like a traffic cop. It coordinates and directs the flow of data and information through the computer system. In doing so, the OS performs several specific functions:

- It provides a way for the user to interact with the computer.
- It manages the processor, or CPU.
- It manages the memory and storage.
- It manages the computer system's hardware and peripheral devices.
- It provides a consistent means for software applications to work with the CPU.

In this section, we look at each of these functions in detail.

The User Interface

How does the operating system control how I interact with my computer? The operating system provides a **user interface** that enables you to interact with the computer. As noted earlier, the first

Figure 5.7

The operating system is the traffic cop of your computer, coordinating its many activities and devices.

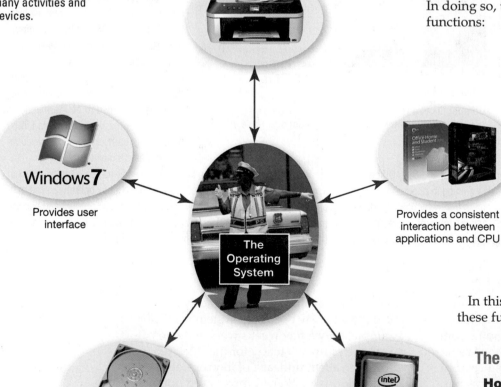

Manages computer hardware and peripherals.

Provides user interface

The Operating System

Provides a consistent interaction between applications and CPU

Manages memory and storage

Manages processor

personal computers had a DOS operating system with a command-driven interface, as shown in Figure 5.8. A **command-driven interface** is one in which you enter commands to communicate with the computer system. The DOS commands were not always easy to understand; as a result, the interface proved to be too complicated for the average user. Therefore, PCs were used primarily in business and by professional computer operators.

The command-driven interface was later improved by incorporating a menu-driven interface, as shown in Figure 5.8. A **menu-driven interface** is one in which you choose commands from menus displayed on the screen. Menu-driven interfaces eliminated the need for users to know every command because they could select most of the commonly used commands from a menu. However, they were still not easy enough for most people to use.

What kind of interface do operating systems use today? Current personal computer operating systems such as Microsoft Windows and Mac OS use a **graphical user interface**, or **GUI** (pronounced "gooey"). Unlike the command- and menu-driven interfaces used earlier, GUIs display graphics and use the point-and-click technology of the mouse and cursor, making them much more user-friendly.

Unlike Windows or Mac OS, Linux does not have a single default GUI interface. Instead, users are free to choose among many commercially available and free interfaces, such as GNOME and KDE, each of which provides a different look and feel. For example, GNOME (pronounced "gah-NOHM")

A Web-Based Operating System

Now that broadband Internet access is becoming commonplace, the concept of a more universal operating system, called a *Web-based OS*, is being discussed, and some prototype sites are in their infancy. So what is a Web-based operating system? Actually, the terms *Web-based operating environment* or *portable desktop* might be more accurate. The concept behind this movement is to make the Web the primary application interface through which users can view content, manage data, and use various services (calendars, e-mail, and picture sharing and storage) on their local machine and on the Web without noticing any difference between interfaces.

Currently, most applications we use have been installed on a specific computer and can be used only on that computer. A Web-based operating environment would allow users access to applications and content via the Web, regardless of the machine they are using. This means business travelers would not need to lug their notebooks everywhere they went. Instead, they would only need to find a computer that had Internet access to be able to work on documents, see their calendar, read their e-mail, and so on. All of their settings and preferences, even a customized desktop image, as well as working documents, could be stored in an individual Web-based account for them to access anywhere and on any machine at any time. Google is the closest to having a complete Web-based system. Its Google Docs application and Chrome browser are the initial components of a completely Web-based operating environment, which is expected to come out by 2011. Because security measures have not been completely worked out, it's advisable that Web-based accounts not be used to store or manipulate personal or proprietary data and information. For more information, or to open your own account, check out the Web sites of the current Web-based OS innovators, including Google, eyeOS (**eyeos.org**), and GoGUI (**gogui.com**).

actually allows you to select which interface (Windows or Mac) you'd like your system to have. This means that if you're using Linux for the first time, you don't have to learn a new interface; you just use the one you're most comfortable with already.

Processor Management

Why does the operating system need to manage the processor? When you use your computer, you are usually asking the CPU to perform several tasks at once. For example, you might be

Figure 5.8

(a) A command-driven interface. (b) A menu-driven interface.

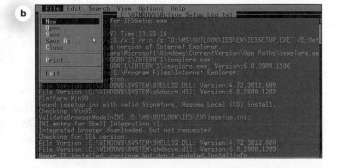

Sugar—The Sweet OS for Every Child

The Internet is a fantastic tool, but only if you can access it. In an effort to give children in developing countries a better opportunity to "learn, share, and create," the One Laptop per Child (OLPC) initiative was founded by Nicholas Negroponte and other faculty from MIT Media Lab, in conjunction with partners such as Google, AMD, and News Corporation. The mission of OLPC (**laptop.org**) is to ensure that all school-aged children in lesser-developed communities receive their own personal computers so that they are no longer excluded from the educational, economic, and entertainment benefits that computers can provide. Laptops have been distributed to children in areas and countries such as the South Pacific, Uruguay, Mongolia, Nigeria, Ethiopia, and Rwanda.

This ambitious project to develop and distribute a low-cost notebook computer (currently, the cost is $199) would provide access to electronic textbooks and other learning aids—and eventually the Internet. The project has expanded to include a wide variety of professionals from academia, business, the arts, and technology. The main thrust of the project is to overcome the so-called digital divide (the gap between people who have access to com-

puters and those who don't) and provide computing resources to everyone regardless of their financial means.

The notebook itself is revolutionary in design (see Figure 5.9). Called the XO-1, the notebook is small and has a comfortable, child-sized, built-in handle. It also has a tablet-like monitor that can twist to turn the notebook into an electronic book (e-book) reader, which is critical in areas where books are hard to come by. The outside of the notebook is rugged and child-friendly. In addition, it is power efficient, running on less than one-tenth the power a standard notebook requires. Because access to electricity is minimal in many of the project's target areas, the notebook is self-powered by an easy-to-use pull-string.

At the core of the project is Sugar, the operating system. It is based on open source code components from Red Hat's Fedora version of the Linux operating system, but has a user interface that is completely different from Windows, Mac OS, or Linux. Credit goes to the developers, who really thought about how the users of the notebook would interact with the device. The OLPC notebooks will most likely be the first computer that many of these children use. Because children have no idea of what to do with the machine and may not have anyone to tell them, the user interface was designed to be as intuitive as possible.

Figure 5.9

The revolutionary design of the XO-1 notebook is rugged yet child-friendly. The XO-1 can be easily converted from a traditional notebook to an e-book. It is extremely power-efficient but can also be self-powered.

---

printing a Word document, chatting with your friends on Facebook, watching a movie using the Blu-ray drive, and working on an Excel spreadsheet—all at the same time, or at least what appears to be at the same time. Although the processor is the powerful brain of the computer, processing all of its instructions and performing all of its calculations, it needs the OS to arrange for the execution of all these activities in a systematic way, creating the appearance that everything is happening simultaneously.

To do so, the operating system assigns a slice of its time to each activity that requires the processor's attention. The OS must then switch among different processes millions of times a second to make it appear that every-

thing is happening seamlessly. Otherwise, you wouldn't be able to watch a movie and print at the same time without experiencing delays in the process.

How exactly does the operating system coordinate all the activities? When you create and print a document in Word while also watching a Blu-ray movie, for example, many different devices in the computer system are involved, including your keyboard, mouse, Blu-ray drive, and printer. Every keystroke, every mouse click, and each signal to the printer and from the Blu-ray drive creates an action, or **event**, in the respective device (keyboard, mouse, Blu-ray drive, or printer) to which the operating system responds.

The operating system focuses on activities rather than on applications. When the machine powers up, the first image is that of the XO man (an O on top of an X) in the middle of a circle. It is surrounded by icons that represent home, friends, and neighborhood. The computer includes a built-in microphone and webcam for children to create their own multimedia. For example, the multimedia tool allows children to add music to their drawings. Other activities include browsing the Internet, chatting, text editing, and playing games. At the core of each activity is the ability to collaborate, which facilitates the community learning experience. To enhance collaboration, the notebooks are all interconnected in a wireless mesh network, providing the potential for every activity to be a networked activity. Browsing, for example, would no longer be an isolated, individual activity; it could also be a collaborative group experience (see Figure 5.10a). Wireless capabilities also help extend the community beyond its physical borders. These computers make it possible for a child in Africa, for example, to connect with another child in Europe.

In addition, the operating system uses a journaling technique for arranging and organizing files (see Figure 5.10b). The file system records what the child has done (rather than just what the student has saved), working as a scrapbook of the student's interactions with the computer as well as with peers. The journal can be tagged, searched, and sorted in a variety of ways.

Another general concept behind the operating system is that children learn through doing, so the software puts an emphasis on tools for exploration and expression, as well as encouraging students to learn by helping each other. Because Sugar is built on an open source platform, it also encourages students to explore how it works and to modify the code to meet their individual preferences.

The OLPC is not the only organization interested in increasing the reach of technology to those in less-developed nations. Intel has gone forward with its own program and produced the Classmate PC. Although the Classmate PC is more closely aligned with the traditional Windows-based PC model—it runs on either Windows or the open source OS Mandriva

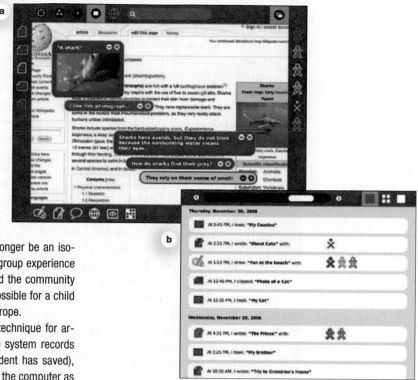

Figure 5.10

(a) One student shares a browsing experience with several others.
(b) The journaling system chronicles what the student saves as well as the student's interaction with the machine and with others.

Discovery 2007 (a version of Linux)—it offers some of the same user-friendly hardware features as the XO-1 machine does, such as the swivel monitor that converts to a tablet PC. Some reviewers and followers of both projects have offered the opinion that the Classmate PC is better suited for the older student user, whereas the XO-1 laptop is geared toward a younger, less sophisticated user. With so many children waiting to be exposed to technology and to a more fun and intuitive learning process, there is most likely room in the market for both machines.

Sometimes these events occur sequentially (such as when you type characters one at a time), but other events involve two or more devices working concurrently (such as the printer printing while you continue to type and watch a movie). Although it looks as though the keyboard, Blu-ray drive, and printer are working at the same time, in fact, the OS switches back and forth among processes, controlling the timing of events the processor works on.

For example, assume you are typing and want to print a document. When you tell your computer to print your document, the printer generates a unique signal called an **interrupt** that tells the operating system that it is in need of immediate attention. Every device has its own type of interrupt, which is associated with an **interrupt handler**, a special numerical code that prioritizes the requests. These requests are placed in the interrupt table in the computer's primary memory (random access memory, or RAM). The operating system processes the task assigned a higher priority before processing a task that has been assigned a lower priority. This is called **preemptive multitasking**.

In our example, when it receives the interrupt from the printer, the operating system pauses the CPU from its typing activity and from the Blu-ray activity, and puts a "memo" in a special location in RAM called a *stack*. The memo is a reminder of what the CPU was doing before it started to work on the printer request. The CPU then retrieves the printer request from the interrupt table and begins to process it. On completion of the printer request, the CPU goes back to the stack, retrieves the memo it placed about the keystroke or Blu-ray activity, and returns to that task until it is interrupted again, in a very quick and seamless fashion.

What happens if there is more than one document waiting to be printed? The operating system also coordinates multiple activities for peripheral devices such as printers. When the processor receives a request to send information to the printer, it first checks with the operating system to ensure that the printer is not already in use. If it is, the OS puts the request in another temporary storage area in RAM, called the *buffer*. The request then waits in the buffer until the **spooler**, a program that helps coordinate all print jobs currently being sent to the printer, indicates the printer is available. If more than one print job is waiting, a line (or *queue*) is formed so that the printer can process the requests in order.

Memory and Storage Management

Why does the operating system have to manage the computer's memory? As the operating system coordinates the activities of the processor, it uses RAM as a temporary storage area for instructions and data the processor needs. The processor then accesses these instructions and data from RAM when it is ready to process them. The OS is therefore responsible for coordinating the space allocations in RAM to ensure that there is enough space for all of the pending instructions and data. It then clears the items from RAM when the processor no longer needs them.

Does the amount of RAM on a system control the type of OS I get? Until recently, the maximum amount of RAM found on most personal computers was 4 GB. That was considered a lot! Now, many personal computer systems that are reasonably priced provide for 8 GB or more of RAM. Systems that offer 4 GB or more of RAM will feature a 64-bit version of Windows. Although there are other factors

> **"You will likely find that the amount of RAM you once found to be sufficient is no longer enough."**

involved in determining what operating system you get, determining the bit-version is important. At the moment, not all applications and devices are compatible with 64-bit systems. If you purchase a 64-bit system, you will need to make sure that all your hardware and software programs are updated to work well with the 64-bit version of your operating system. To assist you in this process, Microsoft has created the Windows 7 Upgrade Advisor. This downloadable free program checks to determine whether your computer is compatible in all respects with Windows 7, including the 64-bit compatibility. If there is incompatibility, Windows 7 allows you the option of running in a compatibility mode to emulate a 32-bit system.

Can my system ever run out of RAM? RAM has limited capacity. Like most users, over time you will expand how you use your computer by adding new software and new peripherals. Most computers sold for home use have between 2 and 12 GB of RAM. If you have an older system with 1 or 2 GB of RAM, it might be sufficient if you're running a few programs at the same time. But, if you start installing and using software with greater RAM requirements (such as Photoshop), your system might not respond well. For example, if you want to upgrade to Windows 7, the minimum requirement for the operating system using minimal capabilities is 1 GB of RAM. Such limited RAM requirements are fine if you are using a netbook that is running Windows 7 Starter edition. However, most other systems that run more robust editions of Windows 7 may be challenged if they have only 1 GB of RAM, especially if you run graphic-intensive programs such as Adobe Photoshop, many gaming applications, or even the latest version of Microsoft Office. If you want to incorporate the translucent Aero user interface themes that are available in some versions of Windows 7, your system should have at least 2 GB of RAM and a video card with at least 256 MB of RAM. As you add and upgrade software and increase your usage of the computer system, you will likely find that the amount of RAM you once found to be sufficient is no longer enough.

What happens if my computer runs out of RAM?

When there isn't enough RAM for the operating system to store the required data and instructions, the operating system borrows from the more spacious hard drive. This process of optimizing RAM storage by borrowing hard drive space is called **virtual memory**. As shown in Figure 5.11, when more RAM is needed, the operating system swaps out from RAM the data or instructions that have not been recently used and moves them to a temporary storage area on the hard drive called the **swap file** (or **page file**). If the data or instructions in the swap file are needed later, the operating system swaps them back into active RAM and replaces them in the hard drive's swap file with less active data or instructions. This process of swapping is known as **paging**.

Can I ever run out of virtual memory?

Only a portion of the hard drive is allocated to virtual memory. You can manually change this setting to increase the amount of hard drive space allocated, but eventually your computer system will become sluggish as it is forced to page more and more often. This condition of excessive paging is called **thrashing**. The solution to this problem is to increase the amount of RAM in your system so that it will not be necessary for it to send data and instructions to virtual memory.

How does the operating system manage storage?

If it weren't for the operating system, the files and applications you save to the hard drive and other storage locations would be an unorganized mess. Fortunately, the OS has a file-management system that keeps track of the name and location of each file you save and the programs you install. We will talk more about file management later in the chapter.

Hardware and Peripheral Device Management

How does the operating system manage the hardware and peripheral devices?

Each device attached to your computer comes with a special program called a **device driver** that facilitates communication between the hardware device and the operating system. Because the OS must be able to communicate with every device in the computer system, the device driver translates the device's specialized commands into commands that the operating system can understand, and vice versa. Devices would not function without the proper device drivers because the OS would not know how to communicate with them.

Do I always need to install drivers?

Today, most devices, such as flash drives, mice, keyboards, and many digital cameras, come with the driver already installed in Windows. The devices whose drivers are included in Windows are called Plug and Play devices. **Plug and Play (PnP)** is a software and hardware standard that Microsoft created with the Windows 95 OS. PnP is designed to facilitate the installation of new hardware in PCs by including in the OS the drivers these devices need in order to run. Because the OS includes this software, incorporating a new device into your computer system seems automatic. Plug and Play enables users to plug a new device into a port on the system unit, turn on the computer, and immediately play (use) the device. The OS automatically recognizes the device and its driver without any further user manipulations of the system.

What happens if the device is not Plug and Play?

Some current devices, such as many types of printers and many older devices are not Plug and Play. When you install a non–PnP device, you will be prompted to insert the driver that was provided with the device. If you obtain a non–PnP device secondhand and do not receive the device driver, or if you are required to update the device driver, you can often download the necessary driver

Data and instructions not recently used

OS

Data and instructions needed now

RAM

Hard drive's swap file

Figure 5.11

Virtual memory borrows excess storage capacity from the hard drive when there is not enough capacity in RAM.

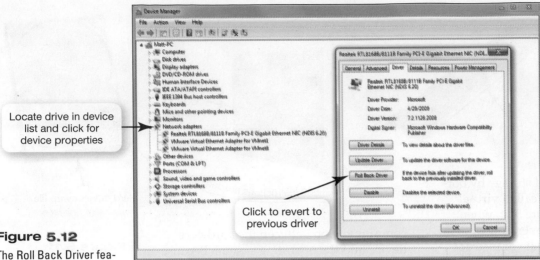

Locate drive in device list and click for device properties

Click to revert to previous driver

Figure 5.12

The Roll Back Driver feature in Windows removes a newly installed driver and replaces it with the last one that worked.

>To access the Device Manager dialog box, click the **Start** button, **Control Panel**, **Hardware** and **Sound Group**; then click the **Device Manager** link.

may stop responding, certain actions may cause a crash, or the device or the entire system may stop working). Although this is uncommon, it can happen. Fortunately, Windows has a Roll Back Driver feature that removes a newly installed driver, and replaces it with the last one that worked, to remedy the problem (see Figure 5.12). Roll Back Driver is found by accessing the Device Manager dialog box under System and Maintenance in the Control Panel.

from the manufacturer's Web site. You can also go to Web sites such as DriverZone.com (**driverzone.com**) or Driver Guide (**driverguide.com**) to locate drivers.

Can I damage my system by installing a device driver? Occasionally, when you install a driver, your system may become unstable (that is, programs

Software Application Coordination

How does the operating system help application software run on the computer? Application software feeds the CPU the instructions it needs to process data. These instructions take the form of computer code. Every computer program, no matter what its type or manufacturer, needs to interact with the CPU. For programs to work with the CPU, they must contain code that the CPU recognizes. Rather than having the same blocks of code for similar procedures in each program, the operating system includes the blocks of code—each called an **application programming interface (API)**—that application software needs in order to interact with the OS. Microsoft DirectX, for example, is a group of multimedia APIs built into the Windows operating system that improves graphics and sounds when you're playing games or watching video on your PC.

What are the advantages of using APIs? To create applications that can communicate with the operating system, software programmers need only refer to the API code blocks when they write an application. They don't need to include the entire code sequence in the application. APIs not only prevent redundancies in software code, but also make it easier for software developers to respond to changes in the operating system.

Large software developers such as Microsoft have many applications under

---

BITS AND BYTES

What Do I Do When My Computer Freezes?

At some point in time, we have all experienced our computers freezing up—nothing seems to respond to a mouse click or a tap on any keyboard key. What should you do? Try following these steps:

1. **Press Ctrl + Alt and then the Delete key** to access the Task Manager. On the Applications tab, close the application that is listed as not responding by clicking on the application and then clicking the End Task button.

2. If the non-responding application will not close from the Task Manager, press Ctrl + Alt and then Delete again to restart the computer. Restarting the computer is called a "soft" or "warm" boot. You might also try using the **Start** menu and choosing **Restart**.

3. If the computer will not restart from the Task Manager or from the Start menu, then **press the power button** one time to try to restart the computer. (Older computers may have a separate Restart button.)

4. If the computer still won't restart, press and hold down the Power button until the power turns completely off. You may have to **hold down the power button** for several seconds.

5. Leave the computer turned off for a minute or so to allow all the internal components to shut down completely. Then turn the computer on again. (Powering the computer on from an off position is called a **"cold" or "hard" boot**.)

6. If you can reproduce what caused the problem in the first place and are running Windows 7, turn on the **Problem Steps Recorder** and work through the steps one more time. This will create documentation that will make your call to technical support more efficient.

---

their corporate umbrella and use the same APIs in all or most of their applications. Because APIs coordinate with the operating system, all applications that have incorporated these APIs have similar interface features, such as toolbars and menus. Therefore, many features of the applications have the same look. An added benefit to this system is that applications sharing these formats can easily exchange data with each other. As such, it's easy to create a chart in Microsoft Excel from data in Microsoft Access and incorporate the finished chart into a Microsoft Word document.

The Boot Process: Starting Your Computer

Many things happen quickly between the time you turn on the computer and the time when it is ready for you to start using it. As you learned earlier, all data and instructions (including the operating system) are stored in RAM while your computer is on. When you turn off your computer, RAM is wiped clean of all its data (including the OS). How does the computer know what to do when you turn it on if there is nothing in RAM? It runs through a special **boot process** (or start-up process) to load the operating system into RAM. The term *boot*, from *bootstrap loader* (a small program used to start a larger program), alludes to the straps of leather, called *bootstraps*, that men used in former times to help them pull on their boots. This is the source of the expression "pull oneself up by the bootstraps."

What are the steps involved in the boot process? As illustrated in Figure 5.13, the boot process consists of four basic steps:

1. The basic input/output system (BIOS) is activated by powering on the CPU.

Figure 5.13

The boot process.

ROM chip

CPU

STEP 1: CPU activates BIOS.

STEP 2: BIOS conducts power-on self-test.

STEP 3: BIOS loads OS to RAM.

STEP 4: Configuration and customization settings checked, and desktop displays.

2. The BIOS checks that all attached devices are in place (called a **power-on self-test** or **POST**).

3. The operating system is loaded into RAM.

4. Configuration and customization settings are checked.

How can I tell if my computer is entering the boot process? As the computer goes through the boot process in a Windows operating system, indicator lights on the keyboard and disk drives may illuminate, and the system may emit various sounds. When you boot up on a PC with Windows or on a Mac, you won't hear any beeps or see any keyboard lights illuminate, but you will most likely see the Windows or Mac OS logo display on the monitor, indicating the progress of the start-up process. Once the boot process has completed these steps, it is ready to accept commands and data. Let's look at each of these steps in more detail.

> **"What's the first thing that happens after I turn on my computer?"**

Step 1: Activating BIOS

What's the first thing that happens after I turn on my computer? In the first step of the boot process, the CPU activates the **basic input/output system (BIOS)**. BIOS (pronounced "bye-OSE") is a program that manages the exchange of data between the operating system and all the input and output devices attached to the system, hence its name. BIOS is also responsible for loading the OS into RAM from its permanent location on the hard drive.

BIOS itself is stored on a special read-only memory (ROM) chip on the motherboard. Unlike data stored in RAM, data stored in ROM is permanent and is not erased when the power is turned off.

Step 2: Performing the Power-On Self-Test

How does the computer determine whether the hardware is working properly? The first job BIOS performs is to ensure that essential peripheral devices are attached and operational. As mentioned already, this process is called the power-on self-test, or POST. The POST consists of a test on the video card and video memory, a BIOS identification process, and a memory test to ensure that memory chips are working properly.

The BIOS compares the results of the POST with the various hardware configurations that are permanently stored in CMOS (pronounced "see-moss"). CMOS, which stands for *complementary metal-oxide semiconductor*, is a special kind of memory that uses almost no power. A little battery provides enough power so that the CMOS contents will not be lost after the computer is turned off. CMOS contains information about the system's memory, types of disk drives, and other essential input and output hardware components. If the results of the POST compare favorably to the hardware configurations stored in CMOS, the boot process continues. If new hardware has been installed, this will cause the POST to disagree with the hardware configurations in CMOS, and you will be alerted that new hardware has been detected.

Step 3: Loading the Operating System

How does the operating system get loaded into RAM? When the previous steps are successfully completed, BIOS goes through a preconfigured list of devices in its search for the drive that contains the **system files**, which are the main files of the operating system. When it is located, the operating system loads into RAM from its permanent storage location on the hard drive.

Once the system files are loaded into RAM, the **kernel** (or **supervisor program**) is loaded. The kernel is the essential component of the operating system. It is responsible for managing the processor and all other components of the computer system. Because it stays in RAM the entire time your computer is powered on, the kernel is said to be *memory resident*. Other parts of the OS that are less critical stay on the hard drive and are copied over to RAM on an as-needed basis so that RAM is not entirely filled. These programs are referred to as *nonresident*. Once the kernel is loaded, the operating system takes over control of the computer's functions.

Step 4: Checking Further Configurations and Customizations

When are the other components and configurations of the system checked?   CMOS checks the configuration of memory and essential peripherals in the beginning of the boot process. In this last phase of the boot process, the operating system checks the registry for the configuration of other system components. The **registry** contains all of the different configurations (settings) used by the OS and by other applications. It contains the customized settings you put into place, such as mouse speed and the display settings, as well as instructions as to which programs should be loaded first.

Why do I sometimes need to enter a login name and password at the end of the boot process?   In a networked environment, such as that found at most colleges, the operating system serves many users. To determine whether a user is authorized to use the system (for example, whether a user is a valid student or college employee), authorized users are given a login name and password. The verification of your login name and password is called **authentication**. The authentication process blocks unauthorized users from entering the system.

On your home computer, you also may need to input a password to log in to your user account on your computer after your computer has completely booted up. Even in a home environment, all users with access to a Windows computer (such as family members or roommates) can have their own user accounts. Users can set up a password to protect their account from being accessed by another user without permission. For more information on selecting a good password, see Chapter 9.

How do I know if the boot process is successful?   The entire boot process takes only a minute or two to complete. If the entire system is checked out and loaded properly, the process completes by displaying the restored screen image. The computer system is now ready to accept your first command.

Handling Errors in the Boot Process

What should I do if my computer doesn't boot properly?   Sometimes problems occur during the boot process.

ACTIVE HELP-DESK

Starting the Computer: The Boot Process

In this Active Helpdesk call, you'll play the role of a helpdesk staffer, fielding calls about how the operating system helps the computer start up.

Fortunately, you have several options for correcting the situation. If you have recently installed new software or hardware, try uninstalling it. (Make sure you use the Add or Remove Programs feature in the Control Panel to remove the software.) If the problem no longer occurs when rebooting, you have determined the cause of the problem and can reinstall the device or software. If the problem does not go away, the first option is to restart your computer in Safe mode.

What is Safe mode?   Sometimes Windows does not boot properly, and you end up with a screen that says "Safe Mode" in the corners, as shown in Figure 5.14. (Alternatively, you can boot directly into Safe mode by pressing the F8 key during the boot process before the Windows logo appears.) **Safe mode** is a special diagnostic mode designed for troubleshooting errors. When the system is in Safe mode, only essential devices—such as the mouse, keyboard, and monitor—function. Even the regular graphics device driver will not be activated in Safe mode. Instead, the system runs in the most basic graphics mode, eliminating any screen images and nonessential icons and resulting in a neutral

Figure 5.14

If there is an error in the boot process, your system might boot into Safe mode. Safe mode offers functionality that is limited but sufficient to allow you to perform diagnostic testing.

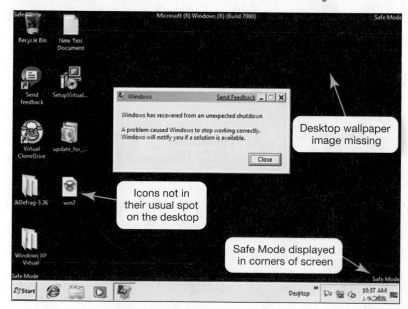

screen. While in Safe mode, you can use the **Device Manager**, a feature in the operating system that lets you view and change the properties of all devices attached to your computer. Safe mode boots Windows with only the original Microsoft Windows drivers that are required to boot the computer.

If Windows detects a problem in the boot process, it will add **Last Known Good Configuration** to the Windows Advanced Options Menu (also accessible by pressing the F8 key during the boot process). Every time your computer boots successfully, a configuration of the boot process is saved. When you choose to boot with the Last Known Good Configuration, the operating system starts your computer by using the registry information that was saved during the last shutdown. Safe mode and Last Known Good Configuration are the two most widely used methods of booting into Windows when a

user cannot do so with the current configuration. Finally, if all other attempts to reboot fail, try a System Restore to roll back to a past configuration. System Restore is covered in more detail later in the chapter.

What should I do if my keyboard or another device doesn't work after I boot my computer? Sometimes during the boot process, BIOS skips a device (such as a keyboard) or improperly identifies it. Your only indication that this sort of problem has occurred is that the device won't respond after the system has been booted. When that happens, you can generally resolve the problem by rebooting. If the problem persists, you may want to check the operating system's Web site for any patches (or software fixes) that may resolve the issue. If there are no patches or the problem persists, then you may want to get technical assistance.

Figure 5.15

(a) The Windows 7 desktop puts the most commonly used features of the operating system at your fingertips. (b) Hover your mouse on a taskbar icon to show thumbnails of the open windows of that application; hover over a thumbnail to display a full size image of that window.

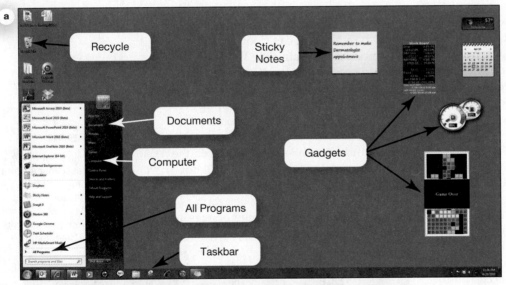

The Desktop and Windows Features

The **desktop** is the first interaction you have with the operating system and the first image you see on your monitor. As its name implies, your computer's desktop puts at your fingertips all of the elements necessary for a productive work session. They are items that are typically found on or near the top of a traditional desk, such as files and folders.

What are the main features of the Windows desktop and Start menu? The very nature of a desktop is that it lets you customize it to meet your individual needs. As such, the desktop on your computer may be different from the desktop on your friend's computer, or even from the desktop of another account user on the same computer. In recent versions of Windows, many features that were once only found on the desktop have moved to the Start menu, including access to documents, programs, and computer drives and devices. You can always create shortcuts on your desktop to these features if you find that's more convenient (see Figure 5.15).

On the desktop you'll find:

- **Recycle Bin:** Location for deleted files and folders from the C: drive only. Deleted files from other locations, such as your flash drive, do not go to the Recycle Bin; instead, they are permanently deleted. Deleted files in the Recycle Bin can be recovered easily before the Recycle Bin is emptied.

- **Gadgets:** A **gadget** is an easy-to-use miniprogram that gives you information at a glance or quick access to frequently used tools including weather information, calendar items, calculators, games, photo albums, and system tools. Sticky Notes, in Windows 7, are not a gadget, but are a convenient accessory that you can use to jot down notes to yourself.

- **Taskbar:** Displays open and favorite applications for easy access. You can point to an icon to preview windows of open files or programs, or move your mouse over a thumbnail to preview a full-screen image. Or right-click an icon to view a Jump List—the most recently or commonly used files for that application. Finally, you can hover your mouse over a Taskbar icon to display thumbnails of open windows, and then you can hover over a thumbnail to display the contents of that window at full size (all other apps are temporarily hidden from view).

In the Windows 7 Start menu, you'll find:

- **Documents:** A convenient organizational tool that enables you to keep all your documents in one place. You can further organize your Documents folder with subfolders, similar to the way a traditional filing system is organized.

- **Computer:** Provides easy access to disk drives and system and network devices.

- **All Programs:** In the Start menu, this provides access to all programs available in the system. To prevent taking up valuable screen space, a limited number of programs displays. Use the scrollbar to gain access to programs not immediately visible. Instant Search can facilitate locating a program.

How does the Mac desktop compare with Windows? Although the Mac OS X and the Windows operating systems are not compatible, they are extremely similar in terms of functionality.

As illustrated in Figure 5.16, both Windows and Mac operating systems use **windows** (rectangular boxes that contain programs displayed on the screen), **menus** (lists of commands that appear on the screen), and **icons** (pictures that represent an object such as a software application or a file or folder).

They both also have streamlined mechanisms to access commonly used applications. Macs feature a Dock and a Dashboard with widgets. A **widget** is a mini-application that enables quick access to frequently used tools and activities (such as stock prices, to-do lists, and games). The latest version of Windows has a taskbar with Dock-like capabilities and *gadgets* that provide functionality similar to that of the Mac widgets.

Figure 5.16

Although not compatible with each other, the Windows OS and the Mac OS have many similar features.

Widgets (Mac)/ Gadgets (Windows)

Files

Icons

Windows

Access to applications

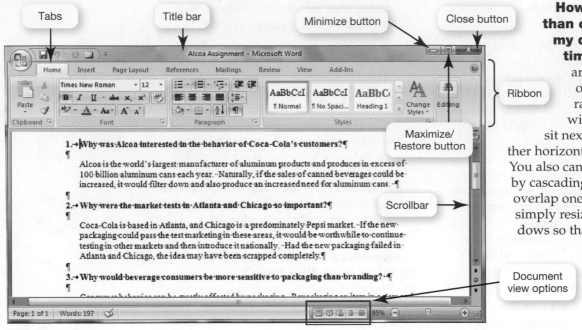

Tabs

Title bar

Minimize button

Close button

Maximize/Restore button

Ribbon

Scrollbar

Document view options

Figure 5.17

Most windows in a graphical user interface have the same common elements.

Figure 5.18

The Windows Flip 3D feature gives you the ability to move through live images of open windows.

What are common features of a window? As noted earlier, one feature introduced in the graphical user interface is windows (with a lowercase *w*), the rectangular panes on your computer screen that display applications running on your system. Most programs have windows that include **toolbars**, which have icons (shortcuts to frequently used tasks) and **scrollbars** (bars that appear at the side or bottom of the screen that control which part of the information is displayed on the screen). As shown in Figure 5.17, the newer versions of Microsoft Office have begun to organize toolbars into a **ribbon** interface. The ribbon is further organized into task-specific tabs with relevant commands. Using the Minimize, Maximize and Restore, and Close buttons, you can open, close, and resize windows.

How can I see more than one window on my desktop at a time? You can easily arrange the windows on a desktop by arranging separate windows so that they sit next to each other either horizontally or vertically. You also can arrange windows by cascading them so that they overlap one another, or you can simply resize two open windows so that they appear on the screen at the same time. Showing windows side by side or stacked on top of each other makes accessing two or more active windows more convenient. To do so, right-click the task bar and select "Show Windows Stacked" or "Show Windows Side by Side." When you want to undo the arrangement, right-click the taskbar again and select "Undo Show Stacked" (or "Side by Side"). To bring a window back to its full size, click the Restore button in the top right corner of the window. Windows 7 introduces the "snap" feature, which is another new way to view windows side by side. Simply drag a window to either the left or right, and Windows will automatically resize and snap them in place.

Windows Vista and 7 offer two more ways to navigate through open windows. To see live thumbnail images of open windows, press Alt + Tab to access Windows Flip. Pressing the Windows key + Tab initiates the Windows Flip 3D feature. You can then "flip" through open windows in a stack by using the scroll wheel on your mouse or the arrow keys on your keyboard. The open windows appear in a three-dimensional configuration as shown in Figure 5.18.

Can I move or resize the windows once they are tiled? Regardless of whether the windows are tiled, you can resize them and move them around the desktop. You can reposition windows on the desktop by using the mouse to point to the title bar at the top of the window and,

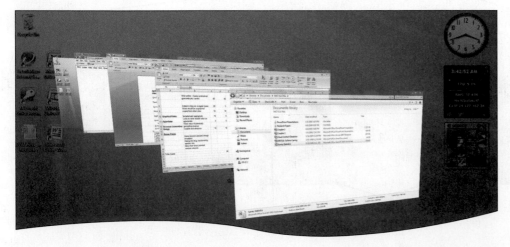

while holding down the left mouse button, drag the window to a different location. To resize a window, place your mouse pointer over any side or corner of a window until it changes to a double-headed arrow [↕]. You can then left-click and drag the window to the new desired size. Aero Shake is a feature that allows you to grab a window by its title bar and "shake" it to minimize all other windows.

Organizing Your Computer: File Management

So far you have learned that the operating system is responsible for managing the processor, memory, storage, and devices, and that it provides a mechanism whereby applications and users can interact with the computer system. An additional function of an operating system is to enable **file management**, which entails providing organizational structure to the computer's contents. The OS allows you to organize the contents of your computer in a hierarchical **directory** structure that includes files, folders, libraries, and drives. In this section, we discuss how you can use this hierarchical structure to make your computer more organized and efficient.

Organizing Your Files

What exactly is a file? Technically, a **file** is a collection of related pieces of information stored together for easy reference. A file in an operating system is a collection of program instructions or data that is stored and treated as a single unit. Files can be generated from an application such as a Word document or an Excel workbook. In addition, files can represent an entire application, a Web page, a set of sounds, or an image. Files are stored on the hard drive, a flash drive, or another permanent storage medium. As the number of files you save increases, it becomes more important to keep them organized in folders and libraries. A **folder** is a collection of files. Windows 7 introduces the concept of libraries. A **library** is a collection that gathers files from different locations and displays them as if they

BITS AND BYTES

Upgrading Your Operating System

If you have had your computer for a year or two, you may be faced with the decision of whether to upgrade to the newest release version of your operating system (such as going from Windows Vista to Windows 7). Here are a few key things to consider before taking the plunge:

- **Are there significant features in the new version that will make your life easier?** If the only features the new version offers are ones you don't need, why bother upgrading?

- **Will your hardware work with the new OS?** Check the minimum operating requirements (required RAM, processor speed, hard drive space, etc.) of the new version to ensure that your computer can handle the workload of the new software. You will also need to make sure drivers for the new OS are available for all your hardware devices and peripherals to ensure they will work properly with the new OS. Microsoft has made this easy with Windows Upgrade Advisor. The Upgrade Advisor scans your hardware, devices, and installed programs for compatibility, advises you on how to resolve any issues found, and recommends what you should do before upgrading.

- **Is your application software compatible with the new version of the OS?** Usually, application software works fine with a new version of an OS. Sometimes it doesn't. Check with the software vendors regarding compatibility, especially if you're upgrading to a 64-bit system. Windows 7 has a compatibility feature that allows you to run your software in an earlier version of the operating system if it is not compatible with Windows 7.

- **Is your current operating system still supported?** When it deploys new versions of operating systems, the company may stop supporting older versions. If your version will not be supported, it's best to upgrade to a newer version.

Before starting the upgrade, you should back up all your data files so you won't lose anything accidentally during the upgrading process. Backup and Restore in Windows 7 makes this job less of a hassle.

were all saved in a single folder, regardless of where they are actually physically stored.

How does the operating system organize files? Windows organizes the contents of your computer in a hierarchical structure comprising drives, folders, subfolders, and files. The hard drive, represented as the C drive, is where you permanently store most of your files. Other storage devices on your computer are also represented by letters. The A drive has traditionally been reserved for a floppy drive, which you may or may not have installed on your computer. Any additional drives (such as flash or DVD drives) found on your computer are represented by other letters (D, E, F, and so on).

How is the hard drive organized? The C drive, or hard drive, is like a large filing cabinet in which all files are stored. As such, the C drive is the top of the filing structure of the computer system and is referred to as the **root directory**. All other libraries, folders, and files are organized within the root directory. There are areas in the root directory that the operating system has filled with files and folders holding special OS files. The programs within these files help run the computer and generally shouldn't be accessed. The Windows operating system creates special folders called *Documents*, *Pictures*, *Music*, and *Videos*, where you may begin to store and organize your text, image, audio, and video files, respectively. However, users do not always carefully save their files in these special folders. Files are often stored all over the PC in various folders. For example, picture files may not just be stored in the Pictures folder, but might also be stored in the temporary folder, in a separate folder within the Documents folder, or even in remote storage, making finding all picture files difficult. Windows 7 tries to remedy this situation with the use of libraries. Recall, libraries gather files from different locations and display the files as if they were all saved in a single folder, regardless of where they are actually physically stored. Some libraries are created already in Windows, and Windows has defined specific folders to include in each standard library, but users can create other libraries to meet their special needs, or can modify the standard libraries, adding or deleting folders to meet their needs.

How can I easily locate and see the contents of my computer? If you use a Windows PC, **Windows Explorer** is the main tool for finding, viewing, and managing the contents of your computer. It shows the location and contents of every drive, folder, and file. As illustrated in Figure 5.19, Windows Explorer is divided into two panes, or sections.

The navigation pane on the left shows the contents of your computer in a traditional hierarchical tree structure. It displays all the drives of the system, as well as other commonly accessed areas such as the Desktop, Libraries, and Documents, Music, Pictures, and Video folders.

How should I organize my files? Creating folders is the key to organizing your files because folders keep related documents together. Again, think of your computer as a big filing cabinet that is filled with many folders. Those folders have the capacity to hold individual files, or even other folders that contain individual files. For example, you might create one folder called Classes to hold all of your class work. Inside the Classes folder, you could create folders for each of your classes (such as CIS110, MGT111, and HIS112). Inside each of those folders, you could create subfolders for each class's assignments, completed homework, research, notes, and so on.

Grouping related files into folders makes it easier for you to identify and find files. Which would be easier—going to the CIS110 folder to find a file or searching through the hundreds individual files in Documents hoping to find the right one? Grouping files in a folder also allows you to move them more efficiently, so you can quickly transfer critical files needing frequent backup, for instance. Sometimes, it's not always possible to put all similar files into one folder. For example, you might have PowerPoint files stored in separate folders that correspond to each particular class. If you want to always have quick access to your PowerPoint files, you could create a PowerPoint Library and specify the folders where the PowerPoint files are located. The PowerPoint Library would then gather the PowerPoint files from the different locations and display them as if they were all saved in a single folder.

Figure 5.19

Windows Explorer lets you see the contents of your computer.

>Click the **Windows Explorer** icon on the taskbar.

Navigation pane

File path

Libraries

Music folder

Files and folders in CIS110

Opened CIS110 folder

Viewing and Sorting Files and Folders

Are there different ways I can view and sort my files and folders? When you open any folder in Windows, the toolbar at the top displays a Views button. Clicking on the Views button offers you different ways to view the folders and files, which are discussed in more detail below. In some views, the folders are displayed as Live Icons, which is a feature that began in Windows Vista. Live Icons allows you to preview the actual contents of a specific file or folder without actually opening the file. Live Icons can be displayed in a variety of views.

- **Tiles view:** Displays files and folders as icons in list form. Each icon represents the application associated with the file, and also includes the name and the size of the file, though the display information is customizable to include other data. The Tiles view also displays picture dimensions, a handy feature for Web page developers.

- **Details view:** The most interactive view. Files and folders are displayed in list form, and the additional file information is displayed in columns alongside the name of the file. You can sort and display the contents of the folder by any of the column headings, so you can sort the contents alphabetically by name or type, or hierarchically by date last modified or by file size (see Figure 5.20).

- **List view:** Another display of icons and names that are even smaller than in Tiles view. This is a good view if you have a lot of content in the folder and need to see most or all of it at once.

- **Small and Medium Icons views:** These views also display files and folders as icons in list form, but the icons are either small- or medium-sized, respectively. Additional file information displays in a ScreenTip (the text that appears when you place your cursor over the file icon).

- **Large and Extra Large Icons views:** Large Icons view (see Figure 5.21) shows the contents of folders as small images. There is also Extra Large Icons view, which shows folder contents and other icons as even larger images. Large Icons and Extra Large Icons views are the best to use if your folder contains

picture files, or for PowerPoint presentations, because the title slide of the presentation will display, making it easier for you to distinguish among presentations. You may use the scale feature to adjust the size of the icons further. Additionally, a preview pane is available in this view. It allows you to view the first page of the selected document without having to open it completely (see Figure 5.21).

For those folders that contain collections of MP3 files, you can download the cover of the CD or an image of the artist to display on any folder to identify that collection further.

What's the best way to search for a file? You've no doubt saved a file and forgotten where you saved it, or have downloaded a file from the Internet and then were not sure where it was saved. What's the quickest way to find a file? Looking through every file stored on your computer could

Sort files and folders by clicking the headers

Figure 5.20

Details view enables you to sort and list your files in a variety of ways to enable quick access to the correct file.

Figure 5.21

The Large Icons view is an especially good way to display the contents of files and folders. The preview pane on the right enables you to see the first page of your document without first opening it.

>To access Large Icons view, from the command bar in any folder dialog box, click the **Views arrow,** and then select **Large Icons** view. To access the Preview Pane, click **Organize,** select **Layout,** and then **Preview Pane.**

Folders with live preview of contents

Preview Pane allows viewing without opening file

Live preview of Excel and PowerPoint files

take hours, even with a well-organized file-management system. Fortunately, the newer versions of Windows include Instant Search, a search feature, found on the Start menu, which searches through your hard drive or other storage device (DVD or flash drive) to locate files that match criteria you provide. Your search can be based on a part of the name of the file or just a word or phrase in the file. You can also narrow your search by providing information about the type of file, which application was used to create the file, or even how long ago the file was saved. (Mac OS Snow Leopard has a similar feature called Spotlight, known as Sherlock in earlier versions.) Instant Search can also find e-mails based on your criteria. Instant Search is found in Windows Explorer, too,

and is used to search the contents of current folders.

Naming Files

Are there special rules I have to follow when I name files? Files have names just like people. The first part of a file, or the **file name**, is similar to your first name, and is generally the name you assign to the file when you save it. For example, "bioreport" may be the name you assign a report you have completed for a biology class.

In a Windows application, an **extension**, or **file type**, follows the file name and a period or dot (.). Like a last name, this extension identifies what kind of family of files the file belongs to, or which application should be used to read the file. For example, if "bioreport" is a document created in Microsoft Works, it has a .wks extension and its name is "bioreport.wks." If the bioreport file is a Word 2007 document, then it has a .docx extension and its name is "bioreport.docx." Figure 5.22 lists some common file extensions and the types of documents they indicate.

Do I need to know the extension of a file to save it? As shown in

Figure 5.22 | COMMON FILE NAME EXTENSIONS

Extension	Type of Document	Application
.doc	Word processing document	Microsoft Word 2003
.docx	Word processing document	Microsoft Word 2007 and 2010
.wpd	Word processing document	Corel WordPerfect
.xlsx	Spreadsheet	Microsoft Excel 2007 and 2010
.accdb	Database	Microsoft Access 2007 and 2010
.pptx	PowerPoint presentation	Microsoft PowerPoint 2007 and 2010
.pdf	Portable Document Format	Adobe Acrobat or Adobe Reader
.rtf	Text (Rich Text Format)	Any program that can read text documents
.txt	Text	Any program that can read text documents
.htm or .html	HyperText Markup Language for a Web page	Any program that can read HTML
.jpg	Joint Photographic Experts Group (JPEG) image	Most programs capable of displaying images
.gif	Graphics Interchange Format (GIF) image	Most programs capable of displaying images
.bmp	Bitmap image	Windows
.zip	Compressed file	WinZip

Figure 5.23, when you save a file created in most applications running under the Windows operating system, you do not need to add the extension to the file name; by default, it is added automatically for you. Mac and Linux operating systems do not require file extensions. This is because the information as to the type of application the computer should use to open the file is stored inside the file itself. However, if you're using these operating systems and will be sending files to Windows users, you should add an extension to your file name so that Windows can more easily open your files. You may need to know the extension of files created in any of the Office 2007 or 2010 applications because they have a different file format than the earlier version. The new versions of Office have an *x* at the end of the extension to represent the XLM file format. For example, files saved in Word 2010 have a .docx file extension, whereas files save in Word 2003 have a .doc file extension. A file created in Office 2007 or 2010 cannot be read with an earlier version of Office unless it is converted or saved in the earlier format.

Are there things I shouldn't do when naming my files? Each operating system has its own naming conventions, or

Figure 5.24 | FILE NAMING CONVENTIONS

	Mac OS	Windows
File and folder name length	As many as 255 characters*	As many as 255 characters
Case sensitive?	Yes	No
Forbidden characters	Colon (:)	" / \ * ? <>	:
File extensions needed?	No	Yes
Path separator	Colon (:)	\

*Note: Although Mac OS X supports file names with as many as 255 characters, many applications running on OS X still support only file names with a maximum of 31 characters.

rules, which are listed in Figure 5.24. Beyond those conventions, it's important that you name your files so that you can easily identify them. A file name such as "research.docx" may be descriptive to you if you're only working on one research paper. However, if you create other research reports later and need to identify the contents of these files quickly, you'll soon wish you had been more descriptive. Giving your files names that are more descriptive, such as bioresearch.docx or, better yet, bio101research.docx, is a good idea.

Keep in mind, however, that all files must be uniquely identified, unless they are saved in different folders or in different locations. Therefore, although files may share the same file name (such as "bioreport.docx" or "bioreport.xlsx") or share the same extension ("bioreport.xlsx" or "budget.xlsx"), no two files stored on the same device and folder can share *both* the same file name and the same extension.

How can I tell where my files are saved? When you save a file for the first time, you give the file a name and designate where you want to save it. For easy reference, the operating system includes default folders where files are saved unless you specify otherwise. In Windows, the default folders are "Documents" for files, "Downloads" for files downloaded from the Internet, "Music" for audio files, "Pictures" for graphic files, and "Videos" for video files. Although you can create your own folders, these default folders are the beginning of a well-organized system.

You can determine the location of a file by its **file path**. The file path starts with the

Type file name

Change file type

Figure 5.23

When you save a file in Microsoft Word 2010, you can select in what format you would like the file to be saved, such as a format compatible with Word 97-2003.

>The Save As features are displayed by selecting the File tab and then selecting Save As.

drive in which the file is located and includes all folders, subfolders (if any), the file name, and the extension. For example, if you were saving a picture of Emily Brontë for a term paper for an English composition course, the file path might be C:\Users\Username\Documents\ English Comp\Term Paper\Illustrations\ EBronte.jpg.

As shown in Figure 5.25, C is the drive on which the file is stored (in this case, the hard drive), and Documents is the file's primary folder. English Comp, Term Paper, and Illustrations are successive subfolders within the Documents main folder. Last is the file name, EBronte, separated from the file extension (in this case, jpg) by a period. Notice that there are backslash characters (\) in between the drive, primary folder, subfolders, and file name. This backslash character, used by Windows and DOS, is referred to as a **path separator**. Mac files use a colon (:), whereas UNIX and Linux files use the forward slash (/) as the path separator.

Working with Files

How can I move and copy files?

Once you've located your file with Windows Explorer, you can perform many other file-management actions such as opening, copying, moving, renaming, and deleting files. You open a file by double-clicking the file from its storage location. Based on the file extension, the operating system then determines which application needs to be started to open the requested file and opens the file

within the correct application automatically. You can copy a file to another location using the Copy command. When you copy a file, a duplicate file is created and the original file remains in its original location. To move a file from one location to another, use the Move command. When you move a file, the original file is deleted from its original location.

Where do deleted files go? The **Recycle Bin** is a folder on the desktop where files deleted from the hard drive reside until you permanently purge them from your system. Unfortunately, files deleted from other drives (such as a DVD drive, flash drive, external hard drive, or network drive) do not go to the Recycle Bin but are deleted from the system immediately. (Mac systems have something similar to the Recycle Bin, called Trash, which is represented by a wastebasket icon. To delete files on a Mac, drag the files to Trash on the Dock.)

How do I permanently delete files from my system? Files in the Recycle Bin or Trash are held only until they are permanently deleted. To delete your files from the Recycle Bin permanently, select Empty the Recycle Bin after right-clicking the desktop icon. On Macs, select Empty Trash from the Finder menu in OS X.

Utility Programs

You have learned that the operating system is the single most essential piece of software in your computer system because it coordinates all the system's activities and provides a means by which other software applications and users can interact with the system. However, there is another set of programs included in system software. Utility programs are small applications that perform special functions.

Some of these utility programs are incorporated into the operating system. For example, Windows has its own firewall and file-compression utilities. Other utility programs, such as antivirus and security programs, are so large and require such

Figure 5.25

Understanding file paths.

frequent updating that they offered as stand-alone programs or as Web-based services. Sometimes utility programs, such as Norton SystemWorks, are offered as software suites, bundled with other useful maintenance and performance-boosting utilities. Still other utilities, like Lavasoft's Ad-Aware, are offered as freeware or shareware programs and are available as downloads from the Web.

Figure 5.27 illustrates some of the various types of utility programs available within the Windows operating system as well as those available as stand-alone programs. In general, the basic utilities designed to manage and tune the computer hardware are incorporated in the operating system. The stand-alone utility programs typically offer more features or an easier user interface for backup, security, diagnostic, or recovery functions.

In this section, we explore many of the utility programs you'll find installed on a Windows 7 operating system. Unless otherwise noted, you can find these utilities in the Control Panel or on the Start menu by selecting All Programs, Accessories, and then System Tools. (We also take a brief look at some Mac utilities.) We will discuss antivirus and personal firewall utility programs in Chapter 9.

Display Utilities

How can I change the appearance of my desktop? Personalization, found in Appearance and Personalization on the Control Panel or by right-clicking any area on the desktop and selecting Personalize, has all the features you need to change the appearance of your desktop. It provides different options for the desktop background, screen savers, and window colors. Although Windows comes with many different background themes and screen saver options preinstalled, hundreds of downloadable options are available on the Web. Just search for "backgrounds" or "screen savers" on your favorite search engine to customize your desktop.

The Programs and Features Utility

What is the correct way to add new programs to the system? When you install a new program, usually the program

A File Type for Everyone

Imagine you are sending an e-mail to a diverse group of individuals. You are not sure what word processing software each of them uses, but you assume that there will be a mix of people who use Word, WordPerfect, and even Writer. How can you be sure that all users will be able to open the attachment regardless of the program installed on their computers? Save the file in Rich Text Format (.rtf), Portable Document Format (.pdf), or Text (.txt) format. Rich Text and Text files can be read by any modern word processing program, although some formatting may be lost when a document is saved in Text (.txt) format. Anyone can read a PDF file by downloading the Acrobat Reader from the Adobe Web site (**adobe.com**). To save files as RTF, PDF, or TXT files, simply change the file type when saving your file. In Microsoft Word, for example, you can select the file type in the Save As menu shown in Figure 5.26.

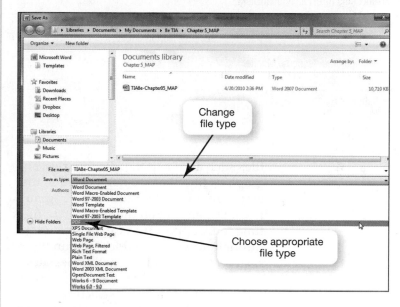

Figure 5.26

By changing a word processing file's type to PDF, RTF, or TXT (plain text), you can ensure that everyone can read your file, no matter which word processing program they use.

automatically runs a wizard (a step-by-step guide) that walks you through the installation process. If a wizard does not start automatically, you should go to the Programs and Features utility found in the Programs folder in the Control Panel. This prompts the operating system to look for the setup program of the new software and starts the installation wizard.

What is the correct way to remove unwanted programs from my system? Some people think that deleting a program from the Program Files folder on the C drive is the best way to remove a program from the system. However, most programs include support

Windows Utility Program	Stand-Alone Windows Utility Program	Function
File Management		
Programs and Features		Properly installs and uninstalls software
Windows Explorer File Compression	WinZip	Reduces file size
Windows System Maintenance and Diagnostics		
Backup and Disk Imaging	Acronis True Image, Norton Ghost, SkyDrive	Backs up important information and makes a complete mirror image of your current computer setup
Disk Cleanup	McAfee Total Protection	Removes unnecessary files from hard drive
Disk Defragmenter	Norton Utilities, iDefrag (for OS X)	Arranges files on hard drive in sequential order
Error-checking (previously ScanDisk)		Checks hard drive for unnecessary or damaged files
System Restore	FarStone Snapshot, Acronis Backup and Security, Norton Ghost	Restores system to a previous, stable state
Task Manager and Resource Monitor		Displays performance measures for processes; provides information on programs and processes running on computer
Task Scheduler		Schedules programs to run automatically at prescribed times

files such as a help file, dictionaries, and graphics files that are not located in the main program folder found in Program Files. Depending on the supporting file's function, support files can be scattered throughout various folders within the system. You would normally miss these files by deleting only the main program file from the system. By selecting the individual program's own uninstall option, or the Windows uninstaller utility found in Programs in the Control Panel, you delete not only the main program file but also all supporting files and most registry entries.

Need to Recover a Deleted File?

Should you move a file to the Recycle Bin in error, you can immediately restore the deleted file by clicking Restore all Items from the Task pane in the Recycle Bin dialog box. Once you empty the Recycle Bin, getting the file back is difficult, but perhaps not impossible.

Because you don't see the file name anymore, it looks as if the file has been erased from the hard drive. However, only the reference to the deleted file is deleted permanently, so the operating system has no easy way to find the file. The file data actually remains on the hard drive until otherwise written over. For those files that have been deleted for awhile, you can use a program such as FarStone's RestoreIT! or Norton Ghost. However, the longer you wait to recover a deleted file, the smaller your chances of a full recovery, because the probability increases that your file has been overwritten by other data.

File Compression Utilities

What is file compression? A file **compression utility** is a program that takes out redundancies in a file to reduce the file size. File compression is helpful because it makes a large file more compact, making it easier and faster to send over the Internet, upload to a Web page, or save onto a disc. As shown in Figure 5.28, Windows has built-in compression (or zip) file support. There are also several stand-alone freeware and shareware programs, such as WinZip (for Windows) and StuffIt (for Windows or Mac), that you can obtain to compress your files.

How does file compression work? Most compression programs look for repeated patterns of letters and replace these patterns with a shorter placeholder. The repeated patterns and the associated

 File Compression

In this Sound Byte, you'll learn about the advantages of file compression and how to use Windows to compress and decompress files. This Sound Byte also teaches you how to find and install file compression shareware programs.

placeholder are cataloged and stored temporarily in a separate file called the *dictionary*. For example, in the following sentence, you can easily see the repeated patterns of letters.

The rain in Spain falls mainly on the plain.

Although this example contains obvious repeated patterns (**ain** and **the**), in a large document the repeated patterns may be more complex. The compression program's algorithm (a set of instructions designed to complete a solution in a step-by-step manner) therefore runs through the file several times to determine the optimal repeated patterns to use to obtain the greatest compression.

How effective are file compression programs? The effectiveness of file compression—that is, how much a file's size is reduced—depends on several factors, including the type and size of the individual file and the compression method used. Current compression programs can reduce text files by 50 percent or more, depending on the file. However, some files, such as PDF files, already contain a form of compression, so they do not need to be compressed further. Other file types, especially some graphics and audio formats, have gone through a compression process that reduces file size by permanently discarding data. For example, image files such as Joint Photographic Experts Group (JPEG), Graphics Interchange Format (GIF), and Portable Network Graphics (PNG) files discard small variations in color that the human eye may not pick up. Likewise, MP3 files permanently discard sounds that the human ear cannot hear. These graphic and audio files do not need further compression.

How do I decompress a file I've compressed? When you want to restore the file to its original state, you need to decompress the file so that the pieces of file that the compression process temporarily removed are restored to the document. Generally, the program you used to compress the file has the capability

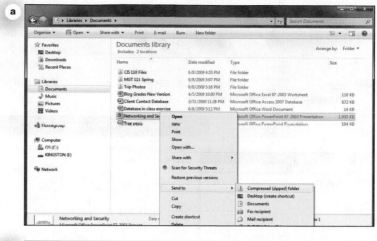

to decompress the file as well (see Figure 5.29).

System Maintenance Utilities

Are there any utilities that make my system work faster? Disk Cleanup is a Windows utility that cleans, or removes, unnecessary files from your hard drive. These include files that have accumulated in the Recycle Bin as well as temporary files, which are files created by Windows to store data temporarily when a program is running. Windows usually deletes these temporary files when you exit the program, but sometimes it forgets to do this, or doesn't have time because your system freezes up or incurs a problem that prevents you from properly exiting a program. Disk Cleanup, found by clicking the Start button, then selecting All Programs, Accessories folder, and then the System Tools folder, also removes temporary Internet files (Web pages stored on your hard drive for quick viewing) as well as offline Web pages (pages stored on your computer so you can view them without being connected to the Internet). If not deleted periodically, these unnecessary files can hinder efficient operating performance.

How can I control which files Disk Cleanup deletes? When you run Disk Cleanup, the program scans your hard drive to determine which folders have files that can be deleted and calculates the amount of

Figure 5.28

(a) File compression is a built-in utility of the Windows operating system. (b) Compressing the PowerPoint document reduced the file size from 1,935 KB to 1,453 KB.

>To access the Windows file compression utility, right-click the file or folder that is to be compressed, select **Send to** from the shortcut menu, and then select **Compressed (zipped) Folder**.

STEP 1: Right-click zipped folder.

STEP 2: Select Extract All...

STEP 3: Browse to storage location.

STEP 4: Extracted file displays in selected location.

Figure 5.29

The Extraction Wizard in Windows makes unzipping compressed folders and files easy.

drive, thereby allowing the OS to work more efficiently. You can find the Windows Disk Defragmenter utility by clicking the Start menu, then All Programs, Accessories, and then System Tools. Using the Windows Disk Defragmenter Analyzer feature, you should check several times a year to determine whether your drive needs to be defragmented. Macs do not have a defrag utility built into the system because developers thought that the file system used by Mac OS X was so efficient that defragging the hard drive would be unnecessary. Those users who feel the need to defrag their Mac can use iDefrag, an external program that can be purchased from Coriolis Systems.

How do I diagnose potential errors or damage on my storage devices? Error-checking, once known as ScanDisk, is a Windows utility that checks for lost files and fragments as well as physical errors on your hard drive. Lost files and fragments of files occur as you save, resave, move, delete, and copy files on your hard drive. Sometimes the system becomes confused, leaving references on the **file allocation table** or **FAT** (an index of all sector numbers in a table) to files that no longer exist or have been moved. Physical errors on the hard drive occur when the mechanism that reads the hard drive's data (which is stored as 1s or 0s) can no longer determine whether the area holds a 1 or a 0. These areas are called *bad sectors*. Sometimes Error-checking can recover the lost data, but more often, it deletes the files that are unnecessarily taking up space. Error-checking also makes a note of any bad sectors so that the system will not use them again to store data.

Where can I find Error-checking? To locate Error-checking, click Computer from the Start menu, right-click the disk

hard drive space that would be freed by doing so. You check off which type of files you would like to delete, as shown in Figure 5.30.

What else can I do if my system runs slowly? Over time, as you add and delete information in a file, the file pieces are saved in scattered locations on the hard drive. Locating all the pieces of the file takes extra time, making the operating system less efficient. Windows **Disk Defragmenter** regroups related pieces of files on the hard

Total space to be freed

Space freed with the selections

Description of folder contents

Figure 5.30

Using Disk Cleanup will help free space on your hard drive.

>Disk Cleanup is accessed by clicking **Start, All Programs, Accessories,** and then **System Tools**.

you want to diagnose, select Properties, and select Tools. On Macs, you can use the Disk Utility to test and repair disks. You will find Disk Utility in the Utilities folder in the Applications folder on your hard drive.

How can I check on a program that has stopped running? If a program has stopped working, you can use the Windows **Task Manager utility** to check on the program or to exit the nonresponsive program. Although you can access Task Manager from the Control Panel, it is more easily accessible by pressing Ctrl + Alt and then the Delete key or by right-clicking an empty space on the taskbar at the bottom of your screen. The Applications tab of Task Manager lists all programs that you are using and indicates whether they are working properly (running) or have stopped improperly (not responding). You can terminate programs that are not responding by clicking the End Task button in the dialog box.

If you need outside assistance because of a program error, Dr. Watson for Windows, a tool that is included in Microsoft Windows XP, and Problem Reports and Solutions, a tool in Windows Vista and Windows 7, gather information about the computer when there is a program error. When an error occurs, these tools automatically create and save a log. The log can then be viewed, printed, or delivered electronically to any technical support professional, who can then use this information to help diagnose the problem.

System Restore and Backup Utilities

Is there an undo command for the system? Say you have just installed a new software program and your computer freezes. After rebooting the computer, when

Making Tech Support Easier

Have you ever been frustrated trying to clearly and accurately describe your problem or an error message you have received to a technical support person? Have you had trouble remembering the steps you took to encounter a problem? Or, are you on the other side, trying to help via the phone a friend or family member with their problems? If so, Windows 7 has a cool new feature called Problem Steps Recorder that you can use to capture all your mouse clicks and keystrokes. In addition to capturing the clicks and keystrokes you make to reproduce the problem or error, the Problem Steps Recorder provides screen shots of your actions. The captured data is stored in a zipped file. You can then send the zipped file to your technical support person.

To start Problem Steps Recorder, click Start, type psr.exe in the search box, and press Enter. When Problem Steps Recorder displays, click the Start Record button and continue the steps to reproduce the problem or error. You can add comments as you go. The end result is a slideshow of all your actions, along with descriptions (in regular English—not code) of what you did.

Figure 5.31

The Problem Steps Recorder captures the clicks and keystrokes you make to reproduce a problem or error.

you try to start the application, the system freezes once again. You uninstall the new program, but your computer continues to freeze after rebooting. What can you do now?

The most recent versions of Windows have a utility called **System Restore** that lets you roll your system settings back to a specific date when everything was working properly. A **system restore point**, which is a snapshot of your entire system's settings, is made every week and prior to certain events, such as installing or updating software. You also can create a custom restore point manually. Should problems occur, if the computer was running just fine before you installed new software or a hardware device, you could restore your computer to the settings that were in effect before the software or hardware installation. System Restore does not affect your personal data files (such as Microsoft Word documents, browsing history, or e-mail), so you won't lose changes made to these files when you use System Restore.

To understand how disk defragmenter utilities work, you must first understand the basics of how a hard disk drive stores files. A hard disk drive is composed of several *platters*, or round, thin plates of metal, that are covered with a special magnetic coating that records the data. The platters are about 3.5 inches in diameter and are stacked onto a spindle. There are usually two or three platters in any hard disk drive, with data stored on one or both sides. Data is recorded on hard disks in concentric circles called tracks. Each **track** is further broken down into pie-shaped wedges, each called a **sector** (see Figure 5.32). The data is further identified by *clusters*, which are the smallest segments within the sectors.

When you want to save (or write) a file, the bits that make up your file are recorded onto one or more clusters of the drive. To keep track of which clusters hold which files, the drive also stores an index of all sector numbers in a table. To save a file, the computer will look in the table for clusters that are not already being used. It will then record the file information on those clusters. When you open (or read) a file, the computer searches through the table for the clusters that hold the desired file and reads that file. Similarly, when you delete a file, you are actually not deleting the file itself, but rather the reference in the table to the file.

How does a disk become fragmented? When only part of an older file is deleted, the deleted section of the file creates a gap in the sector of the disk where the data was originally stored. In the same way, when new information is added to an older file, there may not be space to save the new information sequentially near where the file was originally saved. In that case, the system writes the added part of the file to the next available location on the disk, and a reference is made in the table as to the location of this file fragment. Over time, as files are saved, deleted, and modified, the bits of information for various files fall out of sequential order and the disk becomes fragmented.

Disk fragmentation is a problem because the operating system is not as efficient when a disk is fragmented. It takes longer to locate a whole file because more of the disk must be searched for the various pieces, greatly slowing down the performance of your computer.

How can you make the files line up more efficiently on the disk? At this stage, the disk defragmenter utility enters the picture. The defragmenter tool takes the hard drive through a defragmentation process in which pieces of files that are scattered over the disk are placed together and arranged sequentially on the hard disk. Also, any unused portions of clusters that were too small to save data in before are grouped, increasing the available storage space on the disk. Figure 5.33 shows before and after shots of a fragmented disk that has gone through the defragmentation process.

For more about hard disks and defragmenting, be sure to check out the Sound Byte "Hard Disk Anatomy Interactive."

Track

Sector

Cluster

Figure 5.32
On a hard disk platter, data is recorded onto tracks, which are further broken down into sectors and clusters.

Fragmented files on disk

Defragmented files on disk

Figure 5.33
Defragmenting the hard drive arranges file fragments so that they are located next to each other. This makes the hard drive run more efficiently.

How does the computer remember its previous settings? Every time you start your computer or install a new application or driver, Windows automatically creates a system restore point. You also can create and name your own restore points at any time. Creating a restore point is a good idea before making changes to your computer such as installing hardware or software. If something goes wrong with the installation process, Windows can reset your system to the restore point. As shown in Figure 5.34, Windows includes a Restore Point Wizard that walks you through the process of setting restore points.

How can I protect my data in the event something malfunctions in my system? When you use the Windows **Backup and Restore utility** (found in the Control Panel), you can create a duplicate copy of all the data on your hard drive (or just the folders and files you specify) and copy it to another storage device, such as a DVD or external hard drive. A backup copy protects your data in the event your hard drive fails or files are accidentally erased. Although you may not need to back up every file on your computer, you should back up the files that are most important to you and keep the backup copy in a safe location. Mac OS X Snow Leopard includes a backup utility called Time Machine that will automatically back up your files to a specified location. Apple also offers backup hardware called Time Capsules, which are wireless devices designed to work with Time Machine and record your backup data. Because Time Machine makes a complete image copy of your system, it can also be used to recover your system in the case of a fatal error. (For more information on backing up your files, see Chapter 9.)

If you encounter a non-recoverable error on a Windows machine that System Restore cannot repair, you can recover Windows from a system repair disc. A system repair disc is designed to fix problems with Windows 7. It will let you boot up Windows, and then give you options for repairing your system. It won't reinstall

Windows 7 and it won't reformat your computer; it's just a means to get to the recovery tools that are incorporated into Windows. Sometimes your computer comes with these repair discs, but often they do not. If you do not have a system repair disc, you should create one before problems arise. With Windows 7, it is easy to create a system repair disc. Insert a blank disc into the DVD drive, click Start, and type "System Repair" in the Search box. Then, click on Create a System Repair Disc, make sure the appropriate drive is showing, and click Create disc.

The Task Scheduler Utility

How can I remember to perform all these maintenance procedures? To keep your computer system in top shape, it is important to run some of the utilities described previously on a routine basis. Depending on your usage, you may want to defrag your hard drive or clean out temporary Internet files periodically. However, many computer users forget to initiate these tasks. Luckily, the Windows **Task Scheduler utility**, shown in Figure 5.35, allows you to schedule tasks to run automatically at predetermined times, with no additional action necessary on your part.

Figure 5.34

Setting a restore point is good practice before installing any hardware or software.

>The Restore Point Wizard is found by clicking **Start, All Programs, Accessories, System Tools**. In the System Tools folder, click **System Restore**. The System Restore wizard appears, with Restore Point shown on the first page of the Wizard.

SOUND BYTE — Hard Disk Anatomy Interactive

In this Sound Byte, you'll watch a series of animations that show various aspects of a hard drive, including the anatomy of a hard drive, how a computer reads and writes data to a hard drive, and the fragmenting and defragmenting of a hard drive.

Figure 5.35

To keep your machine running in top shape, use Task Scheduler to schedule maintenance programs to run automatically at selected times and days.

>Task Scheduler is found by clicking **Start, All Programs, Accessories,** and then **System Tools.**

Accessibility Utilities

Are there utilities designed for users with special needs? Microsoft Windows includes an Ease of Access Center, which is a centralized location for assistive technology and tools to adjust accessibility settings. In the Ease of Access Center, you can find tools to help you adjust the screen contrast, magnify the screen image, have screen contents read to you, and display an on-screen keyboard, as more fully explained in the following list. If you're not sure where to start or what settings might help, a questionnaire asks you about routine tasks and

provides a personalized recommendation for settings that will help you use your computer (see Figure 5.36). Some of these features are described below.

- **High Contrast:** Allows you to select a color scheme setting in which you can control the contrast between text and background. Because some visually impaired individuals find it easier to see white text on a dark background, there are color schemes that invert screen colors.

- **Magnifier:** A utility that creates a separate window that displays a magnified portion of the screen. This feature makes the screen more readable for users who have impaired vision.

- **Narrator:** A very basic speech program that reads what is on screen, whether it's the contents of a window, menu options, or text you have typed. The Narrator coordinates with text utilities such as Notepad and WordPad as well as with Internet Explorer, but it may not work correctly with other programs. For this reason, Narrator is not meant for individuals who must rely solely on a text-to-speech utility to operate the computer.

SOUND BYTE

Letting Your Computer Clean Up After Itself

In this Sound Byte, you'll learn how to use the various maintenance utilities within the operating system. In addition, you'll learn how to use Task Scheduler to clean up your hard drive automatically. You'll also learn the best times of the day to schedule these maintenance tasks, and why they should be done on a routine basis to make your system more efficient.

- **On-Screen Keyboard:** Displays a keyboard on the screen. You type by clicking on or hovering over the keys with a pointing device (mouse or trackball) or joystick. This utility, which is similar to the Narrator, is not meant for everyday use for individuals with severe disabilities. A separate program with more functionality is better in those circumstances.
- **Windows Speech Recognition:** An effective tool that allows you to dictate text and control your computer by voice. The Speech Recognition utility is in the Ease of Access folder.

Whether you use Windows, OS X, Linux, or another operating system, a fully featured operating system is available to

Need a System Software Update?

Bugs, or problems, in software occur all the time. Software developers are constantly testing their products, even after releasing the software to the retail market, and as users report errors they find. Windows Update is Microsoft's service (utility) for updating operating system software. Windows Update automatically notifies Windows users when updates are available for download. Mac users can update their system with Software Update, found under System Preferences.

meet your needs. As long as you keep the operating system updated and regularly use the available utilities to fine-tune your system, you should experience little trouble from your OS.

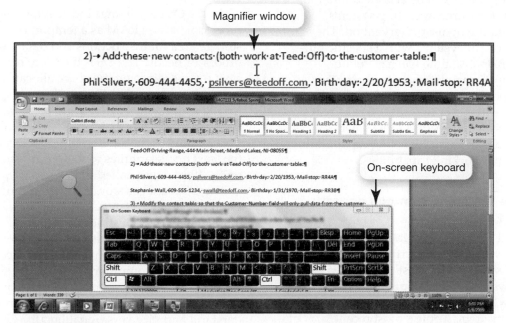

Figure 5.36

Microsoft Windows includes an Ease of Access Center to help users with disabilities. It has handy accessibility features such as a magnifier and an on-screen keyboard.

>The Ease of Access Center is found by clicking **Start, All Programs, Accessories, Ease of Access**.

1. What software is included in system software?

System software is the set of software programs that helps run the computer and coordinates instructions between application software and hardware devices. It consists of the operating system (OS) and utility programs. The OS controls how your computer system functions. Utility programs are programs that perform general housekeeping tasks for the computer, such as system maintenance and file compression.

2. What are the different kinds of operating systems?

Operating systems can be classified into four categories. Real-time operating systems (RTOSs) require no user intervention. They are designed for systems with a specific purpose and response time (such as robotic machinery). Smartphones have their own specific operating systems, the latest of which allow the user to multitask. Current operating systems for desktops, notebooks, and netbooks have multitasking capabilities, as well as networking capabilities.

3. What are the most common operating systems?

Microsoft Windows is the most popular OS. It has evolved into a powerful multiuser operating system. The most recent release is Windows 7. Another popular OS is the Mac OS, which is designed to work on Apple computers. Apple's most recent release, Mac OS X Snow Leopard, is based on the UNIX operating system. There are various versions of UNIX on the market, although UNIX is most often used on networks. Linux is an open source OS based on UNIX and designed primarily for use on personal computers, although it is often found as the operating system on servers.

4. How does the operating system provide a means for users to interact with the computer?

The operating system provides a user interface that enables users to interact with the computer. Most OSs today use a graphical user interface (GUI). Unlike the command- and menu-driven interfaces used earlier, GUIs display graphics and use the point-and-click technology of the mouse and cursor, making the OS more user friendly. Common features of GUIs include windows, menus, and icons.

5. How does the operating system help manage resources such as the processor, memory, storage, hardware, and peripheral devices?

When the OS allows you to perform more than one task at a time, it is multitasking. To provide for seamless multitasking, the OS controls the timing of events the processor works on.

As the OS coordinates the activities of the processor, it uses RAM as a temporary storage area for instructions and data the processor needs. The OS is therefore responsible for coordinating the space allocations in RAM to ensure that there is enough space for the waiting instructions and data. If there isn't sufficient space in RAM for all the data and instructions, then the OS allocates the least necessary files to temporary storage on the hard drive, called *virtual memory*.

The OS manages storage by providing a file-management system that keeps track of the names and locations of files and programs. Programs called *device drivers* facilitate communication between devices attached to the computer and the OS. Device drivers translate the specialized commands of devices to commands that the OS can understand and vice versa, enabling the OS to communicate with every device in the computer system. Device drivers for common devices are included in the OS software, whereas other devices come with a device driver that you must install or download off the Web.

6. How does the operating system interact with application software?

All software applications need to interact with the CPU. For programs to work with the CPU, they must contain code that the CPU recognizes. Rather than having the same blocks of code appear in each application, the OS includes the blocks of code to which software applications refer. These blocks of code are called *application programming interfaces* (APIs).

7. How does the operating system help the computer start up?

When you start your computer, it runs through a special process called the *boot process*. The boot process consists of four basic steps: (1) The basic input/output system (BIOS) is activated when the user powers on the CPU. (2) In the POST check, the BIOS verifies that all attached devices are in place. (3) The operating system is loaded into RAM. (4) Configuration and customization settings are checked.

8. What are the main desktop and windows features?

The desktop provides your first interaction with the OS and is the first image you see on your monitor once the system has booted up. It provides you with access to your computer's files, folders, and commonly used tools and applications. Windows are the rectangular panes on your screen that display applications running on your system. Common features of windows include toolbars, scrollbars, and minimize, maximize and restore, and close buttons.

9. How does the operating system help me keep my computer organized?

The OS allows you to organize the contents of your computer in a hierarchical structure of directories that includes files, folders, libraries, and drives. Windows Explorer helps you manage your files and folders by showing the location and contents of every drive, folder, and file on your computer. Creating folders is the key to organizing files because folders keep related documents together. Following naming conventions and using proper file extensions are also important aspects of file management.

10. What utility programs are included in system software, and what do they do?

Some utility programs are incorporated into the OS; others are sold as stand-alone off-the-shelf programs. Common Windows utilities include those that enable you to adjust your display, add or remove programs, compress files, defragment your hard drive, clean unnecessary files off your system, check for lost files and errors, restore your system to an earlier setting, back up your files, schedule automatic tasks, and check on programs that have stopped running.

key terms

Word Bank

- Disk Defragmenter
- Error-checking
- file compression
- file management
- files
- folders
- Linux
- Mac OS
- platform
- system files
- system software
- Task Manager
- Task Scheduler
- tracks
- utility programs
- Windows
- Windows Explorer
- Windows 7

Instructions: Fill in the blanks using the words from the Word Bank above.

Veena was looking into buying a new computer and was trying to decide what (1) _____ to buy—a PC or a Mac. She had used PCs all her life, so she was more familiar with the (2) _____ operating system. Still, she liked the way the (3) _____ looked and was considering switching. Her brother didn't like either operating system, so he used (4) _____, a free operating system instead.

After a little research, Veena decided to buy a PC. With it, she got the most recent version of Windows, (5) _____. She vowed that with this computer, she'd practice better (6) _____ because she often had a hard time finding files on her old computer. To view all of the folders on her computer, she opened (7) _____. She made sure that she gave descriptive names to her (8) _____ and placed them in organized (9) _____ and libraries.

Veena also decided that with her new computer, she'd pay more attention to the (10) _____, those little special-function programs that help with maintenance and repairs. These special-function programs, in addition to the OS, make up the (11) _____. Veena looked into some of the more frequently used utilities. She thought it would be a good idea to run the (12) _____ on her hard drive regularly so that all the files lined up in sequentially ordered (13) _____ and so that it was more efficient. She also looked into (14) _____ utilities, which would help her reduce the size of her files when she sent them to others over the Internet. Finally, she decided to use the Windows (15) _____ utility to schedule tasks automatically so that she wouldn't forget.

becoming computer literate

Using key terms from the chapter, write a letter to your 14-year-old cousin who just received her first computer, explaining the benefits of simple computer maintenance. First, explain any symptoms her computer may be experiencing (such as a sluggish Internet connection); then include a set of steps she can follow in setting up a regimen to remedy each problem. Make sure you explain some of the system utilities described in this chapter, including but not limited to Disk Defragmenter, Disk Cleanup, and Task Scheduler. Instruct your cousin on how to create a system repair disc and how to back up her files. Include any other utilities she might need, and explain why she should have them.

self-test

Instructions: Answer the multiple-choice and true–false questions below for more practice with key terms and concepts from this chapter.

Multiple Choice

1. Which is *not* an example of a smart-phone operating system?
a. Symbian
b. Android
c. Snow Leopard
d. webOS

2. Which OS does not have a user interface that incorporates point-and-click technology?
a. Windows 7
b. MS-DOS
c. Linux
d. Mac OSX

3. Which is the correct order of the boot process?
a. Check settings, load BOS into RAM, activate BIOS, conduct POST
b. Load OS into RAM, check settings, conduct POST, activate BIOS
c. Activate BIOS, conduct POST, load OS into RAM, check settings
d. Conduct POST, load OS into RAM, activate BIOS, check settings

4. You can determine the location of a file by its
a. name.
b. path.
c. extension.
d. type.

5. Which is *not* a function of the operating system?
a. Providing a means for the user to interact with the computer
b. Enabling the processor to handle multiple operations, seemingly at the same time
c. Carefully shutting the system down when RAM limits have been reached
d. Facilitating installation of peripheral devices with the inclusion of drivers

6. The term that defines excessive swapping of files between RAM and virtual memory is:
a. thrashing.
b. multitasking.
c. caching.
d. paging.

7. Which term describes the pictures that represent an object such as a software application or a folder?
a. Icon
b. Gadget
c. Taskbar
d. Widget

8. Which statement about using APIs is *not* true?
a. APIs prevent redundancies in software code.
b. APIs make it easier for developers to respond to OS changes.
c. APIs allow application software to interact with the OS.
d. APIs make it possible to close non-responding software and restart the computer.

9. Which utility eliminates the inefficiencies of the computer hard drive?
a. System Restore
b. Disk Defragmenter
c. File Compression
d. Disk Cleanup

10. Which utility is *not* a system tools utility?
a. System Restore
b. Disk Defragmenter
c. Windows Explorer
d. File Compression

True–False

_____ 1. Only personal computers need some form of operating system software.

_____ 2. Symbian OS is a common OS for netbooks.

_____ 3. The type of processor helps to determine which OS a computer uses.

_____ 4. Paging is the process of optimizing RAM storage by borrowing hard drive space.

_____ 5. Windows 7 includes a compatibility feature that allows you to run software that is not compatible with Windows 7.

making the
transition to...
next semester

five chapter

making the
transition to...
next semester

1. **Organizing Your Files**

   Despite all the good advice, you have not taken the time to organize your files on your computer. Now you have to plow through all your files to find anything, taking up valuable time. Use the Snipping Tool to show your current organization. Then, using the Hierarchy style of a SmartArt graphic, develop a plan that outlines how you'll set up libraries, folders, and subfolders for your files.

2. **Deciding On a New Computer**

   Your parents are getting you a new computer. Decide whether you want a desktop, notebook, or netbook and then describe how the choice may impact the operating system you get.

   a. Research the advantages of Windows, Mac, and Linux operating systems. Which best fits your needs and why?
   b. Research whether you can use multiple operating systems on a single machine. Why might this be an important feature for you to consider?
   c. Research how your smartphone and PMP would sync with the operating system.
   d. Explain which system would be most useful to you.

3. **Creating a Backup Plan**

   Your computer just shut down unexpectedly but, fortunately, you were able to get it back up and running without any loss of data. However, this was too close of a call, so you decide to back up your precious files once and for all. Research the specific steps you will need to take to initially create a backup and then maintain a current backup as your files change. Include in your research what stand-alone programs or operating system tools you will need to use, as well as any hardware devices or accessories you'll require. Then research the process of creating a disk image. What's the difference between creating a system backup and a disk image?

4. **Upgrading Your OS**

   You have been hearing great things about the newest release of the Windows operating system, Windows 7. Your notebook is running Windows XP, and you'd like to upgrade to Windows 7. Write a brief description of the requirements your notebook must meet in order to successfully run Windows 7. Does the amount of RAM your system has make a difference? Should you upgrade or purchase a full version of Windows 7? What steps will you need to take to install the new operating system onto your computer?

5. **Smartphone OS**

   Your cell phone contract is up in a few weeks, and it's time to upgrade to a smartphone. Which smartphone would you buy, and why? What kind of OS does it have? What are the benefits and disadvantages of this OS compared to that of other smartphones? Is the smartphone OS compatible with the OS on your computer?

making the transition to... the workplace

1. Time to Upgrade?

The small company you work for has been using Windows XP since it came out. The IT department decided not to upgrade to Vista, and because Windows XP is still working well, they are not contemplating an upgrade to Windows 7. However, you have been hearing lots of good things about Windows 7 and think it would be a good idea to upgrade. Write a letter to the head of the IT department informing him or her of the new features of Windows 7 and why they would be beneficial to have. Also, list the things the IT department should consider before upgrading.

2. Top 5 Utility Programs

Create a list of the top five utilities every computer should have. For each utility, list one that can be downloaded for free and one that can be purchased. Then, for each recommendation, include a review of the utility that has been written in the past 6 months—make sure you document your sources. For each utility note whether you would choose the free utility or the one you have to purchase, and include the reasons why.

3. Accessibility Features

Windows offers a lot of great accessibility tools for those needing extra assistance. The vice president for human resources at the company you work for has asked you to research some stand-alone accessibility programs to determine what else, if anything, is available. List software that is available to help those who have special computing needs.

4. Working with More Than One OS

The company you work for, which uses all Windows computers, has just acquired two other smaller companies, one that uses Macs and the other that uses Linux. Your boss, the CIO of the company, needs to decide what to do with all the various computer systems. You have been asked to provide information to your boss so that he can make an informed decision.

a. What are the advantages and disadvantages of letting the acquired companies continue using their current systems?

b. What are the advantages and disadvantages of converting all systems to one common system?

As you research, consider factors such as technical support, training for a new system, compatibility of files and calendars among all employees in the company, cost of new hardware, stability of operating systems, needed frequency of upgrades, and software compatibility.

Instructions: Albert Einstein used *Gedankenexperiments*, or critical thinking questions, to develop his theory of relativity. Some ideas are best understood by experimenting with them in our own minds. The following critical thinking questions are designed to demand your full attention but require only a comfortable chair—no technology.

1. Market Dominance

Microsoft and Apple are large corporations and have control of most of the operating system markets. While there has been some innovative changes to each of their proprietary operating systems, does their size and market dominance prevent more innovation? Why or why not? Linux, as an open source environment, is poised for greater innovation. Why do you think the Linux operating system doesn't have a greater market share?

2. A Web-Based OS

Operating system interfaces have evolved from a text-based console format to the current graphical user interface. Many believe the OS of the future will be on the cloud (the Internet) and Web-based. Discuss the implications of this type of operating system. What would be the advantages and disadvantages of a Web-based operating system?

3. Which Smartphone OS Would You Choose?

In the smartphone market, there are several operating systems such as Android, which runs on Google's Nexus One and the Motorola Droid; Apple OS, which runs on the Apple iPhone; Research in Motion's Blackberry OS, which runs on Blackberry phones; and webOS, which runs on the Palm Pre. When selecting a smartphone, explain which is more important in your decision-making process—the phone or the operating system?

4. Your Own Gadget?

There are plenty of interesting Windows gadgets available on the Web—some for fun, some to aid in productivity, some with specific utilitarian roles. Design or describe what the best gadget for you would be. What features must it have? Why would you need it?

Choosing the Best OS

Problem

You are the owner of a technology consulting firm. Your current assignments include advising several start-up clients on their technology requirements. The companies include a fashion design company, a small financial planning company, and an IT networking firm. The companies are holding off on buying anything until they hear from you as to the platform on which their computers should run. Obviously, one of the critical decisions for each company is the choice of operating system.

Task

Recommend the appropriate operating system for each company.

Process

1. Break up into teams that represent the three primary operating systems: Windows, Mac, or Linux. (Additional teams could be assigned to consider smartphone operating systems).

2. As a team, research the pros and cons of your operating system. What features does it have that would benefit each company? What features does it not have that each company would need? Why (or why not) would your operating system be the appropriate choice for each company? Why is your OS better (or worse) than either of the other options?

3. Develop a presentation that states your position with regard to your operating system. Your presentation should have a recommendation and include facts to back it up.

4. As a class, decide which operating system would be the best choice for each company.

Conclusion

Because the operating system is the most critical piece of software in the computer system, the selection should not be taken lightly. The OS that is best for a fashion design agency may not be best for a financial planning firm. An IT networking firm may have different needs altogether. It is important to make sure you consider all aspects of the work environment and the type of work that is being done to ensure a good fit.

In this exercise, you will research and then role-play a complicated ethical situation. The role you play may or may not match your own personal beliefs, but your research and use of logic will enable you to represent whichever view is assigned. An arbitrator will watch and comment on both sides of the arguments, and together the team will agree on an ethical solution.

Topic: Software Piracy

Software publishers spend millions of dollars developing new products. Illegal copies of software, including operating system software, rob the developers and their shareholders of their rightful profits. In addition, some say that pervasive software piracy, especially in China, could potentially threaten job loss for U.S. software companies. However, some people believe that when they buy the software, they have the right to distribute their copy as they like, thus violating the software license agreement they accepted when installing the software.

Research Areas to Consider

- Software piracy

- Software licensing agreements

- CD piracy

- China antipiracy

Process

Divide the class into teams.

1. Research the areas cited above and devise a scenario in which an individual has been accused of software piracy.

2. Team members should write a summary that provides background information for their character—for example, representative of a software developer, public consumer of the software, or arbitrator—and detail their character's behaviors to set the stage for the role-playing event. Then team members should create an outline to use during the role-playing event.

3. Team members should arrange a mutually convenient time to meet for the exchange, using the collaboration feature of MyITLab, the discussion board feature of Blackboard, or meeting in person.

4. Team members should present their case to the class or submit a PowerPoint presentation for review by the rest of the class, along with the summary and resolution they developed.

Conclusion

As technology becomes ever more prevalent and integrated into our lives, more and more ethical dilemmas will present themselves. Being able to understand and evaluate both sides of the argument, while responding in a personally or socially ethical manner, will be an important skill.

Computing|Alternatives

In this Technology in Focus feature, we explore software and hardware alternatives to working with a PC loaded up with Microsoft products. The world of computing is much broader than that, and many of the options we discuss are less expensive and more flexible. Let's get started by looking at alternatives to Microsoft Office products.

Application Software Alternatives

Corporations such as Microsoft and Apple develop proprietary (or commercial) software to be sold for a profit. Opponents of proprietary software contend that software should be developed without the profit motive and that the source code (the actual lines of instructional code that make the program work) should be made available so that others may modify or improve the software.

Open source software is freely distributed (no royalties accrue to the creators), contains the source code, and can in turn be distributed to others. Therefore, you can download open source software for free from various Web sites, install it on as many computers as you wish, make changes to the source code if you know how to do this, and redistribute it to anyone you wish (as long as you don't charge for distributing it). In this section, we look at some open source software that you can download and use on your computer. For a list of open source resources available on the Web, visit **sourceforge.net**.

PRODUCTIVITY SOFTWARE ALTERNATIVES: OPENOFFICE.ORG

As mentioned in Chapter 4, the OpenOffice.org suite (which we'll refer to as OpenOffice) is a free suite of productivity software programs that provides functionality similar to that of Microsoft Office. Versions of OpenOffice are available for a variety of operating systems, including Windows, Linux, and Mac. Support is offered in more than 100 languages besides English, with more being added all the time by the development community. You can download the installation file you'll need to run OpenOffice at **openoffice.org**. The minimum system requirements for installing OpenOffice 3 in a Windows environment are less than those required for Microsoft Office.

The main components of OpenOffice are word processing (Writer), spreadsheet (Calc), presentation (Impress), and database (Base) programs. These provide functionality similar to that of the Word, Excel, PowerPoint, and Access applications you might be familiar with in Microsoft Office. The OpenOffice 3 suite also includes additional programs. Draw provides the most common tools needed to communicate using graphics and diagrams, and Math creates equations and formulas for your documents.

You won't lose any compatibility with other software by using OpenOffice; it is compatible with most programs. This means that if your friend uses Microsoft Office and you send her an OpenOffice file, she can still read it, and you can read all of her Microsoft Office files, too. OpenOffice 3 is able to open Microsoft Office 2007 or 2010 files without the need for a conversion program. Although the individual applications in OpenOffice are not as fully featured as those in Microsoft Office, and do not have the ribbon interface found in the newest versions of the Office applications, OpenOffice is still a powerful productivity software suite, and the price is right.

One of the biggest advantages of an open source package like OpenOffice is that an incredible number of people continue to develop for it all the time. This means you have a huge library of extensions to select from. These small programs install themselves into OpenOffice and give you additional functions. For example, one extension allows you to import and edit PDF files; another allows Draw to easily create barcodes. The library of extensions includes many hundreds of items with more being added all the time.

When you launch OpenOffice (see Figure 1), you can choose a file type from the list displayed. Once you select the appropriate file type (such as spreadsheet, presentation,

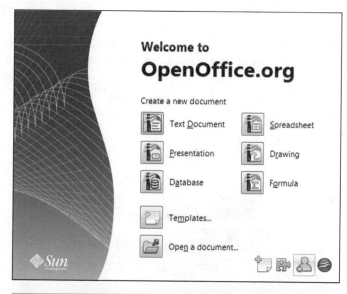

FIGURE 1

Starting OpenOffice.org displays a list of file types from which you can choose to begin working on your project.

or text) and click Open, the appropriate application and a new, blank document will open so that you can begin working.

Writer

Writer, the OpenOffice word processing application, is extremely similar in look and feel to Microsoft Word 2003 (see Figure 2). As is the case in Word, you can easily change text appearance in Writer by altering font type, style, alignment, and color. You can also easily insert graphics (pictures or clip art), tables, and hyperlinks into

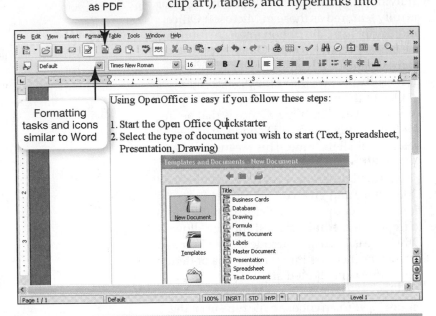

FIGURE 2

Writer provides similar functionality and icons to Microsoft Word.

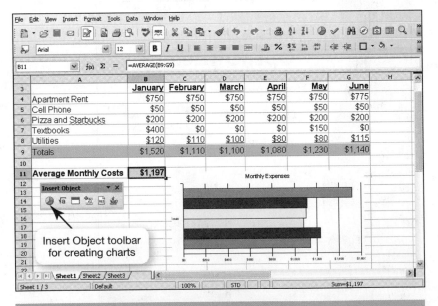

FIGURE 3

Calc offers many of the same features as Microsoft Excel.

documents. Writer's wizards provide you with several templates you can use to create standard documents such as faxes, agendas, and letters. Special tools in Writer also allow you to create bibliographic references, indexes, and tables of contents.

When saving a document in Writer, the default file format has an .odt extension. By using the Save As command, you can save files in other formats, such as various versions of Word (.doc and .docx), Pocket Word (.psw) for mobile devices, Rich Text Format (.rtf), Text (.txt), and HTML Document (.htm). The handy Export Directly as PDF icon in Writer allows you to save documents as PDF files.

Calc

Once you open a Calc spreadsheet, you enter text, numbers, and formulas into the appropriate cells, just as you would in Microsoft Excel. You also can apply a full range of formatting options (font size, color, style, and so on) to the cells, making it easy to create files such as the monthly budget spreadsheet shown in Figure 3. Built-in formulas and functions simplify the job of creating spreadsheets, and Calc's Function Wizard guides you through the wide range of available functions, providing suggestions as to which function to use.

When saving a document in Calc, the default file format has an .ods extension. You can also save files in other formats, such as Excel (.xls and .xlsx) and Pocket Excel (.pxl) for use on mobile devices. The Export Directly as PDF icon is also available in Calc.

Impress

When you select Presentation from the OpenOffice start-up interface, a wizard is displayed that offers you the option of creating a blank Impress presentation or building one from supplied templates. The number of templates shipped with Impress is smaller than those supplied with Microsoft PowerPoint. If you are interested in more templates, be sure to install some of the extensions available. In addition, you can also search Google using the keywords "OpenOffice.org Impress Templates." You'll find a wide variety of templates for Impress that others have created and that you can download free of charge. During the OpenOffice installation you have the option of installing the Google search bar (Web or Desktop), making it easy to access while you

Open source alternatives to Microsoft Office applications are attractive because they are free, and they are also convenient because of their availability. Like most other applications, though, you use these programs on the computer where you installed them. For the ultimate in accessibility and transferability, consider using Web-based Office software alternatives. You can be productive almost anywhere because you access these programs from the Internet without having to install the software on your computer. So if you are at friend's house, you can still get to your files and use the program. Moreover, with Web-based applications you can collaborate on a document online with others, thus avoiding the coordination mess that generally occurs when transferring documents among colleagues or classmates via e-mail. As mentioned in Chapter 4, Google Docs includes Web-based word processing, spreadsheet, and presentation applications. These applications, while useful for sharing and creating basic documents, lack many of the more robust features that Microsoft Office and other proprietary programs have.

Zoho (**zoho.com**) is another great Web-based productivity suite that features project management software, customer relationship management software, and other business solutions in addition to the traditional productivity applications. ThinkFree Office Live (**thinkfree.com**) is an online productivity suite comprising word processing (ThinkFree Write), spreadsheets (ThinkFree Calc), and presentations (ThinkFree Show). ThinkFree also offers ThinkFree Office for desktops and ThinkFree Mobile for smartphones and other mobile devices. Many of the features are available to you without registering and creating an account, and Web services are supported in English and many Asian languages. Like Google and Zoho, ThinkFree applications are fully compatible with Microsoft Office—including the latest formats—and run on Mac, Windows, and Linux platforms.

are working in any of the OpenOffice applications.

Base

If you want to create or just manipulate databases, Base enables you to create and modify tables, forms, queries, and reports by using wizards, design views, and SQL views. Base is similar to Microsoft Access and SQL Server, and it works seamlessly with files created in most database applications, although you will need a separate converter to work with Microsoft Access 2007.

DATABASE SOFTWARE ALTERNATIVES: MYSQL

While Base, the OpenOffice database program described above, is perfectly functional, if you're interested in getting your hands on a free high-end SQL database application, the most popular open source option is MySQL (**mysql.com**). Sporting many of the features contained in SQL Server and Oracle Database 11g, MySQL is a powerful database program you can use to develop serious database applications. The two main

components you should download and install with MySQL are the Database Server and the Query Browser (see Figure 4). You use the Database Server to create tables for your database and enter your data. The Query Browser

FIGURE 4

MySQL is a free open source database alternative to Microsoft Access.

provides a visual interface for the database to display the results of queries you create.

Although it is more difficult to learn and use than Microsoft Access, many books and online tutorials are available to help you get MySQL up and running.

E-MAIL CLIENT ALTERNATIVE: THUNDERBIRD

If you are exploring other choices for Microsoft Office productivity applications, don't overlook other e-mail clients as alternatives to Microsoft Outlook. Mozilla Thunderbird is an open source e-mail client that has many enhancements that allow you to organize e-mail with tagging, folders, search, and saved search features. The latest version, Mozilla Thunderbird 3, has new features like timeline and filtering tools to help find the exact e-mail quickly. Plenty of add-ons, including a blog editor, calendar, calculator, and multimedia tools, are available from the Mozilla Web site (**mozilla.org**). Thunderbird can run on Windows, Mac, and Linux platforms.

DRAWING SOFTWARE ALTERNATIVES: DRAW AND DIA

Microsoft Visio is a popular program for creating flowcharts and diagrams. However, Visio is not inexpensive. As mentioned

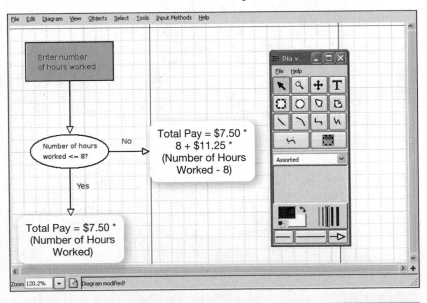

FIGURE 5

With Dia, you can create simple flowcharts, which a computer programmer might use in developing algorithms.

previously, OpenOffice includes a program called Draw that allows you to create simple graphs, charts, and diagrams. Another option is Dia, a free program that allows you to create Visio-like diagrams and charts (see Figure 5). You can download a Windows-compatible version of Dia from **live.gnome. org/Dia**. The Web site also offers a tutorial to get you up and running.

Google offers yet another charting option. SketchUp (**sketchup.google.com**) is a full-featured 3D modeling software application. SketchUp comes in two versions. SketchUp7 is a free program that you can use to create, modify, and share 3D models. SketchUp Pro 7 is more fully featured and is available for about $500.

WEB PAGE AUTHORING SOFTWARE ALTERNATIVES: SEAMONKEY

Although Microsoft Word and OpenOffice Writer can save documents as HTML files, sometimes you need a more versatile tool for creating Web pages, especially for larger sites with many linked pages. Adobe Dreamweaver is a popular commercial package for building Web sites, and Expression Web is a Web authoring application that is complementary to the Microsoft Office 2010 suite. Both of those solutions are proprietary applications that you must purchase. If you are looking for an open source alternative, SeaMonkey Composer, part of the SeaMonkey all-in-one Internet application suite (**seamonkey-project.org**), is a free, open source WYSIWYG ("what you see is what you get") Web authoring application that is compatible with the Windows, Mac, and Linux platforms. SeaMonkey Composer (see Figure 6) supports cascading style sheets, positioned layers, and dynamic image and table resizing. The SeaMonkey suite also includes a Web browser, e-mail and newsgroup client, and IRC chat.

IMAGE EDITING SOFTWARE ALTERNATIVES: GIMP

Do you need to create or edit some digital art but can't afford a high-end package such as Adobe Photoshop, or even a consumer package such as Adobe Photoshop Elements? Download a free copy of GIMP (short for GNU Image Manipulation Program) at

gimp.org and you'll find a set of tools almost as powerful as Photoshop. GIMP is available for systems running Windows, Mac, Linux, and UNIX. Many good tutorials, available at **gimp.org/tutorials**, can turn you into an accomplished user in no time.

Here are some handy things you can do with GIMP in five minutes or less:

- Crop or change the size of an image (see Figure 7).
- Reduce the file size of an image by decreasing its quality.
- Fix perspective distortion.

GIMP also enables you to use advanced techniques such as applying image filters, creating textures and gradients, drawing digital art, creating animated images through layer manipulation, and changing a photo into a painting or sketch.

Operating System Alternatives

Installing open source application software such as OpenOffice on a Windows machine is simple. Changing your OS from Windows to an open source OS such as Linux is a bit more complex. Why would you want to install Linux if you already are running Windows?

Because Windows is the most widely used OS, with more than 90 percent of the market share, it's a prime target for viruses and other annoyances. From a virus creator or hacker's perspective, nuisances that spread via Windows have the greatest chance of causing the most aggravation. A lot of spyware, computer viruses, and other hacker nuisances are designed to take advantage of security flaws in Windows. An open source OS alternative, such as Linux, that is not as widely used as Windows is less of a target for these annoyances.

Another reason to install an open source OS is portability. Depending on which version of Linux you use, you may be able to take it with you on a flash drive and use it on almost any computer. This portability feature appeals to people who use many different computers (such as lab computers at school). Instead of getting used to a new configuration every time you're away from your home computer, wouldn't it be nice to have the same environment you're used to everywhere you go? Such portability also offers an

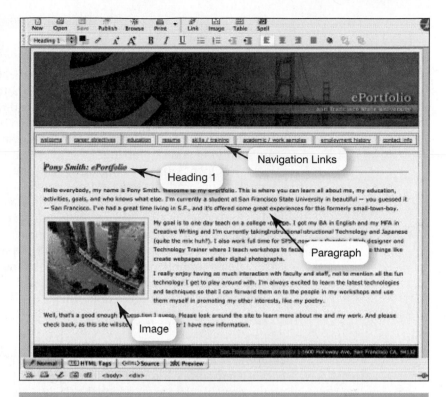

FIGURE 6

SeaMonkey Composer is an open source Web page authoring program that contains many features similar to those of leading commercial packages and is available at no cost.

additional level of protection for users of public computers. As explained in Chapter 9, using an open source OS that's installed on a portable flash drive helps reduce your risk of

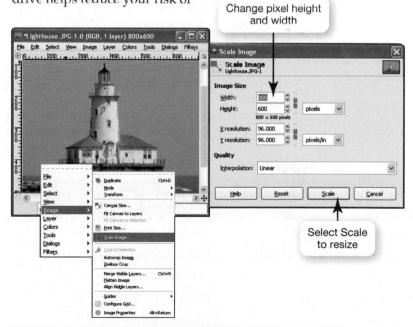

FIGURE 7

GIMP is a freely available software application for image editing.

Open Source Photography

The Open Source Photography group is dedicated to keeping you informed on all of the open source tools that make life easier for photographers. They maintain a wiki page at **wiki.osphoto.org** with tutorials, reviews, and how-to hints for using open source software in your photography projects. There are open source options all along the photography workflow—from image acquisition to processing and editing, printing and displaying, and archiving and organizing.

At the Open Source Photography wiki site, you'll see information on products like F-spot, a personal photo management system to help you share and organize your photos. Inkscape, which is also featured here, is a vector graphics editor like Adobe Illustrator. Pandora manuals and tutorials are here as well. Pandora is a plug-in for GIMP that allows you to create panoramic photos from a series of individual shots. The OSP wiki site is a one-stop shop for all things photographic in the open source community.

picking up viruses and malware from public computers. In addition, it enhances privacy, because temporary Internet files are stored on the portable device on which the OS is installed, rather than on the hard drive of the public computer you are using. Lastly, many users of netbooks, the lightest, smallest category of notebook computers, have opted to install Linux because it takes up less space on the hard drive and runs faster than the proprietary software that was installed originally by the manufacturer. In the next section, we explore the different varieties of Linux and explain how to install them.

WHICH LINUX TO USE

Linux is available for download in various packages known as **distributions**, or **distros**. Think of distros as being like different makes and models of cars. Distros include the underlying Linux kernel (the code that provides Linux's basic functionality) and special modifications to the OS, and may also include additional open source software (such as OpenOffice). Which distro is right for you?

A good place to start researching distros is **distrowatch.com**. This site tracks Linux distros and provides helpful tips for beginners on choosing one. Figure 8 lists some popular Linux distros and their home pages.

Before you can decide which distro is right for you, there are a few things to consider. The overall requirements to run Linux are relatively modest:

- A 1.2 GHz processor
- 256 MB RAM (light on graphics edition) up to 1 GB RAM (standard desktop edition)
- 8 GB of hard drive space
- VGA graphics card capable of 640 × 480 resolution

Just like any other software program, however, Linux performs better with a faster processor and more memory. Depending on how much additional software is deployed in the distro you choose to use, your system requirements may be higher, and you may need more hard drive space. Check the specific recommendations for the distro you're considering on that distro's Web site.

EXPERIMENTING WITH LINUX

Some Linux distros (such as Ubuntu and PCLinuxOS) are designed to run from a

FIGURE 8	Linux Distributions
Distro	**Home Page**
Debian GNU/Linux	**debian.org**
Fedora Core (Red Hat)	**fedoraproject.org**
Gentoo Linux	**gentoo.org**
Mandriva Linux	**mandriva.com**
PCLinuxOS	**pclinuxos.com**
Slackware Linux	**slackware.com**
Ubuntu	**ubuntu.com**

CD/DVD or flash drive. This eliminates the need to install files on the computer's hard drive. Therefore, you can boot up from a flash drive on an existing Windows PC and run Linux without disturbing the existing Windows installation.

Booting your existing computer from a CD/DVD or flash drive-based version of Linux is a low-risk way to experiment with Linux and see how well you like it. Ubuntu, for example, uses an extremely familiar-looking, Windows-like desktop. When you access Ubuntu, you get the Firefox browser as well as GIMP, OpenOffice, and many other software packages, including utilities and games.

Figure 9 shows Ubuntu in action. The computer boots from the Ubuntu disc when it detects it in the optical disc drive. As part of the installation sequence, Ubuntu automatically detects components of the computer (such as the network card) and configures Linux to recognize them. You will have no trouble browsing the Internet because Firefox, a Web browser, is included with the Ubuntu distro. You can also save any files you create with the included OpenOffice suite to a flash drive.

Mandriva Linux offers several versions of its OS. Mandriva Linux 2010 is the company's most recent and most basic product. It is free, remains true to the original open source principles, and is installable. Alternatively, you can try Mandriva in the "live" mode, which doesn't require installation. Other versions with more features are available for a fee, including PowerPack 2010 , which offers a more complete package that includes added multimedia and gaming software. In addition, for a small fee, you can get Mandriva Flash. Flash is Mandriva's portable OS option, and is installed on a convenient 8 GB flash drive. This portable version does not make changes on the host computer, so you can bring your computer environment anywhere you go. Mandriva Flash takes up one-quarter of the flash drive, leaving the remaining 6 GB free so you can conveniently store and take with you all your office work and Internet and multimedia files.

When you install the Mandriva OS, you also get other open source applications, such as OpenOffice, the Firefox browser, and the KMail e-mail manager, as well as several multimedia programs including applications for managing photo albums and digital music collections.

FIGURE 9

The Ubuntu user interface resembles the Windows desktop.

In addition to all this, Mandriva includes security features. The OS divides security levels into five rankings that range from "Poor" to "Paranoid." Your choice depends on how you're using the system. (Select "Paranoid" if you're running business transactions through your computer.) You also can set up a simple-to-configure firewall called Shorewall to prevent unauthorized Internet users from accessing your personal network.

If you don't like Mandriva Linux or Ubuntu, head out to distrowatch.com and find another free Linux distro to install. With hundreds of distros available, you're sure to find one that fits your needs.

Hardware Alternatives

Tired of your Windows-based PC? Is your old computer too slow for your current needs and not worth upgrading? If so, you may be in the market for some new hardware. Before you head off to the Best Buy for yet another Windows-based computer, why not consider two alternatives: (1) moving to an Apple platform or (2) building your own computer.

APPLE COMPUTERS

The best way to decide whether a Mac is right for you is to get your hands on one and take it for a test drive. Chances are that

FIGURE 10

(a) The MacBook Air. (b) The MacBook. (c) The iMac.

desktop units sporting fast Intel Core 2 Duo processors with even a quad-core choice, the Intel Core i5.

Some people are switching to Macs because they love their iPods so much. Many Apple fans think Macs are more user-friendly and stylish than their PC competitors. Professionals such as digital artists and graphic designers who create or edit computer images change to Macs because the applications these users rely on deliver superior features on the Apple platform.

Mac OS X Snow Leopard

Many Mac users have switched from Windows because of the operating system, Mac OS X. The latest version, Snow Leopard, has many slick and innovative features that are tempting to even the most loyal Windows users. If you've been using Windows for a while, you shouldn't have any problem making the transition to Snow Leopard. You'll notice immediately that the Mac OS uses the same desktop metaphors as Windows, including icons for folders and a Trash Can (similar to a Recycle Bin) to delete documents. It also includes a window-based interface like the one you're already accustomed to using in Windows.

Like earlier versions of Mac OS, Snow Leopard is based on the UNIX OS, which is exceptionally stable and reliable. Aside from stability, security and safety are great reasons to switch to the Mac OS because it does not seem as vulnerable as Windows is to the exploitation of security flaws by hackers. This doesn't necessarily mean that the Mac OS is better constructed than Windows; it could just be that because Windows has a lead in market share, it is a more attractive target for hackers. Regardless of the reason, you're probably somewhat less likely to be inconvenienced by viruses, hacking, and spyware if you're running Mac OS. Of course, you won't have any better protection from spam, phishing, or other Internet scams than you would with Internet Explorer, so you still need to stay alert. Snow Leopard offers a 3D desktop environment as well as an automated backup utility called Time Machine (see Figure 11).

someone you know has a Mac. Alternatively, your school might have a Mac lab or have Macs in the library. If not, then Apple has retail stores chock full of employees who are very happy to let you test out the equipment. You also can test Macs at Best Buy. Be sure to check out the full lineup of Macs (see Figure 10). The MacBook Air is Apple's thinnest notebook. It weighs three pounds, and includes a 13-inch screen and a full-sized keyboard. The MacBook weighs in at under five pounds and features the Intel Core 2 Duo processor and a 13-inch screen. The iMac line features sleek, space-saving

When you boot up a Mac, a program called the Finder automatically starts. This program is like Windows Explorer and controls the desktop and the windows with

FIGURE 11

Time Machine, an automated backup and restore utility, is one of the features in Mac OS X.

>To start Time Machine, open the Dock and click the Time Machine icon.

which you interact. It's always running when the Mac is on. With the Quick Look feature, it is possible for you to view the contents of a file without ever opening it. This allows you to flip through multipage documents, watch videos, and view an entire presentation with just a single click of the mouse. Spaces is the name of another feature that helps to keep order when projects pile up. With Spaces, you can group your application windows.

Snow Leopard has kept other features from previous versions, such as Spotlight, a desktop search feature that allows you to find anything on your computer from one spot. The Dashboard and widgets enable you to have easy access to many mini-applications that allow you to perform common tasks and get quick access to real-time information such as weather, stock prices, and sports updates.

At the top of the desktop is the menu bar. The options on the menu bar change according to which program is "active" (that is, foremost on your screen) at the moment. When you click the Apple icon in the upper left corner, a drop-down menu displays, from which you can select several options. The Dock is similar to the Taskbar in Windows and includes a strip of icons that displays across the bottom of the desktop.

Each Finder window has an area on the left known as the Sidebar (see Figure 12). The Sidebar holds any folders you specify (even though the icons don't look like folders). This makes navigation easier and faster. You can choose to view the contents of files and folders in three different views: icon view, list view, and column view. As shown in Figure 12, the sidebar shows that the PageOneEditing folder is selected. The files and subfolders in the PageOneEditing folder display in the next two columns. A display window shows a thumbnail preview of the selected file. Navigating around a Finder window and copying and moving files work almost exactly the same way as they do in Windows.

If you do have some Windows software you need to run, no worries—Mac OS X lets you install Windows Vista or 7 and run them using the built-in utility Boot Camp. With Boot Camp installed, you can fire up your computer in either Windows or Mac OS X. Other software tools like VMware and Parallels let you switch between Mac OS X and Windows without rebooting at all.

FIGURE 12

The Sidebar holds any folders you specify (such as the PageOneEditing folder shown here).

>To access the Sidebar, double-click the hard drive icon on the desktop.

Configuring a Mac

In Windows, you make changes to settings and preferences through the Control Panel. In Mac OS X Snow Leopard, you use System Preferences, which is an option on the Apple menu. Selecting System Preferences from the Apple menu displays the window shown in Figure 13.

FIGURE 13

Much like the Control Panel in Windows, the System Preferences window allows you to customize and configure Mac OS X.

>To get to System Preferences, click the **Apple** menu icon in the top left corner of the screen and choose **System Preferences**.

FIGURE 14

Macs have a firewall, but be sure to configure the firewall before you connect to the Internet.

>Click on the **Security** icon under the **Personal** section of the **System Preferences** window. When the Security window opens, click on the **Firewall** button to display the Firewall configuration screen.

Protecting Your Mac

Although Macs tend to be attacked less frequently by viruses and other hacker nuisances than PCs running Windows are, you can still be vulnerable if you don't take

FIGURE 15

Keeping the Mac OS up to date with the latest software fixes and patches greatly decreases your chances of being inconvenienced by hackers.

>From the **Apple** menu, choose **System Preferences**, and then click **Software Update**.

precautions. Snow Leopard comes with a firewall, but you should take the necessary steps to configure it properly before connecting to the Internet for the first time, because the firewall is set, by default, to allow all incoming connections. As shown in Figure 14, to block all connections except those that are critical to your computer's operation, select "Allow only essential services." If you'd rather set up your firewall on a per-application basis, select the Set access for specific services and applications option.

In addition, hackers may be creating viruses and other nuisances to exploit security holes in the Mac OS. Mac users, like Windows users, should keep their software up to date with the latest fixes and software patches by setting their system to check automatically for software updates on a periodic basis. On Macs, this feature is available through the System Preferences window. Figure 15 shows the options you should choose to keep the Mac OS up to date. The Check Now button enables you to check for immediate updates, which is a great thing to do when you first set up your computer. Then you can choose to have your computer check for updates regularly by scheduling software updates to run automatically at a time convenient to you. Make sure you choose to have the updates downloaded automatically. This feature alerts you when updates are ready to be installed. In addition to these precautions, antivirus software such as Norton is available for Snow Leopard.

Utility Programs

Just like Windows, the Mac OS contains a wide variety of utility programs to help users maintain and evaluate their computers. In Macs, utility programs are located in a folder named Utilities within the Applications folder on the hard drive.

If you're a Windows user, you know that the Windows Task Manager utility can help you determine how your system is performing. In Macs, a similar utility, shown in Figure 16, is called the Activity Monitor. It shows what programs (processes) are currently running and how much memory they're using. The CPU, System Memory, Disk Activity, Disk Usage, and Network buttons indicate the activity in each of these crucial areas.

Like the Systems Properties box in Windows, the Mac OS System Profiler shown in Figure 17 displays all the hardware (and software) installed in a Mac, including the type of processor, the amount of RAM installed, and the amount of VRAM on the video card.

As you can see, operating a Mac is fairly simple and is similar to working in the Windows environment. If you need more help beyond what we provide in this Technology in Focus feature, there are many books that will help you make a smooth transition to using an Apple computer.

DO IT YOURSELF!

There is definitely satisfaction in doing a job yourself, and building a computer is no different. Of course, building a computer isn't for everyone, but for those who enjoy working with their hands and don't mind doing some up-front research, it can be a rewarding experience.

Many Web sites can provide guidance for building your own Windows-based computer. Tom's Hardware (**tomshardware. com/reviews/build-your-own-pc,2601.html**) is a good place to start. Just Google "How to build your own computer" and you'll find plenty of online help and advice. To start, you need a list of parts. Here's what you'll typically need:

1. **Case:** Make sure the case you buy is an ATX-style case, which accommodates the newest motherboards, and that it includes adequate cooling fans. You'll want to decide between a full tower (about 24 inches tall) or a mid- or mini-tower. Also, be sure there are enough drive bays in the case to handle the hard drive and any other peripheral drives (CD/DVD, Blu-ray and so on) you'll be installing.

2. **Motherboard:** Make sure that the motherboard you buy can accommodate the CPU you have chosen. Many motherboards come with integrated sound, video, and network capabilities. These may work fine for you, but be sure to check that they meet your needs. You may want to plug in higher-end graphics and sound cards. The

Running processes and memory usage displayed

Graphical representation of CPU usage

CPU display

FIGURE 16

Similar to the Task Manager in Windows, the Activity Monitor analyzes the performance of a Mac.

>Go to the **Utilities** folder found in the **Applications** folder on your hard drive and double-click **Activity Monitor** to open the utility.

FIGURE 17

The System Profiler is similar to the Systems Properties dialog box in Windows and reveals a wealth of information about the hardware and software in the computer.

>To launch System Profiler, from the **Apple** menu, click **About this Mac**, and then click the **More Info** button.

motherboard needs to have enough PCI expansion slots for the video and sound cards you want to install. Make sure that your motherboard has at least 4 USB ports. Some motherboards now have USB 3.0 ports as well as the older USB 2.0.

3. **Processor (CPU):** Get the fastest one you can afford, because it will help to extend the life of your computer. Many processors come with a fan installed to cool the unit; if not, you'll need to purchase a processor cooling fan.

4. **RAM:** Check your motherboard specifications before buying RAM to ensure you buy the correct type and an amount that will fit into the available slots. In addition, make sure that the amount of RAM you choose is supported by your operating system (32 bit vs. 64 bit).

5. **Hard drive:** Some cases now support up to six drives so you may be able to make a few choices here. SSD drives are more expensive, but they are incredibly fast. In fact, many home system builders are using SSD drives as the boot drives so that the system boots in as little as 10 seconds. The price per gigabyte on mechanical drives has been rapidly coming down in recent years, so consider a large-volume drive. For optimal performance, choose a hard drive spinning at 7,200 rpm or 10,000 rpm.

6. **Power supply:** Make sure to get a power supply with adequate wattage to handle the load generated by all of the computer's components. Don't forget that as time passes you'll probably be adding more peripherals and drives to your system. Be sure to select a power supply wattage that can support that growth.

7. **Video card:** Low-end cards with 512 MB of video memory are fine for normal computer use, but for gaming or displaying high-end graphics or videos, get a card with 1 GB or more, depending on your budget. If you will be using a digital LCD monitor or hooking your gaming system to your computer, make sure that the video card has a DVI connection or an HDMI port.

8. **Sound card:** Make sure to get a PCI card that is compatible with Sound Blaster (the standard for sound cards).

9. **Optical drives (CD/DVD, and Blu-ray):** A CD/DVD drive is necessary for software installation. You may want to install a Blu-ray drive to view your favorite movies using high-definition technology, or a Blu-ray burner to archive large volumes of data.

In addition to these components, you'll need a keyboard, a mouse or other pointing device, a monitor, and OS software.

You can buy these components at reputable Web sites such as Tiger Direct (**tigerdirect.com**) or NewEgg (**newegg.com**). Once you have the components, it is almost as simple as screwing them into the case and connecting them properly. Make sure you read all the installation instructions that come with your components before beginning installation. Don't forget to check YouTube or the Web sites of component manufacturers for handy how-to videos and step-by-step installation guides. Then read a complete installation tutorial such as the one found at the Tech Report Web site (**techreport.com**), which provides an excellent visual guide to assembling a computer. Now, grab your screwdriver and get started. You'll be up and running in no time. The advantages and disadvantages of building your own Windows-based computer are shown in Figure 18.

As you can see, there are many computing options other than a Windows-based computer running commercial software applications. We hope you spread your wings and try a few of them.

FIGURE 18 Considerations When Building Your Own Computer

Advantages	Disadvantages
You get exactly the configuration and features you want.	There is no technical support when things go wrong.
You have the option of using components other than those that are used in mass-produced computers.	You'll need to examine more complex technical specifications (such as which CPU works with the motherboard you want), which may overwhelm the average computer user.
If you succeed, you will get a feeling of satisfaction from a job well done.	You will not necessarily save money.

Multiple Choice

Instructions: Answer the multiple-choice questions below for more practice with key terms and concepts from this Technology in Focus feature.

1. OpenOffice Calc is a
   a. calculator program.
   b. database program.
   c. Web browser.
   d. spreadsheet program.

2. A free alternative to Adobe Photoshop that can be used to edit images is
   a. GIMP.
   c. SeaMonkey.
   b. Thunderbird.
   d. Draw.

3. What kind of software can be installed on as many computers as you wish?
   a. Proprietary software
   c. Apple software
   b. Commercial software
   d. Open source software

4. Which is a popular open source program for creating diagrams and charts?
   a. Visio
   c. SketchUp
   b. Dia
   d. Impress

5. What automated backup utility comes with Mac OS Snow Leopard?
   a. Quick Look
   c. Dashboard
   b. Time Machine
   d. Spotlight

6. By default, files saved in Write use which extension?
   a. .txt
   c. .odt
   b. .docx
   d. .pdf

7. Which statement about Linux is FALSE?
   a. Because so many developers contribute to the OS, Linux is a prime target for hackers.
   b. Linux is used on a lot of netbooks because it takes up less hard drive space than proprietary software.
   c. When stored on a flash drive, Linux provides greater privacy when surfing the Internet on public computers.
   d. Some versions of Linux can be stored on a CD and used on many different computers.

8. What is NOT necessarily an advantage of building your own computer?
   a. Saving money
   b. Getting the exact configuration you want
   c. Using components that aren't mass produced
   d. Getting the features you want

9. One popular Linux distro is
   a. Leopard.
   c. OpenOffice.
   b. Base.
   d. Ubuntu.

10. When building your own computer, make sure the motherboard
    a. has enough PCI expansion slots.
    b. has a processor cooling fan.
    c. can wake up from sleep mode quickly.
    d. has its own drive bay.

six

understanding and assessing hardware:

evaluating your system

objectives

After reading this chapter, you should be able to answer the following questions:

1. How can I determine whether I should upgrade my existing computer or buy a new one? *(pp. 268–272)*

2. What does the CPU do, and how can I evaluate its performance? *(pp. 272–276)*

3. How does memory work in my computer, and how can I evaluate how much memory I need? *(pp. 276–279)*

4. What are the computer's main storage devices, and how can I evaluate whether they match my needs? *(pp. 279–286)*

5. What components affect the output of video on my computer, and how can I evaluate whether they match my needs? *(pp. 286–290)*

6. What components affect my computer's sound quality, and how can I evaluate whether they match my needs? *(pp. 290–291)*

7. How can I improve the reliability of my system? *(pp. 291–294)*

multimedia resources

Active Helpdesk

- Evaluating Your CPU and RAM **(p. 278)**
- Evaluating Computer System Components **(p. 287)**

Sound Bytes

- Using Windows 7 to Evaluate CPU Performance **(p. 276)**
- Memory Hierarchy Interactive **(p. 278)**
- Installing RAM **(p. 279)**
- CD, DVD, and Blu-ray Reading and Writing Interactive **(p. 283)**
- Installing a Blu-ray Drive **(p. 285)**

Companion Website

The Companion Website includes a variety of additional materials to help you review and learn more about the topics in this chapter. Go to: *pearsonhighered.com/techinaction*

how **cool** is this?

how cool is *this?* It used to be that the case for a desktop computer was just a boring rectangular box—but no longer! Consider some of the new designs on the market. On the **Phobos** computer system by BFG Technologies, the front of the case features a **touch-panel LCD** that reports system performance parameters, controls music content, and presents a summary of storage and memory usage. There is also an integrated iPod/iPhone **docking station** on the top of the case. Or consider Falcon NorthWest, which delivers **custom paint** jobs on its system cases—images from its library, your own image, or even a screen from your favorite game.

The Thermaltake Level 10 wins for pure **artistry**. It isolates all the major subsections—motherboard, power supply, hard drives, optical drives—in a separate physical space. Each section is hinged and can swing open for easy access. Made of aluminum, the entire case helps disperse heat . . . and looks cool doing it!

Is It the Computer or Me?

After saving up for a computer, Natalie took the leap a couple of years ago and bought a new desktop PC. Now she is wondering what to do. Her friends with newer computers are burning high-def Blu-ray movies they've made, and they're able to wirelessly connect their phones and synch up music files. They seem to be able to do a hundred things at once without their computers slowing down at all.

Natalie's computer can't do any of these things—or at least she doesn't think it can. Lately it seems to take longer to open files and scroll through Web pages. Making matters worse, her computer freezes often and takes a long time to reboot. Now she's wondering whether she should buy a new computer, but the thought of spending all that money again makes her think twice. As she looks at ads for new computers, she realizes she doesn't know what such things as "CPU" and "RAM" really are, or how they affect her system. Meanwhile, she's heard it's possible to upgrade her computer, but the task seems daunting. How will she know what she needs to do to upgrade, or whether it's even worth it?

Are you in the same situation? How well is your computer meeting your needs? Do you ever wonder whether your computer is fine and you just need more training to get it to work smoothly? Is that true, or do you really need a more sophisticated computer system? In this chapter, you'll learn how to evaluate your computer system to determine whether it is meeting your needs. You'll start by figuring out what you want your ideal computer to be able to do. You'll then learn more about important components of your computer—its CPU, memory, storage devices, audio and video devices, and ports—and how these components affect your system. Along the way, you'll find worksheets to help you conduct a system evaluation, and multimedia Sound Bytes that will show you how to install various components in your system and increase its reliability. You'll also learn about the various utilities available to help speed up and clean up your system. If you don't have a computer, this chapter will provide you with important information you will need about computer hardware to make an informed purchasing decision.

Is now a good time to buy a new computer? There never seems to be a perfect time to buy. It seems that if you can just wait a year, computers will inevitably be faster and cost less. Is this actually true?

As it turns out, it is true. In fact, a rule of thumb often cited in the computer industry, called **Moore's Law**, describes the pace at which CPUs (central processing units)—the small chips that can be thought of as the "brains" of the computer—improve. Named for Gordon Moore, the cofounder of the CPU chip manufacturer Intel, this rule predicts that the number of transistors inside a CPU will increase so fast that CPU capacity will double every 18 months. (The number of transistors on a CPU chip helps determine how fast it can process data.)

As you can see in Figure 6.1, this rule of thumb has held true since 1970, when Moore first published his theory. Imagine finding a bank that would agree to treat your money in this way. If you put 10 cents in that kind of savings account in 1965, you would have a balance of more than $100 million today! Moore himself, however, has predicted that around the year 2020 CPU chips will be manufactured in a different way, thus changing or eliminating the effects of Moore's Law altogether.

In addition to the CPU becoming faster, other system components also continue to improve dramatically. For example, the capacity of memory chips such as dynamic random access memory (DRAM)—the most common form of memory found in personal computers—increases about 60 percent every year. Meanwhile, hard drives have been growing in storage capacity by some 50 percent each year.

Figure 6.1

Moore's Law predicts that CPUs will continue to get faster.

Source: Adapted from the Moore's Law animated demo at Intel.com.

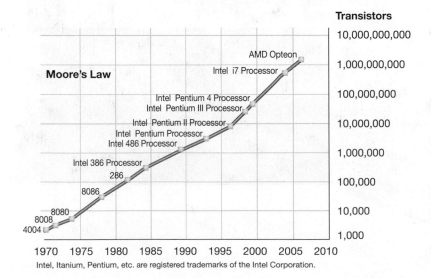

Intel, Itanium, Pentium, etc. are registered trademarks of the Intel Corporation.

So, with technology advancing so quickly, how do you make sure you have a computer that matches your needs? No one wants to buy a new computer every year just to keep up with technology. Even if money weren't a consideration, the time it would take to transfer all of your files and reinstall and reconfigure your software would make buying a new computer every year terribly inefficient. Extending the life of a computer also reduces or postpones the environmental and security concerns involved in the disposal of computers.

No one wants to keep doing costly upgrades that won't significantly extend the life of a system, either. How can you determine if your system is suitable or if it just needs to be upgraded? Moreover, how can you know which is the better option—upgrading or buying a new computer? The first step is figuring out what you want your computer to do for you.

> **To determine your ideal system, consider what you want to be able to do with your computer.**

What Is Your Ideal Computer?

As you decide whether your computer suits you, it's important to know exactly what you would want your ideal computer system to be able to do. Later, as you perform a system evaluation, you can compare your existing system to your ideal system. This will help you determine whether you should purchase hardware components to add to your system or buy a new system.

But what if I don't have a computer? Even if you're a new computer user and are looking to buy your first system, you will still need to evaluate what you want your system to do for you before you purchase a computer. Being able to understand and evaluate computer systems will make you a more informed buyer. You should be comfortable answering questions such as "What kinds of CPUs are there, and how does the CPU affect system performance?" and "How much RAM do I need, and what role will it play in my system?" It's important for you to be able to answer such questions before you buy a computer.

How do I know what my ideal system is? To determine your ideal system, consider what you want to be able to do with

your computer. For example, do you need to bring your computer to school or work with you? Do you want to be able to edit digital photos and video? Do you want to watch and record Blu-ray discs? Or do you mainly use your computer for word processing and Internet access? The worksheet in Figure 6.2 lists a number of ways in which you may want to use your computer. In the second column, place a check next to those computer uses that apply to you. Also, set a priority of high, medium, or low in the rightmost column so that you can determine which features are most important to you.

Next, look at the list of desired uses for your computer and determine whether your current system can perform these activities. If there are things it can't do, you may need to purchase additional hardware or a new computer. For example, if you want to play and burn CDs and DVDs, all you need is a DVD–RW drive. However, you need a Blu-ray burner if you want to burn (record) the higher capacity Blu-ray discs. Likewise, if you plan to edit digital video files or play games that require high video frame rates for smooth in-game motion and have amazing soundtracks, you may want to add more memory, upgrade your video card, and buy a better set of speakers. Depending on the costs of the individual upgrade components, you may be better off buying a new system.

BITS AND BYTES

Moving to a New Computer Doesn't Have to Be Painful

Are you ready to buy a new computer but dread the prospect of transferring all your files and redoing all of your Windows settings? You could transfer all those files and settings manually, but Windows stores much information in the registry files, which can be tricky to update. So what do you do? Windows 7 incorporates Windows Easy Transfer, which lets you migrate files and settings from a Windows Vista system to a Windows 7 system via a network connection by using a flash drive or external hard drive or using optical media such as a CD or DVD.

Alternatively, other PC migration software is available, such as LapLink's PCmover, which is designed to make the transition to a new computer easier. For the latest information on such utilities, search on migration software at PCmag (**pcmag.com**). You'll be ready to upgrade painlessly in no time. If you prefer to avoid the do-it-yourself option, support technicians at retail stores (such as the Geek Squad at Best Buy) will often perform the migration for a small charge.

Figure 6.2 | WHAT SHOULD YOUR IDEAL COMPUTER SYSTEM BE ABLE TO DO?

Computer Uses	Do You Want Your System to Do This?	Can Your System Do This Now?	Priority (High, Medium, Low)
Portability Uses			
Be light enough to carry easily			
Access the Internet wirelessly			
Entertainment Uses			
Access the Internet			
Play and record CDs and DVDs			
Play and record Blu-ray discs			
Record and edit digital videos			
Record and edit digital music			
Edit digital photos			
Play graphics-intensive games			
Transfer files wirelessly to mobile devices and other computers			
Transfer files using flash memory cards			
Upload media to social networking sites			
Have your peripheral devices work easily and speedily with your computer			
Purchase/rent music and videos from the Internet			
Talk with friends and family with live video and audio			
Use the computer to stream television and movies			
Other			
Educational Uses			
Perform word processing tasks			
Use educational software			
Access library and newspaper archives			
Create multimedia presentations			
Create backups of all your files			
Record notes with synchronized audio recordings			
Other			
Business Uses			
Create spreadsheets and databases			
Work on multiple software applications quickly and simultaneously			
Conduct online banking, pay bills online, or prepare your taxes			
Conduct online job searches or post résumés			
Synchronize your mobile device (smartphone or portable media player) with your computer			
Conduct online meetings with video and audio			
Organize business contacts and manage scheduling			
Other			

Note that you also may need new software and training to use new system components. Many computer users forget to consider the training they'll need when they upgrade their computer. Missing any one of these pieces might make the difference between your computer enriching your life and its becoming another source of stress.

Where do I get the training I need? Of course, colleges offer a number of training options from full semester classes, to online modules, to weekend courses. In addition many online tutorials are available for most software products. For specific questions or skills, be sure to check YouTube and podcast directories. Many valuable series exist that answer your questions in step-by-step video demonstrations, such as MrExcel or Photoshop Quicktips. Some manufacturers, like Apple, offer classes at their stores for a yearly fee. Training shouldn't be an afterthought. Consider the time and effort involved in learning about what you want your computer to do before you buy hardware or software. If you don't, you may have a wonderful computer system but lack the skills necessary to take full advantage of it.

Choosing Either a Desktop or Notebook System

The first step in evaluating your system needs is determining whether you want a desktop or a notebook. In this discussion, we'll only be considering full-size desktops and notebooks. If your main need is Internet connectivity, not processing power, and a small screen and small keyboard are acceptable, a netbook may be a workable option. Netbooks are discussed in detail in Chapter 8.

To make the best decision, it's important to evaluate how and where you will use the computer. The main distinction between desktops and notebooks is portability. If you indicated in the chart in Figure 6.2 that you need to take your computer with you to work or school, or even want the flexibility to move from room to room in your house, a notebook is the best choice. If portability is not an absolute requirement, you should consider a desktop.

How does a notebook compare to a desktop for value? Desktop systems are invariably a better value than notebooks in terms of computing power gained for your dollar. Because of the notebook's small footprint (the amount of space it takes up on the desk), you pay more for each component. Each piece has had extra engineering time invested to make sure it fits in the smallest space. In addition, a desktop system offers more expandability options. It's easier to add new ports and devices because of the amount of room available in the desktop computer's design.

If a large monitor is important, desktops have an edge. Although 18-inch screens are now available on some notebooks, the weight of these systems (often more than 10 pounds) makes them really more of a "desktop replacement" than a portable computing solution. Light notebooks typically have 17-inch screens or smaller, while inexpensive 23-inch monitors are readily available for desktop solutions. If you need a large screen and portability, you may end up buying a notebook and a fixed desk monitor to connect to when you are at home, an extra cost.

Desktop systems also are more reliable. Because of the amount of vibration that a notebook experiences and the added exposure to dust, water, and temperature fluctuations that portability brings, notebooks often have a shorter lifespan than desktop computers. Manufacturers offer extended warranty plans that cover accidental damage and unexpected drops; however, such plans may be costly.

BITS AND BYTES

Taking Your System Out of the Box

You just brought your brand-new machine home, and it's loaded up with all kinds of bloat! Here are two steps you can take right away to have that truly fresh beginning you were hoping for.

1. Remove the preinstalled trial programs and advertisements installed by most vendors. A quick way to do this is with the free program PC DeCrapifier. Its wizard walks you through uninstalling the most common annoyances that came preloaded on your new system.

2. Grab the really valuable free software you *will* want to use. Consider loading OpenOffice.org, Firefox, iTunes, Picasa, and Gimp. (These packages are discussed in more detail in the Technology in Focus section titled "Computing Alternatives.")

Now go enjoy your new machine!

Assessing Your Hardware: Evaluating Your System

With a better picture of your ideal computer system in mind, you can make a more informed assessment of your current computer. To determine whether your computer system has the right hardware components to do what you ultimately want it to do, you need to conduct a **system evaluation**. To do this, you look at your computer's subsystems, see what they do, and check how they perform. These subsystems include the following:

- CPU subsystem
- Memory subsystem (the computer's random access memory, or RAM)
- Storage subsystem (hard drive and other drives)
- Video subsystem (video card and monitor)
- Audio subsystem (sound card and speakers)
- Ports

In the rest of this chapter, we will examine each subsystem. At the end of each section, you'll find a small worksheet you can use to evaluate each subsystem on your computer. *Note:* This chapter discusses tools you can use to assess a Windows-based PC. For information on how to assess a Mac, refer to the Technology in Focus feature "Computing Alternatives" on page 252.

Evaluating the CPU Subsystem

Early in the process of determining whether your computer system adequately meets your needs, you'll want to consider the type

How long will a notebook be useful to me? The answer to that question depends on how easy it is to upgrade your system. Take note of the maximum amount of memory you can install in your notebook because that cannot be changed a few years down the road. Internal hard drives are not easy for novices to install in a notebook, but if you have a fast transfer port like an **external SATA (eSATA)** or USB 3.0 on your notebook, you can easily add an external hard drive for more storage space.

Notebooks are often equipped with an ExpressCard slot. **ExpressCard** (shown in Figure 6.3) can add a solid state drive (SSD), eSATA and FireWire ports, and other capabilities to your system. You can add an ExpressCard that allows you to read flash memory cards such as CompactFlash, Memory Sticks, and Secure Digital cards. As new types of ports and devices are introduced, like those for the new USB 3.0 standard, they will be manufactured in ExpressCard formats so you can make sure your notebook does not become obsolete before its time. Figure 6.4 summarizes the advantages and disadvantages of each style of computer.

Figure 6.3

ExpressCards add functionality to your notebook.

Figure 6.4	DESKTOP VERSUS NOTEBOOK COMPUTERS—WHICH FITS YOU?
Notebooks	Desktops
Portable—lightweight, thin	Best value: more processing power, memory, and storage capacity for lower price
Take up less physical space	More difficult to steal, less susceptible to damage from dropping or mishandling
Easier to ship or transport if the system needs repair	Easier to expand and upgrade
Smaller video display (17 inches or smaller)	Large monitors available (19 inches or larger)

of processor in your system. As mentioned in chapter 2, your computer's central processing unit (CPU or processor) is critically important because it processes instructions, performs calculations, manages the flow of information through a computer system, and is responsible for turning raw data into valuable information through processing operations. The CPU is located on the motherboard, the primary circuit board of the computer system. There are several types of processors on the market including Intel processors (such as the Core family with the i7, i5, i3, and the Centrino line) and AMD processors (such as the Athlon and Phenom). The Intel Core i7 is the most advanced desktop CPU ever made by Intel. Figure 6.5 shows the i7 as well as the three-core PowerPC processor used in the Microsoft Xbox 360 gaming console, the Xenon.

Figure 6.5

(a) The Intel i7 is the most advanced desktop CPU ever made by Intel. (b) The Microsoft Xbox 360 gaming console uses a custom PowerPC–based CPU to perform 115 billion calculations per second.

How does the CPU work? The CPU is comprised of two units: the control unit and the arithmetic logic unit (ALU). The control unit coordinates the activities of all the other computer components. The ALU is responsible for performing all the arithmetic calculations (addition, subtraction, multiplication, and division). The ALU also makes logic and comparison decisions such as comparing items to determine if one is greater than, less than, equal to, or not equal to another.

Every time the CPU performs a program instruction, it goes through the same series of steps. First, it fetches the required piece of data or instruction from RAM, the temporary storage location for all the data and instructions the computer needs while it is running. Next, it decodes the instruction into something the computer can understand. Once the CPU has decoded the instruction, it executes the instruction and stores the result to RAM before fetching the next instruction. This process is called a machine cycle. (We will discuss the machine

cycle in more detail in the Technology in Focus feature "Under the Hood" on page 346.)

What makes one CPU different from another? The primary distinction between CPUs is processing power, which is determined by a number of factors. One such factor is the design of the CPU in terms of the number of cores. A **core** is a complete processing section from a CPU embedded into one physical chip. In addition to core design, other factors differentiate CPUs, including how quickly the processor can work (called its **clock speed**) and the amount of immediate access memory the CPU has (called its cache memory).

How will a multiple-core CPU help me? CPUs began to execute more than one instruction at a time quite a while ago, when hyperthreading was introduced. **Hyperthreading** provides quicker processing of information by enabling a new set of instructions to start executing before the previous set has finished. The most recent design innovation for PC processors, an improvement upon hyperthreading, is the use of multiple cores on one CPU chip. With core technology, two or more processors reside on the same chip, enabling the execution of two sets of instructions at the same time. Now applications that are always running behind the scenes, such as virus protection software and your operating system, can have their own processor, freeing the other processor to run other applications such as a Web browser, Word, or iTunes more efficiently. Figure 6.6 shows these different approaches.

In Figure 6.6c, hyperthreading allows two different programs to be processed at one time, but they are sharing the computing resources of the chip. With multiple cores, each program has the full attention of its own processing core (see Figure 6.6a and Figure 6.6b). This results in faster processing

Four cores

Web Browser · Virus Scan · Music · Gaming

Two cores

Video Editing · Virus Scan

Hyperthreading

Web Browser · Virus Scan

Figure 6.6

(a) Some Intel processors have four cores able to run four programs simultaneously. (b) Some Intel processors have two cores. (c) The Intel Pentium 4 Hyperthreading operates with only one core but it hyperthreads (working on two processes at once).

and smoother multitasking. It is possible to design a CPU to have multiple cores *and* hyperthreading. The Intel i7-980x has six cores, each one using hyperthreading, so it simulates having twelve processors!

How do I pick the fastest processor? While clock speed is an important consideration when determining processor performance, CPU performance also is affected by the amount of cache memory and the speed of the front side bus (FSB). **Cache memory** is a form of random access memory that is more accessible to the CPU than regular RAM. Because of its ready access to the CPU, cache memory gets data to the CPU for processing much faster than bringing the data in from RAM.

There are several levels of cache memory. These levels are defined by a chip's proximity to the CPU. Level 1 cache is a block of memory that is built onto the CPU chip for the storage of data or commands that have just been used. Level 2 cache is located on the CPU chip but is slightly farther away from the CPU, or it's on a separate chip next to the CPU and therefore takes somewhat longer to access. Level 2 cache contains more storage area than does level 1 cache. In the same way, some chips continue on to have a third cache, Level 3. Again, this level of cache is slower for the CPU to reach but larger in size.

Another factor that impacts overall performance is the FSB speed. The **front side bus (FSB)** connects the processor (CPU) in your computer to the system memory. Think of the front side bus as the highway on which data travels between the CPU and RAM. With a wider highway, traffic can move faster because more cars can travel at the same time. Consequently, the faster the FSB is, the faster you can get data to your processor. The faster you get data to the processor, the faster your processor can work on it. FSB speed is measured in megahertz (MHz). The speed of the front side bus is an important consideration that determines CPU performance.

Modern processors are defined by the combination of processor speed, front side bus speed, and the amount of cache memory. For example, Intel has several processor families, in a range of clock speeds, cache memory sizes, and FSB speeds, as shown in Figure 6.7. Even within one processor family, there is a variety of choices. For example, the i7-980X processor has six cores, and a 12 MB cache, whereas the i7-860S processor has four cores and an 8 MB L3 cache.

Figure 6.7 | PROCESSOR SPECIFICATIONS

		Number of Cores	Max Clock Speed	Max FSB	Max L3 Cache
Desktop Processors	i3-530	2	2.93 GHz	1333 MHz	4 MB
	i5-750	4	2.66 GHz	1333 MHz	8 MB
	i7-980X	6	3.30 GHz	1600 MHz	12 MB
Notebook Processors	Celeron 585	1	2.16 GHz	666 MHz	1 MB
	i5 mobile 520	2	1.07 GHz	1066 MHz	3 MB
	i7 mobile 820	4	1.73 GHz	1333 MHz	8 MB

There are many factors that influence CPU design, so picking the fastest CPU for the kind of work you do often involves researching some performance benchmarks. **Benchmarks** are measurements used to compare CPU performance between processors. Benchmarks are generated by running software programs specifically designed to push the limits of CPU performance. Articles are often published comparing a number of chips, or complete systems, based on their benchmark performance. Investigate a few, like **cpubenchmark.net**, before you select the chip that is best for you.

Why are there different CPU choices for notebooks and desktops?

Both Intel and AMD make processors that are specifically designed for notebook computers. Notebook processors not only need to perform quickly and efficiently, like their desktop counterparts, but also need better power savings to improve battery life. Processors used in notebooks work to combine low power consumption, to support long battery life, and more flexible wireless connectivity options. AMD features notebook processors like the Turion X2 Mobile and the Mobile AMD Sempron, while Intel has mobile versions of the i5 and i7 series.

What CPU does my current computer have?

You can easily identify the type of CPU in your current system by accessing the System Properties. As shown in Figure 6.8, you can view basic information about your computer, including which CPU is installed in your system as well as its speed. More detailed information, like the FSB speed and the amount of cache memory, is not shown in this screen. You can find those values by checking the manufacturer's Web site for the specific model number of CPU shown. For example, the CPU illustrated here is the Intel i7, version 960.

How can I tell whether my CPU is meeting my needs?

As shown in Figure 6.9, several factors determine whether your CPU is meeting your needs. Even if your CPU meets the minimum requirements specified for a particular software application, if you're running other software at the same time (in addition to the operating system, which is always running), you'll need to check to see how well the CPU is handling the entire load. You can tell whether your CPU speed is limiting your system performance if you periodically watch how busy it is as you work on your computer. Keep in mind that the workload your CPU experiences will vary considerably depending on what you're doing. Even though it might run Word just fine, it may not be able to handle running Word, Photoshop, iTunes, and IM at the same time. The percentage of time that your CPU is working is referred to as **CPU usage**.

A utility that measures information such as CPU usage and RAM usage is incredibly

Figure 6.8

The System Properties window identifies which CPU you have, as well as its speed.

>Click the **Start** button and then click **Computer** on the right panel of the **Start** menu. On the top toolbar, click **System Properties**.

Figure 6.9 | HOW IS YOUR CPU PERFORMING?

	Current System	My Ideal System
What is my computer's CPU speed?		
How much cache memory is on the CPU*?		
What is the FSB speed*?		
What kind of multilevel processing does the CPU have—multiple cores, hyperthreaded, etc.?		
Is the CPU usage value below 90% during most of my daily tasks?		
*You can find these by checking the manufacturer's specifications for your model of CPU.		

CPU usage over time for all eight virtual cores

Total RAM installed

Current CPU usage level

Percentage of RAM in use

Figure 6.10

The Performance tab of the Windows Task Manager utility shows you how busy your CPU actually is.

>In an empty area of the taskbar, right-click, select **Start Task Manager**, and click the **Performance** tab.

useful, both for considering whether you should upgrade and for investigating if your computer's performance suddenly seems to drop off for no apparent reason. On Windows systems, a program called Task Manager gives you easy access to all this data. Mac OS X has a utility similar to Task Manager called Activity Monitor, which is located in the Utilities folder in your Applications folder.

To view information on CPU usage, right-click an empty area of the taskbar, select Start Task Manager, and click the Performance tab, as shown in Figure 6.10. The CPU Usage graph records your CPU usage for the past several seconds. (Note: If you have multiple cores and hyperthreading, you will see several CPUs listed.) Of course, there will be periodic peaks of high CPU usage, but if you see that your CPU usage levels are greater than 90 percent during most of your work session, a faster CPU will contribute a great deal to your system's performance. If you are using the Windows Sidebar, there is a CPU Meter gadget you can add to track both CPU and RAM usage. To see exactly how to use the Task Manager and the Sidebar gadget, watch the Sound Byte "Using Windows 7 to Evaluate CPU Performance."

Will improving the performance of the CPU be enough to improve my computer's performance? You may think that if you have the best processor, you will have a system with the best

performance. However, upgrading your CPU will affect only the processing portion of the system performance, not how quickly data can move to or from the CPU. Your system's overall performance depends on many factors, including the amount of RAM installed as well as hard drive speed. Therefore, your selection of a CPU may not offer significant improvements to your system's performance if there is a bottleneck in processing because of insufficient RAM or hard drive capacity.

Evaluating RAM: The Memory Subsystem

Random access memory (RAM) is your computer's temporary storage space. Although we refer to RAM as a form of storage, it really is the computer's short-term memory. As such, it remembers everything that the computer needs to process the data into information, such as data that has been entered and software instructions, but only when the computer is on. RAM is an example of **volatile storage**. When the power is off, the data stored in RAM is cleared out. This is why, in addition to RAM, systems always include **nonvolatile storage** devices for permanent storage of instructions and data when the computer is powered off. ROM memory, for example, holds the critical startup instructions. Hard drives provide the greatest nonvolatile storage capacity in the computer system.

Why not use a hard drive to store the data and instructions? It's about one million times faster for the CPU to retrieve a piece of data from RAM than from a hard drive. The time it takes the CPU to retrieve data from RAM is measured in

SOUND BYTE Using Windows 7 to Evaluate CPU Performance

In this Sound Byte, you'll learn how to use the utilities provided by Windows 7 to evaluate your CPU's performance. You'll also learn about shareware utilities (software that you can install and try before you purchase it) that expand on the capabilities the Task Manager utility provides.

nanoseconds (billionths of seconds), whereas retrieving data from a fast hard drive takes an average of 10 milliseconds (ms), or thousandths of seconds. Figure 6.11 shows the various types of memory and storage that are distributed throughout your system: CPU registers, cache, RAM, and hard drive. Each of these has its own tradeoff of speed vs. price. Because the fastest memory is so much more expensive, systems are designed with much less of it. This principle is influential in the design of a balanced computer system and can have a tremendous impact on system performance.

Are there different types of RAM? Like most computer components, RAM has gone through a series of transitions. In current systems, the RAM used most often comes in the form of double data rate 2 (DDR2) memory modules. Double data rate 3 memory (DDR3), which has an even faster data transfer rate, is seen in high-performance systems. In older systems, other types of RAM may have been used, including dynamic RAM (DRAM), static RAM (SRAM), and synchronous DRAM (SDRAM). RAM appears in the system on **memory modules** (or **memory cards**), small circuit boards that hold a series of RAM chips and fit into special slots on the motherboard (see Figure 6.12). Most memory modules in today's systems are called *dual inline memory modules* (DIMMs).

Types of RAM are slightly different from each other in how they function and in the speed at which they access memory. On high-end systems, manufacturers may offer an option to purchase Corsair Dominator DDR3 modules. These are tested to high levels to guarantee optimum performance. A special heat exchanger is designed into the RAM module to help it operate at a lower temperature, making it more stable and more reliable. All of these factors boost the performance of the memory and make it popular with demanding video gamers.

If you're adding RAM to any system, you must determine what type your system needs. Consult your user's manual or the manufacturer's Web site. In addition, many online RAM resellers, such as Crucial (**crucial.com**), can help you determine the type of RAM that is compatible with your system by running an automated system scan program on your computer.

How can I tell how much RAM is installed in my computer and how it's being used? The amount of RAM that is actually sitting on memory modules in your computer is your computer's **physical memory**. The easiest way to see how much RAM you have is to look in the System Properties window. (On the Mac, choose the Apple menu and then About This Mac.) This is the same tab you looked in to determine your system's CPU type and speed, and is shown in Figure 6.8. RAM capacity is measured in gigabytes (GB), and most machines sold today, especially those running Windows, have at least 2 GB of RAM. The computer in Figure 6.10 has 12 GB of RAM installed.

Windows 7 uses a memory-management technique known as SuperFetch. SuperFetch monitors which applications you use the

Figure 6.11

A computer system's memory has many different levels, ranging from the small amounts in the CPU to the much slower but more plentiful storage of a hard drive.

Figure 6.12

(a) Memory modules hold a series of RAM chips. (b) This Corsair memory module has an aluminum plate called a heat sink to cool the chips beneath it.

Evaluating Your CPU and RAM

In this Active Helpdesk call, you'll play the role of a helpdesk staffer, fielding calls about what the CPU does and how to evaluate its performance. You'll also field calls about how memory works and how to evaluate how much memory a computer needs.

Figure 6.14 | SAMPLE RAM ALLOCATION

Application	RAM Recommended
Windows 7	2,000 MB (or 2 GB)
Microsoft Office Professional 2010	512 MB
Internet Explorer 8	512 MB
iTunes 9	512 MB to 1,000 MB (1 GB)
Adobe Photoshop Elements 8	1,000 MB (1 GB)
Total RAM required to run all programs simultaneously	4,536 MB to 5,024 MB (or 4.5 GB to 5.0 GB)

most and preloads them into your system memory so that they'll be ready to go. For example, if you have Word running, Windows 7 stores as much of the information related to Word in RAM as it can, which speeds up how fast your application responds, because pulling information from RAM is so much faster than pulling it from the hard drive. This idea of caching the data you need in RAM, having it ready to use quickly when it is asked for, is different from how memory was used in earlier operating systems. You can watch this work using the Resource Monitor, which shows in Figure 6.13 how the 12 GB of installed RAM is being used: 3 GB is running programs, 6 GB is holding cached data and files ready to be quickly accessed, and 3 GB is currently unused.

How much memory does the operating system need to run? The memory that your operating system uses is referred to as **kernel memory**. This memory is listed in a separate Kernel Memory table in the Performance tab. In Figure 6.10, the Kernel Memory table tells you that approximately 555 MB (total kernel memory) of the total 12 GB of RAM is being used to run the operating system.

As you know from Chapter 5, the operating system is the main software application that runs the computer. Without it, the computer does not work. At a minimum, the system needs enough RAM to run the operating system. However, because you run additional applications, you need to have more RAM than the minimum.

How much RAM do I need?
Because RAM is the temporary holding space for all the data and instructions that the computer uses while it's on, most computer users need quite a bit of RAM. In fact, systems running all the new features of Windows 7 should have a minimum of 1 GB of RAM, but for peak performance, systems are recommended to have at least 2 GB of RAM.

To determine how much RAM you need, list all the software applications you might be running at one time. Figure 6.14 shows an example of RAM requirements. In this example, if you are running your operating system, word processing and spreadsheet programs, a Web browser, a music player, and photo editing software simultaneously, then you will need a minimum of 4.5 GB of RAM. It's always best to check the system requirements of any software program

Figure 6.13
The Resource Monitor's Memory tab shows a detailed breakdown of how the computer is using memory.

>In the **Resource Monitor**, click the **Memory** tab.

SOUND BYTE Memory Hierarchy Interactive

In this Sound Byte, you'll learn about the different types of memory used in a computer system.

before you buy it to make sure your system can handle it. System requirements can be found on the software packaging or on the manufacturer's Web site.

It's a good idea to have more than the minimum amount of RAM you need now, so you can use more programs in the future. Remember, too, that "required" means these are the minimum values recommended by the manufacturers, and having more RAM often helps programs run more efficiently. When upgrading RAM, the rule of thumb is to buy as much as you can afford but no more than your system will handle.

Adding RAM

Is there a limit to how much RAM I can add to my computer? Every computer has a maximum limit on the amount of RAM it can support. A motherboard is designed with a specific number of slots into which the memory cards fit, and each slot has a limit on the amount of RAM it can hold. To determine your specific system limits, check your owner's manual or the manufacturer's Web site.

In addition, the operating system running on your machine imposes its own limit. For example, the maximum amount of RAM for the 32-bit version of Windows 7 is 4 GB, while the 64-bit version of Windows 7 Ultimate can address up to 192 GB.

Once you know how much RAM your computer can support, you can determine the best configuration of memory modules to achieve the greatest amount of RAM. For example, say you have a total of four memory card slots: two are already filled with 512 MB RAM cards and the other two are empty. The maximum RAM allowed for your system is 4 GB. This means you can buy two more 512 MB RAM modules for the two empty slots, for a total of 2 GB (4 × 512 MB) of RAM. Alternatively, you could

Figure 6.15 | DO YOU NEED TO UPGRADE YOUR RAM?

	Application	Current System	Ideal System
How much RAM does my system have?			
What is the maximum amount of RAM I need for the applications I currently run?			
What is the maximum amount of RAM the system can hold*?			
Would I be willing to upgrade to a 64-bit operating system and 64-bit CPU to support having 4 GB or more of RAM?			

*Check the manufacturer's specifications for your system.

throw away the 512 MB cards you have and purchase four new 1 GB cards, filling the system up to its capacity of 4 GB.

Review the considerations presented in Figure 6.15 to see if your system could benefit from an upgrade of additional RAM.

Is it difficult or expensive to add RAM? Adding RAM to a computer is fairly easy (see Figure 6.16). RAM comes with installation instructions, which you should follow carefully. RAM is also relatively inexpensive compared with other system upgrade options. Still, the cost of RAM fluctuates in the marketplace as much as 400 percent over time, so if you're considering adding RAM, you should watch the prices of memory in online and print advertisements.

Adding RAM to a personal computer is quite simple and relatively inexpensive. You simply line up the notches and push in the memory module. Just be sure that you're adding a memory module that's compatible with your computer. For a video demonstration and more details, watch the Sound Byte, "Installing RAM."

Evaluating the Storage Subsystem

As you've learned, there are two ways data is stored on your computer: temporary storage and permanent storage. RAM is a form of temporary (or volatile) storage. Thus, anything that resides in RAM is not stored permanently. It's critical to have the means to store data and software applications permanently.

SOUND BYTE Installing RAM

In this Sound Byte, you'll learn how to select the appropriate type of memory to purchase, how to order memory online, and how to install it yourself. As you'll discover, the procedure is a simple one and can add great performance benefits to your system.

Figure 6.16

Adding RAM to a computer is quite simple and relatively inexpensive.

Fortunately, several storage options exist within every computer system. Storage devices for a typical personal computer include the hard drive, USB flash drives, optical drives, and external hard drives. When you turn off your computer, the data that has been written to these devices will be available the next time the machine is powered on. These devices are therefore referred to as *nonvolatile* storage devices.

The Hard Drive

What makes the hard drive the most popular storage device? With storage capacities exceeding 2 terabytes (TB), a **hard drive** has the largest storage capacity of any storage device. The hard drive is also a much more economical device than other storage options, because it offers the most gigabytes of storage per dollar. Most system units are designed to support more than one internal hard drive. The Apple Mac Pro, shown in Figure 6.17, has room for four hard drives. Each one simply slides into place when you want to upgrade.

Another reason the hard drive is so useful for storage is that the hard drive's **access time**, the time it takes a storage device to locate its stored data and make it available for processing, is faster than that of other permanent storage devices, like optical drives. Hard drive access times are measured in milliseconds (ms), meaning thousandths of seconds. For large- capacity drives, access times of approximately 12–13

milliseconds—that's less than one-hundredth of a second—are typical. A DVD drive can take over 150 milliseconds to access data.

Solid state drives offer even faster access times. A **solid state drive (SSD)** uses the same kind of memory that flash drives use, but whereas flash drives have access times of about 1 ms, SSD drives can reach data in only a tenth of that time (around 0.1 ms). Because there are no spinning platters or motors needed, SSDs run with no noise, very little heat, and require very little power. As the storage capacities for SSDs continue to increase and the prices for SSDs continue to drop, you'll start to see them in a wide range of systems.

Figure 6.18 provides a listing of the various storage options and compares their access times.

Another key performance specification for a hard drive is the speed at which it can transfer data to other computer components (such as RAM). This speed of transfer is referred to as **data transfer rate**. Depending on the manufacturer, the rate is expressed in either megabits or megabytes per second.

How is data stored on a hard drive? A hard drive is composed of several coated round, thin plates of metal stacked on a spindle. Each plate is called a **platter**. When data is saved to a hard drive platter, a pattern of magnetized spots is created on the iron oxide coating of each platter. When the spots are aligned in one

New 1 TB
hard drive

Figure 6.17

The Mac Pro allows you to slide a new hard drive into place easily. In all, the Mac Pro can hold up to 4 hard drives.

direction, they represent a 1; when aligned in the other direction, the represent a 0. These 0s and 1s are bits (or binary digits) and are the smallest pieces of data that computers can understand. When data stored on the hard drive platter is retrieved (or read), your computer translates these patterns of magnetized spots into the data you have saved.

How do I know how much storage capacity I need? Typically, hard drive capacity is measured in gigabytes (GB), although hard drives with capacity in the terabytes (TB) are now available. To check how much total capacity your hard drive has, as well as how much is being used, click the Start button and select Computer from the right side of the Start menu. Windows displays the hard drives, their capacity, and usage information, as seen in Figure 6.19. To get a slightly more detailed view, select a drive; then right-click and choose Properties.

To determine the storage capacity your system needs, calculate the amount of storage required by all the types of files you will be keeping on your system. If you have a large digital music library, that alone could require 30 to 50 GB. Do you keep all of your photographs on your hard drive? You may need another 40 GB or more for them. If you store digital video of television shows and movies, that could easily be 100 to 200 GB more, even higher if the videos are all high definition. Of course, the operating system also requires storage space. The demands on system requirements have grown with new versions of operating systems. Windows 7, the latest Microsoft operating system, can require up to 20 GB of available hard drive capacity, depending on the configuration.

In addition to having space for the operating system, you need enough space to store the software applications you use, such as Microsoft Office, music, and games.

Device

Access Time (ms)

Figure 6.18

Access times for non-volatile storage options.

Figure 6.19

In Windows, the free and used capacity of each device in the computer system are shown in the Computer window. The General tab of the Properties dialog box gives you information that is more detailed.

>To view the Computer window, click **Start**, and click **Computer**. To view the pie chart, right-click the C drive, and select **Properties**.

HDTV on Your Notebook

If you are moving through your day with a notebook in tow, why not use it to pull up your favorite television shows? There are now several USB devices that allow your notebook or desktop to receive the high-definition television (HDTV) signals whizzing by in the airwaves.

Devices like the Hauppauge HDTV stick (see Figure 6.20) are USB digital TV tuners. One end plugs into any available USB port. The other end connects to the provided digital antenna. Software is included that allows you to schedule shows to record onto your hard drive, so your notebook essentially becomes a time-shifting digital video recorder. If you are at home, you can remove the antenna and connect to your home cable television signal. It's enough to make you think about buying a larger hard drive on your next computer!

Figure 6.20

The Hauppauge HDTV stick allows you to watch and record high-definition television shows on your computer.

Figure 6.21 shows an example of hard drive requirements for someone storing a few programs on a hard drive. If you plan to have a system backup on the same drive, be sure to budget for that room as well.

How do hard drives compare for speed? There are several types of hard drives. Integrated Drive Electronics (IDE), which is also called *parallel advanced technology attachment (PATA)*, is an older style that uses wide cables to connect the hard drive to the motherboard. **Serial Advanced Technology Attachment (Serial ATA)** hard drives use much thinner cables, and can transfer data more quickly than IDE drives. A slower drive is fine if you use your computer primarily for word processing, spreadsheets, e-mail, and the Internet. However, "power users" such as graphic designers and software developers will benefit from the faster Serial ATA hard drive.

Another factor that affects a hard drive's performance is access time (the speed with which it locates data for processing). As noted earlier, access time is measured in milliseconds. The faster the access time the better, although many hard drives have similar access times.

The latest and fastest hard drive option is the solid state drive (SSD). These are popular in the netbook market because they require so little power to run and are so cool and quiet. With access times of merely a tenth of a millisecond, SSDs can deliver data many times more quickly than mechanical hard drives. SSD drives as large as 1 TB are available, but right now, all SSD drives are still much more expensive than mechanical drives. Currently, some machines compromise by using an SSD just to hold the operating system. This takes advantage of their great speed, making the boot-up time for the system very quick. Watch for further integration of SSD drives into systems as the cost of SSDs continues to drop.

Evaluate hard drive transfer rate when looking for the best performing drive. The data transfer rate is the speed at which a hard drive can transfer data to other computer components (such as RAM). Depending on the manufacturer, the rate is expressed in either megabits or megabytes per second. You can compare the average read and write data transfer rates of hard drives at sites that do performance benchmarking, like Tom's Hardware (**tomshardware.com**).

If you are adding an external hard drive to your system, there are two popular ports to use. Many hard drives use a USB 2.0 port to connect, which limits the transfer rate of data to 400 Mbps. The USB 3.0 standard has raised that limit to 5 Gbps (5,000 Mbps). In addition, some computer systems now offer an eSATA port, shown in Figure 6.22. This is an external SATA port that will connect to some external hard drive models. It allows a data transfer rate of up to 3 Gbps.

Do I want one huge drive or several smaller drives? It depends on what is important to you: speed or security. If you purchase two smaller drives, you can combine them using RAID technology. RAID (redundant array of independent disks) is a set of strategies for using more than one drive in a system. RAID 0 and RAID 1 are the most popular for consumer machines.

In RAID 0 configuration, every time data is written to a hard drive, it is actually spread across two physical drives (see Figure 6.23a). The write begins on the first drive, and while the system is waiting for that write to be completed, the system jumps ahead and begins to write the next block of data to the second drive. This makes writing information to disk almost twice as fast as using just one hard drive. The downside is that if either of these disks fail, you lose all your data, because part of each file is on each drive. So RAID 0 is for those most concerned with performance.

In RAID 1 configuration, all the data written to one drive is perfectly mirrored and written to a second drive (see Figure 6.23b). This provides you a perfect, instant by instant backup of all your work. It also means that if you buy two 1 TB drives, you only have room to store 1TB of data because the second 1 TB drive is being used as the "mirror."

RAID 0 and RAID 1 systems are available on many consumer systems and are even beginning to appear on notebook computers. The Sony Vaio Z is a notebook available with two 256 GB SSDs, connected

Figure 6.22

An eSATA port allows you to connect an external hard drive that can transfer data at speeds faster than USB 2.0 but slower than USB 3.0.

Figure 6.21 | SAMPLE HARD DRIVE SPACE REQUIREMENTS

Application	Hard Drive Space Required
Windows 7	16–20 GB
MS Office 2007 Professional	3.5 GB
Adobe Photoshop Elements 8	2 GB
Roxio Easy Media Creator 2010	3 GB installation space and up to several 10's of GB to copy BDs or DVDs
Total required	At least 24.5 GB

in RAID 0. This gives you access to 500 GB of storage and incredibly quick access speeds, with very little power consumption or noise.

Optical Storage

Optical drives are disc drives that use a laser to store and read data. Data is saved to a compact disc (CD), digital video disc (DVD), or **Blu-ray disc (BDs)** within established tracks and sectors, just like on a hard drive. However, unlike hard drives, which store their data on magnetized platters, optical discs store data as tiny pits that are burned into the disc by a high-speed laser. These pits are extremely small. For CDs and DVDs, they are less than 1 micron in diameter, so nearly 1,500 pits fit across the top of a pinhead. The pits on a Blu-ray disc are only 0.15 microns in diameter, more than twice as small as the pits on a DVD. As

SOUND BYTE — CD, DVD, and Blu-ray Reading and Writing Interactive

In this Sound Byte, you'll learn about the process of storing and retrieving data from CD-RW, DVD, and Blu-ray discs. You'll be amazed to see how much precision engineering is required to burn MP3 files onto a disc.

Figure 6.23

(a) RAID 0 speeds up file read/write time. (b) RAID 1 gives you an instant backup.

you can see in Figure 6.24, data is read from a disc by a laser beam, with the pits and nonpits (called *lands*) translating into the 1s and 0s of the binary code computers understand. CDs and DVDs use a red laser to read and write data. Blu-ray discs get their name because they are read with a blue laser light. All of them collectively are referred to as **optical media**.

Why can I store data on some discs but not others? All forms of optical media come in prerecorded, recordable, and rewritable formats. The prerecorded discs—known as CD-ROM, **DVD-ROM**, and **BD-ROM discs**—are read-only optical discs, meaning you can't save any data onto them. Pre-recorded CDs usually contain audio content, software programs, or games, whereas DVD-ROMs and BD-ROMs typically contain movies or prerecorded TV shows in regular or high definition, respectively. Recordable formats such as CD-R, DVD-R, and BD-R allow data to be written (saved or burned) to them. If

you want to be able to use a form of optical media repetitively, writing and rewriting data to it many times, read/writeable formats such as CD-RW, DVD-RW, and BD-RE are available.

Do I need separate players and burners for CD, DVD, and now BD formats? Although CDs and DVDs are based on the same optical technology, CD drives cannot read DVDs. If your system has only a CD drive, you will need to add a DVD drive to view DVDs. However, if your system has a DVD drive, that is all you need, even just to listen to CDs, because DVD drives can read them. Although Blu-ray discs are read with a different type of laser than CDs and DVDs, most Blu-ray players are backward compatible and can play DVDs and CDs. There are different types of optical drives for playing or recording to discs. If you want to record to CDs, DVDs, or Blu-ray discs, you need to make sure your drive is capable of recording (or burning) and not just playing.

Because recording drives are also backward compatible, you do not need separate burners for each form of media. A DVD burner will also record CDs, and a Blu-ray burner will most likely record both CDs and DVDs (although there may be some compatibility issues).

Are there different standards of optical media? Unfortunately, technology experts have not agreed on a standard DVD format. Currently, there are multiple recognized formats, **DVD-R/RW** (pronounced "DVD dash") and **DVD+R/RW** (pronounced "DVD plus"). **DVD-RAM** is a third format. You can record, erase, and rewrite on DVD-RAM, as you can with the plus and minus formats, but DVD-RAM discs are generally encased in a plastic cartridge. Web sites such as Video Help (**videohelp.com**) list the compatibility of various DVD players with the various DVD formats. However, you must make sure you purchase blank DVD discs that match the type of drive you own. Most new systems come equipped with a DVD +/– RW drive that supports both the plus and minus formats.

There were "format wars" like this for high-definition discs as well. Blu-ray competed against another storage format called HD-DVD (high-definition DVD). Some movie companies would only provide their films on HD discs, while other films were exclusive to Blu-ray. Different players were required to view each kind of disc. In 2008, HD-DVDs were retired, and HD discs and players are no longer in production.

Are some CD and DVD drives faster than others? When you buy an optical drive, knowing the drive speed is important. Speeds are listed on the device's packaging. Record (write) speed is always listed first, rewrite speed is listed second (except for CD-R drives and DVD-R, which cannot rewrite data), and playback speed is listed last. For example, a CD-RW drive may have speeds of 52X32X52X, meaning that the device can record data at 52X speed, rewrite data at 32X speed, and play back data at 52X speed. For CDs, the X after each number represents the transfer of 150 KB of data per second. For example, a CD-RW drive with a 52X32X52X rating records data at 52 times 150 KB per second, or 7,800 KB per second.

DVD drives are much faster than CD drives. For example, a 1X DVD-ROM

To read information stored on a disc, a laser inside the disk drive sends a beam of light through the spinning disc.

Laser beam

Non-scattered reflected light = 1

Scattered reflected light = 0

Laser beam

If the light reflected back is scattered in all directions (which happens when the laser hits a pit), the laser translates this into the binary digit 0.

If non-scattered light is reflected back to the laser (which happens when the laser hits an area in which there is no pit), the laser translates this into the binary digit 1.

Spinning disc

In this way, the laser reads the pits and non-pits as a series of bits (0s and1s), which the computer can then process.

Figure 6.24

Data is read from a disc using focused laser light.

drive provides a data transfer rate of approximately 1.3 MB of data per second, which is roughly equivalent to a CD-ROM speed of 9X. CD and DVD drives are constantly getting faster. If you're in the market for a new CD or DVD burner, then you'll want to investigate the drive speeds on the market and make sure you get the fastest one you can afford.

Blu-ray drives are the fastest optical devices on the market. Blu-ray technology defines 1X speed as 36 MB per second.

SOUND BYTE

Installing a Blu-ray Drive

In this Sound Byte, you'll learn how to install a Blu-ray drive in your computer.

The thin metal platters that make up a hard drive are covered with a special magnetic coating that enables the data to be recorded onto one or both sides of the platter. Hard drive manufacturers prepare the disks to hold data through a process called *low-level formatting*. In this process, concentric circles, each called a **track**, and pie-shaped wedges, each called a **sector**, are created in the magnetized surface of each platter, setting up a gridlike pattern that identifies file locations on the hard drive. A separate process called *high-level formatting* establishes the catalog that the computer uses to keep track of where each file is located on the hard drive. More detail on this is presented in the Dig Deeper feature "How Disk Defragmenter Utilities Work" on page 238.

Hard drive platters spin at a high rate of speed, some as fast as 15,000 revolutions per minute (rpm). Sitting between the platters are special "arms" that contain read/write heads (see Figure 6.25). A **read/write head** moves from the outer edge of the spinning platter to the center, as frequently as 50 times per second, to retrieve (read) and record (write) the magnetic data to and from the hard drive platter. As noted earlier, the average total time it takes for the read/write head to locate the data on the platter and return it to the CPU for processing is called its access time. A new hard drive should have an average access time of approximately 12 ms.

Access time is mostly the sum of two factors: seek time and latency. The time it takes for the read/write heads to move over the surface of the disk, moving to the correct track, is called the **seek time**. (Sometimes people incorrectly refer to this as access time.) Once the read/write head locates the correct track, it may need to wait for the correct sector to spin to the read/write head. This waiting time is called **latency** (or *rotational delay*). The faster the platters spin (or the faster the rpm), the less time you'll have to wait for your data to be accessed. Currently, most hard drives for home systems spin at 7,200 rpm. Some people design their systems to have a faster hard drive run the operating system, such as the Western Digital Velociraptor, which spins at 10,000 rpm. They then add a slower drive with greater capacity for storage.

The read/write heads do not touch the platters of the hard drive; rather, they float above them on a thin cushion of air at a height of 0.5 microinches. As a matter of comparison, a human hair is 2,000 microinches thick and a particle of dust is larger than a human hair. Therefore, it's critical to keep your hard drive free from all dust and dirt, because even the smallest particle could find its way between the read/write head and the disk platter, causing a **head crash**—a stoppage of the hard drive that often results in data loss.

Capacities for hard drives in personal computers can exceed 2000 GB (2 TB). Increasing the amount of data stored in a hard drive is achieved either by adding more platters or by increasing the amount of data stored on each platter. How tightly the tracks are placed next to each other, how tightly spaced the sectors are, and how closely the bits of data are placed affect the measurement of the amount of data that can be stored in a specific area of a hard drive platter. Modern technology continues to increase the standards on all three levels, enabling massive quantities of data to be stored in small places.

Read/write head

Arms

Platters

Figure 6.25

The hard drive is a stack of platters enclosed in a sealed case. Special arms fit in between each platter. The read/write heads at the end of each arm read from and save data to the platters.

Because BD movies require data transfer rates of at least 54 MB per second, most Blu-ray disc players have a minimum of 2X speeds (72 MB per second). Many units are available with 12X speeds.

So how do my storage devices measure up? The table in Figure 6.26 will help you determine if your computer's storage subsystem needs upgrading.

Evaluating the Video Subsystem

How video is displayed depends on two components: your video card and your monitor. It's important that your system have the correct monitor and video card to meet your needs. If you are considering loading Windows 7 on your system, or

Figure 6.26 | DO YOU WANT TO UPGRADE YOUR STORAGE SUBSYSTEM?

	Current System	Ideal System
What is my current hard drive capacity?		
Do I want to have a very fast startup time (i.e., use an SSD drive for my operating system)?		
Do I want to implement multiple drives in RAID 0 for performance?		
Do I want to implement multiple drives in RAID 1 for instant backup?		
Do I have a DVD-ROM drive?		
Can I burn DVDs (i.e., do I have a DVD-/+RW drive)?		
Can I play Blu-ray discs (i.e., do I have a Blu-ray drive)?		
Can I burn my own Blu-ray discs (i.e., do I have a Blu-ray burner installed)?		
Do I have a working data backup solution such as external backup drives or remote data storage?		
Do I use any portable storage devices such as flash drives or external hard drives?		

using your computer system to display files that have complex graphics, such as videos on Blu-ray or from your camcorder, or even playing graphics-rich games with a lot of fast action, you may want to consider upgrading your video subsystem.

Video Cards

What is a video card? A video card (or **video adapter**) is an expansion card that is installed inside your system unit to translate binary data into the images you view on your monitor. Modern video cards like the ones shown in Figure 6.27 and

ACTIVE HELP-DESK

Evaluating Computer System Components

In this Active Helpdesk call, you'll play the role of a helpdesk staffer, fielding calls about the computer's storage, video, and audio devices and how to evaluate whether they match your needs, as well as how to improve the reliability of your system.

Figure 6.27

Video cards have grown to be highly specialized subsystems.

Processor covered by heat sink and fan

Video memory chips

Video memory chip

Clips into motherboard

Connects to VGA monitor

Video memory chip

HDMI port to digital monitor

S-video port to TV, stereo, or VCR

Digital Video Interface (DVI) port to digital monitor

Fan built into graphics card

Figure 6.28

Because of the large amount of graphics memory and the fast graphics processing units on modern video cards, they have their own fan to remove heat.

Figure 6.29

The graphics processing unit (GPU) is specialized to handle processing of photos, videos, and video game images. It frees the CPU to work on other system demands.

Figure 6.28 are extremely sophisticated. They include ports that allow you to connect to different video equipment such as the DVI ports for digital LCDs, HDMI ports to connect to high-definition TVs or gaming consoles, lower-resolution S-video ports for connecting your computer to a TV, and Super VGA ports for CRT and analog LCD monitors. In addition, video cards include their own RAM, called **video memory**. Several standards of video memory are available, including graphics double data rate 3 (GDDR3) memory and the newer graphics double data rate 5 (GDDR5) memory. Because displaying graphics demands a lot of the CPU, video cards also come with their own graphics processing units (GPUs). When the CPU is asked to process graphics, those tasks are redirected to the GPU, significantly speeding up graphics processing.

Is a GPU different from a CPU?
The **graphics processing unit (GPU)** performs the same kind of computational work that a CPU performs. However, a GPU is specialized to handle 3-D graphics and image and video processing with incredible efficiency and speed. Figure 6.29 shows that the CPU can run much more efficiently when a GPU does all of the graphics computation.

Special lighting effects can be achieved with a modern GPU. Designers can now change the type of light, the texture, and the color of objects based on complex interactions. Some GPU designs incorporate dedicated hardware to allow high-definition movies to be decoded.

Does the GPU live on the motherboard or on the video card? Basic video processing is sometimes integrated into the motherboard. However, high-end video cards that have their own GPUs are separate from the motherboard. These sophisticated video cards connect through the ultrafast PCI Express bus. The ATI Radeon HD 5970, a top-end card, is a multi-GPU card with two GPUs that work together to add even more processing punch. Cards like this one carry their own processing RAM space, which can range between 512 MB and 2 GB, depending on the model. Together they provide an unprecedented level of realism and detail in gaming environments.

How can I tell how much memory my video card has? Information about your system's video card can be found in the Advanced Settings of the Screen resolution dialog box. To get to the Screen resolution dialog box, right-click on your desktop and select Screen resolution. In the Screen resolution dialog box, click the Advanced Settings link. A window will appear that shows you the type of graphics card installed in your system, as well as memory information including total available graphics memory, dedicated video memory, system video memory, and shared system memory. The documentation that came with your computer should also contain specifications for the video card, including the amount of video memory it has installed.

How much memory does my video card need? The amount of memory your

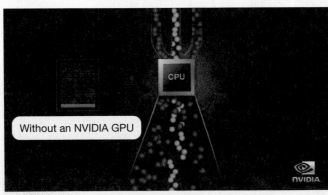

Without an NVIDIA GPU

Without a GPU

With an NVIDIA GPU

With a GPU

video card needs depends on what you want to display on your monitor. If you work primarily in Microsoft Word and conduct general Web searches, 128 MB is a realistic minimum. For the serious gamer, a 512 MB or greater video card is essential, although cards with as much as 1 or 2 GB are available in the market and are preferred. These high-end video cards, which have greater amounts of memory, allow games to generate smoother animations and more sophisticated shading and texture. Before purchasing new software, check the specifications to ensure your video card has enough video memory to handle the load.

How many video cards can I add to a system? For users who are primarily doing text processing or spreadsheet work, one video card is certainly enough. However, computer gamers and users of high-end visualization software often take advantage of the ability to install more than one video card at a time. Two or even three video cards can be used in one system. The two major video card manufacturers, Nvidia and ATI, have each developed their own standards supporting the combining of multiple video cards. For Nvidia this standard is named SLI and for ATI it is called CrossFire. When the system is running at very high video resolutions, such as 1920 × 1200 or higher, multiple video cards working together provide the ultimate in performance. If you are buying a new system and might be interested in employing multiple video cards, be sure to check whether the motherboard supports SLI or CrossFire.

What else does the video card do? The video card also controls the number of colors your monitor can display. The number of bits the video card uses to represent each pixel (or dot) on the monitor, referred to as **bit depth**, defines the color quality of the image displayed. The more bits, the better an image's color detail. A 4-bit

Figure 6.30 | BIT DEPTH AND COLOR QUALITY

Bit Depth	Color Quality Description	Number of Colors Displayed
4-bit	Standard VGA	16
8-bit	256-color mode	256
16-bit	High color	65,536
24-bit	True color	16,777,216
32-bit	True color	16,777,216 plus 8 bits to help with transparency

video card displays 16 colors, the minimum number of colors your system works with (referred to as Standard VGA). Most video cards today are 24-bit cards, displaying more than 16 million colors. This mode is called *true color mode* (see Figure 6.30).

The most recent generation of video cards can add some great features to your computer if you are a TV fan. Multimedia cards such as the ATI All-In-Wonder Radeon HD 3650 can open a live TV window on your screen, including features such as picture-in-picture. Using this video card, you can record programs to your hard drive or pause a live TV broadcast. The card even comes with a wireless remote control.

When is it time to get a new video card? If your monitor takes a while to refresh when you are editing photos, surfing the Web, or playing a graphics-rich game, then the video card could be short on memory or the GPU is being taxed to beyond its capacity.

You also may want to upgrade if added features such as television viewing or importing analog video are important to you. If you want to use multiple monitors at the same time, you also may need to upgrade your video card. Working with multiple monitors is a great advantage if you often have more than one application running at a time (see Figure 6.31). ATI has introduced a

Figure 6.31

Cards like the (a) ATI 5870 Eyefinity support (b) six monitors, which can be combined in any way.

3D Explosions

Most video games produced since 2007 are now ready to be seen in 3D, but the market of 3D monitors has been slow in coming. Currently, several computer monitors and televisions that support 3D are being released. Most video cards that support at least two monitors are capable of running 3D imagery. Sony PlayStation has updated its firmware to support 3D games and movies. So by adding a 3D monitor, and the snazzy glasses that come along, you can move from two dimensions forward into three!

single card that can support up to six monitors. "Surround sight" allows you to merge all six monitors to work as one screen or to combine them into any subset—for example, displaying a movie on two combined screens, Excel on one monitor, Word on another, and a browser spread across the final two.

Review the considerations listed in Figure 6.32 to see if it might be time for you to upgrade. On a desktop computer, replacing a video card is fairly simple: just insert the new video card in the correct expansion slot on the motherboard.

Evaluating the Audio Subsystem

Computers output sound by means of speakers (or headphones) and a sound card. For many users, a computer's preinstalled speakers and sound card are adequate for the sounds produced by the computer itself—the beeps and so on that the computer makes. However, if you're listening to music, viewing DVDs, hooking

into a household stereo system, or playing games with sophisticated sound tracks, you may want to upgrade your speakers or your sound card.

Sound Cards

What does the sound card do? Like a video card, a **sound card**, is an expansion card that attaches to the motherboard inside your system unit. Just as the video card enables your computer to produce images on the monitor, a sound card enables the computer to produce sounds. Most systems have a separate sound card, although low-end computers often have integrated the job of managing sound onto the motherboard itself.

Can I hook up a surround-sound system to my computer? Many computers ship with a basic sound card, which is often a **3D sound card**. The 3D sound technology advances sound reproduction beyond traditional stereo sound (where the human ear perceives sounds as coming from the left or the right of the performance area) and is better at convincing the human ear that sound is omnidirectional, meaning that you can't tell from which direction the sound is coming. This tends to produce a fuller, richer sound than stereo sound. However, 3D sound is not surround sound.

What is surround sound then? **Surround sound** is a type of audio processing that makes the listener experience sound as if it were coming from all directions. The current surround sound standard is from Dolby. There are many formats available, including Dolby Digital EX and Dolby Digital Plus for high-definition audio. Dolby TrueHD is the

Figure 6.32	DO YOU NEED TO UPGRADE YOUR VIDEO CARD?		
		Current System	Ideal System
Is my video card able to refresh the screen fast enough for the videos and games I play?			
What is the total amount of video memory on my video card?			
How many monitors can this card support?			
Can I import video through my video card?			
Can I send a cable television signal to my video card?			
Does my video card support the highest quality port for my monitor—DVI? HDMI?			

Optical Technology: A Free Lunch—Or at Least a Free Copy

Decades ago, when the electronic photocopier made its debut, book publishers and others who distributed the printed word feared they would be put out of business. They were worried that people would no longer buy books and other printed matter if they could simply copy someone else's original. Years later, when audiocassette and VCR players and recorders arrived on the market, those who felt they would be negatively affected by these new technologies expressed similar concerns. Now, with the arrival of CD-RW, DVD-RW, and BD-RE technology, the music and entertainment industries are worried because users can copy CDs, DVDs, and Blu-ray discs in a matter of minutes.

Although photocopiers and VCRs certainly didn't put an end to the industries they affected, some people still say the music and entertainment industries will take a significant hit with CD-RW, DVD-RW, and BD-RE technology. Industry insiders are claiming that these technologies are unethical, and they're pressing for increased federal legislation against such copying. It's not just the CD-RW, DVD-RW, BD-RE technology that's causing problems, either, because "copies" are not necessarily of the physical sort. Thanks to the Internet, file transfers of copyrighted works—particularly music and films—is now commonplace. According to Music United (**musicunited.org**), more than 243 million files are downloaded illegally every month, and about one-quarter of all Internet users worldwide have downloaded a movie from the Internet.

In a separate survey, the Recording Industry Association of America (RIAA), a trade organization that represents the interests of recording giants such as Sony, Capitol Records, and other major producers of musical entertainment, reported that 23 percent of music fans revealed they were buying less music because they could download it or copy a CD-ROM from a friend.

As you would expect, the music and entertainment industries want to be fairly compensated for their creative output. They blame the technology industry for the creation of means by which artists, studios, and the entertainment industry in general are being "robbed." Although technology that readily allows consumers to transfer and copy music and videos exists, the artists who produce these works do not want to be taken advantage of. However, others claim that the technology industry should not bear the complete burden of protecting entertainment copyrights. The RIAA sums up the future of this debate nicely: "Goals for the new millennium are to work with [the recording] industry and others to enable technologies that open up new opportunities but at the same time to protect the rights of artists and copyright owners."

newest standard. It features high-definition and lossless technology, in which no data is lost in the compression process. To create surround sound, Dolby takes digital sound from a medium (such as a DVD-ROM) and reproduces it in eight channels. Seven channels cover the listening field with placement to the left front, right front, and center of the audio stage, as well as the left rear and right rear, and then two extra side speakers are added, as shown in Figure 6.33. The eighth channel holds extremely low-frequency sound data and is sent to a subwoofer, which can be placed anywhere in the room. To set up surround sound on your computer, you need two things: a set of surround-sound speakers and, for the greatest surround-sound experience, a sound card that is Dolby Digital–compatible.

I don't need surround sound on my computer. Why else might I need to buy an upgraded sound card?   Most basic sound cards contain the following input and output jacks (or ports): microphone in, speaker out, and line in. This allows you to hook up a set of stereo speakers and a microphone. But what if you want to hook up a right and left speaker individually, or attach other audio devices to your computer? To do so, you need more ports, which are provided on upgraded sound cards like the one shown in Figure 6.34.

With an upgraded sound card, you can connect portable minidisc players, portable media players, portable jukeboxes, headphones, and CD players to your computer. Musicians also create music on their computers by connecting special devices (such as keyboards) directly to sound card ports. To determine whether your audio subsystem is meeting your needs, review the table in Figure 6.35.

Evaluating System Reliability

Many computer users decide to buy a new system not necessarily because they need a faster CPU, more RAM, or a bigger hard drive, but because they are experiencing problems such as slow performance, freezes, and crashes. Over time, even normal use can cause your computer to build up excess files and to become internally disorganized. This excess, clutter, and disorganization can lead to deteriorating performance or, far worse, system failure. If you think your system is

Front left
speaker

Central
speaker

Front right
speaker

Subwoofer

Computer
system

Side
speaker L

Side
speaker R

Rear left
speaker

Rear right
speaker

Figure 6.33

Dolby Digital 7.1 surround sound gives you better-quality audio output.

unnecessary program and select Delete to remove it from the Startup folder. Make sure you delete *only* programs you are absolutely sure are unnecessary. Another way programs sneak their way in is to load themselves into your system tray. Keep an eye on how many icons are in the system tray and uninstall any that you do not use frequently.

2. **Clear out unnecessary files.** Temporary Internet files can accumulate quickly on your hard drive, taking up unnecessary space. Running the Disk Cleanup utility is a quick and easy way to ensure your temporary Internet files don't take up precious hard drive space. Likewise, you should delete any unnecessary files from your hard drive regularly, because they can make your hard drive run more slowly.

3. **Run spyware and adware removal programs.** These often detect and remove different pests and should be used in addition to your regular antivirus package. You can find more details on how to keep your system safe from spyware, adware, and viruses in Chapter 9.

4. **Run the Disk Defragmenter utility on your hard drive.** When your hard drive becomes fragmented, its storage capacity is negatively affected. When you defragment (defrag) your hard drive, files are reorganized, making the hard drive work more efficiently. For a more complete discussion of the Disk Defragmenter, refer to Chapter 5.

The utilities that need to be run more than once, like Disk Cleanup, Disk Defragmenter, and the antivirus and spyware programs, can be configured to run automatically at any time interval you want. You can set up a sequence of programs to run one after the other every evening while you sleep, and wake up each day to a reliable, secure system.

My system crashes often during the day. What can I do? Computer systems are complex. It's not unusual to have your system stop responding occasionally. If rebooting the computer doesn't help, you'll need to begin troubleshooting:

1. Check that you have enough RAM, which you learned how to do in the section "Evaluating RAM: The Memory Subsystem" earlier in this chapter.

unreliable, see if the problem is one you can fix before you buy a new machine. Proper upkeep and maintenance also may postpone an expensive system upgrade or replacement.

What can I do to ensure my system performs reliably? Here are several procedures you can follow to ensure your system performs reliably:

1. **Clean out your Startup folder.** Some programs install themselves into your Startup folder and run automatically each time the computer starts up, whether you are using them or not. This unnecessary load uses up RAM, leaving less for other programs. To minimize this problem, check your Startup folder by clicking Start > All Programs. Then click on the Startup folder and make sure all the programs listed are important to you. Right-click on any

Systems with insufficient amounts of RAM often crash.

2. Make sure you have properly installed any new software or hardware. If you're using a Windows system, use the System Restore utility to "roll back" the system to a time when it worked more reliably. (To find System Restore, just type "restore" into the Start menu search box.) For Mac systems, Mac OS X Time Machine, shown in Figure 6.36, provides automatic backup and enables you to look through and restore (if necessary) files, folders, libraries, or the entire system.

3. If you see an error code in Windows, visit the Microsoft Knowledge Base (**support.microsoft.com**), an online resource for resolving problems with Microsoft products. This may help you determine what the error code indicates and how you may be able to solve the problem. If you don't find a satisfactory answer in the Knowledge Base, try copying the entire error message into Google and searching the larger community for solutions.

Can my software affect system reliability? Having the latest version of software products makes your system much more reliable. You should upgrade or update your operating system, browser software, and application software as often as new patches (or updates) are reported for resolving errors. Sometimes these errors are performance-related; sometimes they are potential system security breaches.

If you are having a problem that can be replicated, use the Problem Steps Recorder

Analog/Digital Output

Line Input Signal

Microphone Input

Line Output

Rear Speaker Output

FireWire (IEEE 1394)

to capture the exact steps that lead to it. In Windows 7, go to the Start menu and search for "psr." Run the Problem Steps Recorder and go through the exact actions that create the problem you are having. At any particular step, you can click the Annotate button and add a comment about any part of the screen. PSR then produces a documented report, complete with images of your screen and descriptions of each mouse movement you made. You can then e-mail this report, which is compressed in the WinZip format, to customer support to help technicians resolve the problem.

How do I know whether updates are available for my software? You can configure Windows so that it automatically checks for, downloads, and installs any available updates for itself, Internet Explorer, and other Microsoft applications such as Microsoft Office. Many other applications now also include the ability to check

Figure 6.34

In addition to improving sound quality, upgraded sound cards can provide additional ports for your audio equipment.

Figure 6.35 | DO YOU NEED TO UPGRADE YOUR AUDIO SUBSYSTEM?

	Current System	Ideal System
Is the speaker quality high enough for the way I am using my computer?		
Is my sound card capable of 3D sound?		
Does my sound card support Dolby Digital surround sound?		
Do I have 5.1-channel surround sound or 7.1-channel surround sound?		
Do I have an HDMI port on the audio card?		

Figure 6.36

Mac's Time Machine restores files, folders, libraries and, if necessary, the entire system.

for updates. Check under the Help menu of the product, and often you will find a Check for Updates command.

What if none of this helps? Is buying a new system my only option? If your system is still unreliable after these changes, then you have two options:

1. **Upgrade your operating system to the latest version.** There are substantial increases in reliability with each major release of a new operating system. However, upgrading the operating system may require hardware upgrades such as additional RAM, an updated graphics processor, and an even larger hard drive. The Microsoft Windows 7 Upgrade Advisor (a free download from (**microsoft.com**) will scan your

system to determine what upgrades might be required before you convert to Windows 7. Be sure to examine the *recommended* (not required) specifications of the new operating system.

2. **Reinstall the operating system.** As a last resort, you might need to reinstall the operating system. To do so, you'll want to back up all of your data files before the installation and be prepared to reinstall all your software after the installation. Make sure you have all of the original discs for the software installed on your system, along with the product keys, serial numbers, and any other activation codes so that you can reinstall them.

Making the Final Decision

Now that you have evaluated your computer system, you need to shift to questions of *value*. How closely does your system come to meeting your needs? How much would it cost to upgrade the system you have to match what you'd ideally like your computer to do, not only today but also a few years from now? How much would it cost to purchase a new system that meets these specifications?

To decide whether upgrading or buying a new system has better value for you, you need to price both scenarios. Figure 6.37

Figure 6.37 | UPGRADE/NEW PURCHASE COMPARISON WORKSHEET

Needs	Hardware Upgrade Cost	Included on New System?	Additional Expense If Not Included on New System
CPU and Memory Subsystems			
CPU upgrade			
RAM upgrade			
Storage Subsystem			
Hard drive upgrade			
SSD drive			
DVD+/-RW burner			
Blu-ray burner			
Video and Audio Subsystems			
Video card upgrade			
Sound card upgrade			

Computers in Society: How to Donate Your Old Computer Safely

What happened to your last computer? If you threw it away hoping it would be safely recycled with your empty water bottles, think again. Mercury in LCD screens, cadmium in batteries and circuit boards, and flame retardant in plastic housings all are toxic. An alarming, emerging trend is that discarded machines are beginning to create an e-waste crisis.

Instead of throwing your computer away, you may be able to donate it to a nonprofit organization. Many manufacturers, such as Dell, offer recycling programs and have formed alliances with nonprofit organizations to help distribute your old technology to those who need it. Sites like Computers With Causes (**computerswithcauses.org**) organize donations of both working and nonworking computers, printers, and mice. You can also take your computer to an authorized computer recycling center in your area (see Figure 6.38). The Telecommunications Industry Association provides an e-cycling information site you can use to find a local e-cycling center (**eiae.org**).

However, before donating or recycling a computer, make sure you carefully remove all data from your hard drive, or you may end up having your good deed turn bad by becoming the victim of identity theft. Credit card numbers, bank information, Social Security numbers, tax records, passwords, and personal identification numbers (PINs) are just some of the types of sensitive information that we casually record to our computers' hard drives. Just deleting files that contain proprietary personal information is not protection enough. Likewise, reformatting or erasing your hard drive does not totally remove data, as was proved by two MIT graduate students. In 2003, they bought more than 150 used hard drives from various sources. Although some of the hard drives had been reformatted or damaged so the data was supposedly irrecoverable, the two students were able to retrieve medical records, financial information, pornography, personal e-mails, and more than 5,000 credit card numbers!

The U.S. Department of Defense suggests a seven-layer overwrite for a "secure erase." In other words, they suggest that you fill your hard drive *seven times over* with a random series of 1s and 0s. Fortunately, several programs exist for PCs running Windows, such as Active@ Kill Disk, Eraser, and CyberScrub. Wipe is available for Linux, and ShredIt X can be used for OS X.

These programs provide secure hard drive erasures, either of specific files on your hard drive or of the entire hard drive.

Keep in mind that even these data erasure programs can't provide the ultimate level in security. Computer forensic specialists or supercybercriminals can still manage to retrieve some data from your hard drive if they have the right tools. The ultimate level of protection comes from destroying the hard drive altogether. Suggested methods include drilling holes in the hard drive, burning or melting it, or just taking an old-fashioned sledgehammer to it! For large companies that need to upgrade large quantities of computers and have the options of destroying or recycling their old computers, the problem becomes much worse. In these cases, recycling isn't a good option, and throwing the computers away can create an environmental hazard. Companies such as GigaBiter (**gigabiter.com**) eliminate security and environmental risks associated with electronic destruction by first delaminating the hard drive and then breaking down the computer e-waste into recyclable products. The result of the final step is a sandlike substance that is 100 percent recyclable.

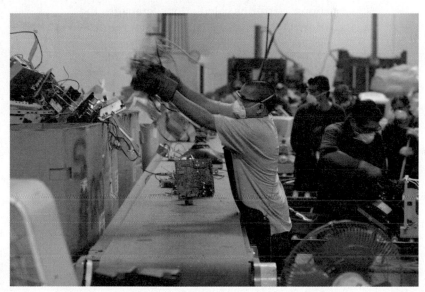

Figure 6.38

An electronics scrap recycler "demanufactures" printers, computers, and other electronics and then resells the usable parts.

provides an upgrade worksheet you can use to evaluate both the upgrade path and the new purchase path. Be sure to consider what benefit you might obtain by having two systems if you were to buy a new computer. Would you have a use for the older system?

Would you donate it to a charitable organization? Would you be able to give it to a family member? Purchasing a new system is an important investment of your resources, and you want to make a well-reasoned, well-supported decision.

six summary

six summary

summary

1. How can I determine whether I should upgrade my existing computer or buy a new one?

To determine whether you need to upgrade your system or purchase a new one, you need to define your ideal system and what you want it to do. Then you need to perform a system evaluation to assess the subsystems in your computer, including the CPU, memory, storage, video, and audio. Finally, you need to determine if it's economical to upgrade, or whether buying a new computer would be better.

2. What does the CPU do, and how can I evaluate its performance?

Your computer's CPU processes instructions, performs calculations, manages the flow of information through the computer system, and is responsible for processing the data you input into information. CPU speed is measured in gigahertz (billions of machine cycles per second). You can tell whether your CPU is limiting your system performance by watching how busy it is as you work on your computer. The percentage of time that your CPU is working is referred to as CPU usage, which you can determine by checking the Task Manager. Benchmarking software offers direct performance comparisons of different CPUs.

3. How does memory work in my computer, and how can I evaluate how much memory I need?

RAM is your computer's temporary memory. It remembers everything that the computer needs to process data into information. However, it is an example of volatile storage. When the power is off, the data stored in RAM is cleared out. The amount of RAM sitting on memory modules in your computer is your computer's physical memory. The memory your OS uses is kernel memory. At a minimum, you need enough RAM to run the OS plus the software applications you're using, plus a bit more to hold the data you will input.

4. What are the computer's main storage devices, and how can I evaluate whether they match my needs?

Storage devices for a typical computer system may include a hard drive, an SSD drive, a flash drive, and CD and DVD drives. Blu-ray drives are gaining in popularity for viewing and burning high-density media. When you turn off your computer, the data stored in these devices remains. These devices are referred to as *nonvolatile* storage devices. Hard drives have the largest storage capacity of any storage device and are the most economical. Newer SSD drives have the fastest access time and data transfer rate of all nonvolatile storage options. CDs and DVDs have capacities from 700 MB to 17 GB, while Blu-ray discs can hold up to 50 GB. Portable flash drives allow easy transfer of 64 GB or more of data from machine to machine. To determine the storage capacity your system needs, calculate the amount of storage your software needs to reside on your computer. To add more storage or to provide more functionality for your system, you can install additional drives, either internally or externally.

5. What components affect the output of video on my computer, and how can I evaluate whether they match my needs?

How video is displayed depends on two components: your video card and your monitor. A video card translates binary data into the images you see. These cards include their own RAM (video memory) as well as ports that allow you to connect to video equipment. The amount of video memory you need depends on what you want to display on the monitor. A more powerful card will allow you to play graphics-intense games and multimedia.

6. What components affect the quality of sound on my computer, and how can I evaluate whether they match my needs?

Your computer's sound depends on your speakers and sound card. A sound card enables the computer to produce sounds. Users upgrade their sound cards to provide for 3D sound, surround sound, and additional ports for audio equipment.

7. How can I improve the reliability of my system?

Many computer users decide to buy a new system because they are experiencing problems with their computer. However, before you buy a new system because you think yours may be unreliable, make sure the problem is not one you can fix. Run a full scan with antispyware software. Make sure you have installed any new software or hardware properly, check that you have enough RAM, run system utilities such as Disk Defragmenter and Disk Cleanup, clean out your Startup folder, remove unnecessary files from your system, and keep your software updated with patches. If you continue to have troubles with your system, reinstall or upgrade your OS, and, of course, seek technical assistance.

key terms

Word Bank

- access time
- Blu-ray disc
- cache memory
- CPU usage
- data transfer rate
- eSATA
- express cards
- front side bus
- GPU
- hard drive
- memory module
- Moore's law
- RAM
- sound card
- SSD
- surround sound
- system evaluation

Instructions: Fill in the blanks using the words from the Word Bank above.

Joe already has a PC but just heard about a great deal on a new one. He decides to perform a(n) (1) _____ on his computer to see whether he should keep it or buy the new one. First, he runs the Task Manager in Windows. By doing so, he can check the history of (2) _____ as he works through his day. Because he is often over 90 percent, he begins to suspect his system is suffering from too little (3) _____. He has room for an additional two (4) _____ on his motherboard. Adding memory is something he learned how to do this semester, but would that be enough to make this machine do all he needs?

He visits the Intel Web site to check two other important factors on his model of CPU: the amount of (5) _____ memory and the speed of the (6) _____. It looks like the newer i7 processor would be much faster overall. It seems each generation of processors is so much faster than the last. That rule, (7) _____, is still holding true!

He continues to evaluate his system by checking out which components he has and which ones he'll need. He notes the storage capacity of the (8) _____. Recently, he has been wishing his system had a(n) (9) _____ port because adding an external hard drive would give him enough space to start to record HD television shows. As it is, he is running out of space to store files. But the (10) _____, or the amount of time it takes to retrieve data from the disk drive, on any mechanical drive is slow compared to the (11) _____ in the new computer he's eyeing, which has no moving parts at all. Joe also notes that he is unable to do a complete backup of his music library onto optical media now that he has 40 GB of music data. His current system can't burn a (12) _____, but the new system could. The new video card would also include several (13) _____ ports so that six digital monitors can be connected simultaneously. It would be great if he could take advantage of the 5.1 (14) _____ that is on the soundtrack of most of the movies he watches on DVD.

He also has a lot of friends who play video games on their computer systems. However, his current system doesn't meet the minimum requirements for a video card. Newer cards have blindingly fast (15) _____, and some cards even have multiple processors. Overall, with prices dropping, it seems like time to go buy that new system!

becoming computer literate

Rebecca has already built five or six PCs and tells you she can make a killer desktop system for you for under $1,300. But you do love the idea of having a light, compact notebook computer that could travel with you around campus and back and forth to work.

Instructions: Using the preceding scenario, write an e-mail to Rebecca describing to her what you need in your new system. Examine the specifications for both notebook and desktop systems in this price range and decide which one is best suited to you. Use key terms from the chapter and be sure your sentences are grammatically correct and technically meaningful.

Instructions: Answer the multiple-choice and true–false questions below for more practice with key terms and concepts from this chapter.

Multiple Choice

1. Which statement about notebook computers is FALSE?
   a. Notebooks typically have a longer lifespan.
   b. Notebooks are typically less reliable.
   c. Notebooks can be docked to larger monitors.
   d. Notebook are more difficult to expand or upgrade.

2. ROM is classified as what type of storage?
   a. Volatile   c. Flash
   b. Nonvolatile   d. Cache

3. To document a problem you are having, you can use
   a. Disk Cleanup.
   b. Problem Step Recorder.
   c. PC DeCrapifier.
   d. Resource Monitor.

4. If you want your system to run reliably, you should
   a. delete all programs from the Startup folder.
   b. save all of your temporary Internet files.
   c. install programs in the system tray.
   d. defragment the hard drive.

5. Which bests describes RAID 0 technology?
   a. Saved data is spread across two hard drives.
   b. Data is written to one drive and mirrored to a second drive.
   c. RAID 0 allows you to store twice the data.
   d. RAID 0 provides an instant backup of your work.

6. What allows two different programs to be processed at one time?
   a. Hyperthreading
   b. SSD
   c. Benchmarking
   d. GPU

7. Which is *not* a type of memory stored in your system?
   a. RAM
   b. Cache
   c. CPU register
   d. ALU

8. The optimal amount of memory for a video card depends on
   a. the quality of video you will be watching.
   b. the resolution of the monitor.
   c. the number of monitors you have.
   d. All of the above.

9. SuperFetch is a memory-management technique that
   a. determines the type of RAM your system requires.
   b. makes the boot-up time for the system very quick.
   c. preloads the applications you use most into system memory.
   d. defragments the hard drive to increase performance.

10. What is the name for the time it takes a storage device to locate its stored data and make it available for processing?
   a. Clock speed
   b. Access time
   c. Data transfer rate
   d. Seek time

True–False

_____ 1. A single CPU can have multiple cores but cannot also use hyperthreading.

_____ 2. The memory that your operating system uses is referred to as kernel memory.

_____ 3. Motherboards are designed with a specific number of memory card slots.

_____ 4. Cache memory is a form of read-only memory that can be accessed more quickly by the CPU.

_____ 5. Solid state drives are faster than hard drives and eSATA drives.

1. Personalize Your System

Likely you spend many hours each day working on your computer using it for school, work, communication, research, and entertainment. Your computer should be a device that fits you, fits your needs, and expresses who you are.

a. Begin with the computer's form. Would you select a notebook or a desktop? What features determine that decision?
b. Next consider performance. Which type of CPU do you need? How much RAM should be installed? What kind of hard drive storage would you select? Give specific price-to-value arguments for each decision.
c. Now consider expandability. If you need this system to last for four years, what kind of ports and expansion capability are necessary?
d. Finally, consider style. What components or design decisions can you make so that this system uniquely suits you and represents you?

2. Desktop Replacement

The line between the capabilities of a desktop system and a powerful notebook have become more and more blurred with the arrival of "desktop replacement" systems. These systems often have 17-inch, 18-inch, or larger monitors, weigh 10 pounds or more, and have a battery life of less than two hours. Research the most current entries in the "desktop replacement" category and evaluate them. What kind of user would find this an ideal solution? Do you anticipate this category of computer becoming more popular?

3. Go Small or Stay Home

Manufacturers are releasing a number of systems that are trying to capitalize on size—or the lack of size! Explore some of the small form factor (SFF) computers appearing on the market.

a. Research the Falcon NorthWest FragBox (falcon-nw.com).
b. Examine the Apple MacMini (apple.com).
c. Compare those systems with the Dell Zino HD (dell.com).

Why are these SFF computers appearing? What role do you see these systems fulfilling? What kind of performance and hardware would you recommend for such a system?

4. Do-It-Yourself Computer Design

Visit NewEgg (**newegg.com**) and do a search on "do it yourself". You will find that NewEgg has created a number of bundles, which are a set of components that cover the categories outlined in this chapter: the computer case, processor, RAM, storage, video, and audio.

a. Which system looks like the best match for your needs for school next semester? Why?
b. What is the price difference between building the system and purchasing a similar unit from a major manufacturer?
c. What skills would you need before you could assemble the computer yourself?
d. What additional components (hardware and software) would you need to complete the system?
e. What kind of support exists to train you in these skills or to help with questions you might have along the way?

5. How Does Your System Measure Up?

A number of tools are available to measure your system's performance. Explore the following tools and use one to gather data on your current system's performance.

a. Windows 7 Gadgets: Visit the Windows 7 Personalization Gallery (**windows. microsoft.com**) and find gadgets to help you monitor system performance.
b. Windows 7 Resource Monitor: Use the Resource Monitor to collect data on CPU utilization and memory usage over a typical school day.
c. Benchmarking suites: Examine a sample of consumer benchmarking programs like the PassMark's PerformanceTest, Primate Lab's Geekbench, and Maxon's Cinebench. Which subsystems do each of these products evaluate? How do they present their results? Which seems easiest to use?

six
making the transition to... the workplace

1. In the "Real World"

As you move from an educational environment to a business environment, how you use your computer will inevitably change. Write a description of your ideal computer system for school and for once you are in the workforce. Defend the position you take with information covered in this chapter. To help you in your decision, fill out the worksheet, similar to Figure 6.2, that is available on the book's companion Website (**pearsonhighered.com/techinaction**).

2. Judging System Performance

As you learned in this chapter, the Resource Monitor provides a detailed breakdown of how the computer is using memory at any given time.

a. Open the Resource Monitor, move to the CPU tab, and open the Processes frame. What is your total CPU Usage? How many "virtual" CPUs does your machine have? Clicking on any of the column titles sorts that column, so clicking the Average CPU column shows you the applications currently using most of the CPU resources. What are the top two most intensive applications?

b. Move to the Memory tab. How much memory is in use? How much is available? Of the memory available, how much has been preloaded with data and files that Windows "thinks" you will need soon?

c. Move to the Disk tab. Click on the Processes With Disk Activity panel. Which programs are making the greatest total demand to read and write to the disk?

3. My Mother(board)

This chapter discussed the qualities of a CPU that are important to consider for system performance. Now examine the features of a motherboard that are critical to the performance and expandability of a system. Visit NewEgg (**newegg.com**) and search for "Intel Motherboards"; then sort by "Best Rated".

a. Which model has the best reviews?
b. How many ports and what type of ports does it have?
c. What kind of CPU does it support?
d. What kind of memory does it use, and what is the maximum memory it supports?
e. How many hard drives can it run? Does it support both RAID 0 and RAID 1?
f. Does it have integrated video? Audio?

4. Room to Move

You are responsible for specifying the storage solution for an accounting customer's computer system. Your customer needs to always have redundancy—that is, multiple copies of the work they are doing—because of the secure nature of the records they keep and the length of time they are required to keep records. Prepare a report that describes the type of hard drive and optical storage you would recommend. Be sure to include performance specifications and price. Devise a list of additional questions you would need to ask your customer to be sure they have a system that meets their expectations.

5. A Picture Is Worth a Thousand Words

You work in a financial analysis firm. It is necessary to watch small fluctuations in many different international monetary funds and markets each day. This data is then fed into your own prediction software, tied to Excel calculations, and then plotted with three different statistical analysis packages. What video solution would be ideal for this environment? Would it require a video card with a single or dual GPU? Multiple video cards? Multiple monitors?

6. Let Me Tell You My Problem

You may be responsible for helping others solve various computer problems. Test out the Problem Steps Recorder in Windows 7 to see how the program can help you help them. Click the Start button and search for "psr". Run the program and click Record. Then just click between different applications, visit the Control Panel, and add an annotation. Save the file to your desktop and close the Problem Steps Recorder. View the annotated report. How could you use the Problem Steps Recorder to describe a problem or to gather information?

Instructions: Albert Einstein used *Gedankenexperiments*, or critical thinking questions, to develop his theory of relativity. Some ideas are best understood by experimenting with them in our own minds. The following critical thinking questions are designed to demand your full attention but require only a comfortable chair—no technology.

1. And Google Says...

In a presentation in Dublin, Ireland in March 2010, Google sales chief Jim Haley stated that desktops would be irrelevant in three years (**SiliconRepublic.com**). Smartphones, notebooks, and the amount of information available online will converge to create a different kind of future than what we've known, according to Haley. Do you agree? Why or why not? What impact would that have on the types of hardware and software that are the most in demand?

2. Emerging Technologies

Touchscreens are now available in a range of sizes, from smartphones to iPads to larger products like the Microsoft Surface. Windows 7 has integrated support for touchscreens. "Surround Sight" and 3D monitors are available in increasing numbers. What new technologies will last and become part of our collective experience? How will these technologies and devices change entertainment and how people interact with information? What future technologies that would be on your wish list?

3. The Early Adopter

We are all aware of the technology price curve: when first introduced, products have the highest prices and the most instability. As these products settle into the market, they become more reliable and the price falls, sometimes very quickly. People who make those first release purchases are called *early adopters*. What are the advantages to being an early adopter? What are the disadvantages? How do you decide at what point you should step into the technology price curve for any given product?

4. A Green Machine

Review the impacts of your computer during its entire lifecycle. How do the production, transportation, and use of the computer impact the increase of greenhouse gas emissions? How does the selection of materials and packaging impact the environment? What restricted substances (like lead, mercury, cadmium, and PVC) are found in your machine? Could substitute materials be used? How would the ultimate "Green Machine" be designed?

5. System Longevity

If you purchase a computer system for business purposes, the Internal Revenue Service (IRS) allows you to depreciate its cost over five years. The IRS considers this a reasonable estimate of the useful lifetime of a computer system. What do you think most home users expect in terms of how long their computer systems should last? How does the purchase of a computer system compare with other major household appliances in terms of cost, value, benefit, life span, and upgrade potential?

six six team time

Many Different Computers for Many Different Needs

Problem

Even within one discipline, there are needs for a variety of types of computing solutions. Consider the Communications department in a large university. Because it is such an interdisciplinary area, there are some groups involved in video production, some groups producing digital music, and some groups responsible for creating scripts and screenplays. The department as a whole needs to decide on a complete computing strategy.

Process

Split your class into teams.

1. Select one segment of the Communications department that your team will represent: video production, digital music, or scripting. The video production team requires their labs to be able to support the recording, editing, and final production and distribution of digital video. The digital music group wants to establish a collegiate recording studio (in the model of the Drexel University recording label, Mad Dragon Records). The scripting group needs to support a collaborative community of writers and voice-over actors.
2. Analyze the computing needs of that division, with particular focus on how they need to outfit their computer labs.
3. Price the systems you would recommend and explain how they will be used. What decisions have you made to guarantee they will still be useful in three years?
4. Write a report that summarizes your findings. Document the resources you used and generate as much enthusiasm as you can for your recommendations.

Conclusion

The range of available computing solutions has never been so broad. It can be a cause of confusion for those not educated in technology. But with a firm understanding of the basic subsystems of computers, it is precisely the pace of change that is exciting. Being able to evaluate a computer system and match it to the current needs of its users is an important skill.

In this exercise, you will research and then role-play a complicated ethical situation. The role you play might or might not match your own personal beliefs; in either case, your research and use of logic will enable you to represent the view assigned. An arbitrator will watch and comment on both sides of the arguments, and together the team will agree on an ethical solution.

Topic: Light Peak

We have seen many dramatic increases in connectivity speed. The USB standard is now in its third revision, with each being many fold faster than its predecessor. Currently, Intel is developing a technology named Light Peak that could replace all of the cables you currently see dangling from computers with one fiber-optic cable—one very fast fiber-optic cable. This technology will allow for smaller notebook computer designs, because they won't need to have a huge set of ports along the side. Intel feels Light Peak could become the universal port, replacing USB, HDMI, FireWire, DVI, and others. And using Light Peak, an entire high-definition movie could be transferred in 30 seconds.

Research Areas to Consider

- Durability of fiber-optic cables for consumers

- Protection of intellectual content as transfer speeds increase

- Building consensus in the market for new technologies

- 2009 Nobel Prize for Physics

Process

Divide the class into teams.

1. Research the areas cited above from the perspective of either an Intel engineer working on Light Peak, a notebook designer, a producer of high-definition videos, or an arbitrator.

2. Team members should write a summary that provides factual documentation for the positions and views their character takes around the issue of increasingly high speed data transfer and intellectual property rights. Then, team members should create an outline to use during the role-playing event.

3. Team members should arrange a mutually convenient time to meet for the exchange, either using the chat room feature of MyITLab, the discussion board feature of Blackboard, or meeting in person.

4. Team members should present their case to the class, or submit a PowerPoint presentation for review by the rest of the class, along with the summary and resolution they developed.

Conclusion

As technology becomes ever more prevalent and integrated into our lives, more and more ethical dilemmas will present themselves. Being able to understand and evaluate both sides of the argument, while responding in a personally or socially ethical manner, will be an important skill.

seven
networking
connecting computing devices

objectives

After reading this chapter, you should be able to answer the following questions:

1. What is a network, and what are the advantages/disadvantages of setting up one? *(pp. 309–310)*

2. What is the difference between a client/server network and a peer-to-peer network? *(pp. 310–312)*

3. What are the main components of every network? *(pp. 312–315)*

4. Which type of network is most commonly found in the home? *(p. 315)*

5. What equipment and software do I need to build a network in my home? *(pp. 319–322)*

6. Besides computers, what other devices would I connect to a home network? *(pp. 322–326)*

7. Why are wireless networks more vulnerable than wired networks, and what special precautions are required to ensure my wireless network is secure? *(p. 327)*

8. How do I configure the software on my computer and set up other devices to get my network up and running? *(pp. 329–334)*

9. What problems might I encounter when setting up a wireless network? *(pp. 334–335)*

multimedia resources

Active Helpdesk
- Understanding Networking **(p. 325)**

Sound Bytes
- Installing a Home Computer Network **(p. 325)**
- Securing Wireless Networks **(p. 327)**

Companion Website
The Companion Website includes a variety of additional materials to help you review and learn more about the topics in this chapter. Go to: *pearsonhighered.com/techinaction*

how cool is *this?*

As you have probably already experienced, wireless connectivity is not always free. Many businesses, such as Starbucks, **charge** customers for each device they want to connect, which can become expensive for groups of friends trying to surf the Internet while waiting to **catch a flight** at the airport. Connectify is free software that takes an existing Internet connection and turns it into a wireless hotspot. So if you are connected to the Internet on your notebook, the **Connectify** software turns your notebook computer into a wireless hotspot so that you and your friends can connect other WiFi-enabled devices such as a cell phone or **gaming** system through the same Internet connection. The hotspot you create features easy connectivity and encryption of data for solid **security**.

Networking Fundamentals

Now that we are into the second decade of the 21st century, most homes have more than one computing device that is capable of connecting to the Internet. A typical family, like the Diaz family (see Figure 7.1), might be engaged in the following: Carlos (the father) is watching a movie, which he downloaded yesterday on the large-screen HDTV in the living room while checking his Gmail

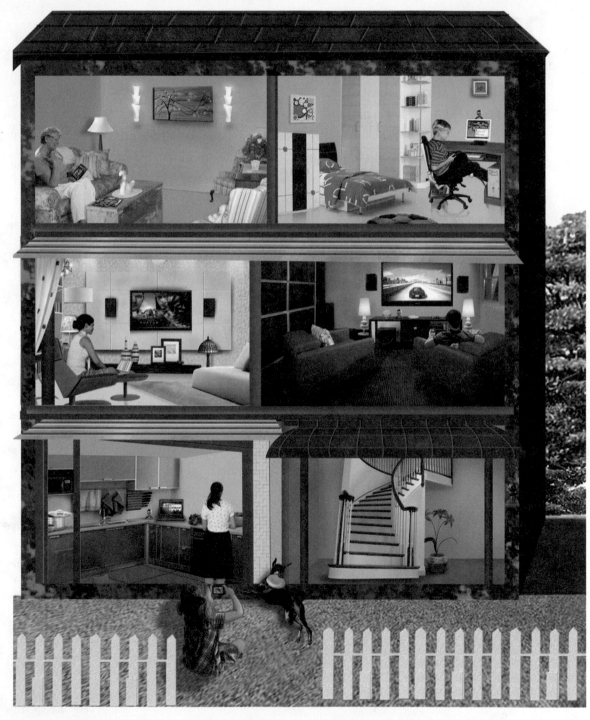

Figure 7.1

By setting up a home network, everyone in the family can connect their computers and others devices whenever and wherever they desire.

on his smartphone. Camila (the mother) is in the kitchen fixing lunch while checking the weather forecast and watching YouTube videos. Antonio, their fifteen-year-old son, is in his bedroom playing an online game with his friends (via his PlayStation) and is uploading a video he made for a class project to a Web site at school. Adriana, Antonio's older sister, is in the den using her notebook computer to finish a report for school. She's also watching a Blu-ray disc of *Avatar*, which is one of her all-time favorite movies. Grandma Cecilia is in the family room viewing pictures from the family's last vacation and is uploading to Facebook the pictures that she took of her grandchildren during their trip to Disneyland last week. And Angel, the youngest daughter, is playing with Sparky in the backyard and uploading video that she took of him with her phone so that everyone can see it in the family room while they eat lunch. And because both Carlos and Camila work outside the home, they use webcams to monitor activities in the house, like ensuring their kids arrive home safely from school, while they are at work. What makes all this technology transfer and sharing possible? A home network!

What is a computer network?
A computer **network** is simply two or more computers that are connected via software and hardware so that they can communicate with each other. You access networks all the time whether you realize it or not. When you use an ATM, get gasoline, or use the Internet (the world's largest network), you are interacting with a network. Each device connected to a network is referred to as a **node**. A node can be a computer, a peripheral (such as an all-in-one printer), a game console (such as a

PlayStation or a Wii), a digital video recorder (such as a TiVo), or a communications device (such as a modem). The main function for most networks is to facilitate information sharing, but networks provide other benefits.

What are the benefits of networks?
There are several benefits to having computers networked. Most home users want a network to facilitate resource sharing. For example, a network allows you to share the high-speed Internet connection coming into your home. Networks also allow you to share peripheral devices, such as printers. Figure 7.2a shows two computers that are not networked. Computer 1 is connected to the printer, but Computer 2 is not. To print files from Computer 2, users have to transfer them using a flash drive or another storage medium to Computer 1, or they have to disconnect the printer from Computer 1 and connect it to Computer 2. By networking Computer 1, Computer 2,

Figure 7.2
(a) Computers 1 and 2 are not networked, and Computer 2 cannot access the printer. (b) Networking allows sharing of the printer.

Inkjet printer

a

Computer 1

Printer cable

Computer 2

b

Computer 1

Wireless connection

Inkjet printer

Computer 2

and the printer, as shown in Figure 7.2b, both computers can print from the printer without transferring files or attaching the printer to a particular computer. Using a wired or wireless network to share a printer saves the cost of buying one printer for each computer.

Besides peripheral and Internet connections, does networking facilitate any other types of resource sharing? You can also easily share files between networked computers without having to use portable storage devices such as flash drives to transfer the files. In addition, you can set sharing options in Windows or OS X that allow the user of each computer on the network to access files (such as music or videos) stored on any other computer on the network, as shown in Figure 7.3.

This Windows network has five computers attached to it. ALAN-DESKTOP, ALAN-NOTEBOOK, and PAT-NOTEBOOK are running the Windows operating system. The two MACBOOKs are running OS X. The Public folders enable file sharing because the user of any computer on the network can access the Public folder's contents. And note the final advantage of networking: computers running different operating systems (such as Windows and OS X) can communicate on the same network.

Are there disadvantages to setting up a network? Networks involve the purchase of additional equipment to set them up, so cost is one disadvantage. Also,

networks need to be administered, at least to some degree. **Network administration** involves tasks such as: 1) installing new computers and devices, 2) monitoring the network to ensure it is performing efficiently, 3) updating and installing new software on the network, and 4) configuring, or setting up, proper security for a network. Fortunately, most home networks do not require a great deal of administration after their initial configuration, and the benefits of using a network usually outweigh the disadvantages.

Network Architectures

The term **network architecture** refers to the design of a network. Network architectures are classified according to the way in which they are controlled and the distance between their nodes.

Describing Networks Based on Network Administration

What different types of control do I have over my network? A network can be administered, or managed, in either of two main ways: locally or centrally. Local administration means that the configuration and maintenance of the network must be performed on each individual computer attached to the network. A peer-to-peer network is the most common example of a locally administered network. Central administration means that tasks can be performed from one computer and affect the other computers on the network. The most common type of centrally administered network is a client/server network.

What is a peer-to-peer network? In a **peer-to-peer (P2P) network**, each node connected to the network can communicate directly with every other node on the network. Thus, all nodes on this type of network are peers (equals). When printing, for example, a computer on a P2P network doesn't have to go through the computer that's connected to the printer. Instead, it can communicate directly with the printer. Figure 7.2b, shown earlier, shows a very small peer-to-peer network.

Figure 7.3

Windows Explorer showing five networked computers set up for sharing.

Shared files on ALAN-NOTEBOOK

Shared files on MACBOOK

Step 1:
Client computer
requests a service.

Computer
A
(client)

Step 2:
Server computer
provides service.

Figure 7.4

In a client/server network, a computer acts either as a client making requests for resources or as a server providing resources.

Because they are simple to set up, P2P networks are the most common type of home network. Very small schools and offices may also use P2P networks. However, most networks that have 10 or more nodes are client/server networks.

What are client/server networks?
A **client/server network** contains two different types of computers: clients and servers. A **client** is a computer on which users accomplish specific tasks (such as construct spreadsheets) and make specific requests (such as printing a file). The **server** is the computer that provides information or resources to the client computers on the network. The server on a client/server network also provides central administration for network functions such as printing. Figure 7.4 illustrates a client/server network in action.

As you learned in Chapter 3, the Internet is

Figure 7.5

At only 8 inches high, the Acer Aspire easyStore server can perform a variety of tasks to simplify media management on a home network.

an example of a client/server network. When your computer is connected to the Internet, it is functioning as a client computer. When it accesses the Internet through an Internet service provider (ISP), your computer connects to a server computer maintained by the ISP. The server "serves up" resources to your computer so that you can interact with the Internet.

Are client/server networks ever used as home networks? Although client/server networks can be configured for home use, P2P networks are more often used in the home because they cost less than client/server networks and are easier to configure and maintain. However, specialized types of servers (such as servers for sharing files) are now appearing on P2P networks in the home.

Nowadays, the individuals in most homes are accumulating vast amounts of media files from digital cameras, camcorders, video downloads, and music downloads. Because users often want to share this media, specialized home network servers such as the Acer Aspire easyStore servers featuring Windows Home Server are now available for home networks. A **home network server** is designed to store media, share media across the network, and back up files on computers connected to the network (see Figure 7.5). All computers connected to the network can access the server.

Even though a server may now be attached to a home network, that does not change the architecture of a home network from a P2P network to a client/server network. Except for the specialized functions of the home network server, all network administration tasks (such as installation of software and changing of configuration settings) must still be performed locally, and all the nodes on the network are still peers to each other.

Describing Networks Based on Distance

How does the distance between nodes define a network? The distance between nodes on a network is another way to describe a network. A **local area network (LAN)** is a network in which the nodes are located within a small geographic area. Examples include a network in a computer lab at school or at a fast-food restaurant. A **home area network (HAN)** is a network located in a home. HANs are used to connect all of a home's digital devices, such as computers, peripherals, phones, gaming devices, digital video recorders (DVRs), and televisions.

Is it possible to connect LANs? A **wide area network (WAN)** is made up of LANs connected over long distances. Say a school has two campuses (east and west) located in different towns. Connecting the

LAN at the east campus to the LAN at the west campus by telecommunications lines would allow the users on the two LANs to communicate. The two LANs would be described as a single WAN.

Are wireless networks that cover large areas like cities considered WANs? Technically, wireless networks like the one deployed in Minneapolis, which provides Internet access to city residents and visitors, are WANs. However, when a network is designed to provide access to a specific geographic area, such as an entire city, the network is usually called a **metropolitan area network (MAN)**. Many cities in the United States are now deploying MANs to provide Internet access to residents and provide convenience for tourists.

Network Components

To function, all networks must include (1) a means of connecting the nodes on the network (cables or wireless technology), (2) special devices that allow the nodes to communicate with each other and to send data, and (3) software that allows the network to run. We discuss each of these components in this section (see Figure 7.6).

Figure 7.6

Network components.

Networking software running on each computer

Computer 2 network node

Printer network node

Transmission media (wires or radio waves) connecting network nodes

Computer 1 network node

External network adapter

Internal network adapter (network interface card)

Router

Wireless access point

Network adapter attached to or inserted in each network node

Specialized network navigation devices (used on some networks)

Transmission Media

How are nodes on a network connected?

All network nodes are connected to each other and to the network by transmission media. **Transmission media** establishes a communications channel between the nodes on a network and can either be wireless or wired.

Wireless networks use radio waves to connect nodes. With the proliferation of portable devices being connected to home networks, a network with at least some wireless connectivity is preferred in most homes.

Wired networks use various types of cable (wires) to connect nodes. **Twisted-pair cable** is made up of copper wires that are twisted around each other and surrounded by a plastic jacket. Normal telephone cable is a type of twisted-pair cable, although phone cable won't work for connecting a home network and a slightly different type of twisted-pair cable is used. **Coaxial cable** consists of a single copper wire surrounded by layers of plastic. If you have cable TV, the cable running into your TV or cable box is most likely coaxial cable. **Fiber-optic cable** is made up of plastic or glass fibers that transmit data at extremely fast speeds. Verizon's FiOS service uses fiber-optic cable to run very fast data connections directly up to your home, although fiber-optic cable is not usually run inside the home. On a FiOS network, twisted-pair or coaxial cable is still used inside the home to transport the network signals.

Does it matter what type of media you use to transfer data?

The media you choose depends on the requirements of a network's users. Using wireless media is critical when portable computing devices (such as smartphones) need to be connected to a network. However, higher speed connections (than can be achieved by wireless connectivity) are required for certain types of network activities, such as downloading large files such as movies. Different types of transmission media transmit data at different speeds.

Data transfer rate (also called **bandwidth**) is the maximum speed at which data can be transmitted between two nodes on a network. **Throughput** is the actual speed of data transfer that is achieved. Throughput is always less than or equal to the data transfer rate. Data transfer rate and throughput are usually measured in megabits per second (Mbps). (A megabit is 1 million bits.) Twisted-pair cable, coaxial cable, and wireless media usually provide enough bandwidth for most home networks.

Network Adapters

How do the different nodes on the network communicate?

Network adapters are devices connected to or installed in network nodes that enable the nodes to communicate with each other and to access the network. All desktop and notebook computers (and many peripherals) sold today contain network adapters installed *inside* the device. This type of adapter is referred to as a **network interface card (NIC)**. Different NICs are designed to use different types of transmission media. Most NICs included in computing devices today are built to use wireless media but many can use wired media as well. Your notebook computer most likely has a wireless NIC in it that allows you to connect to wireless networks (home, school, or the coffee shop). But most notebooks also have a port on the side that accommodates cable for a wired connection to a network.

> **"All computers sold today contain network adapters."**

Why would I ever consider using a wired connection with my notebook computer?

Wired connections can sometimes provide greater throughput than current high-speed wireless networks. Here are some common reasons why wireless signals may have decreased throughput:

- Wireless signals are more susceptible to interference from magnetic and electrical sources.
- Other wireless networks (such as your neighbor's network) can interfere with the signals on your network.
- Certain building materials (such as concrete and cinderblock) and metal (a refrigerator) can decrease throughput.
- Throughput varies depending on the distance from your networking equipment.

Wireless networks usually use specially coded signals to protect their data whereas

ETHICS IN IT

Sharing Your Internet Connection with Your Neighbors: Legal? Ethical? Safe?

With the advances in wireless equipment, signals can travel well beyond the walls of your home. This makes it possible in an apartment or single family home (where homes are close together) for a group of neighbors to share a wireless signal and potentially save money by splitting the cost of one Internet connection among them. However, before jumping into this venture, you need to weigh a few issues carefully.

You probably aren't legally prohibited from sharing an Internet connection, but you should check on the state and local laws. Most laws are designed to prohibit piggybacking, which is using a network without the account holder's consent. However, if you are giving neighbors permission to share your connection, you probably don't violate any piggybacking laws.

Of course, your ISP might not permit you to share your Internet access with anyone. You probably have a personal account that is designed for one household. The terms of your agreement with the Internet provider might prohibit you from sharing your connection with people outside your household. If you aren't allowed to share the type of account you have now, your ISP probably offers a type of account (such as a small business account) that will allow you to share a connection, but it will most likely be more expensive. The ISPs know that the more people that share an account, the more likely that account is to use bandwidth; so they price their accounts accordingly. You might be able to share a personal account without being detected by your ISP, but that certainly would be unethical because you should be paying for a higher level of access. Therefore, make sure to check with your ISP to determine that you have the right type of account.

The next thing you need to consider is whether the shared access should be open to all neighbors, or just to the neighbors that are contributing to the cost of the Internet connection. You could leave the connection open (like the connections at Panera Bread) and let anyone who finds it log on and surf. You might consider this a very ethical action, because you are providing free Internet access for anyone who needs it. You could register your free hot spot with a service like JiWire, and then people would know where it is. However, your neighbors who are helping pay the cost might have a different viewpoint and not want to fund free surfing for everyone. Make sure you work this out before proceeding.

If you are going to host a free and open hot spot, you still need to make sure that you set it up safely. You want to maintain a secure network for you and your neighbors while still allowing the occasional visiting surfer to use the connection. There are WiFi sharing services (see Figure 7.7) such as Fon (**fon.com**), Whisher (**whisher.com**, now owned by **wifi.com**), and WeFi (**wefi.com**) that can provide you with special hardware (a router) or software that allows you to configure your hot spot so your network remains secure.

While offering free access to anyone will earn you lots of good karma, additional risks exist because you don't know what mischief or criminal activities someone might engage in while connected to the Internet through your account. Think very carefully before you proceed down the sharing path, and make sure you set your hot spot up to protect your internal network.

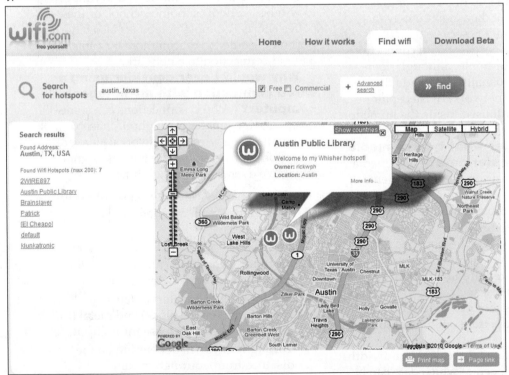

Figure 7.7
At Wifi.com you can search and find free hot spots hosted by other Whisher users.

wired connections don't protect their signals. This process of coding signals can slightly decrease throughput, although once coded, data travels at usual speeds.

Therefore, in situations where you want to achieve the highest possible throughput (transferring a large video), you may want to connect your notebook (or other portable device) to your home network using a wire (at least temporarily). We'll discuss this type of connection in more depth when we talk about home Ethernet networks later in this chapter.

Network Navigation Devices

How is data sent through a network? Network **navigation devices** facilitate and control the flow of data through a network. Data is sent over transmission media in bundles. Each bundle is called a **packet**. For computers to communicate, these packets of data must be able to flow between network nodes. Network navigation devices, which are themselves nodes on a network, enable the transmission of data between other nodes on the network that contain NICs.

> **"Home networks need operating system software that supports P2P networking."**

What network navigation devices will I use on my home network? The two most common navigation devices are routers and switches. A **router** transfers packets of data between two or more networks. For example, if a home network is connected to the Internet, a router is required to send data between the two networks (the home network and the Internet). A **switch** is a "traffic cop" on a network. Switches receive data packets and send them to their intended nodes on the same network (not between different networks). All routers sold for home use have switches integrated into them. We discuss routers for home networks in more detail later in the chapter.

SOUND BYTE

Installing a Home Computer Network

Installing a network is relatively easy if you've seen someone else do it. In this Sound Byte, you'll learn how to install the hardware and configure Windows for a wired or wireless home network.

Networking Software

What software do home networks require? Home networks need operating system (OS) software that supports P2P networking. The Windows, OS X, and Linux operating systems all support P2P networking. You can connect computers running any of these OSs to the same home network (we also cover configuring software for home networks later in the chapter).

Is the same software used in client/server networks? Client/server networks are controlled by centralized servers that have specialized **network operating system (NOS)** software installed on them. This software handles requests for information, Internet access, and the use of peripherals for the rest of the network nodes. As opposed to P2P networks, the nodes on a client server network do not communicate directly with each other but communicate through a server. Communicating through a server is more efficient in a network with a large number of nodes, but requires more complex NOS software than is necessary for P2P networks. Examples of NOS software include Windows Server 2008 R2 and SUSE Linux Enterprise Server.

Home Ethernet Networks

Now that you understand the basic components of a home network, you are probably wondering where to start on installing your home network. In the following sections, we'll discuss the most common types of networks found in the home and how to get the fastest data transfer rates from your home network. We'll also explore the various types of cabling used in wired networks.

Ethernet Home Networks

What type of peer-to-peer network should I install in my home? The vast majority of home networks are Ethernet networks. An **Ethernet network** is so named because it uses the Ethernet protocol as the means (or standard) by which the nodes on the network communicate. The Ethernet protocol was developed by the Institute of

Wake Up Your Computer Remotely

Having your computer on a home network with a shared Internet connection makes it possible to access your computer and its files even when you aren't at home. But if your computer is asleep, you need some way to "wake it up." Otherwise, you can't access it through the Internet. Fortunately for Mac users, there is an application called iNet WOL (Wake on LAN) designed to do this (see Figure 7.8). iNet WOL is compatible with the iPhone, iPod Touch, and iPad. The application allows you to use your portable device to wake up your computer via the Internet. Once your computer is awake, you can then use your remote access software to access it. Think of iNet WOL as an alarm clock for your computer.

Figure 7.8
The application iNet WOL (Wake on LAN) lets you use your iPhone to wake up your computer from a remote location.

Electrical and Electronics Engineers (IEEE). This nonprofit group develops many standard specifications for electronic data transmission that are adopted throughout the world. Each standard the IEEE develops is numbered, with 802.11 (wireless) and 802.3 (wired) being the standards for Ethernet networks. The Ethernet protocol makes Ethernet networks extremely efficient at moving data. Ethernet networks use both wireless and wired transmission media.

What is the current wireless standard for Ethernet networks? The current standard that governs wireless networking for Ethernet networks is the **802.11n standard**, which was ratified in 2009. Establishing standards for networking is important so that devices from different manufacturers will work well together. The

802.11 standard is also known as **WiFi**. Four standards are currently defined under the 802.11 WiFI standard: 802.11a, 802.11b, 802.11g, and 802.11n. Since 802.11n features the fastest data transfer rates, it is now the most desirable choice for home networks. Devices using older standards (such as 802.11g) will still work with 802.11n networks, but they will operate with slower data transfer rates. This accommodation of current devices being able to use previously issued standards in addition to the current standards is known as **backward compatibility**.

How do 802.11n wireless devices work? Wireless routers and network adapters contain transceivers. A **transceiver** is a device that translates the electronic data that needs to be sent along the network into radio waves and then broadcasts these radio waves to other network nodes. Transceivers serve a dual function because they also receive the signals from other network nodes. Devices that use the 802.11n standard achieve higher throughput by using a technology known as Multiple Input Multiple Output (MIMO).

Devices using wireless standards developed prior to the 802.11n standard only utilized one antenna for transmitting and receiving data. Devices that use **Multiple Input Multiple Output (MIMO)** technology are designed to use multiple antennas for transmitting and receiving data. The multiple antennas break the data into multiple data streams and allow for faster transmission of the data. 802.11n devices can achieve throughput of up to 300 Mbps under ideal conditions. But as mentioned previously, many factors can reduce the throughput of a wireless connection.

Throughput Speeds

How can I tell how fast the wireless connection to my network is on my computer? You can install various utilities, such as Net Meter (available at **download.com**), on your computer that will measure your throughput. Net Meter (see Figure 7.9) shows you the throughput you are achieving on your computer's wireless connection to your network over a period of time. Hopefully, you'll achieve throughput in the range of 50 to 200 Mbps on your wireless network, which should be sufficient

Figure 7.9

Net Meter shows this computer is achieving a rather slow maximum connection of 1.65 mbps on a shared wireless network at a hotel.

for most applications (even watching video). However, if you don't achieve acceptable throughput, you might want to consider a wired Ethernet connection.

What kind of throughput is achievable with wired network connections? Up to one gigabit per second (1,000 Mbps) of throughput is possible using the **gigabit Ethernet** standard, which is the most commonly used wired Ethernet standard deployed in devices designed for home networks. Wired Ethernet networks use cables to transmit data as opposed to the radio waves used on wireless networks. Because cabling is much less susceptible to interference, a wired connection can achieve higher rates of throughput.

Network Cabling

What type of cable do I need to connect to a wired Ethernet network? The most popular transmission media option for wired Ethernet networks is **unshielded twisted-pair (UTP) cable**. UTP cable is composed of four pairs of wires that are twisted around each other to reduce electrical interference. You can buy UTP cable in varying lengths with RJ-45 connectors (Ethernet connectors) already attached. RJ-45 connectors resemble standard phone connectors (called RJ-11 connectors) but are slightly larger and have contacts for eight wires (four pairs) instead of four wires (see Figure 7.10). You must use UTP cable with RJ-45 connectors on an Ethernet network because a phone cable will not work.

Do all wired Ethernet networks use the same kind of UTP cable? Figure 7.11 lists the three main types of UTP

cable you would consider using in home-wired Ethernet networks—Cat 5E, Cat 6, and Cat 6a—and their data transfer rates. Although Cat 5E cable is the cheapest and is sufficient for many home networking tasks it was designed for 100 Mpbs wired Ethernet networks that were popular before gigabit Ethernet networks became the popular standard for home networking. Therefore, you should probably not install Cat 5E cable although it is still available in stores. Since **Cat 6 cable** is designed to achieve data transfer rates that support a gigabit Ethernet network, it is probably the best choice for home networking cable. Cat 6a cable is designed for Ultra-Fast Ethernet (10 gigabit Ethernet) networks that run at

---

BITS AND BYTES

Blazingly Fast Wireless Connections on the Horizon

Although most people want wireless connectivity throughout their home, wired connections still provide the best throughput. But a joint effort between the Wireless Gigabit Alliance and the WiFi Alliance aims to change this. The next generation of wireless standards is called Wi-Gig and will be designed to provide up to 7 Gbps of throughput. This speed will blow away current WiFi standards (with a current theoretical maximum transfer rate of 600 Mbps) and wired gigabit connectivity. Whereas WiFi currently operates in the 5 GHz and 2.4 GHz bands, Wi-Gig will operate in the 60 GHz band, which is currently unlicensed by the FCC. This should prevent many of the interference issues that WiFi users currently experience. But don't start looking in the stores for this equipment just yet; this standard will take several years to develop.

Figure 7.10

(a) An RJ-45 (Ethernet) connector, which is used on UTP cables; and (b) a typical RJ-11 connector, which is used on standard phone cords.

Figure 7.11

Data Transfer Rates for Popular Home Network Cable Types

Figure 7.12

Wired and wireless connections in the same home network.

speeds as fast as 10 Gbps. Installing a 10 gigabit Ethernet network in the home is probably unnecessary because today's home applications don't require this rate of data transfer

What precautions should I taken when running UTP cable? UTP cable is no more difficult to install than normal phone cable but there are a few things to avoid. Do not put sharp bends into the cable when running it around corners because this can damage the copper wires inside and lead to breakage. Also, run the cable around the perimeter of the room (instead of under

a rug, for example) to prevent damage to wires from foot traffic.

How long can an Ethernet cable run be? Regardless of the type of Ethernet cable you use, runs for UTP cable can't exceed 100 meters (328 feet) or the signal starts to degrade. Even for short cable runs, you should use continuous lengths of cable. Although two cables can be spliced together with a connecting jack, this creates a point of failure for the cable, because connectors can loosen in the connecting jack and moisture or dust can accumulate on the contacts.

Fortunately, you don't have to choose between a wired or a wireless network. Ethernet networks can handle your wired and wireless needs on the same network. This gives you the best of both worlds (portability and high throughput).

Wired and Wireless on One Network

Can I have wired and wireless nodes on one Ethernet network? Yes, one Ethernet network can support nodes with both wireless and wired connections. Most people will want to connect portable devices (such as notebooks and smartphones) that are constantly being moved around the home wirelessly to their network. However, many of the devices that are connected to a network (such as televisions, DVRs, and Blu-ray players) usually stay in one location. Although these devices probably feature wireless connectivity also, it may be desirable to hook them up to wired connections to take advantage of faster throughput achieved by wired connectivity. Routers sold for home networks facilitate wired and wireless connections. Figure 7.12 shows an example of a network with a wireless/wired router attached.

Are there other types of P2P networks that can be installed in the home? Non-Ethernet networks in the home are extremely rare. Because Ethernet networks 1) are based on a well-established standard, 2) feature easy

Wireless DSL/Cable router

Computer in bedroom with wired connection

Notebook on back porch with wireless connection

Smartphone in kitchen with wireless connection

HDTV with wireless connection

set-up, 3) provide good throughput for home networking needs, and (4) are cost effective, manufacturers of home networking equipment have overwhelmingly embraced Ethernet networks.

Does the type of operating system I'm using affect my choice of a home networking standard? Windows, OS X, and Linux built in P2P networking software will all support connection to an Ethernet network. Therefore, an Ethernet network is appropriate for all computers using these three operating systems.

Home Ethernet Equipment

By now you should have enough information to decide what nodes on your network need be connected wirelessly and which devices would benefit from wired connections. In this section, we'll explore the various types of equipment (such as a router) that you need to obtain to configure your home network. And we'll explore what devices your nodes need to contain to enable them to connect to your network.

Routers and Switches: Moving Data Around Your Network

What equipment do I need for a home Ethernet network?
Ethernet networks need network navigation devices to make them work and therefore the first piece of equipment to consider is a router. Recall that routers are designed to transfer packets of data between two (or more) networks—in this case, your home network and the Internet. A router is essential on a home network to allow sharing of an Internet

connection. For an Ethernet network to function properly, data must also be transmitted efficiently around the network. A switch is the device that is used on Ethernet networks to route the data between nodes on the same network.

Because both a router and a switch are needed on home Ethernet networks, the manufacturers of home networking equipment make devices that are a combination of routers and switches. In most instances, these devices are called *routers* or *broadband routers*. But despite the name, these devices do include integrated switches. Although manufacturers do make routers with only wired capabilities, for the vast majority of home networks, people buy routers with wireless capabilities.

What do switches do on an Ethernet network?
Data is transmitted through the transmission medium of an Ethernet network in packets. Imagine the data packets on an Ethernet network as cars on a road. If there were no traffic signals or rules of the road (such as driving on the right-hand side), we'd see a lot more collisions between vehicles, and people wouldn't get where they were going as readily (or at all). Data packets can also suffer collisions. If data packets collide, the data in them is damaged or lost. In either case, the network doesn't function efficiently. The routers you buy for home networks have a switch integrated into them, so you won't need to buy a standalone switch for your home network.

As shown in Figure 7.13, a switch in an Ethernet network acts like a traffic signal (or a traffic cop) by enforcing the rules of the

Figure 7.13

A simplified explanation is that switches (working in conjunction with NICs) act like traffic signals or traffic cops. They enforce the rules of the data road on an Ethernet network and help prevent data packets from crashing into each other.

Switch

Data packet 1

Data packet 2

Data packet 3

Data packet 4

ETHERNET MEDIA

ETHERNET MEDIA

Figure 7.14

Rear view of typical wireless/wired router.

Antenna for wireless connections

Ethernet ports for wired connections

Modem port

data road on the transmission media. The switch keeps track of the data packets and, in conjunction with network interface cards, helps the data packets find their destinations without running into each other. The switch also keeps track of all the nodes on the network and sends the data packets directly to the node for which they are headed. This keeps the network running efficiently.

In the next section, we'll explore connecting your computing devices to your router.

Connecting Devices to Routers

How many computers and other devices can be connected to a router in a home network? Most home wireless routers can support up to 253 wireless connections at the same time. This number is a theoretical maximum, however—most home networks probably have fewer than ten wireless devices connected to the network. But regardless of how few or how many devices your home network has, those wireless devices share bandwidth when they are connected to a router. Therefore, the more devices actively transmitting data that you connect to a single router, the smaller the portion of the router's bandwidth each device receives.

To look at this another way, consider you have a pizza which represents your router's bandwidth. You can cut the pizza into six or eight pieces (that is, you can connect either six or eight devices to the network). If you cut the pizza into eight pieces, each person who gets a slice receives a smaller portion of pizza than they would if you had cut the pizza into six pieces. (that is, when you connect eight devices to the network, each

device has less bandwidth than it would have if only six devices were connected to the network).

Does my wireless router support wired connections? Most home wireless routers have three or four Ethernet ports on the back of the router to support wired connections via twisted-pair cable (see Figure 7.14). If you have a lot of devices (such as a game console, HDTV, and a notebook) in your home that may be used simultaneously, you might want to consider connecting some of them via a wired connection to increase allocated bandwidth to each wireless device. This will help increase the throughput to each wireless device.

If you find that you need additional ports for plugging in wireless connections to your network, you can buy a standalone switch and plug that into one of the ports on your router. This will give you additional ports for making wired connections to your network. Do not mistakenly buy another router (with an embedded switch) and try adding that to your network because the two routers will cause conflicts as they fight for control over network navigation.

Where do I obtain a router for my home network? You can purchase a router at any store (such as Best Buy) or online stores (**tigerdirect.com**, **newegg.com**) that carry home networking equipment. Also, since networks are so common in homes now, many ISPs offer home subscribers a device that combines a broadband modem and a wireless router. ISPs typically charge either a one-time or a monthly fee for this combination device. If you already have broadband access in your home, you at least have a modem. Check with your ISP if you are not sure whether you also already have a device that contains a router.

How do I know if my router supports wireless networking? If you do have a router provided by your ISP, make sure to ask what wireless networking standard the router supports. If it does not support 802.11n but supports and older standard such as 802.11g, you should consider having your ISP provide you with a new router. You want to have a router that supports the fastest wireless networking standard (802.11n) so that you can achieve the highest possible throughput on your wireless nodes. If all of your wireless devices have 802.11n network adapters, but your router supports 802.11g, you will not achieve the best throughput available to you because 802.11g devices feature much slower transfer rates than 802.11n devices (about four to six times slower).

Where do I place the router on my network? Your router should be connected directly to your broadband modem (see Figure 7.15). The connection is usually an Ethernet cable (Cat 6 cable) running from an Ethernet port on your modem to the modem port on your router.

Are wireless routers for Windows and OS X networks different? All routers that support the 802.11n standard should work with computers running Windows or OS X. However, Apple has designed routers that are optimized for working with Apple computers. So if you are connecting Apple computers to your network, you may wish to consider using an Apple AirPort router. (Windows machines can also connect to the AirPort routers.) The Apple AirPort Extreme (Figure 7.16) is a good choice for a home network. It supports up to 50 simultaneous wireless connections and has three gigabit Ethernet ports for wired connections.

How do I set up my router so that I can use it to connect to the Internet? First, contact your ISP and find out about any special settings that you may need to configure your router to work with your ISP. Next, access your router from Internet Explorer (or another Web browser) by entering the router's IP address or default URL. You can usually find this information in the documentation that came with the router. You'll also need a username and password to log on to the router. You'll probably find these, too, in the documentation that came with the router.

Many routers feature their own wizard (different from the Windows Networking wizards) that takes you through special configuration screens. A sample screen from a router is shown in Figure 7.17. The documentation that came with your router will provide a URL to use to log on to the router. If you're unsure of any information that

DSL/Cable modem

INTERNET

Wireless DSL/ Cable router

Computer #1

All-in-one printer

Computer #2

Figure 7.15

A small network with a wireless router attached.

needs to be entered to configure the router (such as whether IP addresses are assigned dynamically—meaning you are assigned a new IP address by your ISP each time you connect to the Internet), contact your ISP and ask for guidance.

After ensuring that your router is set up properly, you are ready to begin connecting your computing devices to your network. You now need to ensure that all your nodes have the proper equipment to enable them to connect to your network.

USB port   Modem port   Ethernet ports for wired connections

Figure 7.16

The AirPort Extreme router is often used for home networks with Apple computers.

Figure 7.17

Although setups differ from router to router, you will need basic information such as the logon information and the type of IP addressing to configure the router to work with your network and your ISP.

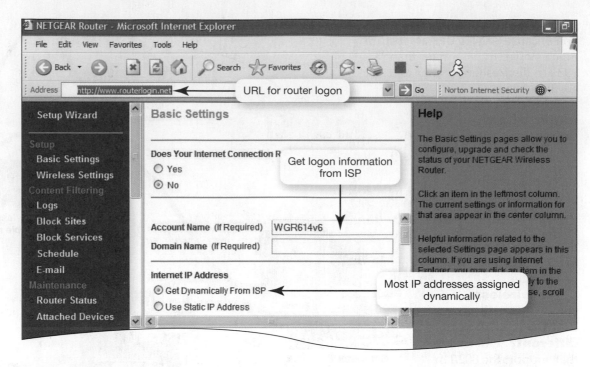

Figure 7.18

This Windows device manager shows a wireless and a wired network adapter installed in a notebook.

>To access Device Manager: Click the **Start Button**, select **Control Panel**, click on the **Hardware and Sound Group**, then click on **Device Manager**.

Connecting Network Nodes

What equipment do my computers need to communicate with wireless media on an 802.11n wireless network? Your computers need to have wireless network interface cards (NICs) installed in them. Notebooks and netbooks sold over the last several years most likely contain 802.11n NICs. For older computers, as long as they have wireless Ethernet adapters that are compatible with a previous standard (802.11g or 802.11b) they will be able to connect to your 802.11n router. However, the throughput will be at the lower 802.11g and b data transfer rates.

How can I tell what network adapters are installed in my computer? To see which network adapter(s) are installed in your Windows computer and to check whether the adapter is working, you should use the Device Manager utility program (see Figure 7.18). The installed adapters will be shown and then you search for information on the Internet to determine the adapter's capability if you aren't sure which wireless standard it supports.

Connecting Other Devices to Networks

Because sharing peripherals is a major benefit of installing a network, many peripheral devices, such as scanners and printers, now come with built-in Ethernet adapters. Also, many home entertainment devices (such as televisions, Blu-ray players, and gaming systems), portable devices (such as smartphones, and iPod Touches and iPads), and power monitoring devices to reduce energy consumption in the home are also designed to attach to home networks. Such devices are usually described as being "network-ready."

a   b

Ethernet port for
easy connection
to a router

Time Machine

Name: My Book
Available: 1.89 TB of 2 TB
Oldest Backup: May 22, 2010
Latest Backup: Today, 3:43 PM
Next Backup: Today, 4:42 PM

Time Machine keeps:
• Hourly backups for the past 24 hours
• Daily backups for the past month
• Weekly backups for all previous months
The oldest backups are deleted when your disk becomes full.

☐ Show Time Machine status in the menu bar

🔒 Click the lock to prevent further changes.

Figure 7.19

(a) The My Book drives from Western Digital feature NAS devices that can store 2 TB of data in a device the size of a small book. (b) Time Machine in conjunction with an external hard drive provides easy backups of Macs on a network.

Network-Ready Devices

What is a network-ready device? A **network-ready device** (or Internet ready) can be connected directly to a router instead of to a computer on the network. Network-ready devices usually contain wireless and/or wired network adapters inside them. A few devices (such as TiVo or the Xbox 360) still have external network adapters that connect to the device via a USB port but these eventually should be phased out in favor of internal adapters. The eventual goal may be to have all electronic devices in your home be nodes on your network.

Why should I connect my peripherals to my home network? There is an advantage to connecting peripherals wirelessly to your network. If a printer were connected directly to another computer (via a cable) on the network instead of being a node on the network, that computer would need to be switched on so other computers could access the printer. With a network-ready printer, only the printer needs to be powered on for any computer on the network to print to it.

What can I attach to my network to facilitate file sharing and back up of data? Network attached storage **(NAS) devices** are specialized computing devices designed to store and manage your data. People are generating tremendous quantities of data today with digital cameras and camcorders, as well as buying music files, and these files need to be stored and shared. Although data can always be stored on individual hard drives in computers on a network, NAS devices provide for centralized data storage and access.

Popular for years on business networks, NAS devices are now being widely marketed for home networks. You can think of them as specialized external hard drives. NAS devices, like the My Book series from Western Digital (see Figure 7.19a), connect directly to the network through a router or switch. Specialized software can then be installed on computers attached to the network to ensure that all data saved to an individual computer is also stored on the NAS as a backup. We'll discuss backing up your data in more detail in Chapter 9.

For Apple computers, the Time Capsule is a wireless router combined with a hard drive for facilitating backups of all computers connected to the network. The Time Capsule looks very similar to the AirPort router and it works in conjunction with the Time Machine backup feature of OS X (see Figure 7.19b). If you buy a Time Capsule, you won't need to buy an AirPort router (or other router) as the Time Capsule fulfills this function on your network also. When the Time Capsule is installed on your network, Macs connected to the network will ask the user if they want to use the Time Capsule as their source for Time Machine backups. The Time Capsule is another type of NAS device.

Besides external hard drives, are their other NAS devices I could use on my network? A more sophisticated type of NAS device is a home network server. Home network servers are specialized devices that are designed to provide a specific set of services to computers on a home network. Home servers do not convert a home peer-to-peer network into a client/server network because these servers only perform only a limited set of functions

Figure 7.20

Windows Home Server remote access interface.

Figure 7.21

Searching for the right remote? New software apps make it easy to just use your phone instead.

instead of all the functions performed on client/server networks.

Home network servers, like the Acer Aspire easyStore server (shown earlier in Figure 7.5), are often configured with Windows Home Server and connect directly as a node on your network. Home servers have the functionality of NAS devices and often handle the following tasks:

- Automatically back up all computers connected to the network.
- Act as a repository for files to be shared across the network (such as music and video files).
- Function as an access gateway to allow any computer on the network to be accessed from a remote location via the Internet (see Figure 7.20).

And you can access the media stored on your Windows Home Server through your Xbox 360 as long as the Xbox is also connected to your home network.

Digital Entertainment Devices on a Network

Why should I connect my digital entertainment devices to my network? The main reason is to access and share digital content. When you attach devices to the Internet, you can purchase (or even obtain for free) more content for you to enjoy such as movies, videos, or music files. You can also use gaming devices to play multi-player games with players all over the world. The content you access is either downloaded or streamed to your entertainment devices. Viewing Netflix movies delivered over the Internet on your computer is an example of streaming media.

When media is *streamed*, it is sent directly to a device (such as a computer or HDTV) without being saved to a hard drive. This requires a lot of bandwidth so a broadband connection is required to effectively view streaming media. Media can also be *downloaded* (saved) to a hard drive for viewing at a later time. Although the Amazon Video on Demand service now offers streaming movies, they still offer the ability to download content to your computer or your TiVo so you can view it later.

What types of digital entertainment devices can I use to view streaming or downloaded media? Network-ready televisions and home theater systems allow for direct connection to your home network (wireless or wired). These devices are configured to receive streaming media directly from the Internet. Waiting for a DVD to come in the mail from Netflix is so passé when you can have it available immediately on your television through your home network!

However, many people prefer to own media and buy it on permanent formats such as Blu-ray discs. Blu-ray disc players, such as the Sony 3D Blu-ray disc players offer not only high-definition resolution but also the capability to display 3D video. These Blu-ray players feature integrated wireless connectivity for connection to your network as well as the ability to receive streaming media from various Internet providers. You can even view videos from YouTube and listen to Pandora Internet Radio right through your Blu-ray player.

In terms of controlling your devices such as televisions and Blu-ray players, more companies are developing applications that enable your handheld devices (such as PSPs or iPhones) to act as remote controls. The BD Remote app by Sonoran Blue (see Figure 7.21) for the iPhone allows you to control Sony Blu-ray players.

Digital video recorders (DVRs), like the TiVo Premiere, are often used in the home to record high-definition television programs. Connecting your TiVo to your network makes it possible to receive downloads of movies directly to your TiVo from services such as Amazon Video on Demand. And some home network servers, like the Hewlett Packard MediaSmart servers, now work in conjunction with TiVo devices to provide additional storage for your TiVo devices. The TiVo Desktop software (see Figure 7.22), which you download from **tivo.com**, allows you to transfer shows recorded on your TiVo to your computer or to portable devices such as an iPod, iPhone, BlackBerry, or PSP.

Can I connect my gaming consoles to my home network? Current gaming systems, like the PlayStation 3, offer much more than just games as they can function as a total entertainment platform when connected to your network (and therefore to the Internet). The PlayStation 3 (PS3) has a built-in Blu-ray drive and can play Blu-ray discs as well as DVDs and music files. You can download movies, games, and videos directly to the PlayStation. It can also be used to share media across your network and import photos or video from cameras and camcorders. And if you have a PSP, you can use an application called Remote Play (see Figure 7.23) to access features of your PlayStation from your PSP. You can use the PSP to turn your PlayStation on and off,

Figure 7.23

The Remote Play feature of the PSP and the PlayStation 3 (PS3) allows users to access PS3 features, like the PlayStation Store, directly from their PSP.

access music and video files, access photos stored on your PlayStation, play games, and browse the Internet. Media is transmitted from your PlayStation and displayed on the PSP screen.

Specialized Home Networking Devices

What if I don't need the full functionality of a PC, but I still want to access Internet content? The launch of the Apple iPad signaled a resurgence of Internet appliances. The main function of an **Internet appliance** is easy access to the Internet, social networking sites, e-mail, video,

Figure 7.22

The TiVo Desktop software facilitates transfer of recorded shows to portable devices so you can enjoy your content on the go.

ACTIVE HELP-DESK

Understanding Networking

In this Active Helpdesk call, you'll play the role of a helpdesk staffer, fielding calls about home networks— their advantages, their main components, and the most common types—as well as about wireless networks and how they are created.

Figure 7.24

Quick access to information and entertainment is the key feature of Internet appliances.

news, and entertainment. These devices fall into a category somewhere between smartphones and full-blown computers. They are light on calculation, but high on easy content delivery. Devices such as the Sony Dash Personal Internet viewer (see Figure 7.24) are popular in kitchens and bedside tables where access to Internet radio stations, short videos, and quick information updates (like Facebook updates and current weather conditions) are needed. Originally, Internet appliances

interface, this frame can access photos stored on your network or on an online photo-sharing site and display them. You can set up an e-mail address for the picture frame so that friends and family can e-mail pictures directly to the frame as soon as they are taken. Wouldn't it be nice to come home to new photos of your friend's trip to Cancun tonight?

How can I use my home network to enhance my home security? Monitoring cameras, both for indoor and outdoor use, are now available for the home and feature wireless connectivity. The cameras can connect to your network and be monitored by software like the Logitech Digital Video Security System (Figure 7.26). Security monitoring software allows you to view real-time images from the cameras at your home. The software can be configured to alert you via e-mail or text message when the cameras detect movement. Some systems also allow you to receive alerts when there is a lack of movement. This can be useful for monitoring an aging relative (who may need help if they stop moving) or for monitoring the arrival of children coming home from school at a certain time.

Figure 7.25

Sending pictures directly to an electronic frame from your phone is possible when the frame is connected to your network.

were marketed toward older computer users since these devices feature easy operation and a shallow learning curve. But the Apple iPad is propelling this category of devices into the hands of much younger users. We discuss the Apple iPad in more detail in Chapter 8.

How can I use my home network to enhance photo sharing? Digital picture frames that display an array of changing digital photos have become quite popular with the rise in digital photography. Now digital picture frames such as the eStarling TouchConnect (see Figure 7.25) come with built-in wireless adapters for easy connection to home networks. Featuring a touch screen

Figure 7.26

Logitech security products can help you remotely monitor your home's security.

As time goes on, many more types of entertainment devices and home gadgets will eventually be connected to your home network.

Securing Wireless Networks

All computers that connect to the Internet (whether or not they are on a network) need to be secured from intruders. This is usually accomplished by using a **firewall**, which is a hardware or software solution that helps shield your network from prying eyes. We discuss firewalls at length in Chapter 9. Wireless networks present special vulnerabilities; therefore, you should take additional specific steps to keep your wireless network safe. It is important to configure your network security before setting up and connecting all the nodes on your network.

Why is a wireless network more vulnerable than a wired network? With a wired network, it is fairly easy to tell if a **hacker** (someone who breaks into computer systems to create mischief or steal valuable information) is using your network. However, wireless 802.11n networks have wide ranges that may extend outside of your house. This makes it possible for a hacker to access your network without your knowledge.

Why should I be worried about someone logging onto my wireless network without my permission? Some use of other people's wireless networks is unintentional. Houses are built close together. Apartments are clustered even closer together. Wireless signals can easily reach a neighbor's residence. Most wireless network adapters are set up to access the strongest wireless network signal detected. If your router is on the east side of your house and you and your notebook are on the west side, then you may get a stronger signal from your neighbor's wireless network than from your own. **Piggybacking** is connecting to a wireless network (other than your own) without the permission of the owner. This practice is illegal in many jurisdictions but often happens inadvertently between neighbors.

Your neighbor probably isn't a hacker, but he might be using a lot of bandwidth—your bandwidth! If he's downloading a massive

movie file while you're trying to do research for a term paper, he's probably slowing you down. In addition, when some less-than-honest neighbors discover they can log onto your wireless network, they may cancel their own Internet service to save money by using yours. Some neighbors might even be computer savvy enough to penetrate your unprotected wireless network and steal personal information, just as any other hackers would.

In addition, because computer criminal activities are traceable, hackers love to work their mischief from public computers (such as those in a library or college) so they can't be identified. If a hacker is sitting in her car outside your house and logging on to your wireless network, any cyberattacks she launches might be traced back to your IP address, and you might find law enforcement officials knocking on your door.

How is my wireless network vulnerable? Packets of information on a wireless network are broadcast through the airwaves. Savvy hackers can intercept and decode information from your transmissions that may allow them to bypass any standard protections, such as a firewall, which you have set up on your network. Therefore, to

SOUND BYTE

Securing Wireless Networks

In this Sound Byte, you'll learn what "war drivers" are and why they could potentially be a threat to your wireless network. You'll also learn some simple steps to secure your wireless network against intruders.

Setup Wizard

Setup
Basic Settings
Wireless Settings
Content Filtering
Logs
Block Sites
Block Services
Schedule
E-mail
Maintenance
Router Status
Attached Devices
Backup Settings
Set Password
Router Upgrade

Wireless Settings

Create and enter unique SSID here

Wireless Network
Name (SSID): Herschell
Region: United States
Channel: 11
Mode: g and b

Security Options
○ Disable
○ WEP (Wired Equivalent Privacy)
⦿ WPA-PSK (Wi-Fi Protected Access Pre-Shared Key) ◄── Select a security protocol

Security Encryption (WPA-PSK)
Passphrase: traSk35wE12SAwY (8-63 characters)
Key Lifetime: 60 (minutes)

Create hard-to-guess passphrase

Figure 7.27

By running your router configuration wizard, you can configure the security protocols available on your router and change the SSID, which helps protect your wireless network.

secure a wireless network, you should take the additional precautions described in the Sound Byte "Securing Wireless Networks" and as summarized below:

1. **Change your network name (SSID).** Each wireless network has its own name to identify it, which is known as the **service set identifier** or **SSID**. Unless you change this name when you set up your router, the router uses a default network name that all routers from that manufacturer use (such as "Wireless" or "Netgear"). Hackers know the default names and access codes for routers. If you haven't changed the SSID, it's advertising the fact that you probably haven't changed any of the other default settings for your router, either.

2. **Disable SSID broadcast.** Most routers are set up to broadcast their SSIDs so that other wireless devices can find them. If your router supports disabling SSID broadcasting, turn it off. This makes it more difficult for a hacker to detect your network and nearly impossible for a neighbor to inadvertently connect to your network.

3. **Change the default password on your router.** Hackers know the default passwords of most routers, and if they can access your router, they can probably break into your network. Change the password on your router to something hard to guess. (Use at least eight char-

acters that are a combination of letters, symbols, and numbers.)

4. **Turn on security protocols.** Most routers ship with security protocols such as Wired Equivalent Privacy (WEP) or WiFi Protected Access (WPA). Both use encryption (a method of translating your data into code) to protect data in your wireless transmissions. WPA is a much stronger protocol than WEP, so enable WPA if you have it; enable WEP if you don't. When you enable these protocols, you are forced to create a security encryption key (passphrase). When you attempt to connect a node to a security-enabled network for the first time, you'll be required to enter the encryption key. The encryption key or passphrase (see Figure 7.27) is the code that computers on your network need to decrypt (decode) data transmissions. Without this key, it is extremely difficult, if not impossible, to decrypt the data transmissions from your network. This prevents unauthorized access to your network because hackers won't know the correct key to use. The Windows 7 Connect to a network dialog box shows all wireless networks within range (see Figure 7.28a). Clicking on one allows you to connect to it, or prompts you for more information such as the SSID name and security key (see Figure 7.28b).

5. **Implement media access control.** Each network adapter on your network has a unique number (like a serial number) assigned to it by the manufacturer. This is called a **media access control (MAC) address**, and it is a number printed right on the network adapter. Many routers allow you to restrict access to the network to only certain MAC addresses. This helps ensure that only authorized devices can connect to your network.

6. **Limit your signal range.** Many routers allow you to adjust the transmitting power to low, medium, or high. Cutting down the power to low or medium could prevent your signal from reaching too far away from your home,

Figure 7.28

(a) The Windows 7 Connect to a network dialog box. (b) Manually connecting to a wireless network allows you to establish a connection if you know the network encryption key and the SSID name.

>You can access the **Connect to a network** dialog box by right-clicking the **Network Connection** icon on the taskbar and selecting **Connect to a network** from the shortcut menu. You can access the **Manually connect to a wireless network** dialog box by accessing the **Control Panel**, clicking on **Network and Internet**, selecting **Network and Sharing Center**, choosing the **Set up a new connection or network** option, and then clicking on **Manually connect to a wireless network**.

making it tougher for interlopers to poach your signal.

7. **Apply firmware upgrades.** Your router has read-only memory that has software written to it. This software is known as **firmware**. As bugs are found in the firmware (which hackers might exploit), manufacturers issue patches, just as the makers of operating system software do. Periodically check the manufacturer's Web site and apply any necessary upgrades to your firmware.

If you follow these steps, you will greatly improve the security of your wireless network. In Chapter 9, we'll explore many other ways to keep your computer safe from malicious individuals on the Internet and ensure that your digital information is secure.

Configuring Software for Your Home Network

Once you install the hardware for your network, you need to configure your operating system software for networking on your computers. In this section, you'll learn how to do just that using special Windows tools. Although configuration is different with Mac OS X, the setup is quick and easy. Linux is the most complex operating system to configure for a home network, though the difficulties are not insurmountable.

Windows Configuration

Is configuring software difficult?
Windows makes configuring software relatively simple if you are using the same version of Windows on all of your

computers. The Windows examples in this section assume you are using Windows 7 on all of your computers. If you are using previous versions of Windows, there is plenty of information on the Internet regarding the connection of previous versions of Windows to a Windows 7 network. In Windows 7, the process of setting up a network is fairly automated by various software wizards. As you learned in Chapter 4, a wizard is a utility program included with software that you can use to help you accomplish a specific task. You can launch the Windows wizards from the Network and Sharing Center, which can be accessed via the Network and Internet group in the Control Panel. Before running any wizards, you should do the following:

> **"The HomeGroup feature in Windows 7 facilitates file and peripheral sharing."**

1. Make sure there are network adapters on each node.

2. For any wired connections, plug all the cables into the router, nodes, and so on.

3. Make sure your broadband modem is connected to your router and that the modem is connected to the Internet.

4. Turn on your equipment in the following order (allowing the modem and the router about one minute each to power up and configure):

   a. your broadband modem,

   b. your router, and

   c. all computers and peripherals (printers, scanners, and so on).

Other devices, such a televisions, Blu-ray players and gaming consoles can be added to the network after configuring the computers.

By completing these steps, you enable the wizards to make decisions about how best to configure your network. After you have completed these steps, open the Network and Sharing Center from the Control Panel (see Figure 7.29a). You can see the network to which you are currently connected on this screen. On the lower portion of the Network and Sharing Center screen, you can set sharing options for your network. Ensure that network discovery is shown as "on," because this allows your computer to locate other computers and peripherals on the network. You should also verify that the options for file and printer sharing and public folder sharing are shown as "on" to enable file and printer sharing with other computers. From the Network and Sharing Center, select the option to Set up a new connection or network to access the Windows networking wizards (see Figure 7.29b).

Select the Connect to the Internet wizard to configure your network to use your broadband modem to connect to the Internet for the first time. This wizard also configures your wired connections on your network (if any). On the information screen (see Figure 7.29c), enter the access information provided by your ISP. Enter a memorable name for your network and check the box to allow other people to use the Internet connection you are establishing. This will allow all users on the network to use the same connection.

After running this wizard, run the Set Up a Wireless Router wizard to configure your wireless connectivity. If you set up a secured wireless network (as detailed in the previous section), use the Manually Connect to a Wireless Network wizard to connect computers to the secure wireless network.

What if I don't have the same version of Windows on all my computers? Computers with various versions of Windows can coexist on the same network. Always set up the computers running the newest version of Windows first (Windows 7). Then consult the Microsoft web site for guidance on how to proceed for configuring computers with previous versions of Windows on a Windows 7 network.

How do I differentiate the computers on my network? When you set up your Windows computer, you gave it a name. Each computer on a network needs a name that is different from the names of all other computers on the network so that the network can identify it. This unique name ensures that the network knows which computer is requesting services and data and can deliver data to the correct computer.

For ease of file and peripheral sharing, Windows 7 created a feature known as HomeGroup. If you have all Windows 7 computers on your network, you simply all join the same HomeGroup. When you set up your first Windows 7 computer on your network, you can set a password for the HomeGroup.

Figure 7.29

(a) The Windows Network and Sharing Center helps you configure your home network. Selecting the appropriate sharing options allow others to share resources on your computer. (b) Selecting the appropriate option provides access to wizards that will assist you. (c) Fill in the information provided by your ISP. The wizard will then set up your connection and connect your computer to the Internet.

>The Windows Network and Sharing Center is found in the Control Panel.

All other computers that subsequently are added to the network will need the password to join the HomeGroup. When you configure a HomeGroup, you have the option of deciding what files and peripherals on your computer will be shared with other computers on the network (see Figure 7.30).

How do Macs connect wirelessly to networks? Generally, connecting Macs to a wireless network is a much easier process than connecting with Windows computers. You set up the security for a router on a Mac network just as was illustrated in the previous section on securing

Figure 7.30

The Change HomeGroup settings screen allows you to configure sharing options for a particular computer.

>The **Change HomeGroup settings** screen can be accessed by clicking the **Computer link** on the **Start** menu, then clicking the **HomeGroup** icon, and then clicking the **View HomeGroup settings** link.

your wireless network. Therefore, logging your Mac onto the network will require knowing the SSID and its passphrase. When you boot up your Mac, the wireless card should be on by default. The network login screen (see Figure 7.31) should appear with a list of available networks (that is, the ones the NIC in your Mac can detect). The locks next to the network names indicate a secure network, which will require a password. Enter the password for the network in the password box and click the Join button to connect to the network. For unsecure networks, the Join button can

Figure 7.31

The OS X available wireless networks dialog box.

be clicked without entering anything in the password box.

Why don't some networks appear as available? But networks with SSID broadcast turned off will not appear on the list of available networks. To join one of these secure networks, click the Other button on the available wireless network dialog box. This will cause the Enter the name of the network dialog box to appear (see Figure 7.32). Then just enter the SSID name for your network in the Network name box and the security passphrase in the password box. Clicking the join button will then connect you to the network. Checking the Remember this network check box will cause the computer to automatically connect to the network when it is available (that is, it becomes one of your preferred networks). You can have multiple preferred networks such as your home, school and local coffee shop networks.

Assuming you installed and configured everything properly, your home network should now be up and running, allowing you to share files, Internet connections, and peripherals. You are now ready to configure other non-computer devices to connect them to your network.

Wireless Node Configuration

How do I hook up devices like a TiVo or gaming console to my network? For a wired connection, you would simply plug a cable into the device and your router. For wireless connections, there is usually a set of steps to follow in the setup menu for the device you are configuring. Assuming you set up a secure wireless network as described in the security section of this chapter, you'll need to know the SSID name of your network and the security passphrase. Although each device's configuration steps will be slightly different, eventually, you will get to a screen where you need to input the SSID name and the

Figure 7.32

The OS X secure wireless networks dialog box.

You probably have a lot of data on your home network such as music and video files. And you probably generate more data every day. But this pales in comparison to the data generated by most businesses. The vast quantities of data on business and government networks also require much higher levels of protection than the data on your home network. With billions of dollars spent on e-commerce initiatives every year, companies have a vested interest in keeping their information technology (IT) infrastructures humming along. The rise in terrorism has shifted the focus slightly—from protecting virtual assets and access, to protecting these plus physical assets and access points. The increased need for virtual and physical security measures means there should be a robust job market ahead for computer security experts.

The National Security Agency and the Office of Homeland Security are both encouraging information security professionals to be proficient in information assurance. As defined by the NSA, *information assurance* is "the set of measures intended to protect and defend information and information systems by ensuring their availability, integrity, authentication, confidentiality, and non-repudiation. This includes providing for restoration of information systems by incorporating protection, detection, and reaction capabilities." The five key attributes of secure information systems are as follows:

1. **Availability:** The extent to which a data-processing system is able to receive and process data. A high degree of availability is usually desirable.

2. **Integrity:** A quality that an information system has if the processing of information is logical and accurate and the data is protected against unauthorized modifications or destruction.

3. **Authentication:** Security measures designed to protect an information system against acceptance of a fraudulent transmission of data by establishing the validity of a data transmission or message, or the identity of the sender.

4. **Confidentiality:** The assurance that information is not disclosed to unauthorized persons, processes, or devices.

5. **Nonrepudiation:** A capability of security systems that guarantees that a message or data can be proven to have originated from a specific person and was processed by the recipient. The sender of the data receives a receipt for the data, and the receiver of the data gets proof of the sender's identity. The objective of nonrepudiation is to prevent either party from later denying having handled the data.

The Global Information Assurance Certification, or GIAC (**giac.org**), is an industry-recognized certification that provides objective evidence (through examinations) that security professionals have mastered key skills in various aspects of information assurance.

What skill sets will be most in demand for security professionals? In addition to information assurance technical skills (with an emphasis on network engineering and data communications), broad-based business experience is also extremely desirable. IT security professionals need to understand the key issues of e-commerce and the core areas of their company's business (such as marketing, sales, and finance). Understanding how a business works is essential to pinpointing and correcting security risks that could be detrimental to a company's bottom line. Because of the large number of attacks by hackers, security and forensic skills and related certifications also are in high demand. Working closely with law enforcement officials is essential to rapidly solving and stopping cybercrime.

Another important attribute of security professionals is the ability to lead and motivate teams. Security experts need to work with diverse members of the business community, including customers, to forge relationships and understanding among diverse groups. Security professionals must conduct skillful negotiations to ensure that large project implementations are not unduly delayed by security initiatives or pushed through with inadequate security precautions. Diplomacy is therefore a sought-after skill.

Look for more colleges and universities to roll out security-based degree and certificate programs as the demand for security professionals increases. These programs will most likely be appropriate for experienced networking professionals who are ready to make the move into the IT security field. If you're just starting to prepare for a career, consider a degree in network engineering, followed by network security training while you're working at your first job. A degree program that is also designed to prepare you for security certification exams is particularly desirable. Networking and security degrees, combined with passing grades on certification exams, should help you make a smooth transition into the exciting world of cybersecurity.

passphrase. The Xbox 360 configuration screens are shown in Figure 7.33.

Once all your devices are connected to your network, you might want to check your Internet connection speed to see what kind of throughput you are achieving. You can check your speed on any device on your network that can access the Internet with a browser.

How can I test my Internet connection speed? Your ISP may have promised you certain speeds of downloading and uploading data. How can you tell if you are getting what was promised? There are numerous sites on the Internet, such as **Speedtest.net** (see Figure 7.34) and **broadband.gov**, where you can test the speed of downloading files to your computer and uploading files to other computers. You can then see how your results compare to those of other users in your state and across the United States. Many factors

Select to enter
SSID name

Enter security
passphrase here
using keys below

Figure 7.33

Xbox 360 wireless
configuration screens.
(a) The Xbox will detect
available networks. Select
the Specify Unlisted
Network option to enter
the SSID name of your
network. (b) Enter the
security passphrase on
the appropriate security
screen.

can influence your Internet speeds, so be
sure to run the test at several different times
during the day over the course of a week before complaining to your ISP about not getting your promised speed.

Troubleshooting Network Problems

**What types of problems can I run
into when installing wireless
networks?** The maximum range of wireless devices under the 802.11n standard is

about 350 feet. But as you go farther away
from your router, the throughput you
achieve will decrease. Obstacles between
wireless nodes also decrease throughput.
Walls, floors, and large metal objects are the
most common sources of interference with
wireless signals. For example, placing a
computer with a wireless network adapter
next to a refrigerator may prevent the signals from reaching the rest of the network.
Similarly, a node that has four walls between it and the Internet connection will

Figure 7.34

Speed test showing a download speed of 20.01 megabits, which is extremely fast for a
home Internet connection.

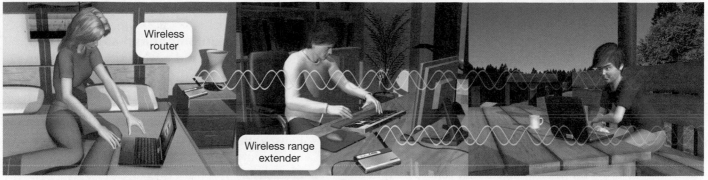

Wireless router

Wireless range extender

Computer A with wireless network adapter   Computer B with wireless range extender   Notebook C with wireless network adapter

most likely have lower-than-maximum throughput.

What if a node on the network can't get adequate throughput? Repositioning the node within the same room (sometimes even just a few inches from the original position) can often affect communication between nodes. If this doesn't work, try moving the device closer to the router or to other rooms in your house. If these solutions don't work, you should consider adding a wireless range extender to your network.

A **wireless range extender** is a device that amplifies your wireless signal to get it out to parts of your home that are experiencing poor connectivity. As shown Figure 7.35, the notebook on the back porch can't connect to the wireless network even though the computer in the den can connect to the network. By placing a range extender in the den, where there is still good connectivity to the wireless network, the wireless signal is amplified and beamed farther out to the back porch. This improves the otherwise poor connectivity on the back porch and allows computer C to make a good connection to the network.

Hopefully, you'll now be able connect all your computing devices to your home network and achieve the throughput you need to move your date efficiently around your home network.

Figure 7.35

Because a wireless range extender is installed in the den, Notebook C on the back porch can now connect to the wireless network generated by the wireless router in the bedroom.

1. What is a network, and what are the advantages/disadvantages of setting up one?

A computer network is simply two or more computers that are connected using software and hardware so that they can communicate. Advantages of networks include allowing users to (1) share an Internet connection, (2) share peripheral devices, and (3) share files. A disadvantage is that the network must be administered.

2. What is the difference between a client/server network and a peer-to-peer network?

In peer-to-peer networks, each node connected to the network can communicate directly with every other node instead of having a separate device exercise central control over the network. P2P networks are the most common type of network installed in homes. Most networks that have 10 or more nodes are client/server networks. A client/server network contains two types of computers: a client computer on which users perform specific tasks and a server computer that provides resources to the clients and central control for the network.

3. What are the main components of every network?

To function, any network must contain four components: (1) transmission media (cables or radio waves) to connect and establish communication between nodes, (2) network adapters that allow the nodes on the network to communicate, (3) network navigation devices (such as routers and switches) that move data around the network, and (4) software that allows the network to run.

4. Which type of network is most commonly found in the home?

Ethernet networks are the most common networks used in home networking. Most Ethernet networks use a combination of wired and wireless connections depending upon the data throughput required. Wired connections usually achieve higher throughput than wireless connections.

5. What equipment and software do I need to build a network in my home?

All computing equipment that will connect to a network has to contain a network adapter. Network adapters allow computers to communicate (either wired or wirelessly) with network navigation devices such as routers and switches. Wired connections are usually made with Cat 6 twisted pair cable. A router is needed to share an Internet connection as it transmits data between two networks (the home network and the Internet).

6. Besides computers, what other devices would I connect to a home network?

Connecting peripherals such as printers directly to a network allow them to be easily shared by all users on the network. Network-attached storage (NAS) devices allow for the storage and sharing of data files such as movies and music as well as providing a central place for file backups. Connecting digital entertainment devices (such as gaming consoles) provides the ability to stream movies and other entertainment directly from the Internet.

7. Why are wireless networks more vulnerable than wired networks, and what special precautions are required to ensure my wireless network is secure?

Wireless networks are even more susceptible to hacking than wired networks because the signals of most wireless networks extend beyond the walls of your home. Neighbors may unintentionally (or intentionally) connect to the Internet through your wireless connection, and hackers may try to access it. To prevent unwanted intrusions into your network, you should change the default password on your router to make it tougher for hackers to gain access, use a hard-to-guess SSID (network name), turn off SSID broadcasting to make it harder for outsiders to detect your network, and enable security protocols such as WPA or WEP.

8. How do I configure the software on my computer and set up other devices to get my network up and running?

Windows features software wizards that facilitate the setup of both wired and wireless networks. Plug in the modem, routers, and all cables, and then switch on the modem, router, and computers (in that order). Run the wizards, which should guide you through the process. Make sure each computer has a distinct name and ensure that all computers are in the same HomeGroup. Devices such as gaming consoles each have their own set-up procedures for connecting to wireless networks but usually require the same information as needed for connecting a computer to a secured wireless network.

9. What problems might I encounter when setting up a wireless network?

You may not get the throughput you need through a wireless connection and therefore you may need to consider a wired connection for certain devices. Distance from the router as well as walls, floors, and large metal objects between a device and the router can interfere with wireless connectivity. Wireless range extenders can amplify signals to improve connectivity in areas of poor signal strength.

Word Bank

- Cat 6 cable
- client/server
- data transfer rate
- hacker(s)
- home network server
- LAN

- network adapter(s)
- network-ready
- peer-to-peer (P2P)
- piggybacking
- router
- switch

- throughput
- twisted pair cable
- WAN
- wired
- wireless
- wireless range expander

Instructions: Fill in the blanks using the words from the Word Bank above.

Cathi needed to network three computers for herself and her roommates, Sharon and Emily. She decided that a(n) (1) _____ network was the right type to install in their dorm suite because a(n) (2) _____ network was too complex. Because they all liked to stream digital movies from the Internet, they needed high a(n) (3) _____ but doubted they would achieve the promised (4) _____ in any network they installed. Although they knew using (5) _____ media would provide the fastest Ethernet networks, they decided to use (6) _____ media so that they could use their notebooks wherever they were in their suite. Therefore they needed to buy a(n) (7) _____ with wireless capability that would allow them to share the broadband Internet connection that Sharon already had through a local ISP. This device would also double as a(n) (8) _____, preventing the need to purchase a separate device. Fortunately, all their computers already had (9) _____ installed, making it easy to connect the computers to the network. Cathi knew they would need to purchase some (10) _____ since the Xbox 360 they wanted to share only had a wired Ethernet adapter in it.

Cathi's roommate Emily wanted to know if they could hook into the (11) _____, or small network, that was already deployed for the students in the dorm. This student network was already hooked into the college's (12) _____, or large network, which spanned all three of the college's campuses. She knew they would need to be careful when connecting to the network, because some students from the dorm had accidentally been illegally (13) _____ on a network from the deli across the street. As the connectivity for notebooks in the lounge at the end of the hall was very poor, they needed to consider purchasing a(n) (14) _____ to extend the range of the wireless signal. As a final detail, Emily suggested they get a(n) (15) _____ printer that would plug right into the router and allow them all to print whenever they needed to do so.

becoming computer literate

Your grandmother has moved into a new retirement community. She is sharing a large living space with three other residents. All four retirees have their own notebook computers. Your grandmother has asked you to advise her and her roommates on an appropriate network to install so that they can share an Internet connection, a laser printer, and movies that they want to stream from Netflix via the Internet. And your grandmother is an avid photographer and has thousands of digital photographs on her computer. She is very concerned about forgetting to back up the photographs after she takes new ones and wants her family to be able to access her photos via the Internet.

Instructions: Using the preceding scenario, draft a networking plan for your grandmother and her roommates using as many of the keywords from the chapter as you can. Be sure that your grandmother, who is unfamiliar with many networking terms, can understand your suggestions.

Instructions: Answer the multiple-choice and true–false questions below for more practice with key terms and concepts from this chapter.

Multiple Choice

1. All of the following are advantages of installing a home network *except* sharing
   a. peripherals.
   b. an Internet connection.
   c. files.
   d. MAC addresses.

2. Which of the following is *not* a reason client/server networks are generally not installed in homes?
   a. Client/server networks can't handle streaming media, which is often required in home networks.
   b. Client/server networks are more difficult to install than peer-to-peer networks.
   c. Client/server networks provide more security than is needed for home networks.
   d. Peer-to-peer networks are less expensive to install than client/sever networks.

3. Which of the following is *not* required on some simple networks?
   a. Network adapters
   b. Networking software
   c. Network navigation devices
   d. Transmission media

4. Which network navigation device is required to move data between two networks?
   a. Repeater   c. Router
   b. Switch   d. Hub

5. If you need very fast throughput in a home network, you should use
   a. an 802.11n wireless Ethernet connection.
   b. a wired power-line network.
   c. a wired gigabit Ethernet connection.
   d. a client/server network.

6. Wireless range expanders
   a. are never used for home networks.
   b. are not needed with 802.11n networks.
   c. improve connectivity in remote areas of a home.
   d. turn devices with wired connections into wireless nodes.

7. Two or more networks connected over long geographic distances to form a single network is usually referred to as a
   a. LAN.   c. HAN.
   b. MAN.   d. WAN.

8. The throughput of a network
   a. is the same on all Ethernet networks.
   b. is usually higher on wireless networks.
   c. is the same in all areas covered by a wireless network.
   d. can vary depending upon the transmission media used.

9. The "name" of a particular wireless network is known as the
   a. NetID.   c. SSID.
   b. HAN-ID.   d. Wifi-ID.

10. The device used to move data around a single network is called a
   a. gateway.
   b. switch.
   c. router.
   d. repeater.

True–False

_____ 1. Actual data throughput is usually higher on wireless networks.

_____ 2. Ethernet networks require each node on the network to be equipped with its own network adapter.

_____ 3. WEP and WPA are popular wired network security protocols.

_____ 4. MANs cover a larger geographic area than HANs.

_____ 5. 802.11n wireless networks provide faster throughput than wired gigabit Ethernet networks.

1. Dormitory Networking

Mikel, Dylan, Sanjay, and Harrison were sitting in the common room of their campus suite and complaining about their wireless network. They inherited the equipment from the last residents of the suite, and unfortunately their router uses the outdated 802.11g standard. They all have notebooks that have 802.11n network adapters, but their throughput is poor. Since they are often all surfing the Internet at the same time and trying to download movies, their network's performance has become unacceptable.

Since they all just sold last semester's books back to the bookstore for a total of $600, they decided this would be a good time to upgrade their network and peripherals. Dylan has an inkjet printer that gobbles up expensive cartridges, and Phil has a laser printer that just broke. The guys figure one good networked all-in-one printer should meet their needs since it would also provide them with photocopying capabilities. Mikel is concerned about backups for his computer. His external hard drive fell on the floor and no longer works reliably. He has a tremendous amount of photos and schoolwork on his computer that he is concerned about losing if his hard drive fails. Since the guys don't know much about networking, the four roommates have asked for your guidance. Consider the following keeping in mind their $600 budget:

a. Research network-ready laser printers on sites such as **hp.com**, **epson.com**, and **brother.com**. What network-ready all-in-one printer would you recommend? Why?

b. Research 802.11n wireless routers at sites such as **netgear.com**, **linksys.com**, and **dlink.com**. What router do you think will meet the roommates' needs? Why?

c. How would you recommend addressing Dave's backup concerns? Would you recommend a NAS device for the network, or do they have enough money left in their budget for a home network server? Research these devices and make an affordable recommendation. Check sites such as **tigerdirect.com** and **newegg.com** for competitive pricing.

2. Connecting Your Computer to Public Networks

You are working for a local coffee shop that offers free wireless access to customers. Your supervisor has asked you to create a flyer for patrons that warns them of the potential dangers of surfing the Internet in public places. Conduct research on the Internet about using public hot spots to access the Internet. Prepare a flyer that lists specific steps that customers can take to protect their data when surfing on publicly accessible networks.

3. Adding a Home Network Server for Backups to Your Network

You know that adding a home network server to your network would facilitate sharing of your digital media and would make backing up your computers easier. You need to consider the following questions when selecting an appropriate home network server:

1. What is the volume of shared media that you need to store? (In other words, how many music files, movies, and other media files do you have?)
2. What are the sizes of the hard drives of the computers on your network (for backup purposes)? What size hard drive would you need on a home network server to ensure you could back up all your computers as well as store your shared media?
3. Would you need to access files on the home network server when you are away from home or allow others (such as your cousins) to access them?

Research home network servers using sites such as **hp.com**, **acer.com**, and **lenovo.com** or use the term "home server" in a search engine. Select a server that is appropriate for your home network. Prepare a summary of your findings and include the reasons for your selection.

1. **Wireless LAN for a Small Business**

   You are working for a local coffee shop. The owner of the shop thinks that adding a wireless network and providing free Internet access to customers would be a good way to increase business. The owner has asked you to research this idea and prepare a report of your findings. Consider the following:

   a. Price out business Internet connectivity with local phone and cable providers. Which vendor provides the most cost effective solution for a coffee shop? Are there any limitations on bandwidth or the number of people that can access the Internet at one time through the business account connection?

   b. What potential problems could you foresee with providing unrestricted free access to the Internet? What policies would you suggest to keep people from abusing the free Internet access? (An example of abuse is someone who sits all day and surfs for free without purchasing any coffee.)

2. **Putting Computers to Work on Research Projects**

   Most computer CPUs only use a fraction of their computing power most of the time. Many medical research companies (such as those seeking cures for cancer and AIDS) could benefit from "borrowing" computer CPU time when computers are not being used or are being under utilized. Virtual supercomputers (which are really networks of computers) can be created using software installed on tens of thousands of computers. This type of computing is also known as *grid* or *distributed computing*. These virtual computing nets can be harnessed to solve complex problems when their owners are not using their computers. Assume that you are working for a business that has 100 computers and you would like to participate in a grid computing project. Investigate IBM's Worldwide Community Grid (**worldcommunitygrid.org**). Prepare a report for your boss that:

   a. Describes the Worldwide Community Grid (WCG) and its objectives

   b. Lists current projects that the WCG is working on.

   c. Describes the process for installing the WCG software on the company's computers.

   d. Suggests a strategy for publicizing the company's participation in the WCG project that will encourage your employer's customers to participate.

3. **Testing Your Internet Connection Speed**

   Visit **speedtest.net** and **speakeasy.net/speedtest** and test the speed of your Internet connection at your home and in the computer lab at your school. Try to repeat the test at two different times during the day.

   a. What did you find out about download speeds at your home? Are you getting as much speed as was promised by your ISP? Would this speed be sufficient for a home-based business? What type of business packages does your ISP offer, and what speeds could you expect when paying for a business package?

   b. How does the connection speed at your school compare to the speed at your home? Where do you think you should have a faster connection—at your school or at your home? Why might the connection speed at your school be slower than you think it should be?

Instructions: Albert Einstein used *Gedankenexperiments*, or critical thinking questions, to develop his theory of relativity. Some ideas are best understood by experimenting with them in our own minds. The following critical thinking questions are designed to demand your full attention but require only a comfortable chair — no technology.

1. **Protecting Your Wireless Home Network**

   Many people have installed wireless networks in their homes. Consider the wireless network installed in your home (or in a friend's home if you don't have wireless).
   a. Is your network set up to provide adequate protection against hackers? If not, what would you need to do to make it secure?
   b. Are there other wireless networks within range of your home? If so, are they set up with an adequate level of security, or can you connect to them easily? How would you go about informing your neighbors that their networks are vulnerable?

2. **Adding Devices to Your Network**

   We discussed adding devices other than computers and computer peripherals to your network in this chapter. Consider the following for your home network:
   a. Do you currently stream or download movies from Netflix, Amazon Video on Demand, or another service? If so, is your storage device sufficient or do you need more capacity? If you don't currently download this type of entertainment, would your family do so if you had a device that was attached to your network? What type of device (DVR, home server, etc.) do you think would be most appropriate for the type of media that you enjoy? How much media would you need to download and view in a month to make purchasing equipment worthwhile?
   b. Do you have a need for a home security system? Would internal and external cameras be appropriate for monitoring your home? Are their people in your house (babysitters, housekeepers, contractors, etc.) on a regular basis that might need monitoring? Would you monitor these people in real time or make recordings for later review?

3. **Evaluating Your Home Networking Needs**

   You might have a network installed in your home already, or perhaps you are still considering whether it is necessary to install one. Consider these issues:
   a. Who uses computing devices in your home? How many computers (notebooks and desktops) are currently in your home? Are the computers networked? If not, should they be networked? What advantages would your family gain by networking its computers?
   b. Which computer peripheral devices does your family own? Which family members need to use which peripherals? Are the peripherals network-ready or are they connected to individual computers? How easy is it to share these peripherals? Are there peripherals that your family doesn't own that would be beneficial? (Make sure to explain why.) How would you go about connecting new peripherals to your network?
   c. Does your home network have network-attached storage or a home server? Would your family benefit from having this technology on your home network? What types of media do your family members routinely share? What other types would they share if they had the means?

4. **Sharing a Home Internet Connection**

   Perhaps you have considered whether sharing a home Internet connection with your neighbors would save you money. Consider the following issues:
   a. How many neighbors would be within range (say, within 350 feet of your router) of an 802.11n signal that came from your house or apartment? Do you think your neighbors would be amenable to sharing the cost of your Internet connection and your bandwidth? Why or why not?
   b. Is it permissible to share an Internet connection with neighbors under your ISP's terms of use for the type of connection you purchased? If not, what type of plan would you need to upgrade to in order to share a connection with your neighbors? Would the increased cost of upgrading your connection still make it economically feasible to share a connection?

Creating a Wireless Network

Problem

Wireless technology is being adopted by leaps and bounds, both in the home and in the workplace. Offering easy access free of physical tethers to networks seems to be a solution to many problems. However, wireless computing also has problems, ranging from poor reception to hijackers stealing your bandwidth.

Task

You are volunteering for a charity that installs wireless networks in homes for needy families. Many of these installations are done in older homes, and some recipients of the networks have reported poor connectivity in certain areas of their residences and extremely low bandwidth at other times. You have volunteered to research the potential problems and to suggest solutions to the director of the program.

Process

Break the class into three teams. Each team will be responsible for investigating one of the following issues:

1. **Detecting poor connectivity:** Research methods that can be used to find areas of poor signal strength, including signal sniffing software (**netstumbler.com**) and handheld scanning devices such as WiFi Finder (**kensington.com**). Investigate maximum distances between access points and network nodes and make appropriate recommendations. (Equipment manufacturers such as **netgear.com** and **linksys.com** provide guidelines.)
2. **Signal boosters:** Research ways to increase signal strength in access points, antennae, and wireless cards. Signal boosters are available for access points. You can purchase or construct replacement antennae or antenna enhancements. WiFi cards that offer higher power than conventional cards are now available.
3. **Security:** "War drivers" (people who cruise neighborhoods looking for open wireless networks from which to steal bandwidth) may be the cause of the bandwidth issues. Research appropriate measures to keep wireless network traffic secure from eavesdropping by hackers. In your investigation, look into the WiFi Protected Access (WPA) standard developed by the WiFi Alliance. Check out the security section of the knowledge center on the WiFi Alliance Web site to start (**wi-fi.org**).

Present your findings to your class and discuss possible causes of and ways to prevent the problems encountered at the residences. Provide your instructor with a report suitable for eventual presentation to the CEO of the charity.

Conclusion

As technology improves, wireless connectivity should eventually become the standard method of communication between networks and network devices. As with any other technology, security risks exist. Understanding those risks and how to mitigate them will allow you to participate in the design and deployment of network technology and provide peace of mind for your network users.

In this exercise, you will research and then role-play a complicated ethical situation. The role you play may or may not match your own personal beliefs, but your research and use of logic will enable you to represent whichever view is assigned. An arbitrator will watch and comment on both sides of the arguments, and together the team will agree on an ethical solution.

Topic: Firing Employees for Expressing Views on Social Media Sites

The largest network, the Internet, provides the capability for vast social interaction. Social media sites such as Facebook, YouTube, and MySpace, as well as blogs and wikis, give everyone convenient ways to express their opinions. However, employers often are intolerant of employees who freely express negative opinions or expose inside information about their employers on social media sites. Given that most jurisdictions in the United States use the doctrine of employment at-will (that is, employees can be fired at any time for any reason, or even no reason), many employers are quick to discipline or terminate employees who express opinions with which the company disagrees. When such cases come to court, the courts often find in favor of the employers. It is clear that individual must exercise extreme care when posting work-related content.

Research Areas to Consider

- Ellen Simonetti and Delta Airlines
- Fired for blogging about work
- Free speech
- Joyce Park or Michael Tunison

Process

Divide the class into teams.

1. Research the areas cited above and devise a scenario in which someone has complained about an employee blogging about a sensitive workplace issue such as cleanliness at a food manufacturing facility or employee romances.
2. Team members should write a summary that provides background information for their character—for example: employee, Human Resources manager, or arbitrator — and details their character's behaviors to set the stage for the role-playing event. Then, team members should create an outline to use during the role-playing event.
3. Team members should arrange a mutually convenient time to meet for the exchange, either using the collaboration feature of MyITLab, the discussion board feature of Blackboard, or meeting in person.
4. Team members should present their case to the class, or submit a PowerPoint presentation for review by the rest of the class, along with the summary and resolution they developed.

Conclusion

As technology becomes ever more prevalent and integrated into our lives, more and more ethical dilemmas will present themselves. Being able to understand and evaluate both sides of the argument, while responding in a personally or socially ethical manner, will be an important skill.

Under the Hood

IN FOCUS

SOME PEOPLE ARE DRAWN TO UNDERSTANDING things in detail, but many folks are happy just to have things work. If you use a computer, you may not have ever been tempted to "look under the hood." However, without understanding the hardware inside, you'll be faced with some real limitations. You'll have to pay a technician to fix or upgrade your computer. This won't be as efficient as fine-tuning it yourself, and you may find yourself buying a new computer sooner than necessary. If you're preparing for a career in information technology, understanding computer hardware will affect the speed and efficiency of the programs you design. And what about all those exciting advances you hear about? How do you evaluate the impact of a new type of memory or a new processor? A basic appreciation of how a computer system is built and designed is a good start.

We'll build on what you've learned about computer hardware in other chapters and go under the hood, looking at the components of your system unit in more detail. Let's begin by looking at the building blocks of computers: switches.

Switches

The **system unit** is the box that contains the central electronic components of the computer. But how, exactly, does the computer perform all of its tasks? How does it process the data you input? The CPU performs functions like adding, subtracting, moving data around the system, and so on using nothing but a large number of on/off switches. In fact, a computer system can be viewed as an enormous collection of on/off switches.

ELECTRICAL SWITCHES

Computers work exclusively with numbers, not words. To process data into information, computers need to work in a language they understand. This language, called **binary language**, consists of just two numbers: 0 and 1. Everything a computer does, such as processing data or printing a report, is broken down into a series of 0s and 1s. **Electrical switches** are devices inside the computer that can be flipped between these two states: 1 and 0, signifying "on" and "off." Computers use 0s and 1s to process data because they are electronic, digital machines. They only understand two states of existence: on and off. Inside a computer these two possibilities, or states, are represented using the binary switches (or digits) 1 and 0.

You use various forms of switches every day. The on/off button on your DVD player is a mechanical switch: pushed in, it represents the value 1 (on), whereas popped out, it represents the value 0 (off). Another switch you use each day is a water faucet. As shown in Figure 1, shutting off the faucet so that no water flows could represent the value 0, whereas turning it on could represent the value 1.

Computers are built from a huge collection of electrical switches. The history of computers is really a story about creating smaller and faster sets of electrical switches so that more data can be stored and manipulated quickly.

Vacuum Tubes

The earliest generation of electronic computers used devices called **vacuum tubes** as switches. Vacuum tubes act as computer switches by allowing or blocking the flow of electrical current. The problem with vacuum tubes is that they take up a lot of space, as you see in Figure 2. The first high-speed digital computer, the Electronic Numerical Integrator and Computer (ENIAC), was deployed in 1945. It used nearly 18,000 vacuum tubes as switches and filled approximately 1,500 square feet of floor space. That's about one-half the size of a standard high school basketball court! In addition to being large, the vacuum tubes produced a lot of heat and burned out frequently. Thus, vacuum tubes are impractical

FIGURE 1

Water faucets can be used to represent binary switches.

to use as switching devices in personal computers because of their size and reliability.

Since the introduction of ENIAC's vacuum tubes, two major revolutions have occurred in the design of switches, and consequently computers, to make them smaller and faster: the invention of the transistor and the fabrication of integrated circuits.

TRANSISTORS

Transistors are electrical switches that are built out of layers of a special type of material called a **semiconductor**, which is any material that can be controlled to either conduct electricity or act as an insulator (to prohibit electricity from passing through). Silicon, which is found in common sand, is the semiconductor material used to make transistors.

By itself, silicon does not conduct electricity particularly well, but if specific chemicals are added in a controlled way to the silicon, it begins to behave like a switch (see Figure 3). The silicon allows electrical current to flow easily when a certain voltage is applied; otherwise, it prevents electrical current from flowing, thus

FIGURE 2

Computers can be constructed using vacuum tubes (see inset). The difference in size achieved by moving from tubes to transistors allowed computers to become desktop devices.

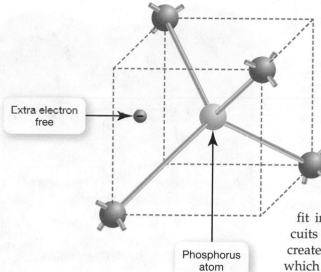

Extra electron
free →

Phosphorus
atom

FIGURE 3

In "doping," a phosphorous atom is put in the place of a silicon atom. Because phosphorous has five electrons instead of four, the extra electron is free to move around.

behaving as an on/off switch. This kind of behavior is exactly what is needed to store digital information, the 0s (off) and 1s (on) in binary language.

Early transistors were built in separate units as small metal rods, with each rod acting as a single on/off switch. These first transistors were much smaller than vacuum tubes, produced little heat, and could quickly be switched from on to off, thereby allowing or blocking electrical current. They also were less expensive than vacuum tubes.

It wasn't long, however, before transistors reached their limits. Continuing advances in technology began to require more transistors than circuit boards could reasonably handle at the time. Something was needed to pack more transistor capacity into a smaller space. Thus, integrated circuits, the next technical revolution in switches, were developed.

FIGURE 4

Integrated circuits use advanced fabrication techniques to fit millions of transistors into a quarter inch of silicon. This is an integrated circuit with areas marked out in black to show memory units, logic sections, and input/output blocks.

Integrated Circuits

Integrated circuits (or **chips**) are tiny regions of semiconductor material such as silicon that support a huge number of transistors (see Figure 4). Along with all the many transistors, other components critical to a circuit board (such as resistors, capacitors, and diodes) are also located on the integrated circuit. Most integrated circuits are no more than a quarter inch in size.

Because so many transistors can fit into such a small area, integrated circuits have enabled computer designers to create small yet powerful **microprocessors**, which are the chips that contain a CPU. The Intel 4004, the first complete microprocessor to be located on a single integrated circuit, was released in 1971, marking the beginning of the true miniaturization of computers. The Intel 4004 contained slightly more than 2,300 transistors. Today, more than 2 billion transistors can be manufactured in a space as tiny as the nail of your little finger!

This incredible feat has fueled an industry like no other. In 1951, the Univac I computer was the size of a large room. The processor memory unit itself, which cost more than one million dollars to produce, was 14 feet long by 8 feet wide by 8.5 feet high and could perform about 1,905 operations per second. Thanks to advances in integrated circuits, the IBM PC released 30 years later took up just 1 cubic foot of space, cost $3,000, and performed 155,000 times more quickly. (For more information about computer history, see the Technology in Focus feature "The History of the PC" on page 34.)

Computers use on/off switches to perform their functions. But how can these simple switches be organized so that they let you use a computer to pay your bills online or write an essay? How can a set of switches describe a number or a word, or give a computer the command to

SOUND BYTE

Where Does Binary Show Up?

In this Sound Byte, you'll learn how to use tools to work with binary, decimal, and hexadecimal numbers. (These tools come with the Windows operating system.) You'll also learn where you might see binary and hexadecimal values when you use a computer.

perform addition? Recall that to manipulate the on/off switches, the computer works in binary language, which uses only two digits, 0 and 1. To understand how a computer works, let's first look at the special numbering system called the *binary number system*.

THE BINARY NUMBER SYSTEM

A **number system** is an organized plan for representing a number. Although you may not realize it, you are already familiar with one number system. The **base 10 number system**, also known as **decimal notation**, is the system you use to represent all of the numeric values you use each day. It's called base 10 because it uses 10 digits, 0 through 9, to represent any value.

To represent a number in base 10, you break the number down into groups of ones, tens, hundreds, thousands, and so on. Each digit has a place value depending on where it appears in the number. For example, using base 10, in the whole number 6,954, there are 6 sets of thousands, 9 sets of hundreds, 5 sets of tens, and 4 sets of ones. Working from right to left, each place in a number represents an increasing power of 10, as shown here:

$$6,954 = 6 * (1,000) + 9 * (100) + 5 * (10) + 4 * (1)$$
$$= 6 * 10^3 + 9 * 10^2 + 5 * 10^1 + 4 * 10^0$$

Note that in this equation, the final number 1 is represented as 10^0 because any number raised to the zero power is equal to 1.

Anthropologists theorize that humans developed a base 10 number system because we have 10 fingers. However, computer systems, with their huge collections of on/off switches, are not well suited to thinking about numbers in groups of 10. Instead, computers describe a number in powers of 2 because each switch can be in one of two

FIGURE 5

The joke here is that the base ten representation of 2 is written as 10 in binary.

positions: on or off. This numbering system is referred to as the **binary number system**.

The binary number system is also referred to as the **base 2 number system**. Even with just two digits, the binary number system can still represent all the values that a base 10 number system can (see Figure 5). Instead of breaking the number down into sets of ones, tens, hundreds, and thousands, as is done in base 10 notation, the binary number system describes a number as the sum of powers of 2. Binary numbers are used to represent every piece of data stored in a computer: all of the numbers, all of the letters, and all of the instructions that the computer uses to execute work.

Representing Integers

In the base 10 number system, a whole number is represented as the sum of ones, tens, hundreds, and thousands—that is, sums of powers of 10. The binary system works in the same way, but describes a value as the sum of groups of 1s, 2s, 4s, 8s, 16s, 32s, 64s, etc—that is, powers of 2: 1, 2, 4, 8, 16, 32, 64, and so on.

Let's look at the number 67. In base 10, the number 67 would be six sets of 10s and seven sets of 1s, as follows:

$$\text{Base 10: } 67 = 6 * 10^1 + 7 * 10^0$$

One way to figure out how 67 is represented in base 2 is to find the largest possible power of 2 that could be in the number 67. Two to the eighth power is 256, and there are no groups of 256 in the number 67. Two to the seventh power is 128, but that is bigger than 67. Two to the sixth power is 64, and there is a group of 64 inside a group of 67.

67 has	1	group of	64	That leaves 3 and
3 has	0	groups of	32	
	0	groups of	16	
	0	groups of	8	
	0	groups of	4	
	1	group of	2	That leaves 1 and
1 has	1	group of	1	And now nothing is left

So, the binary number for 67 is written as 1000011 in base 2:

$$\text{Base 2: } 67 = 64 + 0 + 0 + 0 + 0 + 2 + 1$$
$$=(1 * 2^6) + (0 * 2^5) + (0 * 2^4) + (0 * 2^3) + (0 * 2^2) + (1 * 2^1) + (1 * 2^0)$$
$$=(1000011) \text{ base 2}$$

It is easier to have a calculator do this for you! Some calculators have a button labeled DEC (for decimal) and another labeled BIN (for binary). Using Windows, you can access the Scientific Calculator that supports conversion between decimal (base 10) and binary (base 2) by choosing Start, All Programs, Accessories; then clicking Calculator;

and then clicking the View menu to select Programmer. Instead of the default setting of DEC (decimal), switch to BIN (binary) and enter your calculation.

A large integer value becomes a very long string of 1s and 0s in binary! For convenience, programmers often use **hexadecimal notation** to make these expressions easier to use. Hexadecimal is a base 16 number system, meaning it uses 16 digits to represent numbers instead of the 10 digits used in base 10 or the 2 digits used in base 2. The 16 digits it uses are the 10 numeric digits, 0 to 9, plus six extra symbols: A, B, C, D, E, and F. Each of the letters A through F corresponds to a numeric value, so that A equals 10, B equals 11, and so on (see Figure 6). Therefore, the

FIGURE 6 **Sample Hexadecimal Values**

Decimal Number	Hexadecimal Value	Decimal Number	Hexadecimal Value
00	00	08	08
01	01	09	09
02	02	10	A
03	03	11	B
04	04	12	C
05	05	13	D
06	06	14	E
07	07	15	F

value 67 in decimal is 1000011 in binary or 43 in hexadecimal notation. It is much easier for computer scientists to use the two-digit 43 than the seven-digit string 1000011. The Windows Calculator in Scientific view also can perform conversions to hexadecimal notation. (You can watch a video showing you how to perform conversions between bases using the Windows Calculator in the Sound Byte titled "Where Does Binary Show Up?")

Representing Characters: ASCII

We have just been converting integers from base 10, which *we* understand, to base 2 (binary state), which the computer understands. Similarly, we need a system that converts letters and other symbols that *we* understand to a binary state that the computer understands. To provide a consistent means for representing letters and other characters, certain codes dictate how to represent characters in binary format. Older mainframe computers use Extended Binary-Coded Decimal Interchange Code (EBCDIC, pronounced "Eb-sih-dik"). However, most of today's personal computers use the American National Standards Institute (ANSI, pronounced "An-see") standard code, called the **American Standard Code for Information Interchange** (**ASCII**, pronounced "As-key"), to represent each letter or character as an 8-bit (or 1-byte) binary code.

Each binary digit is called a **bit** for short. Eight binary digits (or bits) combine to create one **byte**. We have been converting base 10 numbers to a binary format. In such cases, the binary format has no standard length.

For example, the binary format for the number 2 is two digits (10), whereas the binary format for the number 10 is four digits (1010). Although binary numbers can have more or fewer than 8 bits, each single alphabetic or special character is 1 byte (or 8 bits) of data and consists of a unique combination of a total of eight 0s and 1s.

The ASCII code represents the 26 uppercase letters and 26 lowercase letters used in the English language, along with many punctuation symbols and other special characters, using 8 bits. Figure 7 shows several examples of ASCII code representation of printable letters and characters.

Representing Characters: Unicode

Because it represents letters and characters using only 8 bits, the ASCII code can assign only 256 (or 2^8) different codes for unique characters and letters. Although this is enough to represent English and many other characters found in the world's languages, ASCII code cannot represent all languages and symbols, because some languages require more than 256 characters and letters. Thus, a new encoding scheme, called **Unicode**, was created. By using 16 bits instead of the 8 bits used in ASCII, Unicode can represent nearly 1,115,000 code points and currently assigns more than 96,000 unique character symbols (see Figure 8). The first 128 characters of Unicode are identical to ASCII, but because of its depth, Unicode is also able to represent the alphabets of all

FIGURE 7 ASCII Standard Code for a Sample of Letters and Characters

ASCII Code	Represents This Symbol	ASCII Code	Represents This Symbol
01000001	A	01100001	a
01000010	B	01100010	b
01000011	C	01100011	c
01011010	Z	00100011	#
00100001	!	00100100	$
00100010	"	00100101	%

Note: For the full ASCII table, see **asciitable.com**.

FIGURE 8

The written languages of the world require thousands of different characters, shown here. Unicode provides a system allowing digital representation of over 1,100,000 unique characters.

modern and historic languages and notational systems, including such languages and writing systems as Tibetan, Tagalog, Japanese, and Canadian Aboriginal syllabics. As we continue to become a more global society, it is anticipated that Unicode will replace ASCII as the standard character formatting code.

Representing Decimal Numbers

The binary number system also can represent a decimal number. How can a string of 1s and 0s capture the information in a value such as 99.368? Because every computer must store such numbers in the same way, the Institute of Electrical and Electronics Engineers (IEEE) has established a standard called the *floating-point standard* that describes how numbers with fractional parts should be represented in the binary number system. Using a 32-bit system, we can represent an incredibly wide range of numbers. The method dictated by the IEEE standard works the same for any number with a decimal point, such as the number –0.75. The first digit, or bit (the sign bit), is used to indicate whether the number is positive or negative. The next eight bits store the magnitude of the number, indicating whether the number is in the hundreds or millions, for example. The standard says to use the next 23 bits to store the value of the number.

Interpretation

All data inside the computer is stored as bits. Positive and negative numbers can be stored using signed integer notation, with the first bit (the sign bit) indicating the sign and the rest of the bits indicating the value of the number. Decimal numbers are stored according to the IEEE floating-point standard, and letters and symbols are stored according to the ASCII code or Unicode. All of these different number systems and codes exist so that computers can store different types of information in their on/off switches. No matter what kind of data you input in a computer—a color, a musical note, or a street address—that data will be stored as a string of 1s and 0s. The important lesson is that the interpretation of 0s and 1s is what matters. The same binary pattern could represent a positive number, a negative number, a fraction, or a letter.

How does the computer know which interpretation to use for the 1s and 0s? When your brain processes language, it takes the sounds you hear and uses the rules of English, along with other clues, to build an interpretation of the sound as a word. If you are in New York City and hear someone shout, "Hey, Lori!" you expect someone is saying hello to a friend. If you are in London and hear the same sound—"Hey! Lorry!"—you jump out of the way because a truck is coming at you! You knew which interpretation to apply to the sound because you had some other information—that you were in England.

Likewise, the CPU is designed to understand a specific language or set of instructions. Certain instructions tell the CPU to expect a negative number next or to interpret the following bit pattern as a character. Because of this extra information, the CPU always knows which interpretation to use for a series of bits.

The CPU Machine Cycle

Any program you run on your computer is actually a long series of binary code describing a specific set of commands the CPU must perform. These commands may be coming from a user's actions or may be instructions fed from a program while it executes. Each CPU is somewhat different in the exact steps it follows to perform its tasks, but all CPUs must perform a series of similar general steps. These steps, illustrated in Figure 9, are referred to as a CPU **machine cycle** (or **processing cycle**).

1. FETCH: When any program begins to run, the 1s and 0s that make up the program's binary code must be "fetched" from their temporary storage location in random access memory (RAM) and moved to the CPU before they can be executed.

2. DECODE: Once the program's binary code is in the CPU, it is decoded into the commands the CPU understands.

3. EXECUTE: Next, the CPU actually performs the work described in the commands.

Specialized hardware on the CPU performs addition, subtraction, multiplication, division, and other mathematical and logical operations at incredible speeds.

4. STORE: The result is stored in one of the **registers**, special memory storage areas built into the CPU, which are the most expensive, fastest memory in your computer. The CPU is then ready to fetch the next set of bits encoding the next instruction.

No matter what program you are running, be it a Web browser or a word processing program, and no matter how many programs you are using at one time, the CPU performs these four steps over and over at incredibly high speeds. Shortly, we'll look at each stage in more detail so that you can understand the complexity of the CPU's design, how to compare different CPUs on the market, and what enhancements you can expect in CPU designs of the future. But first, let's examine a few of the CPU's other components that help it perform its tasks.

THE SYSTEM CLOCK

To move from one stage of the machine cycle to the next, the motherboard uses a built-in **system clock**. This internal clock is actually a special crystal that acts like a metronome, keeping a steady beat and thereby controlling when the CPU will move to the next stage of processing.

These steady beats or "ticks" of the system clock, known as the **clock cycle**, set the pace by which the computer moves from process to process. The pace, known as **clock speed**, is measured in hertz (Hz), a unit of measure that describes how many times something happens per second. Today's system clocks are measured in gigahertz (GHz), each of which represents one billion clock ticks per second. Therefore, in a 3 GHz system, there are three billion clock ticks each second. Computers with older processors would sometimes need one or more cycles to process one instruction. Today, however, CPUs are designed to handle more instructions more efficiently, and are, therefore, capable of executing more than one instruction per cycle.

THE CONTROL UNIT

The CPU, like any part of the computer system, is designed from a collection of switches. How can simple on/off switches

FIGURE 9
The CPU machine cycle.

"remember" the fetch-decode-execute-store sequence of the CPU machine cycle? How can they perform the work required in each of these stages?

The **control unit** of the CPU manages the switches inside the CPU. It is programmed by CPU designers to remember the sequence of processing stages for that CPU and how each switch in the CPU should be set (i.e., on or off) for each stage. With each beat of the system clock, the control unit moves each switch to the correct on or off setting and then performs the work of that stage.

Let's now look at each of the stages in the machine cycle in a bit more depth.

STAGE 1: THE FETCH STAGE

The data and program instructions the CPU needs are stored in different areas in the computer system. Data and program instructions move between these areas as they are needed by the CPU for processing. Programs (such as Microsoft Word) are permanently stored on the hard drive because it offers nonvolatile storage, meaning the programs remain stored there even when you turn the power off. However, when you launch a program (that is, when you double-click an icon to execute the program), the program, or sometimes only the essential parts of a program, is transferred from the hard drive into RAM.

The program moves to RAM because the CPU can access the data and program instructions stored in RAM more than one million times faster than if they are left on the hard drive. In part, this is because RAM is much closer to the CPU than the hard drive is. Another reason for the delay in transmission of data and program instructions from the hard drive to the CPU is that the hard drive is a mechanical device. The hard drive has read/write heads that have to sweep over the spinning platters, which takes time. RAM is faster because it's electronic, not mechanical.

As specific instructions from the program are needed, they are moved from RAM into registers (the special storage areas located on the CPU itself), where they wait to be executed.

The CPU's storage area is not big enough to hold everything it needs to process at the same time. If enough memory were located on the CPU chip itself, an entire program

could be copied to the CPU from RAM before it was executed. This certainly would add to the computer's speed and efficiency, because there would be no delay while the CPU stopped processing operations to fetch instructions from RAM to the CPU. However, including so much memory on a CPU chip would make these chips extremely expensive. In addition, CPU design is so complex that only a limited amount of storage space is available on the CPU itself.

Cache Memory

The CPU doesn't actually need to fetch every instruction from RAM each time it goes through a cycle. There is another layer of storage, called **cache memory**, that has even faster access than RAM. The word *cache* is derived from the French word *cacher*, which means "to hide." Cache memory consists of small blocks of memory located directly on and next to the CPU chip. These memory blocks are holding places for recently or frequently used instructions or data that the CPU needs the most. When these instructions or data are stored in cache memory, the CPU can retrieve them more quickly than would be the case if it had to access the instructions or data in RAM.

Taking data you think you'll be using soon and storing it nearby is a simple idea but a powerful one. This is a strategy that shows up in other places in your computer system. For example, when you are browsing Web pages, it takes longer to download images than text. Your browser software automatically stores images on your hard drive so that you don't have to wait to download them again if you want to go back and view a page you've already visited. Although this cache of files is not related to the cache

FIGURE 10
Modern CPUs have two or more levels of cache memory, which leads to faster CPU processing.

storage space designed into the CPU chip, the idea is the same.

Modern CPU designs include several types of cache memory. If the next instruction to be fetched is not already located in a CPU register, instead of looking directly to RAM to find it, the CPU first searches Level 1 cache. **Level 1 cache** is a block of memory that is built onto the CPU chip to store data or commands that have just been used.

If the command is not located in Level 1 cache, the CPU searches Level 2 cache. Depending on the design of the CPU, **Level 2 cache** is either located on the CPU chip but is slightly farther away from the CPU, or is on a separate chip next to the CPU and therefore takes somewhat longer to access. Level 2 cache contains more storage area than does Level 1 cache. For the Intel Core i7, for example, the Level 1 cache is 64 kilobytes (KB) and the Level 2 cache is 1 megabytes (MB).

Only if the CPU doesn't find the next instruction to be fetched in either Level 1 or Level 2 cache will it make the long journey to RAM to access it.

The current direction of processor design is toward increasingly large multilevel CPU cache structures. Therefore, some newer CPUs, such as Intel's Core i7 processors, have an additional third level of cache memory storage called **Level 3 cache**. On computers with Level 3 cache, the CPU checks this

area for instructions and data after it looks in Level 1 and Level 2 cache, but before it makes the longer trip to RAM (see Figure 10). The Level 3 cache holds between 2 and 12 MB of data. With 12 MB of Level 3 cache, there is storage for some entire programs to be transferred to the CPU for execution.

As an end user of computer programs, you do nothing special to use cache memory. In fact, you are not even able to see that caching is being used—nothing special lights up on your system unit or keyboard. The advantage of having more cache memory is that you'll experience better performance because the CPU won't have to make the longer trip to RAM to get data and instructions as often. Unfortunately, because it is built into the CPU chip or motherboard, you can't upgrade cache; it is part of the original design of the CPU. Therefore, as with RAM, it's important when buying a computer to consider buying the one, everything else being equal, with the most cache memory.

STAGE 2: THE DECODE STAGE

The main goal of the decode stage is for the CPU's control unit to translate (or **decode**) the program's instructions into commands the CPU can understand. A CPU can understand only a tiny set of commands. The collection of commands a specific CPU can execute is called the **instruction set** for that system. Each CPU has its own unique instruction set. For example, the AMD Phenom II X6 six core processor in a Gamer Mage system from iBuyPower has a different instruction set than does the Intel Core i5 used in a Dell Inspiron notebook. The control unit interprets the code's bits according to the instruction set the CPU designers laid out for that particular CPU. Based on this process of translation, the control unit then knows how to set up all the switches on the CPU so that the proper operation will occur.

Because humans are the ones who write the initial instructions, all of the commands in an instruction set are written in a language called **assembly language**, which is easier for humans to work with than binary. Many CPUs have similar assembly commands in their instruction sets, including the commands listed here:

ADD	Add
SUB	Subtract
MUL	Multiply
DIV	Divide
MOVE	Move data to RAM
STORE	Move data to a CPU register
EQU	Check if equal

CPUs differ in the choice of additional assembly language commands selected for the instruction set. Each CPU design team works to develop an instruction set that is both powerful and speedy.

However, because the CPU knows and recognizes only patterns of 0s and 1s, it cannot understand assembly language directly, so these human-readable instructions are translated into long strings of binary code. The control unit uses these long strings of binary code called **machine language** to set up the hardware in the CPU for the rest of the operations it needs to perform. Machine language is a binary code for computer instructions, much like the ASCII code is a binary code for letters and characters. Similar to each letter or character having its own unique combination of 0s and 1s assigned to it, a CPU has a table of codes consisting of combinations of 0s and 1s for each of its commands. If the CPU sees a particular pattern of bits arrive, it knows the work it must do.

Figure 11 shows a few commands in both assembly language and machine language.

STAGE 3: THE EXECUTE STAGE

The **arithmetic logic unit (ALU)** is the part of the CPU designed to perform mathematical operations such as addition, subtraction, multiplication, and division and to test the comparison of values such as *greater than*, *less than*, and *equal to*. For example, in calculating an average, the ALU is where the addition and division operations would take place. The ALU also performs logical OR, AND, and NOT operations. For example, in determining whether a student can graduate, the ALU would need to ascertain whether the student had taken all required courses AND obtained a passing grade in each of them. The ALU is specially designed to execute such calculations flawlessly and with incredible speed.

The ALU is fed data from the CPU's registers. The amount of data a CPU can process at a time is based in part on the amount of data each register can hold. The number of bits a computer can work with at a time is referred to as its **word size**. Therefore, a 64-bit processor can process more information faster than a 32-bit processor.

STAGE 4: THE STORE STAGE

In the final stage, the result produced by the ALU is stored back in the registers. The instruction itself will explain which register should be used to store the answer. Once the entire instruction has been completed, the next instruction will be fetched, and the fetch-decode-execute-store sequence will begin again.

FIGURE 11 Representations of Sample CPU Commands

Human Language for Command	CPU Command in Assembly Language (Language Used by Programmers)	CPU Command in Machine Language (Language Used in the CPU's Instruction Set)
Add	ADD	1110 1010
Subtract	SUB	0001 0101
Multiply	MUL	1111 0000
Divide	DIV	0000 1111

Making CPUs Even Faster

Knowing how to build a CPU that can run faster than the competition can make a company rich. However, building a faster CPU is not easy. A new product launch must take into consideration the time it will take to design, manufacture, and test that processor. When the processor finally hits the market, it must be faster than the competition if the manufacturer hopes to make a profit. To create a CPU that will be released 36 months from now, it must be built to perform at least twice as fast as anything currently available.

Gordon Moore, the cofounder of processor manufacturer Intel, predicted more than 40 years ago that the number of transistors on a processor would double every 18 months. Known as **Moore's Law**, this prediction has been remarkably accurate—but only with tremendous engineering ingenuity. The first 8086 chip had only 29,000 transistors and ran at 5 MHz. Advances in the number of transistors on processors through the 1970s, 1980s, and 1990s continued to align with Moore's prediction.

However, there was a time near the turn of the 21st century when skeptics questioned how much longer Moore's Law would hold true. These skeptics were proved wrong with the microprocessor's continued growth in power. Today's Intel i7 chip has 774 million transistors—more than 18 times the transistor count of the Pentium 4 from the year 2000. Moreover, Intel's Itanium 9300 flaunts a whopping 2.3 billion transistors! How much longer can Moore's prediction hold true? Only time will tell.

Processor manufacturers can increase CPU performance in many different ways. One approach is to use a technique called *pipelining* to boost performance. Another approach is to design the CPU's instruction set so that it contains specialized, faster instructions for handling multimedia and graphics. In addition, some CPUs, such as Intel's i7 980X or the AMD Phenom II x6 processors, now have six independent processing paths inside, with one CPU chip doing the work of six separate CPU units. Some heavy computational problems are attacked by large numbers of computers actually clustered together to work at the same time.

PIPELINING

As an instruction is processed, the CPU runs sequentially through the four stages of processing: fetch, decode, execute, and store. **Pipelining** is a technique that allows the CPU to work on more than one instruction (or stage of processing) at a time, thereby boosting CPU performance.

For example, without pipelining, it may take four clock cycles to complete one instruction (one clock cycle for each of the four

DOES YOUR COMPUTER NEED MORE POWER? TEAM IT UP!

The history of computing shows us that processing power increases tremendously each year. One strategy in use now for continuing that trend is cluster computing. If one computer is powerful, then two are twice as powerful—if you can get them to work together. A *computing cluster* is a group of computers, connected by specialized clustering software, that works together to solve complex equations. Most clusters work on something called the *balancing principle*, whereby computational work is transferred from overloaded (busy) computers in the cluster to computers that have more computing resources available. Computing clusters, although not as fast as supercomputers (single computers with extremely high processing capabilities), can perform computations faster than one computer working alone and are used for complex calculations such as weather forecasting and graphics rendering. You can now rent time on computing clusters through services like PurePowua (**purepowua.com**), where you can upload and remotely control your job from your desktop as it runs on a cluster of computers.

processing stages). However, with a four-stage pipeline, the computer can process four instructions at the same time. Like an automobile assembly line, instead of waiting for one car to go completely through each process of assembly, painting, and so on, you can have four cars going through the assembly line at the same time. When every component of the assembly line is done with its process, the cars all move on to the next stage.

Pipelined architectures allow several instructions to be processed at the same time. The ticks of the system clock (the clock cycle) indicate when all instructions move to the next process. The secret of pipelining is that the CPU is allowed to be fetching one instruction while it is simultaneously decoding another, executing a third, storing a fourth, and so on. Using pipelining, a four-stage processor can potentially run up to four times faster because some instruction is finishing every clock cycle rather than waiting four cycles for each instruction to finish. In Figure 12a, a non-pipelined instruction takes four clock cycles to be completed, whereas in Figure 12b, the four instructions have been completed in the same time using pipelining.

The number of stages in a pipeline depends entirely on design decisions. Earlier we analyzed a CPU that went through four stages in the execution of an instruction. The Intel Pentium 4 with hyperthreading featured a 31-stage pipeline, and the PowerPC G5 processor used a 10-stage pipeline. Thus, similar to an assembly line, in a 31-stage pipeline, as many as 31 different instructions can be processed at any given time, making the processing of information much faster. However, because so many aspects of the CPU design interact, you cannot predict performance based solely on the number of stages in a pipeline.

There is a cost to pipelining a CPU as well. The CPU must be designed so that each stage (fetch, decode, execute, and store) is independent. This means that each stage must be

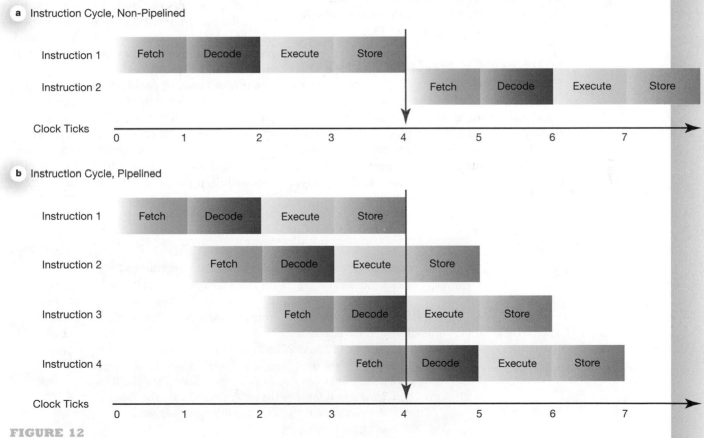

a Instruction Cycle, Non-Pipelined

b Instruction Cycle, Pipelined

FIGURE 12

Instead of (a) waiting for each instruction to complete, (b) pipelining allows the system to work on more than one set of instructions at one time.

able to run at the same time that the other three stages are running. This requires more transistors and a more complicated hardware design.

SPECIALIZED MULTIMEDIA INSTRUCTIONS

Each design team that develops a new CPU tries to imagine what users' greatest needs will be in four or five years. Currently, several processors on the market reflect this consideration by incorporating specialized multimedia instructions into the basic instruction set.

Hardware engineers have redesigned the chip so that the instruction set contains new commands that are specially designed to speed up the work needed for video and audio processing. For example, Intel has integrated the Streaming Single Instruction Multiple Data (SIMD) Extensions 3 set of commands into its processor designs, adding a special group of 157 commands to the basic instruction set. These multimedia-specific instructions work to accelerate video, speech, and image processing in the CPU.

MULTIPLE PROCESSING EFFORTS

Many high-end server systems employ a **quad processor design** that has four completely separate CPU chips on one motherboard. Often, these server systems can later be scaled so that they can accommodate four, six, or even twelve processors. The Cray Jaguar supercomputer has a total of 37,376 independent processors!

Meanwhile, Intel is promoting a technology called *multi-core processing* in its Core processor line of chips. Chips with dual-core processing capabilities have two separate parallel processing paths inside them, so they are almost as fast as two separate CPUs. Dual-core processing is especially helpful because antivirus software and other security programs often run in the background as you use your system. A dual-core processor enables these multiple applications to execute much more quickly than with traditional CPUs. Six-core processors, like the Intel i7 Extreme Edition, are appearing in high-performance home-based systems now as well, executing six separate processing paths.

Multiprocessor systems are often used when intensive computational problems need to be solved in such areas as computer simulations, video production, and graphics processing. Having two processors allows the work to be done almost twice as quickly, but not quite. It is not quite twice as fast because the system must do some extra work to decide which processor will work on which part of the problem and to recombine the results each CPU produces.

Certain types of problems are well suited to a parallel-processing environment. In **parallel processing**, there is a large network of computers, with each computer working on a portion of the same problem simultaneously. To be a good candidate for parallel processing, a problem must be one that can

TODAY'S SUPER-COMPUTERS: THE FASTEST OF THE FAST

Supercomputers are the biggest and most powerful type of computer. Scientists and engineers use these computers to solve complex problems or to perform massive computations. Some supercomputers are single computers with multiple processors, whereas others consist of multiple computers that work together.

The top spot on the June 2010 Top 500 List was won by the Cray Jaguar. It operates at a peak of more than 2,300 teraflops (or 2,300 trillion operations per second). That's almost 23,000 times faster than the fastest personal computer! Second position was the entry from China, the Nebulae.

Check out the current crop of the world's fastest supercomputers at the Top 500 site (**top500.org**).

be divided into a set of tasks that can be run simultaneously. So, for example, a problem where millions of faces are being compared with a target image for recognition is easily adapted to a parallel setting. The target face can be compared at the same time to many hundreds of faces. But if the next step of an algorithm can be started only after the results of the previous step have been computed, parallel processing will present no advantages.

A simple analogy of parallel processing is a laundromat. Instead of taking all day to do five loads of laundry with one machine, you can bring all your laundry to a laundromat, load it into five separate machines, and finish it all in approximately the same time it would have taken you to do just one load on a single machine. In real life, parallel processing is used in complex weather forecasting to run calculations over many different regions around the globe; in the airline industry to analyze customer information in an effort to forecast demand; and by the government in census data compilation.

Thus, what you can continue to expect from CPUs in the future is that they will continue to get smaller and faster and consume less power. This fits with the current demands of consumers for more powerful portable computing devices.

At the most basic level of binary 1s and 0s, computers are systems of switches that can accomplish impressive tasks. By understanding the hardware components that make up your computer system, you can use your system more effectively and make better buying decisions.

Multiple Choice

Instructions: Answer the multiple-choice questions below for more practice with key terms and concepts from this Technology in Focus feature.

1. Which is *not* a typical use of parallel processing systems?
   a. Computer simulations
   b. Word processing
   c. Weather modeling
   d. Graphics processing

2. What is another name for the base 10 number system?
   a. Decimal notation
   b. Binary number system
   c. Hexadecimal notation
   d. Integer system

3. Which encoding scheme can represent the alphabets of all modern and historic languages?
   a. Base 2 number system   c. ASCII
   b. Unicode   d. Scientific

4. Moore's Law is best described as
   a. an observation of the rate of increasing transistor density.
   b. a physical principle.
   c. a legal construct limiting performance.
   d. an advertising campaign by Intel.

5. To regulate the internal timing of a computer system, the motherboard uses
   a. a system clock.   c. RAM.
   b. software simulation.   d. a register.

6. Special areas of memory storage built into the CPU are known as
   a. switches.   c. registers.
   b. semiconductors.   d. integrated circuits.

7. Which is the correct set of steps in the machine cycle?
   a. Execute, store, fetch, decode
   b. Store, fetch, execute, decode
   c. Decode, execute, fetch, store
   d. Fetch, decode, execute, store

8. All data inside the computer is stored as
   a. bytes.   c. switches.
   b. bits.   d. cache memory.

9. Which statement about pipelining is *false*?
   a. Pipelining boosts CPU performance.
   b. Pipeline design is used in many modern CPUs.
   c. Pipelining requires a less complicated hardware design.
   d. The process allows the computer to process multiple instructions simultaneously.

10. From fastest to slowest, which is the fastest sequence of accessing memory?
    a. RAM, Level 1 cache, Level 2 cache, Level 3 cache
    b. Registers, Level 1 cache, Level 2 cache, RAM
    c. Level 1 cache, Level 2 cache, RAM, registers
    d. Level 2 cache, Level 1 cache, registers, RAM

eight
digital lifestyle:
managing digital data and devices

objectives

After reading this chapter, you should be able to answer the following questions:

1. What are the changes that have brought us a digital lifestyle? *(pp. 364–365)*

2. How has the move to digital information affected the communication tools important to both the business world and life outside of work? *(p. 366)*

3. How do cell phone and smartphone components resemble a traditional computer, and how do they work? *(pp. 366–374)*

4. Why would I use VoIP, and what does it offer that is unique? *(pp. 374–376)*

5. How is digital media different from analog? *(p. 377)*

6. What can I carry in a portable media player, and how does it store data? *(pp. 377–381)*

7. What ways are there for me to create and to watch digital video? *(pp. 386–391)*

8. What changes does ubiquitous computing bring to our lifestyles? *(pp. 393–397)*

multimedia resources

Active Helpdesk
- Keeping Your Data on Hand **(p. 376)**
- Using Portable Media Players **(p. 380)**

Sound Bytes
- Smartphones Are Really Smart **(p. 369)**
- Connecting with Bluetooth **(p. 371)**

Companion Website
The Companion Website includes a variety of additional materials to help you review and learn more about the topics in this chapter. Go to: **pearsonhighered.com/techinaction**

how cool

is this?

how cool is *this?* TiVo is not the only game in town! PVR (personal video recorder) software is now available, free of charge, for every style of operating system. Using a PVR, you can record standard or HD television broadcasts on your hard drive and then watch them when you have the time. Free programs like **XBMC** Media Center and **MeediOS** let you pause and rewind live TV shows and include features that allow you to automatically detect and **skip commercials**. You even have access to a TV listings guide and can schedule your **PVR** from any location using the Web.

A Digital Lifestyle

Computers today are central to everyday life. Which part of your life isn't touched by some sort of computer or digital technology? Computer-like devices (such as smartphones and iPods) are everywhere. Much of your entertainment—playing games, watching movies and television, and downloading songs—is probably delivered via the Internet.

Do you really understand how all this digital technology works? Do you know all of your options so you can enjoy the digital devices you purchase to the fullest extent? In this chapter, we explore the key aspects of your digital life—digital communication, digital entertainment, and digital mobility— and help you understand how the related technologies work so you can use them to your best advantage.

When did everything go "digital"? It used to be that everything was analog. Today, no matter what you're interested in—music, movies, television, radio, stock prices—digital information is the key. All forms of entertainment have migrated to the digital domain (see Figure 8.1). MP3 files encode digital forms of music, and digital cameras and video camcorders are now commonplace. In Hollywood, some feature films are now being shot entirely with digital equipment, and many movie theaters use digital projection equipment. Satellite radio systems such as Sirius Satellite Radio and HD Radio are broadcast in digital formats. Phone systems and television signals are now digital streams of data.

What is special about digital? Any kind of information can be digitized (measured and converted to a stream of numeric values). Consider sound. It is carried to your ears by sound waves, which are actually patterns of pressure changes in the air. Images are our interpretation of the changing intensity of light waves around us. These sound and light waves are called **analog** waves or continuous waves. They illustrate the loudness of a sound or the brightness of the colors in an image at a given moment in time. They are continuous signals because you would never have to lift your pencil off the page to draw them; they are just long, continuous lines.

First-generation recording devices such as vinyl records and analog television broadcasts were designed to reproduce these sound and light waves. A needle in the groove of a vinyl record vibrates in the same pattern as the original sound wave. Analog television signals are actually waves that tell an analog TV how to display the same color and brightness as is seen in the production studio. However, it's difficult to describe a wave, even mathematically. The simplest sounds, such as that of middle C on a piano, have the simplest shapes, like the one shown in Figure 8.2. However, something like the word *hello* generates a highly complex pattern, like the one shown in Figure 8.2.

What advantages do digital formats have over analog ones? Digital formats describe signals as long strings of numbers. This digital representation gives us a simple way to describe sound and light waves exactly so that sounds and images can be reproduced perfectly each time. In addition, we already have easy ways to distribute digital information (on CDs and DVDs and using e-mail, for example). Thus, digital information can be reproduced exactly and distributed easily. Both give it huge advantages over analog.

How can a sequence of numbers express complicated analog shapes? The answer is provided by something called *analog-to-digital conversion*. In analog-to-digital conversion, the incoming analog signal is measured many times each second. The strength of the signal at each measurement is recorded as a simple number. The series of numbers produced by

Figure 8.1 | ANALOG VERSUS DIGITAL ENTERTAINMENT

	Analog	Digital
Music	Vinyl record albums and cassette tapes	CDs and MP3 files
Photography	35-mm single lens reflex (SLR) cameras Photos stored on film	Digital cameras, including digital SLRs Photos stored as digital files
Video	8-mm, VHS, and Hi8 camcorders Film stored on tapes	High Definition Digital video (DV) camcorders Film stored as digital files; distributed on DVD and Blu-ray discs and streamed
Radio	AM/FM radio	HD Radio Sirius/XM Radio
Television	Conventional broadcast analog TV	High Definition Digital television (HDTV)

Middle C

"Hello"

the analog-to-digital conversion process gives us the digital form of the wave. Figure 8.3 shows analog and digital versions of the same wave. In Figure 8.3a, you see the original, continuous analog wave. You could draw that wave without lifting your pencil from the page. In Figure 8.3b, the wave has been digitized and is no longer a single line; instead, it is represented as a series of points or numbers.

How has the change from analog to digital technologies affected our lifestyle? When the market for communication devices for entertainment media—like photographs, music, and video—switched over to a digital standard, we began to have products with new and useful capabilities. Small devices can now hold huge collections of a variety of types of information. We can interact with our information any time we like, in ways that, prior to the conversion to digital media, had been too expensive or too difficult to learn. The implications of the shift to digital media are continually evolving. Let's examine the many ways in which digital media has already changed our lifestyles.

Figure 8.2

(a) This is an analog wave showing the simple, pure sound of a piano playing middle C. (b) This is the complex wave produced when a person says "Hello."

Figure 8.3

(a) A simple analog wave. (b) A digitized version of the same wave.

Digital Telephony: Communicating with Bits

Communication has changed radically in the digital age. Chapter 3 discussed the use of wikis, blogs, RSS feeds, and other Web-based tools for connecting people and their ideas. All of these software applications are dependent on digital information.

Hardware devices that support communication also have evolved because of digital technologies. **Telephony**, the use of equipment to provide voice communications over a distance, has shifted from an analog science to a digital one. In this section, we examine cell phones, smartphones, and Voice over Internet Protocol (VoIP) devices to see how they are changing to meet modern communication needs.

Cell Phones and Smartphones

What are cell phones and smartphones? The **cellular phone** (or **cell phone**) has evolved from a clunky, boxlike device to a compact, fully featured communication and information storage device. Cell phones offer all of the features available on a traditional telephone system, including automatic redial, call timers, and voice mail capabilities. Most cell phones also feature voice-activated dialing, which is important for hands-free operation. In addition, many cell phones offer Internet access, text messaging, personal information management (PIM) features, voice recording, GPS services, and digital image and video capture. The most fully featured and powerful cellular phones are found in the **smartphone**

category. A smartphone often requires a data plan from the cell phone provider. This is logical because a smartphone user is likely to spend a lot of time accessing the Internet to upload and download e-mail and data. Some smartphones have enough computing power to run versions of programs like Microsoft Excel and PowerPoint.

How do cell phones use digital signals? When you speak into a cell phone, the sound enters the microphone as a sound wave. Because analog sound waves need to be digitized (that is, converted into a sequence of 1s and 0s that the cell phone's processor can understand), an **analog-to-digital converter chip** converts your voice's sound waves into digital signals. Next, the digital data must be compressed, or squeezed, into the smallest possible space so that it will transmit more quickly to another phone. The processor cannot perform the mathematical operations required at this stage quickly enough, so a specialized chip called the **digital signal processor** is included in the cell phone to handle the compression work. Finally, the digital data is transmitted as a radio wave through the cellular network to the destination phone.

When you receive an incoming call, the digital signal processor decompresses the incoming message. An amplifier boosts the signal to make it loud enough, and it is then passed on to the speaker.

What's "cellular" about a cell phone? A set of connected "cells" makes up a cellular network. Each cell is a geographic area centered on a **base transceiver station**, which is a large communications tower with antennas, amplifiers, receivers, and transmitters. When you place a call on a cell phone, a base station picks up the request for service. The station then passes the request to a central location called a **mobile switching center**. (The reverse process occurs when you receive an incoming call.) A telecommunications company builds its network by constructing a series of cells that overlap in an attempt to guarantee that its cell phone customers have coverage no matter where they are.

As you move during your phone call, the mobile switching center monitors the strength of the signal between your cell phone and the closest base station. When the signal is no longer strong enough between your cell phone and the base station, the mobile switching center orders the next base

BITS AND BYTES

Phoning Home—Accessing Your Home Computer from Your Cell Phone

An estimated 1 billion cellular phones that aren't considered smartphones currently are deployed. But don't count your cheap phone out of the running if it doesn't have advanced software capabilities. You can still use it to access your home computer remotely and retrieve that big presentation you need for this afternoon. Remote access services such as GoToMyPC (**gotomypc.com**) and LogMeIn (**logmein.com**) can help and are free of charge. As long as you have a browser on your cell phone and a data plan with your provider, you can access the files on your computer from your phone without installing any software on the cell phone. You may not have to trade in that low-end cell phone yet. Just try getting it to work a little harder!

station to take charge of your call. When your cell phone "drops out," it may be because the distance between base stations was too great to provide an adequate signal.

Are cell phones and smartphones considered computers? Cell phones and smartphones are so advanced that they have many of the same components as a computer: a processor (central processing unit, or CPU); memory; and input and output devices, as shown in Figure 8.4. Cell/smartphones also require their own operating system (OS) software and have their own application software.

What does the processor inside a cell/smartphone do? Although the processor inside a cell phone is obviously not as fast or as high-powered as a processor in a desktop computer, it is still responsible for a great number of tasks. The processor coordinates sending all of the data among the other electronic components inside the phone. It also runs the cell phone's operating system, which provides a user interface so that you can change phone settings, store information, play games, and so on. Popular processors for cell/smartphones include the Qualcomm Snapdragon, the Texas Instruments OMAP, and the Marvell XScale processor. Some processors use dual-core processing technology, which is also used in some desktop processors.

When shopping for a new phone, be well prepared. Use published smartphone benchmarking results to compare performance. These benchmarks are often published on the *PC Magazine* Web site (**pcmag.com**) or at Wired (**wired.com**).

Is there a standard operating system for cell phones? Each cell phone manufacturer makes its own small changes to the operating system and designs its own user interface. So when moving between different cell phones, you will likely see a different set of commands and icons.

There are a number of operating systems in the cell phone market now. Many smartphones use the Windows Mobile operating system or the newer Windows Phone 7 series. Apple's iPhone uses a version of the OS X operating system that is used in Apple's personal computers, while the Palm Pre uses its own Palm-developed webOS. These operating systems are required to translate the user's commands into instructions for the processor.

Speaker

Liquid crystal display

Keypad

Microphone

Memory chip

CPU

There are several free operating systems that a manufacturer can use as a base for its cell/smartphone operating system. One popular OS is the Symbian, from the Symbian Foundation, which transitioned to an open source product in 2010. The Nokia N8 is one device running a Symbian OS. Another open source project to develop a free cell/smartphone operating system is Openmoko. The most successful open OS is the Android collection developed by Google. The goal of open source mobile operating systems is to leverage the creativity of many developers in creating great applications and new phone designs.

Figure 8.5 illustrates some of the different and creative user interfaces featured among cell phone operating systems.

What does the memory chip inside a cell phone do? The operating system and the information you save in your cell phone (such as phone numbers and addresses) need to be stored in memory. The operating system is stored in read-only memory (ROM) because the phone would be useless without that key piece of software. As you learned earlier, there are two kinds of memory used in computers: volatile memory, which requires power to store data, and nonvolatile memory, which stores data even when the power is turned off. ROM is nonvolatile, or permanent, memory. This means that when you turn off your phone, the data that is stored in ROM

Figure 8.4

Inside your cell phone, you'll find a CPU, a memory chip, input devices such as a microphone and a keypad, and output devices such as a display screen and a speaker.

Figure 8.5

(a) Symbian, (b) Windows Mobile, and (c) Android are all cell/smartphone operating systems.

Figure 8.6

You can insert additional memory by installing a micro SD flash card in a smartphone.

(including the operating system) remains in memory.

Other phone data, such as ring tones, is stored in separate internal memory chips. Full-featured cell phones have as many as 200 MB of internal memory (with some smartphones carrying 1 GB internally) and support additional memory through micro SD flash cards that can store up to 32 GB. Micro SD cards are easy to install in a phone, as shown in Figure 8.6, while some models simply have external slots for an SD card. You can use that storage for contact data, ring tones, images, songs, videos, and even software applications such as a language translators or video games. Not every smartphone allows memory upgrades in this way, however. For example, the iPhone series does not allow you to add any memory.

What input and output devices do cell phones use? The primary input devices for a cell phone are a microphone and a keypad. Some phones, such as the Samsung Impression (see Figure 8.7), feature both a hidden keyboard (to make sending e-mail or text messages more efficient) and a touch-sensitive screen. The Apple iPhone uses its touch-sensitive screen to offer a software-based keyboard (see Figure 8.7) that supports more than 40 languages.

Cell phones often include a digital camera for capturing photos and video. These cameras are catching up to the quality level of standalone point-and-shoot cameras. For example, the Droid Incredible offers a high-quality 8-megapixel (MP) camera with flash and video capture, and the Nokia N8 sports a 12 MP camera with Carl Zeiss lenses. Most cameras on cell phones can record video as well as take still shots. Picture and video messaging is popular with many smartphone users. They can transmit photos and video files via e-mail, post the files to Web sites such as Facebook, or send them directly to other phones.

Cell phone output devices include a speaker and a liquid crystal display (LCD). Higher-end models include full-color, high-resolution LCD screens. Newer on the market are OLED (organic light-emitting diode) displays, which allow very bright, sharp imaging and draw less power. High-resolution displays are becoming increasingly popular because more people are using their cell phones to send and receive the digital images included in multimedia text messages

Figure 8.7

(a) The Samsung Impression includes a touch screen and a built-in QWERTY keyboard. (b) The Apple iPhone has a touch keyboard that supports more than 40 languages and a range of character sets.

NBC, CBS, and PBS are testing this system.

What cell phone and smartphone software is available? Most devices come with a standard collection of software such as a to-do list, contact manager, and calendar. Modified versions of application software such as Microsoft Word, Excel, Outlook, and PowerPoint are available for some high-end smartphones. A variety of games, tools, and reference applications are available from numerous software companies. A good source to locate software applications for your phone is GetJar (**getjar.com**). Many manufacturers have Web-based software stores, like iTunes for the Apple iPhone and the BlackBerry App World for RIM's BlackBerry devices

and e-mail, and even to watch TV (see Figure 8.8). Cell phone and cable providers are teaming up to deliver broadcast TV programs directly to cell phones through services such as Verizon V Cast and Sprint TV. A developing standard named Mobile DTV allows cell/smartphones to receive free broadcasts from television stations using the Mobile DTV technology. At the time of this writing, affiliates of

SOUND BYTE Smartphones Are Really Smart

In this Sound Byte, you'll learn how to use a smartphone as a powerful tool to communicate, calculate, and organize your workload.

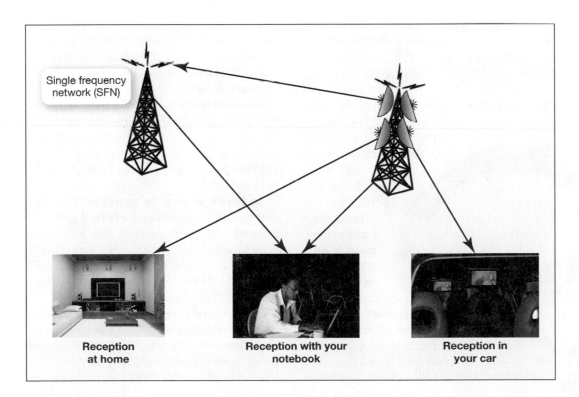

Single frequency network (SFN)

Reception at home

Reception with your notebook

Reception in your car

Figure 8.8

The Mobile DTV system allows local TV stations to broadcast live, digital content to mobile devices.

Figure 8.9

The Blackberry App World is one of many online stores delivering software for smartphones.

Figure 8.10

A USB data synch cable connects your cell phone to your computer for data transfer.

(see Figure 8.9). The Android developer community has held competitions to spur the creation of new software applications for Android-based phones. Many software applications are available for Android through the Web and the Android Market.

How do I move music from my computer to my smartphone? On the 32 GB micro SD cards available for phones, there is room for thousands of songs, videos, or data files. You can transfer files between your phone and your computer easily. Some phones are designed with a flash card that can be easily removed and slipped directly into a flash card reader on the computer. Almost all phones are designed with a USB port. Some have a mini-USB connector, while other models require a special cable to connect the phone to a standard USB port (see Figure 8.10). Once connected using a USB data cable, your phone will appear on your computer like an additional flash drive, and you can drag and drop files to it. You can also charge your phone through the USB cable.

How do I synchronize a cell phone with a computer? Cell phones let you coordinate the changes you make to your to-do lists, schedules, and other files with the files on your home or office computer. This process of updating your data so that the files on your cell phone and computer are the same is called **syncing** or **synchronizing**. To synchronize your computer and the device, simply place the cell phone in its cradle (or attach it to the computer via a USB cable) and touch a "sync" button. This begins the process of data transfer that updates both sets of files to the most current version.

Microsoft has recognized the vast increase in portable computing devices by integrating synchronization into the Windows operating system. The Sync Center (see Figure 8.11), which is accessed from the Control Panel, allows you to set up automatic or manual synchronization. Make sure the device you are trying to set up synchronization parameters for is connected to your computer and then launch the Sync Center. Select the *Set up new sync partnerships* option to view available devices and configure their synchronization options.

Can I transfer files wirelessly?
Bluetooth technology uses radio waves to transmit data signals over short distances (approximately 30 feet for Bluetooth 1 and 60 feet for Bluetooth 2 and 3). Bluetooth 3 devices are expected to hit the market by 2011, with throughput about 8 times faster than Bluetooth 2. Most cell phones on the market today are Bluetooth-enabled, meaning they include a small Bluetooth chip that allows them to transfer data wirelessly to any other Bluetooth-enabled device. One benefit Bluetooth has over infrared, a wireless connection used in the past, is that a direct line of sight does not have to be present between two devices for them to communicate. You also can use Bluetooth to synchronize your device with your computer. Bluetooth accessories such as earpieces, mice, keyboards, and even stereo headsets are now available.

Is there a way to synchronize to my home computer before I get home? Yes, a number of Web services are now available to synchronize your e-mail, files, contacts, and calendars instantly and wirelessly. These Web services follow the model of "cloud computing," where Internet-based services and resources are distributed to users instead of being installed as an application on the user's computer. Some synchronization services charge a fee, like MobileMe from Apple. For a

$99 annual fee, you can make sure the same files are always on your iPhone, your iPad, your home desktop, and your notebook computer. As soon as information is changed on one device, it is automatically "pushed" out to all the other devices, updating their files as well. If you lose your iPhone or iPad, MobileMe lets you log in and display its location on a map. You can then set a password and display a message like "Crazy day! Could you please call me and I'll come pick this up?" If you really can't locate the device, you can use MobileMe to remotely wipe all of the data from the device.

There are other providers of wireless synchronization for mobile devices. Google Sync works with iPhones, Blackberry phones, Symbian and Windows Mobile devices, and it's free. All of your Google e-mail, calendar events, and contacts are automatically backed up online instantly on the Google servers. Even the Amazon Kindle uses wireless synchronization so that if you read a bit further in your e-book on your phone, when you get to your office, the Kindle software on your PC will have automatically updated to bookmark to the new page you're on.

SOUND BYTE

Connecting with Bluetooth

In this Sound Byte, you'll learn what freedoms Bluetooth affords you, how to decide whether you want Bluetooth on equipment that you purchase, and how to use Bluetooth devices.

Text Messaging

What is text messaging? Short message service (SMS)—often just called *text messaging*—is a technology that allows you to send short text messages (comprising up to 160 characters) over mobile networks. To send SMS messages from your cell phone, you use the keypad or a pre-saved template and type your message. You can send SMS messages to other mobile devices or to any e-mail address. You also can use SMS to send short text messages from your home computer to mobile devices such as your friend's cell phone.

How does SMS work? SMS uses the cell phone network to transmit messages. When you send an SMS message, an SMS calling center receives the message and delivers it to the appropriate mobile device using something called *store-and-forward* technology. This technology allows users to send SMS messages to any other SMS device in the world.

Many SMS fans like text messaging because it allows the receivers to read messages when it is convenient for them. Companies now support texting in many ways, so for example, your bank may allow you to text commands to request account balances or details about your last transaction, and the bank will text the requested information back to you. As shown in the table in Figure 8.12, several companies provide useful services based on text messaging.

If you plan to do a lot of texting, check the phone's feature list in advance and look for a phone with a good text prediction algorithm. With such an algorithm, typing a single letter pulls up a list of popular words

Figure 8.11

The Windows Sync Center makes it easy to arrange for synchronization of all your mobile devices.

>To launch Sync Center, click the **Start** button, select **Control Panel**, and double-click the **Sync Center** icon.

Figure 8.12 | TEXT MESSAGING SERVICES

SMS Code	Service Name	Web Site	Description
466453 (google)	Google SMS	**google.com/sms**	Obtains information such as addresses, phone numbers, driving directions, sports scores, and movie listings from the Google search engine.
44636 (4Info)	4INFO	**4info.net**	Similar to Google SMS, but also handles flight information and horoscopes.
242 242 (cha cha)	ChaCha	**chacha.com**	Human "guides" provide answers to any question in conversational English.
3109043113	411sms	**411sms.com**	Offers address and phone listings, turn-by-turn directions, movie show times, stock quotes, hot spot locations, dictionary definitions, horoscopes, and foreign language translations.

beginning with that letter, saving you typing time. For example, the T9 (Text on 9 keys) algorithm also "learns" from your usage patterns and displays the most-used word first.

Can I send and receive multimedia files using a cell phone? SMS technology allows you to send only text messages. However, an extension of SMS called **multimedia message service (MMS)** allows you to send messages that include text, sound, images, and video clips to other phones or e-mail addresses. MMS messages actually arrive as a series of messages; you view the text, then the image, and then the sound, and so on. You can then choose to save just one part of the message (such as the image), all of it, or none of it. MMS users can subscribe to financial, sports, and weather services that will "push" information to them, sending it automatically to their phones in MMS format.

BITS AND BYTES

411 for Answers

Most phone services charge as much as $2.00 for a 411 call for information on a phone listing or address. Now there is competition. The Google 411 service is a free way to find out the address of, directions to, or phone number of a business or person. A call to 1-800-GOOG-411 gets you this information at no charge. If you say "text" into the phone, it kicks back a text message with the address and a map.

If you are looking for a different kind of information, try the ChaCha service. You can either call (1-800-2chacha) or text (242 242) with any kind of question, and real human "guides" will find the answer and send it back to you. So, answers to questions like the following are just a free call or text away!

- How many calories are there in a slice of pizza?
- When is *American Idol* on tonight?
- Is there a way to get acrylic paint out of jeans?

Internet Connectivity

How do I get Internet service for my smartphone? Just as you have an Internet service provider (ISP) for Internet access for your desktop or notebook computer, you must have a **wireless Internet service provider** (or **wireless ISP**) to connect your smartphone to the Internet. Phone companies that provide phone calling plans (such as T-Mobile, Verizon, and AT&T) usually double as wireless ISPs. An Internet connectivity plan or text messaging plan is usually known as a **data plan**. Data charges are separate from phone calling charges and are provided at rates different from voice calls. Most carriers provide separate plans for different levels of texting usage and for various levels of data transfer to and from Internet sites. Before subscribing to a data plan, you should assess your needs: How often do you download new wallpaper, ring tones, or games? Do you use your smartphone's Internet access to download files from e-mails or from your company Web site? Begin by estimating how many kilobytes of data you transfer up and down from the Internet each month. Then select a plan that provides adequate service at a good price.

At what speed is digital information transferred to my smartphone? A smartphone connection often is slower than the one you have at your home. Although broadband speeds of 50 megabits per second (Mbps) are achievable at home using a cable or fiber-optic connection, your smartphone will connect at a much lower speed (see Figure 8.13).

Providers have introduced many smartphones based on two standards that support faster data transfer technologies: EDGE (short for enhanced data rate for global evolution) and 3G. EDGE and 3G have brought mobile devices much faster data transfer—as high as 1.4 Mbps (or more) under ideal conditions. If you use a smartphone that supports EDGE or 3G, and have a phone plan that allows data transfer, both uploading information (such as e-mail messages that include photos) and downloading information (such as from a company intranet or the Internet) can take place much more quickly. Of course if you are in range of a WiFi signal, that is going to be a much faster transfer option. EDGE and 3G have advantages over WiFi, however. They are more reliable and less susceptible to interference. Moreover, you won't have to hunt for a WiFi hot spot, because these technologies are used to blanket major urban areas with connectivity.

4G networks are beginning to be rolled out across the United States. The promise of 4G is incredible: mobile connection speeds of up to 100 Mbps. Currently, most providers can deliver speeds of 3 Mbps to 6 Mbps. The expansion of 4G will usher in a new generation of mobile devices and applications that will continue to expand how we think of mobile computing.

How can I survive when I find I have no WiFi signal? There are devices available that will instantly create a mobile hot spot for you. MiFi (pronounced "my fi") devices, like the Verizon model shown in Figure 8.14, are often available free with a new account from major Internet providers like Verizon and Sprint. The MiFi can fit in a shirt pocket and run for up to four hours on a single charge. It connects to the Internet through the 3G wireless phone network and then distributes the WiFi signal over an area of 30 feet. These personal hot spots can then support up to five WiFi-enabled devices.

An iPhone 3G has a similar capability. It can connect to your notebook computer through wireless Bluetooth, and then provide Internet access through the 3G network signal. This "Bluetooth tethering" makes sure your computer can access the Internet even when it

Figure 8.13 | CELLULAR CONNECTION SPEEDS

Network	Availability	Connection Speed (Mbps)
Edge	13,000 cities	0.1
3G	300 major markets	0.6–2.3
WiFi	WiFi hot spots	4–5
4G	Major cities	5–12

Note: Speeds will vary depending on provider and location.

Figure 8.14

A MiFi device turns your 3G phone signal into a WiFi connection for you and four of your friends.

tells you there are no available wireless networks as long as you have 3G signal.

How do smartphones display content from the Internet? On smartphones that have a limited amount of screen space, it is difficult to view Web pages without a great deal of horizontal scrolling. This is because most Web sites are designed for viewing on desktop monitors, which have much wider pixel widths than mobile screens. To enhance your Internet browsing experience on mobile devices, special micro-browser software runs on your phone. **Microbrowser** software provides a Web browser that is optimized to display Web content effectively on the smaller screen (see Figure 8.15). Popular versions of microbrowser software include Internet Explorer Mobile (included with the Windows Mobile OS), Safari on the iPhone, and Opera Mobile. Opera Mobile uses special small-screen rendering technology to reformat the Web images to fit on your smartphone screen, then zooms in with a simple tap. For the best Web experience, consider a phone that has a large screen, such as the HTC HD2, which boasts a 4.3-inch HD touch screen.

More and more Web sites are being created with content specifically designed for wireless devices. This specially designed content, which is text based and contains no graphics, is written in a format called **Wireless Markup Language (WML)**. Content is designed so that it fits the smaller display screens of handheld mobile devices.

Can I keep my e-mail up to date using my cell phone? A popular feature of cell phones with Internet access lets users check e-mail. BlackBerry handhelds were the first devices that were optimized to check e-mail. BlackBerry pioneered the

Figure 8.15

Microbrowser software for phones like Opera lets you quickly switch between open browser windows.

"push" technology that delivers your e-mail automatically to your phone, whether you want it or not. Now many other systems also offer "push" technology. BlackBerry devices are still an excellent option, but they aren't the only option. With Internet access, users can always e-mail through Web-based e-mail accounts like Gmail or Yahoo!

If checking and sending e-mail while on the go is mission critical for you, check out smartphones with larger displays and integrated keyboards that make it easier to read and respond to messages.

Voice over Internet Protocol

Cell phone service is still not 100 percent reliable. Dropped calls and poor reception are a problem in many areas. In addition, the call quality of landline phone service is often superior to cell phone call quality. Therefore, many people who run home businesses or make business calls from their home maintain a landline to ensure high voice quality of calls. In many instances, landline phone plans can be cheaper than cell phone plans, especially for international calls. Therefore, you may want to consider a style of landline phone service called VoIP (Voice over Internet Protocol).

How is VoIP different from regular telephone service? Voice over Internet Protocol (VoIP) is a form of voice-based Internet communication that turns a standard Internet connection into a means to place phone calls, including long-distance calls. Traditional telephone communications use analog voice data and telephone connections. In contrast, VoIP uses technology similar to that used in e-mail to send your voice data digitally over the Internet.

What do I need to use VoIP? For the simplest and least costly VoIP service, you need speakers, a microphone, an Internet connection, and a VoIP provider (see Figure 8.16). Depending on the provider you choose, you also may need to install software or a special adapter. Creating a VoIP account with Skype (**skype.com**) is similar to creating an instant messaging (IM) account. Skype requires that both callers and receivers have the company's free software installed on their computers. Another similarity to IM is that with Skype you can change your online status, look at your contact list, and decide whom you want to talk to. Other VoIP services, such as Vonage

Figure 8.16

Depending on your VoIP service, you can hold conversations through a computer, a special VoIP telephone, or a regular telephone with an adapter.

advantage of VoIP is it's free or low cost. Portability is another advantage because all you need is an Internet connection. With Internet accessibility so abundant, you can keep in touch with friends and family no matter where you are. As long as you are covered by a WiFi signal, you can plug in your headset or IP phone, sign on to your VoIP service, and make your call.

Although VoIP is affordable and convenient, it does have drawbacks. Some people regard sound quality and reliability issues as VoIP's primary disadvantages. Another drawback is the loss of service if power is interrupted. Although many traditional phones do not depend on electricity, your Internet connection and IP phone do. One serious drawback when VoIP service was first offered to the public was the inability for 911 calls to be traced back to the caller, unlike with a traditional phone. The FCC now requires all VoIP providers to provide traceable 911 services.

Another issue with VoIP is security. Security risks are similar to the risks associated with e-mail (such as spam) and fraud (such as when a hacker breaks into a VoIP system to

(**vonage.com**), are a bit more complicated to set up and are not free. You can use your own telephone by connecting your phone to a special adapter that the company provides, or you can buy a special IP phone that connects to your broadband Internet connection or to a USB port on your computer.

One limitation of VoIP used to be that when you made a call, you had to be at your computer. WiFi (wireless Internet) IP phones, however, make it possible to place VoIP calls from any WiFi hot spot location. And there are Skype applications available for many mobile devices, like the iPhone and the Sony PSP. You can use these devices from any WiFi spot to make free calls to other Skype users or make low-cost calls to non-Skype users.

What are the advantages and disadvantages of VoIP? For people who make many long-distance phone calls, the

How Do You Find Your WiFi?

Detecting a nearby WiFi signal is important If you are looking for Internet connectivity while you are on the move. Some notebooks have a built-in WiFi scanner that displays a row of lights on the case whenever a WiFi signal is available. Keychain fobs that light up when they detect WiFi signals in the vicinity are also available.

If you are running Windows 7, the Connect to a Network dialog box (accessible from the Network and Sharing Center) shows the strength of all wireless networks within range of your computer.

At ThinkGeek (**thinkgeek.com**), you may find the most easy-to-use WiFi detector ever. The WiFi Detector t-shirt has a logo that lights up to indicate the signal strength of a nearby WiFi network (see Figure 8.17). Find your WiFi and look . . . well, look geeky while doing so!

Figure 8.17

The WiFi Detector T-shirt makes a statement—a geeky statement.

make unauthorized calls). These are real risks but they are avoidable if you take proper precautions. In addition, encryption services (similar to those used with e-mail) that convert data into a form that is not easily understood by unauthorized people are being deployed to help protect the very nature of calls made over the Internet. Despite these concerns, VoIP continues to enjoy explosive growth, and the technology will continue to improve.

What new features come with having an Internet-based digital phone at home? Once you are using an Internet-based digital phone system, new features become possible. You can have your telephone messages automatically bundled up as e-mails and sent to your account. If you are watching television and a call comes in, it can be displayed on the screen with caller ID information. Many cable delivery companies are bundling digital phone services in for free if you already purchase cable and television through them, so the price may be attractive.

Cell Phone/Smartphone Security

Can I get a virus on my cell/smartphone? Although viruses can already infect cell phones, manufacturers and software engineers are bracing themselves for a tidal wave of viruses targeted to cell/smartphones. With half of users reporting that they send confidential e-mails using their phones and one-third of users indicating that they access bank account or credit card information, cell/smartphones are the next most likely realm of attack by cybercriminals. The potential of cell/smartphone

"How do I keep my cell/smartphone number private?"

viruses ranges from the mildly annoying (certain features of your phone stop working) to the expensive (your phone is used without your knowledge to make expensive calls).

Symantec, McAfee, and F-Secure are the leading companies currently providing antivirus software for mobile devices. Products are designed for specific cell phone operating systems; for example, Symantec Mobile Security for Symbian is designed for cell phones running the Symbian OS. Often businesses will have their information technology department install and configure an antivirus solution like this for all the phones used in the organization. Although viruses plaguing cell phones have not yet reached the volume of viruses attacking PC operating systems, with the proliferation of mobile devices it is expected that such virus attacks will increase. If no antivirus program is available for your phone's operating system, the best precautions are common sense ones. Check the phone manufacturer's Web site frequently to see whether your cell/smartphone needs any software upgrades that could patch security holes. In addition, remember that you should not download ring tones, games, or other software from unfamiliar Web sites.

How do I keep my cell/smartphone number private? It seems that every time you fill out a Web form someone is asking for your phone number. If you are concerned about widely distributing your cell/smartphone number and potentially inviting lots of unwanted solicitation calls, you should consider using a virtual phone number. A virtual phone number is a phone number you create that can be assigned to ring on existing phone numbers (such as your cell phone). Companies such as Telusion (**tossabledigits.com**) provide these virtual numbers. Then, when you are filling out a registration form for some Web service, you can input your virtual phone number in the Web form instead of giving out your number. When you set up the virtual account, you can restrict the hours that you will receive calls from that number (no more 2 a.m. telemarketing calls), and if you are receiving many unwanted calls, you can disable the virtual number without affecting your cell/smartphone service.

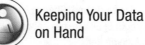

ACTIVE HELP-DESK Keeping Your Data on Hand

In this Active Helpdesk call, you'll play the role of a helpdesk staffer, fielding calls about smartphones—what you can use them for, what internal components and features they have, and how you can synchronize these mobile devices with your computer.

Digital Media and Information

The entertainment industry has become an all-digital field. Today, videos, music, and photographs are created using digital recording devices, processed using digital software systems, and delivered over digital distribution channels. What does this mean for you and your use of music, photography, and video?

How is digital media created? All digital media, whether an image, a song, or a video, has the same basis—digitized information. Figure 8.18 shows the process of creating digital information for a musical selection. This process is described below:

1. Playing music creates analog waves.

2. A microphone feeds the sound waves into a chip called an *analog-to-digital converter (ADC)* inside the recording device.

3. The ADC digitizes the waves into a series of numbers.

4. This series of numbers can be recorded onto CDs and DVDs or sent electronically.

5. On the receiving end, a playback device such as a CD player or DVD player is fed that same series of numbers. Inside the playback device is a digital-to-analog converter (DAC), a chip that converts the digital numbers to a continuous analog wave.

6. That analog wave tells the receiver how to move the speaker cones to reproduce the original waves, resulting in the same sound as the original.

More precisely, the digital wave will be *close* to exact. How accurate it is, or how close the digitized wave is in shape to the original analog wave, depends on the sampling rate of the ADC. The **sampling rate** specifies the number of times the analog wave is measured each second. The higher the sampling rate, the more accurately the original wave can be re-created. However, higher sampling rates also produce much more data, and therefore result in bigger files. For example, sound waves on CDs are sampled at a rate of approximately 44,000 times a second. This produces a huge list of numbers for even a single minute of a song!

When sounds or image waves are digitized, it means that analog data is changed into digital data—from a wave into a series of numbers. The digital data is perfectly reproducible and can be distributed easily on CDs and DVDs or through the airwaves. The data also can be easily processed by a computer.

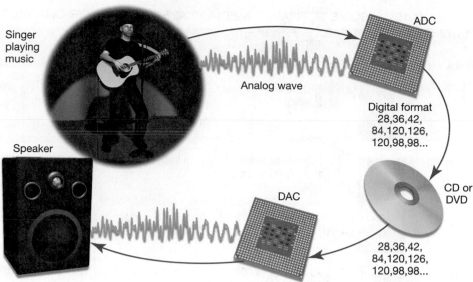

Figure 8.18

During the complete recording process, information changes from analog form to digital data and then back again to analog sound waves.

Digital Music

How can I carry music files easily? **Portable media players (PMPs)** are small portable devices (such as an iPod) that enable you to carry your MP3 files around with you. Many PMPs handle video and still images, as well as music files. Many smartphones are capable of storing and playing media files, but for the best experience, a dedicated media player, such as a portable media player, is often the optimal choice because PMPs tend to offer more features and storage.

Depending on the player, you can carry several hours of music or video—or possibly your entire CD collection—in an incredibly small device. For example, an Apple iPod classic with a 160 GB hard drive is 4.1 inches by 2.4 inches (and only 0.41 inch thick), yet it can hold as many as 40,000 songs, or 200 hours of video. The most compact players are slightly larger than a flash drive

Figure 8.19 | SOME PORTABLE MEDIA PLAYERS AND THEIR CHARACTERISTICS

	Media Capacity	Built-In Flash Memory	Hard Drive Capacity	Connection to Computer	Other Features
Sansa Fuze Player	2000 songs or 24 hours of video	2 GB to 8 GB	None but 16 GB micro SD card supported	USB 2.0 port	FM radio, voice recorder and available "radio" cards prefilled with 1000 songs.
Zune HD	As many as 16,000 songs or 20 hours of HD video	16 to 64 GB	None	USB 2.0 port or wireless	Has HD radio, OLED screen, multitouch navigation.
Apple iPod touch	As many as 14,000 songs or 80 hours of video	8 GB to 64 GB	None	USB 2.0 port	Weighs only 4.05 ounces; flash memory enables skip-free playback.
Apple iPod classic	As many as 40,000 songs or 200 hours of video	None	160 GB	USB 2.0 port	Has calendar feature that syncs with Outlook; can serve as a small, portable hard drive.
Archos 7	As many as 2,000 songs or 24 hours of video	2 GB to 8 GB	None but 32 GB SDHC card supported	USB 2.0 port	Includes 7" screen display, WiFi, and touch screen.

(although they hold far less music than the iPod). Figure 8.19 shows several models of PMPs, all of which connect to computers via USB 2.0 ports.

Are all music files MP3 files? The letters at the end of a file name (the file extension) indicate how the data in the file is organized. MP3 is the name of just one type of file format used to store digital music, but many others exist, such as AAC and WMA. There are also many video formats such as DivX, MPEG-4 (which usually has an .mp4 extension), WMV, and XviD. All file formats compete on sound and video quality and *compression*, which relates to how small the file can be and still provide high-quality playback. If you buy a song from the iTunes Music Store, for example, you receive an .aac format file. AAC files can be played only on iPods but can be converted to the more widely used MP3 or Windows Media Audio (WMA) formats. WMA files can be played on a wide variety of MP3 players. Most PMPs that support video playback can play a wide range of video formats.

Are PMP devices the only choice for portable media management? PMP devices are not the only choice for portable media management. A number of electronic devices now incorporate the capability to carry electronic files and play music and video files. Some models of digital cameras, such as the Samsung NV3, have support for playing both music and videos. Gaming devices such as the Sony PlayStation Portable (PSP) allow you to play video games, play music and videos, and browse the Internet.

How do I know how much digital media a PMP can hold? The number of songs or hours of video a portable media player can hold depends on how much storage space it has. Most PMPs use built-in **flash memory**, a type of nonvolatile memory, to store files. Most PMPs that support video use a hard drive instead of flash memory and can store a much greater amount of music and video. Less expensive PMPs use flash memory (ranging from 1 GB to 32 GB), whereas models that are more expensive use built-in hard drives, which provide as much as 160 GB of storage. Some of the PMPs that use flash memory allow you to add storage capacity by purchasing removable flash memory cards.

Another factor that determines how much music a player can hold is the quality of the MP3 music files. The size of an MP3 file depends on the digital sampling of the song. The same song could be sampled at 320 kbps or 64 kbps. The size of the song file will be five times larger if it is sampled at 320 kbps rather than the lower sampling rate of 64 kbps. The higher the sampling rate, the better quality the sound—but the larger the file size.

How do you control the size of an MP3 file? If you are *ripping*, or converting, a song from a CD into a digital MP3 file, you can select the sampling rate yourself. You decide by considering what quality sound you want, as well as how many songs you want to fit onto your MP3 player. For example, if your player had 1 GB of storage and you have ripped songs at 192 kbps, you could fit about 694 minutes of music onto the player. The same 1 GB could store 2,083 minutes of music if it were sampled at 64 kbps. Whenever you are near your computer, you can connect your player and download a different set of songs, but you always are limited by the amount of storage your player has.

What if I want to store more music or video than the memory on my PMP allows? Some PMPs allow you to add memory by inserting removable flash memory cards. Flash memory cards are quiet and light, use tiny amounts of power, and slide into a special slot in the player. If you've ever played a video game on PlayStation or Xbox and saved your progress to a memory card, then you have used flash memory. Because flash memory is nonvolatile, when you store data on a flash memory card, you won't lose it when you turn off the player. In addition, flash memory can be erased and rewritten with new data. PMPs use a variety of different types of flash cards. Check your manual and then review the coverage on flash media in Chapter 2 for more details.

How do I transfer media files to my portable media player? All portable media players come with software that enables you to transfer audio and video files from your computer to the player. As noted earlier, players that hold thousands of songs and hours of video use internal hard drives to store the files. For example, devices such as Apple iPods can hold several gigabytes of data. To move large volumes of data between your computer and your PMP, you want a high-speed port. Most PMPs use a USB 2.0 port, but some players may use FireWire ports, which provide comparable throughput. Using a USB 2.0 port, you can transfer two dozen MP3 files to the iPod in less than 10 seconds.

What if I want a lot of people to listen to my digital music? PMPs are great for individual listening, but to share music from a PMP, you have to connect it to an alternative device. Many audio receivers now come with a port or a dock so that you can connect a PMP device directly to them as another audio input source, like a CD player or a television. Most new cars are equipped with at least an auxiliary input to the speaker system to support connecting a PMP; others have a fully integrated software system that displays and runs the PMP playlists. There are alarm clocks and home speaker docks that can mate with a PMP and broadcast brilliant sound.

How did the shift to digital music impact the music industry? The initial MP3 craze was fueled by sites such as MP3.com, which originally stored its song

> **"Audio receivers now come with a port to connect a PMP device directly."**

ACTIVE HELP-DESK

Using Portable Media Players

In this Active Helpdesk call, you'll play the role of a helpdesk staffer, fielding calls about portable media players, what they can carry, and how they store data.

files on a public server with the permission of the original artists or recording companies. Therefore, you were not infringing on a copyright by downloading songs from sites such as MP3.com (which still exists and now provides free music in streaming format).

Napster was a file exchange site created to correct some of the annoyances found by users of MP3.com. One such annoyance was the limited availability of popular music in MP3 format. With the MP3 sites, if you found a song you wanted to download, the link to the site on which the file was found often no longer worked. Napster differed from MP3.com because songs or locations of songs were not stored in a central public server, but instead were "borrowed" directly from other users' computers. This process of users transferring files between computers is referred to as **peer-to-peer (P2P) sharing**. Napster also provided a search engine dedicated to finding specific MP3 files. This direct search and sharing eliminated the inconvenience of searching links only to find them unavailable.

The problem with Napster was that it was so good at what it did. Napster's convenient and reliable mechanism to find and download popular songs in MP3 format became a huge success. The rapid acceptance and use of Napster—at one point, it had nearly 60 million users—led the music

industry to sue the site for copyright infringement, and Napster was closed in June 2002. Napster has since reopened as a music site that sells music downloads and is sanctioned by the recording industry.

The reaction of the recording industry was to continue to enforce its absolute ownership over digital forms of its music. The industry even filed legal actions against individuals who had downloaded large amounts of music from Internet sites. This heavy-handed reaction to the new era of digital music ultimately backfired and left the music industry scrambling. Overall music sales in 2009 were about half what they were at the industry's peak. The record industry is still trying to counter losing CD sales to digital forms of music. The approach they took early on did not allow them to adapt quickly enough to the new business models required by the shift to digital technologies.

So if I don't pay for a music download, is it illegal? Although you need to pay for most music you download, some artists post songs for free. Business models are still evolving as artists and recording companies try to meet audience needs while also protecting their own intellectual property rights. Several different approaches exist. One is to deliver something called *tethered downloads* in which you pay for the music and own it, but are subject to restrictions on its use.

Another approach is to offer *DRM-free* music, which is music without any digital rights management. These song files can be moved freely from system to system. For example, Apple's iTunes store currently sells only DRM-free types of music. A DRM-free song can be placed on as many computers or players as you wish. Other sites offer subscription services. For a monthly fee, Napster to Go allows you to download as many songs as you like to your MP3 player. These songs will be usable, however, only as long as you are paying the monthly subscription fee.

Why buy any music if peer-to-peer (P2P) sharing sites are still operating? When Napster was going through its legal turmoil, other P2P Web sites were quick to take advantage of a huge opportunity. Napster was "easy" to shut down because it used a central index server that queried other Napster computers for requested songs. Current P2P protocols (such as LimeWire and BearShare) differ

BITS AND BYTES

Trick Out Your iTouch

With more than 1 billion iTouch/iPhone apps downloaded, the App Store is a proven success. Some apps are games, some are just gimmicks, but many are great tools for a student. iFlipr is an app that connects you to 2.7 million flash cards. You can study for the MCAT exam or build and share your own custom flash card deck. iHomework organizes your teacher contact info, due dates for assignments, and research materials. iProRecorder lets your iTouch record audio using the mic built into the earphones that come with it. Can't find the app you are dreaming of? The iPhone Developer University program is free and supports students and faculty in designing and coding Web apps.

from Napster in that they do not limit themselves to sharing only MP3 files. Video files are obtainable easily on P2P sites. More importantly, these sites don't have a central index server. Instead, they operate in a true P2P sharing environment in which computers connect directly to other computers. This makes them a prime source of unwanted viruses and spyware.

The argument these P2P networks make to defend their legality is that they do not run a central server like the original Napster, but only facilitate connections between users. Therefore, they have no control over what the users choose to trade. Note that not all P2P file sharing is illegal. For example, it is legal to trade photos or movies you have created with other folks over a P2P site.

People who oppose such file-sharing sites contend that the sites know their users are distributing files illegally and breaking copyright laws. Be aware that having illegal content on your computer, deliberately or by accident, is a criminal offense in many jurisdictions.

Will PMPs eliminate radio stations? Radio stations have always had certain advantages: early access to new music, and personalities and conversations that add to the listening experience. However, the Internet allows artists to release new songs to their fans immediately (on sites such as mp3.com) and without relying on radio airtime. This opens up new channels for artists to reach an audience and changes the amount of power radio stations have in the promotion of music. Many radio stations have increased listenership by making their stations available through Internet sites and by broadcasting in high-definition quality.

Another development that competes with radio (and television) is *podcasting*, which allows users to download audio and video content and then listen to those broadcasts on their PMPs whenever they want. Podcasting is paving the way for anyone to create a radio or television show at home and distribute it easily to an audience. Using free software such as Audacity (**audacity.sourceforge.net**) and a microphone, you can record voice-overs, sequence songs, and generate special effects for your recordings. Loyal fans can use podcasting software such as Juice (**juicereceiver.sourceforge.net**) or iTunes (for Windows or Mac) to find a podcast's latest episode and automatically transfer it to their portable media players. Plugging your iPod into a data port on your computer causes the iPod to search iTunes for new content from the podcasters you subscribe to and then automatically transfers the new files to your iPod. Podcasts are easy to subscribe to and download using iTunes (see Figure 8.20).

Digital Navigation

How has digitized information impacted navigation? In the last few years, stand-alone **GPS (global positioning system)** devices have dropped dramatically in price and size. Small, handheld units deliver turn-by-turn instructions and real-time traffic information. GPS units are available with a wide range of features.

Garmin, for example, offers a wide range of services on its line of GPS units. A Map

Figure 8.20

iTunes makes it easy to subscribe to and manage podcasts.

GARMIN nüvi

Figure 8.21

In addition to the driving applications shown, the Garmin Nuvi series GPS devices are also able to provide Internet services.

mode displays your location and the current speed limit on a map that is updated in real time as you drive. When you enter a series of destinations, an optimal route is developed for you. A voice warns you of lane changes and approaching turns, giving you directions using the actual street name (such as "Turn right on Hancock Avenue"). Lane Assist flips into a 3D display mode and shows you how to navigate through lane changes in highway merges. If you miss a turn, the unit automatically recalculates the required route and gives you directions to get back on course. Flip to another screen, and it shows you how far you have to drive to the next gas station, restaurant, or hospital. Some models automatically mark the location of your car when you remove them from the vehicle, and can give you step-by-step directions back to your car.

How do I get GPS in my car? Most automotive companies now offer GPS systems as installed options in their vehicles. Of course, GPS navigation can be added to any vehicle using a portable GPS device or a PDA/smartphone equipped with GPS (see Figure 8.21), or by adding GPS software and accessories to your notebook.

How does the GPS system work? Built and operated by the U.S. Department of Defense, the global positioning system is a network of 21 satellites (plus 3 working spares) that constantly orbits the Earth. GPS devices use an antenna to pick up the signals from these satellites and use special software to transform those signals into latitude and longitude. Using the information obtained from the satellites, GPS devices determine the geographical location anywhere on the planet to within 3 feet (see Figure 8.22). The exact accuracy depends on such things as atmospheric conditions, and interference from obstacles like mountains or buildings. Because they provide such detailed positioning information, GPS devices are now used as navigational aids for aircraft, recreational boats, and automobiles, and they even come in handheld models for hikers.

If I don't have a GPS, how does the 911 system know where I am? By the end of 2005, every cell phone had to include a GPS chip. The Federal Communications Commission (FCC) mandated this to enable the complete rollout of the Enhanced 911 (E911) program. E911 automatically gives dispatchers precise location information for any 911 call. It also means your

Figure 8.22

GPS computes your location anywhere on Earth from a system of orbiting satellites.

phone records may include this precise tracking information, which indicates where you are when you make a call.

Can I use the GPS chip on a child's cell phone? Cellular phone providers offer plans (for a monthly fee) that allow you to track where a phone is at any given time via a Web site. For example, AT&T's service Family Maps allows parents to track all of the phones on their family plan in real time. Locations of all phones are displayed over the Web on a map, or the service will send an automatic text message alert with the phone's location at a specific time each day. So a parent could have a text or e-mail sent with their daughter's phone location each day at 3 p.m. to be sure the she made it home from school. The person being tracked cannot turn off the service.

Do GPS devices carry other information? Full-featured GPS models such as the Garmin Nuvi 705 series include MP3 players, audio book players, and the capability to display photos and connect to the Internet. Using Internet services such as MSN Direct, your GPS can keep you informed about the weather, traffic backups, local movie times, and even local gas prices.

Digital Photography

What is "analog" photography?

Before digital cameras hit the market, most people used some form of 35-mm single-lens reflex (SLR) camera. When you take a picture using a traditional SLR camera, a shutter opens, creating an aperture (a small window in the camera) that allows light to hit the 35-mm film inside. Chemicals coating the film react when exposed to light. Later, additional chemicals develop the image on the film, and the image is printed on special light-sensitive paper. A variety of lenses and processing techniques, special equipment, and filters are needed to create printed photos from traditional SLR cameras.

What is different about digital photography? Digital cameras do not use film. Instead, they capture images on electronic sensors called *charge-coupled device (CCD) arrays* and then convert those images to digital data, long series of

numbers that represent the color and brightness of millions of points in the image. Unlike traditional cameras, digital cameras allow you to see your images the instant you shoot them. Most camera models can now record digital video as well as digital photos.

How do I select a digital camera? With hundreds of models to choose from, where do you begin? The first question to answer is whether you want a compact "point-and-shoot" model camera or a more serious digital SLR. The larger digital SLR cameras allow you to switch among different lenses and offer features important to serious amateur and professional photographers (such as depth-of-field previewing). Although having such flexibility in moving up to a larger zoom lens is a great advantage, these cameras are also larger, heavier, and use more battery power than the tiny point-and-shoot models. Think about how you will be using your camera and decide which model will serve you best in the long run.

"What is smile shutter?"

Next, you'll want to evaluate the quality of the camera on a number of levels. One great resource to use is Digital Photography Review (**dpreview.com**). The site's camera reviews evaluate a camera's construction as well as its features, image quality, ease of use, and value for the cost. In addition, the site provides comparisons to similar camera models by other manufacturers and feedback from owners of those models. Links are provided to several resellers, making it easy to compare prices as well.

Why not just use the camera on my cell/smartphone? Many cell/smartphones include a digital camera. These cameras often provide lower resolutions than stand-alone models and inferior lenses. Many features that photographers rely on are not often available in the cameras included on phones, such as different types of autofocus, image stabilization algorithms, and *smile shutter*, which waits to take a shot until your subject is smiling.

What determines the image quality of a digital camera? The overall image quality is determined by many factors: the quality of the lenses used, the file format and compression used, and the color management software. Another part of what determines the image quality of a digital camera is its **resolution**, or the number of data points it records for each image captured. A digital camera's resolution is measured in megapixels (MP). The prefix *mega* is short for millions. The word *pixel* is short for picture element, which is a single dot in a digital image. Point-and-shoot models typically offer resolutions from 10 MP to 15 MP. Professional digital SLR cameras, such as the Canon EOS-5D Mark II, can take photos at resolutions as high as 21.1 MP, but they sell for thousands of dollars. Figure 8.23 shows some popular digital camera models and the number of pixels they record at their maximum resolution.

If you're interested in making only 5" × 7" or 8" × 10" prints, a lower-resolution camera is fine. However, low-resolution images become grainy and pixelated when pushed to make larger-size prints. For example, if you tried to print an 11" × 14" enlargement from a 2 MP image taken using your cell phone's camera, the image would look grainy; you would see individual dots of color instead of a clear, sharp image. The 10 MP to 15 MP cameras on the market now have plenty of resolution to guarantee sharp, detailed images even with enlargements as big as 11" × 14".

Figure 8.23

Digital camera resolutions.

Panasonic Lumix G2 (12.1 MP)

Kodak V1273 (12 MP)

Canon EOS 5D Mark II (21.1 MP)

Sony Cybershot DSC-T1 (10.2 MP)

Samsung TL225 DualView (12.2 MP)

What file formats are used for digital images? To fit more photos on the same size of flash memory card, digital cameras allow you to choose from several different file types in order to compress, or squeeze, the image data into less memory space. When you choose to compress your images, you will lose some of the detail, but in return, you'll be able to fit more images on your flash card. The most common file types supported by digital cameras are raw uncompressed data (RAW) and Joint Photographic Experts Group (JPEG). Raw files have different formats and extensions depending on the manufacturer of a particular camera. The raw file records all of the original image information, so it is larger than a compressed JPEG file. JPEG files can be compressed just a bit, keeping most of the details, or compressed a great deal, losing some detail. Most cameras allow you to select from a few different JPEG compression levels.

Often cameras also support a very low-resolution storage option, enabling you to create files that you can easily attach to e-mail messages. This low-resolution setting typically provides images that are not useful for printing but are so small in size that they are easily e-mailed. Even people who have slow Internet connections are able to quickly download and view such images on-screen.

How do I move photos to my computer? If you just want to print your photos, you may not need to transfer them to your computer. Many photo printers can make prints directly from your camera or from a flash memory card, and many retailers, like CVS and Walmart, provide photo printing machines that can read directly from your memory card. However, transferring the photos to your computer does allow you to store them and frees your flash card for reuse.

Digital cameras have a built-in USB 2.0 port. Using a USB 2.0 cable, you can connect the camera to your computer and copy the converted images as uncompressed files or in a compressed format as JPEG files. Another option is to transfer the flash card from your camera directly to the built-in memory card reader on your computer. Some camera

Figure 8.24

Scanners are available in a variety of shapes, but all of them can convert paper documents, photo prints, and strips of film negatives into digital data.

models support wireless network connections so that you can transfer the images without the fuss of putting a cable in place. If your model doesn't, you can purchase a memory card with built-in WiFi: the Eye-Fi. Eye-Fi will wirelessly transfer your photos to Google Picasa, Facebook, or one of 30 other Web destinations. It will also back up the photos and videos you take with your camera to your home computer. And when you are away from home, Eye-Fi comes with hot spot access so you can upload for free from any McDonald's, Starbucks, hotel, or airport.

Can I make my old photos digital?   Obviously, not every document or image you have is in an electronic form. What about all the photographs you have already taken? What about an article from a magazine or a hand-drawn sketch? How can these be converted into digital format?

Digital scanners such as the ones shown in Figure 8.24 convert paper text and images into digital formats. You can place any flat material on the glass surface of the scanner and convert it into a digital file. Most scanner software allows you to store the converted images as TIFF files or in compressed form as JPEG files. Some scanners include hardware that allows you to scan film negatives or slides as well or even insert a stack of photos to be scanned in sequence.

Scanner quality is measured by its resolution, which is given in dots per inch (dpi). Most modern scanners can digitize a document at resolutions as high as $4,800 \times 9,600$ dpi, in either color or grayscale mode. You can easily connect a scanner to your computer using USB 2.0 or FireWire ports. Scanners also typically come with software that supports optical character recognition (OCR). OCR software converts pages of handwritten or typed text into electronic files. You can then open and edit these converted documents with traditional word processing programs such as Microsoft Word. In addition, many scanners have a copy function that allows you to scan and print documents, taking the place of a copy machine.

How do I print a digital image?   You can print a digital image using a professional service or your own printer. Most photo printing labs, including the film processing departments at stores such as Walmart and Target, offer digital printing services, as do many high-end online processing labs. The paper and ink used at processing labs are higher quality than what is available for home use and produce heavier, glossier prints that won't fade. You can send your digital photos directly to local merchants such as CVS and Walgreens for printing using Windows Live Photo Gallery. Online services, such as Flickr (**flickr.com**) and Shutterfly (**shutterfly.com**), store your images and allow you to organize them into photo albums or to create hard-copy prints, mugs, T-shirts, or calendars.

Photo printers for home use are available in two technologies: inkjet and dye sublimation (see Figure 8.25). The most popular and inexpensive ones are inkjet printers. As noted in Chapter 2, some inkjet printers are capable of printing high-quality color photos, although they vary in speed and quality. Some include a display window so that you can review the image as you stand at the printer, whereas others are portable, allowing you to print your photos wherever you are. Some printers even allow you to crop the image right at the printer without having to use special image editing software.

Figure 8.25

The Sony DPP-F700 is both a 7-inch digital frame and a dye sublimation printer. With a click of the remote, you can print the image in 45 seconds.

Unlike inkjet printers, which use an inkjet nozzle, dye-sublimation printers produce images using a heating element. The heating element passes over a ribbon of translucent film that has been dyed with bands of colors. Depending on the temperature of the element, dyes are vaporized from a solid into a gas. The gas vapors penetrate the photo paper before they cool and return to solid form, producing glossy, high-quality images. If you're interested in a printer to use for printing only photographs, a dye-sublimation printer is a good choice. However, some models print only specific photo sizes, such as 4" × 6" prints, so be sure the printer you buy will fit your long-term needs.

Transferring images to a printer is similar to transferring them to your computer. If you have a direct-connection camera, you can plug the camera directly into the printer with a cable. Some printers have slots that accept different types of flash memory cards. Of course, you also can transfer your images to the printer from your computer if you have stored them there.

Do I need to print out my photos?
You may decide not to print your photos at all. As noted earlier, online albums let you share your photos without having to print them. There are a number of digital scrapbooking sites that let you electronically design scrapbooks. Portable devices, such as Apple's iPod and cell phones, also enable you to carry and display your photos. The iPod, for example, can be connected to a TV and deliver slide shows of your photographs, complete with musical soundtracks you have selected. As we mentioned in Chapter 7, if you have networked your home, a television connected to your network (or to a network-enabled device like a PlayStation 3 or a networked Blu-ray player) can display all the photos and videos stored on your computer.

Digital Video

Where does digital video come from?
Digital video that you watch comes from several sources, but now people often create their own digital videos. As a video creator, you may purchase dedicated digital camcorders to record digital video. Most cell phones can record video, and digital cameras take video as well as digital still shots. Webcams also work as inexpensive devices for creating digital video.

There are many other sources of digital video available to you now. Television is broadcasting in digitally formatted signals. The Internet delivers a huge amount of digital video through Google Video, YouTube, communities like Vimeo (**vimeo.com**), and webcasting sites like Ustream (**ustream.tv**). Sites like Hulu (**hulu.com**) rebroadcast many current television shows as well as films and movie trailers. Many pay services are available to deliver digital video to you. These include on-demand streaming from cable providers, iTunes, Netflix's Instant Watch films, and Amazon's Video On Demand download service.

How do I record my own digital video? Video equipment for home use stores information in a digital video (DV) format. This allows the cameras to be incredibly small and light. Such cameras don't require any tapes at all; they store hours of video on built-in hard drives or flash cards. Some models even record directly to DVD discs.

You can easily transfer video files to your computer and, using video editing software, edit the video at home, cutting out sections, resequencing segments, and adding titles. To do the same with analog videotape would require expensive and complex audio/video equipment available only in video production studios. You can save (or *write*) your final product on a CD or DVD and play it in your home DVD system or on your computer. For true videophiles, cameras and burners are now available for high-definition video format.

What if I decide to add some special effects and a sound track? Video editing software presents a storyboard or *timeline* with which you can manipulate your video file, as shown in Figure 8.26. You can review your clips frame by frame or trim them at any point. You can order each segment on the timeline in whichever sequence you like and correct segments for color balance, brightness, or contrast.

In addition, you can add transitions to your video such as those you're used to seeing on TV—fades to black, dissolves, and so on. Just select the type of transition you want from the drop-down list and drag that icon into the timeline where you want the transition to occur.

Video editing software also lets you add titles, animations, and audio tracks to your video, including background music, sound effects, and additional narration. You can adjust the volume of each audio track to switch from one to the other or have both

playing together. Finally, you can preview all of these effects in real time.

There is a lot to learn about digital video editing, and with the number of choices available, it is easy to be overwhelmed. Examine online tutorial resources such as Izzy Video podcasts (**izzyvideo.com**) to learn how to make the most impact with the editing and effects you apply to your raw video footage.

What kinds of files will I end up with? Once you're done editing your video file, you can save (or export) it in a variety of formats. Figure 8.27 shows some of the popular video file formats in use today, along with the file extensions they use.

Effects Transitions Titles Themes Clip Art

Video track
Audio track
Music track

Figure 8.26

Adobe Premiere Elements allows you to build a movie from video clips and add sound tracks and special effects.

Figure 8.27 | TYPICAL FILE FORMATS FOR DIGITAL VIDEO

Format	File Extension	Notes
QuickTime	.mov .qt	You can download QuickTime player without charge from **apple.com/quicktime**. The pro version allows you to build your own QuickTime files.
Moving Picture Experts Group (MPEG)	.mpg .mpeg .mp4	MPEG-4 video standard adopted internationally in 2000; recognized by most video player software.
Windows Media Video	.wmv	Microsoft file format recognized by Windows Media Player (included with the Windows OS).
Microsoft Video for Windows	.avi	Microsoft file format recognized by Windows Media Player (included with the Windows OS).
RealMedia	.rm	Format from RealNetworks; popular for streaming video. You can download the player for free at **real.com**.
Adobe Flash Video	.flv	Adobe Flash video format, sometimes embedded in Shockwave files (*.swf).

So you just returned from your trip to the Grand Canyon and all your friends are raving about the quality of the photographs you took. You decide to put the photographs out on Flickr so your friends can see them. You also think that maybe someone might see your photos and want to use them in a commercial publication such as a magazine. Because you own the copyright to your photos, you control how they can be used—and you want to protect your rights. You add a disclaimer to Flickr indicating that all rights are reserved on your photos. Anyone who wants to use them will need to contact you and request permission.

All of a sudden, you are bombarded by dozens of requests for permission to use your photographs for all sorts of purposes. A high school student in Illinois wants to feature one of your photos on her travel blog. A church in Georgia wants to use a photo for their newsletter to illustrate a story about a church member's trip to Arizona. An advertising agency in Seattle wants to modify your sunrise photo by inserting a family on a camping trip into the photo. You want to be ethical and protect your ownership rights as well (maybe the ad agency might even pay you!), but how are you going to manage all these photo permission requests?

Copyleft, a play on the word copyright, is designed for this situation. Copyleft is a term for various licensing plans that enables copyright holders to grant certain rights to the work while retaining other rights. The GNU General Public License is a popular copyleft license that is used for software. For other works, the Creative Commons, a nonprofit organization, has developed a range of licenses that can be used to control rights to works.

Creative Commons has various types of licenses available based on the rights you wish to grant. The company provides a simple form to assist you with selecting the proper license for your work. Creative Commons provides two licenses at **creativecommons.org/about/licenses** that could simplify your life. An *attribution license* permits others to copy, distribute, and display your copyrighted work, but only if they give you credit in the way you specify. Under this license, the high school student could use one of your photos as long as he or she gave you credit.

A *noncommercial license* allows anyone to copy, distribute, and display your work, but only for noncommercial purposes. The church in Georgia could use one of your photos under this license because it is not profiting from its use.

Both of these licenses can also be used to cover **derivative works**. A derivative work is based on the original work (one of your photos) but is modified in some way. The ad agency that wants to modify one of your photos is seeking permission to create a derivative work. If you had used an attribution license, the ad agency could use your work for a derivative purpose, but only if it attributed the original work to you as the author. If you had used a noncommercial license, the ad agency could not use your work to make a profit for itself.

The obvious advantage to using these Creative Commons licenses is that people won't constantly annoy you with permission requests to use your work. These licenses explain exactly how you are willing to have your work be used. Also, many advocates of copyleft policies feel that creativity is encouraged when people are free to modify other people's work instead of worrying about infringing on copyright.

Opponents of Creative Commons licenses often complain that these licenses have affected their livelihoods. If millions of images are out on Flickr with Creative Commons licenses that permit free commercial use, professional photographers might have a tougher time selling their work. Furthermore, Creative Commons licenses are irrevocable. If you make a mistake and select the wrong license for your work, or you later find out a work is valuable and you've already selected a license that allows commercial use, you're out of luck.

Many people find listings of Creative Commons licenses confusing. If there is a Creative Commons disclaimer at the bottom of a group of photos, does that mean all the photos are available under that license, or just some of them? What actually constitutes commercial use? Is displaying Google Adsense ads on your blog commercial use?

Each of us needs to carefully consider the value of our intellectual property and decide how best to conduct our digital livelihood. Understanding the meaning of copyright, and copyleft, is important both so that you respect the rights of others and so that you can simplify your life in granting permission rights to the works you create.

Your choice of file format for your finished video will depend on what you want to do with your video. For example, the QuickTime streaming file format is a great choice if your file is really large and you plan to post it on the Web. The Microsoft AVI format is a good choice if you're sending your file to a wide range of users, because it's extremely popular and is commonly accepted as the standard video format for the Windows Media Player.

You also can try different compression choices to see which one does a better job of compressing your particular file. A **codec** (*co*mpression/*dec*ompression) is a rule, implemented in either software or hardware, that squeezes the same audio and video information into less space. Some information will be lost using compression, and there are several different codecs to choose from, each claiming better performance than its competitors. Commonly used codecs include MPEG-4, H.264, and DivX. There is no one codec that is always superior—a codec that works well for a simple interview may not do a good job compressing a live-action scene.

What if I want a DVD with a menuing system? If you want a DVD with a menuing system, you can use special DVD authoring software such as Pinnacle Studio or Adobe Encore DVD. These DVD software packages often include preset selections for producing video for mobile devices (like the Apple iPod or the Sony PSP). These programs can also create final DVDs that have animated menu systems and easy navigation controls, allowing the viewer to move quickly from one movie or scene to another. Home DVD players as well as gaming systems such as PlayStation and Xbox can read these DVDs.

What is the quickest way to get my video out to viewers? Because of the popularity of videos on the Web, products and services are now available that let you quickly upload your videos. One such product is the Flip SlideHD video camcorder, shown in Figure 8.28.

Flip camcorders, which are priced from $150, can record 1–4 hours of video depending on the model. After recording, simply flip out the USB connector and plug it into your computer. Flip has built-in software that lets you transfer the video file directly to YouTube or several other sites or e-mail the file. It's a simple solution that takes advantage of the easy Web-based distribution of video.

YouTube has a special Mobile Upload Profile that you can set up for your account. Once your unique e-mail address has been assigned, you can submit a video that you have on your phone to YouTube by e-mailing the file to the account address. Of course, it is illegal for you to upload videos you do not own. You also cannot take a piece of a copyrighted video and post it publicly. The Ethics in IT section in this chapter presents several legal and ethical situations that it is important for you to be aware of as a content creator in the digital age.

Webcasting, or broadcasting your video live to an audience, is another option that has become simpler. Inexpensive webcams (costing from $25 to $100) can be easily attached to your desktop or notebook computer. Many models of monitors have built-in webcams. Webcam models that are more expensive have motors that allow you to automatically rotate to track the sound, so you are always in the frame even if you are moving around the room. Services such as YouTube offer Quick Capture buttons, so with one click, your video can be recorded through your webcam and delivered to the Internet.

How can I distribute my video to the greatest number of viewers? Sites like justin.tv or ustream.tv let you quickly set up to webcast your video as it is captured to a live Internet audience. You can also display an interactive chat next to the video feed. Both the chat and the video are captured and archived for viewers who missed the live broadcast. iTunes offers free distribution of video podcasts, so you can build a following there for your video work.

Are the television shows and movies I watch digital? There are a number of ways you can create video content yourself; but probably most of the video you consume in a typical week was created by someone else—movie studios, television studios, or other students. The number of sources we have for video has increased dramatically since digital video appeared. Because the hardware for capturing video and the software for doing professional-level editing have become so inexpensive, there are few barriers to anyone making video. Further, because the opportunities for distributing video have broadened so much and become so instantaneous, there is an ever-growing market for more video.

Is all video digital video now? The switch to digital video as a broadcasting medium has happened over the past few years. In June 2009, all television stations were required to make the move to digital signal broadcasting. **DTV.gov** is a site that keeps consumers current on using conversion boxes to allow older television sets to operate with the new digital signal.

Movie production studios have also been moving toward digital video for many years. George Lucas, a great proponent of digital technology, filmed *Star Wars Episode II: Attack of the Clones* completely in digital format way back in 2002. It played in a special digital release at digital-ready theaters.

Figure 8.28
The Flip SlideHD video camcorder can capture up to 4 hours HD video and quickly post it on Facebook or YouTube.

And in January 2005, the digital film *Rize*, by David LaChapelle, premiered at the Sundance Film Festival. It was streamed from computers in Oregon to a full-size cinema screen in Park City, Utah, beginning a new age of movie distribution.

Since the conversion to digital TV signals, are there any more "free" television signals? Digital television signals now flood the air around you and can be picked up by a digital antenna. If you live in an area with good "over-the-air" (OTA) reception, you can pick up crisp, high-quality digital versions of all the shows on local network affiliates for free.

How is HD different from "plain" digital? HD stands for *high definition*. It is a standard of digital television signal that guarantees a specific level of resolution and a specific *aspect ratio*, which is the rectangular shape of the image. A 1080 HD TV displays 1,920 vertical lines and 1,080 horizontal lines of video on the screen,

which is over six times as many pixels as standard definition. The aspect ratio used is 16:9, which makes the screen wider, giving it the same proportions as the rectangular shape of a movie theater screen (see Figure 8.29). This allows televisions to play movies in the widescreen format that they were created for, instead of "letterboxing" the film with black bars on the top and the bottom of the screen.

What types of connectivity are provided on modern television sets? As video sources have increased, so have the number and types of connectors on a television. A typical HD set has at least three HDMI connectors, allowing game consoles, Blu-ray players, and cable boxes to be connected and produce the highest-quality output. HDMI is a single cable, with just one plug, that carries all of the video and all of the audio information. That means there is one connector, not three for different parts of the video signal and another two for the stereo sound signals!

Many sets have a built-in SD card reader. This allows users to display slide shows of photographs captured by their digital cameras. A PC VGA port is also included on most sets. This allows you to feed your computer's output video signal directly to the television so you can display an Internet browser or work on your files on the big screen. Some sets are now incorporating a wireless network adapter so the set can stream video from the Internet without having a separate computer connected. Several manufacturers are offering TV sets that stream Internet content. Sony Bravia Internet Video link can deliver content on demand from a number of free sources (see Figure 8.30), and the Panasonic Viera Cast feature works in a similar fashion. Google announced that it is working with Sony and Logitech to offer Google TV. Google TV is built into some sets and also available as a set top box add-on. It allows a single search utility to check for content on the Internet, on your stored recorded programs, and on the TV guide listing.

What advantages are there to watching digital video? Because the signal can be stored into computer memory as it is delivered, a digital video

Figure 8.29

(a) Standard definition television has a more "square" aspect ratio, while (b) high-definition television matches the 16:9 ratio used in the motion picture industry without resorting to (c) letterboxing.

NTSC

HDTV

Extra image area

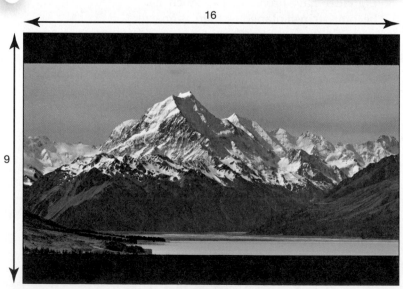

Letterbox

television show can be paused, or can be rewound in real time. Other information services can be integrated with the broadcast; so if a telephone call came through during the show, a pop-up could appear identifying the caller. The Sony Bravia series of televisions, for example, has Internet video capabilities that let you select "widgets" you can position on the screen to display the latest news, weather, sports, or other Internet downloads. In the future, there will be more interactivity integrated so you can participate in live polls or chats on-screen as the show is broadcast.

In movie studios, digital video is ushering in the age of "remixable" films. The components of these feature films—from production footage to soundtrack, dialogue, and sound effects—are available to the audience online, and each person is able to interact with and modify the film, creating a new plotline or a different ending. The MOD Films site (**modfilms.com**) is one place where remixers gather.

Can I record the digital video that comes over my television? There are a variety of digital video recorders (DVRs) available to record the digital video from your television. These can record in either standard or HD quality and store the information on a hard drive. Useful features include being able to record two shows at once, being able to download movie purchases or rentals from the Internet directly to the DVR unit, and easily moving stored content to a mobile device like an iPod or a notebook. Using a DVR, you can pause live TV or set up a schedule to capture every episode of a series, no matter when it airs. Models like TiVo even recommend new shows you might like based on what you have been watching. If you don't want to purchase a DVR or pay the monthly subscription fee for DVR service, you can install PVR (personal video recording) software on your computer. When connected to your cable signal, programs like BeyondTV (**snapstream.com**) and SageTV (**sagetv.com**) turn your computer itself into a DVR.

How else can I get digital video to my TV? In addition to the broadcast content coming in to your TV, there are a number of streaming sources of digital video. Cable providers offer a wide range of on-demand video services. Many older films, as well as shows such as exercise classes, are offered free of charge. Other

Figure 8.30

Sony Bravia televisions use a wireless network adapter to stream digital video from a number of online sources.

premium content, like new-release movies, is offered for a fee. Just one click and you can instantly watch any offered movie for 24 hours, with full control—stopping, starting, and rewinding. Other providers, like Netflix, also offer streaming video content. While Netflix's basic business model is to ship members DVDs physically in the mail, they now also offer Watch Instantly. Thousands of movies and TV series are available with just a click. You can view these shows on a television through any gaming console, a PC, an iPad, or a specialized device like the Roku digital video player.

Can I get digital video to watch on my portable device? Yes. Many DVR units, like TiVo, support software that allows you to transfer recorded shows to files on your PC and format them for viewing on an iPod, a PlayStation Portable, or another mobile device. There are also devices like Slingbox that take the video from your television and broadcast it to you over the Internet. With Slingbox, you can be in another room, or another country, and control and watch your home television on your notebook or your smartphone (see Figure 8.31).

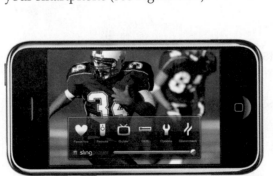

Figure 8.31

Slingbox can send your digital television content to your notebook or phone, wherever you may be.

Digital Mobility and Access

Once you are comfortable with digital communication and digital media, you'll want to be able to communicate and to access your music, files, and videos whether you are in front of a desktop at home or in an airport while traveling. Access to your digital assets is required in a modern business environment and is a great benefit in your personal life. Earlier chapters discussed expensive solutions like notebook computers; but now there is a much wider range of devices that grant you access to your media and data wherever you are.

Selecting the Right Device

How do I select the right device for my needs? There are a wide range of computing devices on the market today that give you varying access to digital communication and digital media. A **netbook** runs a fully featured operating system but weighs in at 2 pounds or less. An **Internet tablet** is another type of very light, very portable

device. Internet tablets do not offer full-size keyboards. Netbooks and Internet tablets can carry files, music, and videos as well as provide specialized services. Then there is the full range of notebooks and tablet computers, and new blends of various features are appearing in new devices all the time. Figure 8.32 lists the main features of several different mobile devices.

What if I don't need a phone but do need Internet access? Tiny, lightweight Internet-enabled devices are appearing that don't bother to include cell phone features at all. The Nokia N810 Internet tablet series (see Figure 8.33), for example, uses Skype or Gizmo for voice communications instead of a cell phone service. It has a high-resolution screen and WiFi connectivity so you can stream audio and video, use Web e-mail clients, and access Web sites. It features an RSS reader so you can peruse the latest from the sites you are following. Memory expands with SD expansion cards.

The Sony PlayStation Portable (PSP) can play video games but also includes a Web browser, Skype, and an RSS reader. It uses Sony Memory Sticks to store data

Figure 8.32 | MOBILE DEVICES: PRICE, SIZE, WEIGHT, AND CAPABILITIES

Device	Relative Price	Approximate Size	Approximate Weight	Standard Capabilities
Cell phone	$$ (Includes cost for the phone, a monthly plan, and Internet access)	5″ × 2″ × 0.5″	0.25 lb.	Voice, e-mail, some application software, and Internet connectivity
PMP	$$–$$$	4″ × 2″ × 0.5″	0.25 lb. or more	Storage of digital music, video, and other digital files
Smartphone	$$–$$$	4.5″ × 2″ × .75″	0.25 lb.	PIM capabilities, access to application software, and access to the Internet
Internet tablet	$$	6″ × 3″ × 0.5″	0.5 lb	Webcam, GPS, phone calls using Skype, sharp resolution, and widescreen display
Netbook	$$$$	10″ × 7″	1–2 lbs.	8″ to 10″ screens and run full-featured operating systems and applications
Tablet PC	$$$$$	10″ × 8″ × 1″	3 lbs.	PIM capabilities, access to application software, access to the Internet, and special handwriting- and speech-recognition capabilities
Notebook	$$$$–$$$$$	10″ × 13″ × 2″	5 to 8 lbs.	All the capabilities of a desktop computer plus portability

files, videos, music, and images. The screen is a 4.3" widescreen design with great clarity and brightness. The PSP can even connect over the Internet to your PlayStation 3 system at home and display the videos or music stored there for you wherever you are.

What if I need a larger screen and keyboard? If you require a larger screen and more processing power, then look at a category of emerging computer systems known as *netbooks*. Examples include the Asus Eee PC and the Dell Inspiron Mini 10 (see Figure 8.34). Netbooks pack major computing power into a tiny package, and manufacturers try to extend battery life as long as possible. Screen sizes are typically between 8" to 10", and keyboards are less than full sized. No optical drive is integrated but one can be connected as a separate peripheral via the USB port. Netbooks often come with a Windows operating system. Some users opt to install a flavor of Linux, however, because Linux requires fewer resources than Windows. Solid-state hard drives are a good choice for netbooks because they use less power and produce less heat. Many models include integrated webcams as well as Bluetooth, so while netbooks are small and light, they still can serve many functions.

New tablet entries also fall into this category. The Apple iPad has a touch keyboard that is almost full size in landscape mode. It has a 9.7" multitouch screen and weighs in at only 1.5 pounds. Although the iPad

Figure 8.33

The Nokia N810 series Internet tablet features a touch screen and keypad and is designed primarily for Web surfing and sending e-mail.

does not have a fully featured operating system, it can run mobile touch versions of popular Apple software like Pages, Numbers, and Keynote.

What if all I really need is to bring my books with me? For avid readers of e-books (books stored as electronic files), the Amazon Kindle DX or the Sony Reader Digital Book could be what you are looking for. These feature internal RAM, but also support flash memory cards for more storage. You can get approximately 7,500 turned pages on one charge, so on long plane flights this may be the device you use most. The Apple iPad supports reading e-books as well, with the Amazon Kindle software app and with Apple's own iBooks bookstore. The iPad is full color, however, whereas both of the other readers display content in shades of gray. The iPad also supports video viewing, music, Internet browsing and thousands of apps on its 9.7" multitouch screen (see Figure 8.35).

Ubiquitous Computing

What is in the future for our digital lifestyles? Mark Weiser, a researcher at Xerox's PARC laboratories, has predicted that "computing will be woven into the fabric of everyday life until it is indistinguishable from it." This concept is called **ubiquitous computing** (or *ubicom*). More and more styles of digital devices are being

Figure 8.34

Subnotebooks like the Asus Eee PC weigh in at less than two pounds but run fully featured operating systems.

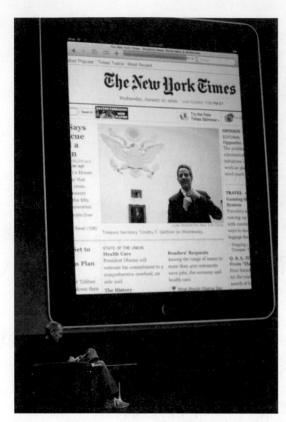

Figure 8.35

The Apple iPad has a color 9.7" screen and lasts more than 10 hours on a single battery charge.

introduced, but there is a second force at work. Digital computing devices are increasingly embedded in appliances, clothing, cars—all the items we physically interact with in our day. The era of "smart things" is just beginning.

How will our lifestyles change as computing becomes everywhere and invisible? While we can't predict the future, there are trends in design that give us hints. Researchers and inventors like Mike Kuniavsky of ThingM are creating devices that exploit the new digital nature of our world to make tasks easier. The WineM product from ThingM is a good example (see Figure 8.36). WineM is a "smart" wine rack. Each bottle is labeled with a radio frequency identification (RFID) tag when it is stored by the owner. When it is time to pick the perfect bottle for dinner, the owner can ask the wine rack to show just the Chardonnay, and LEDs light up just those

bottles. WineM can also display which wines are ready to drink, or if any of your friends has a similar wine collection, or if the winery is having a sale. It updates information automatically and will e-mail or text you an alert when a bottle of wine is removed from the rack.

How is shopping changing with increased access to digital information? Recent studies show that 93% of adults in the U.S. ages 18–29 now have a cell phone. Combined with the explosion in popularity of social networking sites, consumers' experiences are changing. Shopping now begins with price comparison tools like ShopSavvy and RedLaser. These "location aware" tools compare prices between nearby stores and then also compare the prices with the best prices available online. Once you've selected a store, many different mobile apps let you take advantage of mobile coupons, called *mobicoupons*. A smartphone can simply read the barcode on the item, and then will display a barcode for a coupon. The cashier scans the mobicoupon right at the register. More and more sites are appearing that offer some type of mobile coupon, including Zavers, Yowza, mobiOpons, and Cell Fire. Future trends in this area include a tighter integration with the information customer loyalty programs already store about you. Based on location and your past buying preferences, specialized coupons could be designed and delivered through the mobicoupon system.

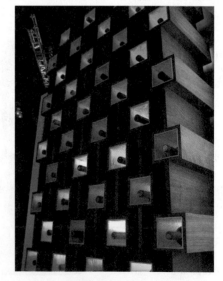

Figure 8.36

The smart wine rack uses WineM technology and answers queries from its controller, (a) like "Show me all of the California wines I have that are ready to drink and under $50 in value." (b) In response WineM lights up the bottles that fit the criteria.

How is marketing changing because of ubiquitous computing?

New strategies in marketing and communications are counting on the fact that so many people have a cell phone with a camera and Internet access. A new technology from Microsoft called Microsoft Tag transforms everyday things in the real world into live links to online information and entertainment. From your smartphone, simply snap a Tag image (see Figure 8.37) anywhere you see it—on a product, in an advertisement, on a sign or storefronts—and your phone takes you directly to a display of information. It might be a Web site, video, or a schedule, or a social network. To use Tag just download the free Tag reader on your Web-enabled camera phone.

Marketers also have to be aware of the phenomenon of "crowdsourcing"—checking in with the voice of the crowd. Consumers are using apps like MobileVoice to let you check in on what the verdict of the crowd is on the quality of an item. Forward-thinking companies are using this input to improve their products and services. TaxiHack, for example, allows phone users to comment on NYC cab drivers, and AT&T has an app to let customers report locations of coverage gaps.

How will our "ownership" of objects change with the new access to information?

The evolution of information to a digital form is allowing us to change our relationship to objects. Items like bicycles and cars can become "subscriptions" instead of large one-time purchases. Call a Bike is a program run in Germany. At most major street corners, there is a rack of Call a Bikes (see Figure 8.38). Place a call to the phone number printed on the bike, and it texts you a code you can use to unlock the bike lock. Ride the bike to where you're going. When you arrive, re-lock it. The amount of time you rode it automatically is billed (by the minute) to your phone.

City CarShare is another system using the digital communication of information to change our lifestyle habits. Many cities, like San Francisco and Philadelphia, now offer a City CarShare program. Residents sign up for the program and receive a key that has an RFID chip in it. All cars are connected to a central network. You can open a City CarShare car and start the engine only when your specific key is scheduled to open and start it. GPS technology is used to track

When you photograph this tag, the image on the right displays on your phone.

where the car is, whether it has been dropped off at the right location, and how far it has been driven. The entire process is transparent to City CarShare members. Members have 24/7 access to a vehicle—a truck, a hybrid, a convertible—when they need it, with very little advance notice, for a cost of about $6.00 an hour (gas and insurance included!).

Could ubiquitous computing technology improve the world?

The notion of an instantly connected population is an

Figure 8.37

In print advertising, Microsoft Tag technology can quickly take a reader to a display on their cell phone that includes more information and a mobile coupon.

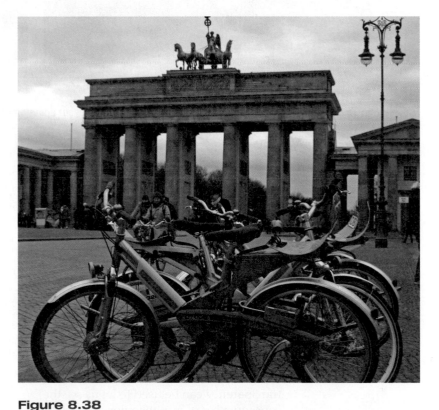

Figure 8.38

Call a Bike uses digital technology to change our lifestyle from one of ownership to one of "subscription."

Computers in Society: "Ecosystem" of New Tools—Augmented Reality

We are familiar with digital data—comfortable with carrying around music, some files, contact lists, and calendars. But where is your data when you need it? Today, your information is locked in your cell phone, your iPad, or your notebook computer. This mobility is revolutionary compared to the access of any prior generations, but it still requires you to take out your notebook, open it up, boot it up, and initiate a request for information. What lies ahead?

The Media Lab of MIT provides some great clues. The Fluid Interfaces group works to develop new tools to bring our data more directly into the physical world. One of the most promising of these new tools is called Sixth Sense. It is a wearable device hanging around your neck consisting of a camera, a projector, and a mirror that can communicate with the Internet over wireless Bluetooth via the cell phone in your pocket. What Sixth Sense can do is augment your experience of reality by adding the information you need as you need it.

Say you are on your way to the airport and pull out your boarding pass. Sixth Sense uses pattern recognition to realize you are holding an airline

ticket. It then goes out to the Internet to check if the flight is on time or if a gate change has been issued. If it has, the words *Delayed: 20 Minutes* suddenly appear on the top of the boarding pass (see Figure 8.39a). The information is no longer trapped in your mobile device—it is part of your environment. Or say you are in a bookstore and select the title *Ambient Findability*. As you hold the book, its Amazon rating appears on the cover (see Figure 8.39b). You open to the inside sleeve, and the comments from readers at Amazon begin to scroll over the page. Then you can tap any one of those comments for more detail.

Sixth Sense is the product of work by Pranav Mistry and his advisor Patti Maes. The product can also respond to gestures, so when you make a rectangle with your fingers, it takes a photograph. When you reach your destination, any flat surface such as a wall or table can be used to "dump" your photos into a "pile." Using your hands, you can shuffle the images, or resize or rotate an image. Or draw a watch-sized circle on your wrist, and Sixth Sense displays an analog watch face on your arm.

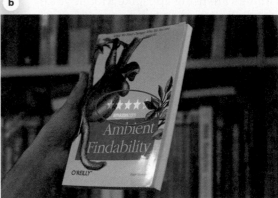

Figure 8.39

Sixth Sense recognizes what information you need added to your environment and displays it automatically.

idea that has appealed to futurists throughout time. Writer and futurist Jamais Cascio has presented ideas of how such a setting might bring all citizens into a more engaged role in changing the world. In his TED talk "The Future We Will Create" (**ted.com**), Cascio discusses how a smartphone-carrying population can work to create a better world—more sustainable, more secure, and more desirable.

Having an international population armed with cameras and a means to quickly distribute their video allows the invisible to become visible in many ways (see Figure 8.42). This transparency can be used to let us see the consequences of our behavior directly—and make changes. The Witness Project, founded by Peter Gabriel, uses this strategy to stop

human rights abuses throughout the world (**witness.org**). Their slogan is "See it. Film it. Change it." Similar efforts are aimed at documenting the environmental state of the world. Environmental successes can be collected together along with evidence to document ecological crimes.

What if each of the cell phones distributed around the world had integrated atmospheric sensors? Then millions of points around the world would be "reporting" in on quality of air and water. And what if these sensors could monitor for flu viruses? Tagged with geographical information, the data could be combined with maps for easy viewing and analysis. Ideas like these are being explored by UCLA researcher Dr. Deborah Estrin, the

Figure 8.40

Any surface can become an input device using Sixth Sense.

In fact your hand is as good a flat surface as any to Sixth Sense (see Figure 8.40). Need to make a phone call? Sixth Sense will display a keypad on your palm. Tap out the number on the virtual keypad, and one touch of the red CALL button that appears on your palm places your call.

The shirt of the person walking toward you will also work as a projection surface. When a person walks up to us, we don't often pull out our cell phone and Google them before speaking, but as a person approaches a Sixth Sense wearer, it recognizes their face, heads off to their Facebook page or blog, and scans the most recent entries. It then projects the keywords that describe the person and their interests on their clothing as you watch them approach. Currently the Sixth Sense is small but not very stylish. The product is constructed from off-the-shelf components costing about $350. Within a few years its inventors believe it can be produced as a button-sized device, costing less than a cell phone costs now. You can monitor the progress of this device at **pranavmistry.com/ projects/sixthsense**.

There are a number of iPhone apps available right now that use the integrated compass and camera of iPhone to add information to your environment. BionicEye is a $1 app that "augments" reality. When you point the camera's lens at a building, it shows you the nearest subway lines or restaurants, along with which direction you need to go in to get there (see Figure 8.41).

This kind of direct integration of digital information with the physical world around us is a hallmark of our digital future. Augmented reality combines the digital information we have accumulated in an immediate and spontaneous manner. So where will your new reality take you?

Figure 8.41

Augmented reality apps let you look through your phone's camera and see the world with extra information superimposed.

director of the Center for Embedded Network Sensing.

There is no exaggerating the range and severity of problems facing us, from environmental threats to dangers brought on by how we treat each other. Technological advances, like cell phones equipped with cameras and Internet access, could provide the means to change the course of our future. It will be our job to focus the direction of that change, using it as a response to the challenging problems facing us.

Figure 8.42

Using mobile devices we could document the environmental dangers and successes around the world.

1. What are the changes that have brought us a digital lifestyle?

The increased use of digital information has led to a period of greater creativity and control of our data. In a digital format, information is easy to carry, manipulate, and exchange. This has led to revolutionary changes in communication, entertainment media, and mobile computing.

2. How has the move to digital information affected the communication tools important to both the business world and life outside of work?

The age of digital information has brought new opportunities and challenges to businesses. Some have had to struggle to shift their business models to the new style of information. Because information can be shared so easily, issues of copyright and intellectual property have become critical. In our personal lives, we see products that allow us to interact with information in ways that had been too expensive or difficult before.

3. How do cell/smartphone components resemble a traditional computer, and how do they work?

Like a traditional computer, a cell/smartphone has a central processor, memory, and an operating system. These components work in the same way as in a computer to process information and support communications, software applications, and other services.

4. Why would I use VoIP, and what does it offer that is unique?

VoIP allows inexpensive communication using a computer or a WiFi-enabled phone. Because it is based on a digital format for information, it can support services like automatic delivery of phone messages to an e-mail account or texts to a mobile device.

5. How is digital media different from analog?

Digital media is based on a series of numeric data comprising number values that were measured from the original analog waveform. As a string of numbers, a digital photo or video file can be easily processed by modern computers.

6. What can I carry in a portable media player, and how does it store data?

Most PMPs can store any kind of digital information—photos, videos, or music files for example. Some PMPs store data on a hard drive, while others use flash memory. Some also allow the amount of memory to be upgraded, while others have a fixed amount of memory.

7. What ways are there for me to create and to watch digital video?

You can create digital video using any digital camera, webcam, or digital camcorder. Digital editing software allows you to add transitions, effects, and sound tracks. There are a great many sources of digital video, including free sources like YouTube and JustIn, as well as pay-per-view services like Amazon Video On Demand or cable providers' streaming video options.

8. What changes does ubiquitous computing bring to our lifestyles?

As computers become smaller and less obvious, they will begin to integrate into our life-like appliances rather than be complicated tools. Ubiquitous computing is beginning to allow us to move some objects from an ownership model to a subscription service model.

key terms

Word Bank

- analog-to-digital converter
- Bluetooth
- cell phone
- GPS
- Internet tablet
- microbrowser

- MMS
- netbook
- P2P
- PMP
- sampling rate
- smartphone

- SMS
- synchronize
- telephony
- ubiquitous computing
- VoIP
- WML

Instructions: Fill in the blanks using the words from the Word Bank above.

Elizabeth knows that everything seems to be "digital" these days. In the past, she carried a traditional SLR camera but now she uses her simple (1) _____ to take photos. She can connect wirelessly to the computer to transfer the images because the phone supports (2) _____. Sometimes she doesn't bother to do that because she has already sent a(n) (3) _____ message to a friend with the image. Her old phone couldn't do that because it only supported (4) _____. If she upgraded to a(n) (5) _____, she could actually make many refinements and edits to the image without transferring it to the computer at all.

Pete is a real fan of technology, and so he has selected a(n) (6) _____ instead of a cell phone. He's always near a WiFi signal, so he doesn't need an actual phone. He doesn't even pay for traditional phone service at home, where he uses (7) _____ instead of a landline. He's fallen in love with his new device for many reasons. It can give him driving directions with its built-in (8) _____. The (9) _____ software displays full HTML Web pages right on the device. To keep this device coordinated with the data on his computer, he makes sure to (10) _____ the data each night.

Niti can't quite decide what device will work best for his new life. He's moving to California and plans to be outside a lot, so he wants something very light. He thinks the two-pound (11) _____ might be ideal because he doesn't really need a full keyboard or a huge screen. When he's out biking, he'll just wear his (12) _____ on his arm to keep the tunes flowing. He downloads free songs offered by bands that are just starting out from a(n) (13) _____ site. The songs have a much lower (14) _____ than he usually demands, but at least they don't take up much space on his hard drive. He's heard that electronics are merging with clothing more and more, so maybe soon (15) _____ will lead to a T-shirt that can take care of his mobile music needs!

becoming computer literate

Instructions: Write a report providing answers to the question posed below, using as many of the key terms from the chapter as you can. Be sure the sentences are grammatically and technically correct.

You have a limited budget to spend on technology tools and toys in the years you will be a student. You are considering communication, entertainment media, and your need to be able to work and connect with your information when you are not at home. Which digital media services and products would you definitely invest in? How would you justify their value? What kinds of services and products would you use that are free or low cost? Has the migration to a digital lifestyle given you more freedom and creativity or just caused you more annoyance and expense?

Instructions: Answer the multiple-choice and true–false questions below for more practice with key terms and concepts from this chapter.

Multiple Choice

1. Which is *not* a factor that determines the quality of images taken with a digital camera?
   a. Lens quality   c. Resolution
   b. File format   d. EyeFi

2. Which is the process of ensuring that two computer devices have the same data?
   a. Mapping
   b. Standardizing
   c. Synchronizing
   d. Transferring

3. The operating system of your cell phone is stored in
   a. read-only memory.
   b. the display.
   c. the digital signal processor.
   d. random-access memory.

4. If you want the lightest, most portable computing solution, you would purchase
   a. a netbook.
   b. a tablet PC.
   c. an Internet tablet.
   d. a notebook.

5. P2P is an acronym for
   a. packet-to-packet networking.
   b. peer-to-peer sharing.
   c. person-to-person texting.
   d. power-to-power delivery.

6. What software makes it possible to view Web pages on a cell phone?
   a. Microbrowser
   b. Extension

   c. Push technology
   d. 3G standard

7. Flash memory is a type of
   a. nonvolatile memory.
   b. hard drive memory.
   c. SSD memory,
   d. volatile memory.

8. VoIP is phone service that
   a. works even when the electricity goes out.
   b. works over an Internet connection.
   c. requires no special setup for a secure connection.
   d. has extremely high quality and is very reliable.

9. Which of the following is *not* true about modern televisions?
   a. They incorporate wireless connectivity.
   b. They allow other services, like caller ID, to be integrated.
   c. They can use widgets to display sports and news updates.
   d. They run word processing and slide presentation software.

10. Which service allows you use your cell phone to send messages that contain images?
    a. MMS
    b. ISP
    c. SMS
    d. MiFI

True–False

_____ 1. All smartphones allow you to add more memory.

_____ 2. Digital music files must be converted to the MP3 format if they are transferred to a mobile device.

_____ 3. A codec is the algorithm that compresses and decompresses video files.

_____ 4. If your digital camera doesn't support wireless connectivity, you can use a memory card with built-in WiFi.

_____ 5. Some Internet-enabled devices like the Nokia N810 Internet tablet use Skype for voice communications instead of cell phone service.

1. Choosing Mobile Devices to Fit Your Needs

As a student, which devices discussed in this chapter would have the most immediate impact on the work you do each day? Which would provide the best value (that is, the greatest increase in productivity and organization per dollar spent)? Consider the full range of devices, from cell phones to notebook systems.

2. Ready... Set... Act!

As a student, you often give presentations or take on student teaching assignments. What would be the steps for creating a digital video recording of one of your presentations? What tools would you need to record? What kind of file would you end up producing? How would you make a DVD from that? How would you distribute the video to a live Internet audience?

3. Do You Still Need a Phone?

Explore Skype (**skype.com**) as an alternative to paid telephone service. What equipment would you need to use Skype as your everyday communication medium? When would this be useful? What telephone services and features would you lose if you went to Skype?

4. Choosing the Best Phone

Your friend wants to trim down the number of different devices that she carries. Visit the most popular cellular providers' Web sites and research options. Which phone would you recommend to your friend, and why? Compare at least three different models of phones and list their price, music storage capacity, built-in memory, and expandability options.

a. Which of the three models you compared is the best value for your friend?
b. What special features does the phone you chose have? What accessories would you recommend your friend buy to make the phone more useful?
c. Would you suggest buying a refurbished phone? Why or why not?

5. iTunes U

Download a free copy of iTunes software. In the iTunes Store, explore the iTunes U podcast directory, which contains free audio and video lectures published by major universities.

a. Look for the MIT Open Courseware video podcasts. How many lectures are available from MIT (Massachusetts Institute of Technology)?
b. If each lecture were 90 minutes on average and approximately 200 MB in size, how much storage would it take to save all of the video lectures in every course published by MIT?
c. Is there a mobile device that can store and play that much content? What devices could store the lectures from all of the courses in mathematics offered by MIT Open Courseware?

eight
making the transition to... the workplace

making the transition to... the workplace

1. Corporate Mobile Communications Needs

Imagine your company is boosting its sales force and looking to the future of mobile technology. Your manager has asked you to research the following issues surrounding mobile communications for the company:

a. Do mobile communication devices present increased security risks? What would happen if you left a cell phone at a meeting and a competitor picked it up? Are there ways to protect your data on mobile devices?

b. Can viruses attack cell phones? Is there any special software on the market to protect mobile devices from viruses? How much would it cost to equip 20 devices with virus protection?

c. Is there a role for mobile communication devices even if employees don't leave the building? Which devices would be important for a company to consider for use within corporate offices? Are there software solutions that would work as well?

d. Should employees be allowed to use smartphones provided by the company for personal use even though files related to personal use might eat up potentially valuable memory and space? What restrictions should be put on personal use to protect the privacy of proprietary company information contained on the devices?

2. 4G Communications

The most recent generation of telecommunications (nicknamed "4G" for fourth generation) allows the speed of cellular network transmissions to hit 3-6 Mbps. How does that compare to dial-up and broadband access over wired networks? What implications does it have for information access and e-commerce? What download speed would be ideal? Upload speed? How would it change how you communicate?

3. Subscription versus Ownership

Consider the examples of Call-a-Bike and CarShare. Are there other businesses you can identify that would be able to take advantage of digital information and become subscription services instead of vendors of a physical product? What are the advantages to the consumer of subscription over ownership? What are the drawbacks?

4. Too Much Media?

Imagine you are a manager of 18 employees, all of whom work with constant Internet access. As a manager, what concerns might you have about their use of corporate bandwidth to download and view media files? Do you think it would benefit your business to block any MP3 file transfers? Should you put in place a block to prevent access to sites that store huge numbers of streaming videos? As a manager, are there concerns you might have if employees have digital cameras on their cell phones? Would your answers be different in an academic setting?

5. Mobile Devices on the Highway

Mobile devices used in vehicles are becoming the norm in today's society. Consider the following:

a. Several car manufacturers provide Bluetooth option packages for their vehicles. What advantages are there to having Bluetooth connectivity in your car? Are there any disadvantages?

b. Examine the Microsoft Sync software package. List the features and services it provides. If you were a salesperson with a territory that you covered by car, how would Sync help you?

Instructions: Albert Einstein used *Gedankenexperiments*, or critical thinking questions, to develop his theory of relativity. Some ideas are best understood by experimenting with them in our own minds. The following critical thinking questions are designed to demand your full attention but require only a comfortable chair—no technology.

1. Digital Entertainment

Can you name a style of media that has not made the shift to digital? What advantages does digital photography offer? Digital video? What disadvantages come along with a digital format for entertainment media? Has the growth in digital media promoted an increased understanding between people or has it created more isolation?

2. The Ultimate Style

As ubiquitous computing continues to evolve, devices become lighter and smaller, and we are beginning to see a convergence of computing and clothing.

a. What would the ultimate convergent mobile clothing be for you? Is there a limit in weight, size, or complexity?

b. Can you imagine uses for technology in fashion that would support better health? Better social relationships? A richer intellectual life?

c. What other applications can you think of for a device like Sixth Sense? What kind of information needs to be displayed in our environment to be helpful?

3. Ubiquitous Means Everywhere

As we continue to see computing power distributed throughout all of our environment, there are shifts happening in how we relate to objects, how we shop, and how marketing is done. Consider three other areas of our lives—professional sports, buying a house, and staying healthy. How will ubiquitous computing change those activities? How would just knowing that every participant has a smartphone change the activity?

4. Too Much Information?

Consider the following questions:

a. Your rent a car that has a GPS installed. After you return it, the rental company uses the GPS data to determine whether you have driven the car at speeds above the speed limit. They then issue fines for violations of the rental contract. Does this lead to safer highways? Is it an infringement of your privacy?

b. Would you agree to insert a GPS-enabled tracking chip into your pet? Your child? What legislation do you think should be required regarding use of the tracking data from your phone records? Would you be willing to sell that information to marketing agencies? Should that data be available to the government if you were suspected of a crime?

5. Electronic Publishing

Explore the specifications of the Sony Portable Reader, the Barnes & Noble NOOK, the Amazon Kindle, and the Apple iPad. How would your study habits change if your textbooks were only delivered to you in electronic format on one of these devices? What unique advantages would there be? What disadvantages would there be? How would using such a device compare with just receiving the book as an electronic file, such as a PDF document, to your notebook computer?

eight team time

Convergence? Any Time Soon?

Problem

There are so many different mobile devices saturating the market that many people are left in a state of confusion. Either they are buying too many devices and not using them, or they are refusing to buy anything because of the dilemma of too many choices.

Task

Each team will assign a member to become the expert resource in one of the digital areas presented in this chapter: digital communication, digital media, or digital mobility. For each scenario described by a client, the group will select the minimum set of devices that would support and enhance the client's life.

Process

1. Consider the following three clients:
   - A retired couple who now travel for pleasure a great deal. They want to be involved in their grandchildren's lives and will need support for their health and personal care as they age.
   - A young family with two children, two working parents, and a tight budget.
   - A couple in which each individual is a physician and both adore technology.
2. Make two recommendations for your client in terms of digital technologies that will enhance their business or their lifestyle. Discuss the advantages and disadvantages of each technology. Consider value, reliability, computing needs, training needed and communication needs, as well as expandability for the future.
3. As a group, prepare a final report that considers the costs, availability, and unique features of the recommendations you have made for each client.
4. Bring the research materials from the individual team meetings to class. Looking at the clients' needs, make final decisions as to which digital technologies are best suited for each client.

Conclusion

Digital information has allowed the development of a new style of living, both at home and at work. With so many digital solutions on the market today, recommending digital communication, media management, and mobility options needs to focus on converging to the minimum set of tools that will enhance life without adding complication to it.

In this exercise, you will research and then role-play a complicated ethical situation. The role you play might or might not match your own personal beliefs; in either case, your research and use of logic will enable you to represent the view assigned. An arbitrator will watch and comment on both sides of the arguments, and together the team will agree on an ethical solution.

Topic: When Everyone Has a Voice

In the near future much of the world's population could be equipped with Internet-ready camera phones. Sensors on these phones could report location, measure for viruses, and compute pollution indexes, while the cameras could be used to document a range of human behavior. This could create changes in political movements, art, and culture as everyone's experience is documented and shared.

Research Areas to Consider

- Ted.com
- Mobilebehavior.com
- Witness project
- Center for Embedded Network Sensing

Process

Divide the class into teams.

1. Research the sources cited above and devise a scenario in which mobile access could make an impact politically or environmentally.
2. Team members should write a summary that provides background information for their character—for example: business owner, politician, reporter, and arbitrator—and details their character's behaviors to set the stage for the role-playing event. Then, team members should create an outline to use during the role-playing event.
3. Team members should arrange a mutually convenient time to meet for the exchange, either using the collaboration feature of MyITLab, the discussion board feature of Blackboard, or meeting in person.
4. Team members should present their case to the class, or submit a PowerPoint presentation for review by the rest of the class, along with the summary and resolution they developed.

Conclusion

As technology becomes ever more prevalent and integrated into our lives, more and more ethical dilemmas will present themselves. Being able to understand and evaluate both sides of the argument, while responding in a personally or socially ethical manner, will be an important skill.

securing your system

protecting your digital data and devices

objectives

After reading this chapter, you should be able to answer the following questions:

1. From which types of viruses do I need to protect my computer? *(pp. 411–414)*

2. What can I do to protect my computer from viruses? *(pp. 414–417)*

3. How can hackers attack my computing devices, and what harm can they cause? *(pp. 417–421)*

4. What is a firewall, and how does it keep my computer safe from hackers? *(pp. 421–425)*

5. How do I create secure passwords and manage all of my passwords? *(pp. 425–428)*

6. How can I surf the Internet anonymously and use biometric authentication devices to protect my data? *(pp. 428–429)*

7. How do I manage online annoyances such as spyware and spam? *(pp. 429–434)*

8. What data do I need to back up, and what are the best methods for doing so? *(pp. 435–438)*

9. What is social engineering, and how do I avoid falling prey to phishing and hoaxes? *(pp. 438–441)*

10. How do I protect my physical computing assets from environmental hazards, power surges, and theft? *(pp. 441–445)*

multimedia resources

Active Helpdesk

- Avoiding Computer Viruses **(p. 414)**
- Understanding Firewalls **(p. 421)**

Sound Bytes

- Protecting Your Computer **(p. 416)**
- Installing a Personal Firewall **(p. 424)**
- Surge Protectors **(p. 443)**

Companion Website

The Companion Website includes a variety of additional materials to help you review and learn more about the topics in this chapter. Go to: *pearsonhighered.com/techinaction*

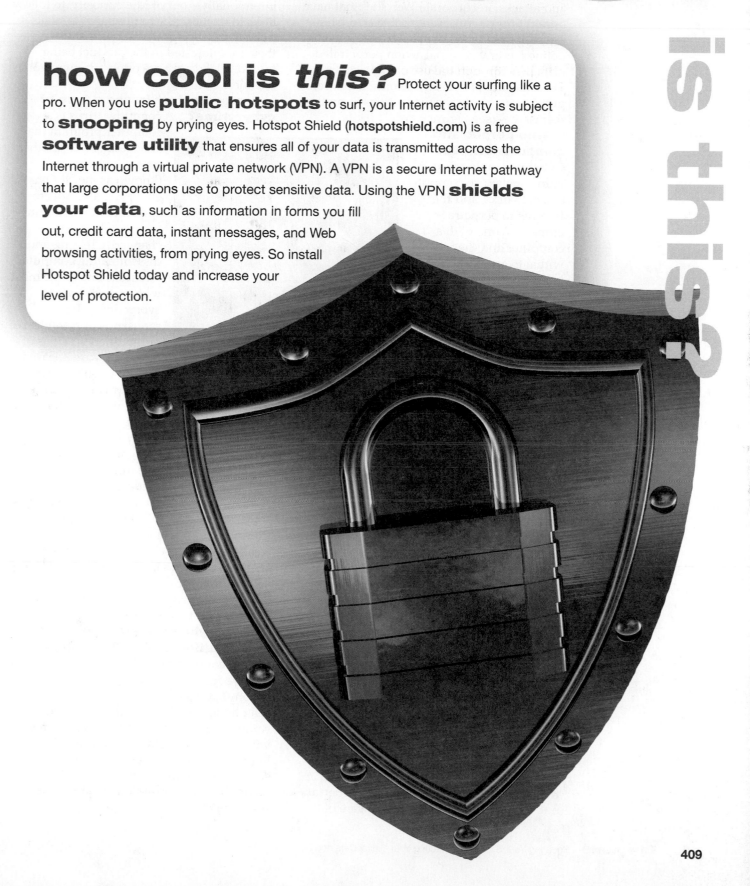

how cool

is this?

how cool is *this?* Protect your surfing like a
pro. When you use **public hotspots** to surf, your Internet activity is subject
to **snooping** by prying eyes. Hotspot Shield (**hotspotshield.com**) is a free
software utility that ensures all of your data is transmitted across the
Internet through a virtual private network (VPN). A VPN is a secure Internet pathway
that large corporations use to protect sensitive data. Using the VPN **shields
your data**, such as information in forms you fill
out, credit card data, instant messages, and Web
browsing activities, from prying eyes. So install
Hotspot Shield today and increase your
level of protection.

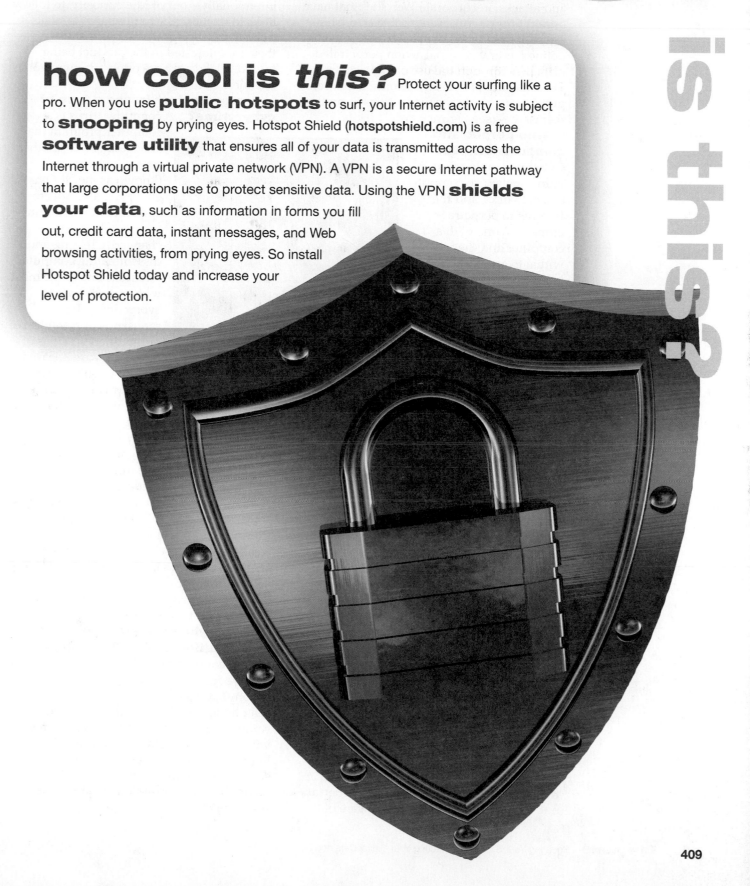

409

Keeping Your Data Safe

The media is full of stories about malicious computer programs damaging computers, criminals stealing people's identities online, and attacks on corporate Web sites that have brought major corporations to a standstill. These are examples of **cybercrime**, which is defined as any criminal action perpetrated primarily through the use of a computer. The existence of cybercrime means that computer users must take precautions to protect themselves (see Figure 9.1).

Who perpetrates computer crimes? **Cybercriminals** are individuals who use computers, networks, and the Internet to perpetrate crime. Anyone with a computer and the wherewithal to arm him- or herself with the appropriate knowledge can be a cybercriminal.

What kinds of cybercrimes are conducted over the Internet? The Internet Crime Complaint Center (IC3) is a partnership between the Federal Bureau of Investigation (FBI) and the National White Collar Crime Center (NW3C). In 2009, the latest year for which data is available, IC3 processed more than 336,000 complaints related to Internet crime, an increase of 22 percent over 2008. Many complaints were fraud related, such as auction fraud, nondelivery of ordered items, credit and debit card fraud, and advanced fee scams. Complaints not related to fraud still pertained to serious issues such as computer intrusions, unsolicited e-mail, and child pornography. Much of the credit card fraud was perpetrated when credit card numbers were stolen by criminals tricking people into revealing sensitive information or by computer programs that gather credit card data.

With all the news coverage about cybercrimes, aren't people being more cautious? Unfortunately, they are not. Although most people are aware of

spam, a recent survey by the Messaging Anti-Abuse Working Group (MAAWG) found that half of e-mail users in North American and Europe have opened spam. And the MAAWG discovered that 46 percent of people who opened spam did so intentionally—out of idle curiosity, to follow links to unsubscribe to unwanted e-mails (which only brings more spam), or because they are interested in the product being touted. Clearly, we are often our own worst enemies!

Are computer viruses a type of cybercrime? A computer **virus** is a computer program that attaches itself to another computer program (known as the *host program*) and attempts to spread to other computers when files are exchanged. Creating and disseminating computer viruses is one of the most widespread types of cybercrimes. Tens of thousands of new viruses or modified versions of old viruses are released each year. Some viruses cause only minor annoyances, while others cause destruction of data. Many viruses are now designed to gather sensitive information such as credit card numbers. The Conficker virus was the most widespread in 2009 and infected millions of computers in a few weeks of its release, which illustrates how serious a threat a virus can pose to your digital security. You need to make sure your data is protected from viruses and other malicious software attacks.

Does cybercrime include the theft of computing devices? Although theft of computer equipment is not classified as a cybercrime (rather, it is considered larceny), the theft of notebook computers, cell phones, iPods, and other portable computing devices is on the rise. The resale value for used electronic equipment is high, which contributes to demand for stolen merchandise. The ease with which equipment can be sold online also fuels this problem.

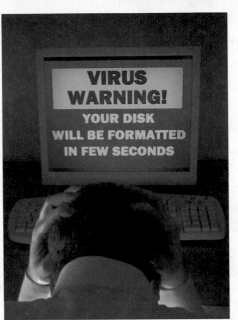

Figure 9.1

Cybercrimes, including virus attacks, are a serious problem for Web surfers.

In this chapter, we discuss serious threats to your digital security (such as computer viruses and other activities of cybercriminals), less serious annoyances (such as spyware and spam), and good security practices to keep yourself from undermining your digital security. We also discuss methods for protecting your digital assets from attacks and damage.

Computer Threats: Computer Viruses

Computer viruses are threatening because they are engineered to evade detection. Viruses normally attempt to hide within the code of a host program to avoid detection. And viruses are not just limited to computers. Any computing device such as a smartphone, notebook, netbook, or iPad can be infected with a virus. Even your car, which now contains embedded computer systems, could catch a virus, especially if it connects to the Internet for software updates.

"Viruses are not just limited to computers."

What do computer viruses do? A computer virus's main purpose is to replicate itself and copy its code into as many other files as possible. Although virus replication can slow down networks, it is not usually the main threat. The majority of viruses have secondary objectives or side effects, ranging from displaying annoying messages on the computer screen to destroying files or the contents of entire hard drives. Because computer viruses cause disruption to computer systems, including data destruction and information theft, virus creation and deployment is a form of cybercrime.

How does my computer catch a virus? If your computer is exposed to a file infected with a virus, the virus will try to copy itself and infect a file on your computer. If you never expose your computer to new files, then it will not become infected. However, this would be the equivalent of a human being living in a bubble to avoid catching viruses from other people—quite impractical.

Downloading infected audio and video files from peer-to-peer file sharing sites is a major source of virus infections. Shared flash drives are also a common source of

virus infection, as is e-mail, although many people have misconceptions about how e-mail infection occurs. Just opening an e-mail message will not usually infect your computer with a virus, although some new viruses are launched when viewed in the preview pane of your e-mail software. Downloading or running a file that is attached to the e-mail is a common way that your computer becomes infected. Thus, be extremely wary of e-mail attachments, especially if you don't know the sender. Figure 9.2 illustrates the steps by which computer viruses are often passed from one computer to the next:

1. An individual writes a virus program disguised as a music file of a popular music group's new hit song and posts it to a file sharing site.

2. Unsuspecting Bill downloads the "music file" and infects his computer.

3. Bill sends his cousin Fred an e-mail with the infected "music file" and contaminates Fred's computer.

4. Fred saves the MP3 file to a flash drive and then copies it to his work computer and infects that machine as well.

5. Everyone who copies files from Fred's infected computer at work, or whose computer is networked to Fred's computer, risks spreading the virus.

Types of Viruses

Although thousands of computer viruses and variants exist, they can be grouped into six broad categories based on their behavior and method of transmission.

Boot-Sector Viruses

What are boot-sector viruses? A **boot-sector virus** replicates itself into a hard drive's master boot record. The **master boot record** is a program that executes whenever a computer boots up, ensuring that the virus will be loaded into memory immediately, even before some virus protection programs can load. Boot-sector viruses are often transmitted by a flash drive left in a USB port. When the computer boots up with the flash drive

Step 1: Virus creation.

Hacker's computer

Step 2: Initial virus infection.

File sharing server

Bill's computer

Coworker's computer

Step 3: Virus spreads to another computer.

Coworker's computer

Fred's work computer

Step 4: Virus spreads to work computer.

Step 5: Other computers susceptible to infection.

Fred's home computer

Figure 9.2

Computer viruses are passed from one unsuspecting user to the next.

connected, the computer tries to launch a master boot record from the flash drive, which is usually the trigger for the virus to infect the hard drive.

Logic Bombs and Time Bombs

What is a logic bomb? A logic bomb is a virus that is triggered when certain logical conditions are met—such as opening a file or starting a program a certain number of times. A **time bomb** is a virus that is triggered by the passage of time or on a certain date. For example, the Michelangelo virus was a famous time bomb that was set to trigger every year on March 6, Michelangelo's birthday. The BlackWorm virus (otherwise known as Kama Sutra, Mywife, or CME-24), another time bomb, spreads through e-mail attachments. Opening the attachment infects the computer, and on the third day of every month, the virus seeks out and deletes certain file types (such as executable or .EXE files) on Windows

computers. The effects of logic bombs and time bombs range from the display of annoying messages on the screen to reformatting of the hard drive, which causes complete data loss.

Worms

What is a worm? A **worm** is slightly different from a virus in that a worm attempts to travel between systems through network connections to spread an infection. A virus infects a host file and waits until that file is executed on another computer to replicate. A worm, however, works independently of host file execution and is much more active in spreading itself. When the Conficker worm broke out, it quickly infected an estimated 9 million to 15 million individual computers. This worm spread through vulnerabilities in the Windows code and compromised computers by disabling certain software services and utility programs (such as Windows Update). Fortunately, it is easy to protect yourself from most worms.

Installing **antivirus software**, which is software specifically designed to detect viruses and protect your computer and files from harm, is a good start. You also should apply software patches (updates issued by the manufacturers of software such as Windows that repairs known security problems) to your computer whenever they are issued. We discuss protective measures later in the chapter.

Script and Macro Viruses

What are script and macro viruses? Some viruses are hidden on Web sites in the form of scripts. A **script** is a series of commands—actually, a miniprogram—that is executed without your knowledge. Scripts are often used to perform useful, legitimate functions on Web sites such as collecting name and address information from customers. However, some scripts are malicious. For example, say you receive an e-mail encouraging you to visit a Web site full of useful programs and information. When you click a link to display a video on the Web site you were directed to, a script runs that infects your computer with a virus without your knowledge

A **macro virus** is a virus that attaches itself to a document (such as a Word or Excel file) that uses macros. A macro is a short series of commands that usually automates repetitive tasks. However, macro languages are now so sophisticated that viruses can be written with them. The Melissa virus became the first major macro virus to cause problems worldwide.

The Melissa virus was also the first practical example of an e-mail virus. **E-mail viruses** use the address book in the victim's e-mail system to distribute the virus. Anyone opening an infected document triggered the virus, which infected other Word documents on the victim's computer. Once triggered, the Melissa virus sent itself to the first 50 people in the address book on the infected computer. This helped ensure that Melissa became one of the most widely distributed viruses ever released.

Encryption Viruses

What are encryption viruses? When **encryption viruses** infect your computer, they run a program that searches for common types of data files (such as Microsoft Word and Excel files) and compresses them using a complex encryption key that renders

CAPTCHA: Keeping Web Sites Safe From Bots

Automated programs called *bots* (or *Web robots*) are used to make tasks easier on the Internet. Search engines use bots in a technique called *spidering* to search and index Web pages. Unfortunately, bots can also be used for malicious or illegal purposes because these bots can perform some computing tasks much faster than humans. For example, bots can be used on ticket ordering sites to try to buy large blocks of high-demand concert tickets or to make repeated entries into contests in attempts to increase the chances of winning sweepstakes or prizes. Frequently, bots are used to post spam in the comments sections of blogs. Fortunately, Web site owners can easily deploy software known as a *CAPTCHA program* (see Figure 9.3) to prevent such bot activities.

CAPTCHA (Completely Automated Public Turing Test to Tell Computers and Humans Apart) programs generate distorted text and require that it be typed into a box. Because bots can't yet be programmed to read distorted text, which most people usually can, the CAPTCHA program is used to verify that a human is performing whatever task is being tested. The program helps Web site owners defend against all types of automated scams. If you want to try integrating a CAPTCHA program into your Web site (to protect your e-mail address), go to **recaptcha.net**, which offers free CAPTCHA tools to help you protect your data.

Figure 9.3

CAPTCHA programs like this one verify that a human, not a bot being used for malicious purposes, is performing the requested task.

your files unusable. You then receive a message that asks you to send money to an account if you want to receive the program to decrypt your files. The flaw with this type of virus, which keeps it from being widespread, is that law enforcement officials can trace the payments to an account and may possibly be able to catch the perpetrators. Still, we see these types of viruses from time to time.

Virus Classifications

How else are viruses classified? Viruses can also be classified by the methods they take to avoid detection by antivirus software:

- A **polymorphic virus** changes its own code (or periodically rewrites itself) to avoid detection. Most polymorphic

BITS AND BYTES

Virus Symptoms

If your computer displays any of the following symptoms, it may be infected with a virus:

1. Existing program icons or files suddenly disappear. (Viruses often delete specific file types or programs.)
2. Changes appear in your browser. If you start your browser and it takes you to an unusual home page (one you didn't set) or it has new toolbars, then you may have a virus.
3. Odd messages, pop-ups, or images are displayed on the screen or strange music or sounds play.
4. Data files become corrupt. Although files become corrupt for many reasons, a virus is one cause.
5. Programs don't work properly. This could be caused by either a corrupted file or a virus.
6. Your system slows down or takes a long time to boot up.

If you think you have a virus, boot up your computer with an antivirus software CD in your DVD/CD drive. This allows you to run the antivirus software before potential viruses load on the computer. Are you looking for free antivirus software? Consider downloading AVG Anti-Virus Free Edition (**free.avg.com**) or Microsoft Security Essentials (**microsoft.com/security_essentials**).

viruses infect a particular type of file (.EXE files, for example).

- A **multipartite virus** is designed to infect multiple file types in an effort to fool the antivirus software that is looking for it.
- **Stealth viruses** temporarily erase their code from the files where they reside and then hide in the active memory of the computer. This helps them avoid detection if only the hard drive is being searched for viruses. Fortunately, current antivirus software scans memory as well as the hard drive.

Given the creativity of virus programmers, you can be sure we'll see other types of viruses emerge in the future. In the next section, we discuss preventing virus infections.

ACTIVE HELP-DESK

Avoiding Computer Viruses

In this Active Helpdesk call, you'll play the role of a helpdesk staffer, fielding calls about different types of viruses and what users should do to protect their computer from them.

Computer Safeguard: Antivirus Software and Software Updates

Certain viruses merely present minor annoyances, such as randomly sending an ambulance graphic across the bottom of the screen, as is the case with the Red Cross virus. Other viruses can significantly slow down a computer or network, or destroy key files or the contents of entire hard drives. The best defense against viruses is to install antivirus software. Symantec, Kaspersky, AVG, and McAfee are among the companies that offer highly rated antivirus software packages.

Although you can buy stand-alone antivirus software, antivirus protection is included in comprehensive Internet security packages such as Norton Internet Security, Kaspersky Internet Security, or McAfee Total Protection. These software packages will help protect you from other threats as well as from computer viruses.

Antivirus Software

How often do I need to run antivirus software? Although antivirus software is designed to detect suspicious activity on your computer at all times, you should run an active virus scan on your entire system at least once a week. By doing so, all files on your computer will be checked for undetected viruses. Because these checks take time, you can configure the software to run them automatically when you aren't using your system—for example, late at night (see Figure 9.4). Alternatively, if you suspect a problem, you can launch a scan and have it run immediately.

How does antivirus software work? Most antivirus software looks for virus signatures in files. A **virus signature** is a portion of the virus code that is unique to a particular computer virus. Antivirus software scans files for these signatures and thereby identifies infected files and the type of virus that is infecting them.

The antivirus software scans files when they're opened or executed. If it detects a virus signature or suspicious activity (such as the launch of an unknown macro), it stops the execution of the file and virus and notifies you that it has detected a virus. It also places the virus in a secure area on your hard drive so that it won't spread infection to other files. This procedure is known as **quarantining**. Usually the antivirus software then gives you the choice of deleting or repairing the infected file. Unfortunately, antivirus programs can't always fix infected files to make them usable again. You should keep backup copies of critical files so that you can restore them in case a virus damages them irreparably.

Most antivirus software will also attempt to prevent infection by inoculating key files on your computer. In **inoculation**, the antivirus software records key attributes about files on your computer (such as file size and date created) and keeps these statistics in a safe place on your hard drive. When scanning for viruses, the antivirus software compares the files to the attributes it previously recorded to help detect attempts by virus programs to modify your files.

Does antivirus software always stop viruses? Antivirus software catches known viruses effectively. Unfortunately, new viruses are written all the time. To combat unknown viruses, modern antivirus programs search for suspicious virus-like activities as well as virus signatures. However, virus authors know how antivirus software works. They take special measures to disguise their virus code and hide the effects of a virus until just the right moment. This helps ensure that the virus spreads faster and farther. Thus, your computer can be attacked by a virus that your antivirus software doesn't recognize. To minimize this risk, you should keep your antivirus software up to date.

How do I make sure my antivirus software is up to date? Most antivirus programs have an automatic update feature that downloads updates for virus signature files every time you go online (see Figure 9.5).

What should I do if I think my computer is infected with a virus? Boot up your computer using the antivirus installation disc. (*Note:* If you download your antivirus software from the Internet, it is a good idea to copy your antivirus software to a DVD in case you have problems in the future.) This should prevent most virus

programs from loading and will allow you to run the antivirus software directly from your disk drive. If the software does detect viruses, you may want to research them further to determine whether your antivirus software will eradicate them completely or whether you will need to take additional manual steps to eliminate the virus. Most antivirus company Web sites, such as the Symantec site (**symantec.com**), contain archives of information on viruses and provide step-by-step solutions for removing viruses.

Figure 9.4

In Norton Internet Security, complete virus scans can be set up to run automatically. This computer will be scanned every Tuesday at 8 P.M.

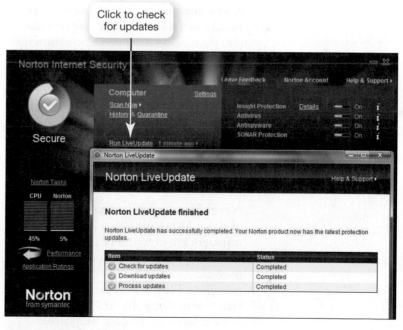

Figure 9.5

Antivirus software, such as Norton Internet Security, provides for automatic updates to the software installed on the computer.

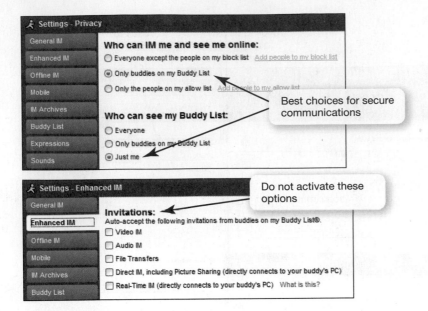

Figure 9.6

When you use instant messenger programs, check all of the preference screens for appropriate settings.

Are instant messenger programs safe from virus attacks? Virus attacks and other forms of malicious hacking can be perpetrated via instant messenger (IM) programs such as Google Talk, Skype, Facebook Chat, and iChat. Even if you have antivirus protection installed, people still could contact you for the purposes of trying to trick you into revealing sensitive information. Therefore, you should try to hide your instant messaging activity from everyone except people you know. To keep your IM sessions safe, follow these precautions:

1. **Allow contact only from users on your Buddy or Friends List.** This prevents you from being annoyed by unknown parties. On Facebook, you should restrict your profile information to be viewed only by friends and only accept friend requests from people you know and trust. On the settings screen for your IM program (Figure 9.6), select Allow only users on my Buddy List. And, of course, don't put anyone you don't know and trust on your buddy list.

2. **Never automatically accept transfers of data.** Although video IMs and file transfers are potentially useful for swapping files over IM (see Figure 9.6), they are a common way of transmitting malicious files, which can then infect your computer with viruses. Enabling auto-acceptance of data transfers is never a good idea.

3. **Avoid using instant messaging programs on public computers.** If you use

a shared computer, such as one in a computer lab at school, be sure you don't select any features that remember your password or connect you automatically. The next person who uses the computer might be able to connect to the instant messaging service with your screen name (or your Facebook account) and impersonate you.

Software Updates

Is there anything else I should do to protect my system? Many viruses exploit weaknesses in operating systems. Malicious Web sites can be set up to attack your computer by downloading harmful software onto your computer. According to research conducted by Google, this type of attack, known as a **drive-by download**, is common and affects almost 1 in 1,000 Web pages. To combat these threats, make sure your antivirus software and your operating system are up to date and contain the latest security patches. You can update your Windows operating system with an automatic update utility called *Windows Update*. When you enable automatic updates, your computer searches for updates on the Microsoft Web site every time it connects to the Internet. OS X has a similar utility for gathering updates.

Do updates only happen automatically? Although many people decide to receive updates automatically, there are several options you can choose from in Windows, as shown in Figure 9.7. The following options are noteworthy.

- Option 1: **Install updates automatically**. Selecting this option will automatically download and install updates at a time you have specified. We strongly recommend that you select this option.

- Option 2: **Download updates but let me choose whether to install them**. Although this option automatically

SOUND BYTE Protecting Your Computer

In this Sound Byte, you'll learn how to use a variety of tools to protect your computer, including antivirus software and Windows utilities.

downloads updates, they are not installed until you instruct Windows to install them. We don't usually recommend this option because you may forget to install important updates.

- Option 3: **Check for updates but let me choose whether to download and install them**. This is an appropriate choice if you have low bandwidth Internet access. Because downloads over dial-up can take a long time due to low bandwidth, you need to control when downloads will occur so they don't interrupt your workflow.

- Option 4: **Give me recommended updates**. This option ensures you receive recommended (optional) updates as well as critical (necessary) updates.

- Option 5: **Microsoft Update**, This option ensures you receive updates for other Microsoft products besides Windows (such as Microsoft Office).

In the next section, we explore another major threat to your digital security—hackers.

Computer Threats: Hackers

Although there is a great deal of disagreement as to what a hacker actually is (especially among hackers themselves), a **hacker** is most commonly defined as anyone who unlawfully breaks into a computer system—either an individual computer or a network (see Figure 9.8).

Are there different kinds of hackers? Some hackers are offended by being labeled as criminals and therefore attempt to classify different types of hackers. A hacker who breaks into systems just for the challenge of it (and who doesn't wish to steal or wreak havoc on the systems) may refer to him- or herself as a **white-hat hacker**. These individuals tout themselves as experts who are performing a needed service for society by helping companies uncover the vulnerabilities in their systems.

White-hat hackers look down on those hackers who use their knowledge to destroy information or for illegal gain. A term for these more villainous hackers is **black-hat hacker**. (The terms *white hat* and *black hat* are references to old Western movies in which the heroes wore white hats and the outlaws wore

black hats.) Regardless of the hackers' opinions, the laws in the United States and in many other countries consider any unauthorized access to computer systems a crime.

What about the teenage hackers who are caught every so often? These amateur hackers are often referred to as **script kiddies**. Script kiddies don't create the programs they use to hack into computer systems; instead, they use tools created by skilled hackers that enable unskilled novices to wreak the same havoc as professional hackers.

Fortunately, because the users of these programs are amateurs, they're usually not proficient at covering their electronic tracks. Therefore, it's relatively easy for law enforcement officials to track them down and prosecute them. Script kiddies nevertheless can cause a lot of disruption and damage to computers, networks, and Web sites.

Why would a hacker be interested in breaking into my home computer? Some hackers just like to snoop. They enjoy the challenge of breaking into systems and seeing what information they can find. Other hackers are hobbyists seeking information about a particular topic wherever they can find it. Because many people keep proprietary business information on their home computers, hackers bent on industrial espionage may break into home computers. For other hackers, hacking is a way to pass time.

What Hackers Steal

Could a hacker steal my credit card number? If you perform financial transactions online, such as banking or buying

Figure 9.7

The Windows Update screen makes it easy for users to configure Windows to update itself.

>To enable automatic updates, click **Start**, select **Control Panel**, select **System** and **Security**, click the **Windows Update** link, and then click the **Change Settings** link.

BRINGING CIVILIZATION TO ITS KNEES...

Goths

Vandals

Huns

Geeks

Figure 9.8
Although they do not necessarily destroy civilization, hackers can cause problems for corporations and individuals alike.

goods and services, then you probably do so using a credit (or debit) card. Credit card and bank account information can thus reside on your hard drive and may be detectable by a hacker. Also, many sites require you to provide a login ID and password to gain access. Even if this data is not stored on your computer, a hacker may be able to capture it when you're online by using a packet sniffer or a keylogger (a program that captures all keystrokes made on a computer).

What's a packet sniffer? Data travels through the Internet in small pieces, each called a **packet**. The packets are identified with an IP address, in part to help identify the computer to which they are being sent. Once the packets reach their destination, they are reassembled into cohesive messages. A **packet sniffer** is a computer program deployed by hackers that looks at (or sniffs) each packet as it travels on the Internet—not just those that are addressed to a particular computer, but all packets. Some packet sniffers are configured to capture all the packets into memory, whereas others capture only packets that contain specific content (such as credit card numbers). Wireless networks can be particularly vulnerable to this type of exploitation because many people do not enable encryption of data when they set up their wireless

networks (covered in Chapter 7). A hacker might sit in a coffee shop connected to a wireless network and run a packet sniffer to capture data from other patrons who are using the wireless network. This makes it easy for hackers to intercept and read sensitive information transmitted without encryption, such as credit card numbers or the contents of e-mails.

What do hackers do with the information they "sniff"? Once a hacker has your credit card information, he or she can either use it to purchase items illegally or sell the number to someone who will. If a hacker steals the login ID and password to an account where you have your credit card information stored (such as eBay or Amazon), he or she can also use your account to purchase items and have them shipped to him- or herself instead of to you. If hackers can gather enough information in conjunction with your credit card information, they may be able to commit identity theft. **Identity theft** is characterized by someone using personal information about you (such as your name, address, or Social Security number) to assume your identity for the purpose of defrauding others.

Although this sounds scary, you can easily protect yourself from packet sniffing by installing a firewall (which we discuss later in this chapter) and using data encryption on a wireless network (which was covered in Chapter 7).

Trojan Horses

Besides stealing information, what other problems can hackers cause if they break into my computer? Hackers often use individuals' computers as a staging area for mischief. To commit widespread computer attacks, for example, hackers need to control many computers at the same time. To this end, hackers often use Trojan horses to install other programs on computers. A **Trojan**

horse is a program that appears to be something useful or desirable (like a game or a screen saver), but while it runs does something malicious in the background without your knowledge. The term *Trojan horse* derives from Greek mythology and refers to the wooden horse that the Greeks used to sneak into the city of Troy and conquer it. Therefore, computer programs that contain a hidden (and usually dreadful) "surprise" are referred to as Trojan horses.

What damage can Trojan horses do? Often, the malicious activity perpetrated by a Trojan horse program is the installation of a **backdoor program** that allows hackers to take almost complete control of your computer without your knowledge. Using a backdoor program, hackers can access and delete all the files on your computer, send e-mail, run programs, and do just about anything else you can do with your computer. A computer that a hacker controls in this manner is referred to as a **zombie**. Zombies are often used to launch denial-of-service attacks on other computers.

Denial of Service Attacks

What are denial-of-service attacks?
In a **denial-of-service (DoS) attack**, legitimate users are denied access to a computer system because a hacker is repeatedly making requests of that computer system through a computer he or she has taken over as a zombie. A computer can handle only a certain number of requests for information at one time. When it is flooded with requests in a denial-of-service attack, it shuts down and refuses to answer any requests for information, even if the requests are from a legitimate user. Thus, the computer is so busy responding to the bogus requests for information that authorized users can't gain access.

Couldn't a DoS attack be traced by to the computer that launched it? Launching a DoS attack on a computer system from a single computer is easy to trace. Therefore, most savvy hackers use a **distributed denial-of-service (DDoS) attack**, which launches DoS attacks from more than one zombie (sometimes thousands of zombies) at the same time. Figure 9.9 illustrates how a DDoS attack

Figure 9.9

Zombie computers are used to facilitate a distributed denial-of-service (DDoS) attack.

Hacker launches DDoS by activating zombies (red lines)

Hacker's computer

Academic computer (zombie)

Government computer (zombie)

Home computer (zombie)

Corporate computer (zombie)

ISP computer (zombie)

Zombie computers attack target system (blue lines)

Victim of DDoS

works. A hacker creates many zombies and coordinates them so that they begin sending bogus requests to the same computer at the same time. Administrators of the victim computer often have a great deal of difficulty stopping the attack because it comes from so many computers. Often the attacks are coordinated automatically by botnets. A **botnet** is a large group of software programs (called *robots* or *bots*) that runs autonomously on zombie computers. Some botnets have been known to span 1.5 million computers.

DDoS attacks are a serious problem. In April 2009, the International Federation of the Phonographic Industry (IFPI) and Motion Picture Association of America (MPAA) Web sites were subjected to DDoS attacks in protest of the conviction of the owners of The Pirate Bay (a notorious file-sharing site) on charges of assisting in copyright infringement. In August 2009, social networking sites including Twitter and Facebook were subjected to a DDoS attack that was apparently aimed at a blogger. Twitter and Facebook users experienced problems accessing the sites for hours during the attack. Because many Web sites receive revenue from users, either directly (such as via subscriptions to online games) or indirectly (such as when Web surfers click on advertisements), DDoS attacks can be financially distressing for the owners of the affected Web sites.

How Hackers Gain Access

How exactly does a hacker gain access to a computer? Hackers can gain access to computers directly or indirectly. Direct access involves sitting down at a computer and installing hacking software. It is unlikely that such an attack would occur in your home. However, to deter unauthorized use, you may want to lock the room that your computer is in or remove key components (such as the power cord) when strangers such as repair personnel are in your house and may be unobserved for periods of time. You might also set up your computer so that it requires a password for a user to gain access to your desktop.

The most likely method a hacker will use to access a computer is to enter indirectly through its Internet connection. When connected to the Internet, your computer is potentially open to attack by hackers. Many people forget that their Internet connection is a two-way street. Not only can you access the Internet but also people on the Internet can access your computer.

Think of the computer as a house. Common sense tells you to lock your doors and windows to deter theft when you aren't home. Hooking your computer up to the Internet is like leaving the front door to your house wide open. Anyone passing by can access your computer and poke around for valuables. Your computer obviously doesn't have doors and windows like a house, but it does have logical ports.

What are logical ports? Logical **ports** are virtual—that is, not physical—communications gateways or paths that allow a computer to organize requests for information (such as Web page downloads or e-mail routing) from other networks or computers. Unlike physical ports (USB, FireWire, and so on), you can't see or touch a logical port; it is part of a computer's internal organization.

Logical ports are numbered and assigned to specific services. For instance, logical port 80 is designated for hypertext transfer protocol (HTTP), the main communications protocol (or standard) for the World Wide Web. Thus, all requests for information from your browser to the Web flow through logical port 80. E-mail messages sent by simple mail transfer protocol (SMTP), the protocol used for sending e-mail on the Internet, are routed through logical port 25. Open logical ports, like open windows in a home, invite intruders, as illustrated in Figure 9.10. Unless you take precautions to restrict access to your logical ports, other people on the Internet may be able to access your computer through them.

Fortunately, you can thwart most hacking problems by installing a firewall.

Restricting Access to Your Digital Assets

Keeping hackers at bay is often just a matter of keeping them out. This can be achieved either by preventing them from accessing your computer (usually through your Internet connection), by protecting your digital information in such a way that it can't be accessed (with passwords, for example), or by hiding your activities from prying eyes. In the next section, we explore strategies for protecting access to your digital assets and keeping your Internet surfing activities from being seen by the wrong people.

Firewalls

A **firewall** is a program or hardware device designed to protect computers from hackers. A firewall specifically designed for home networks is called a **personal firewall**. Personal firewalls are made to be easy to install. By using a personal firewall, you can close open logical ports to invaders and potentially make your computer invisible to other computers on the Internet.

Firewalls are named after a housing construction feature. When houses were first being packed densely into cities, they were attached to each other with common walls. Fire was a huge hazard because wood burns readily. An entire neighborhood could be lost in a single fire. Thus, builders started building common walls of nonflammable or slow-burning material to stop, or at least slow, the spread of fire. These came to be known as *firewalls*.

Types of Firewalls

What kinds of firewalls are there? As noted earlier, firewalls can be configured using either software or hardware devices. Although installing either a software or a hardware firewall on your home network is probably sufficient, you should consider installing both for maximum protection.

What software firewalls are there? Most current operating systems include reliable firewalls. Many security suites such as Norton Internet Security, McAfee Internet Security, and ZoneAlarm Internet Security Suite also include firewall software. Although the firewalls that come with Windows 7 and OS X will protect your computer, firewalls included in security suites often come with additional features such as monitoring systems that alert you if your computer is under attack.

If you are using a security suite (say, for virus protection and parental controls) that includes a firewall, you should disable the firewall that came with your operating system. Two firewalls running at the same time can conflict with each other and can cause your computer to slow down or freeze up.

What are hardware firewalls? You can also buy and configure hardware firewall devices. Many routers sold for home networks include firewall protection. Just like software firewalls, the setup for hardware firewalls is designed for novices, and the default configuration on most routers keeps unused logical ports closed. Documentation accompanying routers can assist users with more experience in adjusting the settings to allow access to specific ports if needed.

FTP (Port 21) YOUR COMPUTER DNS (Port 53)

HTTP (Port 80)

E-mail (Port 25) Telnet (Port 23)

WEB SITE REQUEST

Figure 9.10

Open logical ports are an invitation to hackers.

ACTIVE HELP-DESK

Understanding Firewalls

In this Active Helpdesk call, you'll play the role of a helpdesk staffer, fielding calls about how hackers can attack networks and what harm they can cause, as well as what a firewall does to keep a computer safe from hackers.

Firewalls are designed to restrict access to a network and its computers. Firewalls protect you in two major ways: by blocking access to logical ports and by keeping your computer's network address secure.

To block access to logical ports, firewalls examine data packets that your computer sends and receives. Data packets contain information such as the address of the sending and receiving computers and the logical port the packet will use. Firewalls can be configured so that they filter out packets sent to specific logical ports. This process is referred to as **packet filtering**.

For example, file transfer protocol (FTP) programs are a typical way in which hackers access a computer. Hackers can disguise their requests for information as legitimate packets that appear to be FTP requests authorized by your computer. If a firewall is configured to ignore *all* incoming packets that request access to port 21 (the port designated for FTP traffic), no FTP requests will get through to your computer. This process is referred to as **logical port blocking**.

If port 21 were a window at your home, you would probably lock it so that a burglar couldn't get in. If you needed port 21 for a legitimate purpose, you could instruct the firewall to allow access to that port for a specified period of time or by a certain user.

For the Internet to share information seamlessly, data packets must have a way of getting to their correct locations. Therefore, every computer connected to the Internet has a unique address called an **Internet Protocol address** (or **IP address**). As noted earlier, data packets contain the IP address of the computer to which they are being sent. Routing servers on the Internet make sure the packets

get to the correct address. This is similar to the way addresses work on a conventional letter. A unique street address (such as 123 Main St., Anywhere, CA 99999) is placed on the envelope, and the postal service routes it to its correct destination. Without such addressing, data packets, like letters, would not reach their intended recipients.

IP addresses are assigned in a procedure known as **dynamic addressing** when users log on to their Internet service provider (ISP), as shown in Figure 9.11). The dynamic host configuration protocol (DHCP) server assigns IP addresses out of a pool of available IP addresses licensed to the ISP in this manner:

1. When you connect to your ISP, your computer requests an IP address.
2. The ISP's DHCP server consults its list of available IP addresses and selects one.
3. The selected IP address is communicated to your computer. The address remains in force for as long as you are connected to the ISP.
4. Once on the Internet, your Web browser requests access to ABC Company's Web site.
5. The ABC Company server consults an IP address listing and determines that the IP address of your computer is assigned to your ISP. It then forwards the requested information to the ISP's router.
6. The ISP knows to whom it assigned the IP address and, therefore, routes the requested information to your computer.

Because hackers use IP addresses to find victims and come back to their computers for more mischief, frequently switching IP addresses helps make users less vulnerable to attacks. Periodically switching off your modem and rebooting it will cause a different IP address to be assigned dynamically

Figure 9.11

How dynamic addressing works.

Knowing Your Computer Is Secure

How can I tell if my computer is at risk?
For peace of mind (and to ensure that your firewall setup was successful), you can visit several Web sites that offer free services that test your computer's vulnerability. One popular site is Gibson Research (**grc.com**). The company's ShieldsUP and LeakTest programs are free, easy to run, and can pinpoint security vulnerabilities in a system that is connected to the Internet. If you get a clean report from these programs,

your system is probably not vulnerable to attack. Figure 9.13 shows the results screen from a ShieldsUP port probe test, which checks which logical ports in your computer are vulnerable. This test was run on a computer connected to the Internet with no firewall installed. Ports reported as closed or in stealth mode are safe from attack. Ports reported as open (such as port 1025) are subject to exploitation by hackers. Installation of a hardware or software firewall should close any open ports.

Step 1

Step 4

Router IP address:
111.22.3.44

Step 2

Step 3

Your computer's internal
IP address: 192.11.4.123

Hacker

ABC Company
Web server

Figure 9.12

Network address
translation in action.

to your modem by your ISP. This tends to enhance your security.

However, because many broadband users leave their modems on for long periods of time (consecutive days or weeks), their IP addresses tend to change less frequently than those of dial-up users. This is similar to having an IP address assigned by **static addressing**. In static addressing, your IP address is always the same and is assigned by your ISP. This process is often used by businesses who are hosting a Web site. When a broadband user has a static address, the user is more vulnerable to hackers because the hackers have a more permanent IP address with which to locate the computer. It also makes it easier for hackers to make repeated visits to a computer.

To combat the problems associated with static addressing, firewalls use a process called **network address translation (NAT)** to assign internal IP addresses on a network. These internal IP addresses are only shared with devices that are part of the network, so the addresses are safe from hackers. Figure 9.12 shows how NAT works. Your computer's internal IP address is assigned to your computer by the router. This IP address is used only on the internal network and therefore cannot be detected by other Internet users. Here's how it works:

1. Your computer's Web browser requests access to the ABC Company's Web site. This request travels through the router, which is configured as a firewall.

2. The router forwards the browser request to the ABC Company Web server and directs that server to send the data back to the router's

external IP address (in this example, 111.22.3.44). The internal IP address of your computer (assigned by NAT) is not revealed to computers outside your network.

3. The ABC Company Web server processes the request and sends the data back to the router's external IP address (111.22.3.44). This is the IP address the ISP assigned to your router, and it can be detected by other users on the Internet.

4. The router then passes the requested data to the IP address of the computer that requested it (in this example, 192.11.4.123).

The router's IP address is assigned by your ISP. Only the router's external IP address can be detected by other users on the Internet. For hackers to access your computer, they must know your computer's internal IP address. With a NAT-capable router/firewall installed on your network, hackers are unable to access the internal IP address assigned to your computer, so your computer is safe.

You can use NAT in your home by purchasing a hardware firewall with NAT capabilities. As noted earlier, many routers sold for home use are also configured as firewalls, and many feature NAT as well.

Figure 9.13

ShieldsUP common ports
test results.

143	IMAP	Closed	Your computer has responded that this port exists but is currently closed to connections.
389	LDAP	Closed	Your computer has responded that this port exists but is currently closed to connections.
443	HTTPS	Closed	Your computer has responded that this port exists but is currently closed to connections.
445	MSFT DS	Stealth	There is NO EVIDENCE WHATSOEVER that a port (or even any computer) exists at this IP address!
1002	ms-ils	Closed	Your computer has responded that this port exists but is currently closed to connections.
1024	DCOM	Closed	Your computer has responded that this port exists but is currently closed to connections.
1025	Host	OPEN!	One or more unspecified Distributed COM (DCOM) services are opened by Windows. The exact port(s) opened can change, since queries to port 135 are used to determine... As is the rule for all exposed Intern... close this port to external access so tha... ...curity or privacy exploits can not succeed against your system.

Ports safe from attack

Port subject to attack

Figure 9.14 | COMMON LOGICAL PORTS

Port Number	Protocol Using the Port
21	FTP (file transfer protocol) control
23	Telnet (unencrypted text communications)
25	SMTP (simple mail transfer protocol)
53	DNS (domain name system)
80	HTTP (hypertext transfer protocol)
443	HTTPS [HTTP protocol with transport layer security (TLS) encryption]

What if I don't get a clean report from the testing program? If the testing program detects potential vulnerabilities and you don't have a firewall, you should install one as soon as possible. If the firewall is already configured and common ports (such as those shown in Figure 9.14) are identified as being vulnerable, consult your firewall documentation for instructions on how to close or restrict access to those ports.

Preventing Bluetooth Attacks

What are the security vulnerabilities of Bluetooth devices? Bluetooth is a transmission medium for exchanging data wirelessly over short distances. Most smartphones are Bluetooth enabled. Although progress is being made, Bluetooth hardware and software still are riddled with security holes, especially on smartphones. If you have a Bluetooth-enabled device, you are susceptible to two severe types of mischief: bluesnarfing and bluebugging.

- Bluesnarfing involves exploiting a flaw in the Bluetooth access software for the purpose of accessing a Bluetooth device and stealing the information contained on it. Think how much valuable information is contained on your smartphone

SOUND BYTE — Installing a Personal Firewall

Firewalls provide excellent protection against hackers on a home network. In this Sound Byte, you'll learn how to install and configure software firewalls to protect your computer.

(names, contact information, and meeting notes) that might be valuable to a business competitor. Unfortunately, Bluesnarfing is relatively easy (and cheap) because a lot of Bluesnarfing software is available on the Internet. A twist on this attack is Car Whisperer software, which is specifically designed to eavesdrop on conversations taking place in your car when you are using a hands-free device (such as a cell phone or GPS).

- Although much more difficult and expensive to execute, Bluebugging presents more serious dangers. The process involves a hacker actually taking control of a Bluetooth-enabled device. Once a hacker gains control of the device, he or she can make phone calls, establish Internet connections, read phonebook entries, set call forwarding, or send, receive, and read short message service (SMS) messages.

  Bluebugging is a major risk in Europe because Bluetooth and SMS are wildly popular there, but the rise of Bluetooth usage in the United States is making it a risk here as well. Many Europeans use their phones to make micropayments (small purchases from merchants that eventually appear on their cell phone bill) by a process known as *reverse* SMS. If a hacker Bluebugs your phone, he or she could potentially send payments to fake accounts he or she controls, using reverse SMS.

How can I protect myself from Bluetooth attacks? Most devices with Bluetooth capability give you the option of making your device invisible to unauthorized Bluetooth devices. This does not affect your ability to use two Bluetooth devices you own together (such as a wireless headset paired with a phone). When you pair your headset with your phone, the headset (which has a unique serial number) becomes an authorized Bluetooth device for your phone. Moreover, by making your device invisible to unauthorized devices (such as hackers' headsets), you prevent hackers from connecting to your equipment (your phone) because their headsets are not authorized devices for your phone. When vulnerabilities are discovered, cell phone manufacturers issue software patches. Antivirus software is also available for mobile devices, so you may wish to purchase this for your phone. You must ensure that you update the software in your mobile devices just as you do your computer's OS and antivirus software. For more information on securing your Bluetooth devices, go to the Bluetooth technology Web site (**bluetomorrow.com**).

Password Protection and Password Management

Passwords, used in conjunction with login IDs, are the major way we restrict access to computers, networks, and online accounts. You no doubt have many passwords that you need to remember to access your digital life. However, creating strong passwords—ones that are difficult for hackers to guess—is an essential piece of security that individuals sometimes overlook. Password cracking programs have become more sophisticated lately. In fact, some commonly available programs, such as John the Ripper, can test more than 1 million password combinations per second! Creating a secure password is therefore more important than ever.

Many people use extremely weak passwords. The Imperva Application Defense Center (a computer security research organization) conducted a review of 32 million passwords that were used at the Web site **rockyou.com**. More than 345,000 people were using "12345," "123456," or "123456789" as their password. And almost 62,000 people were using "password"! Passwords such as these are extremely easy for hackers to crack.

Creating Passwords

What constitutes a strong password? Strong passwords are difficult for someone to guess. They should not contain easily deduced components related to your life such as parts of your name, your pet's name, your street address, or your telephone number. To create strong passwords, follow the basic guidelines shown here:

- Your password should contain at least 14 characters and include numbers, symbols, and upper- and lowercase letters.
- Your password should not be a single word or any word found in the dictionary.

- Ideally, it should be a combination of several words with strategically placed uppercase characters.
- Your password should not be easily associated with you (such as your birth date, the name of your pet, or your nickname).
- Use a different password for each system or Web site you need to access. This prevents access to other accounts you maintain if one of your passwords is discovered.
- Never tell anyone your password or write it down in a place where others might see it.
- Change your password on a regular basis (say, every month) and change it sooner if you think someone may know it.

Figure 9.15 shows some possible passwords and explains why they are strong or weak candidates.

How can I check the strength of my passwords? You can use online password strength testers, such as The Password Meter (**passwordmeter.com**) or Microsoft's test (**microsoft.com/protect/ yourself/password/checker.mspx**), to

BITS AND BYTES

Connecting to Wireless Networks on the Road? Beware of "Evil Twins"!

When you are at the airport or coffee shop, you may need to connect to a wireless network and check your e-mail. You switch on your notebook, and the wireless network adapter finds a network called "free wifi" or "airport wireless." You connect, enter your credit card information to pay for your airtime, and start merrily surfing away. Three days later, your credit card company calls asking about the $2,400 big-screen TV you just bought at the local electronics store and the $3,200 of power tools charged at the home improvement store. You didn't make either of these purchases; you probably fell prey to an "evil twin" wireless hotspot.

Hackers know the areas where people are likely to seek access to wireless networks. They will often set up their own wireless networks in these areas with sound-alike names to lure unsuspecting Web surfers and get them to enter credit card information to gain access. Other times these "evil twins" offer free Internet access, and the hackers monitor traffic looking for sensitive information they can use.

So how can you protect yourself? Check with authorized personnel at places where you will be connecting to hotspots to determine the names of the legitimate hotspots. If you run across "free" access to a hotspot that isn't provided by a legitimate merchant, then you are better off not connecting at all because you can't be sure your information won't be used against you or that malicious files won't be downloaded to your computer.

Figure 9.15 | STRONG AND WEAK PASSWORD CANDIDATES

Strong Password	Reason
L8t2meGaNDalf351	Uses letters and numbers to come up with memorable phrase "Late to me" and adds it to a character name from *Lord of the Rings* plus a random number.
IwaLR8384GdY	First initials of first line of Green Day song *I Walk a Lonely Road* plus a random number and an abbreviation for Green Day.
P1zzA244WaterShiPDowN	Easily remembered word with mix of alphanumeric characters and upper- and lowercase letters, your locker number at your gym, plus the title of a book that you like (with upper- and lowercase letters).
S0da&ICB3N&J3RRY	Mix of numbers, symbols, and letters. Stands for soda and ice cream and the names of famous ice cream makers with the number 3 instead of the letter E.

Weak Password	Reason
Jsmith	Combination of first initial and last name.
4smithkids	Even though this has alphanumeric combination, it is too descriptive of a family.
Brown5512	Last name and last four digits of phone number are easily decoded.
123MainSt	A street address is an easily decoded password.

evaluate your passwords (see Figure 9.16). The Password Meter provides guidelines for good passwords and shows you how integrating various elements (such as symbols) affects the strength score for your password.

You should make sure you change your passwords on a regular basis (such as monthly or quarterly). Your school or your employer probably requires you to change your password regularly. This is also a good idea for your personal passwords. You should also not use the same password for every account that you have. Because remembering constantly changing strong passwords for numerous accounts can be

a challenge, you should use password-management tools, as described in the next section, to make the process easier to handle. If you have trouble thinking of secure passwords, there are many password generators available for free, such as Perfect Passwords (**grc.com/passwords.htm**) and the Bytes Interactive Password Generator (**goodpassword.com**).

Can I use a password to restrict access to my computer? Windows has built-in password protection for files as well as the entire desktop. If your computer is set up for multiple users with password protection, the Windows login screen requires you to enter a password to gain access to the desktop. You are also asked to enter a password hint to remind you in case you forget your password. The computer can be set to default back to the Welcome screen after it is idle for a set period of time. This forces a user to reenter a password to regain access to the computer. If someone attempts to log on to your computer without your password, that person won't be able to gain access. It is an especially good idea to use passwords on notebook computers or any computer that may be unattended for periods of time. Figure 9.17 shows the Control Panel screen used to set up a password on a user account.

There are two types of users in Windows: administrators and standard users. Setting up a password on a standard user account

Figure 9.16

The Password Meter objectively evaluates your passwords.

prevents other standard users from being able to access that user's files. However, users with administrator privileges can still see your files if you are a standard user. So be aware that your files may not be safe from all prying eyes!

Managing Your Passwords

How can I remember all of my complex passwords? Good security practices suggest that you have different passwords for different Web sites that you access and that you change your passwords frequently. The problem with well-constructed passwords is that they can be hard to remember. Fortunately, password-management tools are now widely available. This takes the worry out of forgetting passwords because the password-management software does the remembering for you.

Where can I obtain password-management software? Most current Internet security suites and Web browsers make it easy to keep track of passwords by providing password-management tools. For

example, to set up the password manager in Firefox, from the Tools menu, select Options, and then click the Security icon (the closed padlock) shown in Figure 9.18. In the Passwords section, check **Remember passwords for sites** to have Firefox remember passwords when you log onto Web sites. Check **Use a master password**, which causes a dialog box to appear, and enter a well-designed, secure password. The next time

Figure 9.17

Windows provides additional security for your files by locking unauthorized users out of your account.

>Click **Start**, click **Control Panel**, click **User Accounts** and **Family Safety**, click **UserAccounts**, and then click **Create a Password** for your account.

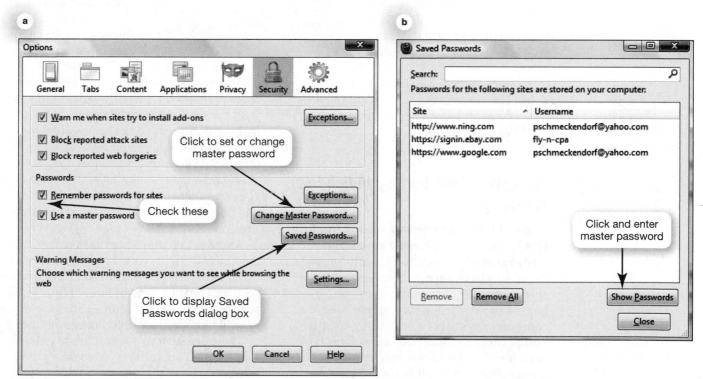

Figure 9.18

(a) The security tab in the Firefox browser options screen provides access to password-management tools. (b) The Firefox Saved Passwords dialog box displays all sites for which login information is saved.

>From the **Tools** menu, select **Options**. In the **Options** dialog box, click the **Show Passwords** button.

you go to a Web site that requires a login, Firefox will display a dialog box prompting you to have Firefox remember the login name and password for this site. Then, when you return to the site and select a login option, enter the master password and the Firefox Password Manager will fill in the login and password information for you.

You also can see a list of sites maintained by the Firefox Password Manager by clicking the Show Passwords button, which displays the Saved Passwords dialog box (see Figure 9.18). Passwords for each site are displayed after you click the Show Passwords button and enter the master password.

Even though you only need to remember the master password, you still need to make sure that it is a secure password (according to the rules we discussed earlier) and that you change it on a regular basis. Password managers are useful on the machine that you use on a regular basis. However, if you need to access your accounts from another computer (such as one at school), you will still need to know the individual passwords for each site you wish to access.

So start using secure passwords and let your browser (on your main computer) relieve you of the problem of trying to remember them all.

Anonymous Web Surfing: Hiding from Prying Eyes

Should I be concerned about surfing the Internet on shared or public computers? If you use shared computers in public places such as libraries, coffee shops, or college student unions, you should be concerned about a subsequent user of a computer spying on your surfing habits. You never know what nefarious tools have been installed by hackers on a public computer. When you browse the Internet, traces of your activity are left behind on that computer, often as temporary files. A wily hacker can glean sensitive information long after you have finished your latte and your surfing session.

What tools can I use to protect myself when using public computers? The current versions of Google Chrome, Firefox, and Internet Explorer include privacy tools that help you surf the Internet anonymously. Google Chrome's Incognito feature allows you to open a special version of the Google browser window. When surfing in this window, records of Web sites you visit and files you download do not appear in the Web browser's history files. Furthermore, any temporary files that were generated in that browsing session are deleted when you exit the Incognito window. The InPrivate Browsing feature of Internet Explorer and the Private Browsing feature of Firefox offer similar security features.

Portable privacy devices, such as the IronKey (**ironkey.com**) shown in Figure 9.19, provide an even higher level of surfing privacy. Simply plug the device into an available USB port on the machine on which you will be working. All sensitive Internet files, such as cookies, Internet history, and browser caches, will be stored on the privacy device, not on the computer you are using. Privacy devices such as these often come preloaded with software designed to shield your IP address from prying eyes, making it difficult (if not impossible) for hackers to tell where you are surfing on the Internet. These privacy devices also have password-management tools that store all of your login information and encrypt it so it will be safe if your privacy device falls into someone else's hands.

Another free practical solution is to take the Linux OS with you on a flash drive and avoid using the public computer's operating system. The interfaces of many Linux builds, such as Ubuntu (see Figure 9.20), look almost exactly like Windows and are easy to use.

There are several advantages to using a Linux-based operating system on a public computer. First, your risk of picking up viruses and other malicious programs is significantly reduced because booting a public computer from a flash drive completely eliminates any interaction with the public computer's operating system. This, in turn,

Figure 9.19

Portable privacy devices help to protect your privacy when you work on computers away from your home or office.

Figure 9.20

Ubuntu is a version of Linux that has a Windows-like interface and familiar browser tools like Firefox.

significantly reduces the chance that your flash drive will become infected by any malware running on the public computer.

Next, virus and hacking attacks against Linux are far less likely than attacks against Windows. Because Windows has more than 90 percent of the operating system market, people who write malware tend to target Windows systems. Finally, when you run software from your own storage medium (flash drive), you avoid reading and writing to the hard disk of the public computer. This significantly enhances your privacy because you don't leave traces of your activity behind.

Pendrivelinux.com (**pendrivelinux.com**) is an excellent resource that offers many different versions of Linux for download and includes step-by-step instructions on how to install them on your flash drive. If you are a Mac user, there is an option for you, too! The gOS version of Linux provides a close approximation of OS X, so you can feel right at home.

Biometric Authentication Devices

Besides passwords, how else can I restrict the use of my computer? A **biometric authentication device** is a device that reads a unique personal characteristic such as a fingerprint or the iris pattern in your eye and converts its pattern to a digital code. When you use the device, your pattern is read and compared to the one stored on the computer. Only users having an exact fingerprint or iris pattern match are allowed to access the computer.

Because no two people have the same biometric characteristics (fingerprints and iris patterns are unique), these devices provide a high level of security. They also eliminate the human error that can occur in password protection. You might forget your password, but you won't forget to bring your fingerprint to the computer! Some notebooks feature built-in fingerprint readers, and companies like SecuGen produce computer mice and keyboards (see Figure 9.21) that include built-in fingerprint readers. Other biometric devices, which include voice authentication and face pattern–recognition systems, are now widely offered in notebook computers.

Make sure to utilize some (or all) of these methods to keep your activities from prying eyes and to restrict access to your digital information.

Managing Online Annoyances

Surfing the Web, sending and receiving e-mail, and chatting online have become a common part of most of our lives. Unfortunately, the Web has become fertile ground

Figure 9.21

(a) The SecuGen OptiMouse Plus is a two-button mouse with a scroll wheel that includes a digital fingerprint reader. (b) The SecuGen Keyboard Plus features a fingerprint reader.

Fingerprint reader

Fingerprint reader

for people who want to advertise their products, track our Web browsing behaviors, or even con people into revealing personal information. In this section, we'll look at ways in which you can manage, if not avoid, these and other online headaches.

Malware, Adware, and Spyware

What is malware? **Malware** is software that has a malicious intent (hence the prefix *mal*). There are three primary forms of malware: adware, spyware, and viruses (which we have already discussed). Adware and spyware are not physically destructive like viruses and worms, which can destroy data. Known collectively as *grayware*, most are intrusive, annoying, or objectionable online programs that are downloaded to your computer when you install or use other online content such as a freeware program, game, or utility.

What is adware? **Adware** is software that displays sponsored advertisements in a section of your browser window or as a pop-up ad box. It is considered a legitimate (though sometimes annoying) means of generating revenue for those developers who do not charge for their software or information. Pop-up windows (small boxes that open up automatically on your screen) have been referred to as the billboards of the Internet because they appear and display advertisements or other promotional information when you install freeware programs or access certain Web sites. At one point, these pop-up windows were so common that they were incredibly irritating and annoying.

Some pop-ups, however, are legitimate and increase the functionality of the

Figure 9.22

Internet Explorer's Pop-up Blocker Settings dialog box.

>Pop-up Blocker is found in the **Tools** menu on the **Internet Explorer** toolbar.

originating site. For example, your account balance may pop up on your bank's Web site. Fortunately, because Web browsers such as Firefox, Safari, and Internet Explorer have pop-up blockers built into their browsers, the occurrence of annoying pop-ups has been greatly reduced. You can access the pop-up blocker settings in your browser (see Figure 9.22) and add Web sites for which you will allow pop-ups. Whenever a pop-up is blocked, the browser displays an information bar at the top of the browser window or plays a sound to alert you. If you feel the pop-up is legitimate, you can then choose to accept it.

What is spyware? **Spyware** is an unwanted piggyback program that usually downloads with other software you want to install from the Internet. It runs in the background of your system. Without your knowledge, spyware transmits information about you, such as your Internet surfing habits, to the owner of the program so that the information can be used for marketing purposes. Many spyware programs use tracking cookies (small text files stored on your computer) to collect information, whereas others are disguised as benign programs that are really malicious programs (such as Trojan horses). One type of spyware program known as a **keystroke logger** monitors keystrokes with the intent of stealing passwords, login IDs, or credit card information.

Can I prevent spyware? Many Internet security suites now include antispyware software. However, you can also obtain stand-alone spyware removal software and run it on your computer to delete unwanted spyware. Because there are so many variants of spyware, your Internet security software may not detect all types that attempt to install themselves on your

Think you aren't being closely watched by your employer? Think again! A survey of employers by the American Management Association and the ePolicy Institute revealed that, of the employers surveyed:

- 73 percent monitored e-mail messages
- 66 percent monitored Web surfing
- 48 percent monitored activities using video surveillance
- 45 percent monitored keystrokes and keyboard time
- 43 percent monitored computer files in some other fashion

There is a high probability that you are being monitored while you work and when you access the Internet via your employer's Internet connection (see Figure 9.23).

The two most frequently cited reasons for employee monitoring are to prevent theft and to measure productivity. Monitoring for theft isn't new, because monitoring cameras have been around for years, and productivity monitoring has been a consistent process for assembly line workers for decades. However, the Internet has led to a new type of productivity drain that is of concern to employers: **Cyberloafing**, or cyberslacking, means doing anything with a computer, while you are being paid to do your job, that is *not* an approved function of your job. Examples of cyberloafing activities are playing games, reading personal e-mail, checking sports scores, watching videos, and buying personal-use products on e-commerce sites. Estimates of business productivity losses due to cyberloafing top $50 billion annually.

Like most other Americans, you probably feel you have a right to privacy in the workplace. Unfortunately, the laws in the United States don't support a worker's right to privacy. Laws such as the 1986 Electronic Communications Privacy Act (ECPA), which prohibits unauthorized monitoring of electronic communications, have been interpreted by the courts in favor of employers. The bottom line is that employers who pay for equipment and software have the legal right to monitor their usage.

But just because an action is *legal* doesn't mean it is *ethical*. It is difficult to argue that an employer doesn't have the right to take measures to prevent theft and detect low productivity. The ethical issue here is whether or not the employees are made aware of monitoring policies. An ethical employer should treat employees with respect and dignity and inform employees of any monitoring. Employers have an ethical

responsibility (and a legal one as well, depending on the jurisdiction) not to place monitoring devices in sensitive locations such as bathrooms and dressing areas. However, in many states, the employer does not need to inform the employees in advance that they are being monitored. Conscientious employers include monitoring disclosures in published employee policies to avoid confusion and conflict.

Employers use a variety of software programs to monitor employee computer usage. Certain software packages keep track of every Web site you visit and the duration of your stay. Checking the baseball scores might take only three seconds and go unnoticed, but spending two hours updating your fantasy football team may be flagged. Keystroke loggers were originally used to monitor performance for people with input-intensive jobs like clerks and secretaries. Now these programs have the potential to be used to invade your privacy because they can record everything you type, even that nasty e-mail about the boss that you decided to delete!

Computer software can also be used to monitor the contents of your hard drive, so you don't want to collect 4,823 illegal MP3 files on your work computer. Some programs even track how long your computer is idle, which can give your manager a good idea of whether you were working or taking a three-hour lunch.

Since your employer might not tell you that your computer use is being monitored, you should assume that anything you do on your company-provided computer is subject to scrutiny. If you need to do personal work on your lunch hour or other breaks, you may be able to use your personal notebook computer to avoid the monitoring. Check with your employer to be sure you can connect personal computers to the corporate network or Internet connection. Note that courts in some jurisdictions have ruled that e-mails sent from third-party systems, such as Yahoo! and Gmail, are subject to monitoring if they are sent from employer-provided computer systems. Instant messaging is also subject to monitoring.

People who monitor employees have a duty to protect their right to privacy and not to disclose any information that they may inadvertently see during the course of monitoring. The acceptable computer use policies at most companies include guidelines for network administrators and other people who have high levels of access to sensitive information. When monitoring employees' work habits, management must ensure that compliance with the policies is tested periodically. Periodic reviews of procedures and compliance help ensure that established company policies are working as designed. An ethical employer strives to prevent misuse of personal data and accidental data loss. However, you can't always be certain that everyone who monitors you will behave ethically. Therefore, you need to think very carefully about exactly what personal tasks you are willing to risk engaging in on company computer systems.

So, do your employers have an ethical right to monitor your activities? Certainly, they have a right to ensure they are getting a fair day's work from you, just as you have an ethical obligation to provide a fair effort for a fair wage. However, employers should also be willing to respect the privacy rights of their employees and treat them as professionals, unless there is some indication of wrongdoing. Because employers may have a legal right to monitor you in the workplace, you should work under the assumption that everything you do on your work computer is subject to scrutiny and behave accordingly. Do your online shopping at home!

Figure 9.23

Big Brother might really be watching you at work.

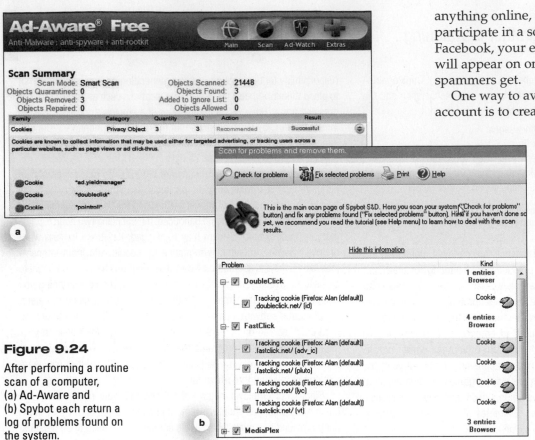

Figure 9.24

After performing a routine scan of a computer, (a) Ad-Aware and (b) Spybot each return a log of problems found on the system.

computer. Therefore, it is a good idea to install one or two additional stand-alone antispyware programs on your computer.

Because new spyware is created all the time, you should update and run your spyware removal software regularly. Windows comes with a program called Windows Defender, which scans your system for spyware and other potentially unwanted software. Malwarebytes Anti-Malware, Ad-Aware, and Spybot–Search & Destroy (all available from **download.com**) are other programs that are easy to install and update. Figure 9.24 shows an example of Ad-Aware and Spybot in action. They detect unwanted programs and allow you to delete the offending software easily.

Spam

How can I best avoid spam?

Companies that send out **spam**—unwanted or junk e-mail—find your e-mail address either from a list they purchase or with software that looks for e-mail addresses on the Internet. (Unsolicited instant messages are also a form of spam, called *spim*.) If you've used your e-mail address to purchase

anything online, open an online account, or participate in a social network such as Facebook, your e-mail address eventually will appear on one of the lists that spammers get.

One way to avoid spam in your primary account is to create a free Web-based e-mail address that you use only when you fill out forms or purchase items on the Web. For example, both Windows Live Mail and Yahoo! allow you to set up free e-mail accounts. If your free Web-based e-mail account is saturated with spam, then you can abandon that account with little inconvenience. It's much less convenient to abandon your primary e-mail address.

Another way to avoid spam is to filter it. A **spam filter** is an option you can select in your e-mail account that places known or suspected spam messages into a folder other than your inbox. Most Web-based e-mail services, such as Office Live Mail and Yahoo!, offer spam filters (see Figure 9.25). Files perceived to be spam are segregated in a special folder (often named "Spam" or "Junk Mail"). Microsoft Outlook also features a spam filter. Third-party programs that provide some control over spam include SPAMfighter and Cactus Spam Filter, both of which can be obtained at **download.com**.

How do spam filters work? Spam filters and filtering software can catch as much as 95 percent of spam by checking incoming e-mail subject headers and senders' addresses against databases of known spam. Spam filters also check your e-mail for frequently used spam patterns and keywords (such as "for free" and "over 21"). E-mail that the filter identifies as spam does not go into your inbox but rather to a folder set up for spam. Spam filters aren't perfect, and you should check the spam folder before deleting its contents because legitimate e-mail might end up there by mistake. Most programs provide you with a tool to reclassify e-mails that have been misidentified as spam.

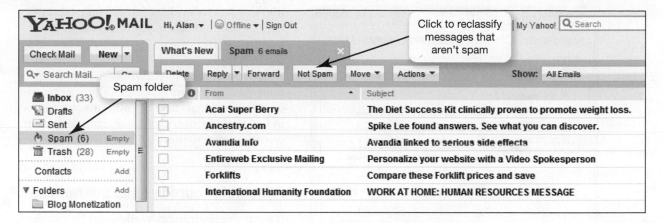

Figure 9.25

In Yahoo! Mail, messages identified as spam are directed into a folder called "Spam" for review and deletion.

How else can I prevent spam?

There are several additional ways you can prevent spam.

1. Before registering on a Web site, read its privacy policy to see how it uses your e-mail address. Don't give the site permission to pass on your e-mail address to third parties.

2. Don't reply to spam to remove yourself from the spam list. By replying, you are confirming that your e-mail address is active. Instead of stopping spam, you may receive more.

3. Subscribe to an e-mail forwarding service such as Emailias (**emailias.com**) or Sneakemail.com (**sneakemail.com**). These services screen your e-mail messages, forwarding only those messages you designate as being okay to accept.

Cookies

What are cookies?   Cookies (also known as *tracking cookies*) are small text files that some Web sites automatically store on your computer's hard drive when you visit them. When you log on to a Web site that uses cookies, a cookie file assigns an ID number to your computer. The unique ID is intended to make your return visit to a Web site more efficient and better geared to your interests. The next time you log on to that site, the site marks your visit and keeps track of it in its database.

What do Web sites do with cookie information?   Cookies can provide Web sites with information about your browsing habits, such as the ads you've opened, the products you've looked at, and the time and duration of your visits. Companies use this information to determine the traffic flowing through their Web site and the effectiveness of their marketing strategy and placement on Web sites. By tracking such information, cookies enable companies to identify different users' preferences.

Can companies get my personal information when I visit their sites?   Cookies do not go through your hard drive in search of personal information such as passwords or financial data. The only personal information a cookie obtains is the information you supply when you fill out forms online.

Do privacy risks exist with cookies?   Some sites sell the personal information their cookies collect to Web advertisers who are building huge databases of consumer preferences and habits, collecting personal and business information such as phone numbers, credit reports, and the like. The main concern is that advertisers will use this information indiscriminately, thus infiltrating your privacy. And you may feel your privacy is being violated by tracking cookies that monitor where you go on a Web site.

Should I delete cookies from my hard drive?   Because cookies pose no security threat (it is virtually impossible to hide a virus or malicious software program in a cookie), take up little room on your hard drive, and offer you small conveniences on return visits to Web sites, there is no great reason to delete them. Deleting your cookie files could actually cause you the inconvenience of reentering data you have entered into Web site forms. However, if you're uncomfortable with the accessibility of your personal information, you can periodically delete cookies or configure your browser to block certain types of cookies, as shown in Figure 9.26. Software such as

Figure 9.26

Tools are available, either through your browser (Internet Explorer is shown here) or as separate applications, to distinguish between cookies you want to keep and cookies you don't want on your system.

>On the Internet Explorer menu toolbar, click **Tools**, and then click **Internet Options**. The cookie settings are on the **Privacy** tab.

Cookie Pal (**kburra.com**) also can help you monitor cookies.

Protecting Yourself . . . from Yourself!

People are often too trusting or just plain careless when it comes to protecting private information about themselves or their digital data. When was the last time you created a copy of your digital data (such as the thousands of photographs you have stored on your hard drive)? The hard drive in your computer is likely to fail at some point, which may render all the data on it useless. What strategy do you have in place to protect your data from damage?

If you have a Facebook or Twitter account, you are probably constantly revealing information about your likes and dislikes, such as what movie you saw this weekend or the presents you received for your birthday. You might even be revealing information about where you live. Have you ever filled out an online form to enter a contest? Have you ever applied for a customer loyalty card at your local supermarket or electronics store? Think about how much information you voluntarily give up all the time in the course of running your digital

life. Con artists and scammers take advantage of people's tendency to reveal information freely to compromise their privacy and commit theft.

In this section, we discuss ways to keep your data safe from damage (either accidental or intentional) and to keep unscrupulous individuals from tricking you into revealing sensitive information.

Protecting Your Personal Information

If a complete stranger walked up to you on the street and asked you for your address and phone number, would you give it to them? Of course you wouldn't! But many people are much less careful when it comes to sharing sensitive information online. And often people inadvertently share information that they really only intended to share with their friends. With cybercrimes like identify theft rampant, you need to take steps to protect your personal information.

What information should I never share on Web sites? Your Social Security number, phone number, and street address are three key pieces of information that identity thieves need to steal an identity. This information should never be shared in a public area on any Web site.

Many sites, such as Facebook, ask for other potentially sensitive information when you sign up. This information might include your real name, e-mail address, birth date, zip code, and gender. After you register, social networking sites then encourage you to add profile details such as your school, your employer, your personal interests and hobbies, and who your friends are. Although it is fine to share this information with people you know, you need to be careful that your information isn't visible to everyone.

How can I tell who can see my information in a social network? Social networking sites, like Facebook, make privacy settings available in their account menus. If you have never changed your privacy settings in Facebook, you are probably sharing information more widely than you should. Since Facebook is designed to foster social interaction, the default privacy settings make it easy to search for people. Someone with nefarious intentions could glean quite a bit of information from your Facebook profile, including your contact information, which they might use to trick you into revealing other information that would lead to them stealing your identity.

How can I protect my information on Facebook? To begin, you need to change your privacy settings from some of the default options. On the upper right-hand side of the Facebook page, click Account and then click Privacy Settings. On the Privacy Settings page, select Profile Information to display the screen shown in Figure 9.27a. It's a good idea to set most of the options on this screen to Only Friends because, presumably, you are only friending people you trust.

The other screen you need to address is Contact Information Privacy Settings (see Figure 9.27b), which you can also reach from the Privacy Settings page. Restricting this information only to friends or to yourself is imperative. You don't want scammers contacting you via phone and trying to trick you into revealing sensitive information. So use discretion and keep your information as private as possible.

Backing Up Your Data

How might I damage the data on my computer? The data on your computer faces three major threats: unauthorized access, tampering, and destruction. As noted earlier, a hacker can gain access to your computer and steal or alter your data. However, a more likely scenario is that you will lose your data unintentionally. You may accidentally delete files. You may drop your notebook on the ground, causing the hard drive to break, resulting in complete data loss. A virus from an e-mail attachment you opened may destroy your original file. Your house or dorm may catch fire and destroy your computer. Because many of these possibilities are beyond your control, you should have a strategy for backing up your files, which is especially important if you are running a small business. (The backup strategy for small businesses is quite similar to the procedures recommended for individuals.)

What exactly is meant by "backing up data"? Backups are copies of files that you can use to replace the originals if they are lost or damaged. To be truly secure, backups must be stored away from where

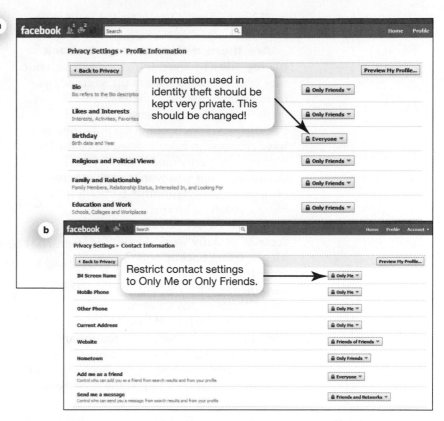

your computer is located. You wouldn't want a fire or a flood destroying the backups along with the original data. Removable storage media, such as external hard drives, DVDs, and flash drives have been popular choices for backing up files because they hold a lot of data and can be transported easily.

What types of files do I need to back up? Two types of files need backups—program files and data files.

A **program file** is used to install software and usually comes on CDs or DVDs or is downloaded from the Web. If any programs came preinstalled in your computer, then you may have received a CD or DVD that contains the original program. As long as you have the original media in a safe place, you shouldn't need to back up these files. If you have downloaded a program file from the Internet, however, you should make a copy of the program installation files on a removable storage device as a backup. If you didn't receive discs for installed programs with your computer, then see the next section for suggested strategies for backing up your entire computer.

A **data file** is a file you have created or purchased. Data files include such files as research papers, spreadsheets, music files, movies, contact lists, address books, e-mail

Figure 9.27

You should review the (a) Profile Information and (b) Contact Information privacy settings in Facebook to ensure you aren't sharing too much information.

archives, and your Favorites list from your browser.

Are there different ways to back up my files? Even with modest use, your files change. To back them up, you can perform an incremental backup.

An **incremental backup** (or **partial backup**) involves backing up only files that have changed or been created since the last backup was performed. Many of the key documents that you want to protect change only periodically: monthly banking statements, yearly tax returns, weekly employee payment records, or daily work documents. Using backup software that has an option for incremental backups will save a tremendous amount of time because backing up files that haven't changed is redundant.

An **image backup** (or **system backup**) means that all system, application, and data files are backed up, not just the files that changed. While incremental backups are more efficient, an image backup ensures you capture changes to application files, such as automatic software updates, that an incremental backup might not capture. The idea of imaging is to make an exact copy of the setup of your computer so that in the event of a total hard drive failure, you could copy the image to a new hard drive and have your computer configured exactly the way it was before the crash. This is a quick way to get up and running again.

How often should I back up my files? You should back up your data files frequently. How frequently depends on how much work you cannot afford to lose. You should always back up data files when you make changes to them, especially if those changes involve hours of work. It may not seem important to back up your history term paper file when you finish it, but do you really want to do all that work again if your computer crashes before you have a chance to turn in your paper?

Because your program and operating system files don't change as often as your data files, you can perform image backups on a less frequent basis. Most backup software can be configured to do backups automatically so you don't forget to perform them. You might consider scheduling backups of your data files on a daily basis and an image

> **"How often should I back up my files?"**

backup of your entire system on a weekly basis.

To make backups easier, store all your data files in one folder on your hard drive. For example, in Windows and most other operating systems, on your hard drive you will find a folder called Documents. You can create subfolders (such as History Homework, Music Files, and so on) within the Documents folder. If you store all your data under one main folder on your hard drive, you simply configure your backup software to back up that folder and all subfolders beneath it.

Where do the backups of my files reside? This location is a decision that you need to make. You have three main choices:

1. **Online sites.** In essence, online storage is like using the Internet as an alternative to a portable storage device (such as an external hard drive or flash drive). The beauty of online storage is that your data is available anywhere you are; you do not need to be at your computer or have to lug around your external hard drive to access the information. More important, because the information is stored online, it is in a secure, remote location, so data is much less vulnerable to all the potential disasters (such as a flood) that could harm data stored in your computer or external hard drive. If you are taking advantage of one of these free online storage services, selectivity is the key because of cost. Although you might have hundreds of gigabytes of data sitting on your computer, perhaps you only need to store several gigabytes online so that they are always available.

   A convenient free storage option for Windows users is Windows Live SkyDrive (**skydrive.live.com**), which provides 25 GB of storage space. For non-Windows users or those needing even more storage space, check out ADrive (**adrive.com**) and its 50 GB of free storage! Fee-based plans at ADrive give users access to tools that allow them to schedule automatic backups of files and folders. However, image backups probably won't fit within the storage limits offered by free providers. For a fee, companies such as Iron Mountain (**backup.ironmountain.com**) and IBackup (**ibackup.com**) provide larger storage capacity.

If you store a backup of your entire system on the Internet, then you won't need to buy an additional hard drive for backups. This method also takes the worry out of finding a safe place to keep your backups because they're always stored in an area far away from your computer (on the backup company's server). However, the yearly fees can be expensive, so a cheaper option may be to buy an external hard drive.

2. **Local drives.** External hard drives are popular options for performing backups of data files and for complete image backups. Affordable external drives are available with capacities of 3 TB or more. These drives are usually connected to a single computer and often come with their own backup software (although you could still use the backup software included with your operating system). Although convenient and inexpensive, using external hard drives for backups still presents the dilemma of keeping the hard drive in a safe location. You need to keep the hard drive connected to your computer to perform scheduled backups, but for ultimate safety the hard drive should be stored in a location separate from the computer in case of catastrophic events, such as a fire. Therefore, using an external hard drive for backups is best done in conjunction with an online backup strategy for added safety.

3. **Network-attached storage devices and home servers.** Manufacturers such as HP, Seagate, and Buffalo Technology now make network-attached storage (NAS) devices and servers designed for home networks. The NAS devices are essentially large hard drives that are connected to a network of computers instead of one computer, and they can be used to back up multiple computers simultaneously. Home servers are not really servers like those found in client/server networks. Home servers act as high-capacity NAS devices for automatically backing up data and

sharing files. Both NAS devices and home servers are easy to configure and are very useful if you have multiple computers within a single household that need backing up.

How do I actually perform a file backup? Windows 7 includes the Backup and Restore utility, which provides a quick and easy way to schedule file backups, restore files from backups, or perform image (system) backups. You can access Backup and Restore from the Control Panel. Before starting this utility, make sure your external hard drive or NAS device is connected to your computer or network and is powered on.

When you start the Backup and Restore utility for the first time, no backups will have ever been configured. Select the Set up backup option to launch the Set up backup dialog box (see Figure 9.28a) and display a list of available backup devices. Select a device and click Next to proceed. On the next screen, you have the option to let Windows choose what to back up or to choose for

Figure 9.28

The Windows 7 Backup and Restore utility. (a) Select your backup destination. (b) Choose locations to back up. (c) Review your scheduled backups, restore files, and start wizards for system image and repair disc creation.

yourself what you want to back up. If you select the Let me choose option, the screen shown in Figure 9.28b displays. You can then click the appropriate check boxes to select the libraries you wish to back up. Click Next to proceed. On the following screen, you can review your settings and set up a schedule for the backups. When you click the Save settings and exit button, you are returned to the Back up or restore your files screen (see Figure 9.28c), which now shows the scheduled backup. You can also choose to restore backed-up files you have backed up from this screen.

From the Back up or restore your files screen, you also have two other options. If you click the Create a system image link, you will be walked through a series of steps to configure an image backup of your system. The Create a system repair disc link helps you create a DVD repair disc that can be used to boot your computer in case of a serious Windows error. This disc is also used when you need to restore your computer from an image backup, so it is a good idea to create the repair disc before you begin using your computer heavily.

> **"Should I back up files on my school's network?"**

For Mac OS X users, backups are very easy to configure. The Time Machine feature (in Mac OS X Leopard and subsequent versions) detects when an external hard drive is connected to the computer or a NAS device is connected to your network. You are then asked if you want this to be your backup drive. If you answer yes, all of your files (including operating system files) are automatically backed up to the external drive or NAS device. You even have the option to go back in time and see what your computer looked like on a specific date. This is very handy for recovering a file that you wish you hadn't deleted.

No matter what backup strategy you choose, be sure to perform them on a regular basis because nearly everyone has need to access backup files at one time or another.

Should I back up my files that are stored on my school's network?
Most likely, if you're allowed to store files on your school's network, these files are backed up on a regular basis. You should check with your school's network administrators to determine how often they're backed up and how you would go about requesting that files be restored from the backup media if they're damaged or deleted. But don't rely on these network backups to bail you out if your data files are lost or damaged. It may take days for the network administrators to get around to restoring your files. It is better to keep backups of your data files yourself (especially homework and project files) so that you can immediately restore them. Buy a large-capacity flash drive and carry it with you!

Social Engineering: Fooling the Unwary

What is social engineering?
Social engineering is any technique that uses social skills to generate human interaction that entices individuals to reveal sensitive information. Social engineering often doesn't involve the use of a computer or face-to-face interaction. For example, telephone scams are a common form of social engineering because it is often easier to manipulate someone when you don't have to look at them.

How does social engineering work?
Most social engineering schemes use a pretext to lure their victims. **Pretexting** involves creating a scenario that sounds legitimate enough that someone will trust you. For example, you might receive a phone call during which the caller says he is from the bank and that someone tried to use your account without authorization. The caller then tells you he needs to confirm a few personal details such as your birth date, Social Security number, bank account number, and whatever other information he can get out of you. The information he obtains can then be used to empty your bank account or commit some other form of fraud. Often pretexting is used to gain access to corporate computer networks. People will sometimes call random extensions in a large business, claiming to be from technical support. Eventually, the caller will find someone who has a problem and is happy that someone is willing to help. The scam artist will then elicit information such as

Computers in Society: Identity Theft—Is There More Than One of You Out There?

You've no doubt heard of identity theft. A thief steals your name, address, Social Security number, bank account and credit card information and runs up debts in your name. This leaves you holding the bag, and you're hounded by creditors collecting on the fraudulent debts. It sounds horrible—and it is. In fact, one of the authors of this textbook had his identity stolen and spent about 50 hours filing police reports, talking to credit agencies, closing bogus accounts, and convincing companies that the $25,000 of debt run up on six phony credit card accounts was done by an identity thief. Many victims of identity theft spend months (or even years) trying to repair their credit and eliminate fraudulent debts. Worse yet, if an identity thief uses your identity to obtain medical services at a hospital, you may be denied coverage at a later date because the thief's treatment has exceeded the limit of covered services on your policy.

Stories of identity thieves—such as the New York man accused of stealing more than 30,000 identities—abound in the media and should serve to make the public wary. However, many media pundits would have you believe that the only way your identity can be stolen is by a computer. This is simply not true. The Federal Trade Commission (**ftc.gov**) has identified other methods thieves use to obtain others' personal information. These include (1) stealing purses and wallets, in which people often keep unnecessary valuable personal information such as their ATM PIN codes; (2) stealing mail or looking through trash for bank statements and credit card bills, which provide valuable personal information; and (3) posing as bank or credit card company representatives and tricking people into revealing sensitive information over the phone.

Obviously, you're at risk from online attacks, too, such as phishing. Once identity thieves obtain your personal information, they can use it in many different ways. Identity thieves often request a change of address for your credit card bill or bank statement. By the time you realize that you aren't receiving your statements, the thieves have rung up bogus charges on your account or emptied your bank account. The thieves can open new credit card and bank accounts in your name. They then will write bad checks and not pay the credit card bills, which will ruin your credit rating.

Even worse, the identity thieves may counterfeit debit cards or checks for your legitimate accounts and empty them of funds. They might even take out a mortgage in your name and then disappear with the proceeds, leaving you with the debt.

Although foolproof protection methods don't exist, there are precautions that will help you minimize your risk. You should never reveal your password or your PIN code to anyone or place it in an easy-to-find location. Also, never reveal personal information unless you're sure that a legitimate reason exists for a business to know the information, and you can confirm you're actually dealing with a legitimate representative (don't fall for phishing schemes). If someone calls or e-mails asking you for personal information, decline and call the company with which you opened your account.

Obviously, you should create secure passwords for your online accounts. When shopping online, be wary of unfamiliar merchants that you can't contact through a mailing address or phone number, or businesses whose prices are too good to be true. These can be attempts to collect your personal information for use in fraudulent schemes.

If you have been the victim of identity theft, most states now allow you to freeze your credit history so that no new accounts can be opened until you lift the credit freeze. Even if you live in a state where you can't freeze your account, you can still place an extended fraud alert on your credit history for seven years, which also warns merchants that they should check with you (at your home address or phone number) before opening an account in your name.

Using common sense and keeping personal information in the hands of as few people as possible are the best defenses against identity theft. For additional tips on preventing identity theft or for procedures to follow if you are a victim, check out the Identity Theft Resource Center (**idtheftcenter.org**).

---

logins and passwords from the victim as part of the process for "solving the problem." The most common form of pretexting in cyberspace is phishing.

Phishing and Pharming

How are phishing schemes conducted? Phishing (pronounced "fishing") lures Internet users to reveal personal information such as credit card numbers, Social Security numbers, or other sensitive information that could lead to identity theft. The scammers send e-mail messages that look like they are from a legitimate business such as an online bank. The e-mail states that the recipient needs to update or confirm his or her account information. When the recipient clicks the provided link, he or she goes to a Web site. The site looks like a legitimate site but is really a fraudulent copy the scammer has created. Once the e-mail recipient confirms his or her personal information, the scammers capture it and can begin using it.

Is pharming a type of phishing scam? Pharming is much more insidious than phishing. Phishing requires a positive action by the person being scammed, such as going to a Web site mentioned in an e-mail and typing in your bank account information. **Pharming** is when malicious code is planted on your computer that alters your browser's ability to find Web addresses. Users are directed to bogus Web sites even when they enter the correct address of the real Web site or follow a bookmark that they previously had established for the Web site. So instead of ending up at your bank's Web site when you type in its address, you end up at a fake Web site that looks like your bank's site but is expressly set up for the purpose of gathering information.

How can I avoid being caught by phishing and pharming scams? You should never reply directly to any e-mail asking you for personal information. Never click on a link in an e-mail to go to a Web site. Instead, type the Web site address in the browser. Check with the company asking for the information and only give the information if you are certain it is needed.

Also, never give personal information over the Internet unless you know the site is secure. Look for the closed padlock, https, or a certification seal such as VeriSign to help reassure you that the site is secure. The latest versions of Firefox, Chrome, and Internet Explorer have phishing filters built in, so each time you access a Web site, the phishing filter checks for the site's legitimacy and warns you of possible Web forgeries. Finally, make sure you have Internet security software installed on your computer and that it is constantly being updated. Most Internet security packages can detect and prevent pharming attacks. The major Internet security packages—for example, McAfee and Norton (see Figure 9.29)—also offer phishing-protection tools. When you have the Norton Toolbar displayed in your browser, you are constantly informed about the legitimacy of the site you are visiting.

Another way to protect yourself is never to use your credit card number when you

Figure 9.29

Not sure whether you are on the Amazon Web site or a cleverly disguised phishing site? Norton Site Safety reassures you that all is well.

shop online. Although it sounds impossible, credit card providers such as Citibank are offering services such as "Virtual Account Numbers" for their customers. Before purchasing a product online, you visit an online site, where you are assigned a new virtual account number each time you visit. This number looks like a regular credit card number and is tied to your real credit card account. However, the virtual account number can be used only once. That means that if the number is stolen, it's no good to thieves. They can't use the virtual account number, because you've already used it.

Hoaxes

What is a hoax? A **hoax** is an attempt to make someone believe something that is untrue. Hoaxes target a large audience and are generally perpetrated as practical jokes, instruments of social change (which poke fun at an established norm in an effort to change it), or merely ways to waste people's valuable time. Although there are hoax Web sites such as Pacific Northwest Tree Octopus (**zapatopi.net/treeoctopus**), most cyberspace hoaxes are perpetrated by e-mail.

Why do people concoct e-mail hoaxes? As opposed to garnering financial rewards (like in a phishing fraud), the motives of e-mail hoax creators can be more complex. Many people start an e-mail hoax just for the challenge of seeing if their "brainchild" can be spread globally. Other hoaxes start as innocent practical jokes between friends that take on lives of their own via the fast communication available on the Internet. Many hoaxes become so well known that they are accepted by society as true events even though they are false. Once this happens to a hoax, it becomes known as an **urban legend**. An example is the phony story about the man who woke up in a bathtub full of ice water and found he had had his kidney stolen. Hoaxes may be compared to acts of real-world vandalism like graffiti. Graffiti artists "make their mark" on the world, physically; hoaxers may consider they are making a similar mark when a bogus e-mail they have created becomes widespread.

Sometimes hoaxes are based on misinformation or are a way to vent frustration. An e-mail hoax that reappears every time there is a spike in gasoline prices is the Gas Boycott (Gas War) hoax. To boost the scheme's credibility, the e-mail touts it as having been invented by reputable business-people. The e-mail explains how boycotting certain gasoline companies will drive the price of gasoline down and urges recipients of the e-mail to join the fight. The originator of this hoax was probably frustrated by high gas prices and, armed with a poor understanding of economics, distributed this brainstorm. Unfortunately, this tactic can have no effect on gasoline prices because it only shifts demand for gasoline from certain oil companies to other sources. Because it does not reduce the overall demand for gasoline, the price of gas will not decline. Did you receive this e-mail and think it sounded like a plausible idea? How many people did you forward it to?

How can I tell if an e-mail is a hoax? Sometimes it is difficult to separate fact from fiction. Many hoax e-mails are well written and crafted in such a way that they sound very real. Before using the Forward button and sending an e-mail to all your friends, check it out at one of the many Web sites that keep track of and expose e-mail hoaxes. Check sites such as Snopes (**snopes.com**), Hoax-Slayer (**hoax-slayer.com**, shown in Figure 9.30), or TruthOrFiction.com (**truthorfiction.com**). These sites are searchable, so you can enter a few keywords from an e-mail you suspect may be a hoax and quickly find similar e-mails and explanations of whether they are true or false. Checking out e-mails before forwarding them on to friends, family, and co-workers will save other people's time and help end the spread of these time wasters.

Protecting Your Physical Computing Assets

Your computer isn't useful to you if it is damaged. Therefore, it's essential to select and ensure a safe environment for it. This includes protecting it from environmental factors, power surges, power outages, and theft.

Environmental Factors

Why is the environment critical to the operation of my computer equipment? Computers are delicate devices and can be damaged by the adverse effects of abuse or a poor environment. Sudden movements (such as a fall) can damage your notebook computer or mobile device's internal components. You should make sure that your computer sits on a flat, level surface, and, if it is a notebook, carry it in a padded case to protect it. If you do drop your computer, have it professionally tested by a computer repair facility to check for any hidden damage.

Electronic components do not like excessive heat or excessive cold. Unfortunately, computers generate a lot of heat, which is why they have fans to cool their internal components. Make sure that you place your desktop computer where the fan's input vents (usually found on the rear of the system unit) are unblocked so that air can flow inside. Chill mats that contain cooling fans and sit underneath notebook computers are useful accessories for dissipating heat. And don't leave computing devices in a car during especially hot or cold weather because components can be damaged by extreme temperatures. Naturally, a fan drawing air into a computer also draws in dust and other particles, which can wreak havoc on your system. Therefore, keep the room in which your computer is located as clean as possible. Even in a clean room, the fan ducts can become packed with dust, so vacuum it periodically to keep a clear airflow into your computer. Finally, because food crumbs and liquid can damage keyboards and other computer components, consume food and beverages away from your computer.

Figure 9.30

Sites like Hoax-Slayer help you research potential hoaxes.

Metal-oxide varistors (MOVs) bleed off excess current

Fuse blows during major surges

Figure 9.31

Anatomy of a surge protector.

Power Surges

What is a power surge? Power surges occur when electrical current is supplied in excess of normal voltage (120 volts in the United States). Old or faulty wiring, downed power lines, malfunctions at electric company substations, and lightning strikes can all cause power surges. A **surge protector** is a device that protects your computer against power surges (see Figure 9.31). To use a surge protector, you simply plug your electrical devices into the outlets of the surge protector, which in turn plugs into the wall.

How do surge protectors work? Surge protectors contain two components that are used to protect the equipment that is connected to them. Metal-oxide varistors (MOVs) bleed off excess current during minor surges and feed it to the ground wire, where it harmlessly dissipates. The MOVs can do this while still allowing normal current to pass through the devices plugged into the surge protector. Because the ground wire is critical to this process, it is important to plug the surge protector into a grounded (typically, three-prong) power outlet.

During major surges that overwhelm the MOVs, a fuse inside the surge protector blows, which stops the flow of current to all devices plugged into the surge protector. After a major surge, the surge protector will no longer function and must be replaced.

Over time, the MOVs lose their ability to bleed off excess current, which is why you should replace your surge protectors every two to three years. Buy a surge protector that includes indicator lights. Indicator lights illuminate when the surge protector is no longer functioning properly. (Don't be fooled by old surge protectors—although they can still function as multiple-outlet power strips, they deliver power to your equipment without protecting it.) A power surge could ruin your computer and other devices if you don't protect them. At $20 to $40, a quality surge protector is an excellent investment.

Besides my computer, what other devices need to be connected to a surge protector? All electronic devices in the home that have solid state components, such as TVs, stereos, printers, and phones, should be connected to a surge protector. Printers and other computer peripherals all require protection. However, it can be inconvenient to use individual surge protectors on everything. A more practical method is to install a **whole-house surge protector** (see Figure 9.32). Whole-house surge protectors function like other surge protectors, but they protect *all* electrical devices in the house. Typically, you will need an electrician to install a whole-house surge protector, which will cost $200 to $300 (installed).

Is my equipment 100 percent safe when plugged into a surge protector? Surge protectors won't necessarily guard against all surges. Lightning strikes can generate such high voltages that they can overwhelm a surge protector. As tedious as it sounds, unplugging

Surge protector

Figure 9.32

A whole-house surge protector usually is installed at the breaker panel or near the electric meter.

computers and peripherals during an electrical storm is the only way to achieve absolute protection.

How can I prevent my computers from losing power during a power outage? Computers can develop software glitches caused by a loss of power if not shut down properly. Mission-critical computers such as Web servers often are protected by an **uninterruptible power supply (UPS)**, as shown in Figure 9.33, which is a device that contains surge protection equipment and a large battery. When power is interrupted (such as during a blackout), the UPS continues to send power to the attached computer from its battery. Depending on the battery capacity, you have between about 20 minutes and 3 hours to save your work and shut down your computer properly.

Figure 9.33

A UPS device should not be mistaken for a fat surge protector!

Deterring Theft

Because they are portable, notebooks are easy targets for thieves. Even though they are not considered portable, desktop computers are also subject to theft. Three approaches to deterring computer theft include alarming them, locking them down, or installing devices that alert you (or destroy data) when the computer is stolen.

Alarms

What type of alarm can I install on my notebook computer? To prevent your notebook from being stolen, you can attach a motion alarm to it (see Figure 9.34).

SOUND BYTE Surge Protectors

In this Sound Byte, you'll learn about the major features of surge protectors and how they work. You'll also learn about the key factors you need to consider before buying a surge protector, and you'll see how easy it is to install one.

When you leave your notebook, you use a small device called a *key fob activator* or punch in a code to activate the alarm. If your notebook is moved while the alarm is activated, it emits a wailing 100-decibel sound. The fact that the alarm is visible acts as an additional theft deterrent, just like a "Beware of Dog" sign in a front yard.

Locks and Surrounds

How can I lock up a notebook computer? Chaining a notebook to your work surface can be another effective way to prevent theft. As shown in Figure 9.35, a special locking mechanism is attached to the notebook (some notebooks are even manufactured with locking ports), and a hardened steel cable is connected to the locking mechanism. The other end of the cable is looped around something large and heavy, such as a desk. The cable lock requires the use of a key or combination to free the notebook. You should consider taking a cable lock with you when traveling to help deter theft from hotel rooms.

Software Alerts

How can my computer alert me when it is stolen? You've probably heard of LoJack, the theft-tracking device used in cars. Car owners install a LoJack transmitter somewhere in their vehicle. If the vehicle is stolen, police activate the transmitter and use its signal to locate the car. Similar

Figure 9.34

A notebook alarm sends out an ear-piercing sound if your notebook is moved before you deactivate the alarm.

Figure 9.35

Cable locks are an effective deterrent to theft.

systems now exist for computers. Tracking software such as Computrace LoJack for Laptops (**absolute.com**), PC PhoneHome, and Mac PhoneHome (**pcphonehome.com**) enables the computer to alert authorities to the computer's location if it is stolen. This software can be installed in either notebook or desktop computers.

To enable your computer to help with its own recovery, install the tracking software on your hard drive. The software contacts a server at the software manufacturer's Web site each time you connect to the Internet. If your computer is stolen, you notify the software manufacturer. The software manufacturer instructs your computer to transmit tracking information (such as an IP address) that will assist authorities in locating and retrieving the stolen computer.

What if the thieves find the tracking software and delete it? The files and directories holding the software are not visible to thieves looking for such software, so they probably won't know the software is there. Furthermore, the tracking software is written in such a way that even if the thieves tried to reformat the hard drive, it would detect the reformat and hide the software code in a safe place in memory or on the hard drive. (Some sectors of a hard drive are not rewritten during most reformattings.) That way, it can reinstall itself after the reformatting is completed.

Are there ways to protect data contained on mobile devices? Smartphones can be vulnerable to unauthorized access if they are left unattended or are stolen. Although some devices offer basic protection features (such as password protection), sensitive business information often requires an additional level of protection. Security software such as TealLock from TealPoint Software (**tealpoint.com**) offers additional protection features such as data encryption and protection against attempts to break into a device through "brute force" attacks (running a program to guess all possible passwords). Most programs feature optional data self-destruct modes (sometimes known as **bomb software**) that destroy data on both internal memory and external data cards if repeated attempts are made to crack passwords.

Figure 9.36 | COMPUTER SECURITY CHECKLIST

	Yes	No
Virus and Spyware Protection		
Is antivirus and antispyware software installed on all your computers?		
Is the antivirus and antispyware software configured to update itself automatically and regularly?		
Is the software set to scan your computer on a regular basis (at least weekly) for viruses and spyware?		
Firewall		
Do all your computers have firewall software installed and activated before connecting to the Internet?		
Is your router also able to function as a hardware firewall?		
Have you tested your firewall security by using the free software available at **grc.com**?		
Wireless Security (see Chapter 7 for additional details)		
Have you changed the default password for your router?		
Have you changed the name (SSID) of your network and turned off SSID broadcasting?		
Have you enabled WPA or WEP encryption for your network?		
Software Updates		
Have you configured your operating systems (Windows, OS X) to install new software patches and updates automatically?		
Is other software installed on your computer (such as Microsoft Office) configured for automatic updates?		
Is the Web browser you are using the latest version?		

How can I ensure that I've covered all aspects of protecting my computer? The checklist in Figure 9.36 is a guide to ensure you didn't miss any critical aspects of security. If you've addressed all of these issues, then you can feel reasonably confident that your Internet access will be secure and free from problems.

Taking a few precautions regarding your data security can provide huge benefits such as peace of mind and the avoidance of time spent correcting problems. So enjoy your computing experiences, but do so safely.

summary

1. From which types of viruses do I need to protect my computer?

A computer virus is a program that attaches itself to another program and attempts to spread to other computers when files are exchanged. Computer viruses can be grouped into five categories: (1) boot-sector viruses, (2) logic bombs and time bombs, (3) worms, (4) scripts and macros, and (5) encryption viruses. Once run, they perform their malicious duties in the background and are often invisible to the user.

2. What can I do to protect my computer from viruses?

The best defense against viruses is to install antivirus software. You should update the software on a regular basis and configure it to examine all e-mail attachments for viruses. You should periodically run a complete virus scan on your computer to ensure that no viruses have made it onto your hard drive.

3. How can hackers attack my computing devices, and what harm can they cause?

A hacker is defined as anyone who breaks into a computer system unlawfully. Hackers can use software to break into almost any computer connected to the Internet (unless proper precautions are taken). Once hackers gain access to a computer, they can potentially (1) steal personal or other important information, (2) damage and destroy data, or (3) use the computer to attack other computers.

4. What is a firewall, and how does it keep my computer safe from hackers?

Firewalls are software programs or hardware devices designed to keep computers safe from hackers. By using a personal firewall, you can close open logical ports to invaders and potentially make your computer invisible to other computers on the Internet.

5. How do I create secure passwords and manage all of my passwords?

Secure passwords contain a mixture of upper- and lowercase letters, numbers, and symbols, and are at least 14 characters long. Passwords should not contain words that are in the dictionary or easy-to-guess personal information (like your pet's name). Online password checkers can be used to evaluate the strength of your passwords. Utilities built into Web browsers and Internet security software can be used to manage your passwords and alleviate the need to remember numerous complex passwords.

6. How can I surf the Internet anonymously and use biometric authentication devices to protect my data?

The current versions of the popular browsers include tools (such as Chrome's Incognito feature) that hide your surfing activities by not recording Web sites that you visit, or files that you download, in your browser's history files. Biometric authentication devices use a physical attribute (such as a fingerprint) that is not easily duplicated to control access to data files or computing devices. Some notebooks today feature fingerprint readers and facial recognition software to control access.

7. How do I manage online annoyances such as spyware and spam?

The Web is filled with annoyances such as spam, pop-ups, cookies, spyware, and scams such as phishing that make surfing the Web frustrating and sometimes dangerous. Software tools help to prevent or reduce spam, adware, and spyware, while exercising caution can prevent serious harm caused by phishing, pharming, and other Internet scams and hoaxes.

8. What data do I need to back up, and what are the best methods for doing so?

Data files created by you (such as Word and Excel files) or purchased by you (such as music files) need to be backed up in case they are inadvertently deleted or damaged. Application software (such as Microsoft Office) may need to be reinstalled if files are damaged, so backups (usually the DVDs or CDs the application came on) must be maintained. Web sites such as Adrive and Skydrive are great for backing up individual files. External hard drives are popular choices for holding image backups of your entire system. Windows 7 and OS X contain solid backup tools that help automate backup tasks.

9. What is social engineering, and how do I avoid falling prey to phishing and hoaxes?

Social engineering schemes use human interaction, deception, and trickery to fool people into revealing sensitive information such as credit card numbers and passwords. Phishing schemes usually involve e-mails that direct the unwary to a Web site that appears to be legitimate (such as a bank site) but is specifically designed to capture personal information for committing fraud. To avoid phishing scams, you should never reply directly to any e-mail asking you for personal information, and never click on a link in an e-mail to go to a Web site. You can research topics you believe to be hoaxes at sites such as Snopes (**snopes.com**).

10. How do I protect my physical computing assets from environmental hazards, power surges, and theft?

Computing devices should be kept in clean environments free from dust and other particulates and should not be exposed to extreme temperatures (either hot or cold). You should protect all electronic devices from power surges by hooking them up through surge protectors, which will protect them from most electrical surges that could damage the devices. Notebook computers can be protected from theft either by attaching alarms to them or by installing software that will help recover the computer, if stolen, by reporting the computer's whereabouts when it is connected to the Internet.

Word Bank

- adware
- antivirus software
- backup(s)
- distributed denial-of-service (DDoS)
- firewall
- hacker(s)
- identity theft
- keystroke logger(s)
- logical port(s)
- phishing
- social engineering
- spyware
- surge protector
- virus
- zombie(s)

Instructions: Fill in the blanks using the words from the Word Bank above.

Emily learned a lot about computer security in her computer literacy class. She already knew it was important to exercise caution when using the Internet because she had been the victim of (1) _____, which destroyed her credit rating. A(n) (2) _____ had obtained her credit card information by posing as an employee of her bank, using a method known as (3) _____. In her class, Emily learned that hackers could install (4) _____, a type of software that will capture everything she types, to steal her personal information. And one of Emily's classmates received a (5) _____ e-mail that directed her to a fake Web site that looked like her bank's Web site and resulted in her bank account information being stolen. The computers in the lab at school had just been cleaned of (6) _____ software that was displaying annoying pop-up advertisements. The computer technician who fixed this problem indicated that (7) _____ software, which was monitoring computer user activity, was often inadvertently installed on lab computers by students downloading files.

Emily found out that her router could be configured as a(n) (8) _____ to repel malicious hacking mischief. Turning off the unused (9) _____ would repel most attacks on her home network. With this protection, it was unlikely that a hacker would turn her PC into a(n) (10) _____ to launch (11) _____ attacks. However, after the scare with the Conficker (12) _____, Emily was careful to warn her family not to open files from untrusted sources. She also made sure all of the computers in her home had (13) _____ installed to protect them from viruses. For extra security, Emily installed an external hard drive so that she could create (14) _____ of her data files, and she replaced her power strip with a(n) (15) _____ to make sure power spikes didn't ruin her computer after all of the other precautions she'd taken.

becoming computer literate

While attending college, you are working at a company that manufactures industrial adhesives. Recently, the company computers have been behaving strangely and running slowly. Your investigation revealed that although antivirus software was initially installed on the company computers, the subscriptions have lapsed and the software is out of date. It also appears that no antispyware software was ever deployed. Your boss heard that you are taking a computer course and has asked you to run a seminar to educate management about the potential problems and solutions.

Instructions: Using the preceding scenario, draft an antivirus and antispyware plan for the company using as many of the keywords from the chapter as you can. Be sure that the company managers, who are unfamiliar with many computer terms, can understand the report.

Instructions: Answer the multiple-choice and true–false questions below for more practice with key terms and concepts from this chapter.

Multiple Choice

1. Computer viruses that hide in memory to escape detection are known as
   a. logic bombs.
   b. Trojan horses.
   c. stealth viruses.
   d. multipartite viruses.

2. Viruses that that feature a series of commands hidden on a web site are called
   a. boot-sector viruses.
   b. script viruses.
   c. polymorphic viruses.
   d. time bombs.

3. Antivirus software segregates infected files to prevent further spread in a process known as
   a. inoculation. c. disinfection.
   b. quarantine.   d. eradication.

4. Hackers without sophisticated computer knowledge who use tools developed by others to break into systems are called
   a. black-hat hackers.
   b. script kiddies.
   c. amateur hackers.
   d. white-hat hackers.

5. Which are programs that pretend to be a useful program but do something malicious on your computer?
   a. Trojan horses
   b. Backdoor programs
   c. Zombies
   d. Spyware

6. Large groups of software programs that run automatically on many computers at the same time often

   to perpetrate DoS attacks are known as
   a. Trojan horses.
   b. backdoor programs.
   c. zombie webs.
   d. botnets.

7. When hackers use many zombie computers to launch an attack on another computer or Web site, the attack is known as a
   a. zombie infestation.
   b. distributed denial-of-service attack.
   c. phishing attack.
   d. pharming plague.

8. Which are the virtual pathways into a computer that firewalls close?
   a. Packet gateways
   b. IP addresses
   c. Logical ports
   d. Data paths

9. Programs that download to your computer, usually without your knowledge, for the purpose of collecting information, is a type of cyberannoyance known as
   a. pharmware.
   b. adware.
   c. spyware.
   d. bloatware.

10. A backup of the entire contents of your hard drive is knows as
    a. a system backup.
    b. an incremental backup.
    c. an image backup.
    d. an incremental backup.

True–False

_____ 1. An incremental backup back ups all files on your computer in a specified location.
_____ 2. Even a properly installed surge protector may fail to protect a computer from all power surges.
_____ 3. Phishing is a form of social engineering.
_____ 4. When malicious code is planted on your computer that interferes with your browser's ability to find Web addresses, it is known as *phishing*.
_____ 5. If a password includes numbers, symbols, and upper- and lowercase letters, it is considered to be a strong password.

1. Backup Procedures

After reading this chapter, you know you should have a good backup strategy in place for your key data. Consider the following and prepare answers in an appropriate format as directed by your instructor.

a. How often do you back up critical data files such as homework files? What type of device do you use for backing up files? Where do you store the backups to ensure they won't be destroyed if a major disaster (such as a fire) destroys your computer? Do you use online sites for file backups?

b. List the applications (such as Microsoft Office) that are currently installed on your computer. Where is the media (DVDs) for your application software stored? For any software you purchased in an Internet download, have you burned a copy of the installation files to DVD in case you need to reinstall the software?

c. Have you ever made an image backup of your entire system? If so, what software do you use for image backups, and where are the image backups stored? If not, research image backup software on the Internet and find an appropriate package to use. Will you need to purchase an additional backup device to hold your image backup or does your current device have room for an image backup? If you need a new device, find one on the Internet that is appropriate. What is the total cost of the software and hardware you will need to implement your image backup strategy?

2. Connecting Your Computer to Public Networks

In the course of your education, you are constantly connecting your notebook to various wireless public networks such as those in the school library and neighborhood coffee shop. As you know from reading this chapter, you are more vulnerable to hackers when connected to a wireless network in a public place. Conduct research on the Internet about surfing at public hot spots and prepare a list of sensible precautions for you and your classmates to take when surfing on an open network.

3. Botnet Awareness

Botnets are serious computer infestations that affect large numbers of computers at one time. Still, many students are unaware of this threat even as botnets strike college campuses. Using the Internet, research botnets and prepare a short flyer for your fellow students that explains the threats posed by botnets and software that can be used to detect botnets.

4. Internet Security Suites

Full-featured Internet security suites offer comprehensive protection for your computer. But how do you know which suite meets your needs? Research the features of three Internet security suites such as Norton Internet Security, AVG Internet Security, Kaspersky Internet Security, Trend Micro Internet Security, or McAfee Internet Security. Prepare a document for your instructor comparing the features and prices of each security suite for a home with four computers. Explain which security suite you would choose for your home and why you would choose it.

nine

making the
transition to...
the workplace

1. File Backup Strategies

Your employer was recently the victim of a break-in, and all three dozen of its computers were stolen. Your company lost invaluable data because there was no comprehensive backup strategy in place for its computers. Your boss has asked you to prepare a report outlining a new file backup plan for the company. While preparing your report, consider the following:

a. How often should computer data be backed up? Should full backups or incremental backups be performed? Are image backups necessary?

b. Eighteen employees have notebook computers that they take off company premises. How will backups for notebooks be handled?

c. Research companies that provide online backup solutions for businesses. Which one provides the most cost effective solution for backing up three dozen computers? Can backups be performed automatically as employees change data files?

2. Securing Customer Data

Many corporations are collecting vast amounts of sensitive data (such as credit card numbers, birth dates, etc.) about their customers. Assume you are working for a business that accepts orders for merchandise through a Web site. Answer the following questions:

a. What types of information should you collect from your customers? What information couldn't you justify collecting from your customers using a valid business reason (i.e., Social Security number)?

b. Your company would like to send e-mails to customers on their birthdays, offering them a special discount on merchandise purchased within one week of their birthday. How would you explain to customers why you are collecting their birth dates, and what measures would you need to take to keep this data secure?

c. How would you ensure that information shared with third parties (such as delivery companies) is kept secure?

d. If your computer system was compromised and customer data was stolen, what would you say to customers regarding the loss of their personal data? What steps would you recommend your customers take to prevent identity theft due to your losing control of their data?

3. Is Your Computer Vulnerable?

Visit Gibson Research (**grc.com**) and run the company's ShieldsUP and LeakTest programs on your personal computer.

a. Did your computer get a clean report? If not, what potential vulnerabilities did the testing programs detect? If ports were shown as being vulnerable, research what these ports do and explain what steps you will take to protect them.

b. A properly configured firewall protects your computer from port vulnerabilities. Use the Internet to research firewall products and find three free firewall products. Which one appears to provide the best protection?

c. Besides adding a firewall to your system, what other measures should you take to protect your system from exploitation by hackers?

4. Computer Security Careers

Computer security professionals are among the highest paid employees in information technology organizations. Using employment sites such as **Monster.com**, **computerjobs.com**, and **dice.com**, research computer security jobs available in the state where your school is located (try searching "computer security"). Select three entry-level computer security jobs from different employers and prepare a document comparing the following: What are the educational requirements for computer security jobs? What job skills are required? How much prior work experience are firms looking for? Are programming skills required? With cloud computing becoming more popular, how will that affect the outlook for computer security jobs?

Instructions: Albert Einstein used *Gedankenexperiments*, or critical thinking questions, to develop his theory of relativity. Some ideas are best understood by experimenting with them in our own minds. The following critical thinking questions are designed to demand your full attention but require only a comfortable chair—no technology.

1. Protecting Your Home Network

Many people have networks in their homes. Consider the network installed in your home (or in a friend's home if you don't have a network).

a. Is your network set up to provide adequate protection against hackers? If not, what would you need to do to make it secure?

b. Are the computers on your home network protected against viruses and malware? What software do you use for protection and how often is it updated? Have you ever had problems from a virus or spyware infestation? If so, how did you resolve the problem?

2. Password Protection

You know from reading this chapter that secure passwords are essential to protecting your digital information. Consider the following:

a. How many online accounts do you have that have passwords? List them. Are the passwords for these accounts secure, based on the suggestions proposed in this chapter? Do you change your passwords on a regular basis?

b. How do you keep track of all of your passwords? Do you use password-management software? If so, what product are you using? How often do you change your master password? If you don't use password-management software, what methodology do you use for remembering and tracking your passwords?

3. Shouldn't Protection Be Included?

The Uniform Commercial Code, which governs business in every state except Louisiana, covers the implied warranty of merchantability. This warranty's basic premise is that a company selling goods guarantees that their products will do what they are designed to do (i.e., a car will transport you from place to place) and that there are no significant defects in the product. But computers are routinely sold with only trial versions of antimalware software.

a. Does the failure of OS manufacturers to include antimalware tools constitute a breach of the implied warranty of merchantability? Why or why not? Microsoft does have an antimalware product (Security Essentials), but it requires a separate download. Should Microsoft be required to include Security Essentials as part of the Windows product?

b. Computer hardware manufacturers don't make OS software, but they sell computers that would be unusable without an OS. What responsibility do they have in regard to providing antimalware protection to their customers?

4. Restricting Information to Keep You Safe

Many countries, such as China, have laws that control the content of the Internet and restrict their citizens' access to information. The United States, with the exception of specific areas such as cyberbullying and pornography, does not currently take steps to restrict its citizens' access to the Internet. Unfortunately, this freedom of information does carry some cost because some information on the Web can be potentially dangerous to the general public.

a. Do you think the U.S. government should censor information on the Web, such as instructions for making weapons, to protect the general public? Why or why not? If you think there should be some censorship, do you think such a law would violate the First Amendment right to free speech? Explain your answer.

b. Would you be willing to live with a lower level of information access to increase your sense of well being? What topics do you feel would make you feel more secure if they were censored?

Protecting Your Local Real Estate Office

Problem

Computer networks with high-speed connections to the Internet are common in most businesses today. However, along with easy access to computing devices and the Web comes the danger of theft of digital assets.

Task

A recent graduate of your school has opened a 15-person real estate office in a neighboring town. He approached your instructor for help in ensuring that his computers are adequately protected from viruses, malware, and hackers. Because he is currently low on funds, he is hoping that there may be free software available that can adequately shield his company from harm.

Process

Break the class into three teams. Each team will be responsible for investigating one of the following issues:

1. **Firewalls**. Research free firewall software and locate at least three software options that can be deployed at the business. Be sure to concentrate on software that is easy to configure and requires little or no user interaction to be effective.
2. **Antivirus software**. Research alternatives that can be used to protect the computers in the office from virus infection. Find at least three alternatives and support your recommendations with reviews (from publications such as *PC Magazine* or *Consumer Reports*) that evaluate the free packages and compare them to commercial solutions.
3. **Antimalware software**. Research free packages that will offer protection from malware. Locate at least three alternatives and determine whether the recommended software can be updated automatically. (Many free versions require manual updates.) Most companies that provide free malware protection also offer commercial packages (for a fee) that provide automatic updates. You may need to recommend that the company purchase software to ensure that a minimum of employee intervention is needed to keep the software up to date.

Present your findings to your class and discuss the pros and cons of free and commercial software. Provide your instructor with a report suitable for eventual presentation to the owner of the real estate office.

Conclusion

With the proliferation of viruses and malware, it is essential to protect business (and home) computers and networks from destruction and disruption. Free alternatives might work, but you should ensure that you have done adequate research to determine the best possible protection solution for your particular situation.

In this exercise, you will research and then role-play a complicated ethical situation. The role you play may or may not match your own personal beliefs, but your research and use of logic will enable you to represent whichever view is assigned. An arbitrator will watch and comment on both sides of the arguments, and together the team will agree on an ethical solution.

Topic: Content Control (Censorship) to Protect Children

Many parents use Web filtering software (also known as content-control software) to protect their children from objectionable content on the Internet. However, the software is also widely used in libraries, schools, and other public places where people other than parents are making decisions about what information to restricted. In 2000, the U.S. federal government began requiring libraries to use content filtering software as a condition to receiving federal funds under the provisions of the Children's Internet Protection Act (CIPA). Libraries that don't receive federal funds still do not have to install filtering software unless their state (like Virginia in 2007) passes laws requiring them to do so to receive state funding. Upon installation of the software, it is up to the library administrators to decide what content is restricted (as guided by the provisions of laws such as CIPA). Therefore, content restriction can vary widely from library to library.

Research Areas to Consider

• United States Supreme Court case *United States v. American Library Association* (2003)

• Content-filtering software and First Amendment rights

• Violating children's free speech rights

• Children's Internet Protection Act (CIPA)

Process

Divide the class into teams.

1. Research the areas cited above and devise a scenario in which parents have complained about their child not being able to access a certain Web site needed for school research.
2. Team members should write a summary that provides background information for their character—for example, parent, library administrator, and arbitrator—and details their character's behaviors to set the stage for the role-playing event. Then, team members should create an outline to use during the role-playing event.
3. Team members should arrange a mutually convenient time to meet for the exchange, using the chat room feature of MyITLab, the discussion board feature of Blackboard, or meeting in person.
4. Team members should present their case to the class or submit a PowerPoint presentation for review by the rest of the class, along with the summary and resolution they developed.

Conclusion

As technology becomes ever more prevalent and integrated into our lives, more and more ethical dilemmas will present themselves. Being able to understand and evaluate both sides of the argument, while responding in a personally or socially ethical manner, will be an important skill.

Careers in IT

It's hard to imagine an occupation in which computers are not used in some fashion. Even such previously low-tech industries as waste disposal and fast food use computers to manage inventories and order commodities. In this Technology in Focus feature, we explore various information technology (IT) career paths open to you.

What to Consider First: Job Outlook

If you want to investigate a career with computers, the first question you probably have is, "Will I be able to get a job?" With all the media reports surrounding the loss of IT jobs to other countries, many people think the boom in computer-related jobs is over. However, current projections by the U.S. Department of Labor's Bureau of Labor Statistics report that 2 out of the top 15 fastest-growing occupations from 2008 through 2018 are still in computer fields (see Figure 1). Recently, CNBC rated the top 10 best jobs in the United States; software engineers came in at number 2, and computer systems analysts were number 3! A recent survey by MSNBC showed that prospects for college graduates were improving especially in the fields of accounting, engineering, mathematics, and computer science.

After years of declining enrollment, students pursuing computer science degrees are continuing to increase extending trends seen over the

past several years. In 2010, computer science enrollment was up another 5.5% per the Web site Ars Technica. This marks a reversal of a trend that developed mainly because of the intense media discussion about the demise of Internet start-up companies in the early 2000s. Because of low enrollment during the past decade, shortages of computing professionals in the United States are projected over the next 5 to 10 years. In terms of job outlook, this is a perfect time to consider an IT career.

Regardless of whether you choose to pursue a career in IT, you should visit the Bureau of Labor Statistics site (**bls.gov**). One of the site's most useful features is the *Occupational Outlook Handbook*. Aside from projecting job growth in various career fields, it describes typical tasks that workers perform, the amount of training and education needed, and salary estimates.

In the global economy in which we now operate, job outlook also includes the risk of jobs being outsourced, possibly to other countries (a process known as *offshoring*). **Outsourcing** is a process whereby a business hires a third-party firm to provide business services (such as customer-support call centers) that were previously handled by in-house employees. **Offshoring** occurs when the outsourcing firm is located (or uses employees) outside the United States. India was the first country to offer its workforce and infrastructure for offshoring, and countries such as China, Romania, and other former Eastern Bloc countries now vie for a piece of the action. The big lure of outsourcing and offshoring is cost savings: The outsourcing firm can do the work more cheaply than in-house employees can. Considering that the standard of living and salaries are much lower in many countries than they are in the United States, offshoring is an attractive option for many U.S. employers. It may also be faster to hire outside assistance if a business does not already employ workers with the required skill set.

However, outsourcing and offshoring do not always deliver the vast cost savings that chief executive officers (CEOs) envision. TPI, a global sourcing advisory firm, conducted a survey that showed that the average cost savings from outsourcing was only 15 percent. Furthermore, other less-tangible factors can outweigh the cost savings from outsourcing. Some helpdesk jobs are being brought back to the United States because companies have experienced a backlash from

FIGURE 1 According to the Bureau of Labor Statistics, huge growth is expected in two categories of high-paying computer occupations.

Occupations with the Fastest Growth

Occupations	Percent change	Number of new jobs (*in thousands*)	Wages (May 2008 median)	Education/training category
Biomedical engineers	72	11.6	$ 77,400	Bachelor's degree
Network systems and data communications analysts	53	155.8	71,100	Bachelor's degree
Home health aides	50	460.9	20,460	Short-term on-the-job training
Personal and home care aides	46	375.8	19,180	Short-term on-the-job training
Financial examiners	41	11.1	70,930	Bachelor's degree
Medical scientists, except epidemiologists	40	44.2	72,590	Doctoral degree
Physician assistants	39	29.2	81,230	Master's degree
Skin care specialists	38	14.7	28,730	Postsecondary vocational award
Biochemists and biophysicists	37	8.7	82,840	Doctoral degree
Athletic trainers	37	6.0	39,640	Bachelor's degree
Physical therapist aides	36	16.7	23,760	Short-term on-the-job training
Dental hygienists	36	62.9	66,570	Associate degree
Veterinary technologists and technicians	36	28.5	28,900	Associate degree
Dental assistants	36	105.6	32,380	Moderate-term on-the-job training
Computer software engineers, applications	34	175.1	85,430	Bachelor's degree

consumers who have had difficulty understanding the employees with foreign accents who staff the support lines. Communications problems can arise between internal and external employees, for example, and cultural differences between the home country and the country doing the off-shoring can result in software code that needs extensive rework by in-house employees to make it usable. Data also can be less secure in an external environment, or during the transfer between the company and an external vendor. A study by Deloitte Consulting found that 70 percent of survey participants had "negative experiences" with overseas outsourcing. And a survey in *CFO* magazine indicated that 22 percent of CFOs were planning to increase their outsourcing within the United States. Although outsourcing and offshoring won't be going away, companies are approaching it with more caution and looking more to U.S. companies to provide resources.

So, what IT jobs will be staying in the United States? According to *InformationWeek* magazine, most of the jobs in these three categories (see Figure 2) will stay put:

FIGURE 2 Jobs That Should Remain Onshore

Customer Interaction	Software and Systems	Hardware/Networking
Web application developers	Business process analysts	Network security
Web interface designers	Application developers (when customer interaction is critical)	Network installation technicians
Database and data warehouse designers/developers	Project managers (for systems with customers and business users who are located predominantly in the United States)	Network administrators (engineers)
Customer relationship management (CRM) analysts		Wireless infrastructure managers and technicians
Enterprise resource planning (ERP) implementation specialists		Disaster recovery planners and responders

1. **Customer interaction:** Jobs that require direct input from customers or that involve systems with which customers interface daily.

2. **Enablers:** Jobs that involve getting key business projects accomplished, often requiring technical skills beyond the realm of IT and good people skills.

3. **Infrastructure jobs:** Jobs that are fundamental to moving and storing the information that U.S.–based employees need to do their jobs.

Common Myths About IT Careers

Many people have misconceptions about pursuing a career in IT that scare them away from considering a career in computing or convince them to pursue a computing career for the wrong reasons. Review the myths listed in the boxed feature shown on the next page. Do you share any of these misconceptions?

Is an IT Career Right for Me?

A career in IT can be a difficult path. Before preparing yourself for such a career, consider the following.

1. **Salary range:** What affects your salary in an IT position? Your skill set and your experience level are obvious answers, but

the size of an employer and its geographic location are also factors. Large companies tend to pay more, so if you're pursuing a high salary, set your sights on a large corporation. But remember that making a lot of money isn't everything—be sure to consider other quality-of-life issues such as job satisfaction.

2. **Gender bias:** Many women view IT departments as *Dilbert*-like microcosms of antisocial geeks and don't feel they would fit in. Unfortunately, some mostly male IT departments do suffer from varying degrees of gender bias. Although some women may thrive on the challenge of enlightening these male enclaves and bringing them into the 21st century, others find it difficult to work in such environments.

3. **Location:** In this case, *location* refers to the setting in which you work. IT jobs can be office based, field based, project based, or home based. Not every situation is perfect for every individual. Figure 3 summarizes the major job types and their locations.

4. **Changing nature of the work:** In IT, the playing field is always changing. New software and hardware are constantly being developed. It's almost a full-time job to keep your skills up to date. You can expect to spend a lot of time in training and self-study trying to learn new systems and techniques.

COMMON MYTHS ABOUT IT CAREERS

MYTH 1: Getting an information technology degree means you're going to be rich. Computer-related careers often offer high salaries, but choosing a computer career isn't a guarantee you'll get a high-paying job. Just as in other professions, you probably will need years of training and on-the-job experience to earn a high salary. However, starting salaries in certain IT professions are robust.

MYTH 2: You have three professional certifications—so you're ready to work. Many freshly minted technical school graduates sporting IT certifications feel ready to jump into a job. However, employers routinely cite experience as being more desirable than certification. Experience earned through an internship or a part-time job will make you much more marketable when your certification program is complete.

MYTH 3: Women are at a disadvantage in an IT career. Currently, women make up less than 20 percent of the IT workforce and about 4 percent of senior-level IT positions (per the Anita Borg Institute). This presents a huge opportunity for women who have IT skills because many IT departments are actively seeking to diversify their workforces. In addition, although a salary gender gap (the difference between what men and women earn for performing the same job) exists in IT careers, it's smaller than in many other professions.

MYTH 4: People skills don't matter in IT jobs. Despite what many people think, IT professionals are not locked in lightless cubicles, basking in the glow of their monitors. Most IT jobs require constant interaction with other workers, often in team settings. People skills are important, even when you work with computers.

MYTH 5: Mathematically impaired people need not apply. It is true that a career in programming involves a fair bit of math, but even if you're not mathematically inclined, you can explore other IT careers. IT employers also value such attributes as teamwork, creativity, leadership ability, and artistic style.

MYTH 6: Working in IT means working for a computer company or in an IT department. Computers and information systems are used across all industries and in most job functions. For example, as an accounting major, if you minor in IT, employers may be more willing to consider hiring you because working in accounting today means constantly interfacing with management information systems and manipulating data.

MYTH 7: All of the jobs are going offshore. Although many IT jobs have been lost to international competition over the past decade, most networking, analyst (business, systems, and database) and creative (digital media creation and game development) jobs have stayed in the United States. As demand for IT professionals has increased overseas, foreign wages have been driven up, making offshoring of jobs less attractive. The bottom line is that plenty of IT jobs remain in the United States.

Resolving myths is an important step toward considering a job in IT. However, you need to consider other issues related to IT careers before you decide to pursue a particular path.

FIGURE 3 Where Do You Want to Work?

Type of Job	Location and Hours	Special Considerations
Office based	Report for work to the same location each day and interact with the same people on a regular basis Requires regular hours of attendance (such as 9 A.M. to 5 P.M.)	May require working beyond "normal" working hours May also require workers to be on call 24/7
Field based	Travel from place to place as needed and perform short-term jobs at each location	Involve a great deal of travel and the ability to work independently
Project based	Work at client sites on specific projects for extended periods of time (weeks or months) Examples: contractors and consultants	Can be especially attractive to individuals who like workplace situations that vary on a regular basis
Home based (telecommuting)	Work from home	Involve very little day-to-day supervision and require an individual who is self-disciplined

HOW MUCH WILL I EARN?

Like many other professionals, IT employees can earn a very good living. Although starting salaries for some IT positions (computer desktop support and helpdesk analysts) are in the modest range ($38,000 to $42,000), starting salaries for students with bachelor's degrees in information technology are fairly robust. CNBC recently profiled the 10 best jobs in the United States. Coming in at second and third place were software engineer (median salary $79,780) and computer systems analyst with median salaries of $79,780 and $69,760 respectively.

IT salaries vary widely, depending on experience level, the geographic location of the job, and the size of the employer. To obtain the most accurate information, research salaries yourself. Job posting sites such as **Monster.com** can provide guidance, but **Salary.com** provides a wizard to help you determine what IT professionals in your area are making compared with national averages. Figure 4 shows that for an entry-level programming position in Portland, Oregon, you could expect to earn a median salary of between $42,500 and $57,000 depending on the size of the company.

FIGURE 4

The salary wizard at Salary.com is easy to tailor to your location and company size.

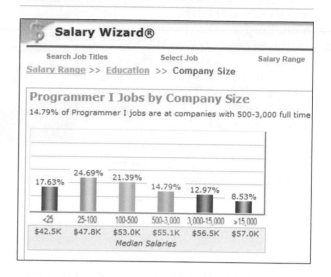

Hundreds of IT job titles are listed so that you can fine-tune your search to the specific job in which you're interested.

5. **Stress:** Whereas the average American works 42 hours a week, a survey by *InformationWeek* shows that the average IT staff person works 45 hours a week and is on call for another 24 hours. On-call time (hours an employee must be available to work in the event of a problem) has been increasing in recent years because more IT systems (such as e-commerce systems) require 24/7 availability.

The good news is that despite the stress (see Figure 5) and changing nature of the IT environment, most computing skills are portable from industry to industry. A networking job in the clothing manufacturing industry uses the same primary skill set as a networking job for a

FIGURE 5

Stress comes from multiple directions in IT jobs.

MATCHING A CAREER TO YOUR SKILLS

Are you unsure about what career you would like to pursue? There are many online tools such as the Skill Profiler from America's Career InfoNet (**careerinfonet.org**) that can help you identify careers based on your skills. This tool asks you to identify your skills (see Figure 6) in seven categories and then rate your skills in each area you selected. The program then compiles a skills profile for you and suggests job titles for you to explore.

FIGURE 6

"Basic Skills" is one of seven categories on the Skills Profiler, a survey that you can complete to help you assess which career paths match your talents.

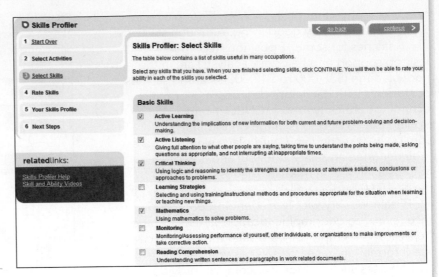

supermarket chain. Therefore, if something disastrous happens to the industry you're in, you should be able to switch to another industry with little trouble.

What Realm of IT Should I Work In?

Figure 7 provides an organizational chart for a modern IT department that should help you understand the careers currently available and how they interrelate. The chief information officer (CIO) has overall responsibility for the development, implementation, and maintenance of information systems and infrastructure. Usually the CIO reports to the chief operating officer (COO).

The responsibilities below the CIO are generally grouped into two units: development and integration (responsible for the development of systems and Web sites) and technical services (responsible for the day-to-day operations of the company's information infrastructure and network, including all hardware and software deployed).

In large organizations, responsibilities are distinct and jobs are defined more narrowly. In medium-sized organizations, there can be overlap between position responsibilities. At a small shop, you might be the network administrator, database administrator, computer support technician, and helpdesk analyst all at the same time. Let's look at the typical jobs found in each department.

Working in Development and Integration

Two distinct paths exist in this division: Web development and systems development. Because everything involves the Web today, there is often a great deal of overlap between these paths.

Web Development

When most people think of Web development careers, they usually equate them with being a **webmaster**. However, today's webmasters usually are supervisors with responsibility for certain aspects of Web development. At smaller companies, they may also be responsible for tasks that the other individuals in a Web development group usually do:

* **Web content creators** generate the words and images that appear on the Web. Journalists, other writers, editors, and marketing personnel prepare an enormous amount of Web content, whereas **video producers**, **graphic designers**, and **animators** create Web-based multimedia. **Interface designers** work with graphic designers and animators to create a look and feel for the site and make it easy to navigate. Content creators have a thorough understanding of their own fields as well as HTML/XHTML, PHP, and JavaScript. They also need to be familiar with the capabilities and limitations of modern Web development tools so that they know what the Web publishers can accomplish.

FIGURE 7

This is a typical structure for an IT department at a large corporation.

- **Web publishers** build Web pages to deploy the materials that the content creators develop. They wield the software tools (such as Adobe Dreamweaver and Microsoft Expression) that develop the Web pages and create links to databases (using products such as Oracle and SQL Server) to keep information flowing between users and Web pages. They must possess a solid understanding of client- and server-side Web languages (HTML/XHTML, XML, Java, JavaScript, ASP, PHP, and PERL) and development environments such as the Microsoft .NET Framework.

- **Customer interaction technicians** provide feedback to a Web site's customers. Major job responsibilities include answering e-mail, sending requested information, funneling questions to appropriate personnel (technical support, sales, and so on), and providing suggestions to Web publishers for site improvements. Extensive customer service training is essential to work effectively in this area.

- **Social media directors** are responsible for directing the strategy of the company on all social media sites where the company maintains a presence. Often supervising customer interaction technicians, these people make sure that customers have a quality experience while interacting with company employees and customers on sites such as Facebook, Twitter, and MySpace. Responding to comments left on sites, developing promotional strategies, and designing functionality of the company's social media sites are common job responsibilities.

FIGURE 8

As you can see, it takes a team to create and maintain a Web site.

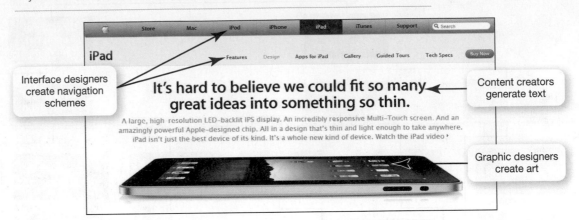

As you can see in Figure 8, many different people can work on the same Web site. The education required varies widely for these jobs. Web programming jobs often require a four-year college degree in computer science, whereas graphic designers often are hired with two-year art degrees.

Systems Development

Ask most people what systems developers do and they will answer, "programming." However, programming is only one aspect of systems development. Because large projects involve many people, there are many job opportunities in systems development. An explanation of each key area follows.

- **Systems analysts** spend most of their time in the beginning stages of the system development life cycle (SDLC). They talk with end users to gather information about problems and existing information systems. They document systems and propose solutions to problems. Having good people skills is essential to success as a systems analyst. In addition, systems analysts work with programmers during the development phase to design appropriate programs to solve the problem at hand. Therefore, many organizations insist on hiring systems analysts who have both solid business backgrounds and previous programming experience (at least at a basic level). For entry-level jobs, a four-year degree is usually required. Many colleges and universities offer degrees in management information systems (MIS) that include a

mixture of systems development, programming, and business courses.

- **Programmers** participate in the SDLC, attending meetings to document user needs and working closely with systems analysts during the design phase. Programmers need excellent written communication skills because they often generate detailed systems documentation for end-user training purposes. Because programming languages are mathematically based, it is essential for programmers to have strong math skills and an ability to think logically. Programmers should also be proficient at more than one programming language. A four-year degree is usually required for entry-level programming positions.

- **Project managers** usually have years of experience as programmers or systems analysts. This job is part of a career path upward from entry-level programming and systems analyst jobs. Project managers manage the overall systems development process: assigning staff, budgeting, reporting to management, coaching team members, and ensuring deadlines are met. Project managers need excellent time management skills because they are pulled in several directions at once. Many project managers obtain master's degrees to supplement their undergraduate degrees in computer science or MIS.

In addition to these key players, the following people are also involved in the systems development process:

- **Technical writers** generate systems documentation for end users and for programmers who may make modifications to the system in the future.

- **Network engineers** help the programmers and analysts design compatible systems, because many systems are required to run in certain environments (UNIX or Windows, for instance) and must work well in conjunction with other programs.
- **Database developers** design and build databases to support the software systems being developed.

Large development projects may have all of these team members on the project. Smaller projects may require an overlap of positions (such as a programmer also acting as a systems analyst). The majority of these jobs require four-year college degrees in computer science or management information systems. As shown in Figure 9, team members work together to build a system.

It is important to emphasize that all systems development careers are stressful. Deadlines are tight for development projects, especially if they involve getting a new product to market ahead of the competition. Nevertheless, if you enjoy challenges and can endure a fast-paced, dynamic environment, there should be plenty of opportunities for good systems developers in the decade ahead.

FIGURE 9

This is a flowchart of a ticket ordering system. Each member of the systems development team performs functions critical to the development process (as shown in the red boxes).

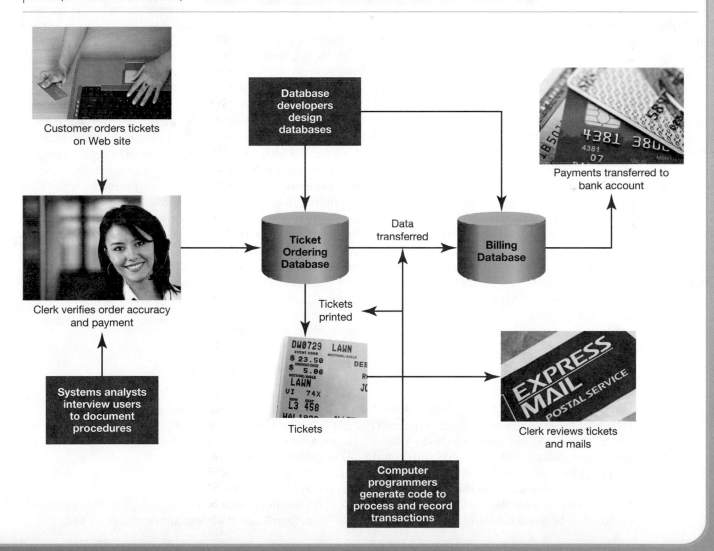

Customer orders tickets on Web site

Clerk verifies order accuracy and payment

Systems analysts interview users to document procedures

Database developers design databases

Ticket Ordering Database

Data transferred

Billing Database

Payments transferred to bank account

Tickets printed

Tickets

Computer programmers generate code to process and record transactions

Clerk reviews tickets and mails

GET IN THE GAME: CAREERS IN GAME DEVELOPMENT

The video gaming industry in the United States has surpassed the earning power of the Hollywood movie industry. In 2009, U.S. consumers bought almost $20 billion worth of video games and accessories, whereas Hollywood took in just over $10 billion. Although some aspects of game development, such as scenery design and certain aspects of programming, are being sent offshore, the majority of game development requires a creative team whose members need to work in close proximity to each other. Therefore, it is anticipated that most game development jobs will stay in the United States. Consoles such as the Xbox 360 and the PlayStation 3 generate demand for large-scale games, but the popularity of mobile devices such as phones, iPads, and netbooks is driving demand for lower-end, casual game applications. Casual games are games that can be played relatively quickly, often puzzle games. Demand for family-friendly games without violence, sex, and profanity is on the rise (see Figure 10). With all this demand, there are many opportunities for careers in game development.

Game development jobs usually are split along two paths: designers and programmers. Game designers tend to be artistic and are responsible for creating 2D and 3D art, game interfaces, video sequences, special effects, game levels, and scenarios. Game designers must master software packages such as Autodesk 3ds Max, Autodesk Maya, NewTek LightWave 3D, Adobe Photoshop, and Adobe Flash. Programmers are then responsible for coding the scenarios developed by these designers. Using languages such as C, C++, Assembly, and Java, programmers build the game and ensure that it plays accurately.

Aside from programmers and designers, play testers and quality assurance professionals play the games with the intent of breaking them or discovering bugs within the game interfaces or worlds. **Play testing** is an essential part of the game development process because it assists designers in determining which aspects of the game are most intriguing to players and which parts of the game need to be repaired or enhanced.

No matter what job you may pursue in the realm of gaming, you will need to have a two- or four-year college degree. If you're interested in gaming, then look for a school with a solid animation or 3D art program or a computer game programming curriculum. Programming requires a strong background in mathematics and physics to enable you to realistically program environments that mimic the real world. Proficiency with mathematics (especially geometry) also helps with design careers. For more information on gaming careers, check out the International Game Developers Association site (**igda.org**) and Game Career Guide (**gamecareerguide.com**).

FIGURE 10
Although Puzzle Pirates involves pirating activities, all major aspects of the game are displayed as puzzles with no violence, making it suitable for children. Check it out at www.puzzlepirates.com.

Working in Technical Services

Technical services jobs are vital to keeping IT systems running. The people in these jobs install and maintain the infrastructure behind the IT systems and work with end users to make sure they can interact with the systems effectively. These also are the *least likely* IT jobs to be outsourced because hands-on work with equipment and users is required on a regular basis. The two major categories of technical services careers are information systems and support services.

Information Systems

The information systems department keeps the networks and telecommunications up and

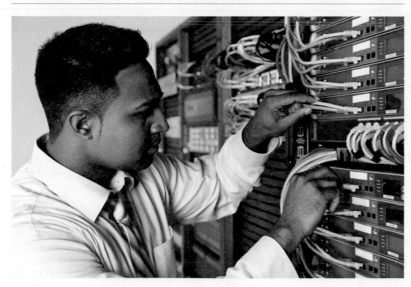

running at all times. Within the department, you'll find a variety of positions.

- **Network administrators** (sometimes called *network engineers*) install and configure servers, design and plan networks, and test new networking equipment (see Figure 11).
- **Database administrators (DBAs)** install and configure database servers and ensure that the servers provide an adequate level of access to all users.
- **Web server administrators** install, configure, and maintain Web servers and ensure that the company maintains Internet connectivity at all times.
- **Telecommunications technicians** oversee the communications infrastructure, including training employees to use telecommunications equipment. They are often on call 24 hours a day.

Support Services

As a member of the support services team, you interface with users (external customers or employees) and troubleshoot their computer problems. These positions include the following:

- **Helpdesk analysts** staff the phones, respond to Internet live chat, or respond to e-mail and solve problems for customers or employees, either remotely or in person. Often helpdesk personnel are called upon to train users on the latest software and hardware.
- **Computer support technicians** go to a user's physical location and fix software and hardware problems. They also often have to chase down and repair faults in the network infrastructure.

As important as these people are, they often receive a great deal of abuse by angry users whose computers are not working. When working in support services, you need to be patient and not be overly sensitive to insults!

Technical services jobs often require two-year college degrees or training at trade schools or technical institutes. At smaller companies, job duties tend to overlap between the helpdesk and technician jobs. These jobs are in demand. A survey of more than 1,400 chief information officers sponsored by Robert Half Technology identified network administration, desktop support and Windows administration as the top skills needed by U.S. IT departments.

How Should I Prepare for a Job in IT?

A job in IT requires a robust skill set and formal training and preparation. Most employers today have an entry-level requirement of a college degree, a technical institute diploma, appropriate professional certifications, experience in the field, or a combination of these. How can you prepare for a job in IT?

1. **Get educated.** Two- and four-year colleges and universities normally offer three degrees to prepare students for IT careers: computer science, MIS, and information technology (although titles vary). Alternatives to colleges and universities are privately licensed technical (or trade) schools. Generally, these programs focus on building skill sets rapidly and qualifying

SO YOU WANT TO BE A NETWORK ADMINISTRATOR?

You know that network administrators are the people who design, install, and maintain the network equipment and infrastructure. But what *exactly* do they do?

Network administrators are involved in every stage of network planning and deployment. They decide what equipment to buy and what type of media to use, and they determine the correct topology for the network. They also often develop policies regarding network usage, security measures, and hardware and software standards.

After the planning is complete, network administrators help install the network (either by supervising third-party contractors or by doing the work themselves). Typical installation tasks include configuring and installing client computers and peripherals,

running cable, and installing wireless media devices. Installing and configuring security devices and software are also critical jobs.

When equipment and cables break, network administrators must locate the source of the trouble and fix the problem. They also obtain and install updates to network software, and evaluate new equipment to determine whether the network should be upgraded. In addition, they monitor the network performance to ensure that users' needs are met.

Because of the importance of the Internet to most organizations, network administrators ensure that the Internet connection is maintained at all times, which usually is a high priority on their to-do list. Finally, network administrators plan disaster recovery strategies (such as what to do if a fire destroys the server room).

for a job in a specific field. The main advantage of technical schools is that their programs usually take less time to complete than college degrees. However, to have a realistic chance of employment in IT fields other than networking or Web development, you should attend a degree-granting college or university.

2. **Investigate professional certifications.** Certifications attempt to provide a consistent method of measuring skill levels in specific areas of IT. Hundreds of IT certifications are available, most of which you get by passing a written exam. Software and hardware vendors (such as Microsoft and Cisco) and professional organizations (such as the Computing Technology Industry Association) often establish certification standards. Visit **microsoft.com**, **cisco.com**, **comptia.org**, and **sun.com** for more information on certifications.

   Employees with certifications generally earn more than employees who aren't certified. However, most employers don't view a certification as a substitute for a college degree or a trade school program. You should think of certifications as an extra edge beyond your formal education that will make you more attractive to employers. To ensure you're pursuing the right certifications, ask employers which certifications they respect, or explore online job sites to see which certifications are listed as desirable or required.

3. **Get experience.** In addition to education, employers want you to have experience, even for entry-level jobs. While you're still completing your education, consider getting an internship or part-time job in your field of study. Many colleges will help you find internships and allow you to earn credit toward your degree through internship programs.

4. **Do research.** Find out as much as you can about the company and the industry it is in before going on an interview. Start with the company's Web site and then expand your search to business and trade publications such as *Business Week* and *CIO* magazines.

How Do I Find a Job in IT?

Training for a career is not useful unless you can find a job at the end of your training. Here are some tips on getting a job.

1. **Visit your school's placement office.** Many employers recruit at schools, and most schools maintain a placement office to help students find jobs. Employees in the placement office can help you with résumé preparation and interviewing skills, and provide you with leads for internships and jobs.

2. **Visit online employment sites.** Most IT jobs are advertised online at sites such as **Monster.com** and **Dice.com**. Most of these

FIGURE 12
Employment sites such as Dice.com enable you to search for specific jobs within a defined geographic area.

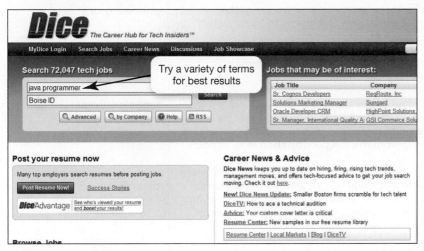

sites allow you to store your resume online, and Dice (see Figure 12) allows employees to browse resumes to find qualified employees.

Other sites also offer career resources, including **computerjobs.com**, **jobcircle.com**, **techcareers.com**, **justtechjobs.com**, **linkedin.com**, **computerwork.com**, **careerbuilder.com**, and **gamasutra.com**. Begin looking at job postings on these sites early in your education, because these job postings detail the skill sets employers require. Focusing on coursework that will provide you with desirable skill sets will make you more marketable.

3. **Start networking.** Many jobs are never advertised but instead are filled by word of mouth. Seek out contacts in your field and discuss job prospects with them. Find out what skills you need, and ask them to recommend others in the industry with whom you can speak. Professional organizations such as the Association for Computing Machinery (ACM) offer one way to network. These organizations often have chapters on college campuses and offer reduced membership rates for students.

The contacts you make there could lead to your next job. Local user groups that are made up of working professionals with similar interests (such as Microsoft programmers or Linux administrators) also are good sources of contacts. Figure 13 lists major professional organizations you should consider investigating.

FIGURE 13 Professional Organizations

Organization Name	Purpose	Web Site
Association for Computing Machinery (ACM)	Oldest scientific computing society. Maintains a strong focus on programming and systems development.	acm.org
Association for Information Systems (AIS)	Organization of professionals who work in academia and specialize in information systems.	aisnet.org
Association of Information Technology Professionals (AITP)	Heavy focus on IT education and development of seminars and learning materials.	aitp.org
Institute of Electrical and Electronics Engineers (IEEE)	Provides leadership and sets engineering standards for all types of network computing devices and protocols.	ieee.org
Information Systems Security Association (ISSA)	Not-for-profit, international organization of information security professionals and practitioners.	issa.org

FIGURE 14 Resources for Women in IT

Organization Name	Purpose	Web Site
Anita Borg Institute for Women and Technology	Organization whose aim is to "increase the impact of women on all aspects of technology."	anitaborg.org
Association for Women in Computing (AWC)	A not-for-profit organization dedicated to promoting the advancement of women in computing professions.	awc-hq.org
Center for Women and Information Technology (CWIT)	Established at the University of Maryland, Baltimore County (UMBC), the organization is dedicated to providing global leadership in achieving women's full participation in all aspects of IT.	umbc.edu/cwit
Diversity/Careers in Engineering & Information Technology	An online magazine whose articles cover career issues focused on technical professionals who are members of minority groups, women, or people with disabilities.	diversitycareers.com
Women in Technology International (WITI)	A global trade association for tech-savvy, professional women.	witi.com

If you are a woman and are thinking about pursuing an IT career, there are many resources and groups that cater to female IT professionals and students. The oldest and best-known organization is the Association for Women in Computing, founded in 1978. Figure 14 provides a list of resources to investigate.

4. **Check corporate Web sites for jobs.** Many corporate Web sites list current job opportunities. For example, Google provides searchable job listings by geographic location (see Figure 15). Check the sites of companies in which you are interested and then do a search on the sites for job openings or, if provided, click their Employment links.

The outlook for IT jobs should continue to be positive in the future. We wish you luck with your education and job search.

FIGURE 15
Corporate Web sites often list available jobs. The Google site arranges jobs by location and then by broad categories to help you zero in on the right job.

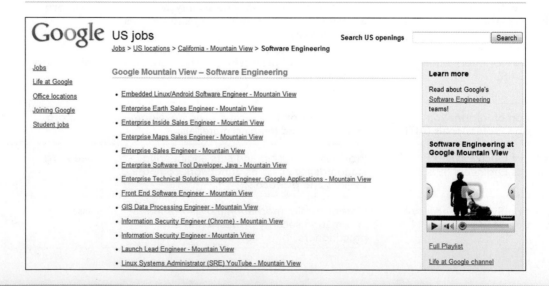

Multiple Choice

Instructions: Answer the multiple-choice questions below for more practice with key terms and concepts from this Technology in Focus feature.

1. The individuals responsible for making a Web site easy to navigate are referred to as
   a. network engineers.
   b. graphic designers.
   c. Web programmers.
   d. interface designers.

2. What type of job involves a great deal of travel and the ability to work independently?
   a. Field based
   b. Project based
   c. Office based
   d. Home based

3. Which position is *not* typically a part of the information systems department?
   a. Helpdesk analysts
   b. Telecommunications technicians
   c. Network administrators
   d. Web server administrators

4. Outsourcing is thought to be an attractive option for many companies because of
   a. the emphasis on employee training.
   b. the cost savings that can be realized.
   c. increased data security.
   d. the opportunity to experience new cultures and ideas.

5. Which role best describes those employees who design solutions to problems?
   a. Project managers
   b. Network engineers
   c. Systems analysts
   d. Database developers

6. Which of the following statement about IT careers is *true*?
   a. IT employers typically prefer certification to experience.
   b. Women who have IT skills have limited opportunities.
   c. Most IT jobs are being moved offshore.
   d. IT jobs require frequent interaction with others.

7. Which task is *not* typically performed by a network administrator?
   a. Developing network usage policies
   b. Installing networks
   c. Planning for disaster recovery
   d. Web site programming

8. Social media directors are the people who are responsible for
   a. orchestrating the company strategy in online venues.
   b. providing feedback to Web site customers.
   c. creating the look and feel of a Web site.
   d. deploying the materials prepared by content creators.

9. The oldest scientific computing organization is the
   a. Institute of Electrical and Electronics Engineers.
   b. Association for Computing Machinery.
   c. Information Systems Security association.
   d. Association for Women in Computing.

10. Which position is part of the Web development department?
    a. Systems analyst
    b. Web content creator
    c. Programmer
    d. Technical writer

objectives

After reading this chapter, you should be able to answer the following questions:

1. What is a system development life cycle, and what are the phases in the cycle? *(pp. 474–476)*
2. What is the life cycle of a program? *(p. 478)*
3. What role does a problem statement play in programming? *(pp. 478–480)*
4. How do programmers create algorithms? *(pp. 480–486)*
5. How do programmers move from algorithm to code, and in what categories of language might they code? *(pp. 486–487)*
6. How does a programmer move from code in a programming language to the 1s and 0s the CPU can understand? *(pp. 487–493)*
7. How is a program tested? *(pp. 493–494)*
8. What steps are involved in completing the program? *(pp. 494–495)*
9. How do programmers select the right programming language for a specific task? *(pp. 495–502)*
10. What are the most popular programming languages for Windows and Web applications? *(pp. 502–505)*

multimedia resources

Active Helpdesk

- Understanding Software Programming **(p. 495)**
- Selecting the Right Programming Language **(p. 497)**

Sound Bytes

- Programming for End Users **(p. 479)**
- Looping Around the IDE **(p. 493)**
- 3D Programming the Easy Way **(p. 503)**

Companion Website

The Companion Website includes a variety of additional materials to help you review and learn more about the topics in this chapter. Go to: *pearsonhighered.com/techinaction*

how cool

how cool is *this?*

Microsoft has a tool to make gaming programming simpler for all of us. The tool is called **XNA Game Studio**. This platform uses the C# programming language to develop video games for both Windows and the Xbox 360 game system. When the game is complete, the "developer" can distribute his or her creation to other players using the **Xbox Live** network. Windows Phone 7, the operating system for Windows-based mobile devices like the Microsoft Zune, now also supports XNA. So you can open up the Platformer Starter Kit and start creating your own 2D game in an afternoon!

Tour the XNA **Creators Club** (creators.xna.com/en-US) to see the types of games players from all over the world have created!

Understanding Software Programming

Every day we face a wide array of tasks. Some tasks are complex and need a human touch; some require creative thought and high-level organization. However, some tasks are routine, such as alphabetizing a huge collection of invoices. Tasks that are repetitive, work with electronic information, and follow a series of clear steps are candidates for automation with computers.

Why would I ever need to create a program? Well-designed computer programs already exist for many tasks. For example, if you want to write a research paper, Microsoft Word allows you to do just that. The program has already been designed to translate the tasks you want to accomplish into computer instructions. To do your work, you need only be familiar with the interface of Word; you do not have to create a program yourself.

However, for users who cannot find an existing software product to accomplish a task, programming is mandatory. For example, imagine that a medical company comes up with a new smart bandage that is designed to transmit medical information about a wound directly to a diagnostic computer. (These devices are currently under development.) No existing software product on the market is designed to accumulate and relay information in just this manner. Therefore, a team of software programmers will have to create smart-bandage software.

If I'm not going to be a programmer, why do I need to know some programming? Even if you'll never create a program of your own, knowing the basics of computer programming is still helpful. For example, most modern software applications enable you to customize and automate various features by using custom-built miniprograms called *macros*. By creating macros, you can ask the computer to execute a complicated sequence of steps with a single command. Understanding how to program macros enables you to add custom commands to Word or Excel, for example, and lets you automate frequently performed tasks, providing a huge boost to your productivity.

> **"Why do I need to know some programming?"**

Understanding programming is therefore an important piece of getting the most out of your computer system. If you plan to use only off-the-shelf (existing) software, having a basic knowledge of programming enables you to understand how application software is constructed and to add features that support your personal needs. If you plan to create custom applications from scratch, having a detailed knowledge of programming will be critical to the successful completion of your projects. In this chapter, we explore the stages of program development and survey the most popular programming languages.

The Life Cycle of an Information System

Generally speaking, a system is a collection of pieces working together to achieve a common goal. Your body, for example, is a system of muscles, organs, and other organized groups of cells working together. The college you attend is a system, too, in which administrators, faculty, students, and maintenance personnel work together. An **information system** includes data, people, procedures, hardware, and software. You interact with information systems all the time, whether you are at a grocery store, bank, or restaurant. In any of these instances, the parts of the system work together toward a similar goal. Because teams of individuals are required to develop such systems, they need to follow an organized process (set of steps) to ensure that development proceeds in an orderly fashion.

This set of steps is usually referred to as the **system development life cycle (SDLC)**. Systems theory came long before programming: Everything is a part of something larger and something smaller. If you change one part of a system, other parts of the system also change. In this section, we provide you with an overview of systems development and show you how programming fits into the cycle.

System Development Life Cycle

Why do I need a process to develop a system? To create a modern software package, an entire team of people is needed, and a systematic approach is necessary.

Those programs are generally far more complex than the ones you would write yourself, and they require many phases to make the product complete and marketable. They need to be available for multiple operating systems, work over networked environments, and be free of errors and well supported. Therefore, a process often referred to as the *system development life cycle (SDLC)* is used.

What steps constitute the SDLC?
There are six steps in a common SDLC model, as shown in Figure 10.1. This system is sometimes referred to as a "waterfall" system because each step is dependent on the previous step being completed first. A brief synopsis of each step follows.

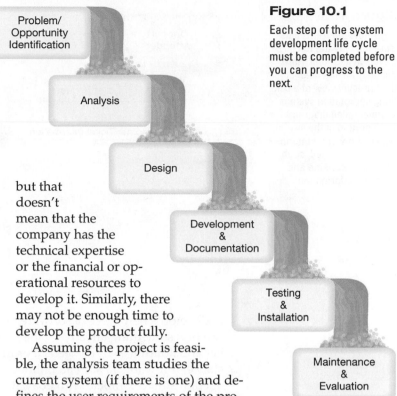

Figure 10.1

Each step of the system development life cycle must be completed before you can progress to the next.

Problem/Opportunity Identification

Analysis

Design

Development & Documentation

Testing & Installation

Maintenance & Evaluation

1. **Problem and Opportunity Identification:** Corporations are always attempting to break into new markets, develop new sources of customers, or launch new products. For example, when the founders of eBay developed the idea of an online auction community, they needed a system that could serve customers and allow them to interact with each other. At other times, systems development is driven by a company's desire to serve its existing customers more efficiently or to respond to problems with a current system. For example, when traditional brick-and-mortar businesses want to launch e-commerce sites, they need to develop systems for customers to purchase products.

    Whether solving an existing problem or exploiting an opportunity, corporations usually generate more ideas for systems than they have the time and money to implement. Large corporations typically form a development steering committee to evaluate systems development proposals. The committee reviews ideas and decides which projects to take forward based on available resources such as personnel and funding.

2. **Analysis:** In this phase, analysts explore in depth the problem to be solved and develop a program specification. The program specification is a clear statement of the goals and objectives of the project. It is also at this stage that the first feasibility assessment is performed. The feasibility assessment determines whether the project should go forward. You might have a great idea, but that doesn't mean that the company has the technical expertise or the financial or operational resources to develop it. Similarly, there may not be enough time to develop the product fully.

    Assuming the project is feasible, the analysis team studies the current system (if there is one) and defines the user requirements of the proposed system. Finally, the analysts recommend a solution or plan of action, and the process moves to the design phase.

3. **Design:** Before a house is built, blueprints are developed so that the workers have a plan to follow. The design phase of the SDLC has the same objective: generating a detailed plan for programmers to follow. The current and proposed systems are documented using flowcharts and data-flow diagrams. **Flowcharts** are visual diagrams of a process, including the decisions that need to be made along the way. **Data-flow diagrams** trace all data in an information system from the point at which data enters the system to its final resting place (storage or output). The data-flow diagram in Figure 10.2 shows the flow of concert ticket information.

    The ultimate goal of the design phase with respect to system software development is to design a system that details the software, inputs and outputs, backups and controls, and processing requirements of the problem. It is also in this phase that the "make or buy" decision is made. Once the system plan is designed, a company evaluates existing software packages (off-the-shelf software) to determine whether it needs

Figure 10.2

Data-flow diagrams illustrate the way the data travels in a system. Here the diagram documents the top-level view of a ticketing information system. More detailed diagrams for each portion of the system would show other information being tracked, such as customer name and payment information.

to develop a new piece of software or can buy something already on the market and adapt it to fit its needs. For instance, if it wants to start an online auction site to compete with eBay, it might not have to build its own system. Numerous online auction software packages are for sale. If the company cannot find an existing package that will work, then it would have to develop its own system. Alternatively, it could outsource (hire someone outside the corporation) to develop the program it needs.

4. **Development and Documentation:** It is during this phase that actual programming takes place. This phase is also the first part of the program development

life cycle (PDLC), described in detail in the rest of the chapter.

5. **Testing and Installation:** The next step in the SDLC is testing the program to ensure it works properly and then installing the program so that it can be used.

6. **Maintenance and Evaluation:** Once the system is installed, its performance must be monitored to determine whether it is still meeting the needs of the end users. Bugs (errors) that were not detected in the testing phase but that the users discover subsequently must be corrected. Additional enhancements that users request are evaluated so that appropriate program modifications can be made.

The waterfall model is an idealized view of software development. Most developers follow some variation of it, however. For example, a design team may "spiral," so a group that is supporting the work of another group will work concurrently with that group on development. (This contrasts with workflows in which the groups work independently, one after the other.) Often there is a "backflow" up the waterfall, because even well-designed projects can require redesign and specification changes midstream.

Some people criticize the waterfall model for taking too long to provide actual working software to the client. This may contribute to scope creep, an ever-changing set of requests from the clients for additional features as they wait longer and longer to see a working prototype. Other developmental models are

The More Minds the Better

In each phase of software program creation, a style of interaction named *joint application development* (JAD) is useful in creating successful, flexible results. JAD is popular because it helps designers adapt to changes in program specifications quickly. In JAD, the customer is intimately involved in the project right from the beginning. Slow communication and lengthy feedback time make the traditional development process extremely time consuming. In JAD "workshops," there are no communication delays. Such workshops usually include end users, developers, subject experts, observers (such as senior managers), and a facilitator. The facilitator enforces the rules of the meeting to make sure all voices are heard and agreement is reached as quickly as possible. Also called *accelerated design* or *facilitated team techniques*, JAD's goal is to improve design quality by fostering clear communication. For more details, refer to the articles located on The Facilitator Web site (**thefacilitator.com/htdocs/article11.html**).

When Software Kills

Building a software application is a process that involves many people and requires many decisions. But what happens when the released product is defective—tragically defective?

The most infamous example of this was the computerized radiation therapy machine called the Therac-25 (see Figure 10.3). Between June 1985 and January 1987, six known accidents in the United States and Canada led to massive radiation overdoses by the Therac-25, resulting in the death of three patients and serious injuries to three others. This error has been described as the worst series of radiation accidents in the history of medical accelerators.

The software was responsible for monitoring the machine's status, accepting input about the treatment desired, and setting the machine up for treatment. It turned on the beam in response to an operator command and turned off the beam when treatment was completed, when an operator commanded it, or when a malfunction was detected.

In the first accident, a 61-year-old woman was receiving follow-up radiation after surgery for breast cancer. When the machine turned on, she said that she felt a "tremendous force of heat . . . this red-hot sensation." When the technician came in and the patient said that she had been burned, the technician replied that it was not possible. The patient went home but was soon in so much pain that she went to the local hospital. Hospital staff determined that the patient was experiencing a normal reaction to the radiation therapy and advised her to continue treatments.

Although the therapeutic dose was expected to be about 200 rads, it was later estimated that the patient had received one or two doses of radiation in the 15,000- to 20,000-rad range (doses of 1,000 rads can be fatal). The hospital explained that part of the confusion happened because staff members had never seen a radiation overdose of that magnitude before. Eventually the patient lost her breast, lost the use of her shoulder and arm, and was in constant pain. Other patients had similar incidents, some dying as a result of complications from the error in the dosage.

In the years since these accidents, much analysis has been done to see how the tragedy could have been avoided. One notable item is that remarkably little software documentation was produced by the two manufacturing companies involved during development. A memo by the Food and Drug Administration reviewing the incident said, "Unfortunately, the company response also seems to point out an apparent lack of documentation on software specifications and a software test plan."

In addition, testing was not done in a rigorous manner. A "small amount" of software testing was done on a simulator, but most testing was done at the system level rather than by examining software and hardware separately. It appears that machine and software testing was minimal, with most effort directed at the integrated system test.

Although the basic mistakes involved poor software engineering practices, many different factors explained the full set of accidents including:

- Simple programming errors
- Inadequate safety engineering
- Poor human–computer interaction design
- Too little focus on safety by the manufacturing organization
- Inadequate reporting structure at the company level and as required by the U.S. government

In events such as this one, who should be held responsible for producing defective software? Is it the corporate management that did not institute a defined software process? Is it the production managers, who forced tight schedules that demanded risky software engineering practices? What about the software engineers who wrote the defective code? The very first article of the code of ethics of the Institute of Electrical and Electronic Engineers (IEEE) states, "[We] accept responsibility in making engineering decisions consistent with the safety, health, and welfare of the public, and to disclose promptly factors that might endanger the public or the environment." What about users of the software? Can they be held responsible for accidents? What if they made changes to the system?

The Association for Computing Machinery (ACM) and the IEEE have established eight principles for ethical software engineering practices:

1. **Public:** Software engineers shall act consistently with the public interest.
2. **Client and Employer:** Software engineers shall act in a manner that is in the best interests of their client and employer consistent with the public interest.
3. **Product:** Software engineers shall ensure that their products and related modifications meet the highest professional standards possible.

4. **Judgment:** Software engineers shall maintain integrity and independence in their professional judgment.
5. **Management:** Software engineering managers and leaders shall subscribe to and promote an ethical approach to the management of software development and maintenance.
6. **Profession:** Software engineers shall advance the integrity and reputation of the profession consistent with the public interest.
7. **Colleagues:** Software engineers shall be fair to and supportive of their colleagues.
8. **Self:** Software engineers shall participate in lifelong learning regarding the practice of their profession and shall promote an ethical approach to the practice of the profession.

Only through constant vigilance on the part of each software programmer, manager, and testing professional will situations such as the Therac-25 be prevented.

Figure 10.3

The Therac-25 incident reminds us of the responsibilities incumbent on programmers, system designers, and system users.

being used in the industry to address these issues (see the Bits and Bytes sidebar, "The More Minds the Better" on page 476.)

The Life Cycle of a Program

Programming often begins with nothing more than a problem or a request, such as "We can't get our budget reports out on time," or "Can you tell me how many transfer students have applied to our college?" When problems or requests such as these arise, someone realizes that computer programs could solve these problems more efficiently and reliably than the procedures currently in place. A proposal will be developed for a system to solve this problem and, as you recall from the earlier section, programming is part of the development stage for the overall project.

What is programming? Once a project has been deemed feasible and a plan is in place, the work of programming begins. **Programming** is the process of translating a task into a series of commands a computer will use to perform that task. It involves identifying which parts of a task a computer can perform, describing those tasks in a highly specific and complete manner, and, finally, translating this description into the language spoken by the computer's central processing unit (CPU).

How do programmers tackle a programming project? Just as an information system has a development life cycle, each programming project follows several stages from conception to final deployment. This process, described below, is sometimes referred to as the **program development life cycle (PDLC)**.

1. **Describing the Problem:** First, programmers must develop a complete description of the problem. The problem statement identifies the task to be automated and describes how the software program will behave.

2. **Making a Plan:** The problem statement is next translated into a set of specific, sequential steps that describe exactly what the computer program must do to complete the work.

The steps are known as an **algorithm**. At this stage, the algorithm is written in natural, ordinary language (such as English).

3. **Coding:** The algorithm is then translated into programming code, a language that is friendlier to humans than the 1s and 0s that the CPU speaks but is still highly structured. By coding the algorithm, programmers must think in terms of the operations that a CPU can perform.

4. **Debugging:** The code then goes through a process of debugging in which the programmers find and repair any known errors in the code.

5. **Finishing the Project:** The software is tested by both the programming team and the people who will use the program. The results of the entire project are documented for the users and the development team. Finally, users are trained so that they can use the program efficiently.

Figure 10.4 illustrates the steps of a program's life cycle.

Now that you have an overview of the process involved in developing a program, let's look at each step in more detail.

Describing the Problem: The Problem Statement

The **problem statement** is the starting point of programming work. It is a clear description of what tasks the computer program must accomplish and how the program will execute these tasks and respond to unusual situations. Programmers develop problem statements so that they can better understand the goals of their programming efforts.

What kind of problems can computer programs solve? Not every problem is well suited to a computerized solution. The strengths of computing machines are that they are fast and work without error. Unlike humans, computers don't introduce mistakes because they're tired or stressed. Thus, as mentioned earlier, tasks that are repetitive, work with electronic information, and follow a series of clear steps are good candidates for computerization.

This might sound as if computers only help us with the dullest and most simplistic tasks. However, many sophisticated problems

Figure 10.4

The stages followed by each programming project from conception to final deployment are collectively referred to as the *program development life cycle.*

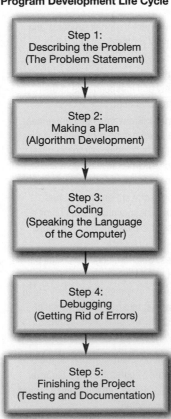

Program Development Life Cycle

Step 1:
Describing the Problem
(The Problem Statement)

Step 2:
Making a Plan
(Algorithm Development)

Step 3:
Coding
(Speaking the Language of the Computer)

Step 4:
Debugging
(Getting Rid of Errors)

Step 5:
Finishing the Project
(Testing and Documentation)

can be broken down into a series of easily computerized tasks. For example, pharmaceutical companies design drugs using complex computer programs that model molecules. Using simulation software to perform "dry" chemistry, chemists can quickly "create" new drugs and determine whether they will have the desired pharmacological effects. Scientists then select the most promising choices and begin to test those compounds in the "wet" laboratory.

Still, computers cannot yet act with intuition or be spontaneously creative. They can attack highly challenging problems such as making weather predictions or playing chess, but only in a manner that takes advantage of what computers do best—making fast, reliable computations.

How do programmers create problem statements? Most computer users understand what jobs (or problems) they want to computerize but not the details of the programming process. Therefore, the goal in creating a useful problem statement is to have programmers interact with users to describe three things relevant to creating a useful program: data, information, and method.

1. **Data** is the raw input that users have at the start of the job. It will be fed into the program.

2. **Information** is the result, or output, that the users require at the end of the job. The program produces this information from data.

3. **Method**, described precisely, is the process of how the program converts the inputs into the correct outputs.

For example, say you want to compute how much money you'll earn working at a

> **"Users understand the jobs they want done, but not the programming behind them."**

parking garage. Your salary is $7.50 per hour for an eight-hour shift, but if you work more than eight hours a day, you will get time and a half, which is $11.25 per hour, for the overtime work. To determine how much money you make in any given day, you could multiply this in your mind, write it on a piece of paper, or use a calculator; alternatively, you could create a simple computer program to do the work for you. In this example, what are the three elements of the problem statement?

1. **Data (Input)**: The data you have at the beginning of the problem, which is the number of hours you worked and the pay rate.

2. **Information (Output)**: The information you need to have at the end of the problem, which is your total pay for the day.

3. **Method (Process)**: The set of steps that will take you from your input to an output. In this case, the computer program would check if you worked more than eight hours. (That is important because it determines if you are paid overtime.) If you did not work overtime, then the output would be $7.50 multiplied by the total number of hours you worked ($60.00 for eight hours). If you did work overtime, then the program would calculate your pay as eight hours at $7.50 per hour for the regular part of your shift, plus an additional $11.25 multiplied by the number of overtime hours you worked. This processing thereby transforms your input into your desired output.

How do programmers handle bad inputs? In the problem statement, programmers also must describe what the program should do if the input data is invalid or just gibberish. (Users do make mistakes.) This part of the problem statement is referred to as **error handling**. The problem statement also includes a **testing plan** that lists specific input numbers the program would typically expect the user to enter. It then lists the precise output values that a perfect program would return for those input values. Later, in a testing process, programmers use the input and output data

SOUND BYTE

Programming for End Users

In this Sound Byte, you'll be guided through the creation of a macro in the Microsoft Office 2010 suite. You'll learn how Office enables you to program with macros to customize and extend the capabilities it offers.

Figure 10.5 | COMPLETE PROBLEM STATEMENT FOR PARKING GARAGE EXAMPLE

Problem Statement			
Program Goal	Compute the total pay for a fixed number of hours worked at a parking garage.		
Input	Number of hours worked (a positive number)		
Output	Total pay earned (a positive number)		
Process	Total pay earned is computed as $7.50 per hour for the first 8 hours worked each day. Any hours worked beyond the first 8 are calculated at $11.25 per hour.		
Error Handling	The input (number of hours worked) must be a positive real number. If it is a negative number or other unacceptable character, the program will force the user to re-enter the information.		
Testing Plan	**Input**	**Output**	**Notes**
	8	8*7.50	Testing positive input
	3	3*7.50	Testing positive input
	12	8*7.50 + 4*11.25	Testing overtime input
	−6	Error message/ask user to re-enter value	Handling error

values from the testing plan to determine whether the program they created works in the way it should. (We discuss the testing process later in this chapter.)

Does the testing plan cover every possible use of the program? The testing plan cannot list every input that the program could ever encounter. Instead, programmers work with users to identify the categories of inputs that will be encountered, find a typical example of each input category, and specify what kind of output must be generated. In the preceding parking garage pay example, the error-handling process would describe what the program would do if you happened to enter "-8" (or any other nonsense character) for the number of hours you worked. The error handling would specify whether the program would return a negative value, prompt you to re-enter the input, or yell at you and shut down (well, maybe not exactly). We could expect three categories of inputs in the parking garage example. The user might enter:

- A negative number for hours worked that day
- A positive number equal to or less than eight
- A positive number greater than eight

The testing plan would describe how the error would be managed or how the output would be generated for each input category.

Is there a standard format for a problem statement? Most companies (and instructors) have their own format for documenting a problem statement. However, all problem statements include the same basic components: the data that is expected to be provided (inputs), the information that is expected to be produced (outputs), the rules for transforming the input into output (processing), an explanation of how the program will respond if users enter data that doesn't make sense (error handling), and a testing plan. Figure 10.5 shows a sample problem statement for our parking garage example.

Making a Plan: Algorithm Development

Once programmers understand exactly what the program must do and have created the final problem statement, they can begin developing a detailed algorithm, a set of specific, sequential steps that describe in natural language exactly what the computer program must do to complete its task. Let's look at some ways in which programmers design and test algorithms.

Do algorithms appear only in programming? Although the term *algorithm* may sound like it would fall only under the domain of computing, you design and execute algorithms (or problem-solving procedures) in your daily life. For example, say you are planning your morning. You know you need to (1) get gas for your car, (2) swing past the café and pick up a mocha latté, and (3) stop by the bookstore and buy a textbook before your 9 A.M. accounting lecture. You quickly think over the costs and decide it will take $80 to buy all three. In what order will you accomplish all these tasks? How do you decide? Should you try to minimize the distance you'll travel or the time you'll spend driving? What happens if you forget your credit card?

Figure 10.6 presents an algorithm you could develop to make decisions about how

Figure 10.6

An algorithm you might use to plan your morning would include several steps that encapsulate all of the decisions you might need to make and show the specific sequence in which these steps would occur.

to accomplish these tasks. This algorithm lays out a specific plan that encapsulates all of the choices you need to make in the course of completing a particular task and shows the specific sequence in which these tasks will occur. At any point in the morning, you could gather your current data (your inputs)—"I have $20 and my Visa card, but the ATM machine is down"—and the algorithm would tell you unambiguously what your next step should be.

What are the limitations of algorithms? The deterministic nature of an algorithm enables us to describe it completely on a simple piece of paper. An algorithm is a series of steps that is completely known: At each point we know *exactly* what step to take next. However, not all problems can be described as a fixed sequence of predetermined steps; some involve random and unpredictable events. For example, although the program that computes your parking garage take-home pay each day works flawlessly, programs that predict stock prices are often wrong because many random events (inputs), such as a flood in Costa Rica or a shipping delay in California, can change the outcomes (outputs).

How do programmers represent an algorithm? Programmers have several visual tools at their disposal to help them document the decision points and flow of their algorithm.

Flowcharts provide a visual representation of the patterns the algorithm comprises. Figure 10.6 presents an example of a flowchart used to depict the flow of an algorithm. Specific shape symbols indicate program behaviors and decision types. Diamonds indicate that a yes/no decision will be performed, and rectangles indicate an instruction to follow. Figure 10.7 lists additional flowcharting symbols and explains what they indicate.

Many software packages make it easy for programmers to create and modify flowcharts. Microsoft Visio is one popular flowcharting program.

Pseudocode is a text-based approach to documenting an algorithm. In pseudocode, words describe the actions that the algorithm will take. Pseudocode is organized like an outline, with differing levels of indentation to indicate the flow of actions within the program. There is no standard set of vocabulary for pseudocode. Programmers use a combination of common words in their

Figure 10.7

Standard symbols used in flowcharts.

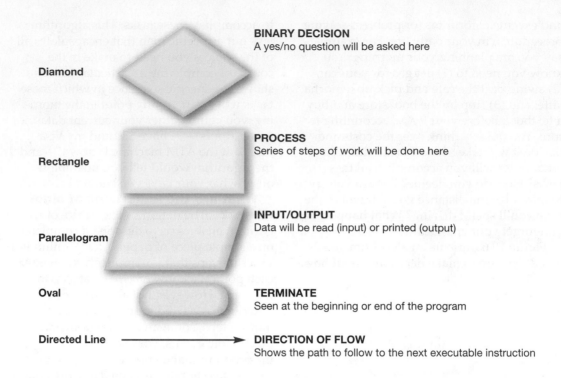

Diamond — **BINARY DECISION** — A yes/no question will be asked here

Rectangle — **PROCESS** — Series of steps of work will be done here

Parallelogram — **INPUT/OUTPUT** — Data will be read (input) or printed (output)

Oval — **TERMINATE** — Seen at the beginning or end of the program

Directed Line — **DIRECTION OF FLOW** — Shows the path to follow to the next executable instruction

natural language and the special words that are commands in the programming language they are using.

Developing an Algorithm: Decision Making and Design

How do programmers develop an algorithm? When programmers develop an algorithm, they convert the problem statement into a list of steps (or actions) the program will take. For simple problems, this list is straightforward: The program completes this action first, that action second, another action third, and so on. However, only the simplest algorithms execute the same series of actions every time they run.

Problems that are more complex involve choices and, therefore, cannot follow a sequential list of steps to generate the correct output. Instead, the list of steps created for complex problems includes **decision points**, places where the program must choose from an array of different actions based on the value of its current inputs. For example, a binary decision (shown in a flowchart as a diamond) will have two possible paths that can be taken, depending on the value of the inputs. Programmers convert a problem into an algorithm by listing the sequence of actions that must be taken and recognizing the places where decisions must be made.

In our parking garage example, if the number of hours you worked in a given day is eight or less, the program performs one simple calculation: It multiplies the number of hours worked by $7.50. If you worked more than eight hours in a day, then the program takes a different path and performs a different calculation, as shown in Figure 10.8.

What kinds of decision points are there? Two main types of decisions change the flow of an algorithm. One decision point that appears often in algorithms is like a "fork in the road" or a branch. Such decision points are called **binary decisions**

Figure 10.8

Decision points force the program to travel down one branch of the algorithm or another.

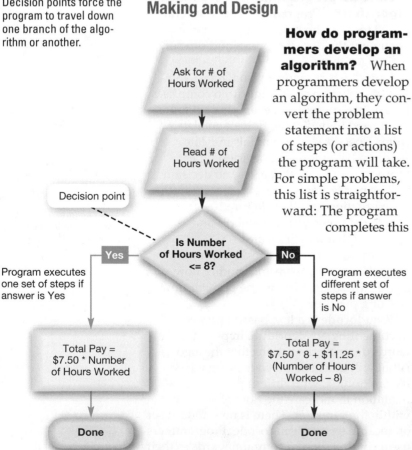

Ask for # of Hours Worked

Read # of Hours Worked

Decision point

Is Number of Hours Worked <= 8?

Yes — Program executes one set of steps if answer is Yes

No — Program executes different set of steps if answer is No

Total Pay = $7.50 * Number of Hours Worked

Total Pay = $7.50 * 8 + $11.25 * (Number of Hours Worked − 8)

Done

Done

because they can be answered in one of only two ways: *yes* (true) or *no* (false). For example, the answer to the question, "Did you work at most eight hours today?" (Is number of hours worked <= 8 hours?), shown in Figure 10.8, is a binary decision because the answer can be only *yes* or *no*. The result of the decision determines which path the algorithm follows. If the answer is *yes*, the program follows one sequence of steps; if the answer is *no*, it follows a different path.

A second decision point that often appears in algorithms is a repeating loop. In a **loop**, a question is asked, and if the answer is *yes*, a set of actions is performed. Once the set of actions has finished, the question is asked again, creating a loop. As long as the answer to the question is *yes*, the algorithm continues to loop around and repeat the same set of actions. When the answer to the question is *no*, the algorithm breaks free of the looping and moves on to the first step that follows the loop.

In our parking garage example, the algorithm would require a loop if you wanted to compute the total pay you earned in a full week of work rather than in just a single day. For each day of the week, you would want to perform the same set of steps. Figure 10.9 shows how the idea of looping would be useful in this part of our parking garage program. On Monday, the program would set the Total Pay value to $0.00. It would then perform the following set of steps:

1. Read the number of hours worked that day.

2. Determine whether you qualified for overtime pay.

3. Compute the pay earned that day.

4. Add that day's pay to the total pay for the week.

On Tuesday, the algorithm would loop back, repeating the same sequence of steps it performed on Monday, adding the amount you earned on Tuesday to the Total Pay amount. The algorithm would continue to perform this loop for each day (seven times) until it hits Monday again. At that point, the decision "Are we still in the same week?" would become false. The program would stop, calculate the total pay for the entire week of work, and print the weekly paycheck. As you can see, there are three important features to look for in a loop:

1. A beginning point, or **initial value**. In our example, the Total Pay for the week starts at an initial value of $0.00.

2. A **set of actions** that will be performed. In our example, the algorithm computes the daily pay each time it passes through the loop.

3. A check to see whether the loop is completed, or a **test condition**. In our example, the algorithm should run the loop seven times, no more and no fewer.

Almost every higher-level programming language supports both making binary yes/no decisions and handling repeating loops. **Control structures** is the general term used for keywords in a programming language that allow the programmer to control (redirect) the flow of the program based on a decision.

Start on Monday
Start with Total Pay for Week = 0.00 - - - - Initial value

Test condition

Are we still in the same week? - - - - **No**

If test condition passes, loop continues

Yes

If test condition fails, break out of loop and move to next step

Calculate Pay for the Day

Calculate Total Pay for Week So Far

Bump to Next Day - - - Update

Print Weekly Paycheck

Figure 10.9

In this example of a loop, we stay in the loop until the test condition is no longer true. We then break free from the loop and move on to the next step in the algorithm, which is outside of the loop.

How do programmers create algorithms for specific tasks? It's difficult for human beings to force their problem-solving skills into the highly structured, detailed algorithms that computing machines require. Therefore, several different methodologies have been developed to support programmers, including top-down design and object-oriented analysis.

Top-Down Design

What is top-down design? Top-down design is a systematic approach in which a problem is broken into a series of high-level tasks. In top-down design, programmers apply the same strategy repeatedly, breaking each task into successively more detailed subtasks. They continue until they have a sequence of steps that are close to the types of commands allowed by the programming language they will use for coding. (Previous coding experience helps programmers know the appropriate level of detail to specify in an algorithm generated by top-down design.)

How is top-down design used in programming? Let's consider our parking garage example again. Initially, top-down design would identify three high-level tasks: Get Input, Process Data, and Output Results (see Figure 10.10a).

Applying top-down design to the first operation, Get Input, we'd produce the more detailed sequence of steps shown in Figure 10.10b: Announce Program, Give Users Instructions, and Read the Input NumberHoursWorkedToday. When we try to refine each of these steps, we find that

they are at the level of commands that most programming languages support (that is, they tell the computer to print and read statements). Therefore, the operation Get Input has been converted to an algorithm.

Next, we move to the second high-level task, Process Data, and break it into subtasks. In this case, we need to determine whether overtime hours were worked and compute the pay accordingly. We continue to apply top-down design on all tasks until we can no longer break tasks into subtasks, as shown in Figure 10.10c.

Object-Oriented Analysis

What is object-oriented analysis? A very different approach to generating an algorithm is object-oriented analysis. With **object-oriented analysis**, programmers first identify all of the categories of inputs that are part of the problem the program is trying to solve. These categories are called **classes**. For example, the classes in our parking garage example might include a TimeCard class and an Employee class.

Classes are further defined by information (data) and actions (methods or behaviors) associated with the class. For example, data for an Employee would include a Name, Address, and Social Security Number, whereas the methods for the Employee would be GoToWork(), LeaveWork(), or CollectPay(). Think of classes as the things around you in your world—books, accounts, shopping carts. The data of the class describes the class, so classes are often characterized as nouns, whereas methods are

Figure 10.10

In this figure, (a) a top-down design is applied to the highest level of task in our parking garage example, (b) the tasks are further refined into subtasks, and (c) subtasks are refined into a sequence of instructions—an algorithm.

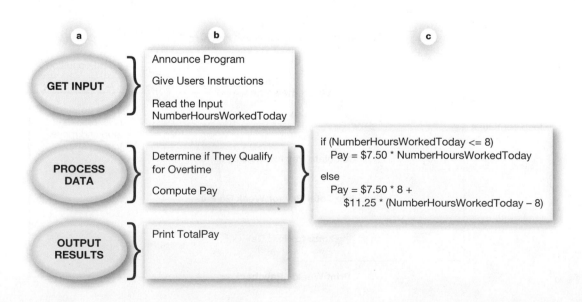

often characterized as verbs—the ways that the class acts and communicates with other classes. Figure 10.11 shows the data and methods the Employee class would contain.

In the object-oriented approach, programmers identify and define each class, as well as their data and methods. Programmers then determine how classes interact with each other. For example, when an Employee does GoToWork(), the Employee class must "talk" to the TimeCard class and punch in for the day, setting the StartTime on the TimeCard.

Programmers may need to create several different examples of a class. Each of these examples is an **object**. In Figure 10.11, John Doe, Jane Doe, and Bill McGillicutty are each Employee objects (specific examples of the Employee class). Each object from a given class is described by the same pieces of data and has the same methods; for example, John, Jane, and Bill are all Employees and can use the GoToWork, LeaveWork, and CollectPay methods. However, because John and Jane have different pay grades (PayGrade 5 and PayGrade 10, respectively), and because they all have different Social Security numbers, they are all unique objects.

Why would a developer select the object-oriented approach over top-down design? Object-oriented analysis forces programmers to think in general terms about their problem, which tends to lead to more general and reusable solutions. An important aspect of object-oriented design is that it leads to **reusability**. Because object-oriented design generates a family of classes for each project, programmers can easily reuse existing classes from other projects, enabling them to produce new code quickly.

To take advantage of reuse, programmers must study the relationships between objects. Hierarchies of objects can be built quickly in object-oriented languages using the mechanism of inheritance. **Inheritance** means that a new class can automatically pick up all of the data and methods of an existing class, and then extend and customize those to fit its own specific needs.

The original class is called the **base class**, and the new, modified

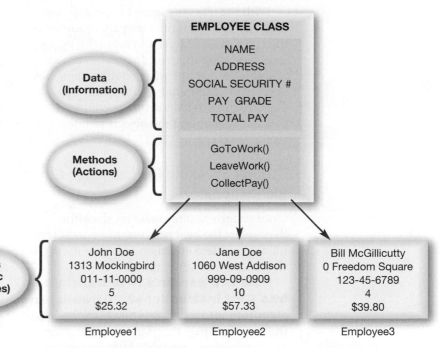

class is called the **derived class**, as illustrated in Figure 10.12. You can compare this with making cookies. For example, you have a basic recipe for sugar cookies (base class: sugar cookies). However, in your family, some people like chocolate-flavored sugar cookies (derived class: chocolate cookies), and others like almond-flavored sugar cookies (derived class: almond cookies). All the cookies share the attributes of the basic sugar cookie. However, instead of creating two entirely new recipes—one for chocolate cookies and one for almond cookies—the two varieties inherit the basic sugar cookie (base class) recipe; the recipe is then customized to make the chocolate- and almond-flavored sugar cookies (derived classes).

Figure 10.11

The Employee class includes the complete set of information (data) and actions (methods or behaviors) that describe an Employee.

Figure 10.12

In object-oriented programming (OOP), a single base class—for example, **Shape**—helps you quickly create many additional derived classes, such as **Polygon** and **Ellipse**.

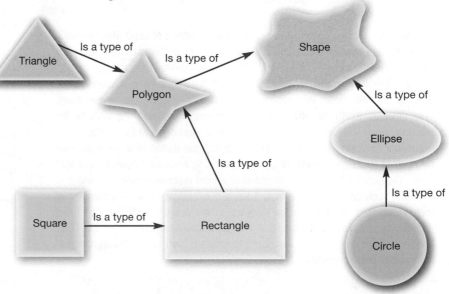

With the object-oriented approach, the majority of design time is spent in identifying the classes required to solve the problem, modeling them as data and methods, and thinking about what relationships they need to be able to have with each other. Constructing the algorithm becomes a process of enabling the objects to interact.

Coding: Speaking the Language of the Computer

Once programmers create an algorithm, they select the best programming language for the problem and then translate the algorithm into that language.

How is a person's idea translated into CPU instructions? Translating an algorithm into a programming language is the act of **coding**. Programming languages are (somewhat!) readable by humans but then are translated into patterns of 1s and 0s to be understood by the CPU.

Although programming languages free programmers from having to think in binary language (the 1s and 0s that computers understand), they still force programmers to translate the ideas of the algorithm into a highly precise format. Programming languages are quite limited, allowing programmers to use only a few specific words while still demanding a consistent structure.

How exactly do programmers move from algorithm to code? Once programmers have an algorithm, in the form of either a flowchart or a series of pseudocode statements, they scan the algorithm and identify the key pieces of information it uses to make decisions. What steps are required for the calculation of new information? What is the exact sequence of the steps? Are there points where decisions have to be made? What kinds of decisions are made? Are there places where the same steps are repeated several times? Once the programmer identifies the required information and the flow of how it will be changed by each step of the algorithm, he or she can begin converting the algorithm into computer code in a specific programming language.

Categories of Programming Languages

What exactly is a programming language? A **programming language** is a kind of "code" for the set of instructions the CPU knows how to perform. Computer programming languages use special words and strict rules so programmers can control the CPU without having to know all of its hardware details.

What kinds of programming languages are there? Programming languages are classified in several major groupings, sometimes referred to as *generations*. With each generation in language development, programmers have been relieved of more of the burden of keeping track of what the hardware requires. The earliest languages—assembly language and machine languages—required the programmer to know a great deal about how the computer was constructed internally and how it stored data. Programming is becoming easier as languages continue to become more closely matched to how humans think about problems.

How have modern programming languages evolved? A first-generation language (1GL) is the actual **machine language** of a CPU, the sequence of bits (1s and 0s) that the CPU understands. A **second-generation language (2GL)** is also known as an **assembly language**. Assembly languages allow programmers to write their programs using a set of short, English-like commands that speak directly to the CPU and give the programmer direct control of hardware

BITS AND BYTES

My Algorithm Can Beat Your Algorithm!

Programming became a competitive sport with the advent of LEGO MINDSTORMS. The First Lego League conducts a programming competition each year using the LEGO MINDSTORMS series of LEGO kits. These kits include gears, wheels, motors, and a motorized, programmable LEGO "brick" that contains a microprocessor. Sensors feed the robots information such as sounds, images, and temperatures. Teams then use ROBOLAB software to develop programs and send them to the brick's microprocessor. You can try out this software in a small demo at the ROBOLAB site (**robolabonline.com**). The unit can be told to turn the motor on or off, switch the direction of a wheel's rotation, or turn on sensors to measure temperature or light levels. The ROBOLAB software even allows beginning programmers to drag and drop elements such as "if" statements and loops. Synthesizing their understanding of motors and their talent for logical thinking, teams design robots that can travel through mazes, cross bridges, and deliver packages—whatever tasks the LEGO League has come up with for that year's tournament (**usfirst.org/firstlegoleague/ community/homepage.html**).

resources. A **third-generation language (3GL)** uses symbols and commands to help programmers tell the computer what to do. This makes 3GL languages easier for humans to read and remember. Most programming languages today, including BASIC, FORTRAN, COBOL, C/C++, and Java, are considered third generation.

Structured Query Language (SQL) is a database programming language that is an example of a **fourth-generation language (4GL)**. Many other database query languages and report generators are also 4GLs. The following single SQL command would check a huge table of data on the employees and build a new table showing all those employees who worked overtime:

```
SELECT * EMPLOYEES WHERE
"TotalHours" TOTAL MORE THAN 8
```

But programmers must always work from algorithms, correct? Not if they are using a **fifth-generation language (5GL)**. Fifth-generation languages are considered the most "natural" of languages. In a 5GL, a problem is presented as a series of facts or constraints instead of as a specific algorithm. The system of facts can then be queried (asked) questions. PROLOG (PROgramming LOGic) is an example of a 5GL. A PROLOG program could be a list of family relationships and rules such as "Mike is Sally's brother. A brother and a sister have the same mother and father." Once a user has amassed a huge collection of facts and rules, she can ask for a list of all Mike's cousins, for example. PROLOG would find the answers by repeatedly applying the principles of logic, instead of by following a systematic algorithm that the programmer provided. Figure 10.13 shows small code samples of each generation of language.

Do programmers have to use a higher-level programming language to solve a problem with a computer? No, experienced programmers sometimes write a program directly in the CPU's assembly language. However, the main advantage of higher-level programming languages—C or Java, for example—is that they allow programmers to think in terms of the problem they are solving rather than worrying about the internal design and specific instructions available for a given CPU. In addition, higher-level programming languages have the capability to produce a program easily that will run on differently configured CPUs. For example, if programmers wrote directly in the assembly language for an Intel i7 CPU, then they would have to rewrite the program completely if they wanted it to run on a Sun workstation with the UltraSPARC CPU. Thus, higher-level programming languages offer **portability**—the capability to move a completed solution easily from one type of computer to another.

Creating Code: Writing the Program

What happens first when you write a program? All of the inputs a program receives and all of the outputs the program produces need to be stored in the computer's RAM while the program is running. Each

Figure 10.13 | SAMPLE CODE FOR DIFFERENT LANGUAGE LEVELS AND GENERATIONS

Level	Generation	Example	Sample Code
Low	1GL	Machine	**Bits** describe the commands to the CPU 1110 0101 1001 1111 0000 1011 1110 0110
	2GL	Assembly	**Words** describe the commands to the CPU ADD Register 3, Register 4, Register 5
High	3GL	FORTRAN, BASIC, C, Java	**Symbols** describe the commands to the CPU Total Pay = Pay + Overtime Pay
	4GL	SQL	**More powerful commands** allow complex work to be done in a single sentence SELECT isbn, title, price, price*0.06 AS sales_tax FROM books WHERE price>100.00 ORDER BY title;
Natural	5GL	PROLOG	Programmers can build applications **without specifying an algorithm**. Find all the people who are Mike's cousins as: ?-cousin (Mike, family)

The Building Blocks of Programming Languages: Syntax, Keywords, Data Types, and Operators

Programming languages are evolving constantly. New languages emerge every year, and existing languages change dramatically. Therefore, it would be extremely difficult and time consuming for programmers to learn every programming language. However, all languages have several common elements: rules of syntax, a set of keywords, a group of supported data types, and a set of allowed operators. By learning these four concepts, a programmer will be better equipped to approach any new language.

The transition from a well-designed algorithm to working code requires a clear understanding of the rules (syntax) of the programming language being used. **Syntax** is an agreed-upon set of rules defining how a language must be structured. The English language has a syntax that defines which symbols are words (for example, *poodle* is a word but *oodlep* is not) and what order words and symbols (such as semicolons and commas) must follow.

Likewise, all programming languages have a formal syntax that programmers must follow when creating code **statements**, which are sentences in a code. Syntax errors are violations of the strict, precise set of rules that defines the language. In a programming language, even misplacing a single comma or using a lowercase letter where a capital letter is required will generate a syntax error and make the program unusable.

Keywords are a set of words that have predefined meanings for a particular language. Keywords translate the flow of the algorithm into the structured code of the programming language. For example, when the algorithm indicates a *decision point*—a location where a binary decision must be made—the programmer translates that binary decision into the appropriate keyword or keywords from the language.

To illustrate further, in the programming language C++, the binary decision asking whether you worked enough hours to qualify for overtime pay would use the keywords **if else**. At this point in the code, the program can follow one of two paths: *If* you indicated through your input that you worked fewer than or equal to eight hours, it takes one path; if not (*else*), it follows another. Figure 10.14 shows the binary decision in the algorithm and the lines of C++ code for this decision using the *if else* keywords.

Loops are likewise translated from algorithm to code by using the appropriate keyword from the language. For example, in the programming language Visual Basic, programmers use the keywords **For** and **Next** to implement a loop. After the keyword *For*, an input or output item is given a starting value. Then the statements, or "sentences," in the body of the loop are executed. When the command *Next* is run, the program returns to the For statement and increments the value of the input or output item by 1. It then tests that the value is still inside the range given. If it is, the body of the loop is executed again. This continues until the value of the input or output item is outside the range listed. The loop is then ended, and the statement that follows the loop is run. If we think back to the parking garage example, the following lines of Visual Basic code loop to

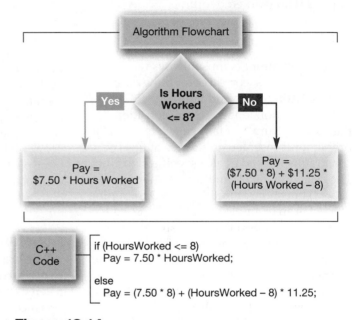

Figure 10.14

The binary decision in the algorithm has been converted into C++ code.

input and each output item that the program manipulates, also known as a **variable**, needs to be announced early in the program so that memory space can be set aside. A **variable declaration** tells the operating system that the program needs to allocate storage space in RAM. The following line of code is a variable declaration in the language Java:

```
int Day;
```

This variable's name is *Day*. The "int" that precedes the Day variable indicates that this variable will always be an integer (a whole number such as 15 or –4). This statement asks for enough RAM storage space to hold an integer. After the RAM space is found, it is reserved. As long as the program is running, these RAM cells will be saved for the Day variable, and no other program can use that memory until the program ends. From that point on, when the program encounters the symbol Day, it will access the memory it reserved as Day and find the integer stored there.

The following line of C++ code asks that a decimal number (represented by the keyword *float*) be stored in RAM:

```
float TotalPay;
```

sum up the total pay for the entire week. In this statement, the starting value of the input item Day is 1, and the program loops until Day equals 7:

```
For Day = 1 to 7
   Total Pay = Total Pay + Pay;
Next Day
```

Often, a quick overview of a language's keywords can reveal the unique focus of that language. For example, the language C++ includes the keywords *public*, *private*, and *protected*, which indicate that the language includes a mechanism for controlling security. Although people who are new to a language might not immediately understand how these keywords are used, examining the keywords of a language you are learning will often tell you what special features the language has and will help you ask important questions about it.

Each time programmers want to store data in their program, they must ask the operating system for storage space at a random access memory (RAM) location. **Data types** describe the *kind* of data that is being stored at the memory location. Each programming language has its own data types (although there is some degree of overlap among languages). For example, C++ includes data types that represent integers, real numbers, characters, and Boolean (true–false) values. These C++ data types show up in code statements as *int* for integer, *float* for real numbers, *char* for characters, and *bool* for Boolean values.

Because it takes more room to store a real number such as 18,743.23 than it does to store the integer 1, programmers use data types in their code to indicate to the operating system how much memory it needs to allocate. Programmers must be familiar with all of the data types available in the language so that they can assign the most appropriate data type for each input and output value, without wasting memory space.

Operators are the coding symbols that represent the fundamental actions of the language. Each programming language has its own set of operators. Many languages include common algebraic operators such as +, –, *, and / to represent the mathematical operations of addition, subtraction, multiplication, and division, respectively. Some languages, however, introduce new symbols as operators. The language A Programmer's Language (APL) was designed to solve multidimensional mathematical problems. APL includes less familiar operators such as rho, sigma, and iota, each representing a complex mathematical operation. Because it contains many specialized operators, APL requires programmers to use a special keyboard (see Figure 10.15).

Programming languages sometimes include other unique operators. The C++ operator >>, for example, is used to tell the computer to read data from the keyboard or from a file. The C++ operator && is used to tell the computer to check whether two statements are both true. "Is your age greater than 20 AND less than 30?" is a question that requires the use of the && operator.

In the following C++ code, several operators are being used. The > operator checks whether the number of hours worked is greater than 0. The && operator checks that the number of hours worked is simultaneously positive AND less than or equal to 8. If that happens, then the = operator sets the output Pay to equal the number of hours paid at $7.50 per hour:

```
if (Hours > 0 && Hours <= 8)
   Pay = Hours * 7.50;
```

Knowing operators such as these, as well as the other common elements described earlier, helps programmers learn new programming languages.

APL keyboard

Figure 10.15

APL requires programmers to use an APL keyboard that includes the many specialized operators in the language.

This line asks the operating system to find and reserve enough storage space for one real number. It then associates the symbol TotalPay with the address of the memory cell where that value will be stored.

Can programmers leave notes to themselves inside a program?
Programmers often insert a **comment** (or **remark**) into program code to explain the purpose of a section of code, to indicate the date they wrote the program, or to include other important information about the code so that fellow programmers can more easily understand and update it should the original programmer no longer be available.

Comments are written into the code in plain English. The *compiler*, a program that translates codes into binary 1s and 0s, just ignores comments. Comments are intended to be read only by human programmers. Languages provide a special symbol or keyword to indicate the beginning of a comment. In C++, the symbol // at the beginning of a line indicates that the rest of the line is a comment. In Visual Basic, a single apostrophe or the keyword *REM*, short for *remark*, does the same thing.

What would completed code for a program look like? Figure 10.16, presents a completed C++ program for our

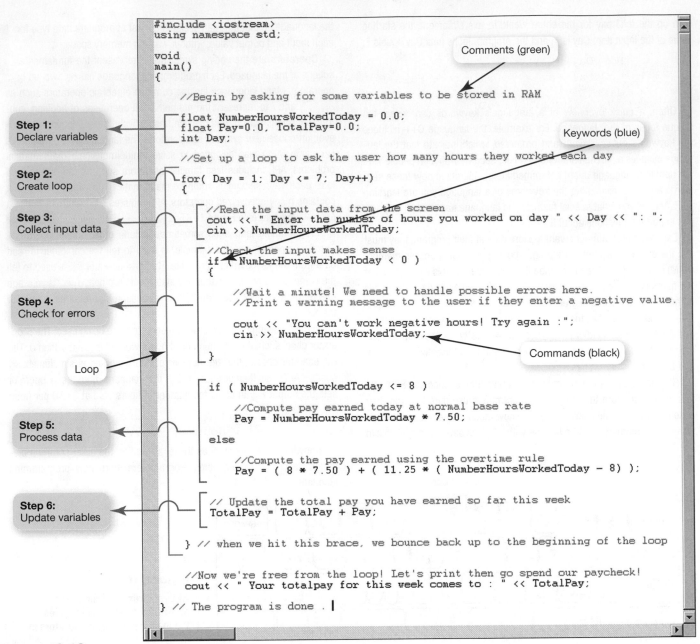

```
#include <iostream>
using namespace std;

void
main()
{

    //Begin by asking for some variables to be stored in RAM

    float NumberHoursWorkedToday = 0.0;
    float Pay=0.0, TotalPay=0.0;
    int Day;

    //Set up a loop to ask the user how many hours they worked each day

    for( Day = 1; Day <= 7; Day++)
    {
        //Read the input data from the screen
        cout << " Enter the number of hours you worked on day " << Day << ": ";
        cin >> NumberHoursWorkedToday;

        //Check the input makes sense
        if ( NumberHoursWorkedToday < 0 )
        {

            //Wait a minute! We need to handle possible errors here.
            //Print a warning message to the user if they enter a negative value.

            cout << "You can't work negative hours! Try again :";
            cin >> NumberHoursWorkedToday;

        }


        if ( NumberHoursWorkedToday <= 8 )

            //Compute pay earned today at normal base rate
            Pay = NumberHoursWorkedToday * 7.50;

        else

            //Compute the pay earned using the overtime rule
            Pay = ( 8 * 7.50 ) + ( 11.25 * ( NumberHoursWorkedToday - 8) );

        // Update the total pay you have earned so far this week
        TotalPay = TotalPay + Pay;

    } // when we hit this brace, we bounce back up to the beginning of the loop


    //Now we're free from the loop! Let's print then go spend our paycheck!
    cout << " Your totalpay for this week comes to : " << TotalPay;

} // The program is done . |
```

Comments (green)

Keywords (blue)

Commands (black)

Step 1:
Declare variables

Step 2:
Create loop

Step 3:
Collect input data

Step 4:
Check for errors

Loop

Step 5:
Process data

Step 6:
Update variables

Figure 10.16

A complete C++ program that solves the parking garage pay problem.

parking garage example. We'll discuss later how you would actually enter this program on your system. This program, which is written in a top-down style, does not make use of objects. Each statement in the program is executed sequentially (that is, in order from the first statement to the last) unless the program encounters a keyword that changes the flow. In the figure, the program begins by declaring the variables needed to store the program's inputs and outputs in RAM (step 1). Next, the *for* keyword begins a looping pattern (step 2). All of the steps between the very first bracket ({) and the last one (}) will be repeated seven times to gather the total pay for each day of the week.

The next section (step 3) collects the input data from the user. The program then checks that the user entered a reasonable value (step 4). In this case, a positive number for hours worked must be entered. Next, the program processes the data (step 5). If the user worked eight or fewer hours, he or she is paid at the rate of $7.50, whereas hours exceeding eight are paid at $11.25.

The final statement (step 6) updates the value of the TotalPay variable. The last bracket indicates that the program has reached the end of a loop. The program will repeat the loop to collect and process the information for the next day. When the seventh day of data has been processed, the Day variable will be bumped up to the next value, 8. This causes the program to fail the test (Day <= 7?). At that point, the program exits the loop, prints the results, and quits.

Are there ways in which programmers can make their code more useful for the future? One aspect of converting an algorithm into good code is the programmer's ability to design general code that can adapt easily to new settings. Sections of code that will be used repeatedly, with only slight modification, can be packaged into reusable "containers" or components. Depending on the language, these reusable components are referred to as *functions, methods, procedures, subroutines, modules,* or *packages.*

In our program, we could create a function that implements the overtime pay rule. As it stands in Figure 10.16, the code works only in situations in which the hourly pay is exactly $7.50 and the bonus pay is exactly $11.25. However, if we rewrote this part of the processing rules as a function, we could have code that would work for any base pay rate and any overtime rate. If the base pay rate or overtime rate changed, the function would use whichever values it was given as input to compute the output pay variable. Such a function, as shown in Figure 10.17, may be reused in many settings without changing any of the code.

Compilation

How does a programmer move from code in a programming language to the 1s and 0s the CPU can understand? Compilation is the process by which code is converted into machine language—the language the CPU can understand. A **compiler** is a program that understands both the syntax of the programming language and the exact structure of the CPU and its machine language. It can "read" the **source code**, which comprises the instructions programmers have written in the higher-level language, and translate the source code directly into machine language—the binary patterns that will execute commands on the CPU. You can learn more about the details of the binary number system in the "Under the Hood" Technology in Focus section.

Each programming language has its own compiler. It is a program that you purchase and install just like any other software on your system. Separate versions of the compiler are required if you want to compile code that will run on separate processor types. One version of a compiler would create finished programs for a Sun UltraSPARC processor, for example, and another version of the compiler would create programs for an Intel i7 CPU.

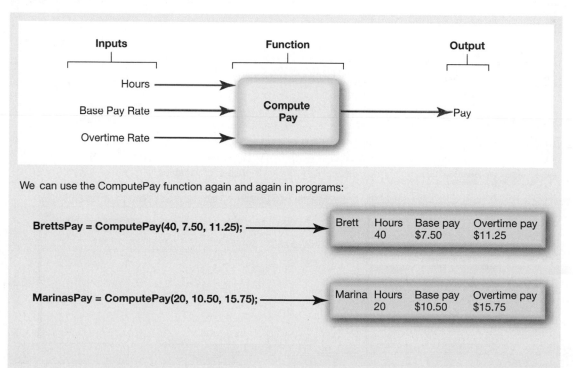

Figure 10.17

A *function* is a reusable component that can be used in different settings.

Inputs   Function   Output

Hours ⟶

Base Pay Rate ⟶ **Compute Pay** ⟶ Pay

Overtime Rate ⟶

We can use the ComputePay function again and again in programs:

BrettsPay = ComputePay(40, 7.50, 11.25); ⟶

Brett	Hours	Base pay	Overtime pay
	40	$7.50	$11.25

MarinasPay = ComputePay(20, 10.50, 15.75); ⟶

Marina	Hours	Base pay	Overtime pay
	20	$10.50	$15.75

At this stage, programmers finally have produced an **executable program**, the binary sequence that instructs the CPU to run their code. Executable programs cannot be read by human eyes because they are pure binary codes. They are stored as *.exe or *.com files on Windows systems.

Does every programming language have a compiler? Some programming languages do not have a compiler, but use an interpreter instead. An **interpreter** translates the source code into an intermediate form, line by line. Each line is then executed as it is translated. The compilation process takes longer than the interpretation process because in compilation all of the lines of source code are translated into machine language before any lines are executed. However, the finished compiled program runs faster than an interpreted program because the interpreter is constantly translating and executing as it goes.

If producing the fastest executable program is important, programmers will choose a language that uses a compiler instead of

an interpreter. For development environments in which many changes are still being made to the code, interpreters have an advantage because programmers do not have to wait for the entire program to be recompiled each time they make a change. With interpreters, programmers can immediately see the results of their program changes as they are making them.

Coding Tools: Integrated Development Environments

Are there any tools that make the coding process easier? Modern programming is supported by a collection of tools that make the writing and testing of software easier. Compiler products feature an **integrated development environment (IDE)**, a developmental tool that helps programmers write, compile, and test their programs. As is the case with compilers, every language has its own specific IDE. Figure 10.18 shows the IDE for Microsoft Visual Studio using C++.

Figure 10.18

The IDE for Microsoft Visual C++ helps the programmer when he or she is entering the code and when logical errors are found.

How does an IDE help programmers when they are typing the code? The IDE includes tools that support programmers at every step of the coding process. **Code editing** is the step in which a programmer physically types the code into the computer. An IDE includes an **editor**, a special tool that helps programmers as they enter the code, highlighting keywords and alerting them to typos. Modern IDE editors also automatically indent the code correctly, align sections of code appropriately, and apply color to code comments to remind programmers that these lines will not be executed as code. In addition, IDEs provide help files that document and provide examples of the proper use of keywords and operators.

How does the IDE help programmers after code editing is finished? Editing is complete when the entire program has been keyed into the editor. At that time, the programmer clicks a button in the IDE, and the compilation process begins. A pop-up window shows how the compilation is progressing, which line is currently being compiled, how many syntax errors have been identified, and how many warnings have been generated. A warning is a suggestion from the compiler that the code might not work in the way the programmer intended, although there is no formal syntax error on the line.

As mentioned earlier, a **syntax error** is a violation of the strict, precise set of rules that define the language. Programmers create syntax errors when they misspell keywords (such as typing BEEGIN instead of BEGIN) or use an operator incorrectly (such as typing x = y ++ 2 instead of x = y + 2). Once compilation is finished, the IDE presents all of the syntax errors in one list. The programmer can then click any item in the list to see a detailed explanation of the type of error. When the programmer double-clicks an item in the list, the editor jumps to the line of code that contains the error, enabling the programmer to repair syntax errors quickly.

Debugging: Getting Rid of Errors

Once the program has compiled without syntax errors, it has met all of the syntax rules of the language. However, this doesn't mean that the program behaves in a logical way or that it appropriately addresses the task the algorithm described. If programmers made errors in the strategy used in the algorithm or in how they translated the algorithm to code, problems will occur. The process of running the program over and over to find errors and to make sure the program behaves in the way it should is termed **debugging** (see Figure 10.19).

How do programmers know whether there is anything wrong with their program? At this point in the process, the testing plan that was documented as part of the problem statement becomes critically important to programmers. The testing plan clearly lists input and output values, showing how the users expect the program to behave in each input situation. It is important that the testing plan contain enough specific examples to test every part of the program.

In the parking garage problem, we want to make sure the program calculates the correct pay for a day when you worked eight or fewer hours and for a day when you worked more than eight hours. Each of these input values forces the program to make different decisions in its processing path (the sequence of steps that turns inputs into outputs). To be certain the program works as intended, programmers try every possible path.

For example, once we can successfully compile the example code for the parking

Figure 10.19

Debugging—the process of correcting errors in a program—combines logic with an understanding of the problem to be solved.

garage problem, we can begin to use our testing plan. The testing plan indicates that an input of 3 for NumberHours WorkedToday must produce an output of Pay = 3 * $7.50 = $22.50. In testing, we run the program and make sure that an input value of 3 yields an output value of $22.50. To check that the processing path involving overtime is correct, we input a value of 12 hours. That input must produce Pay = 8 * $7.50 + (12 − 8) * $11.25 = $105.00.

A complete testing plan includes sample inputs that exercise all of the error handling required as well as all of the processing paths. Therefore, we would also want to check how the program behaves when NumberHoursWorkedToday is entered as –2.

If the testing plan reveals errors, why does the program compile? The compiler itself is a program. It cannot think through code or decide whether what the programmer wrote is logical. The compiler only can make sure that the specific rules of the language are followed, that all of the keywords are spelled correctly, and that the operators being used are meaningful to that language.

For example, if in the parking garage problem we happened to type the if statement as

```
if (NumberHoursWorkedToday > 88)
//Use the Overtime Pay rule
```

instead of

```
if (NumberHoursWorkedToday > 8)
//Use the Overtime Pay rule,
```

the compiler would not see a problem. It doesn't seem strange to the compiler that you only get overtime after working 88 hours a day. These **logical errors** in the problem are caught only when the program executes. Another kind of error caught when the program executes is a **runtime error**. For example, it is easy for a programmer to

accidentally write code for a loop that loops one time too many or one time too few. This can lead to a problem such as dividing a number by zero, a big "no-no" mathematically! That kind of forbidden operation generates a runtime error message.

Are there tools that help programmers find logic errors? Most IDEs include a tool called a **debugger** that helps programmers dissect a program as it runs. The debugger pauses the program while it is executing and allows the programmer to examine the values of all the variables. The programmer can then run the program in slow motion, moving it forward just one line at a time. Working through the program in this way lets the programmer see the exact sequence of steps being executed and the outcome of each calculation. He or she can then isolate the precise place in which a logical error occurs, correct the error, and recompile the program.

Finishing the Project: Testing and Documentation

Once debugging has detected all of the runtime errors in the code, it is time for users to test the program. This process is called *internal testing*. In internal testing, a group within the software company uses the program in every way it can imagine—including how it was intended to be used and in ways only new users may think up. The internal testing group makes sure the program behaves as described in the original testing plan. Any differences in how the program responds are reported back to the programming team, which makes the final revisions and updates to the code.

The next round of testing is external testing. In this testing round, people like the ones that eventually will purchase and use the software must work with it to determine whether it matches their original vision.

What other testing does the code undergo? Before its final commercial release, software is often provided free or at a reduced cost in a **beta version** to certain test sites or to interested users. By providing users with a beta version of software, programmers can collect information about the remaining errors in the code and make a final round of revisions before officially releasing the program. Often, popular software packages like Microsoft Windows and Microsoft

Office are available for free beta download for months before the official public release.

What happens if problems are found after beta testing? The manufacturer will make changes before releasing the product to other manufacturers, for installation on new machines for example. That point in the release cycle is called **RTM** (or **release to manufacturers**). After the RTM is issued, the product is in **GA** (or **general availability**) and can be purchased by the public.

Users often uncover problems in a program even after its commercial release to the public. These problems are addressed with the publication of **software updates** or **service packs**. Users can download these software modules to repair errors identified in the program code. For example, the original Windows Vista operating system had a revision released as Service Pack 1 that added many bug fixes and security fixes and extended its compatibility so that instead of working with 40,000 devices, it could interact effectively with more than 80,000 devices.

After testing, is the project finished? Once testing is completed, but before the product is officially released, the work of **documentation** is still ahead. At this point, technical writers create internal documentation for the program that describes the development and technical details, how the code works, and how the user interacts with the program. In addition, the technical publishing department produces all of the necessary user documentation that will be distributed to the program users. User training begins once the software is distributed. Software trainers take the software to the user community and teach others how to use it efficiently.

Programming Languages: Many Languages for Many Projects

In any programming endeavor, programmers want to create a solution that meets several competing objectives. They want the software to run quickly and reliably and to

be simple to expand later when the demands on the system change. They also want it to be completed on time and for the minimum possible cost, and to use the smallest amount of system resources possible.

Because it will always be difficult to balance these conflicting goals, a wide variety of programming languages has been developed. Earlier in the chapter, you learned about the five main categories (generations) of programming languages. In this section, we discuss the specific programming languages that are members of these different generations.

Although programming languages often share many common characteristics, each language has specific traits that allow it to be the best fit for certain types of projects. Sometimes a language builds a loyal following, and that pushes a programmer to apply the same language to every situation.

> "What programming languages are popular today?"

The ability to understand enough about each language to match it to the appropriate style of problem is an exceptionally powerful skill for programmers.

What languages are popular today? There are far too many languages for one person to become expert at them all, but understanding the range of languages and how they relate to one another is especially useful. One quick way to determine which languages are popular is to examine job postings for programmers. As of this writing, the languages most in demand include C/C++ and Java. In specific industries, certain languages tend to dominate the work. In the banking and insurance industries, for example, the programming language COBOL is still common, although most other industries rarely use it any more.

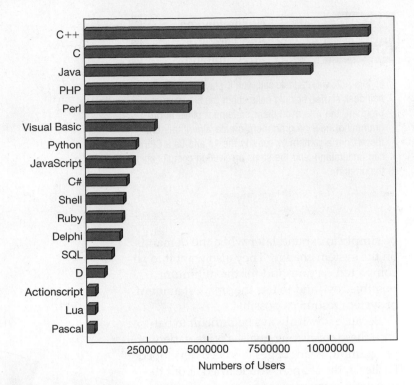

Figure 10.20

When attacking a problem, you can choose from many different programming languages. This chart from **langpop.com** shows how popular certain languages are right now.

The Web site **Langpop.com** uses a number of different techniques to get a feel for which languages are popular in the software industry at the moment (see Figure 10.20).

How do I know which language to study first? A good introductory programming course will emphasize many skills and techniques that will carry over from one language to another. You should find a course that emphasizes design, algorithm development, debugging techniques, and project management. All of these aspects of programming will help you in any language environment. **Pascal** is the only modern language that was specifically designed as a teaching language, but it is no longer often taught at the college level. Many colleges and universities have opted to have students begin with Java or C++.

How does anyone learn so many languages? Professional programmers can work in a great number of different languages. They become proficient at learning new languages because they have become familiar with the basic components, discussed in this chapter's Dig Deeper feature, that are common to all languages: syntax, keywords, operators, and data types. The Bits and Bytes piece "Many Languages on Display" earlier in this chapter directs you to a site that displays an old song in more than 1,300 different languages. Although

Figure 10.21 pokes fun at one stereotype about learning to program, the experience has become much more manageable in recent years.

Selecting the Right Language

How do programmers know which language to select for a specific project? A programming team considers several factors before selecting the language it will use for a specific project.

- **Space available:** Not all languages produce code that takes up the same amount of space. Therefore, the target language should be well matched to the amount of space available for the final program. For example, if the program will be embedded in a chip for use in a cell phone, then it is important for the language to create space-efficient programs.

- **Speed required:** Although poorly written code executes inefficiently in any language, some languages can execute more quickly than others can. Some projects require a focus on speed rather than size. These projects require a language that produces code that executes in the fastest possible time.

- **Organizational resources available:** Another consideration is the resources available in a manager's group or organization. Selecting a language that is easy to use and will be easy to maintain if there is a turnover in programmers is an important consideration. Managers also may factor in the existing pool of talent available for the project. Having to train five programmers to tackle a project in a new language would have significant disadvantages over allowing them to work in a familiar language.

- **Type of target application:** Certain languages are customized to support a specific environment (UNIX or Windows, for instance). Knowing which languages are most commonly used for which environments can be helpful.

Windows Applications

What languages do programmers use if they want to build a Windows application? Software programs that run under the Windows OS are extremely popular. These programs often have a number of common features—scroll bars, title bars, text boxes, buttons, and expanding or collapsing menus, to name a few. Several languages include customized controls that make it easy for programmers to include these features in their programs.

Can I just point and click to create a Windows application? In languages that support Windows programming, programmers can use the mouse to lay out on the screen where the scroll bars and buttons will be in the application. The code needed to explain this to the computer is then written automatically when the programmer says the layout is complete. This is referred to as **visual programming**, and it helps programmers produce a final application much more quickly. In this section, we'll discuss a few languages that are used to develop Windows applications and that take advantage of visual programming.

Visual Basic

What if programmers want to have a model of their program before it's fully developed? Earlier in the chapter, you read about how information systems are developed through the system development life cycle (SDLC). Although the SDLC has

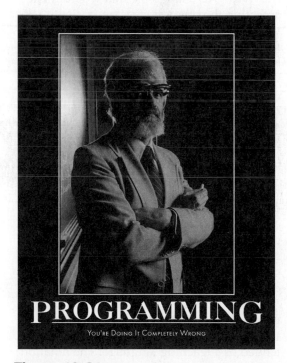

Figure 10.21

This poster mocks the image of a harsh, difficult road to learning programming. Modern tools allow programming to be fun to learn.

been around for quite some time, it doesn't necessarily work for all environments and instances. Programmers often like to build a **prototype**, or small model, of their program at the beginning of a large project.

Although an entire project may not be finished for several months, it can be useful to have a simple shell or skeleton of what the final program will look like to help with design. Prototyping is a form of **rapid application development (RAD)**, an alternative to the waterfall approach of systems development described at the beginning of this chapter. Instead of developing detailed system documents before they produce the system, developers create a prototype first, then generate system documents as they use and remodel the product.

Prototypes for Windows applications are often coded in Microsoft **Visual Basic (VB)**, a powerful programming language used to build a wide range of Windows applications. One strength of VB is its simple, quick interface, which is easy for a programmer to learn and use. It has grown from its roots in the language BASIC (short for Beginner's All-purpose Symbolic Instruction Code) to become a sophisticated and full-featured object-oriented language. It is often used in the creation of graphical user interfaces for Windows.

Visual Basic 2010 is the current version of Visual Basic and is designed for building object-oriented applications for Windows, the Web, and mobile devices. Figure 10.22 shows how the interface of Visual Basic makes it easy to drag and drop entire programming components into an application. Visual Basic 2010 provides a multitude of features that are new or an improvement on the previous versions. These changes make development with Visual Basic easier and produce more efficient code than with any earlier version. Visual Basic 2010 and the .NET Framework are both part of Visual Studio 2010, which provides a complete set of developer tools.

Figure 10.22

The Toolbox in Visual Basic 2010 allows the programmer to drag and drop any of these items into a program.

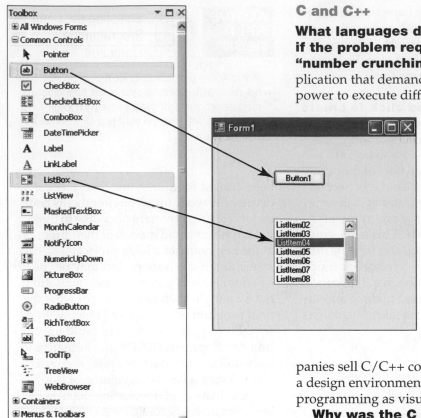

C and C++

What languages do programmers use if the problem requires a lot of "number crunching"? A Windows application that demands raw processing power to execute difficult repetitive numerical calculations is most often a candidate for C/C++. For example, applications that simulate human cells and drug interactions have to solve elaborate mathematical equations many thousands of times each second, and are, therefore, excellent candidates for programming using C/C++. Several companies sell C/C++ compilers equipped with a design environment that makes Windows programming as visual as with VB.

Why was the C language developed? The predecessor of C++, C, was originally developed for system programmers. It was defined by Brian Kernighan and Dennis Ritchie of AT&T Bell Laboratories in 1978 as a language that would make accessing the operating system easier. It provides higher-level programming language features (such as *if* statements and *for* loops) but still allows programmers to manipulate the system memory and CPU registers directly. This mix of high- and low-level access makes C highly attractive to "power" programmers. Most modern operating systems (Windows Vista, Windows 7, Mac OS X, and Linux) were written in C.

The **C++** language takes C to an object-oriented level. Bjarne Stroustrup, the developer of C++, used all of the same symbols and keywords as C, but he extended the language with additional keywords, better security, and more support for the reuse of existing code through object-oriented design.

Are C and C++ natural choices when I'm looking to learn my first language? Neither C nor C++ was intended as a teaching language. The notation and compactness of these languages make them relatively difficult to master. They are in demand in industry, however, because C/C++ can produce fast-running code that

How does the Microsoft .NET Framework help programmers? Too often, computer systems cannot exchange information—perhaps because they have different operating systems or use different rules for packaging data. The Microsoft .NET (pronounced "dot net") Framework is a software development environment designed to let Web sites "talk" to each other easily. The .NET Framework introduces Web services, which provide a standard way for software to interact. A **Web service** is a program that a Web site uses to make information available to other Web sites. For example, your Web site could use the Google Web service to search for information or to check the spelling of a word. The Google Web service returns the requested information to your program in a standard package that you then decode. Before Web services, programs needed a human being to submit a search to Google and read over the results. Now the programs themselves can do this.

The power of .NET and Web services will continue to grow as more companies make some or all of their data available this way. The VB.NET programming tool has many supports for the Visual Basic programmer who is interested in using Web services.

```
for (i = 1; i < 20; i++)
{
    System.out.println(i);
}
```

uses a small amount of memory. Programmers often choose to learn C/C++ because their basic components (operators, data types, and keywords) are common to many other languages.

Java and C#

What language do programmers use for applications that need to collect information from networked computers? Imagine that an insurance company with many locations wants a program that will run each night and will communicate with networked computers in many offices around the country, collecting policy changes and updates from that day's business and updating the company's main records. The team that writes this program would want to use a language that already provides support for network communications.

Java would be a good choice. James Gosling of Sun Microsystems introduced Java in the early 1990s. It quickly became popular because its object-oriented model enables Java programmers to benefit from its large set of existing classes. For example, a Java programmer could begin to use the existing "network connection" class with little attention to the details of how that code itself was implemented. Classes exist for many graphical objects, such as windows and scroll bars, and for network objects such as connections to remote machines. Observing Java's success, Microsoft released a language named **C#** (pronounced "see sharp") that competes with Java.

Can a Java application work on any type of computer? An attractive feature of Java is that it is architecture neutral. This means that Java code needs to be compiled only once, after which it can run on many CPUs (see Figure 10.23). The Java program does not care which CPU, operating system, or user interface is

Figure 10.23

Java programs can be compiled once and run on many different platforms.

 BITS AND BYTES

Really Want to Learn? Work for Free!

The open source software movement is a grassroots collection of developers who believe that software projects can be managed start to finish by groups of individuals instead of companies. Open source software is developed and maintained at no charge by groups of people who are brought together by common interests such as photo editing. When completed, the software product and its source code are distributed free of charge.

The development, testing, and maintenance of the open source code are managed through resources such as SourceForge (**sourceforge.net**), a development Web site that hosts more than 100,000 programs. To support development of open source projects, SourceForge provides services to its more than 1 million users in support of their development of projects. For example, version control tools allow specific versions of a project to be "checked in" or "checked out," as in a library, allowing many people to work on the project at the same time. Communication tools and publicity tools are also provided to help the project succeed in reaching its audience.

Most types of software in the marketplace have an open source equivalent. (See the Technology in Focus section called "Computing Alternatives" on page 252 for more information.) If you are looking to learn about software development by doing it, investigate SourceForge and volunteer for a project!

running on the machine on which it lands. This is possible because the target computer runs a Java Virtual Machine (VM), software that can explain to the Java program how to function on any specific system. A Java VM installed with Microsoft Internet Explorer, for example, allows Internet Explorer to execute any **Java applet** (small Java-based program) it encounters on the Internet. Although Java code does not perform as fast as C++, the advantage of needing to compile only once before it can be distributed to any system is extremely important.

Web Applications: HTML/XHTML and Beyond

What is the most basic language for developing Web applications? A document that will be presented on the Web must be written using special symbols called *tags*. Tags control how a Web browser will display the text, images, and other content tagged in the **HyperText Markup Language (HTML)** or **eXtensible HyperText Markup Language (XHTML)**. Although knowledge of HTML or XHTML is required to program for the Web, they are not in themselves programming languages. HTML and XHTML are just series of tags that modify the display of text. HTML was the original standard defining these tags. XHTML is a newer standard that corrects some of the inconsistencies found in HTML. To see more detail of HTML/XHTML tags, flip to the "HTML/XHTML" section in Chapter 13 (page 621). Many good HTML and XHTML tutorials are available on the Web at sites

such as Learn the Net (**learnthenet.com**), Web Monkey (**webmonkey.com**), and the World Wide Web Consortium (**w3c.org**). These sites include lists of the major tags that can be used to create HTML and XHTML documents.

Are there tools that help programmers write in HTML and XHTML? Several different programs are available to assist in the generation of HTML and XHTML. Adobe Dreamweaver and Microsoft Expression Web present Web page designers with an interface that is similar to a word processing program. Web designers can quickly insert text, images, and hyperlinks, as shown in Figure 10.24. The program automatically inserts the corresponding HTML or XHTML tags. For simple, static (nonchanging) Web pages, no programming is required.

Scripting Languages for the Web

Which programming languages do programmers use to make complex Web pages? To make their Web pages more visually appealing and interactive, programmers use scripting languages to add more power and flexibility to their HTML code. A **scripting language** is a simple programming language that is limited to performing a set of specialized tasks. Scripts allow decisions to be made and calculations to be performed. Several popular scripting languages work well with HTML, including JavaScript, VBScript, and PHP (Hypertext Preprocessor).

JavaScript is a scripting language that is often used to add interactivity to Web pages. JavaScript is not as fully featured as Java, but its syntax, keywords, data types, and operators are subsets of Java's. In addition, JavaScript has a set of classes that represent the objects often used on Web pages: buttons, check boxes, and drop-down lists.

The JavaScript button class, for example, describes a button with a name and a type—for example, whether it is a regular button or a Submit or Reset button. The language includes behaviors, such as click (), and can respond to user actions. For example, when a user moves his or her mouse over a button and clicks to select it, the button "knows" the user is there and jumps in and performs a special action (such as playing a sound).

Figure 10.24

Adobe Dreamweaver is a popular tool for creating Web pages.

STEP 1: User requests information on red bikes.

STEP 2: Server sends request to database computer.

STEP 3: Database computer returns list.

Customer's computer

ABC Bike Company server

ABC Bike Company database

12345
45678
98764
54321
11223
22334

STEP 4: Server's ASP program writes HTML page.

Figure 10.25

An online store is an example of the three-tier client/server type of Internet application.

Are there other scripting languages besides JavaScript?

Programmers who are more familiar with Visual Basic than Java or C++ often use **VBScript**, a subset of Visual Basic, to introduce dynamic decision making into Web pages. **Dynamic decision making** means that the page can decide how to display itself based on the choices the reader makes. PHP, discussed below, is another scripting language that has become extremely popular. It is a free, open source product that runs very efficiently on multiple platforms, including Windows, UNIX, and Linux.

ASP, JSP, and PHP

How are interactive Web pages built? To build Web sites with interactive capabilities, programmers use **Active Server Pages (ASP)**, **Java Server Pages (JSP)**, or the scripting language **PHP (Hypertext Preprocessor)** to adapt the HTML or XHTML page to the user's selections. The user supplies information that is translated into a request by the main computer at the company that owns the Web site, often using a database query language such as SQL. Scripting code in ASP, JSP, or PHP controls the automatic writing of the custom HTML/XHTML page that is returned to the user's computer.

What does additional programming bring to a Web page? The most advanced Web pages interact with the user, collecting information and then customizing the content displayed based on the user's feedback. For example, as shown in Figure 10.25, the ABC online store's Web page will collect a customer bicycle inquiry for red bikes. It then asks ABC's main server for a list of red bicycles sold by the company. An ASP program running on the server creates a new HTML/XHTML page and delivers that to the user's browser, telling the customer what red bicycles (including details such as model and size) are currently sold by ABC.

Thus, ASP programs can have HTML/XHTML code as their output. They use what the user has told them (via the list boxes, check boxes, and buttons on the page) to make decisions. Based on those results, the ASP program decides what HTML/XHTML to write. A small example of ASP writing its own HTML/XHTML code is shown in Figure 10.26.

Flash and XML

What if a programmer wants to create a Web page that includes sophisticated animation? Many Web sites feature elaborate animations that interact with visitors. These sites include buttons and hyperlinks, along with animation effects. These components can be designed with **Adobe Flash**, a software product for developing Web-based multimedia. Flash includes its own programming language, named **ActionScript**, which is similar to JavaScript in its keywords, operators, and classes.

Figure 10.26

An ASP program can (a) write HTML/XHTML code as its (b) output. This image illustrates how the HTML/XHTML page would (c) show up in a browser.

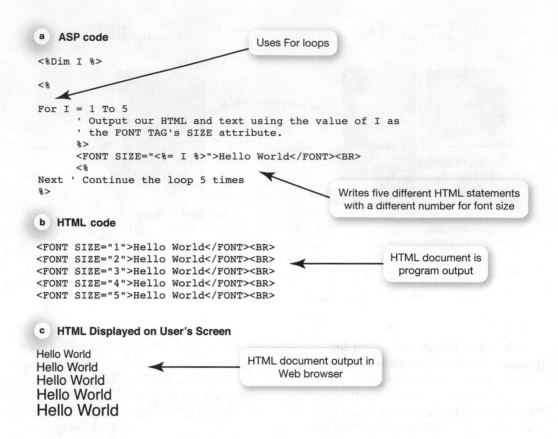

a ASP code

```
<%Dim I %>

<%

For I = 1 To 5
        ' Output our HTML and text using the value of I as
        ' the FONT TAG's SIZE attribute.
        %>
        <FONT SIZE="<%= I %>">Hello World</FONT><BR>
        <%
Next ' Continue the loop 5 times
%>
```

Uses For loops

Writes five different HTML statements with a different number for font size

b HTML code

```
<FONT SIZE="1">Hello World</FONT><BR>
<FONT SIZE="2">Hello World</FONT><BR>
<FONT SIZE="3">Hello World</FONT><BR>
<FONT SIZE="4">Hello World</FONT><BR>
<FONT SIZE="5">Hello World</FONT><BR>
```

HTML document is program output

c HTML Displayed on User's Screen

Hello World
Hello World
Hello World
Hello World
Hello World

HTML document output in Web browser

Microsoft has unveiled a competing product named *SilverLight* that supports the development of rich multimedia and interactive Web applications. Other advances, like the collection of technologies referred to as **AJAX (Asynchronous JavaScript And XML)**, allow the creation of Web applications that can update information on a page without requiring the user to do a page refresh or leave the page. By using existing technologies to do more processing in the browser, users have a more responsive experience.

Is HTML/XHTML the only markup language for the Web? When Web sites communicate with humans, HTML/XHTML work well because the formatting they control is important. People respond immediately to the visual styling of textual information; its layout, color, size, and font design all help to transfer the message of the page to the reader. When computers want to communicate with each other, however, all of these qualities just get in the way. A third markup language, called **eXtensible Markup Language (XML)**, enables designers to define their own data-based tags, making it much easier for a Web site to

transfer the key information on its page to another site.

Without XML, a Web site that wanted to look up current stock pricing information at another site would have to retrieve the HTML/XHTML page, sort through the formatting information, and try to recognize which text on the page identified the data needed. With XML, groups can agree on standard systems of tags that represent important data elements. For example, the XML tags <stock> and </stock> might delimit key stock quote information. Mathematicians have created a standardized set of XML tags named MathML for their work, and biometrics groups are developing an XML standard to describe and exchange data such as DNA and face scans. We discuss HTML/XHTML and XML in more detail in Chapter 13.

Figure 10.27 shows a table of popular programming tools with their features and the typical settings in which they are used.

The Next Great Language

What will be the next great language? It is never easy to predict which

Figure 10.27 | POPULAR PROGRAMMING TOOLS

Programming Language	Features	Typical Setting
C/C++ and C#	Can create compact code that executes quickly Provides high- and low-level access	Used in industrial applications such as banking and engineering
Objective C	Has a framework for writing iTouch/iPhone/ iPad applications	Used to create applications for Mac OS X and Apple mobile devices
Flash ActionScript	Is similar in syntax to JavaScript but customized for the Flash animation environment	Used to control Flash animations
Microsoft SilverLight	Is a competitor to Adobe Flash, and supports rich multimedia capabilities	Used to deliver audio and video to Web pages
Java	Is architecture neutral Is object-oriented	Used to create applets that can be delivered over the Web
JavaScript	Is similar in syntax to Java Has classes that represent buttons, drop-down lists, and other Web page components	Creates code that lives on the client machine and supports interaction with Web pages
VBScript	Is similar in syntax to Visual Basic Has classes that represent buttons, drop-down lists, and other Web page components	Creates code that lives on the client machine and adds interaction to Web pages
Visual Basic	Is easy to learn and use Is object-oriented Has a drag-and-drop interface	Used in prototype development Used to design graphical user interfaces
Web Technologies		
ASP, JSP, PHP	Has a set of rules and standards that allow Web sites to create their own HTML code based on user actions	Controls the automated writing of HTML pages
HTML/XHTML	Provide a set of tags that control the display of text on a Web page	Control layout and style of information presented on a Web page
XML	Enables users to define their own tags Facilitates exchange of information between Web sites	Used in the construction of Web services
AJAX	Uses a combination of existing technologies like JavaScript, CSS, and XML	Creates Web sites that can update without the user refreshing the page

language will become the next "great" language. For example, as the popularity of Apple's mobile devices increases, programming for the iPhone, iTouch, and iPad is becoming much more popular. The language required to develop these application is a flavor of object-oriented C known as *Objective C*. Objective C has been used to develop applications for Mac OS X for quite a few years but is seeing a huge increase in interest with the explosion of new devices.

Software experts predict that as software projects continue to grow in size, the amount of time needed to compile a completed project will also grow. It is not uncommon for a large project to require

SOUND BYTE 3D Programming the Easy Way

In this Sound Byte, you'll create a three-dimensional game using the visual drag-and-drop interface provided by Alice, a free software package. This program teaches all the concepts of programming with none of the pain of learning syntax.

Emerging Technologies: Will It Blend? Writing Your First Video Game in Blender

Blender is a free, open source application that supports home video game production by combining many tools into one package. Blender gives you what you need for each stage of beginning 3D video game development, allowing you to create three-dimensional objects with textures and move them around a 3D world with realistic physics.

First, Blender allows you to construct three-dimensional models (see Figure 10.28). Meshes are used to begin any model and can be customized to represent any 3D shape or object. You can add specific textures and shading to make the model more realistic. Blender then allows you to animate the object. That animation can be saved as a movie or connected to specific control keys or movements. You can also play a complete video game within Blender by using the built-in game engine. Finally, Blender incorporates a physics engine that understands basic concepts such as particle collisions and gravity modeling. This is useful, for example, when a game character tosses a plasma grenade toward a target!

The programming rules used to describe object behavior in the game are made simpler by Blender's Logic Bricks. For example, using Logic Bricks you can, in just a few clicks, create a rule that makes one object disappear when it collides with another. You can also use Logic Bricks to map key movements to control objects or cameras in the environment.

Blender is available as a free download (**blender.org**). You will also find an active community to support you as you learn. The Blender Foundation is involved in releasing games to the public that were developed for free using Blender. These open source games include titles such as Yo! Frankie and Apricot. These are available for anyone to learn from and reuse.

Many resources are available for Blender, including free books such as *Blender 3D: Noob to Pro* on Wiki Books (**en.wikibooks.org/wiki/**

Blender) and a blog of everything Blender at **blendernation.com**. In addition, YouTube has numerous video tutorials on working with Blender, and libraries of Blender routines and objects are freely distributed on the Internet.

If you are interested in video game development, three-dimensional art, or just creating animations, download Blender and realize the power of the open source software movement.

Figure 10.28

Blender allows you to design 3D models, animate them, and apply real physics to create playable video games.

---

30 minutes or more to compile. Interpreted languages, however, have virtually no compile time because compilation occurs while the code is being edited. As projects get larger, the capability to be compiled instantaneously will become even more important. Thus, interpreted languages such as Python, Ruby, and Smalltalk could become more important in the coming years.

Will all languages someday converge into one? Certain characteristics of modern programming languages correspond well with how programmers actually think. These traits support good programming practices and are emerging as common features of most modern programming languages. The object-oriented paradigm is one example. Both Visual Basic and COBOL have moved toward supporting objects.

There will always be a variety of programming languages, however. Figure 10.29, in which the artist tries to give

each language a "personality," illustrates that idea in lighthearted fashion.

Forcing a language to be so general that it can work for any task also forces it to include components that make it slower to compile, produce larger final executables, and require more memory to run. Having a variety of languages and mapping a problem to the best language creates the most efficient software solutions.

So what do I do if I want to learn languages that will be relevant in the future? No particular set of languages is best to learn, and there is no one best sequence in which to learn them. The Association for Computing Machinery (**acm.org**), encourages educators to teach a core set of mathematical and programming skills and concepts, but school and university departments are free to offer a variety of languages.

When you are selecting which programming languages to study, some geographical

Figure 10.29

There will always be a variety of languages, each with its own personality.

and industry-related considerations come into play. For example, in an area in which a large number of pharmaceutical companies exist, there may be a demand for Massachusetts General Hospital Utility Multi-Programming System (MUMPS). This language is often used to build clinical databases, an important task in the pharmaceutical industry. Review the advertisements for programmers in area newspapers and investigate resources such as ComputerJobs (**computerjobs.com**) to identify languages in demand in your area.

Whether or not you pursue a career in programming, having an understanding of how software is created will help you in many IT careers. Software is the set of instructions that allows us to make use of our hardware. Programming skills give you the power to understand, create, and customize a computer system.

ten summary

1. What is a system development life cycle, and what are the phases in the cycle?

An information system includes data, people, procedures, hardware, and software. Teams of individuals are required to develop systems. Those teams need to follow an organized process (or set of steps) to ensure that development proceeds in an orderly fashion. This set of steps is usually referred to as the system development life cycle (SDLC). There are six steps in the SDLC waterfall model discussed earlier in this chapter: (1) A problem or opportunity is identified. (2) The problem is analyzed, and a program specification document is created to outline the project objectives. (3) A detailed plan for programmers to follow is designed using flowcharts and data-flow diagrams. (4) Using this plan, the program is developed and documented. (5) The program is tested to ensure that it works properly and is installed so that it can be used. (6) Ongoing maintenance and evaluation ensure a working product.

2. What is the life cycle of a program?

Each programming project follows several stages from conception to final deployment. The problem statement identifies the task to be computerized and describes how the software program will behave. An algorithm is developed that specifies the sequence of steps that the program must take to complete the work. The algorithm is then translated into highly structured programming code. The code goes through the processes of debugging, in which the programmers find and repair any errors in the code; testing by the programming team; and further testing by the people who will use the program. The results of the entire project are documented for the users and the development team. Finally, users are trained so that they can use the program efficiently.

3. What role does a problem statement play in programming?

The problem statement is an explicit description of what tasks the computer program must accomplish and how the program will execute these tasks and respond to unusual situations. It describes the input data that users will have at the start of the job, the output that the program will produce, and the exact processing that converts these inputs to outputs. In addition, the problem statement identifies potential errors and plans to address these errors.

4. How do programmers create algorithms?

For simple problems, programmers create an algorithm by converting a problem statement into a list of steps (or actions) the program will take. For more complex problems, programmers must identify where decision points occur in the list of steps. Some decisions are yes/no (binary), whereas others create a repeating action (loop). Algorithms are documented in the form of a flowchart or in pseudocode. Programmers use either top-down or object-oriented analysis to produce the algorithm.

5. How do programmers move from algorithm to code, and in what categories of language might they code?

Computer code uses special words and strict rules to enable programmers to control the CPU without having to know all of its hardware details. Programming languages are classified in several major groupings, sometimes referred to as *generations*, with the first generation being machine language—the binary code of 1s and 0s that the computer understands. Assembly language is the next generation; it uses short, English-like commands that speak directly to the CPU and give the programmer direct control of hardware resources. Each successive generation in language development has relieved programmers of some of the burden of keeping track of what the hardware requires and more closely matches how humans think about problems.

6. How does a programmer move from code in a programming language to the 1s and 0s the CPU can understand?

Compilation is the process by which code is converted into machine language, the language the CPU can understand. A compiler is a program that understands both the syntax of the programming language and the exact structure of the CPU and its machine language. It can translate the instructions written by programmers in the higher-level language into machine language, the binary patterns that will execute commands on the CPU. Each programming language has its own compiler. Separate versions are required to compile code that will run on each different type of processor.

7. How is a program tested?

If programmers make errors in the algorithm or in translating the algorithm to code, problems will occur. Programmers debug the program by running it constantly to find errors and to make sure the program behaves in the way it should. Once debugging has detected all the code errors, users, both within the company and outside the company, test the program in every way they can imagine—both as it was intended to be used and in ways only new users may think up. Before its commercial release, software is often provided at a reduced cost or no cost in a beta version to certain test sites or to interested users for a last round of testing.

8. What steps are involved in completing the program?

Once testing is complete, technical writers create internal documentation for the program and external documentation that will be provided to users of the program. User training, which begins once the software is distributed, teaches the user community how to use the software efficiently.

9. How do programmers select the right programming language for a specific task?

A programming team reviews several considerations before selecting the language. First, certain languages are best used with certain problems. Second, the target language should be well matched to the amount of space available for the final program. Third, some projects require the selection of a language that can produce code that executes in the fastest possible time. Finally, selecting a language with which the programmers are familiar is also helpful.

10. What are the most popular programming applications for Windows and Web applications?

Visual Basic, C/C++, and Java are languages that enable programmers to include Windows control features such as scroll bars, title bars, text boxes, buttons, and expanding and collapsing menus. Programmers use HTML/XHTML tags to structure for Web pages. For more complex Web development, scripting programs such as JavaScript and VBScript are popular. Web page animations are done with ASP, JSP, PHP, Flash, and XML.

Word Bank

- algorithm
- beta version
- C/C++
- classes
- compiler
- debugger

- documentation
- HTML/XHTML
- inheritance
- interpreter
- JavaScript
- machine language

- object-oriented
- problem statement
- testing plan
- top-down
- Visual Basic

Instructions: Fill in the blanks using the words from the Word Bank above.

Things are not running smoothly at the Whizgig factory. We need to keep track of how many Whizgigs are made every hour and how many are defective. We begin by calling in the programming team to work with users. Together team members begin to build a software solution by creating a(n) (1) _____. All of the input and output information required is identified as well as the (2) _____, which lists specific examples of what outputs the program will produce for certain inputs. The team then begins to design the (3) _____ by listing all the tasks and subtasks required to complete the job. This approach is called (4) _____ design.

An alternative to this design method is the (5) _____ design model, which develops the program based on objects. Objects that have similar attributes and behaviors can be grouped into (6) _____. The benefit of using this type of design approach is that objects and classes can be reused easily in other programs. If necessary, new classes can be made by first "borrowing" the attributes of an existing class and then adding differentiating attributes. This concept is known as (7) _____.

To select the best language for this problem, the team considers the resources at Whizgig. Although many of the programmers know the visual programming language of (8) _____, the most important factors for this application will be how fast it runs, so the language (9) _____ is selected. Once Whizgig has started to take off, the plan is to expand into a strong Web presence. Then there will be a round of hiring programmers who know (10) _____. For now, the program to track production and quality control has been written in programming language; the (11) _____ translates it to (12) _____, or the binary code that the CPU understands. After that step, the program is ready to be tested.

The (13) _____ helps identify errors in the program code. Then the programmers put together the necessary (14) _____ that explains the program and how to use it. However, because this is a program that is to be used internally, the program does not need to go through a test of the (15) _____ by a group of potential outside users.

becoming computer literate

Your new manager wants to design and deploy an iPad application to collect marketing information about potential customers. She wants to gather data and analyze it in one report, which can be shipped to the marketing department.

Instructions: Write a memo to the manager describing what will have to be considered in the creation of this project. Write the memo using as many of the key terms from the chapter as you can. Consider what languages will need to be used, and what features will be critical to the application's success.

Instructions: Answer the multiple-choice and true–false questions below for more practice with key terms and concepts from this chapter.

Multiple Choice

1. In the SDLC, which is the phase in which the program specification is developed?
   a. Problem and opportunity identification
   b. Analysis
   c. Design
   d. Development and documentation

2. The step of the SDLC in which the "make or buy" decision is made is the
   a. problem and opportunity phase.
   b. analysis phase.
   c. design phase.
   d. development and document phase.

3. The steps that describe exactly what the computer program must do to complete the work is
   a. a debugger.
   b. a problem statement.
   c. an algorithm.
   d. the SDLC.

4. What do companies provide to repair code errors for a program that has been released to the public?
   a. Beta versions
   b. Service packs
   c. Documentation updates
   d. Maintenance programs

5. Which language is best for executing numerically intensive calculations?
   a. C/C++
   b. Objective C
   c. Java
   d. ASP

6. A yes/no decision point in an algorithm is called
   a. a loop.
   b. a binary decision.
   c. a test condition.
   d. a control structure.

7. In object-oriented analysis, classes are defined by their
   a. objects and data.
   b. data and methods.
   c. operators and objects.
   d. behaviors and keywords.

8. Which is NOT an advantage of Java?
   a. Java is architecture neutral.
   b. Java needs to compile only once prior to distribution.
   c. Java supports network communications.
   d. Java performs faster than C++.

9. Which is TRUE about XML?
   a. XML supports the development of rich multimedia.
   b. XML makes it possible to update Web pages without refreshing.
   c. XML enables designers to define their own data-based tags.
   d. XML has classes that represent drop-down lists and other Web elements.

10. Which helps programmers write, compile, and test programs?
    a. IDE
    b. RAD
    c. JAD
    d. PDLC

True–False

_____ 1. When producing the fastest executable program is essential, programmers use a language with an interpreter.

_____ 2. Companies release service packs to repair problems after software has been made commercially available.

_____ 3. Comments that programmers insert to explain the purpose of the code are written in binary.

_____ 4. Each step of the SDLC must be completed before moving on to the next.

_____ 5. Programmers often use ActionScript to code prototypes for Windows applications.

1. Learning to Program

Research the core programming sequence at the college you are attending.

a. What languages does the core sequence cover? Are there any introductory courses that use languages with less syntax, like Alice or Visual Logic?

b. How do the languages in the programming sequence reflect the popularity of the languages used in today's workplace?

c. How many sections of each of the classes are offered?

d. What can you infer about the percentage of students that stay in the programming track over time?

e. What does that result mean to the future of your community and your country?

2. Learn and Earn

Investigate summer internship positions for student programmers. Be sure to check into companies like FogCreek, university programs like the University of Pennsylvania's SUNFEST, and sites like **onedayoneinternship.com**. What is the common set of requirements? What kind of projects do interns produce? What internships are available in your local area?

3. A Ruby, a Perl, and a Python

Perl is an especially useful and convenient language to use for specific types of programming problems. Ruby and Python are other programming languages, each with their own specific advantages. Research Ruby, Perl, and Python, and identify the key features of these languages. Determine which programming situations call for using Ruby and which would be best suited for Perl or Python.

4. Deal or No Deal

There is a famous mathematical game named Googol, invented by Martin Gardner in his column in *Scientific American* in 1960. The rules are as follows: Player 1 writes 10 different numbers on cards, and the cards are turned face down and shuffled. Player 2 flips the cards over one by one until he decides to stop. Player 2 wins if the number on the last opened card is the largest of all the cards; otherwise Player 1 wins. There is a mathematical strategy that gives Player 2 the best chance of winning, but without using any mathematics, think about the game and describe what rule you would use to decide when to stop flipping cards.

5. Reuse, Reuse, Reuse

One key to being an efficient programmer is to reuse code. Programmers often use collections of prewritten code modules named application programming interfaces (APIs) to add functionality to their program with very little work. Research the set of APIs available from Google by visiting Google Code and the API Code Playground.

1. Programming Is Not Just for Programmers

Think about the range of jobs at the place where you currently work.

a. How many of the employees use computers?
b. How many individuals create macros, scripts, or shortcuts for doing their work in a faster, more automated fashion?
c. How many people actually program in a modern programming language?

2. Algorithm Design

Identify the most commonly performed task at your place of business. Think of a way to document it as an algorithm. Then study it to see if you can find a way to make it even more efficient. A small improvement to the most often performed task means big productivity gains. Review the Jolt Award winners at **joltawards.com** to see examples of the kinds of efficiencies that have been introduced in the software field this year to boost productivity.

3. Choosing the Best Language

Using resources from the Web, determine which programming languages would be best to learn if you were going to program for the following industries:

a. Animated movies
b. Computer games for mobile devices and Web deployment
c. Database management
d. Robotics

4. Software Development . . . in PowerPoint?

The tool MockApp (**mockapp.com/download**) is a template for the presentation tools PowerPoint or Keynote. It provides an interface that allows you to drag and drop all of the visual components of an iPhone, iTouch, or iPad application onto a simulated screen. You can link button clicks and other interactions from one screen to the next and create a "working" simulation or prototype of a new iPhone, iTouch, or iPad application. Investigate this tool using either PowerPoint or Keynote. Design an iPhone application that would be useful for you or successful in the marketplace.

5. Accessibility

Web designers and programmers can take specific steps to allow visually impaired users to access Web sites more easily. Examine the information on accessibility at Adobe's Accessibility Resource Center (**adobe.com**). What does accessibility mean in a software context? Explore the details of existing assistive technologies, such as screen readers. What are the legal requirements with which Web sites must comply in order to meet the needs of persons with disabilities? Why is maximizing accessibility important to everyone?

Instructions: Albert Einstein used *Gedankenexperiments*, or critical thinking questions, to develop his theory of relativity. Some ideas are best understood by experimenting with them in our own minds. The following critical thinking questions are designed to demand your full attention but require only a comfortable chair—no technology.

1. Using Data and Methods

Think about what classes would be important in modeling a band that is about to go on a national concert tour. The band already has a Web site, a presence on Twitter and Facebook, and a local following at area clubs. The band signed a new manager last year, and the members have all been with the group for awhile now. They hope to get on bills with other independent-label bands. What data and methods would each class need? How would the classes be related to each other?

2. Class Hierarchy

A common test for deciding the structure of a class hierarchy is the "is a" versus "has a" test. For example, a motorcycle "has a" sidecar, so Sidecar would be a data field of a Motorcycle object. However, a motorcycle "is a" kind of vehicle, so Motorcycle would be a subclass of the base class Vehicle. Use the "is a" versus "has a" test to decide how a class structure could be created for computer peripherals. For example, consider that printers are a type of peripheral and there are laser printers, inkjet printers, 3D printers, color printers, black-and-white printers, and thermal printers. Work to separate the unique features into objects and to extract the most common features into higher-level classes.

3. First Programming Languages

By watching children learn language, we know that language acquisition is much easier at an early age. What if learning a programming language works the same way? What kinds of learning strategies would make a young child curious about programming? What kinds of games would illustrate developing algorithms?

4. Something for Nothing

The open source software movement depends on the participation of a number of people from all over the world. Some individuals donate time by writing code; others do testing or documentation. Projects are then made available free to users. Does the open source movement threaten or strengthen the software industry? Could it replace the existing business model for distributing software? Are there any benefits to working for free and giving your intellectual property away?

5. Language Popularity

At the site **Langpop.com**, results of many different surveys are combined to decide which programming languages are the most popular today. Where would you go to conduct a survey on which programming languages are popular? What individuals would you survey? How would you expect their answers to differ from one another?

Working Together for Change

Problem

You and your team have just been selected to write a software program that tells a vending machine how to make proper change from the bills or coins the customer inserts. The program needs to deliver the smallest possible amount of coins for each transaction.

Task

Divide the class into three teams: Algorithm Design, Coding, and Testing. The responsibilities of each team are outlined as follows.

Process

1. The Algorithm Design team must develop two documents. The first document should present the problem as a top-down design sequence of steps. The second document should use object-oriented analysis to identify the key objects in the problem. Each object needs to be represented as data and behaviors. Inheritance relationships between objects should be noted as well. You can use flowcharts to document your results.

    Consider using a product such as Microsoft Visio or the open source program Dia to create a visual representation of your objects and their relationships to each other.

2. The Coding team needs to decide which programming language would be most appropriate for the project. This program needs to be fast and take up only a small amount of memory. Use the Web to collect information about the language you select and be sure you have enough information to defend your selection.

    You may also consider using a product such as Visual Logic to try to develop the code for a prototype of the system. (**VisualLogic.org** offers a free demo version.) This language, based on Visual Basic, allows you to write code free from many constraints of syntax. Programs in Visual Logic look like flowcharts but actually execute!

3. The Testing team must create a testing plan for the program. What set of inputs would you test with to be sure the program is completely accurate? Develop a table listing combinations of inputs and correct outputs.

4. As a group, discuss how each team would communicate its results to the other teams. Once one team has completed its work, are the team members finished or do they need to interact with the other teams? How would the tools of a site such as SourceForge (**sourceforge.net**) help your development team across the life of the project?

Conclusion

Any modern programming project requires programming teams to produce an accurate and efficient solution to a problem. The interaction of the team members within the team as well as with the other teams is vital to successful programming.

In this exercise, you will research and then role-play a complicated ethical situation. The role you play may or may not match your own personal beliefs, but your research and use of logic will enable you to represent whichever view is assigned. An arbitrator will watch and comment on both sides of the arguments, and together the team will agree on an ethical solution.

Topic: Software That Kills

Re-examine the Ethics in IT section on page 477 of this chapter about the Therac-25 incident. The error-prone software remained on the market was for more than 18 months before the problem was recognized, acknowledged, and solved. During that time six people were killed or badly harmed. Does this situation indicate criminal conduct? Is this a situation that needs to be resolved in civil court, for monetary damages, but does not constitute a criminal act? Should this incident be seen as an example of the price society pays for using complex technology and no blame should be assigned?

Research Areas to Consider

• Therac-25 case resolution

• 2010 Toyota recalls for unanticipated acceleration

• Software errors in avionic software systems

• ACM Ethical Guidelines

Process

Divide the class into teams.

1. Research the areas cited above from the perspective of one of the following people: a software developer, the injured or noninjured patients, and the arbitrator.

2. Team members should write a summary that provides factual support for their character's position regarding the fair and ethical design of medical equipment and a policy for handling fair restitution for injured patients. Then, team members should create an outline to use during the role-playing event.

3. Team members should arrange a mutually convenient time to meet for the exchange, using the collaboration features of MyITLab, the discussion board feature of Blackboard, or meeting in person.

4. Team members should present their case to the class or submit a PowerPoint presentation for review by the rest of the class, along with the summary and resolution they developed.

Conclusion

As technology becomes ever more prevalent and integrated into our lives, more and more ethical dilemmas will present themselves. Being able to understand and evaluate both sides of the argument, while responding in a personally or socially ethical manner, will be an important skill.

objectives

After reading this chapter, you should be able to answer the following questions:

1. What is a database, and why is it beneficial to use databases? *(pp. 518–520)*

2. What components make up a database? *(pp. 520–524)*

3. What types of databases are there? *(pp. 524–526)*

4. What do database management systems do? *(pp. 526–534)*

5. How do relational databases organize and manipulate data? *(pp. 534–539)*

6. What are data warehouses and data marts, and how are they used? *(pp. 539–542)*

7. What is an information system, and what types of information systems are used in business? *(pp. 542–549)*

8. What is data mining, and how does it work? *(pp. 549–551)*

multimedia resources

 Active Helpdesk

- Understanding Database Management Systems **(p. 525)**
- Using Databases **(p. 527)**
- Data Warehouses, Data Marts, and Information Systems **(p. 550)**

 Sound Bytes

- Creating an Access 2010 Database **(p. 532)**
- Improving an Access 2010 Database **(p. 538)**

 Companion Website

The Companion Website includes a variety of additional materials to help you review and learn more about the topics in this chapter. Go to: *pearsonhighered.com/techinaction*

how cool is *this?*

Most useful sites on the Internet have databases integrated into them (or are actually databases themselves). One popular example is Twitter. But with the **millions** of Twitter users Tweeting about all sorts of different things, how can you find Twitter users that generate Tweets about subjects that fit your interests?

Justtweetit.com is a **database of Twitter** users that groups users by **logical topics of interest**. Are you an artist interested in following what other artists are Tweeting about? Just click on the Artists link to find more than 250 active Twitter users who discuss art. What if you regularly Tweet on a topic, such as fashion or video gaming, and want to have **more potential followers** find you? You can easily add yourself to the Justtweetit directory in the most appropriate of the hundreds of categories featured on the site. So start finding **more relevant Tweets** today!

Life Without Databases

A **database** is a collection of related data that can be easily stored, sorted, organized, and queried. By creating an organized structure for data, we hope to make data more meaningful and therefore more useful. In other words, we are attempting to turn data into information. But why should you learn about databases?

Although you may never be called upon to construct a database, you probably use databases every day. For example, you might search a database in an attempt to extract relevant information. A key attribute of databases is that information can be filtered so that you only see the information you really want. Understanding how databases work and what you can do with a database will help you use them more effectively. Let's look at two examples.

Have you checked Facebook today? If so, you used a database even though you probably didn't realize it. When you load your Facebook page, you see a news feed of items your friends have posted on their Facebook pages. Facebook is using your list of friends to comb through their databases to provide you with what it thinks is relevant information—in other words, what your friends are saying today.

Now suppose the top entry on your news feed is yet another post related to a game you don't play (like Mafia Wars or Farmville). You can click on the Hide button next to that entry and then you have the choice of hiding all information from that friend or hiding all information from all friends related to the application (Mafia Wars). When you choose to hide items on your feed in this manner, you are actually instructing the database to filter out information that is not useful to you.

Or, suppose you are looking for a new netbook computer. When you search for netbooks on the Best Buy site (see Figure 11.1), you get results showing more than 50 different products. Perhaps you are on a limited budget, so you select an option to sort the products with the lowest price first. But maybe you are also interested in seeing netbooks that many other people have purchased. You then have the option of re-sorting the products by how well they sell. Sorting data by criteria you specify is also a very useful aspect of databases.

Filtering and sorting information to enhance its usefulness to you are just two useful aspects of databases. In the rest of this chapter, you'll learn about the inner workings of databases and other ways that they can be used to provide relevant information quickly and easily.

Should I use databases for managing all types of data? Not every situation in which related data needs to be turned into organized information demands the complexity of a database. For simple tasks, lists are adequate. Often, word processing or spreadsheet software works for creating simple lists. A table you create in Microsoft Word can serve as a list, as can a spreadsheet you create in Microsoft Excel.

Figure 11.2 shows a simple "Books to Buy" list you might create in Excel before beginning college. This list works well because it is simple and suited to just one purpose: to provide you with a list of the books you need to buy for a particular semester. If all the information that needed to be tracked were as simple as the information in Figure 11.2, there would be no need for databases.

When is a list not appropriate? If complex information needs to be organized or more than one person needs access to it, a list is not an efficient solution. For example, when you enrolled in college, you provided information about yourself to a number of people. This information included your name, your address, the classes you wished to take, and the meal plan you selected. Your

Figure 11.1

On Best Buy's site, sorting results of a product search gives you information that is more useful. You can also further filter the data such as restricting your results to one manufacturer.

	A	B	C	D
1	**Books To Buy**			
2				
3	**Class**	**Title**	**Author**	**Bought**
4	Western Civilizations	The Western Heritage: Volume 1	Kagen, Ozment, Turner	
5	Intro to Business	Better Business	Solomon, Poatsy, Martin	Yes
6	Intro to Sociology	Sociology	Macionis	
7	Computer Programming 1	Introduction to Java Programming	Liang	Yes
8	Intro to Psychology	Psychology	Wade, Tarvis	Yes

Figure 11.2

A simple list created as a spreadsheet in Microsoft Excel or as a table in Microsoft Word is often sufficient to organize simple tasks.

school also tracks other information about you, such as your residence hall address. Consider the two lists shown in Figure 11.3. Figure 11.3a is a list the registrar's office uses to keep track of students, the classes they are taking, and the meal plan they selected. Figure 11.3b is a list the residence hall manager uses to track where students are housed.

What's the problem with having two lists? First, there is a great deal of duplicated data between the two lists in Figure 11.3. For example, each time Donald Lopez registers for a class, his name and address are entered. He needs to provide the same data to the residence hall manager when he receives his residence hall assignment. This **data redundancy**, though not a problem in the small lists in Figure 11.3, can be problematic when a college or university has 10,000 students. Imagine the time wasted by entering data multiple times, semester after semester. Imagine, too, the increased likelihood that someone will make a mistake.

Second, each time the information in the list changes, multiple lists must be updated. If Li Chan moves, his data will need to be updated in all the lists that contain his address. It would be easy to overlook one or more lists or even one or more rows in the same list. This would lead to a state of **data inconsistency**. It would not be possible to tell easily which data was correct. In addition, notice that Jennifer Evans's last record in Figure 11.3a contains a different street address than that shown in her other records. It's impossible to tell which address is correct, again resulting in data inconsistency.

In addition, correct data can be entered into a list but in an inconsistent format. Look at students Jennifer Evans and Donald Lopez in Figure 11.3a. Both are registered for PSY 110, but two different course names appear: Intro to Psychology and Intro to Psych. Are these the same course? Which name is the correct one? Confusion arises when data is inconsistently entered. Establishing data consistency is difficult to do with a list.

Aside from data redundancy and inconsistency, are there any other problems with using lists instead of databases? What if someone accidentally entered Jennifer Evans's enrollment data twice in the list in Figure 11.3a? Any reports (such as student bills) that are generated based on this list will be inaccurate because of the duplicate data. For example, Jennifer would be sent two separate bills for her classes, resulting in confusion and headaches.

In Figure 11.3a, each student has selected one of the college's meal plans, and this data must be entered into each row. What if someone enters a nonexistent meal plan in one of the rows pertaining to Donald Lopez?

Figure 11.3

(a) A class registration list and (b) a list of residence hall assignments are two lists that a college might create to keep track of student information.

a

Class Registration List - Fall

SID #	Last Name	First Name	Home Address	City	State	Zip Code	Class Code	Class Name	# Of Credits	Meal Plan #
234567891	Chan	Li	123 Main Street	Tuba City	NV	49874-7643	LAN 330	Japanese 1	3	2
234567891	Chan	Li	123 Main Street	Tuba City	NV	49874-7643	REL 216	Early Buddhism	3	2
234567891	Chan	Li	123 Main Street	Tuba City	NV	49874-7643	ENG 102	English Comp 2	3	2
456789123	Coyle	Diane	745 Station Drive	Springfield	MA	18755-5555				
123456789	Evans	Jennifer	123 Oak Street	Gotham City	PA	19999-8888	CIS 111	Programming	3	1
123456789	Evans	Jennifer	123 Oak Street	Gotham City	PA	19999-8888	ENG 101	English Comp 1	3	1
123456789	Evans	Jennifer	123 Oak Street	Gotham City	PA	19999-8888	HIS 103	Western Civ	3	1
123456789	Evans	Jennifer	123 Oak Street	Gotham City	PA	19999-8888	CHE 140	Chemistry	4	1
123456789	Evans	Jennifer	124 Oak Street	Gotham City	PA	19999-8888	PSY 110	Intro to Psychology	3	1
567891234	Lopez	Donald	3421 Lincoln Court	Spalding	ND	87564-2546	HIS 401	16th Century Europe	3	1
567891234	Lopez	Donald	3421 Lincoln Court	Spalding	ND	87564-2546	SOC 310	Interpersonal Relationships	3	1
567891234	Lopez	Donald	3421 Lincoln Court	Spalding	ND	87564-2546	PSY 110	Intro to Psych	3	1
345678912	Wallace	William	654 Front Street	Locust Glen	MI	67744-3584	HIS 204	Scottish History	3	3
345678912	Wallace	William	654 Front Street	Locust Glen	MI	67744-3584	PEH 125	Fencing 1	3	3
345678912	Wallace	William	654 Front Street	Locust Glen	MI	67744-3584	SOC 220	The Art of Negotiation	2	3

b

Residence Hall Assignment List - Fall

SID #	Last Name	First Name	Home Address	City	State	Zip Code	Residence Hall Name	Room Number
234567891	Chan	Li	123 Main Street	Tuba City	NV	49874-7643	Wilson Hall	218
456789123	Coyle	Diane	745 Station Drive	Springfield	MA	18755-5555	Montgomery Hall	231
123456789	Evans	Jennifer	123 Oak Street	Gotham City	PA	19999-8888	Montgomery Hall	312
567891234	Lopez	Donald	3421 Lincoln Court	Spalding	ND	87564-2546	Stone House	102
345678912	Wallace	William	654 Front Street	Locust Glen	MI	67744-3584	Forsman Quad	124

This is not only wrong, but also can be confusing to anyone viewing the list. With a list, anything can be entered in a row or column, even if that information is incorrect.

In addition, information can be organized in many ways. Consider the list of residence hall assignments in Figure 11.3b, which is organized alphabetically by last name. This works well for the accounting clerk, who needs to generate bills for student housing. However, for the residence manager who wants to see which residence hall rooms are still vacant, it would be more useful to have the data organized by residence hall and room number. Reorganizing multiple lists in this way can be labor intensive.

A final problem with lists is how to handle incomplete data. In Figure 11.3a, Diane Coyle has enrolled in the college but has not yet selected a meal plan or registered for courses. Her known information has been entered, but it's impossible to tell by looking at her record whether data relating to her course registrations and meal plans is available and just was not entered, or is truly missing.

Can't I just exercise caution and set rules for updating lists? Carefully following the rules when you update a list like the ones shown in Figure 11.3 can address many of the problems mentioned, but there is still room for error. Being careful does not avoid the most pressing problems of lists: (1) the inability of the data to be shared and (2) data redundancy. Even if you could surmount all of these problems, you cannot easily change a list to accommodate the disparate needs of many users.

How can I solve the problems associated with lists? For single topics, a list is sufficient. However, for any complex data that needs to be organized or shared, using a database is the most practical and efficient way to avoid the pitfalls associated with using lists.

Database Building Blocks

Almost any kind of data that needs organization and analysis can be put into a database. For example, Yahoo! maintains an online database (called Yahoo! People Search) that helps users find a person's street address or e-mail address. Media providers such as Netflix, which rents DVDs and streams video content to consumers, store subscribers' mailing addresses and payment information in a database. In this section, we explore the advantages of using databases as well as the terminology databases use to categorize data.

Advantages of Using Databases

How do databases make our lives easier? Without databases, you could not store and retrieve large quantities of information easily. Consider airline reservation systems. Thousands of people fly across the United States on any given day. Without a database, it would be extremely difficult to keep track of such a large number of airline reservations. In addition, although you can look up information fairly quickly in a list, even extremely large electronic databases can provide the information you request in seconds. Databases provide three main advantages: They enable information sharing, they promote data integrity, and they allow the flexible use of data.

How do databases make information sharing possible? Consider student records at a college. As noted earlier, without databases, financial aid, admissions, and student housing would all need their own student lists (files). The information in these lists might not match because each department would maintain its own records. If a change had to be made in a student's address, all three lists (the financial aid file, the admissions file, and the student housing file) would have to be changed.

As shown in Figure 11.4, with a database only one file is maintained, which reduces the possibility of errors when data is entered or updated. It also increases efficiency, because there are no files to reconcile with each other. A database therefore provides for data centralization. There is no need for multiple lists. Each department that needs to use student information accesses it from the same set of data.

> "How do databases make information sharing possible?"

How do databases promote data integrity?
Data integrity means that the data contained in the database is accurate and reliable. **Data centralization** goes a long way toward ensuring data integrity. Instead of being in multiple lists that have to be maintained, your name and address information is maintained in only one place. If you move, your address must be changed only once.

How do databases provide flexibility?
Another significant advantage of databases is that they are flexibly organized, enabling you to reorganize the information they contain in a variety of ways to suit the needs of the moment. Think back to the earlier example regarding lists. The registrar and housing manager need to see different information. With a list, you can organize information in only one way. If information is in a database, the registrar can easily view just the information she needs (such as the courses the student is taking). Likewise, the housing manager can easily view just the information she needs (such as the residence hall to which the student is assigned).

Data flexibility also makes information dissemination tasks easier. Suppose your school wants to send out a mailing about a new course to all business majors. Having the contact information of students available in a database makes it easy to merge the data, using an application such as Microsoft Word, and create personalized letters and address labels. Obviously, this would be much faster than generating these items manually, and the results should contain fewer errors. Thus, databases can manage larger amounts of data and process that data more efficiently.

Are there any disadvantages associated with databases?
Databases are

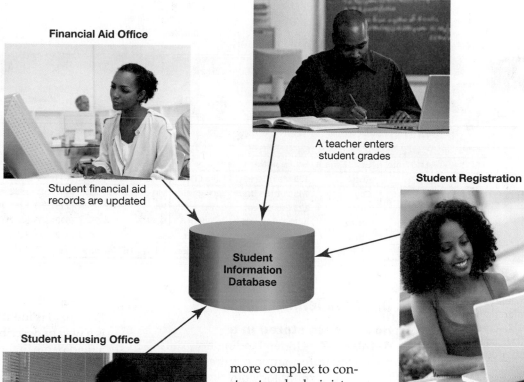

Financial Aid Office
Student financial aid records are updated

A teacher enters student grades

Student Registration
A student registers for classes and checks her grades

Student Housing Office
A student is assigned to a residence hall

Student Information Database

Figure 11.4

Using a database lets data be centralized, so that only one copy of relevant data must be maintained. All database users therefore access the same up-to-date information.

more complex to construct and administer than lists. They also can be time-consuming and expensive to set up. Great care must be exercised in the design of databases to ensure they will function as intended. Although average individuals can design small databases, it is helpful to have an experienced **database administrator** (or **database designer**), an individual trained in the design and building of databases, to assist with the construction of large databases.

Data privacy concerns also arise when using databases. Think about how much information you've provided to your school. The school probably has records of your Social Security number, birth date, address, and credit card information. These are things an identity thief would love to get their hands on. For this reason, many colleges and universities no longer use Social Security numbers as student identification (ID) numbers. Instead, they create a unique student ID number when you register, which helps protect your Social Security number from falling into the wrong hands. Despite the increased complexity of databases and the issues surrounding privacy, however, the advantages of databases far outweigh the administrative disadvantages.

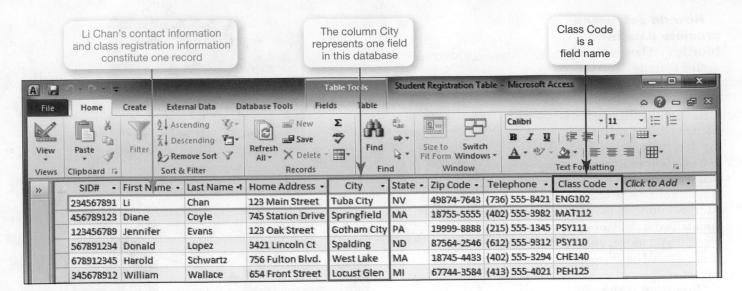

Li Chan's contact information and class registration information constitute one record

The column City represents one field in this database

Class Code is a field name

Class Code is a field name

Figure 11.5

In a database, a category of information is stored in a field. A group of related fields is called a record, and a group of related records is called a table (or file). This is a table that contains records for all students registered for classes in the current semester.

Database Terminology

How is data stored in a database?
Understanding how databases store information requires knowing the unique terminology developed to describe databases. As shown in Figure 11.5, databases have three main components: fields, records, and tables (or files).

Fields

What is a field? A database stores each category of information in a **field**. Fields are displayed in columns. The city where a student lives can be found in the City field in the class registration list shown in Figure 11.5. Each field is identified by a **field name**, which is a way of describing the field. Class Code is a field name in the class registration list database in Figure 11.5. In a database, fields have other characteristics to describe them, including field data types and field size.

What are data types? When fields are created in the database, the user assigns those fields a **data type** (or **field type**). The data type indicates what type of data can be stored in the field.

Common data types are listed and illustrated in Figure 11.6 and described in the remainder of this section.

Figure 11.6 COMMON DATA TYPES AND ILLUSTRATIVE DATA

Data Type	Used to Store	Examples
Text	Alphabetic or alphanumeric data	Mirabel CIS 110
Numeric	Numbers	256 1.347 $5,600
Computational	Computational formulas	Credit hours × per-credit tuition charges
Date	Dates in standard date notation	4/15/2014
Memo	Long blocks of text	Four score and seven years ago, our fathers brought forth on this continent a new nation, conceived in liberty, and dedicated to the proposition that all men are created equal.
Object	Multimedia files or documents	MP3 file AVI file
Hyperlink	A hyperlink to a Web page	pearsonhighered.com/techinaction

- A **text field** can hold any combination of alphanumeric data (letters or numbers), but is most often used to hold words. Although text fields can contain numbers (such as telephone numbers), they are stored as text and therefore cannot be used in calculations.
- A **numeric field** stores numbers. Unlike values in text fields, values in numeric fields can be used to perform calculations. For instance, the numbers stored in numeric fields can be used to calculate tuition owed.
- A **computational field** (or **computed field**) is a numeric field that stores the contents of a calculation, which is generated with a formula in the numeric field. This is similar to a formula computation in a spreadsheet cell.
- A **date field** holds data such as birthdays and due dates.
- A **memo field** is like a text field but can hold long pieces of text. For example, a paragraph describing your high school achievements would be stored in a memo field.
- An **object field** holds items such as pictures, video clips, or documents.
- A **hyperlink field** stores hyperlinks to Web pages.

What is meant by field size? Field size defines the maximum number of characters or numbers that a field can hold. If a numeric field has a size of 5, it can hold a number as high as 99999. As a rule, you should tailor the field size to the length of the data it contains. If you define a field size of 50, space is reserved for 50 characters in that field, whether or not all 50 characters are used. Therefore, if you know that a character field will have a maximum of two characters, defining the field size as 50 wastes space and makes the files unnecessarily large. This can cause decreased database performance, especially in large databases.

Records and Tables

What are records and tables in databases? A group of related fields is called a **record**. For example, a student's name, address, and class registration information comprise a record. A group of related records is called a **table** (or **file**). Tables usually are organized by a common subject. Figure 11.5 shows a table that contains records for all students registered for classes in the current semester.

Primary Keys

Can fields have the same values in the same table? Yes, they can. It is possible that two students may live in the same town or have the same last name. However, to keep records distinct, each record must have one field that has a value unique to that record. This unique field is called a **primary key** or a **key field**. For example, as shown in Figure 11.7, in student records, the primary key is the student ID number (field name SID#). Establishing a primary key and ensuring that it is unique make it impossible to duplicate records.

Figure 11.7

Unique student ID numbers make ideal primary keys because even students with the same name won't have the same ID number.

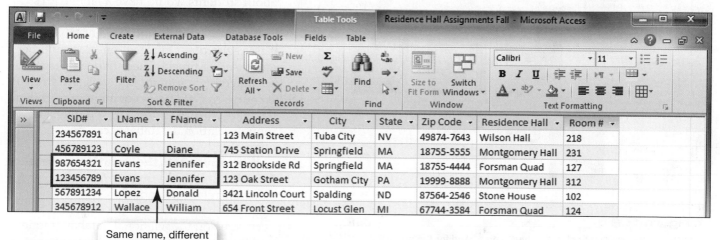

Same name, different primary keys

What makes a good primary key? We already have many numbers that follow us through our lives that make excellent primary keys. In the past, Social Security numbers were often selected as primary keys in databases containing data about individuals. More recently, concerns about identity theft have led many businesses to abandon Social Security numbers as the primary means of identifying individuals. Driver's license numbers are unique within a particular state, as are the license plate numbers on cars. State government agencies often use these numbers to track individuals and their transactions.

Primary keys don't have to be numbers that already represent something. For example, when you place an order with **Amazon.com**, your transaction gets a unique order number. This number is the Amazon database's primary key. You refer to this number when checking your order status, returning merchandise, and so on. It is essential to have a unique number for each order because it would be difficult to keep track of it without one.

Database Types

Many different types of electronic databases have been used since the invention of the computer. The three major types of databases currently in use are relational, object-oriented, and multidimensional. Of these three, relational databases have the largest market share, but the market share of multidimensional databases is growing at a fast pace.

Relational Databases

What is a relational database? A **relational database** organizes data in table format by logically grouping similar data into a **relation** (a table that contains related data). As discussed earlier, each record in a database table is assigned a primary key to ensure that the record is unique. In relational databases, tables are logically linked to each other by including their primary keys in other tables with related information.

For example, at your college, a database about students would have a table with student contact information (name, address, and phone number) and another table with class registration information (class number and meeting times). These two tables would be linked by a primary key such as a student ID number. Data types common in relational databases are text, numeric, and date, although relational databases can possess other data types.

Who invented the relational database? E. F. Codd first significantly defined the relational model in 1970. Since then, much research and development have been done on the relational database model, and the model has proven to be extremely reliable for storing and manipulating data.

Object-Oriented Databases

What is an object-oriented database?
An **object-oriented database** stores data in objects, rather than in tables. The models on which these databases are formed derive from the object-oriented programming paradigm, discussed in Chapter 10, which was catching on in the programming community in the late 1980s. Objects contain not only data, but also methods for processing or manipulating that data. This allows object-oriented databases to store more types of data than relational databases and to access that data faster.

For example, a "student" object that contains data about the courses a student is taking might also store the instructions for generating a bill for the student based on his or her course load. Because object-oriented databases store the instructions for doing computations in the same place as they store the data, they can usually process requests for information faster than can relational databases (which would only store the student information).

Why would I use an object-oriented database?
Whereas relational databases excel in the storage of **structured (analytical) data** (such as "Bill" or "345"), object-oriented databases are more adept at handling unstructured data. **Unstructured data** includes nontraditional data such as audio clips (including MP3 files), video clips, pictures, and extremely large documents. Data of this type is known as a **binary large object (BLOB)** because it is actually encoded in binary form.

Object-oriented databases are based on complex models for manipulating data. These models are much more complex than relational database models. Because businesses today need to store a greater variety of data, object-oriented databases are becoming more popular. Many relational database systems have been expanded to include object-oriented components. For a business to use its data in an object-oriented database, it needs to undergo a costly conversion process. However, once this initial cost is overcome, the faster access and reusability of the database objects can provide advantages for large businesses.

Object-oriented databases also need to use a query language to access and manage data. Many object-oriented databases use **object query language (OQL)**, which is similar in many respects to SQL (structured query language), a standard language used to construct queries to extract data from databases.

Multidimensional Databases

What is a multidimensional database?
A **multidimensional database** stores data in more than two dimensions. This distinguishes it from a relational database, which stores data in two-dimensional tables. Multidimensional databases organize data in a cube format. Each data cube has a *measure attribute*, which is the main type of data that the cube is tracking. Other elements of the cube are known as *feature attributes*, which all describe the measure attribute in some meaningful way. For example, sales of automobiles (measure attribute) could be categorized by various dimensions such as region, automobile color, automobile model, time period (such as current month), or salesperson—all feature attributes (see Figure 11.9). In addition, the database could be constructed to define different levels within a particular feature attribute (such as state and town within a region).

What are the advantages of multidimensional databases?
The two main advantages of multidimensional databases are that they can easily be

Figure 11.9

Multidimensional databases describe data in at least three dimensions.

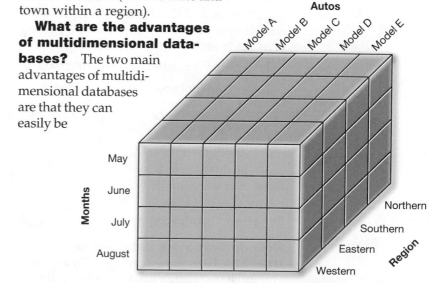

customized to provide information to a variety of users (based on their need), and they can process data much faster than pure relational databases can. The need for processing speed is especially critical when deploying a large database that will be accessed via the Internet. Therefore, large databases such as eBay that are accessed by many users needing to view data in different ways are usually designed as multidimensional databases. Oracle Corporation has slowly morphed its tried-and-true relational database into a multidimensional database in response to customer demand. This was primarily in response to customers who were using an Oracle database for applications deployed on the Web and needed better ways of storing and accessing image, audio, and video files. With multidimensional databases such as the current Oracle Database 11g, businesses do not have to abandon the proven relational database model, because multidimensional databases are based on proven relational database theory.

Database Management Systems: Basic Operations

Databases are created and managed using a **database management system (DBMS)**. A DBMS is specially designed application software (such as Oracle Database or Microsoft Access) that interacts with the user, other applications, and the database to capture and analyze data. The four main operations of a DBMS are

1. Creating databases and entering data.
2. Viewing (or browsing) and sorting data.
3. Querying (extracting) data.
4. Outputting data.

In the next section, we look at each of these operations in detail.

Creating Databases and Entering Data

How do I create a database with a DBMS? To create a database with a DBMS, you must first define the data to be captured.

Therefore, you must create a description of the data. This description is contained in the database's files and is referred to as the **data dictionary** or the **database schema**. The data dictionary defines the name, data type, and length of each field in the database. Describing the data helps to categorize and analyze it and sets parameters for entering valid data into the database (such as a 10-digit number in a phone number field).

How do I know what fields are needed in my database? Careful planning is required to identify each distinct piece of data you need to capture. Each field should describe a unique piece of data and should never combine two separate pieces of data.

> "Each field should describe a unique piece of data."

For example, for student registration at a college, capturing the student's name, street address, city, state, and zip code is important. But should a student's name be placed in one field or two? Because first and last names are separate pieces of data, you would want to create a separate field for each. For instance, suppose you wish to send an e-mail message to students addressing all of them by their first names (such as "Dear Susan"). If Susan's first and last names are in the same field in the database, it will be difficult to extract just her first name for the salutation.

What does a data dictionary look like, and how do I create one? In Microsoft Access, the data dictionary is called the Field Properties box. Figure 11.10a shows the Field Properties box for a database table in Access. The first step in creating an entry in the data dictionary is to create a field name. Field names should be unique within a table. In the table in Figure 11.10a, the field name State is used to store the abbreviation for the state where the student lives.

Second, you must define a data type for each field. For the State field, you use a text data type because names are expressed using characters. Third, you should set a maximum field size (in this case, two characters) for the field. Data in the field can be shorter than the maximum but can never exceed it. Sometimes the field name may not be meaningful to the user of the database even though it makes sense to the designer. The Caption value allows you to display a name of your choice on forms and reports.

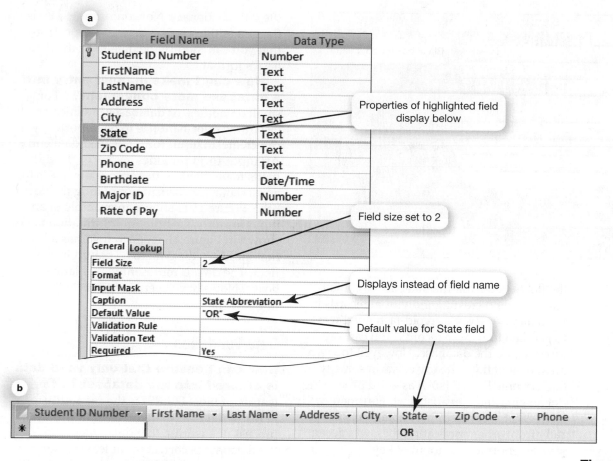

a

Field Name	Data Type
Student ID Number	Number
FirstName	Text
LastName	Text
Address	Text
City	Text
State	Text
Zip Code	Text
Phone	Text
Birthdate	Date/Time
Major ID	Number
Rate of Pay	Number

Properties of highlighted field display below

General Lookup

Field Size	2
Format	
Input Mask	
Caption	State Abbreviation
Default Value	"OR"
Validation Rule	
Validation Text	
Required	Yes

Field size set to 2

Displays instead of field name

Default value for State field

b

Student ID Number ▾	First Name ▾	Last Name ▾	Address ▾	City ▾	State ▾	Zip Code ▾	Phone ▾
*					OR		

Figure 11.10

(a) The Field Properties box, shown for the Student Information table in an Access database, represents the database's data dictionary. (b) The Student Information table, ready for data input, results from setting up the data dictionary in Figure 11.10a.

Finally, you can set a **default value** for a field. A default value is the value the database uses for the field unless the user enters another value. Though not appropriate for first names, because they vary widely, default values are useful for field data that is frequently the same. For example, setting a default value for a State field saves users from having to enter it for each student if most students live in one state.

You need to repeat these steps for each field in the table. When completed, the resulting Student Information table, shown in Figure 11.10b, is ready for data entry.

The attributes (such as data type and field size) shown in Figure 11.10a and 11.10b are **metadata**: data that describes other data. Metadata is an integral part of the data dictionary. You need to build the data dictionary for each table you will use in a database before you enter data into the database. This also has the benefit of forcing you to consider up front the data you need to capture and the metadata that describes it.

What happens if I forget to define a field in the data dictionary or if I want to add another one later? Databases are extremely flexible. You can

add additional fields as needed but this does not negate the need for proper planning and design of a database. You will need to populate (enter data into) into any new fields that are added to your database. This could be difficult if you suddenly need to add a Birth Date field to a database that already contains records for 10,000 individuals. If you plan to use the Birth Date field to analyze the data, you need to have a plan for accumulating birth dates to ensure the completeness of the data.

Inputting Data

How do I get data into the database?
After you create a data dictionary for each table (or file) in the database and establish

ACTIVE HELP-DESK — Using Databases

In this Active Helpdesk call, you'll play the role of a helpdesk staffer, fielding calls about databases, their benefits, their components, and how relational databases organize and manipulate data.

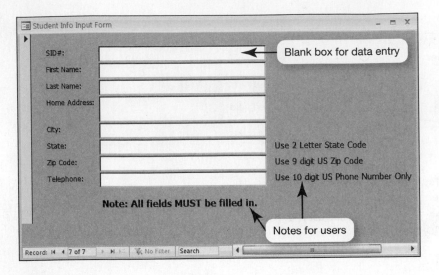

Figure 11.11

The input form used for entering data into the Student Information table.

Figure 11.12

A validation rule set to restrict rates of pay to a certain range.

the fields you want the database to contain, you can begin creating individual records in the database. There's an old-fashioned way to get data into these records: you can key it directly into the database. However, today, a great deal of data already exists in some type of electronic format (such as word processing documents and spreadsheets). Fortunately, most databases can import data electronically from other application files, which can save an enormous amount of keying.

When importing data, most databases usually apply filters to the data to determine that it is in the correct format as defined by

the data dictionary. Nonconforming data is flagged (either on-screen or in a report) so that you can modify the data to fit the database's format.

How can I make manual entry into a database more convenient? For small databases, or databases in which no electronic information is to be imported, you can create an input form to speed data entry. An **input form** provides a view of the data fields to be filled, with appropriate labels to assist database users in populating the database. Figure 11.11 shows an example of an input form for the Student Information table shown in Figure 11.10. Each field has a label that indicates the data to be placed in the field. The data is represented by blank boxes. Notes have been added to the form to guide the users.

Data Validation

How can I ensure that only valid data is entered into the database? One feature of most DBMSs is the capability to perform data validation. **Validation** is the process of ensuring that data entered into the database is correct (or at least reasonable) and complete. When you registered for college, for example, the admissions clerk most likely asked you for your phone number. A phone number in the United States usually comprises 10 digits formatted in the following fashion: (610) 555-1234. A **validation rule** is set up in the student database to alert the user if a clearly wrong entry, such as "Joh-nSm-ythe" or "2345," is entered in the phone number field instead of a valid 10-digit phone number.

Validation rules are generally defined as part of the data dictionary. Violations of validation rules usually result in an error message being displayed on the screen so that the error can be addressed. Common types of validation checks include range, completeness, consistency, and alphabetic and numeric checks.

How does a range check work? A **range check** ensures that the data entered into the database falls within a certain range of numbers. For instance, rates of pay for student jobs usually fall within a certain range. Therefore, in a student pay database, you could set a **field constraint** (a property that must be satisfied for an entry to be accepted into the field) to restrict pay rates to a range you define.

Figure 11.13

A database completeness check, like this one shown for Amazon, ensures that all fields defined as "required" have data in them.

Figure 11.12 shows how you set up a range check in a data dictionary (in the Field Properties box) for an Access database. A validation rule restricts the entries for the Rate of Pay field to amounts between $7.25 (minimum rate of pay) and $20.00 (the maximum rate of pay for students at the college). If users tried to enter a rate of pay less than $7.25 or greater than $20.00, they would be notified of an invalid range error and the input would not be accepted.

What does a completeness check accomplish? If you have ever bought anything online, you have probably encountered error messages generated by completeness checks. In database systems, fields can be defined as "required," meaning data must be entered into them. A **completeness check**, such as the one shown in Figure 11.13, ensures that all fields defined as "required" have data entered into them. When a user submits this form, the database performs a completeness check and, in this case, notices that the required "Address Line 1" field was left blank. An error message then displays to alert the user of the omission.

What is the function of a consistency check? A consistency check compares the values of data in two or more fields to see if these values are reasonable. For example, your birth date and the date you enrolled in school are often in a college's database. It is not possible for you to have enrolled in college before you were born. Further, most college students are at least 16 years old. Therefore, a consistency check on these fields might ensure that your birth date is at least 16 or more years before the date when you enrolled in college.

How are alphabetic and numeric checks used? You may want to restrict fields to only alphabetic or numerical data (such as for names and student ID numbers). An **alphabetic check** confirms that only textual characters (such as "Gwen") are entered in a field. A **numeric check** confirms that only numbers are entered in the field. With these checks in place, "St3v3" would not be accepted as a first name or a zip code. Figure 11.14 shows how you can set such checks and customize error messages in Access.

Figure 11.14

Although several types of validation rules have been activated here, you probably wouldn't find it necessary to use all of them at once.

DIG DEEPER

Structured Query Language (SQL)

To extract records from a database, you use a query language. Almost all relational and object relational databases today use **structured query language**, or **SQL**. Oracle, Microsoft SQL Server, Microsoft Access, IBM DB2, and MySQL are examples of popular databases that use SQL.

When relational databases were first developed in the early 1970s, each DBMS software product contained its own query language. This meant that database administrators had to learn a new language whenever they worked with a different DBMS. The early query languages were mathematically based and often difficult to master. E. F. Codd, who has been called the father of relational databases, proposed a standardized query language when he worked at IBM in the mid-1970s.

The original language was called SEQUEL, short for *structured English query language*. The idea was to make queries easy by using English language–like sentence structure. Database software designers enthusiastically accepted the concept, developing a modified version of the original SEQUEL language, named SQL. Oracle first introduced SQL in

a commercial database product in 1979. It has been the unofficial standard language for relational databases since then.

SQL uses relational algebra to extract data from databases. **Relational algebra** is the use of English-like expressions that have variables and operations, much like algebraic equations. Variables include table names, field names, or selection criteria for the data you wish to display. Operations include directions such as *select* (which enables you to pick variable names), *from* (which tells the database which table to use), and *where* (which enables you to specify selection criteria). The two most common queries used to extract data using relational algebra are select queries and join queries.

A **select query** displays a subset of data from a table (or tables) based on the criteria you specify. A typical select query has the following format:

SELECT (Field Name 1, Field Name 2,…)
FROM (Table Name)
WHERE (Selection Criteria)

Figure 11.15

When the query on the left is applied to the (a) Student Information table, it restricts the output to (b) only a phone list. The query on the right, which uses a WHERE statement, further restricts the phone list to (c) only students from Massachusetts.

The first line of the query contains variables for the field names you want to display. The FROM statement enables you to specify the table name from which the data will be retrieved. The last line (the WHERE statement) is used only when you wish to specify which records need to be displayed (such as all students with GPAs greater than 3.2). If you wish to display all the rows (records) in the table, then you do not use the WHERE statement. (See Figure 11.15.)

Suppose you want to create a telephone list that includes all students from the Student Information table In Figure 11.15a. The SQL query you would send to the database would look like this:

SELECT (First Name, Last Name, Telephone)

FROM (Student Information Table)

Figure 11.15b shows the output from this query.

What if you want a phone list that only shows students from Massachusetts? In that case, you would add a WHERE statement to the query as follows:

SELECT (First Name, Last Name, Telephone)

FROM (Student Information Table)

WHERE (State = MA)

This query restricts the output to students who live in Massachusetts, as shown in Figure 11.15c. Notice that the State field in the Student Information table can be used by the query (in this case, as a limiting criterion),

but the contents of the State field are not required to be displayed in the query results. This explains why the output shown in Figure 11.15c doesn't show the State field.

When you want to extract data that is in two or more tables, you use a **join query**. The query actually links (or joins) the two tables using the common field in both tables and extracts the relevant data from each. The format for a simple join query for two tables is as follows:

SELECT (Field Name 1, Field Name 2)

FROM (Table 1 Name, Table 2 Name)

WHERE (Table 1 Name. Common Field Name = Table 2 Name. Common Field Name)

AND (Selection Criteria)

Notice how similar this is to a select query, although the FROM statement must now contain two table names. In a join query, the WHERE statement is split into two parts. In the first part (right after WHERE), the relation between the two tables is defined by identifying the common fields between the tables. The second part of the statement (after AND) is where the selection criteria are defined.

The AND means that both parts of the statement must be true for the query to produce results (i.e., the two related fields must exist and the selection criteria must be valid). Figure 11.16 illustrates using a join query for the Student Information and Roster Master tables to produce a class roster for students.

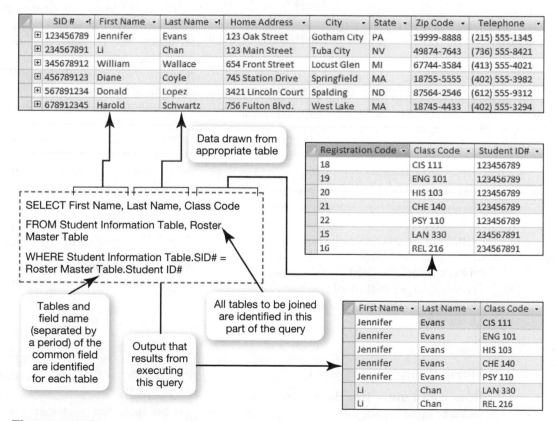

Figure 11.16

This join query will display a student roster for each student in the Student Information table. Notice that the WHERE statement creates the join by defining the common fields (in this case SID # and Student ID#) in each table.

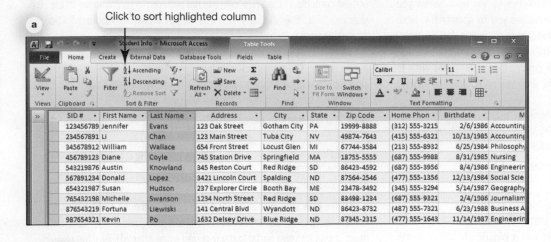

a

Click to sort highlighted column

SID #	First Name	Last Name	Address	City	State	Zip Code	Home Phon	Birthdate	M
123456789	Jennifer	Evans	123 Oak Street	Gotham City	PA	19999-8888	(312) 555-3215	2/6/1986	Accounting
234567891	Li	Chan	123 Main Street	Tuba City	NV	49874-7643	(415) 555-6321	10/13/1985	Accounting
345678912	William	Wallace	654 Front Street	Locust Glen	MI	67744-3584	(213) 555-8932	6/25/1984	Philosophy
456789123	Diane	Coyle	745 Station Drive	Springfield	MA	18755-5555	(687) 555-9988	8/31/1985	Nursing
543219876	Austin	Knowland	345 Reston Court	Red Ridge	SD	86423-4592	(687) 555-3956	8/4/1986	Engineerin
567891234	Donald	Lopez	3421 Lincoln Court	Spalding	ND	87564-2546	(477) 555-1356	12/13/1984	Social Scie
654321987	Susan	Hudson	237 Explorer Circle	Booth Bay	ME	23478-3492	(345) 555-3294	5/14/1987	Geography
765432198	Michelle	Swanson	1234 North Street	Red Ridge	SD	83498-1284	(685) 555-9321	2/4/1986	Journalism
876543219	Fortuna	Liewiski	141 Central Blvd	Wyandott	ND	86423-8732	(487) 555-7321	6/23/1988	Business A
987654321	Kevin	Po	1632 Delsey Drive	Blue Ridge	ND	87345-2315	(477) 555-1643	11/14/1987	Engineerin

b

SID #	First Name	Last Name	Address
234567891	Li	Chan	123 Main Street
456789123	Diane	Coyle	745 Station Drive
123456789	Jennifer	Evans	123 Oak Street
654321987	Susan	Hudson	237 Explorer Circle
543219876	Austin	Knowland	345 Reston Court
876543219	Fortuna	Liewiski	141 Central Blvd
567891234	Donald	Lopez	3421 Lincoln Court
987654321	Kevin	Po	1632 Delsey Drive
765432198	Michelle	Swanson	1234 North Street
345678912	William	Wallace	654 Front Street

Figure 11.17

(a) Shown is an unsorted table. Notice that the Last Name column is selected (highlighted) for sorting. Selecting the highlighted sorting option (Ascending) produces the sorted output (b) with the records sorted in ascending alphabetical order by last name.

The field properties table for the State field in Access is shown in Figure 11.14. The expression "Like??" tells Access to restrict entries for the State field to two alphabetic characters. Selecting "Yes" for the required attribute means that Access will not allow the field to be left blank. Error messages that display when validation checks fail can be customized by the user.

Viewing and Sorting Data

How can I view the data in a database? Displaying the tables on-screen and **browsing** through the data (viewing records) is an option with most databases. In many instances you'll only want to view the data, not display the entire table. For example, if you want to register for an

additional course for the current semester, the admissions clerk would browse the roster database to determine which courses you are already taking. However, browsing through a large database is time consuming unless the records are in an order that makes your task easy.

How can I reorder records in a database? You can easily **sort** a database into the order that you need. Sorting a database involves organizing it in a new fashion. Figure 11.17a shows an Access data table in which the records were input in no particular order. By highlighting a column (in this case Last Name) and then clicking the Sort Ascending button, the database displays the records in alphabetical order by last name, as shown in Figure 11.17b.

What if I want to find a particular piece of data in a database? Browsing records works for small databases, but if the amount of data you are managing is small, then you probably will just maintain it in a list anyway. To find data in a large database quickly and efficiently, you need to be able to request only the data you are seeking. Therefore, database management systems let you query the data to enable you to find what you're looking for.

Extracting or Querying Data

What is a query? A **query** is a question or inquiry. A **database query** is a question

SOUND BYTE

Creating an Access 2010 Database

In this Sound Byte, you'll learn how to create an Access database to catalog a collection of CDs and DVDs. The Sound Byte will take you through a systematic process that will result in a fully functional small database.

you ask the database so that it provides you with the records you wish to view. When you query a database, you instruct it to search for a particular piece of data, such as a student's grade point average (GPA). Queries also enable you to have the database select and display records that match certain criteria, such as all of the students who have GPAs of 3.2 or higher.

Is querying a database as simple as just asking the proper question? All modern DBMSs contain a **query language** that the software uses to retrieve and display records. A query language consists of its own vocabulary and sentence structure, which you use to frame the requests. Query languages are similar to full-blown programming languages but are usually much easier to learn. The most popular query language today is structured query language, or SQL (pronounced "sequel").

Do I have to learn a query language to develop queries for my database? Modern database systems provide wizards to guide you through the process of creating queries. Figure 11.18 shows an example of an Access wizard being used to create a query. Highlighting an available field and then clicking the arrow button adds the field to the selected fields list. Selected fields display in the query. Highlighting a field on the selected fields list and clicking the back arrow removes the field from the list. The wizard speeds up the process of creating queries, and also removes the need to learn a query language.

The Query Wizard can be found on the Create tab, in the Macros & Code group. Click Query Wizard and select Simple Query Wizard. When you use the Simple Query Wizard, you're actually using SQL commands without realizing it. The Simple Query Wizard takes the criteria you specify

and creates the appropriate SQL commands behind the scenes.

However, you may want to create your own SQL queries in Access, modify existing queries at the SQL language level, or view the SQL code that the wizard created. To do so, open a query and select SQL View from the View drop-down box on the Ribbon. This displays the SQL code that makes up the query. Figure 11.19 shows the SQL code that the query in Figure 11.18 created.

Outputting Data

How do I get data out of a database?
The most common form of output for any database is a viewable (or printable) electronic report. Businesses routinely summarize the data within their databases and compile summary data reports. For instance, at the end of each semester your school generates a grade report for you that shows the classes you took and the grades you received.

Figure 11.18

(a) The Simple Query Wizard displays all fields available in your table so that you can select the ones you need. (b) This information is displayed when you run the query defined in (a).

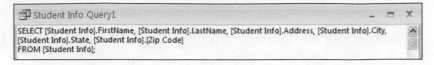

```
Student Info Query1                                    _  □  x
SELECT [Student Info].FirstName, [Student Info].LastName, [Student Info].Address, [Student Info].City,
[Student Info].State, [Student Info].[Zip Code]
FROM [Student Info];
```

Figure 11.19

The SQL View window shows the SQL code that the wizard created for the query in Figure 11.18. Although it is a relatively simple SELECT statement, it is much easier to create with the wizard.

Can I transfer data from a database to another software application? Database systems also can be used to **export** data to other applications. Exporting data involves putting it into an electronic file in a format that another application can understand. For example, the query shown in the wizard in Figure 11.18 may be used to generate a list of recipients for a form letter. In that case, the query output would be directed to a file that could be easily imported into Microsoft Word so that the data could be used in a mail merge process to generate letters.

In the next section, we look at the operation of relational databases and explore how

 ## iTunes Smart Playlists—They're Just Queries!

Ever built a smart playlist in iTunes? If so, you've created a database query. iTunes is just a relational database that manages your media. A smart playlist (see Figure 11.20) allows you to define multiple criteria to create a playlist. Say you want all songs in the genre Celtic, except for the artist Allison Barber and the album Scythian Live. When you define these criteria as "match all" in the smart playlist creation window, you will get a smart playlist that contains the music you want. You have built a query that tells iTunes exactly what music to extract from the database and include in your playlist.

Figure 11.20

The iTunes smart playlist creation box.

Relational Database Operations

As explained earlier, relational databases operate by organizing data into various tables based on logical groupings. For example, all student address and contact information (phone numbers, e-mail addresses, and so on) would be grouped into one table. Because not all of the data in a relational database is stored in the same table, a methodology must be implemented to link data between tables.

In relational databases, a link between tables that defines how the data is related is referred to as a **relationship**. To establish a relationship between two tables, both tables must have a common field (or column). Common fields contain the same data (such as student ID numbers), as shown in Figure 11.21. The fields do not have to have the same field name as long as they contain the same data.

Relationships in databases can take three forms: one-to-one, one-to-many, or many-to-many. A **one-to-one relationship** indicates that for each record in a table there is only one corresponding record in a related table. For example, a parking space can be occupied by only one car at a time, so a table that links assigned parking spaces to a table of faculty members (who are assigned parking spaces) would have a one-to-one relationship.

One-to-many relationships occur most frequently in relational databases. A **one-to-many relationship** is characterized by a record in one table (such as the student information table in Figure 11.21). There is only one instance of a student ID in the Student Information table, but there can be many instances of the same student ID in the Master Roster table. Students can register for many classes, but each registration record can relate to only one student.

A **many-to-many relationship** is characterized by records in one table being related to multiple records in a second table and vice versa. For instance, a table of students could be related to a table of student employers. The employers could employ many students, and students could work for more than one employer.

Normalization of Data

How do I decide which tables I need and what data to put in them? You create database tables (or files) for two reasons: to hold unique data about a person or thing and to describe unique events or transactions. In databases, the goal is to reduce data redundancy by recording data only once. This process is called **normalization** of the data. Yet the tables must still work well enough together to enable you to retrieve the data when you need it. Tables should be grouped using logical data that can be identified uniquely.

Let's look at an example. In Figure 11.22, the Class Registration—Fall table contains a great deal of data about individual students and their course registration. However, each table in a relational database should contain a related group of data on a single topic. There are two distinct topics in this list: student contact information and student registration information. Therefore, this list needs to be divided into two tables so that the distinct data (contact data and registration data) can be categorized appropriately. Data about each student is

SID #	First Name	Last Name	Home Address	City	State	Zip Code	Telephone
⊞ 234567891	Li	Chan	123 Main Street	Tuba City	NV	49874-7643	(736) 555-8421
⊞ 456789123	Diane	Coyle	745 Station Drive	Springfield	MA	18755-5555	(402) 555-3982
⊞ 123456789	Jennifer	Evans	123 Oak Street	Gotham City	PA	19999-8888	(215) 555-1345
⊞ 567891234	Donald	Lopez	3421 Lincoln Court	Spalding	ND	87564-2546	(612) 555-9312
⊞ 678912345	Harold	Schwartz	756 Fulton Blvd.	West Lake	MA	18745-4433	(402) 555-3294
⊞ 345678912	William	Wallace	654 Front Street	Locust Glen	MI	67744-3584	(413) 555-4021

Common field in each table

Registration Code	Class Code	Student ID#
18	CIS 111	123456789
19	ENG 101	123456789
20	HIS 103	123456789
21	CHE 140	123456789
22	PSY 110	123456789
15	LAN 330	234567891
16	REL 216	234567891
17	ENG 102	234567891
28	HIS 204	345678912
29	PEH 125	345678912
30	SOC 220	345678912
23	HIS 401	567891234
24	SOC 310	567891234
25	PSY 110	567891234
26	ENG 102	678912345
27	PSY 110	678912345

Figure 11.21

(a) The Student Information table and (b) the Roster Master table share the common field of student ID number. This allows a relationship to be established between the two tables.

duplicated in this table. Normalizing the data eliminates this duplication.

Class Registration - Fall

SID #	Last Name	First Name	Home Address	City	State	Zip Code	Class Code	Class Name	# of Credits
234567891	Chan	Li	123 Main Street	Tuba City	NV	49874-7643	LAN 330	Japanese 1	3
234567891	Chan	Li	123 Main Street	Tuba City	NV	49874-7643	REL 216	Early Buddhism	3
234567891	Chan	Li	123 Main Street	Tuba City	NV	49874-7643	ENG 102	English Comp 2	3
456789123	Coyle	Diane	745 Station Drive	Springfield	MA	18755-5555			
123456789	Evans	Jennifer	123 Oak Street	Gotham City	PA	19999-8888	CIS 111	Programming	3
123456789	Evans	Jennifer	123 Oak Street	Gotham City	PA	19999-8888	ENG 101	English Comp 1	3
123456789	Evans	Jennifer	123 Oak Street	Gotham City	PA	19999-8888	HIS 103	Western Civ	3
123456789	Evans	Jennifer	123 Oak Street	Gotham City	PA	19999-8888	CHE 140	Chemistry	4
123456789	Evans	Jennifer	124 Oak Street	Gotham City	PA	19999-8888	PSY 110	Intro to Psychology	3
567891234	Lopez	Donald	3421 Lincoln Court	Spalding	ND	87564-2546	HIS 401	16th Century Europe	3
567891234	Lopez	Donald	3421 Lincoln Court	Spalding	ND	87564-2546	SOC 310	Interpersonal Relationships	3
567891234	Lopez	Donald	3421 Lincoln Court	Spalding	ND	87564-2546	PSY 110	Intro to Psych	3
678912345	Schwartz	Harold	756 Fulton Blvd.	West Lake	MA	18745-4433	ENG 102	English Comp 2	3

Figure 11.22

The column headings in blue are related to student contact data, whereas the column headings in red relate to enrollment information. To construct an efficient database, these topics should be contained in separate tables.

Computers in Society: User-Populated Databases

Web 2.0 applications are mostly about enhancing communications and encouraging making it easy for users to create and disseminate their own content. So if you have a database that needs populating, why not seek help from the Web community to populate it, especially if it is designed as a resource for the masses.

The economy in the United States is largely a service-based economy. Businesses based in the U.S. tend to provide services to individuals or other businesses as the business climate has shifted away from manufacturing. Everyone needs haircuts and health care services, and many Americans love to eat out. But how do you find reliable service providers and good restaurants? Recommendations from friends and family are reliable, but what if no one in your circle of acquaintances knows of a good personal trainer or a great dentist? Why shouldn't the Internet be used to harness the power of millions of people's experiences to recommend reliable service providers? Two companies that have successfully plunged into this arena are Yelp and Angie's List.

Yelp (**yelp.com**) was conceived as the "yellow pages" for the 21st century. Yelp is free to use, and anyone can write a review of a business and post it to the site. The site has more than 11 million reviews of all types of businesses. Users can easily search the site, find service providers in their geographic area, and see what ratings (both good and bad) consumers gave them. Thinking about going to a Chinese restaurant in the Minneapolis area that you have never visited (see Figure 11.23)? A quick search on Yelp found 149 restaurants that fit this broad criteria. Surely you'll be able to find one that fits your budget and that other people enjoyed visiting.

However, Yelp.com is not without its critics. Because Yelp allows anonymous posting, some people are afraid that businesses may try to up their ratings by using shill reviewers. And Yelp actively markets to businesses to pay for placement of ads on their site that some users may mistake for unsponsored reviews. An alternative to Yelp that addresses these concerns is Angie's list.

Angie's List (**angieslist.com**) has the same basic premise as Yelp: to have individuals recommend businesses based on their experiences. However, whereas Yelp derives its revenue from advertising, Angie's List is a subscription service. Members pay a monthly fee to access the reviews on Angie's list. So what do you get for your fees that you don't get on Yelp? Angie's List does not permit anonymous reviews. This is a big benefit for business owners because it makes it easier to contact dissatisfied customers and try to resolve issues. Angie's list also has a verification process with reviewers to ensure that businesses do not report on themselves. And businesses do not pay to advertise on Angie's list; they make the list only when they are reviewed by a consumer.

Both Yelp and Angie's List are searchable databases just like the other examples in this chapter. But whereas most companies usually populate databases with data that they generate or collect themselves, these Web sites rely on users to create their content. The databases still need to be well designed to capture this content, and there needs to be processes in place to review the data entered for appropriateness. For instance, both Yelp and Angie's List would want to delete reviews that contained racist comments or hate speech, for example. By harnessing the power of large groups of users to populate a database, the database owners can reap the rewards of saving time, effort, and money.

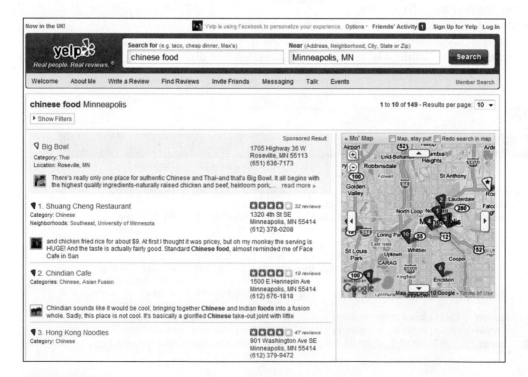

Figure 11.23

Yelp's database is populated with reviews created by users.

The Student Informa-tion table in Figure 11.24 organizes all of the stu-dent contact information found in Figure 11.22, into a separate table. Notice that the information for each student needs to be

SID#	First Name	Last Name	Home Address	City	State	Zip Code	Telephone
234567891	Li	Chan	123 Main Street	Tuba City	NV	49874-7643	(736) 555-8421
456789123	Diane	Coyle	745 Station Drive	Springfield	MA	18755-5555	(402) 555-3982
123456789	Jennifer	Evans	123 Oak Street	Gotham City	PA	19999-8888	(215) 555-1345
567891234	Donald	Lopez	3421 Lincoln Court	Spalding	ND	87564-2546	(612) 555-9312
678912345	Harold	Schwartz	756 Fulton Blvd.	West Lake	MA	18745-4433	(402) 555-3294
345678912	William	Wallace	654 Front Street	Locust Glen	MI	67744-3584	(413) 555-4021

shown only once, instead of multiple times (as in the list in the figure). The unique pri-mary key for this table is the student's ID number. Student information might be needed in a variety of instances and by a va-riety of departments, but it needs to reside only in this one database table, which many departments of the school can share.

Next, we could put the registration data found in Figure 11.22 for each student in a separate table, as shown in Figure 11.25. There is no need to repeat student name and address data in this table. Instead, each stu-dent can be identified by his or her student ID number. However, there are problems with this table. Each class name and class code has to be repeated for every student taking the course, Also, there is no unique field that can be used as a primary key for this table. Student ID # cannot be used because it will be entered on multiple records when a student enrolls in more than one course. This presents another opportunity to normalize the data further.

What can be done to fix the table in Figure 11.25? In Figure 11.25, we have identified more data that should be grouped logically into another separate table: class code and class name. Therefore, we should create another table for just this information. This enables us to avoid repeating class names and codes. Figure 11.26 shows the Course master table. Note that the class code is unique for every course and acts as a primary key in this table.

To solve the other problems with the table in Figure 11.25, we need a way to identify uniquely each student registered for a spe-cific course. This can be solved by creating a course registration number that will be unique and assigned by the database as records are entered. Figure 11.27 shows the resulting Roster master table. Only three fields are needed: the registration code num-ber (the unique primary key), the class code,

and the student's ID number. This approach greatly minimizes duplicate data.

How do I get the data in the tables to work together now that it is split up? The entire premise behind relational databases is that relationships are estab-lished among the tables to allow the data to be shared. As noted earlier, to establish a relationship between two tables, the

Figure 11.24

Student contact data is grouped in the Student Information table and needs to be entered only once for each student. The primary key for each record is a unique student ID number.

Student ID #	Class Code	Class Name	# Of Credits
123456789	PSY 110	Intro to Psychology	3
123456789	CIS 111	Programming	3
123456789	ENG 101	English Comp 1	3
123456789	HIS 103	Western Civ	3
123456789	CHE 140	Chemistry	4
234567891	LAN 330	Japanese 1	3
234567891	ENG 102	English Comp 2	3
234567891	REL 216	Early Buddhism	3
345678912	SOC 220	The Art of Negotiation	2
345678912	HIS 204	Scottish History	3
345678912	PEH 125	Fencing 1	3
567891234	PSY 110	Intro to Psychology	3

Student ID# not unique

Duplicate data

Figure 11.25

Although it contains related data (registration information), this table still contains a great deal of duplicate data and no usable primary key.

Class Code	Class Name	Credits
CHE 140	Chemistry	4
CIS 111	Programming	3
ENG 101	English Comp 1	3
ENG 102	English Comp 2	3
HIS 103	Western Civ	3
HIS 204	Scottish History	3
HIS 401	16th Century Europe	3
LAN 330	Japanese 1	3
PEH 125	Fencing 1	3
PSY 110	Intro to Psychology	3
REL 216	Early Buddhism	3
SOC 220	The Art of Negotiation	2
SOC 310	Interpersonal Relationships	3

Figure 11.26

Related information about courses (class code, class name, and the credits for the class) is grouped logically in one table. The unique class code is the primary key.

tables must have a common field (column). This usually involves the primary keys of a table.

For instance, to track registrations by student in the Roster master table in Figure 11.27, the student ID number is the logical piece of data to use. The student ID number is the primary key in the Student Information table in Figure 11.24; however, in the Roster master table, the student ID number is called a **foreign key**—the primary key of another table that is included for purposes of establishing relationships with that other table. Figure 11.28 shows the relationships that exist among the Course Master, Roster Master, and Student Information tables. Join lines indicate established relationships between tables. Tables must contain fields with common data; this establishes relationships between them. Notice that foreign keys in related tables do not have to have the same field names as the primary keys in the other table; they merely have to contain the same data. Relationships among tables can be established whenever you need them.

Because relationships are vital to the operation of the database, it is important to ensure that there are no inconsistencies in the data entered in the common fields of two tables. Each foreign key (Student ID# in the Roster master table in Figure 11.27) entered into a table must be a valid primary key from the related table (SID# from the Student Information table in Figure 11.24).

For instance, if 392135684 is not a valid student ID number for any student listed in the Student Information table, then it should not be entered into the Roster master table. Each entry in the Roster master table must correspond to a student (linked by his or her SID#) in the Student Information table. If this requirement is not applied to foreign keys, then a relationship cannot be established between tables.

How do I ensure that a foreign key field contains a valid primary key from the related table? To apply this restraint, when defining a relationship in a database, you have the option of enforcing referential integrity for that relationship. **Referential integrity** means that for each value in the foreign key of one table, there is a corresponding value in the primary key of the related table.

For instance, if you attempt to enter a record in the Roster Master table with an SID# of 156784522 and referential integrity is being enforced, the database checks to ensure that a record with SID# 156784522 exists in the Student Information table. If the corresponding record does not exist, then an error message displays. Establishing referential integrity between two tables helps prevent inconsistent data from being entered.

Who manages the data in a database? All of the data that is collected in databases needs to be stored and managed. Database administrators (DBAs) are the IT professionals responsible for designing, constructing, and maintaining databases. They review and manage data on an ongoing basis to ensure data is flowing smoothly in and out of the database. Figure 11.29 shows a view of the MySQL Enterprise Dashboard screen, a tool that is used primarily by DBAs when reviewing the performance of a database. Database administrators can monitor table usage and CPU utilization to help determine if database performance is acceptable.

Registration Code	Class Code	Student ID#
18	CIS 111	123456789
19	ENG 101	123456789
20	HIS 103	123456789
21	CHE 140	123456789
22	PSY 110	123456789
15	LAN 330	234567891
16	REL 216	234567891
17	ENG 102	234567891
28	HIS 204	345678912
29	PEH 125	345678912
30	SOC 220	345678912
23	HIS 401	567891234

Figure 11.27

The Roster master table shows only pertinent data related to a student's registration.

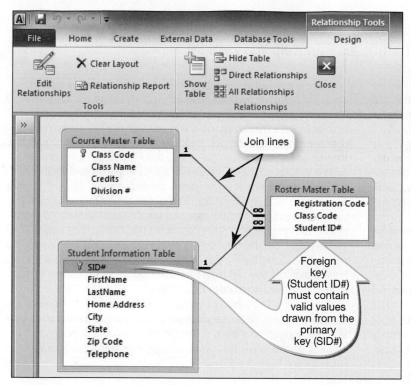

Figure 11.28

The Relationships screen in Microsoft Access visually represents the relationships established between tables.

In the next section, we explore the types of systems where databases are typically used today.

Data Storage

At the simplest level, data is stored in a single database on a database server, and you retrieve the data as needed. This works fine for small databases and simple enterprises where all of the data you are interested in is in a single database. Problems can arise, however, when the data you need is in multiple places. Large storage repositories called *data warehouses* and *data marts* help solve this problem.

Data Warehouses

What is a data warehouse? A **data warehouse** is a large-scale electronic repository of data that contains and organizes all the data related to an organization in one place. Individual databases contain a wealth of information, but each database's information usually pertains to one topic.

For instance, the order database at **Amazon.com** contains such information about book orders as the buyer's name, address, and payment information, and the book's name. However, the order database does not contain information on inventory levels of books, nor does it list suppliers from which out-of-stock books can be obtained. Data warehouses, therefore, consolidate information from disparate sources to present an enterprise-wide view of business operations.

Is data in a data warehouse organized the same way as in a normal database? Data in the data warehouse is organized by subject. Most databases focus on one specific operational aspect of business operations. For example, insurance companies sell many types of insurance, such as life, automobile, and homeowners' insurance. Different divisions of the insurance company are responsible for each type of insurance and track the policies they

Figure 11.29

The Enterprise Dashboard in MySQL helps DBAs review database performance.

Emerging Technologies: Can Your Business Partner Deliver the Goods? Enhanced Databases Can Help You Decide!

You watch a weather forecast on television to gain information about the weather. The weather forecaster tells you that it will be sunny. When you get out of your car to go to class, rain is pouring down. Yes, you gathered relevant information. Too bad that it was inaccurate information!

Data and information stored in databases can be just as unhelpful as an inaccurate weather forecast if the information is incorrect or distorted. Although a poor weather report is probably nothing more to you than an inconvenience, accurate data in business is mission critical. Businesses rely on information in databases every day just to accomplish even routine tasks.

Developed to respond to business needs, **Alibaba.com** is one of the world's largest online business-to-business databases. **Alibaba.com** specializes in matching suppliers with buyers for all types of manufactured goods and raw materials. With the global nature of business, databases such as those maintained by **Alibaba.com** are essential tools that assist businesspeople in managing their global business. Figure 11.30 shows a search for cotton fabric supplies in mainland China. You could also google Chinese fabric manufacturers, and would probably find many leads. The information in the leads available online may be factually correct, but how do you determine how reliable these suppliers are?

There is a wealth of information online, provided by various sources, which you can use to evaluate potential suppliers before you use them. However, it can be difficult for an individual to tell if the data has been altered or falsified. **Panjiva.com** is a Web site that also has a searchable database of suppliers. However, the founders of Panjiva decided to make their database different. They gather data that indicates reliability of suppliers from sources such as government agencies, independent certification companies, nonprofit organizations, and customers.

Using the reliability information, Panjiva then creates ratings for companies (on a scale of 1 to 100) based on specific business performance criteria such as number of shipments to the U.S. market, their environmental record, and their capability to deliver shipments within promised time frames. Subscribers to Panjiva's database (companies such as The Home Depot) can then feel more comfortable about doing business with suppliers that Panjiva has rated for reliability.

Databases with enhanced information are the wave of the future in the business world. So, before you make that next crucial business decision, ask yourself how much you really know about your prospective business partner. If you don't know enough, then find a database that can make you feel more at ease.

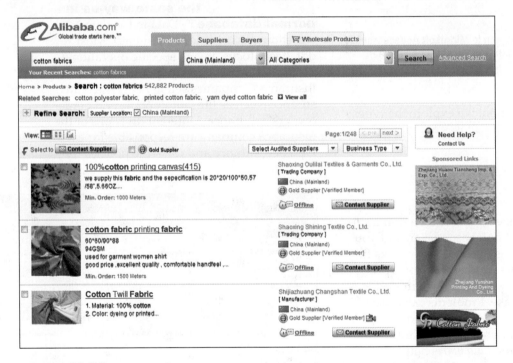

Figure 11.30

Using the database on **Alibaba.com**, a search for cotton fabric suppliers in China results in more than 200 pages of links to vendors selling some type of cotton cloth.

sell in different databases (one for automobile insurance policy sales and one for life insurance policy sales, for example), as shown in Figure 11.31.

These databases capture specific information about each type of policy. The Automobile Policy Sales database captures information about driving accident history, car model, and the age and gender of the drivers because this information is pertinent to the pricing of car insurance policies. The Life Insurance Policy Sales database captures information about the age and gender of the policyholder and notes whether he or she smokes, but it does not include details about cars or driving records.

However, data on total policies sold (and the resulting revenue generated) is critical to the management of the insurance company no matter what type of policy is involved. Therefore, an insurance company's data warehouse would have a subject called Policy Sales Subject (see Figure 11.28) that would contain information about *all* policies sold throughout the company. The Policy Sales Subject is a database that contains information from the other databases the company maintains. However, all data in the Policy Sales Subject database is specifically related to policy sales.

From the Policy Sales Subject database, it is easy for managers to produce comprehensive reports such as the Total Policy Sales Report, as shown in Figure 11.31, which can contain information pertaining to all policy sales.

Are data warehouses much larger than conventional databases? Data warehouses, like conventional warehouses, are vast repositories of information. The data contained within them is not operational in nature, but rather archival. Data warehouse data is **time-variant data**, meaning it doesn't all pertain to one period in time.

The warehouse contains current values, such as amounts due from customers, as well as historical data. If you want to examine the buying habits of a certain type of customer, then you need data about both current and prior purchases. Having time-variant data in the warehouse enables you to analyze the past, examine the present in light of historical data, and make projections about the future.

Populating Data Warehouses

How are data warehouses populated with data? Source data for data warehouses can come from three places:

- Internal sources (such as company databases).
- External sources (suppliers, vendors, and so on).
- Customers or visitors to a company's Web site.

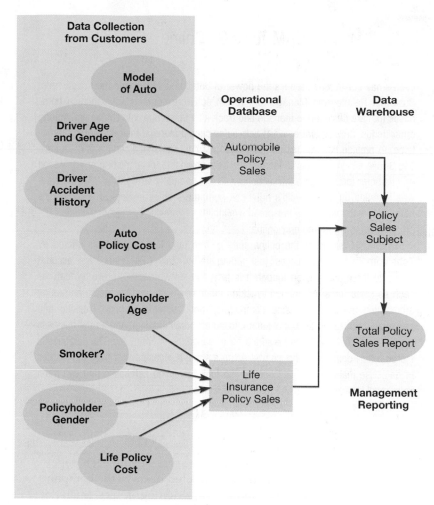

Internal data sources are obvious. Sales, billing, inventory, and customer databases all provide a wealth of information. However, internal information is not contained exclusively in databases. Spreadsheets and other ad hoc analysis tools may contain data that needs to be loaded into the warehouse.

External data sources include vendors and suppliers that often provide data regarding product specifications, shipment methods and dates, electronic billing information, and so on. In addition, a virtual wealth of customer (or potential customer) information is available by monitoring the clickstream of the company Web site.

What is a clickstream, and why is it important? Companies can use software on their Web sites to capture information about each click that users make as they navigate through the site. This information is referred to as **clickstream data**. Monitoring the clickstream helps managers assess the effectiveness of a Web site. Using clickstream data capture tools, a company can determine which pages users visit most

Figure 11.31

Data from individual databases is drawn together under appropriate subject headings in a data warehouse. Managers can then produce comprehensive reports that would be impossible to create from the individual databases.

nature and complexity of the source data determine the complexity of the data staging process.

Once the data is stored in the data warehouse, how can it be extracted and used? Managers can query the data warehouse in much the same way you would query an Access database. However, because there is more data in the warehouse, much more flexible tools are needed to perform such queries. Online analytical processing (OLAP) software provides standardized tools for viewing and manipulating data in a data warehouse. The key feature of OLAP tools is that they enable flexible views of the data, which the software user can easily change.

Data Marts

Is finding the right data in a huge data warehouse difficult? Looking for the data you need in a data warehouse can be daunting when there are terabytes of data. Therefore, small slices of the data warehouse, each called a **data mart** are often created. Whereas data warehouses have an enterprise-wide depth, the information in data marts pertains to a single department.

For instance, if you work in the sales department, you need accurate sales-related information at your fingertips—and you do not want to wade through customer service data, accounts payable data, and product shipping data to get it. Therefore, a data mart that contains information relevant only to the sales department can be created to make the task of finding this data easier. An overview of the data-warehousing process is illustrated in Figure 11.32. Data staging is vital because different data must be extracted and then reformatted to fit the data structure defined in the data warehouse's DBMS. Data can be extracted using powerful OLAP query tools, or it can be stored in specialized data marts for use by specific employee groups.

often, how long users stay on each page, which sites directed users to the company site, and the user demographics. Such data can provide valuable clues to what a company needs to improve on its site to stimulate sales.

Data Staging

Does all source data fit into the warehouse? No two source databases are the same. Although two databases might contain similar information (such as customer names and addresses), the format of the data is most likely different in each database. Therefore, source data must be "staged" before entering the data warehouse. **Data staging** consists of three steps:

1. Extraction of the data from source databases
2. Transformation (reformatting) of the data
3. Storage of the data in the warehouse

Many different software programs and procedures may have to be created to extract the data from varied sources and to reformat it for storage in the data warehouse. The

Managing Data: Information Systems

Making intelligent decisions about developing new products, creating marketing strategies, and buying raw materials requires timely, accurate information. An

Figure 11.32

An overview of the data warehouse process.

Source Data (Internal & External Sources)
- Supplier Database
- Customer Order Database
- Billing Database

Web Users — Clickstream Data

Data Extraction

Data Extraction

Data Staging — Data Reformatting

Reformatted Data Stored

Data Warehouse DBMS

OLAP Query

Information Systems (To Extract Data)

Data Marts
- Sales Department Data Mart
- Customer Service Data Mart

---

information system is a software-based solution used to gather and analyze information. A system that delivers up-to-the-minute sales data on books to the computer of **Amazon.com**'s president is one example of an information system. Databases, data warehouses, and data marts are integral parts of information systems because they store the information that makes information systems functional.

All information systems perform similar functions, including acquiring data, processing that data into information, storing the data, and providing the user with a number of output options with which to make the information meaningful and useful (see Figure 11.33). Most information systems fall into one of five categories: (1) office support systems, (2) transaction-processing systems, (3) management information systems, (4) decision support systems, and (5) enterprise resource planning (ERP) systems. Each type of system almost always involves the use of one or more databases.

Office Support Systems

What does an office support system accomplish?
An **office support system (OSS)** is designed to improve

Data Acquisition
- Tele-Salesperson
- Supplier Shipments
- Online Shopping

Data Processing Procedures

Information Storage

Information Retrieval and Dissemination

Output Methods
- Online Data Retrieval
- Reports

Figure 11.33

All information systems perform similar functions, including acquiring data, processing that data into information, storing the data, and providing the user with a number of output options with which to make the information meaningful and useful.

communications and assist employees in accomplishing their daily tasks. Microsoft Office is an example of an OSS because it assists employees with routine tasks such as maintaining an employee phone list in Excel, designing a sales presentation in PowerPoint, and writing customer letters using Word.

Modern OSSs include software tools with which you are probably familiar, including e-mail, word processing, spreadsheet, database, and presentation programs. Office support systems have their roots in manual, paper-based systems that were developed before computers. After all, maintaining a company phone listing was necessary long before computers were invented. A paper listing of employee phone extensions typed by an administrative assistant is an example of an early OSS. A modern OSS might publish this directory on the company's intranet (its internal network).

Transaction-Processing Systems

What is a transaction-processing system?
A transaction-processing system (TPS) keeps track of everyday business activities. For example, at your college, transactions that occur frequently include registering students for classes, accepting tuition payments, mailing advertisements, and printing course catalogs. Your college has TPSs in place to track these types of activities.

When computers were introduced to the business world, they often were first put to work hosting TPSs. Computers were much faster at processing large chunks of data than previous manual systems had been. Imagine having clerks type up tuition invoices for each student at a 10,000–student university. Obviously, a computer can print invoices much quicker from a database.

How do transactions enter a TPS?
Transactions can be entered manually or electronically. When you call a company and order a sweater, for example, the call taker enters your data into a TPS. When you purchase gasoline at a pay-at-the-pump terminal, the pump captures your credit card data and transmits it to a TPS, which automatically records a sale (gallons of gasoline and dollar value). Transactions are processed either in batches or in real time. Various departments in an organization then access the TPSs to extract the information they need to process additional transactions, as shown in Figure 11.34.

What is batch processing?
Batch processing means that transaction data is accumulated until a certain point is reached, and then several transactions are processed all at once. Batch processing is appropriate for activities that are not time sensitive, such as developing a mailing list to mail out the new course catalogs that students have requested. The college could print a mailing label each time someone requests a catalog, but it is more efficient to batch the requests and process them all at once when the catalogs are ready to be addressed.

How does real-time processing work?
For most activities, processing and recording transactions in a TPS occur in real time. Real-time processing means that the database is queried and updated while the transaction is taking place. For instance, when you register for classes, the registration clerk checks to make sure seats are still

Figure 11.34

TPSs help capture and track critical business information needed for successful completion of business transactions such as selling merchandise over the telephone.

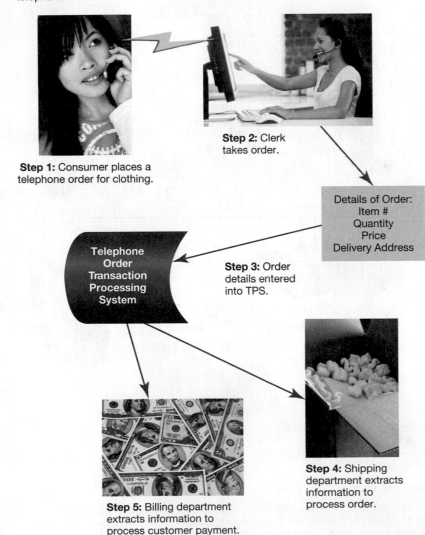

Step 1: Consumer places a telephone order for clothing.

Step 2: Clerk takes order.

Details of Order:
Item #
Quantity
Price
Delivery Address

Telephone Order Transaction Processing System

Step 3: Order details entered into TPS.

Step 4: Shipping department extracts information to process order.

Step 5: Billing department extracts information to process customer payment.

Daily Enrollment Report

Class Code	Class Name	Student ID#
CHE 140	Chemistry	123456789
CIS 111	Programming	123456789
ENG 101	English Comp 1	123456789
ENG 102	English Comp 2	234567891
ENG 102	English Comp 2	678912345
HIS 103	Western Civ	123456789
HIS 204	Scottish History	345678912
HIS 401	16th Century Europe	567891234

Enrollment Summary Report

Division Name	Total Credits
Chemistv	4
Computer Information Systems	5
English	9
History	9
Languages	3
Physical Education	3
Psychology	9
Religion	3
Sociology	3
Grand Total Credits	48

Class Sections Fully Enrolled Fall Semester

Class Code	Class Name
CHE 140	Inorganic Chemistry
ENG 101	English Comp 1
SOC 310	Interpersonal Relationships

Figure 11.35

The three types of management information system reports are (a) detail report, (b) summary report, and (c) exception report.

available for the classes you want and immediately records your registration in the class. This **online transaction processing (OLTP)** ensures that the data in the TPS is as current as possible.

Management Information Systems

What is a management information system? A **management information system (MIS)** provides timely and accurate information that enables managers to make critical business decisions. MISs were a direct outgrowth of TPSs. Managers quickly realized that the data contained in TPSs could be an extremely powerful tool only if the information could be organized and output in a useful form. Today's MISs are often built in as a feature of TPSs.

What does an MIS provide that a TPS does not? The original TPSs were usually designed to output detail reports. A **detail report** provides a list of the transactions that occurred during a certain time period. For example, during registration periods at your school, the registrar might receive a detail report that lists the students who registered for classes each day. Figure 11.35a shows an example of a detail report on daily enrollment.

Going beyond the detail reports provided by TPSs, MISs provide summary reports and exception reports. A **summary report** provides a consolidated picture of detailed data. These reports usually include some calculation (totals) or visual displays of information (such as charts and graphs). Figure 11.35b shows an example of a summary report displaying total daily enrollment.

An **exception report** shows conditions that are unusual or that need attention by users of the system. The registrar at your college may get an exception report when all sections of a course are full, indicating that it may be time to schedule additional sections. Figure 11.35c shows an example of such an exception report.

Decision Support Systems

What is a decision support system? A **decision support system (DSS)** is designed to help managers develop

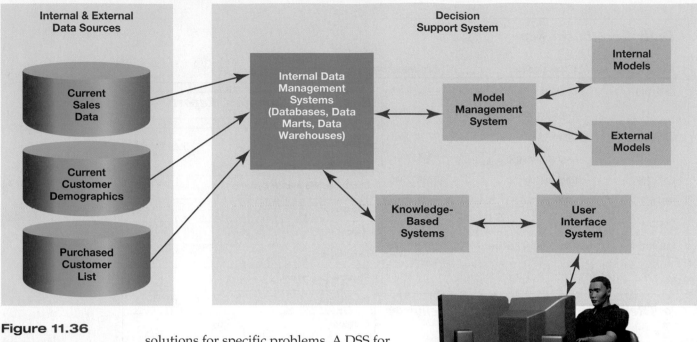

Figure 11.36

Major components of a DSS. Through the user interface, models are analyzed and manipulated to provide information on which management decisions are based.

solutions for specific problems. A DSS for a marketing department might provide statistical information on customer attributes (such as income levels, buying patterns, and so on) that would assist managers in making decisions regarding advertising strategy. A DSS not only uses data from databases and data warehouses, but also enables users to add their own insights and experiences and apply them to the solution.

What does a decision support system look like? Database management systems, while playing an integral part of a DSS, are supplemented by additional software systems in a DSS. In a DSS, the user interface provides the means of interaction between the user and the system. An effective user interface must be easy to learn. The other major components of a DSS are internal and external data sources, model management systems, and knowledge-based systems. As shown in Figure 11.36, all of these systems work together to provide the user of the DSS with a broad base of information on which to base decisions.

Internal and External Data Sources

What are internal and external data sources for decision support systems? Data can be fed into the DSS from a variety of sources. Internal data sources are maintained by the same company that operates the DSS. For example, internal TPSs can provide a wealth of statistical

data about customers, ordering patterns, inventory levels, and so on. An **external data source** is any source not owned by the company that owns the DSS, such as customer demographic data purchased from third parties, mailing lists, or statistics compiled by the federal government. Internal and external data sources provide a stream of data that is integrated into the DSS for analysis.

Model Management Systems

What function does a model management system perform? A **model management system** is software that assists in building management models in DSSs. A management model is an analysis tool that, through the use of internal and external data, provides a view of a particular business situation for the purposes of decision making. Models can be built to describe any business situation, such as the classroom space requirements for next semester or a listing of alternative satellite campus locations.

Internal models (such as a spreadsheet that shows current classroom use on a college campus) are developed inside an organization. External models (such as statistics about populations of students at two-year colleges in the United States) are purchased from third parties. Model management systems typically contain financial and statistical analysis tools used to analyze the data provided by models or to create additional models.

Knowledge-Based Systems

What is a knowledge-based system, and how is it used in decision support systems? A knowledge-based system provides additional intelligence that supplements the user's own intellect and makes the DSS more effective. It can be an **expert system** that tries to replicate the decision-making processes of human experts to solve specific problems. For example, an expert system might be designed to take the place of a physician in a remote location such as a scientific base in Antarctica. A physician expert system would ask the patient about symptoms just as a live physician would, and the system would make a diagnosis based on the algorithms programmed into it.

Another type of knowledge-based system is a **natural language processing (NLP) system**. NLP systems enable users to communicate with computer systems using a natural spoken or written language instead of using a computer programming language. Individuals with disabilities who cannot use a keyboard benefit greatly from NLP systems because they can just speak to the computer and have it understand what they are saying without using specific computer commands. Using an NLP system can simplify the user interface, making it much more efficient and user friendly. The speech-recognition feature of Microsoft Windows is a type of NLP system.

All knowledge-based systems fall under the science of artificial intelligence. **Artificial intelligence (AI)** is the branch of computer science that deals with the attempt to create computers that think like humans. To date, no computers have been constructed that can replicate the thinking

> **"All knowledge-based systems fall under the science of artificial intelligence."**

patterns of a human brain because scientists still do not fully understand how humans store and integrate knowledge and experiences to form human intelligence.

How does a knowledge-based system help in the decision-making process? Databases and the models provided by model management systems tend to be extremely analytical and mathematical in nature. If we relied solely on databases and models to make decisions, then the answers would be derived with a "yes or no" mentality, allowing no room for human thought. Fortunately, human users are involved in these types of systems, providing an opportunity to inject human judgment and experience into the decision-making process.

The knowledge-based system also provides an opportunity to introduce experience into the mix. Knowledge-based systems support the concept of fuzzy logic. Normal logic is highly rigid: If "x" happens, then "y" will happen. **Fuzzy logic** enables the interjection of experiential learning into the equation by considering probabilities. Whereas an algorithm in a database has to be specific, an algorithm in a knowledge-based system could state that if "x" happens, 70 percent of the time "y" will happen.

For instance, managers at **Amazon.com** would find it extremely helpful if their DSSs informed them that 40 percent of customers who bought a certain book also bought the sequel. This could suggest that designing a discount program for sequels bought with the original book might spur sales. Fuzzy logic enables a system to be more flexible and to consider a wider range of possibilities than would conventional algorithmic thinking.

Enterprise Resource Planning Systems

What is an enterprise? An enterprise is any business entity, large or small. It could be the pizza shop on the corner or a Fortune 500 manufacturer of sports apparel. All businesses have data and information to

As databases have become commonplace, an ever-increasing amount of information about you and your habits has gone into various databases. Every time you purchase something with a credit card, there is a record of that transaction, and both the merchant from whom you purchased the item and the credit card company have information about your buying habits (see Figure 11.37).

Have you used a toll service that allows you to pay your tolls electronically by just driving through a lane without stopping? Toll records are routinely subpoenaed in court cases. Toll records were used in an Illinois court by a husband in a divorce case to prove his wife was rarely home and therefore unfit for custody of their son. All banking transactions are handled by computers (and hence databases) in the United States, and there is a high probability that your employer is electronically transferring your pay to your bank by direct deposit. If you engage in online banking and bill paying, yet another electronic trail of your financial life is being generated in databases.

Do you think you can avoid scrutiny by paying cash? Not if you are a member of a frequent shopper "club" (a popular promotion used by supermarkets and drug stores) and provide the checkout clerk with your personal information in exchange for coupons or a few dollars off your purchases. Remember, you never can be sure of how this data might be used. In October 2004, a firefighter was arrested after his supermarket purchase records revealed he had purchased the same type of fire starters used in an arson case. After three months, the charges were dropped when another person pleaded guilty to committing the arson.

Financial information isn't the only sensitive information that is tracked. The majority of physicians and hospitals in the United States track medical records in electronic databases. Your entire prescription history (and hence hints about your medical history) is in a database at the local pharmacy. Have you applied for insurance lately? Your doctor was probably able to provide (with your permission, of course) your entire medical history to the insurance company with a few clicks of a mouse. All of the data that exists in the world around us should give us pause, and we need to stop and consider the ethical implications of the electronic society we live in.

Figure 11.37

Workmen disassembling a house reveal the contents hidden inside. This is a metaphor for the erosion of our privacy rights. If our personal information is in multiple databases and viewable by many people, is the information still private?

Data Convergence—The Perfect Storm of Privacy Invasion?

Discrete pieces of data, such as that you filled your gas tank last Thursday or bought a copy of *War and Peace* last month, don't mean much in and of themselves. However, with so much data in electronic form, it is getting much easier to combine data from various data sources and build a powerful profile of an individual to which manage, and large, complex organizations can benefit from managing that information with a central piece of software.

What does an enterprise resource planning system do? An **enterprise resource planning (ERP) system** is a broad-based software system that integrates multiple data sources and ties together the various processes of an enterprise to enable information to flow more smoothly. ERP systems use a common database to store and integrate information. This enables the information to be used across multiple areas of an enterprise.

For instance, human resource functions (such as the management of hiring, firing, promotions, and benefits) and accounting functions (such as payroll) are often the first processes integrated into an ERP system. Historically, human resource records and accounting records were kept in separate databases, but having the information reside in one database makes the management and paying of employees more streamlined. If manufacturing operations were then integrated into the ERP system, the data that was already in place regarding the employees and payroll could be easily used for determining data-mining techniques can be applied. For instance, suppose a marketing company purchased data about your buying habits from your credit card company and the supermarket, pharmacy, and bookstore where you shop. In addition, the marketing company purchased information about you from the company where you bought your lawn mower (it got that from your credit card information). What information did the lawn mower company have about you? The personal information you gave when you filled out your warranty card online (household income, age, whether you rent or own your home, and so on)! By combining all of this information into one database, the marketing company is able to build an extremely detailed picture of who you are.

For example, based on your purchases at the pharmacy, a marketing company might determine that there are both males (shaving gel) and females (cosmetics) living in your home. It also might notice that you have been buying pregnancy test kits once a month for 18 months and conclude you are trying to have a baby (and not having much luck, by the way). By your address and the car you drive (you had charges on your credit card at a Lexus dealer), the company estimated that you have a household income of more than $100,000 per year, making you affluent. It also noticed you shop at many stores that feature outdoor apparel and sports equipment and recently bought a mountain bike, so the company has concluded that you have an active lifestyle. Based on this analysis, you start receiving mail and phone solicitations for canoes, baby clothing, fertility treatments, and plasma TVs. Just because this type of analysis can be done, should we be doing it? Do you want people marketing to you based on sensitive personal information? Where does marketing stop and invasion of privacy begin?

What Can You Do?

Providing information and having it recorded in databases are part of our way of life now. Because refusing to give information out at all is bound to be impractical, you should ask the following questions related to data you are providing:

- **For what purpose is the data being gathered?** When the clerk at the electronics superstore asks for your zip code, ask why she wants it. (It is probably for some marketing purpose).
- **Are the reasons for gathering the data legitimate or important to you?** When you purchase a DVD, is asking for your zip code really a legitimate request? However, to validate the warranty on a

large-screen TV, you may need to give a clerk your address and zip code. Similarly, disclosing medical information to key people (such as your pharmacist) may be important to receiving good care and therefore is extremely important to you. If you don't see the advantage, then ask more questions or don't reveal the information.

- **How will the information gathered be protected once it has been obtained?** Ask about data protection policies before you give information. Most Web sites provide access to their data protection policies—readily available through clickable links or pop-up boxes—when they ask for information. If an organization doesn't have a data protection policy, then be wary of giving them sensitive information unless there is a compelling advantage to doing so (such as receiving good medical care). Data protection doesn't just refer to keeping data secure. It also means restricting access to the data to employees of the organization that need to use that data. A shipping clerk might need to see your address, for example, but doesn't need to see your credit card information.
- **Will the information collected be used for purposes other than the purpose for which it was originally collected?** This might be covered in a data protection policy. If it isn't, then ask about it. Will your information be sold to other companies? Will it be used for marketing other products to you?
- **Could the information asked for be used for identity theft?** Identity thieves usually need your Social Security number and your birth date to open credit card accounts in your name. Be especially wary when asked for this information, and make sure there is a legitimate need for this information. Most organizations and businesses are shying away from using Social Security numbers to track customers because of the risk of identity theft.
- **Are organizations that already have your data safeguarding it?** Don't just consider new requests for information. Think about organizations, such as banks, that already have your information and monitor their performance. Have they been in the news lately because of a major data breach (inadvertently exposing information to inappropriate or unauthorized individuals)? You might want to consider switching institutions if yours has a poor record of data security.

Think carefully before providing information and be vigilant about monitoring your data when you can. It may make the difference between invasion of privacy and peace of mind.

---

the cost of running an assembly line (because the workers on the assembly line get paid) or for scheduling workers to run the assembly line. The objective of ERP systems is to accumulate all information relevant to running a business in a central location and make it readily available to whoever needs that information to make decisions.

Almost all Fortune 500 companies have implemented ERP systems, and many medium-sized companies are implementing them also. Although the corner pizza shop probably does not need an ERP system, it would be difficult to coordinate the

activities of a multinational corporation without one.

Data Mining

Just because you have captured data in an organized fashion and have stored it in a format that seems to make sense doesn't mean that an analysis of the data will automatically reveal everything you need to know. Trends can sometimes be hard to spot if the data is not organized or analyzed in a particular way. To make data work

ACTIVE HELP-DESK

Data Warehouses, Data Marts, and Information Systems

In this Active Helpdesk call, you'll play the role of a helpdesk staffer, fielding calls about data warehouses, data marts, and information systems.

harder, companies employ data-mining techniques.

Data mining is the process by which great amounts of data are analyzed and investigated. The objective is to spot significant patterns or trends within the data that would otherwise not be obvious. For instance, through mining student enrollment data, a school may discover that 40 percent of new nursing degree students are Latino.

Why do businesses mine their data? The main reason businesses mine data is to understand their customers better. If a company can better understand the types of customers who buy its products and can learn what motivates their customers to do so, it can market effectively by concentrating its efforts on the populations that are most likely to buy.

How do businesses mine their data? Data mining enables managers to sift through data in several ways. Each method produces different information that managers can then base their decisions on. Managers make their data meaningful through the following activities:

> **"Often, the purpose of data mining is to describe data so that managers can visualize it."**

- **Classification:** To analyze data, managers need to classify it. Therefore, before mining, managers define data classes that they think will be helpful in spotting trends. They then apply these class definitions to all unclassified data to prepare it for analysis. For example, "good credit risk" and "bad credit risk" are two data classes that managers could establish to determine whether to grant mortgages to applicants. Managers would then identify factors (such as credit history and yearly income) that they could use to classify applicants as good or bad risks.

- **Estimation:** When managers classify data, the record either fits the classification criteria or it doesn't. Estimation enables managers to assign a value to data based on some criterion. For example, assume a bank wants to send out credit card offers to people who are likely to be granted a credit card. The bank may run the customers' data through a program that assigns them a score based on where they live, their household income, and their average bank balance. This provides managers with an estimate of the most likely credit card prospects so that they can include them in the mailing.

- **Affinity grouping (or association rules):** When mining data, managers also can determine which data goes together. In other words, they can apply affinity grouping or association rules to the data. For example, suppose analysis of a sales database indicates that two items are bought together 70 percent of the time. Based on this data, managers might decide that these items should be pictured on the same page in their next mail-order catalog.

- **Clustering:** Clustering involves organizing data into similar subgroups, or clusters. It is different from classification in that there are no predefined classes. The data-mining software makes the decision about what to group, and it is up to managers to determine whether the clusters are meaningful. For example, the data-mining software may identify clusters of customers with similar buying patterns. Further analysis of the clusters may reveal that certain socioeconomic groups have similar buying patterns.

- **Description and visualization:** Often, the purpose of data mining is merely to describe data so that managers can visualize it. Sometimes having a clear picture of what is going on with the data helps people to interpret it in new and different ways. For example, if large amounts of data revealed that left-handed males who live in suburban environments never take automotive technology courses, it would most likely spark a heated discussion about the reasons why. It would certainly provide plenty of opportunities for additional study on the part of psychologists, sociologists, and college administrators!

You may have noticed that products are frequently moved around in supermarkets. This is usually the result of data mining. With electronic scanning of bar codes, each customer's purchase is recorded in a database. By classifying the data and using cluster analysis, supermarket managers can determine which products people usually purchase with other products. The store then places these products close to each other so that shoppers can find them easily. For instance, if analysis shows that people often buy coffee with breakfast cereal, it makes sense to place these items in the same aisle.

As the human race continues to accumulate data, the development of faster and bigger databases will be a necessity. You can expect to interact with more and more databases every year, even if you don't realize you are doing so. While you may never have to create a database, understanding how databases work will enable you to interact with them more effectively.

1. What is a database, and why is it beneficial to use databases?

Databases are electronic collections of related data that can be organized so that it is more easily accessed and manipulated. Properly designed databases cut down on data redundancy and duplicate data by ensuring relevant data is recorded in only one place. This also helps eliminate data inconsistency, which comes from having different data about the same transaction recorded in two different places. When databases are used, multiple users can share and access information at the same time. Databases are used any time complex information needs to be organized or more than one person needs to access it. In these cases, lists (which are used to keep track of simple information) are no longer efficient.

2. What components make up a database?

The three main components of a database are fields, records, and tables. A category of information in a database is stored in a field. Each field is identified by a field name, which is a way of describing the field. Fields are assigned a data type that indicates what type of data can be stored in the field. Common data types include text, numeric, computational, date, memo, object, and hyperlink. A group of related fields is a record. A group of related records is a table or file. To keep records distinct, each record must have one field that has a value unique to that record. This unique field is a primary key (or a key field).

3. What types of databases are there?

The three major types of databases currently in use are relational, object-oriented, and multidimensional. Relational databases are characterized by two-dimensional tables of data in which a common field is maintained in each of two tables and the information in the tables is linked by this field.

Object-oriented databases store data in objects, not in tables. The objects also contain instructions about how the data is to be manipulated or processed. Multidimensional databases represent data in three-dimensional cubes to enable faster retrieval of information from the database.

4. What do database management systems do?

Database management systems (DBMSs) are specially designed applications (such as Oracle or Microsoft Access) that interact with the user, other applications, and the database itself to capture and analyze data. The main operations of a DBMS are creating databases, entering data, viewing (or browsing) data, sorting (or indexing) data, extracting (or querying) data, and outputting data. A query language is used to extract records from a database. Almost all relational databases today use structured query language, or SQL. However, most DBMSs include wizards that enable you to query the database without learning a query language. The most common form of output for any database is a printed report.

5. How do relational databases organize and manipulate data?

Relational databases operate by organizing data into various tables based on logical groupings. Because not all of the data in a relational database is stored in the same table, a methodology must be implemented to link data between tables. In relational databases, the links between tables that define how the data is related are referred to as relationships. To establish a relationship between two tables, both tables must have a common field (or column). Once linked, information can be drawn from multiple tables through the use of queries (for on-screen viewing of data) or report generators (used to produce printed reports).

6. What are data warehouses and data marts, and how are they used?

A data warehouse is a large-scale electronic repository of data that contains and organizes in one place all the relevant data related to an organization. Data warehouses often contain information from multiple databases. Because it can be difficult to find information in a large data warehouse, small slices of the data warehouse called *data marts* are often created. The information in data marts pertains to a single department within the organization, for example. Data warehouses and data marts consolidate information from a wide variety of sources to provide comprehensive pictures of operations or transactions within a business.

7. What is an information system, and what types of information systems are used in business?

Information systems are software-based solutions that are used to gather and analyze information. Information systems fall into one of five categories. An office support system (OSS) is designed to assist employees in accomplishing their day-to-day tasks and improve communications. A transaction-processing system (TPS) is a system that is used to keep track of everyday business activities. A management information system (MIS) provides timely and accurate information that enables managers to make critical business decisions. A decision support system (DSS) is a system designed to help managers develop solutions for specific problems. An enterprise resource planning (ERP) system is a large software system that gathers information from all parts of a business and integrates it to make it readily available for decision making.

8. What is data mining, and how does it work?

Data mining is the process by which large amounts of data are analyzed to spot otherwise hidden trends. Through processes such as classification, estimation, affinity grouping, clustering, and description (visualization), data is organized so that it provides meaningful information that can be used by managers to identify business trends.

key terms

Word Bank

- data dictionary
- data inconsistency
- data mining
- data warehouse
- decision support system
- field
- join query
- memo field
- metadata
- numeric field
- object field
- primary key
- relational algebra
- select query
- structured query language (SQL)
- table
- text field
- transaction-processing system (TPS)

Instructions: Fill in the blanks using the words from the Word Bank above.

When constructing a database (1) _____, it is important to ensure each record is identified uniquely. A(n) (2) _____ should be established as a unique field that will be included with each record. In a database, numbers such as 1234 are normally stored in a(n) (3) _____, but they also could be stored in a(n) (4) _____ if calculations do not need to be performed on the number. Extremely lengthy textual data is stored in a(n) (5) _____, whereas video files are appropriately stored in a(n) (6) _____. The (7) _____ fully describes each field in the database and its attributes. Data used to describe other data in this manner is referred to as (8) _____.

Queries are used to prepare data for viewing or printing. A(n) (9) _____ usually displays requested information from only one table. For displaying related information that is stored in multiple tables, a(n) (10) _____ must be used. The most popular query language in use today is (11) _____. Queries generated by this language make use of English-language statements driven by the mathematical principles of (12) _____.

When individual databases are not sufficient to maintain all the data that needs to be tracked, a(n) (13) _____ should be created. Databases are often key components of (14) _____, which record routine business activities. A(n) (15) _____ utilizes databases and other related systems to assist management with building business models and making critical decisions.

becoming computer literate

Everyone loves the handbags that your best friend, Linh, makes, and she has decided to start selling them to the general public. Linh has a few existing customers already (mostly family and friends), but she plans to put her work in a few art shows, make some deals with area stores to feature it, and sell it online at **Etsy.com**. Keeping track of all this information is going to be important, but she is not computer literate.

Linh has approached you to be her database consultant and to design a database for her new business. Write a proposal that outlines what you intend to do for your friend. What kind of database will you create? What kind of information will your friend need in the database to run her business? How should that information be organized? Can the database be created and stored online so that Linh can access it from her phone? As her business grows, how do you imagine the database will grow with the business?

Instructions: Answer the multiple-choice and true–false questions below for more practice with key terms and concepts from this chapter.

Multiple Choice

1. Having the different birthdates for the same person on two different lists is an example of
  a. data redundancy.
  b. data inconsistency.
  c. data disparity.
  d. data duplication errors.

2. Which of the following is NOT one of the three main advantages of using databases?
  a. Promotion of data integrity.
  b. Data can be easily shared.
  c. Elimination of data recording errors.
  d. Flexible use of data.

3. A group of related fields in a relational database is called a
  a. primary key.   c. record.
  b. field string.   d. table.

4. An example of a good primary key is a(n)
  a. order number.
  b. person's first name combined with their last name.
  c. name of a pet.
  d. street address.

5. A primary key
  a. should always contain only numbers.
  b. is always unique for each record in a database.
  c. does not have to be unique for every record in a database.
  d. is only used in object-oriented databases.

6. A(n) _____ database organizes data in a cube format.
  a. relational
  b. object-oriented
  c. rectangular
  d. multidimensional

7. Which is NOT one of the four main operations of a DBMS?
  a. Consolidating data
  b. Entering data
  c. Sorting data
  d. Querying data

8. Comparing data values to ensure reasonableness is an example of a(n)
  a. alphabetic check.
  b. completeness check.
  c. range check.
  d. consistency check.

9. A data system that is a subset of a larger system is known as (a)n
  a. data mart.
  b. office support system.
  c. data warehouse.
  d. transaction-processing system.

10. An electronic system used to keep track of everyday business activities is an example of a(n)
  a. transaction-processing system.
  b. decision support system.
  c. expert system.
  d. knowledge-based system.

True-False

_____ 1. A query is used to transfer information into a database.

_____ 2. Completeness checks ensure that only reasonable data values are entered into a database.

_____ 3. Reducing incorrect or incomplete data by recording data in only one place is called data optimization.

_____ 4. An expert system attempts to replicate the decisions made by a live person.

_____ 5. Data mining cannot be used to spot customer trends.

1. Understanding Database Design

Go out to **ebay.com** and look at some items that are for sale. eBay uses a very sophisticated database to process transactions. But every good database starts with good design by creating a field for each unique piece of data. List as many fields as you can identify used to record information for an item for sale on eBay. Assign each field you identify a data type and suggest a reasonable field length.

2. Privacy Settings on Facebook

Facebook is a large database. It is important to protect personal information that is contained in a database, and with Facebook you are responsible for making decisions about sharing your information. The owners of Facebook are constantly tweaking the privacy settings on the site. If you have not checked your privacy settings lately, you may not be aware of the personal information that you are sharing with anyone who can access Facebook.

a. Log in to your Facebook account and access your privacy settings. Which information about you is accessible to everyone? Is any of your information only visible to your friends? What types of information is viewable by friends of your friends?

b. Did any of the privacy settings surprise you? Which privacy settings do you think you need to change? Why? If you don't think any changes to your setting are necessary, explain why you feel secure with your current privacy settings.

3. Designing Your Own Database

Suppose you wish to create a database to facilitate the buying and selling of used textbooks for students at your campus. Determine the following:

a. What fields do you need in your database for identifying and categorizing the books? What would be a good primary key to use for the "book inventory" table? Why would it be a good primary key?

b. What fields do you need to capture information about the customers (students) who are buying the books? What would be the primary key of the "customer" table? Why would it be a good primary key?

c. Design a table that tracks the selling transactions. What fields from the other two tables would need to be included in the "sales transaction" table? Justify your answer.

4. Comparing Databases

Amazon.com and **eCampus.com** are two sites students frequently use to buy textbooks. On both sites you interact with a database to search for and purchase your textbooks. Visit both sites and search for several textbooks such as the ones you are using this semester. Compare your experiences on both sites. Consider the following (and make sure you fully explain each answer):

a. Which site is easier to use?

b. Which site offers better options for refining the results of your search (query) for a textbook?

c. What fields did you search on to find your textbooks? Would searching on another field have produced more accurate results?

d. What enhancements would you suggest the owners of both sites to improve your shopping experience?

making the
transition to...
the workplace

1. Data Marts

You are a summer intern in the information technology group of a regional chain of sandwich shops. The company has been in business for fifteen years and operates 200 locations in eight states. The 200 locations are organized into five regions (A, B, C, D, and E) of 40 stores each. Regional managers are responsible for inventory management, procurement of inventory, sales, and marketing for their particular region. The company has been processing all transactions electronically (with customers and suppliers), and it has captured all the data in a large data warehouse. Unfortunately, the regional managers are complaining that there is now so much information in the data warehouse that it has become somewhat difficult to sort through it and extract meaningful data. You have just been placed on the team that will be designing a new data strategy for the company.

a. Setting up data marts would probably help with the accessibility of information. What type of data marts would you suggest setting up for this company? Make sure you explain who will benefit from the data marts you suggest.

b. For the data marts you identified in the previous question, list the data that should be stored in each data mart and explain how the regional managers could make use of that information to manage their group of stores.

2. Creating a Data Access Policy

You have an internship in the information technology department at the regional office of Mammoth Insurance Company, which sells automobile, life, and medical insurance. Colossal Insurance Company, one of your firm's competitors, was recently raked over the coals in the news media because a few employees were looking up medical records of insurance customers for the purpose of developing a mailing list for people with certain illnesses. The employees were then using the list to market a new mail-order prescription drug Web site (owned by the employees, not Colossal) directly to Colossal's customers. Many customers were upset by the solicitations, which they viewed as an invasion of their privacy. The Colossal employees contended that no one ever told them they couldn't use the company records for this purpose.

The CIO of Mammoth wants to ensure that such a controversy doesn't happen to her company. She has asked your supervisor (who in turn drafted you to help) to prepare a data access policy for Mammoth. Prepare a draft of the policy and consider the following:

a. Who should have access to the medical information of insurance company customers? The insurance underwriters (the people who approve or disapprove policies) need the information. Does anyone else?

b. Should marketing personnel be granted access to medical and driving records for the purposes of marketing Mammoth's products? If so, who should approve the access? Should customers be informed before conducting marketing campaigns using their "sensitive" information? Who should be responsible for notifying customers?

c. Describe the types of uses of customer information that would be deemed inappropriate by the company. What should the penalties be for violating the policy?

Instructions: Albert Einstein used *Gedankenexperiments*, or critical thinking questions, to develop his theory of relativity. Some ideas are best understood by experimenting with them in our own minds. The following critical thinking questions are designed to demand your full attention but require only a comfortable chair—no technology.

1. Database Privacy Policies

Most likely you have provided quite a bit of personal information to various companies when you became their customer. Companies have an ethical responsibility to protect sensitive data obtained from customers. Consider the following:

a. Think about a retailer (such as Walmart) that you have done business with recently. What personal information did you provide to that retailer? What personal information should a company be precluded from disclosing to others? What information does the company have of yours that you don't care if they share with (or sell to) other companies?

b. Most retailers have privacy policies that describe how your information will be used and safeguarded. Have you ever read a privacy policy from a retailer that you have done business with? If so, summarize the provisions of the policy. If not, review a privacy policy from a major online retailer and summarize its provisions. In your opinion, is the privacy policy you reviewed sufficient to protect your sensitive data?

2. Social Security Database

The U.S. Social Security Administration (SSA) maintains a large database containing a great deal of information on the personal income of individuals. The information in this database could be easily sorted and categorized by attributes such as geographic location and age. This information would be of great value to marketing professionals for targeting marketing programs to consumers. Currently, the SSA is prohibited from selling this information to third parties. However, the SSA and other government agencies face increasing pressure to find ways to generate revenue or decrease expenses.

a. Do you favor a change in the laws that would permit the SSA to sell names and addresses with household income information to third parties? Why or why not?

b. Would it be acceptable for the SSA to sell income information to marketing firms if it did not include personal information, but only included income statistics for certain geographic areas? How is this better (or worse) than selling personal information?

c. How would you feel about the SSA marketing financial products (such as investment opportunities and retirement plans) directly to consumers? Would this be a conflict of interest with the SSA's main mission, which is the collection of retirement taxes and the provision of old-age pensions?

3. Information About You

There are many databases such as **411.com** and **spokeo.com** on the Web, and some of them probably contain your personal information. Using Google (or other search engines), perform a Web search on your name. Because many people have the same name, you may need to use some other identifying attributes (such as your address, employer, high school attended, and so on) to ensure that the search returns results about you. Consider the following:

a. What information did you find about yourself? What was the most surprising piece of information you located?

b. Did you find enough information about yourself to enable a criminal to steal your identity?

c. Repeat this same exercise but instead use the name of one of your friends. What obligation do you have to your friend to inform him or her of any potentially sensitive information you located?

eleven team time

Redesigning Facebook

Problem

Facebook is the most popular social media site. But as with any product, there is always room for improvement. Facebook management has made decisions about what data they require from users who create Facebook accounts. They also have set up specific areas to display what management considers to be pertinent information on a user's main Facebook page. But perhaps you as a user would have designed Facebook differently.

Task

Your class has volunteered to work as a focus group for Facebook as part of a nationwide project to assess the usefulness of the information gathered by Facebook. Users often provide unique perspectives, and they should be consulted whenever possible during the design, implementation, and updates of Web sites. As heavy users of Facebook, management feels that student input is invaluable to ensuring currency and usability of its features.

Process

Divide the class into small groups.

1. Your group members should examine their individual Facebook accounts. If anyone in your group does not have a Facebook account, they should set one up. If you all have Facebook accounts, you might want to consider going through the process of setting up an account to reacquaint yourselves with the information that is required (or can be entered) when a Facebook account is first set up. Pay particular attention to the profile area of your account. What fields in the profile do you consider to be most useful? Which fields do you think are totally unnecessary and could be eliminated? What fields are missing from the profile that you think would be useful to you and your friends?

2. Investigate your account settings and application settings paying particular attention to items that are displayed on the main page of your account. What changes would you make to these settings? Are options missing that you would find helpful to configuring your Facebook page?

3. Present your group's findings to the class. Compare your suggestions to those of other groups. Be sure to think about the needs of other groups of users (such as your parents or your grandparents) because they probably use Facebook in ways that you might not.

4. Prepare a list of recommendations for improvements to the current Facebook home page and settings pages. Clearly indicate how the proposed changes will benefit both users and the management of Facebook (retaining users, being able to better target advertising to users, and so on).

Conclusion

Facebook will most likely experience competition in the future from other social networking sites that will want to poach its huge base of users. To remain competitive, Facebook needs to consider the input of users like you to ensure that it delivers a cutting-edge product that delivers the features its customers want and need. Facebook's best chance of remaining on top of the social media heap is to be sensitive to the needs of its current users.

In this exercise, you will research and then role-play a complicated ethical situation. The role you play might or might not match your own personal beliefs; in either case, your research and use of logic will enable you to represent the view assigned. An arbitrator will watch and comment on both sides of the arguments, and together the team will agree on an ethical solution.

Topic: Private Information on Public Databases

As more tasks in our lives are conducted online, there is a tremendous amount of data that is accumulated about us in online databases. Unfortunately, much of this material is accessible in databases that are searchable by anyone with Internet access or to anyone willing to pay a small fee. Web sites such as **Spokeo.com** and **411.com** comb through publicly accessible databases such as social networking sites (Facebook or MySpace), online phone books, business sites where you have accounts (Yahoo! or MSN), and government (federal, state, and local) Web sites to compile information on individuals. There is probably a lot of information available about you available on sites such as these that could expose you to risks such as identify theft.

Research Areas to Consider

- Electronic information privacy
- Electronic privacy information center (**epic.org**)
- Protecting your online privacy
- Protecting yourself on Facebook

Process

Divide the class into teams.

1. Research the areas cited above and devise a scenario in which someone has complained about a Web site (such as **spokeo.com**) providing information that lead to their identity being stolen.
2. Team members should write a summary that provides background information for their character—for example: victim of identity theft, Web site owner, or arbitrator—and details their character's behaviors to set the stage for the role-playing event. Then, team members should create an outline to use during the role-playing event.
3. Team members should arrange a mutually convenient time to meet for the exchange, either using the collaboration feature of MyITLab, the discussion board feature of Blackboard, or meeting in person.
4. Team members should present their case to the class, or submit a PowerPoint presentation for review by the rest of the class, along with the summary and resolution they developed.

Conclusion

As technology becomes ever more prevalent and integrated into our lives, more and more ethical dilemmas will present themselves. Being able to understand and evaluate both sides of the argument, while responding in a personally or socially ethical manner, will be an important skill.

twelve

behind the scenes:

networking and security in the business world

multimedia resources

Active Helpdesk

- Using Servers **(p. 572)**
- Selecting a Network Topology and Cable **(p. 577)**
- Selecting Network Navigation Devices **(p. 589)**

Sound Bytes

- Network Topology and Navigation Devices **(p. 574)**
- What's My IP Address? (And Other Interesting Facts about Networks) **(p. 586)**
- A Day in the Life of a Network Technician **(p. 589)**

Companion Website

The Companion Website includes a variety of additional materials to help you review and learn more about the topics in this chapter. Go to: *pearsonhighered.com/techinaction*

how cool is *this?* Planning a meeting

with classmates to work on a **group project** can be **difficult**. E-mail is not an efficient planning tool because it is difficult to coordinate numerous messages. Even using threaded message postings on Facebook can be cumbersome. A simple free tool that solves this problem is Doodle (**doodle.com**).

With **Doodle**, you can quickly set up a grid with possible meeting dates and times. You then provide the URL of the meeting poll to the other members of the group. As members come to the meeting site, they enter their names and indicate their availability for various meeting times (**yes, no, or maybe**) as indicated by the colors green, red, and yellow. Doodle then provides a visual summary of all input from the group so you can easily select a meeting time that works for the majority of the participants.

So stop **tearing your hair out** about getting your group together and use Doodle to simplify your planning!

Networking Advantages

You learned about peer-to-peer networks in Chapter 7, and we'll expand your knowledge of networks in this chapter. Recall that a **network** is a group of two or more computers (or nodes) that are configured to share information and resources such as printers, files, and databases. Essentially, a network enables computers and other devices to communicate with each other. But why do we network computers? Home networks enable users to share an Internet connection, share peripherals, and share media. Businesses, such as your college or an insurance company, also gain advantages from deploying networks.

What advantages do businesses gain from networks?   Large business networks provide advantages similar to those of home networks, and therefore have advantages over individual stand-alone computers:

- **Networks increase productivity.** Computers are powerful stand-alone resources. However, to increase productivity, people need to be able to share data and peripherals with co-workers and communicate with them efficiently. Without a network, only one person at a time can access information because it resides on a single computer. Information sharing is therefore the largest benefit gained by installing a network.

- **Networks enable expensive resources to be shared.** Networks enable people to share peripherals such as printers, eliminating the need for duplicate devices.

You probably have a printer hooked up to your home computer. Think about how often it sits idle. Compound that by having 20 students in a lab, all with their own printers. Having 20 printers sitting idle 95 percent of the time is a tremendous waste of money. Installing a network that enables one printer (working most of the time) to serve all 20 students saves money.

- **Networks facilitate knowledge sharing.** The databases you learned about in Chapter 11 become especially powerful when deployed on a network. Networked databases can serve the needs of many people at one time and increase the availability of data. Your college's databases are much more useful when all college employees can look up student records at the same time.

- **Networks enable software sharing.** Installing a new version of software on everyone's desktop in a college with 500 employees can be time consuming. However, if the computers are networked, all employees can access the same copy of a program from the server. Although the college must still purchase a software license for each employee, with a network it can avoid having to install the program on every computer. This also saves space on individual computers, because the software doesn't reside on every computer.

- **Networks facilitate Internet connectivity.** Most college students need to connect to the Internet to complete class work. Providing each computer on a network with its own dedicated connection to the Internet is costly. Through a network, large groups of computers can share one Internet connection, reducing Internet connectivity expenses.

- **Networks enable enhanced communication.** Social networking tools, e-mail, and instant messaging are extremely powerful applications when deployed on a network (especially one that is connected to the Internet). College students can easily exchange information with each other and their professors, and can share valuable data by transferring files to other users.

Are there disadvantages to using networks?   Because business (or college) networks are often complex, additional

---

BITS AND BYTES

Print Documents Anywhere . . . From Your Phone!

You have plenty of information on your smartphone, but what do you do when you need print something and you're nowhere near your printer? Using a free software program called PrinterShare (**printeranywhere.com**), you can print a document from your smartphone to any local WiFi connected printer.

The PrinterShare software helps your smartphone detect nearby printers connected via a WiFi connection (such as a printer in the business center at your hotel) and print documents (such as your boarding pass for an airline fight) from your phone to that printer. PrinterShare also works on smartphones such as the iPhone or phones using the Android operating system. Check it out for yourself—it could save you some aggravation in the future.

personnel are usually required to maintain them. These people, called **network administrators**, have training in computer and peripheral maintenance and repair, networking design, and the installation of networking software.

Another disadvantage is that operating a network requires special equipment and software. However, most companies feel that the cost savings of peripheral sharing and the ability to give employees simultaneous access to information outweigh the costs associated with network administrators and equipment.

Aside from the smallest networks, such as peer-to-peer networks, which are typically used in homes and small businesses, the majority of computer networks are based on the client/server model of computing.

Client/Server Networks

As you've learned, a server is a computer that both stores and shares resources on a network, whereas a **client** is a computer that requests those resources. A **client/server network** (also called a **server-based network**) contains servers as well as client computers. The inclusion of servers is what differentiates a client/server network from a typical peer-to-peer (P2P) network. Each node connected to a P2P network can communicate directly with every other node on the network instead of having a separate device exercise control over the network. Figure 12.1 illustrates the client/server relationship.

The main advantage of a client/server relationship is that it makes data flow more efficiently than in peer-to-peer networks. Servers can respond to requests from a large number of clients at the same time. In addition, servers can be configured to perform specific tasks (such as handling e-mail or database requests) efficiently.

Say you are hungry and go to a fast-food restaurant. In your role as the customer ordering food, you are the client making a request. The cook, in the role of the server, responds to the request and prepares the meal. Certainly, you could go to the restaurant and cook your own meal, but this hardly would be efficient. You would be floundering around in the kitchen with other customers as they try to cook their own meals. If the manager assigns specialized tasks to a fast-food cook (the server), many customers (clients) can be served efficiently at the same time. This is how servers work: One server can provide services efficiently to a large number of clients at one time.

Does my home network have a server? Your home P2P network does not need a server. Peer-to-peer networks, which are typically set up in homes or very small businesses, do not require servers (although some home networks now have specialized media servers for sharing media) to function efficiently. In these networks, computers act as both clients and servers when appropriate.

When shouldn't a peer-to-peer network be used? P2P networks become difficult to administer when they are expanded beyond 10 users. Each individual computer may require updating if there are changes to the network, which is not efficient with large numbers of computers. In addition, security can't be implemented centrally on a P2P network but instead must be handled by each individual user. Client/server networks contain at least

Figure 12.1

Basic client/server interaction.

Step 1: Client computer requests service from server computer.

What are the names of the customers who bought more than 500 television sets this month?

Query submitted from client

Answer provided by server

Mega-Discount Appliances
Wall-To-Wall Televisions, Inc.
Televisions-R-Us

Computer A
(client)

Computer B
(server)

Step 2: Server computer provides requested service to client computer.

Wireless connection

Cable

INTERNET

Client Computer #1

High-speed communications line

Switch

Server

Client Computer #2

Client Computer #3

Laser printer

Figure 12.2

This small client/server network enables users to share a printer and an Internet connection.

one server that provides shared resources and services (including security) to the client computers that request them.

In addition, client/server networks move data more efficiently than P2P networks, making them appropriate for large numbers of users. For example, Figure 12.2 shows a small client/server arrangement. The server in this figure provides printing and Internet connection services for all the client computers connected to the network. The server is performing tasks that would need to be done by the client computers in a P2P network. This frees resources on the client computers for more efficiently performing processor-intensive tasks such as viewing a movie or playing video games.

Besides having a centralized server, what makes a client/server network different from a peer-to-peer network? The main difference is that client/server networks have increased scalability. **Scalability** means that more users can be added easily without affecting the performance of the other network nodes (computers or peripherals). Because servers handle the bulk of tasks performed on the network (printing, Internet access, and so on), it is easy to accommodate more users by installing additional servers to help with the

increased workload. Installing additional servers on a network is relatively simple and can usually be done without disrupting services for existing users.

In addition, peer-to-peer networks are **decentralized**. This means that users are responsible for creating their own data backups and for providing security for their computers. In client/server networks, all clients connect to a server that performs tasks for them. Therefore, client/server networks are said to be **centralized**. Many tasks that individual users must handle on a P2P network can be handled centrally at the server.

For instance, data files are normally stored on the server. Therefore, backups for all users on a college's network can be performed by merely backing up all the files on the server. Security, too, can be exercised over the server instead of on each user's computer; this way, the server, not the individual user, coordinates data security.

Classifications of Client/Server Networks: LANs, WANs, and MANs

Networks are generally classified according to their size and the distance between the physical parts of the network. Four popular classifications are local area networks, wide area networks, metropolitan area networks, and personal area networks.

A **local area network (LAN)** is a (generally small) group of computers and peripherals linked together over a relatively small geographic area. The computer lab at your school or the network serving the floor of the office building where you work is probably a LAN.

Wide area networks (WANs) comprise large numbers of users over a wider physical area or separate LANs that are miles apart. For example, a large college campus might have a WAN that spans all of its lecture halls, residence halls, and administrative offices.

Corporations often use WANs to connect two or more geographically distant branches. For example, ABC Shoe Company has manufacturing plants and administrative offices all over the globe. The LAN at each ABC Shoe Company office is connected to other ABC Shoe Company LANs, forming a global ABC Shoe Company WAN.

Figure 12.3 shows an example of what part of the ABC Shoe Company WAN might look like.

Sometimes government organizations or civic groups establish WANs to link users in a specific geographic area (such as within a city or county). This special type of WAN is known as a **metropolitan area network (MAN)**. San Diego's Traffic Management Center (TMC) uses a MAN to analyze traffic patterns. You can check out the traffic maps they generate at **dot.ca.gov/sdtraffic**.

What sort of network connects devices such as smartphones and Bluetooth headsets? A **personal area network (PAN)** is a network used to connect wireless devices (such as Bluetooth-enabled devices) that are in close proximity to each other. (Bluetooth technology uses radio waves to transmit data over short distances.) PANs are wireless and work within the

Figure 12.3

A WAN comprises several LANs in different geographic locations connected by telecommunications media. Satellite communication is often used to transmit data over long distances.

Microwaves   Microwaves

High-speed Communications Line   Satellite   High-speed Communications Line

Microwave Tower   Microwave Tower

Modem   Modem

Client Computer   Client Computer

Wireless connection   Client Computer

Server   Server

Client Computer   Client Computer

Printer   Printer

LAN at ABC Shoe Company Beaverton, Oregon

LAN at ABC Shoe Company Hilversum, Netherlands

PAN Clothing—Organization and Power for Portable Gear

Now that people carry so many portable computing devices, clothing designers are starting to offer clothing that facilitates the storage, transportation, charging, and networking of their digital gadgets. The Scottevest (see Figure 12.4a) is one of a line of vests and jackets designed to hold iPods, smartphones, and even iPads. It also features a built-in PAN to help maintain connectivity of your devices. And because all the devices in your PAN need power, accessories such as the Voltaic Backpack (see Figure 12.4b) help recharge your digital devices using renewable energy sources. So don't forget to consider the perfect fashion accessory for your latest digital acquisition!

Figure 12.4

(a) Shown here with an X-ray, the Scottevest has a convenient spot for all of your gadgets. (b) The Voltaic Backpack recharges your mobile devices using solar cells.

personal operating space of an individual, which is generally defined to be within 30 feet (or 10 meters) of one's body. Today, PANs free you from having wires running to and from the devices you're using. One day, though, PANs may use your body to transmit and receive signals.

What other sort of networks do businesses use? An **intranet** is a private network set up by an entity (such as a business, charity, or government organization) that is used exclusively by a select group of individuals (employees, customers, suppliers, volunteers, supporters, etc.). It can facilitate information sharing, database access, group scheduling, videoconferencing, and other employee collaborations. Intranets are usually deployed using Transmission Control Protocol/Internet Protocol (TCP/IP), which is discussed in Chapter 13, networks and generally include links to the

Internet. An intranet is not accessible by unauthorized individuals; a firewall protects it from unauthorized access through the Internet.

One of the first main uses of intranets was to run groupware (software that enables users to share and collaborate on documents). One example, Lotus Notes, facilitates information sharing and solving problems through brainstorming. Most groupware programs also support messaging and group calendaring. Now, many organizations supplant groupware applications by deploying Web 2.0 tools such as blogs, wikis, and social networks on an intranet.

An area of an intranet that only certain corporations or individuals can access is called an **extranet**. The owner of an extranet decides who will be permitted to access it. For example, a company's customers and suppliers may be permitted to access information on the company's extranet. Extranets are useful for enabling electronic data interchange (EDI). EDI allows the exchange of large amounts of business data (such as orders for merchandise) in a standardized electronic format. Other uses of extranets include providing access to catalogs and inventory databases and sharing information among partners or industry trade groups.

What security tools do intranets and extranets use? Because of security concerns, intranets and extranets often use virtual private networks to keep information secure. A **virtual private network (VPN)** uses the public Internet communications infrastructure to build a secure, private network among various locations. Although WANs can be set up using private leased communications lines, these lines are expensive and tend to increase in price as the distance between points increases. VPNs use special security technologies and protocols that enhance security, enabling data to traverse the Internet as securely as if it were on a private leased line. Installing and configuring a VPN requires special hardware such as VPN-optimized routers and firewalls. In addition, VPN software must be installed on users' PCs.

The main technology for achieving a VPN is, in fact, called *tunneling*. In tunneling, data packets are placed inside other data packets. The format of these external data packets is encrypted and is understood only by the sending and receiving hardware, which is

Denver, CO branch office LAN

VPN enabled router

Data flow

INTERNET

VPN secure tunnel through the Internet

VPN enabled router

Phoenix, AZ branch office LAN

Wireless connection

Switch

Data flow

Switch

Computer #1

Computer #2

Computer #3

Computer #4

Computer #5

Computer #6

known as a *tunnel interface*. The hardware is optimized to seek efficient routes of transmission through the Internet. This provides a high level of security and makes information much more difficult to intercept and decrypt.

Imagine you have to deliver a message to a branch office. You could have one of your employees drive to the other office and deliver the message. But suppose he has to go through a bad neighborhood or has never been to the office before? The messenger could be waylaid by a carjacker or become hopelessly lost. Using a VPN (as shown in Figure 12.5) is the equivalent of hiring a limousine and an armed guard to drive your employee through a private tunnel directly to the destination. Of course, a VPN avoids the enormous cost associated with this method!

Constructing Client/ Server Networks

Client/server networks have many of the same components that P2P networks do, as well as some components specific to client/ server networks:

- **Server**: Unlike peer-to-peer networks, client/server networks contain at least one computer that functions solely as a server.
- **Network topology:** Because client/ server networks are more complex than peer-to-peer networks, the layout and structure of the network, which is called the **network topology**, must be carefully planned.

- **Transmission media:** Data needs a way to flow between clients and servers on networks. Therefore, an appropriate type of transmission media (cable or wireless communications technology) based on the network topology is needed. Client/server networks use a wider variety of cable types than do simpler P2P networks. Although business networks also feature wireless connectivity, they tend to use a lot more cabling than home networks. Cabling is used to achieve higher throughput because many network nodes tend to stay in fixed locations (such as an employee's cubicle).
- **Network operating system (NOS) software:** All client/server networks require network operating system (NOS) software, which is specialized software that is installed on servers and client computers and enables the network to function. Most modern operating systems (such as Windows 7 and Mac OS X) include the software computers need to function as clients on a network.
- **Network adapter:** As is the case with peer-to-peer networks, all nodes on the network must contain adapters (network interface cards). These adapters enable a computer (or peripheral) to communicate with the network using

Figure 12.5

Local area networks (LANs) in different cities can communicate securely over the Internet using VPN technology.

Network interface card
(NIC)
Installed in each
client

Client Computer #3

Network interface card
(NIC)
Installed in server

Cable
(transmission media)

Client Computer #2

Switch
(Network navigation device)

Server

Client Computer #1

Network operating software
Often included in operating
system software for client computers

Network operating
software
Installed on server

Figure 12.6

The basic components of
a typical client/server
network.

a common data communication language, or protocol.

• **Network navigation device**: Because of the complexity of client/server networks, specialized network navigation devices (such as routers, switches, and bridges) are needed to move data signals around the network.

Figure 12.6 shows the components of a simple client/server network. In the following sections, we will explore each component in more detail.

Servers

Servers are the workhorses of the client/server network. They interface with many different network users and assist them with a variety of tasks. The number and types of servers on a client/server network depend on the network's size and workload. Small networks (such as the one pictured in Figure 12.2) would have just one server to handle all server functions, such as file storage, delivery of applications to the clients, printing, and so on.

What types of servers are found on larger client/server networks? A **dedicated server** is a server used to fulfill one specific function, such as handling e-mail. When more users are added to a network, dedicated servers are also added to reduce the load on the main server. Once dedicated servers are deployed, the original server can become merely an authentication server or a file server.

What are authentication and file servers? An **authentication server** is a server that keeps track of who is logging on to the network and which services on the network are available to each user. Authentication servers also act as overseers for the network. They manage and coordinate the services provided by any other dedicated servers located on the network. A **file server** is a server that stores and manages files for network users. On the network at your workplace or school, you may be provided with space on a file server to store files you create.

What functions do dedicated servers handle? Any task that is repetitive or demands a lot of time from

Client Computer #1

Wireless connection

Wireless access point

Client Computer #2

Client Computer #3

Print server

Laser printer 1

Laser printer 2

Switch

Database server

Authentication/ file server

Web server

Communication server

Application server

E-mail server

INTERNET

Figure 12.7

This is a typical large-scale client/server network with several dedicated servers installed.

a computer's processor (CPU) is a good candidate to relegate to a dedicated server. Common types of dedicated servers are print servers, application servers, database servers, e-mail servers, communications servers, and Web servers. Servers are connected to a client/server network so that all client computers that need to use their services can access them, as shown in Figure 12.7.

Print Servers

How does a print server function?
Printing is a function that takes a large quantity of CPU time and that most people do quite often. **Print servers** manage all client-requested printing jobs for all printers on a network, which helps client computers to complete more productive work by relieving them of printing duties. When you tell your computer to print a document, it passes off the task to the print server. This frees the CPU on your computer to do other jobs.

How does the printer know which documents to print? A print queue is a software holding area for print jobs. When the print server receives a job (a printing

request) from a client computer, it puts the job into a print queue on the print server. Normally, each printer on a network has its own uniquely named print queue. Jobs receive a number when they enter the queue and go to the printer in the order in which they were received. Print queues thus function like the "take a number" machines at a supermarket deli. Thus, print servers organize print jobs into an orderly sequence to make printing more efficient on a shared printer. Another useful aspect of print servers is that network administrators can set them to prioritize print jobs. Different users and types of print jobs can be assigned different priorities so higher-priority jobs will be printed first. For instance, in a company in which documents are printed on demand for clients, you would want these print jobs to take precedence over routine employee correspondence.

Application Servers

What function does an application server perform? In many networks, all users run the same application software

(such as Microsoft Office) on their computers. In a network of thousands of personal computers, installing application software on each individual computer is time consuming. An **application server** acts as a repository for application software.

When a client computer connects to the network and requests an application, the application server delivers the software to the client computer. Because the software does not reside on the client computer itself, this eases the task of installation and upgrading. The application needs to be installed or upgraded only on the application server, not on each network client.

Database Servers

What does a database server do? As its name implies, a **database server** provides client computers with access to information stored in databases. Often, many people need to access a database at the same time. For example, multiple college advisers can serve students at the same time because the advisers all have access to the student information database. This is made possible because the database resides on a database server that each adviser's computer can access through the network. If the database were on a stand-alone computer instead of a network, only one adviser could use it at a time, making the process of serving students terribly inefficient.

E-Mail Servers

How is e-mail handled on a large client/server network? The volume of e-mail on a large network could quickly overwhelm a server that was attempting to handle other functions as well. The sole function of an **e-mail server** is to process and deliver incoming and outgoing e-mail. On a network with an e-mail server, when you send an e-mail from your computer, it

goes to the e-mail server, which then handles the routing and delivery of your message. The e-mail server functions much like a postal carrier, who picks up your mail and sees that it finds its way to the correct destination.

Communications Servers

What types of communications does a communications server handle? A **communications server** handles all communications between the network and other networks, including managing Internet connectivity. All requests for information from the Internet and all messages being sent through the Internet pass through the communications server. Because Internet traffic is substantial at most organizations, the communications server has a heavy workload.

The communications server often is the only device on the network connected to the Internet. E-mail servers, Web servers, and other devices needing to communicate with the Internet usually route all their traffic through the communications server. Providing a single point of contact with the outside world makes it easier to secure the network from hackers.

Web Servers

What function does a Web server perform? A **Web server** is used to host a Web site so it will be available through the Internet. Web servers run specialized software such as Apache HTTP Server (open source server software) and Microsoft Internet Information Services (IIS) that enable them to host Web pages. Not every large network has a Web server. Many colleges and businesses use a third-party Web hosting company to host their Web sites instead.

Network Topologies

Just as buildings have different floor plans depending on their uses, networks have different blueprints denoting their layout. *Network topology* refers to the physical or logical arrangement of computers, transmission media (cable), and other network components. *Physical topology* refers to the layout of the "real" components of the network,

ACTIVE HELP-DESK — Using Servers

In this Active Helpdesk call, you'll play the role of a helpdesk staffer, fielding calls about various types of servers and client/server software.

A cable break here
cuts off Computer #1 and
Computer #2 from
peripherals

Computer #1

Computer #4

Computer #3

Terminator

Terminator

Computer #2

Laser printer

Scanner

Figure 12.8

A linear bus topology.

whereas *logical topology* refers to the virtual connections among network nodes. Logical topologies usually are determined by network protocols instead of the physical layout of the network or the paths electrical signals follow on the network.

Because networks have different uses, not all networks have the same topology. For example, assume that your class has to send a message to the class next door. You decide to arrange your class in a straight line from your classroom to the other classroom. Each student will whisper the message to the next student in the line until the message is eventually passed to a student in the other classroom. The arrangement of the students in a straight line is the topology. The passing of the message from student to student using the English language is the protocol.

In this section, we will explore the most common network topologies (bus, ring, and star) and discuss when each topology is used. As you'll see, the type of network topology used is important because it can affect a network's performance and scalability. Knowing how the basic topologies work, and the strengths and weaknesses of each one, will help you understand why particular network topologies were chosen on the networks you use.

Bus Topology

What does a bus topology look like?

In a **bus** (or **linear bus**) **topology**, all computers are connected in sequence on a single cable, as shown in Figure 12.8. This topology was deployed most often in peer-to-peer networks (not client/server networks). It has largely become legacy technology due to the decreased cost of Ethernet networks (which use a star topology) and because a bus topology is not designed to easily support wireless connections. However, bus topologies are still found in some manufacturing facilities when connecting groups of computer-controlled machines.

Each computer on the bus network can communicate directly with every other computer on the network. **Data collisions**, which happen when two computers send data at the same time and the sets of data collide somewhere in the media, are a problem on all networks. When data collides, it is often lost or irreparably damaged. A limitation of bus networks is that data collisions can occur fairly easily because a bus network is essentially comprised of one main communication medium (a single cable).

Think of a data collision as having a group of three people (e.g., Emily, Reesa, and Luis) sitting in a room having a conversation. For the conversation to be effective, only one person can speak at a time; otherwise, they would not be able to hear and understand each other. Therefore, if Emily is speaking, Reesa and Luis must wait until she finishes before presenting their ideas, and so on.

Because two signals transmitted at the same time on a bus network may cause a data collision, an **access method** has to be established to control which computer is allowed to use the transmission media at a certain time. Computers on a bus network behave like a group of people having a conversation. The computers "listen" to the network data traffic on the media. When no other computer is transmitting data (that is, when the "conversation" stops), the computer knows it is allowed to transmit data on the media. This means of taking turns "talking" prevents data collisions.

How does data get from point to point on a bus network? When it is safe to send data (that is, when no other computers are transmitting data), the sending computer broadcasts the data onto the media. The data is broadcast throughout the network to all devices connected to the network. The data is broken into small segments, each called a **packet**. Each packet contains the address of the computer or peripheral device to which it is being sent. Each computer or device connected to the network listens for data that contains its address. When it "hears" data addressed to it, it takes the data off the media and processes it.

For example, say your computer needs to print something on the printer attached to the network. Your computer "listens" to the network to ensure no other nodes are transmitting. It then sends the print job out onto the network. When the printer "hears" a job

addressed to it (here, the print job your computer just sent), it pulls the data off the network and executes the job.

The devices (nodes) attached to a bus network do nothing to move data along the network. This makes a bus network a **passive topology**. The data travels the entire length of the medium and is received by all network devices. The ends of the cable in a bus network are capped off by terminators (as shown in Figure 12.8). A **terminator** is a device that absorbs a signal so that it is not reflected back onto parts of the network that have already received it.

What are the advantages and disadvantages of bus networks? The simplicity and low cost of bus network topology were the major reasons it was deployed most often in P2P networks. The major disadvantage is that if there is a break in the cable, the bus network is effectively disrupted because some computers are cut off from others on the network. Only one computer can communicate at a time, so adding a large number of nodes to a bus network limits performance and causes delays in sending data. Because Ethernet networks don't suffer from these limitations, you rarely see bus topologies today.

> **"What are the advantages and disadvantages of bus networks?"**

Ring Topology

What does a ring topology look like? Not surprisingly, given its name, the computers and peripherals in a **ring** (or **loop**) **topology** are laid out in a configuration resembling a circle, as shown in Figure 12.9. Data flows around the circle from device to device in one direction only. Because data is passed using a special data packet called a **token**, this type of topology is commonly called a *token-ring topology*. The original token-ring networks could achieve a **data transfer rate** (bandwidth) of either 4 Mbps or 16 Mbps, but more recent token technologies can deliver speeds as high as 100 Mbps.

How does a token move data around a ring? A token is passed from computer to computer around the ring until it is grabbed by a computer that needs to transmit data. The computer "holds onto" the token until it has finished transmitting data. Only one computer on the ring can

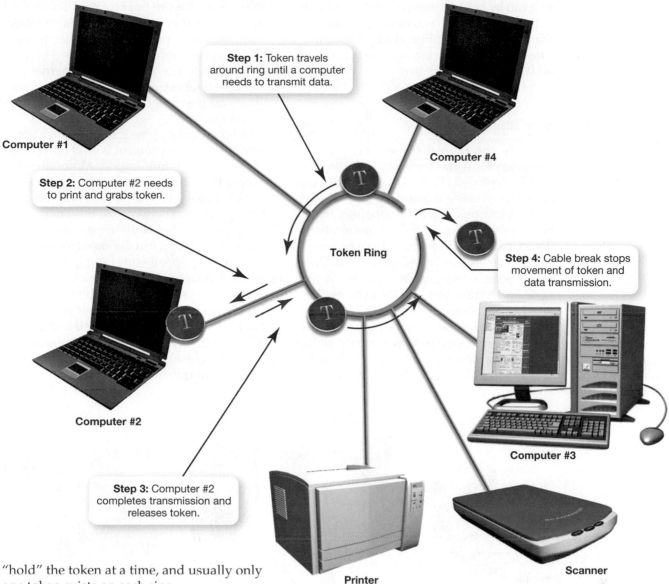

Step 1: Token travels around ring until a computer needs to transmit data.

Computer #1

Computer #4

Step 2: Computer #2 needs to print and grabs token.

Token Ring

Step 4: Cable break stops movement of token and data transmission.

Computer #2

Computer #3

Step 3: Computer #2 completes transmission and releases token.

Printer

Scanner

"hold" the token at a time, and usually only one token exists on each ring.

If a node (a computer or device) has data to send, such as a document that needs to go to the printer, it waits for the token to be passed to it. The node then takes the token out of circulation and sends the data to its destination. When the receiving node receives a complete transmission of the data (in this example, when the document is received by the printer), it transmits an acknowledgment to the sending node. The sending node then generates a new token and starts it going around the ring again. This is called the **token method** and is the access method ring networks use to avoid data collisions.

A ring topology is an **active topology**, which means that nodes participate in moving data through the network. Each node on the network is responsible for retransmitting the token or the data to the next node on the ring. Large ring networks have the capability to use multiple tokens to help move more data faster.

Is a ring topology better than a bus topology?   A ring topology provides a fairer allocation of network resources than does a bus topology. By using a token, a ring network enables all nodes on the network to have an equal chance to send data. One "chatty" node cannot monopolize the network bandwidth as easily as in a bus topology because it must pass the token on after sending a batch of data. In addition, a ring topology's performance will remain acceptable even with large numbers of users.

One disadvantage of a ring network is that if one computer fails, it can bring the entire network to a halt because that computer is unavailable to retransmit tokens and data. Another disadvantage is that problems in the ring can be hard for network administrators to find. It's easier to expand a ring topology than a bus topology, but adding a node to a ring does cause the ring to cease to function while the node is installed.

Star Topology

What is the layout for a star topology?

A **star topology** is the most widely deployed client/server network layout today because it offers the most flexibility for a low price. In a star topology, the nodes connect to a central communications device called a *switch* in a pattern resembling a star, as shown in Figure 12.10. The switch receives a signal from the sending node and retransmits it to the node on the network that needs to receive the signal. Each network node picks up only the transmissions addressed to it. Because the switch retransmits data signals, a star topology is an active topology. (We discuss switches in

more detail later in this chapter.) The only drawback is that if the switch fails, the network no longer functions. However, it is relatively easy to replace a switch.

Many star networks use the Ethernet protocol. Networks using the Ethernet protocol are by far the most common type of network in use today.

A topology is a physical design of a network, whereas a **protocol** is a set of rules for exchanging communication. Although many people think that Ethernet is a type of network topology, it is actually a communications protocol. Therefore, an Ethernet network could be set up using a bus, a ring, or a star topology. Most computers sold today are equipped with 1-gigabit wired network adapters. For businesses that need even more speed, the 10-gigabit standard supports a transfer rate of up to 10 Gbps, but the equipment supporting this standard is still relatively expensive and therefore small businesses do not use it unless very high bandwidth is required.

Figure 12.10

In a star topology, network nodes are connected through a central switch.

A cable break here means Computer #1 cannot communicate with the network. However, all other computers and devices can still communicate with each other.

Step 1: When two nodes transmit simultaneous data signals, a data collision occurs and is detected.

Computer #1 — Signal #1
Computer #2
Computer #3 — Collision Detected
Computer #4 — Signal #4

Signal #1 — Collision! — Signal #4

Step 2: The detecting node sends a jam signal.

Computer #1 — Jam Signal
Computer #2 — Jam Signal
Computer #3 — Jam Signal Sent
Computer #4 — Jam Signal

Jam Signal — Jam Signal — Jam Signal

Step 3: The two nodes that sent simultaneous data signals retransmit their signals after a random amount of time.

Computer #1 — Retransmit Signal #1
Computer #2
Computer #3
Computer #4 — Retransmit Signal #4

14 nanoseconds later   **18 nanoseconds later**

Figure 12.11

Avoiding data collisions on an Ethernet network.

How do computers on a star network avoid data collisions? Because most star networks are Ethernet networks, they use the method used on all Ethernet networks to avoid data collisions: **CSMA/CD** (short for *carrier sense multiple access with collision detection*). With CSMA/CD, a node connected to the network uses carrier sense (that is, it "listens") to verify that no other nodes are currently transmitting data signals. If the node doesn't hear any other signals, it assumes that it is safe to transmit data. All devices on the network have the same right (that is, they have multiple access) to transmit data when they deem it safe. It is therefore possible for two devices to begin transmitting data signals at the same time. If this happens, the two signals collide.

What happens when the signals collide? As shown in Figure 12.11, when two nodes (Computer 1 and Computer 4) begin transmitting data signals at the same time, signals collide, and a node on the network (Computer 3) detects the collision (Step 1). That node (Computer 3) then sends a special signal called a **jam signal** to all network nodes, alerting them that a collision has occurred (Step 2). The original nodes (Computer 1 and Computer 4) then stop transmitting and wait a random amount of time before retransmitting their data signals (Step 3). The wait times need to be random; otherwise, both nodes would start retransmitting at the same time and another collision would occur.

ACTIVE HELP-DESK

Selecting a Network Topology and Cable

In this Active Helpdesk call, you'll play the role of a Helpdesk staffer, fielding calls about how a client/server network differs from a peer-to-peer network, the different classifications of client/server networks, various network topologies, and the types of transmission media used in client/server networks.

What are the advantages and disadvantages of a star topology?

The main reason a star topology generally is considered to be superior to a ring topology is that if one computer on a star topology fails, it doesn't affect the rest of the network. This is extremely important in a large network in which having one disabled computer affect the operations of several hundred other computers would be unacceptable.

Another advantage is that it is easy to add nodes to star networks. Furthermore, performance remains acceptable even with large numbers of users. In addition, centralizing communications through a switch makes troubleshooting and repairs on star networks easier for network technicians. Technicians can usually pinpoint a communications problem just by examining the switch, as opposed to searching for a particular length of cable that broke in a ring network.

The disadvantage of star networks used to be cost. Because of the complexity of the layout of star networks, they require more cable and used to be more expensive than bus or ring networks. Because the price of cable has fallen, this has ceased to be a barrier in most cases.

Comparing Topologies

Which topology is the best one?

Figure 12.12 lists the advantages and disadvantages of bus, ring, and star topologies. Star topologies are the most common, mainly because large networks are constantly adding new users. The ability to add new users simply—by installing a new switch—without affecting users already on the network is the deciding factor. The networks you'll encounter at school and in the workplace will almost certainly be laid out in a star topology. Bus topologies have become all but extinct now that most home networks utilize a star topology. Ring topologies are still popular in certain businesses where fair allocation of network access is a major requirement of the network.

Can topologies be combined within a single network? Because each topology has its own unique advantages, topologies are often combined to construct business networks. Combining multiple topologies into one network is known as constructing a **hybrid topology**. For instance, fair allocation of resources may be critical for reservation clerks at an airline (thereby requiring a ring network), but the airline's purchasing department may require a star topology. One disadvantage of hybrid topologies is that hardware changes must usually be made to switch a node from one topology to another.

Transmission Media

A variety of building materials are available for constructing a house; the ones chosen will depend on the needs of the builder. Similarly, when building a network, network engineers can use different types of

Figure 12.12 | ADVANTAGES AND DISADVANTAGES OF BUS, RING, AND STAR TOPOLOGIES

Topology	Advantages	Disadvantages
Bus	It uses a minimal amount of cable. Installation is easy, reliable, and inexpensive.	Breaks in the cable can disable the network. Large numbers of users will greatly decrease performance because of high volumes of data traffic.
Ring	Allocates access to the network fairly. Performance remains acceptable even with large numbers of users.	Adding or removing nodes disables the network. Failure of one computer can bring down the entire network. Problems in data transmission can sometimes be difficult to find.
Star	Failure of one computer does not affect other computers on the network. Centralized design simplifies troubleshooting and repairs. High scalability: adding computers or groups of computers as needed is easy. Performance remains acceptable even with large numbers of users.	Requires more cable (and possibly higher installation costs) than a bus or ring topology. The switch is a single point of failure. If it fails, all computers connected to that switch are affected.

media. **Transmission media**, whether for wired or wireless communications technology, comprise the routes data takes to flow between devices on the network. Without transmission media, network devices would be unable to communicate.

Why are wired connections used in business networks? Wired connections are popular in business networks because wired connections generally provide higher throughput than wireless connections. And although most home users purchase notebooks instead of desktop computers, desktop computers still provide more computing power for less money than notebooks, which makes desktop computers popular choices for business networks. Because desktops aren't moved around, they are usually connected to a network with a wired connection.

Wired Transmission Media

What types of cable are commonly used for networks? Most home networks use twisted-pair cable as wired transmission media. For business networks, the three main cable types that are used today are twisted pair, coaxial, and fiber optic.

What are the important factors in choosing a cable type? Although each cable type is different, the same criteria always need to be considered when choosing a cable type:

- **Maximum run length:** Each type of cable has a maximum run length over which signals sent across it can be "heard" by devices connected to it. Therefore, when designing a network, network engineers must accurately measure the distances between devices to ensure that they select an appropriate cable.
- **Bandwidth:** As you learned in earlier chapters, **bandwidth** is the amount of data that can be transmitted across a transmission medium in a certain amount of time. Each cable is different and is rated by the maximum bandwidth it can support. Bandwidth is measured in bits per second, which represents how many bits of data can be transmitted along the cable each second.
- **Bend radius (flexibility):** When installing cable, it is often necessary to bend the cable around corners, surfaces,

and so on. The bend radius of the cable defines how many degrees a cable can be bent in a one-foot segment before it is damaged. If many corners need to be navigated when installing a network, network engineers use cabling with a high bend radius.

- **Cable cost:** The cost per foot of different types and grades of cable varies widely. Cable selection may have to be made based on cost if adequate funds are not available for the optimal type of cabling.
- **Installation costs:** Certain types of cable (such as twisted pair) are easy and inexpensive to install. Fiber-optic cable requires special training and equipment to install, which increases the installation costs.
- **Susceptibility to interference:** Signals traveling down a cable are subject to two types of interference. Electromagnetic interference (EMI), which is caused when the cable is exposed to strong electromagnetic fields, can distort or degrade signals on the cable. Fluorescent lights and machinery with motors or transformers are the most common sources of EMI emissions. Cable signals also can be disrupted by radio frequency interference (RFI), which is

 BITS AND BYTES ViFi—WiFi for Those on the Move!

With the proliferation of portable computing devices, demand for connectivity is increasing exponentially. To meet the demand, technologies such as WiFi are now deployed even in moving vehicles. Numerous cities in the United States, including San Francisco, California; Cincinnati, Ohio; and Austin, Texas offer WiFi connectivity on city buses. Initiatives like Aspirnaut, in Kentucky, provide rural children with school bus rides in excess of one hour with free WiFi access and computing devices to use while riding the bus. However, WiFi connectivity is tricky to achieve while on the move because you can connect to only one wireless access point at a time, and the access points have limited range. As you drive along and get out of range, you need to change to other access points. As you switch from one access point to another, connectivity speeds drop dramatically or connectivity is lost altogether.

A joint initiative among the University of Massachusetts, the University of Washington, and Microsoft may be close to solving the problem. They have developed a new technology called Vehicle WiFi (ViFi) that allows a device to connect to more than one access point at the same time. The software your device runs determines which access point has the best signal strength and sends data packets through it. By connecting with multiple access points at once, it makes switching from point to point less likely to sever your Internet connection. Perhaps you'll be able to take advantage of ViFi in the next new car you buy, and your passengers can surf effortlessly while you whiz along at 55 miles per hour!

usually caused by broadcast sources (television and radio signals) located near the network. Cable types are rated as to how well they resist interference.

- **Signal transmission methods:** Both coaxial cable and twisted-pair cable send electrical impulses down conductive material to transmit data signals. Fiber-optic cable transmits data signals as pulses of light.

In the sections that follow, we will discuss the characteristics of each of the three major types of cable. We will also discuss the use of wireless media as an alternative to cable.

Twisted-Pair Cable

What does twisted-pair cable look like? Twisted-pair cable should be familiar to you because the telephone cable (or wire) in your home is one type of twisted-pair cable. **Twisted-pair cable** consists of pairs of copper wires twisted around each other and covered by a protective sheath (jacket). The twists are important because they cause the magnetic fields that form around the copper wires to intermingle, which makes them less susceptible to outside interference. The twists also reduce the amount of crosstalk interference (the tendency of signals on one wire to interfere with signals on a wire next to it).

If the twisted-pair cable contains a layer of foil shielding to reduce interference, it is known as **shielded twisted-pair (STP) cable**. If it does not contain a layer of foil shielding, it is known as **unshielded twisted-pair (UTP) cable**. This type is more susceptible to interference. Figure 12.13

shows illustrations of both types of twisted-pair cable. Because of its lower price, UTP is more widely used, unless significant sources of interference must be overcome (such as in a production environment where machines create magnetic fields).

What types of UTP cable are available? There are different standard categories of UTP cable from which to choose. The two most common types of UTP cable used in business networks today are Category 6 (Cat 6) and Category 6a (Cat 6a). Cat 6 cable can handle a bandwidth of 1 gigabit per second (Gbps), whereas Cat 6a can handle a bandwidth of 10 Gbps.

Unless severe budget constraints are in place, network engineers usually install the highest-bandwidth cable possible because reinstalling cable later (which often requires tearing up walls and ceilings) can be very expensive. Therefore, new cable installed on business networks will usually be Cat 6a cable. Home networks that use twisted-pair cable generally use Cat 6 cable because it's less expensive and most home networks don't need 10 Gbps of throughput.

Coaxial Cable

What does coaxial cable look like? **Coaxial cable** should be familiar to you if you have cable television, because most cable television installers use coaxial cable. Coaxial cable (as shown in Figure 12.14) consists of four main components:

1. The core (usually copper) is in the very center and is used for transmitting the signal.

2. A solid layer of nonconductive insulating material (usually a hard, thick plastic) surrounds the core.

3. A layer of braided metal shielding covers the insulation to reduce interference with signals traveling in the core.

4. An external jacket of lightweight plastic covers the internal cable components to protect them from damage.

Figure 12.13

Anatomy of (a) unshielded twisted-pair (UTP) cable and (b) shielded twisted-pair (STP) cable.

Twisted pairs of copper wires

a

Protective sheath

b

Protective sheath

Foil shielding

Twisted pairs of copper wires

Although coaxial cable used to be the most widely used cable in business networks, advances in twisted-pair cable shielding and transmission speeds, as well as twisted pair's lower cost, have reduced the popularity of coaxial cable. However, coaxial cable is still used in some manufacturing facilities where machinery creates heavy electrical interference.

Figure 12.14

Coaxial cable consists of four main components: the core, an insulated covering, a braided metal shielding, and a plastic jacket.

Fiber-Optic Cable

What does fiber-optic cable look like?   As shown in Figure 12.15, the core of **fiber-optic cable** is comprised of a glass (or plastic) fiber (or a bundle of fibers) through which the data is transmitted. A protective layer of glass or plastic cladding is wrapped around the core to protect it. Finally, for additional protection, an outer jacket (sheath) is added, often made of a durable material such as Kevlar (the substance used to make bulletproof vests). Data transmissions can pass through fiber-optic cable in only one direction. Therefore, at least two cores are located in most fiber-optic cables to enable transmission of data in both directions.

How does fiber-optic cable differ from twisted-pair and coaxial cable? As we noted earlier, the main difference between fiber-optic cable and other types of cable is the method of signal transmission. Twisted-pair and coaxial cable use copper wire to conduct electrical impulses. In a fiber-optic cable, electrical data signals from network devices (client computers, peripherals, and so on) are converted to light pulses before they are transmitted. Because EMI and RFI do not affect light waves, fiber-optic cable is virtually immune to interference.

Figure 12.15

Fiber-optic cable is made up of a glass or plastic fiber (or a bundle of fibers), a glass or plastic cladding, and a protective sheath.

Wireless Media Options

What wireless media options are there?   Although the word *wireless* implies "no wires," in businesses, **wireless media** are usually add-ons that extend or improve access to a wired network. In the corporate environment, wireless access is often provided to give employees a wider working area. For instance, if conference rooms offer wireless access, employees can bring their notebooks (laptops) to meetings and gain access to the network during the meeting. However, when they go back to their offices, they may connect to the network through a wired connection. Accordingly, corporate networks are often a combination of wired and wireless media.

Are there standards defined for wireless communication?   Wireless devices must use the same communications standard to communicate with each other. Wireless networks in the United States are currently based on the **802.11 standard**, also known as **WiFi**, established by the Institute of Electrical and Electronics Engineers (IEEE). Wireless devices attached to networks using the 802.11 standard communicate with each other using radio waves.

Comparing Transmission Media

So who decides which medium is best for client/server networks? Network engineers specialize in the design and deployment of networks and are responsible for selecting network topology and media types. Their decision as to which

DIG DEEPER — The OSI Model: Defining Protocol Standards

The Institute of Electrical and Electronics Engineers (IEEE) has taken the lead in establishing recognized worldwide networking protocols, including a standard of communications called the Open Systems Interconnection (OSI) reference model. The OSI model, which has been adopted as a standard throughout the computing world, provides the protocol guidelines for all modern networks. All modern network operating system (NOS) protocols are designed to interact in accordance with the standards set out in the OSI model.

The OSI model divides communications tasks into seven distinct processes called layers. Each layer of an OSI network has a specific function and knows how to communicate with the layers above and below it. Figure 12.16 shows the layers of the OSI model and their functions.

This layering approach makes communications more efficient because specialized pieces of the NOS perform specific tasks. The layering approach is akin to assembly-line manufacturing. Producing thousands of cars per day would be difficult if one person had to build a car on his or her own. However, by splitting up the work of assembling a car into specialized tasks (such as installing the engine or bolting on the bumpers) and assigning them to people who perform exceptionally well at certain tasks, greater efficiency is achieved. This is how the OSI layers work. By handling specialized tasks and communicating only with the layers above and below them, OSI layers make communications more efficient.

Let's look at how each OSI layer functions by following an e-mail you create and send to your friend:

- **Application layer:** Handles all interaction between the application software and the network. It translates the data from the application into a format that the presentation layer can understand. For example, when you send an e-mail, the application layer takes the e-mail message you created in Microsoft Outlook, translates it into a format your network can understand, and passes it to the presentation layer.
- **Presentation layer:** Reformats the data so that the session layer can understand it. It also handles data encryption (changing the data into a format that makes it harder to intercept and read the message) and compression, if required. In our e-mail example, the presentation layer notices that you selected an encryption option for the e-mail message and encrypts the data before sending it to the session layer.

- **Session layer:** Sets up a virtual (not physical) connection between the sending and receiving devices. It then manages the communication between the two. In our e-mail example, the session layer would set up the parameters for the communications session between your computer and the Internet service provider (ISP) where your friend has her e-mail account. The session layer then tracks the transmission of the e-mail until it is satisfied that all the data in the e-mail was received at your friend's ISP.
- **Transport layer:** Breaks up the data into packets and sequences them appropriately. It also handles acknowledgment of packets (that is, it determines whether the packets were received at their destination) and decides whether packets need to be sent again. In our e-mail example, the transport layer breaks up your e-mail message into packets and sends them to the network layer, making sure that all the packets reach their destination.
- **Network layer:** Determines where to send the packets on the network and identifies the best way to route them there. In our e-mail example, the network layer examines the address on the packets (the address of your friend's ISP) and determines how to route the packets so they get to your ISP and can ultimately get to the receiving computer.
- **Data link layer:** Responsible for assembling the data packets into frames (a type of data packet that holds more data), addressing the frames, and delivering them to the physical layer so they can be sent on their way. It is the equivalent of a postal worker who reads the address on a piece of mail and makes sure it is sent to the proper recipient. In our e-mail example, the data link layer assembles the e-mail data packets into frames, which are addressed with appropriate routing information that it receives from the network layer.
- **Physical layer:** Takes care of delivering the data. It converts the data into a signal and transmits it over the network so that it can reach its intended address. In our e-mail example, the physical layer sends the data over the Internet to its ultimate destination (your friend's ISP).

By following standardized protocols set forth by the OSI model, NOS software can communicate happily with the computers and peripherals attached to the network as well as with other networks.

Figure 12.16 | LAYERS OF THE OSI MODEL AND THEIR FUNCTIONS

Application layer	Handles all interfaces between the application software and the network Translates user information into a format the presentation layer can understand
Presentation layer	Reformats data so that the session layer can understand it Compresses and encrypts data
Session layer	Sets up a virtual (not physical) connection between the sending and receiving devices Manages communications sessions
Transport layer	Creates packets and handles packet acknowledgment
Network layer	Determines where to send the packets on the network
Data link layer	Assembles the data into frames, addresses them, and sends them to the physical layer for delivery
Physical layer	Transmits (delivers) data on the network so it can reach its intended address

Figure 12.17 | CHARACTERISTICS OF MAJOR CABLE TYPES

Cable Characteristics	Twisted Pair (Cat 6)	Twisted Pair (Cat 6a)	Fiber-Optic
Maximum run length	328 feet (100 m)	328 feet (100 m)	Up to 62 miles (100 km)
Bandwidth	Up to 1 Gbps	Up to 10 Gbps	10 to 40 Gbps
Bend radius (flexibility)	No limit	No limit	30 degrees/foot
Cable cost	Extremely low	Low	High
Installation cost	Extremely low	Extremely low	Most expensive because of installation training required
Susceptibility to interference	High	High	None (not susceptible to EMI or RFI)

transmission medium a network will use is based on the topology selected, the length of the cable runs needed, the amount of interference present, and the need for wireless connectivity. Coaxial cable has been made largely obsolete by advances in twisted-pair cabling throughput and decreases in its cost.

Figure 12.17 compares the attributes of the major cable types. Most large networks have a mix of media. For example, fiber-optic cable may be appropriate for the portion of the network that traverses the factory floor, where interference from magnetic fields is significant. However, unshielded twisted-pair cable may work fine in the general office area. Wireless media may be required in conference rooms and other areas where employees are likely to connect their notebooks or where it is impractical or expensive to run cable.

Network Operating Systems

Merely using media to connect computers and peripherals does not create a client/server network. Special software known as a **network operating system (NOS)** needs to be installed on each client computer and server connected to the network to provide the services necessary for them to communicate. Many modern operating systems, such as Windows 7 and Mac OS X, include NOS client software as part of the basic installation. However, if your operating system does not include NOS client software, it must be installed on each client. The NOS provides a set of common rules (a protocol) that controls communication among devices on the network. The major NOSs on the market today include Windows Server 2008 R2, Linux, UNIX, and Novell SUSE Linux Enterprise.

Do peer-to-peer networks need special NOS software? The software that P2P networks require is built into the Windows and Macintosh operating systems. Therefore, if you have a simple P2P network, there is no need to purchase specialized NOS software. When a peer-to-peer network won't suffice (such as in a network with more than 10 computers), you can't use the networking software included in Windows and Mac OS X. Instead, you will need to purchase additional NOS software.

How does NOS software differ from operating system software? Operating system (OS) software is designed to facilitate communication between the software and hardware components of your computer. NOS software is specifically designed to provide server services, network communications, management of network peripherals, and storage. To provide network communications, the client computer must run a small part of the NOS in addition to the OS. Windows 7 is an OS and is installed on home computers. As noted above, because it also has some NOS functionality, client computers (in a client/server network) that have Windows 7 installed as the OS do not need an additional NOS. Windows Server 2008 R2 is a NOS that is deployed on servers in a client/server network.

How does the NOS control network communications? Each NOS has its own proprietary communications language, file-management structure, and device-management structure. The NOS also sets and controls the protocols (rules) for all devices wishing to communicate on the network. Many different proprietary networking protocols exist, such as Novell Internetwork Packet Exchange (IPX),

Microsoft NetBIOS Extended User Interface (NetBEUI), and the Apple File Protocol (AFP). These protocols were developed for a specific vendor's operating system. For example, IPX was developed for networks running the Novell NOS. Proprietary protocols such as these do not work with another vendor's NOS.

However, because the Internet uses an open protocol (called TCP/IP) for communications, many corporate networks use TCP/IP as their standard networking protocol regardless of the manufacturer of their NOS. All modern NOSs support TCP/IP. (We discuss TCP/IP in more detail in Chapter 13.)

Can a network use two different NOSs? Many large corporate networks use several different NOSs at the same time. This is because different NOSs provide different features, some of which are more useful in certain situations than others are. For instance, although the employees of a corporation may be using a Microsoft Windows environment for their desktops and e-mail, the file servers and Web servers may be running a Linux NOS.

Because NOSs use different internal software languages to communicate, one NOS can't communicate directly with another. However, if both NOSs are using the same protocol (such as TCP/IP), they can pass information between the networks and it can be interpreted by the receiving network.

Figure 12.18

A NIC is responsible for breaking down data into packets, preparing packets for transmission, receiving incoming data packets, and reconstructing them.

Network Adapters

As we noted in Chapter 7, client computers and peripherals need an interface to connect with and communicate on the network.

Network adapters are devices that perform specific tasks to enable computers to communicate on a network. Most network adapters are installed *inside* computers and peripherals. These adapters are referred to as network interface cards (NICs).

What do network adapters do? Network adapters perform three critical functions:

1. **They generate high-powered signals to enable network transmissions.** Digital signals generated inside the computer are fairly low powered and would not travel well on network media (cable or wireless technology) without network adapters. Network adapters convert the signals from inside the computer to higher-powered signals that have no trouble traversing the network media.

2. **They are responsible for breaking the data into packets and preparing the packets for transmission across the network.** They also are responsible for receiving incoming data packets and, in accordance with networking protocols (rules), reconstructing them, as shown in Figure 12.18.

3. **They act as gatekeepers for information flowing to and from the client computer.** Much like a security guard in a gated community, a network adapter is responsible for permitting or denying access to the client computer (the community) and controlling the flow of data (visitors).

You should note that there will not always be the same number of response

Step 1: You request information from network database.

Step 2: NIC breaks request into packages and sends packets to server.

Request packet #1

Request packet #2

Request packet #3

Server

Response packet #1

Response packet #2

Network interface card

Your computer (client)

Step 4: NIC reassembles response packets and displays information on your screen.

Step 3: Server executes request, assembles response into package, and sends packets to client.

Desktop computer

Cat 6 cable

Notebook computer
with wireless NIC

Smartphone
with wireless NIC

Radio waves

Switch

Wireless access point

Server

Figure 12.19

This small corporate
network has an added
wireless access point.

packets as there are request packets. The
number of packets depends on the volume
of the data being sent. A simple response
may have less data than a complex one.

**Are there different types of
network adapters?** Although there are
different types of network adapters, almost
without exception, Ethernet (either wired or
wireless) is the standard communications
protocol used on most client/server networks. Therefore, the adapter cards that
ship with computers today are Ethernet
compliant. The majority of Ethernet
adapters provide connection ports that accept RJ-45 (Ethernet) connector plugs for
connection to twisted-pair cable. However,
adapters that provide other types of connectors for direct connections to other types of
network media (such as fiber-optic cables)
are available.

**Do wireless networks require
network adapters?** Most corporate networks are not entirely wireless, but they do
provide wireless connectivity to some computers and to portable devices such as
smartphones. A computer that connects to
the network using wireless access needs to
have a special network adapter card, called
a **wireless network interface card (wireless
NIC)**, installed in the system unit. Notebook
computers and other portable computing
devices contain wireless NICs. To allow
wireless connections, the network must be
fitted with devices called *wireless access*

points. A **wireless access point (WAP)** gives
wireless devices a sending and receiving
connection point to the network.

Figure 12.19 shows an example of a typical corporate network with a wireless access
point. The access point is connected to the
wired network through a conventional
cable. When a notebook (or other device
with a wireless NIC) is powered on near a
wireless access point, it establishes a connection with the access point using radio
waves. Many devices can communicate
with the network through a single wireless
access point.

**Do network adapters require
software?** Because the network adapter
is responsible for communications between
the client computer and the network, it
needs to speak the same language as the network's special operating system software.
Therefore, special communications software
called a **device driver** is installed on all client
computers in the client/server network.
Device drivers enable the network adapter
to communicate with the server's operating
system and with the operating system of the
computer in which the adapter is installed.

**What are my options if I'm not
located in range of a wireless
network?** You can bring your own
wireless network with you! Most cellular
telephone companies, such as AT&T and
Sprint, offer broadband PC adapters for
your notebook that will keep you connected

(for a fee, of course). A PC adapter plugs into a USB port on your notebook and enables it to send and receive data using your cellular provider's wireless network. Broadband download speeds now can reach more than 50 Mbps with 4G networks, making this a viable option if you need to ensure you have connectivity everywhere you go—or virtually everywhere. Check with the cellular provider to ensure they have coverage in most places you will travel through.

Network Navigation Devices

To flow through a network, data is broken into small segments called packets. Data packets are like postal letters. They don't get to their destinations without some help. In this section, we explore the various conventions and devices that help speed data packets on their way through the network.

MAC Addresses

How do data packets know where to go on the network? Each network adapter has a physical address similar to a serial number on an appliance. This is called a **media access control (MAC) address**, and it is made up of six two-position characters such as 01:40:87:44:79:A5. (Don't confuse this MAC with the Apple computers of the same name.) The first three sets of characters (in this case, 01:40:87) specify the manufacturer of the network adapter, whereas the second set of characters (in this case, 44:79:A5) makes up a unique address. Because all MAC addresses must be unique, there is an IEEE committee responsible for allocating blocks of numbers to network adapter manufacturers.

SOUND BYTE

What's My IP Address? (And Other Interesting Facts about Networks)

In this Sound Byte, you'll learn how to determine your IP address, which is commonly required to set up online gaming. You'll also explore several Web sites that can reveal interesting information about your connection to the Internet.

Are MAC addresses the same as IP addresses? MAC addresses and Internet Protocol (IP) addresses are not the same thing. A MAC address is used for identification purposes *internally* on a network, which is similar to giving people different names to differentiate them. An IP address is the address *external* entities use to communicate with your network and is similar to your home street address. Think of it this way: The postal carrier delivers a package (data packet) to your dorm building based on its street address (IP address). The dorm's mail clerk delivers the package to your room because it has your name on it (MAC address) and not that of your neighbor. Both pieces of information are necessary to ensure that the package (or data) reaches its destination.

How does a data packet get a MAC address? Data packets are not necessarily sent alone. Sometimes groups of data packets are sent together in a group called a frame. A **frame** is a container that can hold multiple data packets. This is similar to placing several letters going to the same postal address in a big envelope. While the data packets are being assembled into frames, the NOS software assigns the appropriate MAC address to the frame. The NOS keeps track of all devices and their addresses on the network. Much like a letter that is entrusted to the postal service, the frame is delivered to the MAC address that the NOS assigned to the frame.

What delivers the frames to the correct device on the network? In a small bus network, frames just bounce along the wire until the correct client computer notices the frame is addressed to it and pulls the signal off the wire. This is inefficient in a larger network. Therefore, many types of devices have been developed to deliver data to its destination efficiently. These devices are designed to route signals and exchange data with other networks.

Are MAC addresses useful for anything besides identifying a particular network device? On networks with wireless capabilities, MAC addresses can be used to enhance network security. Most wireless routers and access points can be used to filter MAC addresses and eliminate addresses of unauthorized devices. Because each MAC address is unique, you can input a list of authorized MAC addresses into the router. If someone who is using an unauthorized network adapter

Message for
Computer #3

Switch

Computer #1

Server

Broadcast of
message for
Computer #3

Computer #2

Computer #4

Computer #3

Figure 12.20

Switches rebroadcast
messages—but only to
the devices to which the
messages are addressed.

(one with an unauthorized MAC address) attempts to connect to the network, he or she will be unable to make a connection. Although it would be impractical for a large organization, in which employees constantly are being hired and leaving, MAC address filtering is a useful security tool on home networks and small business networks.

Switches and Bridges

Which devices are used to route signals through a single network?

Switches and bridges are used to send data on a specific route through the network. A **switch** makes decisions, based on the MAC address of the data, as to where the data is to be sent and directs it to the appropriate network node. This improves network efficiency by helping to ensure that each node receives only the data intended for it.

Do all networks need a switch?

Switches are needed on Ethernet networks whether installed in the home or a business. Routers sold for home use have switches built into them. Figure 12.20 shows a switch being used to rebroadcast a message.

Are switches sufficient for moving data efficiently across all sizes of networks?

When a corporate network grows in size, performance can decline because many devices compete for transmission time on the network media. To solve this problem, a network can be broken into multiple segments known as collision domains. A **bridge** is a device that is used to send data between these different collision domains. A bridge sends data between collision domains, depending on where the recipient device is located, as indicated in Figure 12.21. Signals received by the bridge from collision domain A are forwarded to collision domain B only if the destination computer is located in that domain. Most home networks contain only one segment and therefore do not require bridges.

Routers

What device does a network use to move data to another network?

Whereas switches and bridges perform their functions within a single network, a **router** is designed to send information between two networks. To accomplish this, the router must look at higher-level network addresses (such as IP addresses), not MAC addresses. When the router notices data with an address that does not belong to a device on the network from which it originated, it

Figure 12.21

Bridges are devices used to send data between different network collision domains.

sends the data to another network to which it is attached (or out onto the Internet).

Network Security for Client/Server Networks

A major advantage that client/server networks have over peer-to-peer networks is that they offer a higher level of security. With client/server networks, users can be required to enter a user ID and a password to gain access to the network. The security can be centrally administered by network administrators, freeing individual users of the responsibility of maintaining their own data security (as they must do on a peer-to-peer network).

In the next section, we will explore the challenges network administrators face in keeping a client/server network secure. We use a college network as our example, but note that the same principles apply to all client/server networks.

What sources of security threats do all network administrators need to watch for? Threats can be classified into three main groups: human errors and mistakes, malicious human activity, and natural events and disasters.

- **Human errors and mistakes:** Everyone makes mistakes. For example, the clerk processing your tuition payment could accidentally delete your records. A member of the computer support staff could mistakenly install an old database on top of the current one. Even physical accidents fall into this category; for example, someone could lose control of a car and drive it through the wall of the main server room.

- **Malicious human activity:** Malicious actions can be perpetrated by current employees, former employees, or third parties. For example, a disgruntled employee could introduce a virus to the network. A hacker could break into the student database server to steal credit card records. A former employee who feels he or she was unjustly fired could deliberately destroy data.

- **Natural events and disasters:** Some events—such as broken water pipes or fire, or disasters such as hurricanes, floods, earthquakes, and other acts of nature—are beyond human control. All can lead to the inadvertent destruction of data.

Who and what does a college network need to be secure against? A college network, like any network, is vulnerable to unauthorized users and manipulation or misuse of the data contained on it. The person who sat next to you last semester in English class—and failed—may be interested in changing his or her grade to an A. Hackers may be interested in the financial and personal information (such as Social Security numbers and credit card numbers) stored in college financial office databases on the network. Thus, one of the network administrator's key functions is to keep network data secure.

Authentication

How does a college ensure that only authorized users access its network? Authentication is the process whereby users prove they have authorization to use a computer network. The type of authentication most people are familiar with consists of providing a user ID and password. However, authentication can also be achieved through the use of biometric devices (discussed later in this chapter) and through possessed objects. A **possessed object** is any object that a user carries to identify himself and that grants him access to a computer system or computer facility. Examples include identification badges, magnetic key cards, and smart keys (similar to flash drives).

How do most colleges handle authentication on their networks? As mentioned earlier, to gain access to a typical college client/server network, you have to go through authentication by entering a user ID and a password. By correctly inputting your ID and password, you prove who you are to the network and show that you have authorized access. The access is authorized because the ID was generated by a network administrator when you became a student.

Can hackers use my account to log on to the network? If a hacker knows your user ID and password, he or she can log on and impersonate you. (Impersonation can also happen if you fail to log out of a terminal on the college network and someone comes along and uses your account.) Sometimes network user IDs are easy to figure out because they have a certain pattern (such as your last name and the first initial of your first name). If a hacker can deduce your user ID, he might use a software program that tries millions of combinations of letters and numbers as your password in an attempt to access your account. Attempting to access an account by repeatedly trying different passwords is known as a **brute force attack**. To prevent these attacks from succeeding, network administrators often configure accounts so that they will disable themselves after a set number of logon attempts using invalid passwords have been made. If a network account isn't set to disable itself after a small number of incorrect passwords is tried, a brute force attack may eventually succeed.

Access Privileges

How can I gain access to everything on the college network? The simple answer is that you can't! When your account was set up, certain access privileges were granted to indicate which systems you were allowed to use. For example, your access privileges probably include the ability to access the Internet. You also might have access privileges to view your transcript and grades online, depending on the sophistication of your college network. However, you definitely were not granted access to the grade reporting system, because this would enable you to change your grades. Likewise,

Bought anything at WalMart or Best Buy lately? If so, there is a good chance that you brought home a **radio frequency identification tag (RFID tag)** with your purchase. Originally, RFID tags were used to keep track of cattle, but now they've moved into the retail sector to keep track of products. What are RFID tags, how did they end up in retail stores, and why should you care about them?

RFID tags can look like stickers or labels, or like the thin plastic wristbands you get when you check into a hospital. The tags are attached to batches of merchandise (usually cases or pallets), and all tags contain a microchip that holds a unique sequence of numbers used to identify the product to which it is attached. The tags also contain a tiny antenna that broadcasts information about the merchandise, such as its date of manufacture or price. Think of RFID tags as the next generation of UPC codes.

Two types of tags are in use: active and passive. Active tags are equipped with a battery and constantly transmit information. Passive tags don't have their own power source but instead get their energy from tag readers. Passive tags are more common because they are cheaper. Tag readers are devices that scan the information on the tags as the tags are passed by the reader. They do this through antennas that generate magnetic fields, which the passive tags sense. In response, the passive tags transmit their product code to the tag reader. The reader then sends the digital information to a computer network, and most likely into a database.

So how do RFID tags help retailers? For large retailers, inventory can be daunting to manage. Retailers such as WalMart have tens of thousands of suppliers sending hundreds of thousands of products to their warehouses and stores. The use of RFID tagging allows the recording of inventory receipts and shipments to stores to be largely automated, resulting in fewer mistakes, fewer instances of merchandise being lost and forgotten in the warehouse, and tighter control over stock levels. This helps retailers and their suppliers ensure that the correct inventory levels are maintained at all times, resulting in fewer shortages of merchandise

and, ultimately, increased sales because the product is on the shelf when you go to buy it.

Retailers also can use the product serial number information, which can be embedded in tags, to speed repair or return service. This process is shown in Figure 12.22. As merchandise equipped with RFID tags enters the warehouse, the tags are scanned, and the inventory database is updated. When merchandise is moved to the sales floor, scanning updates the inventory database again for the new stock location. One last scan occurs when customers purchase items, which triggers the stock ordering system to place another order with a supplier if inventory is too low.

RFID can provide huge benefits for consumers. Imagine if all products in your local grocery store had RFID tags. When you entered the store and grabbed a shopping cart, you could swipe your credit card through a reader on the cart. After you finished shopping, you could just walk out the door, at which time an RFID reader would take an inventory of the contents of your cart and charge your credit card for what you purchased. No more waiting in checkout lines! This streamlining of payment could result in lower costs for consumers. After you got home, if your refrigerator was equipped with RFID equipment, it could scan your purchases and keep track of your groceries, including expiration dates. Your refrigerator might contact your smartphone (via the Internet) and let you know that your milk was out of date so you could buy more on the way home. Now that's a smart fridge!

All this convenience could come with a price. There is concern that people might gather information about consumers' buying habits without their knowledge, similar to the concerns people have about spyware on computers today, because the RFID tags would be operational outside of the retail store. For example, someone could sit in the parking lot with a tag reader and detect exactly what you had purchased as you pushed your shopping cart by his or her car. If this person were from a competing retailer, this information could be especially valuable to that

you did not receive access to the financial systems; otherwise, you might be able to change your account, indicating that your bill was paid when it had not been.

How does restricting access privileges protect a network?
Because network access accounts are centrally administered on the authentication server, it is easy for the network administrator to set up accounts for new students and grant them access only to the systems and software they need. The centralized nature of the creation of access accounts and the ability to restrict access to certain areas of the client/server network make it more secure than a peer-to-peer network. If you shouldn't go somewhere (such as into the files that record student grades), you can't get there on your school network!

Aside from improper access, how else do data theft and destruction occur?
Data storage devices are becoming smaller even as their capacities are increasing. One problem that devices such as flash drives pose is theft of data or intellectual property. Because these devices are so portable and have such large memory capacity, it is easy for a disgruntled employee to walk out the front door with stacks of valuable documents tucked in his or her pants pocket. Industrial espionage has never been easier—and no spy cameras are needed!

Flash drives can also introduce viruses or other malicious programs to a network, either intentionally or unintentionally. Just Secure Network Technologies, a security consulting firm, decided to test a client's

Figure 12.22
RFID tags are scanned multiple times at a retail store.

Truck — Pallets of merchandise being unloaded at the dock

Data being scanned as boxes go into the warehouse

Warehouse — Data being scanned as boxes go into the retail space

Sales Floor — Data being scanned as customers take boxes out to their cars

Customer

company. Alternatively, this person could be from a government enforcement agency trying to determine whether underage consumers were purchasing alcoholic beverages. Some pundits have speculated that if the tags had a long enough range, thieves could drive by houses and scan for desirable items to steal, such as large-screen TVs. However, this is unlikely given the state of current RFID technology.

Many consumers resent any potential invasion of their privacy. Therefore, retailers will need to educate consumers about RFID tags and their benefits. Retailers also will need to ensure that consumers have the option to deactivate or remove tags to protect their privacy.

security procedures by leaving 20 flash drives at random locations around the client's office. By the end of the day, employees had picked up 15 of the flash drives and plugged them into computers on the company network. The flash drives contained a simple program to display images as well as a Trojan horse program. While the employees were viewing the images, the Trojan horse program enabled the consultants to access the company network (if they wanted to do so) and steal or compromise data. It isn't hard to imagine hackers leaving flash drives around your company that could act as "skeleton keys" to your company's network.

How should network administrators protect their networks from portable storage devices? First,

educate employees to the dangers posed by portable media devices and other untrusted media. Second, create policies regulating the use of media in the workplace. Third, install security measures such as personal firewalls or antivirus software on all computers in the company. The firewalls should be able to prevent malicious programs from running, even if they are introduced to a computer via a flash drive. Last, lock down and monitor the use of USB devices. Although Microsoft networking software allows network administrators to shut off access to the USB ports on computers, this prevents employees from using flash drives and other USB devices for legitimate purposes.

Other software products, such as DeviceLock and Safend, can be deployed on a network to provide options such as

Network Technicians' Access to Networks—Who Is Watching the Watchers?

According to **Salary.com**, the majority of employers report monitoring their employees in some fashion. The monitoring of phone calls, e-mail, and Internet usage by employers is legal in almost all jurisdictions in the United States even if employees are not told they are being monitored. Employers that suspect employees are goofing off can install spyware to monitor employee computer keystrokes and keep track of Web sites visited, down to the individual computer level. Naturally, network administrators are often involved in employee monitoring.

Consider the case of Vernon Blake, a system administrator at the Alabama Department of Transportation. His boss was constantly playing computer games at work. This was common knowledge, yet no action was taken. Vernon installed software on his boss's computer and captured screen images that verified the boss was playing solitaire about 70 percent of the time. When Blake reported the results to management, the boss was reprimanded and Blake was fired! The company cited Blake's lack of authority or permission to install the monitoring software.

Or consider the spying scandal in Lower Merion School District in Pennsylvania. In the spring of 2010, it came to light that software that was installed on notebook computers (provided to students by the school district) was being used by network administrators to capture photos through the computers' webcams and to capture students' on-screen activities. The software was only supposed to be activated when a student reported the notebook stolen, and the parents and students were not sufficiently notified as to the capabilities of the tracking software installed when the notebooks were issued to the students. Despite some students and parents complaining about the potential for invasion of privacy (after they became aware of the software), the school administrators did not lay down strict guidelines for use of the software. When a student was disciplined for behavior that occurred off of school property, which was supported by a picture taken from the webcam on his computer, his parents filed a lawsuit alleging invasion of privacy. Subsequent investigation revealed that the software had been used numerous times by network administrators to capture images of students even when the computers were not reported missing or stolen. It appears the use of the software was left up to the discretion of the network administrators instead of being delineated in a written policy.

So who is in charge of monitoring network administrators so that they don't abuse their access to sensitive information or fail to exercise proper safeguards over sensitive data? Savvy companies put written policies in place for employees regarding computer usage. These policies need to include guidelines for network administrators who have higher levels of access than normal employees do. Procedures for safeguarding data and guidelines for investigating employee misuse of computers must be clearly explained, and management needs to periodically review the activities of the network administrators to ensure compliance with polices. Although all employees need to follow approved company procedures regarding computer usage, it is especially important to ensure that employees with high levels of access and critical security responsibilities are adhering to company guidelines.

detailed security policies. Such products can also monitor USB device connections and track which users have connected devices to the network (including devices other than flash drives).

Don't forget to inform the employees that their use of these devices is being monitored. That alone will be enough to scare many employees from connecting untrusted devices to the network.

Physical Protection Measures

Can any physical measures be taken to protect a network? Restricting physical access to servers and other sensitive equipment is critical to protecting the network. Where are the servers that power your college network? They are most likely behind locked doors to which only authorized personnel have access. Do you see any routers or switches lying about in computer labs? Of course you don't. These devices are securely tucked away in ceilings, walls, or closets, safe from anyone who might tamper with them in an attempt to sabotage the network or breach its security.

As shown in Figure 12.23, access to sensitive areas must be controlled. Many different devices can be used to control access. An **access card reader** is a relatively cheap device that reads information from a magnetic strip on the back of a credit card–like access card (such as your student ID card). The card reader, which can control the lock on a door, is programmed to admit only authorized personnel to the area. Card readers are easily programmed by adding authorized ID card numbers, employee numbers, and so on.

Biometric authentication devices are becoming more popular, although they are still prohibitively costly for many organizations, especially colleges. A **biometric authentication device** uses some unique characteristic of human biology to identify authorized users. Some devices read fingerprints or palm prints when you place your hand on a scanning pad. Other devices shine a beam of laser light into your eye and read the unique

Biometric
Authentication
Device

Biometric
Authentication
Device

Biometric
Authentication
Device

IT
Manager's
Office

Wiring
Closet

Server Room

General IT
Office Area

Access
Card
Reader

Figure 12.23

Access card readers can be used to limit access to semisensitive areas such as the IT office. Higher-security areas, such as the server room, may deserve the additional protection that biometric authentication devices offer.

patterns of your retina to identify you. Facial recognition systems store unique characteristics of an individual's face for later comparison and identification. All of these devices are programmable. When an authorized individual uses a device for the first time, his or her fingerprints, face patterns, or retinal patterns are scanned and stored in a database.

Financial institutions and retail stores are considering using such devices to attempt to eliminate the growing fraud problems of identity theft and counterfeiting of credit and debit cards. If fingerprint authorization were required at the supermarket to make a purchase, a thief who stole your wallet and attempted to use your credit card would be unsuccessful.

The biometric devices currently on the market don't always function as intended. Facial recognition and retinal scanning systems can sometimes be fooled by pictures or videos of an authorized user. Researchers

have fooled biometric fingerprint readers by using fingers made out of modeling clay, using the fingers of cadavers, or having unauthorized persons breathe on the sensor, which makes the previous user's fingerprint visible. (Fingers leave an oily residue behind when they touch a surface.) Research institutions, such as Clarkson University in New York, are designing next-generation fingerprint readers that are much more difficult to fool. These will use specially designed algorithms that will detect moisture patterns on a person's fingers. Another approach may involve readers that detect an electrical current when a finger touches the reader, which is possible because the human body conducts electrical current. Future retinal readers may check whether a person blinks (or his or her pupils contract) when a bright light shines on him or her. Suffice it to say, these devices have a way to go before they are foolproof.

Firewalls

Is the college Internet connection vulnerable to hackers? Just like a home network, a college network that is connected to the Internet can create an attractive nuisance. A college network will most likely have a high-bandwidth connection to the Internet that will attract hackers. For this reason, a well-defended college network, just like a well-defended home network, includes a firewall. Firewalls can be comprised of software or hardware, and many sophisticated firewalls include both. Routers are often equipped to act as hardware firewalls.

Does the firewall on my college's network work the same way as a personal firewall installed on a home network does? Although the firewall at your school may contain a few extra security options, making it even harder to breach than a personal firewall, the school's firewall works on the same basic principles as a home network. At a minimum, most firewalls work as packet screeners. **Packet screening** involves examining incoming data packets to ensure that they originated from or are authorized by valid users on the internal network. The router is the device that performs the packet screening. Unauthorized or suspect packets are discarded by the firewall before they reach the network.

Packet screening also can be configured for outgoing data to ensure that requests for information to the Internet are from legitimate users. This helps detect Trojan horse programs that may have been installed by hackers. As you learned in Chapter 9, Trojan horses masquerade as harmless programs but have a more sinister purpose. They often try to disguise where they are sending data from by using bogus IP addresses on the packets the programs send instead of using an authorized IP address belonging to the network.

If packet screening is working, packets going into and out of the network are checked to ensure they are either from or addressed to a legitimate IP address on the network. If the addresses are not valid addresses on the network, the firewall discards them.

What other security measures does the firewall on a client/server network use? To increase security even further, most large networks add a **bastion host**, which is a heavily secured server located on a special perimeter network between the company's secure internal network and the firewall. A bastion host gets its name from the fortified towers (called *bastions*), located along the outer walls of medieval castles, which were specifically designed to defend the castles against attackers.

To external computers, the bastion host gives the appearance of being the internal network server. Hackers can waste a lot of time and energy attacking the bastion host. However, even if a hacker breaches the bastion host server, the internal network is not vulnerable because the bastion host is not on the internal network. Moreover, during the time the hackers spend trying to penetrate the bastion host, network administrators can detect and thwart their attacks.

Bastion hosts are often configured as proxy servers. A **proxy server** acts as a go-between, connecting computers on the internal network with those on the external network (the Internet). All requests from the internal network for Internet services are directed through the proxy server. Similarly, all incoming requests from the Internet must pass through the proxy server. It is much easier for network administrators to maintain adequate security on one server than it is to ensure that security is maintained on hundreds or thousands of computers in a college network. Figure 12.24 shows a network secured by a firewall, a bastion host, and a screening router.

Now that you know a bit more about business network computing, you should be able to comfortably navigate the network at your college or your place of employment and understand why certain security measures have been taken to protect network data.

> **"Firewalls can be comprised of software or hardware, and many sophisticated firewalls include both."**

INTERNET

Firewall

Packets to/from the Internet

Rejected packets from unauthorized users

External screening router
External screening routers examine all incoming and outgoing packets to/from the Internet. Only packets to/from authorized internal users are permitted into the perimeter network. Packets from unauthorized users are rejected.

Accepted packets from authorized users

Perimeter Network

Authorized requests for Internet services

Bastion host & proxy server
The bastion host/proxy server acts as the single point of contact for all incoming and outgoing Internet traffic. Even if this server is breached, because it is not located on the internal network, the computers on the internal network are still secure.

Valid Internet services

Internal screening router
Internal screening routers can be set to only allow certain types of Internet services (such as e-mail and Web browsing) and to reject all other requests.

Secure Internal Network

Computer #1

Computer #2

Figure 12.24

A typical college network firewall layout.

1. What are the advantages of a business network?

A network enables employees to communicate with each other more easily, even over large distances. Networks also enable resources, such as printers, to be shared, avoiding the cost of providing these resources to individual employees. Software can be deployed from a network server, thereby reducing the costs of installation on each user's computer. Finally, networks enable employees to share an Internet connection, avoiding the cost of providing each employee with a dedicated Internet connection.

2. How does a client/server network differ from a peer-to-peer network?

A client/server network requires at least one server to be attached to the network. The server coordinates functions such as file sharing and printing. In a peer-to-peer network, each node connected to the network can communicate directly with every other node on the network. In a client/server network, a separate device (the server) exercises control over the network. Data flows more efficiently in client/server networks than in peer-to-peer networks. In addition, client/server networks have increased scalability, meaning users can be added to the network easily.

3. What are the different classifications of client/server networks?

Local area networks (LANs) are small groups of computers (as few as two) and peripherals linked together over a small geographic area. A group of computers on the floor of the office building where you work is most likely a LAN. Wide area networks (WANs) comprise large numbers of users (or of separate LANs) that are miles apart and linked together. Corporations often use WANs to connect two or more branches (such as an office in California and one in Ohio). Sometimes government organizations or civic groups establish WANs to link users in a specific geographic area (such as within a city or county). These special WANs are known as metropolitan area networks (MANs).

4. What components are needed to construct a client/server network?

Client/server networks have many of the same components of peer-to-peer networks as well as some components specific to client/server networks, including servers, a network topology, transmission media, network operating system (NOS) software, network adapters, and network navigation devices.

5. What do the various types of servers do?

Dedicated servers are used on large networks to increase efficiency. Authentication servers control access to the network and ensure that only authorized users can log on. File servers provide storage and management of user files. Print servers manage and control all printing jobs initiated on a network. Application servers provide access to application software (such as Microsoft Office). Database servers store database files and provide access to users who need the information in the databases. E-mail servers control all incoming and outgoing e-mail traffic. Communications servers are used to control the flow of information from the internal network to outside networks (such as the Internet). Web servers are used to host a Web site.

6. What are the various network topologies (layouts), and why is network topology important in planning a network?

In a bus topology, all nodes are connected to a single linear cable. Ring topologies are made up of nodes arranged roughly in a circle. The data flows from node to node in a specific order. In a star topology, nodes are connected to a central communication device (a switch) and branch out like points of a star. A hybrid topology blends two or more topologies in one network. Each topology has its own advantages and disadvantages. Topology selection depends on two main factors: (1) the network budget, and (2) the specific needs of network users (such as speed or fair allocation of resources).

7. What types of transmission media are used in client/server networks?

In addition to wireless media, three main cable types are used: twisted-pair cable, coaxial cable, and fiber-optic cable. Twisted-pair cable consists of four pairs of wires twisted around each other to reduce interference. Coaxial cable is the same type of cable used by your cable TV company to run a signal into your house. Fiber-optic cable uses bundles of glass or plastic fiber to send signals using light waves. It provides the largest bandwidth but is expensive and difficult to install. Wireless media uses radio waves to send data between nodes on a network.

8. What software needs to run on computers attached to a client/server network, and how does this software control network communications?

Network operating system (NOS) software needs to be installed on each computer and server connected to a client/server network to provide the services necessary for the devices to communicate. The NOS provides a set of common rules (called a *protocol*) that controls communication between devices on the network.

9. How do network adapters enable computers to participate in a client/server network?

Without a network adapter, a computer could not communicate on a network. A network adapter provides three critical functions. First, it takes low-power data signals generated by the computer and converts them into higher-powered signals that can traverse network media easily.

Second, it breaks the data generated by the computer into packets and packages them for transmission across the network media. Last, it acts as a gatekeeper to control the flow of data to and from the computer.

10. What devices assist in moving data around a client/server network?

Switches are devices that read the addresses of data packets and retransmit a signal to its destination instead of to every device connected to the switch. Bridges are devices used to send data between two different segments (collision domains) of the same network. Routers are used to route data between two different networks (such as between a corporate network and the Internet).

11. What measures are employed to keep large networks secure?

Access to most networks requires authentication procedures (such as having users enter a user ID and password) to ensure that only authorized users access the network. The system administrator defines access privileges for users so that they can access only specific files. Network equipment is physically secured behind locked doors, which are often protected by biometric authentication devices. Biometric devices, such as fingerprint and palm readers, use unique physical characteristics of individuals for identification purposes. Firewalls are employed to keep hackers from attacking networks through Internet connections. Packet screeners review traffic going to and from the network to ascertain whether the communication was generated by a legitimate user.

key terms

Word Bank

- application server
- bastion host
- bridges
- bus
- database server
- fiber-optic
- file server
- LAN
- network administrator
- packet screener
- packets
- router
- scalable
- star
- switches
- twisted pair
- WAN
- wireless access points

Instructions: Fill in the blanks using the words from the Word Bank above.

As a(n) (1) _____ Susan's first task was to configure her college's new network. Because the college had campuses in three different towns, she knew it would be necessary to configure the network as a(n) (2) _____ . However, to handle all of the wireless devices the students carried, (3) _____ would need to be installed throughout the buildings. Software would need to be shared among 500 employees, so a robust (4) _____ would be a necessity. Because the college was experiencing rapid growth, the network would have to be highly (5) _____ , which would require the selection of a(n) (6) _____ topology instead of a(n) (7) _____ topology, which would only work for a very small network.

The transfer of large files by the digital media department would mean that using (8) _____ cabling would be an absolute necessity in the fine arts building, whereas (9) _____ cabling would be sufficient for other areas of the campus. Because the college had experienced hacking on its old network, Susan insisted that a(n) (10) _____ be installed to bolster the network defenses further by filtering unauthorized transmissions of data. Combined with a(n) (11) _____ installed as part of the perimeter network, she felt they would be adequately protected from wily hackers.

(12) _____ would be necessary to shift data (13) _____ between collision domains on the network. For transferring data from the network to the Internet, a(n) (14) _____ would need to be installed. If a star topology was to be used, many (15) _____ would need to be deployed to handle all 500 network users.

becoming computer literate

Ginormous State University is constructing a new building to house its Fine Arts and Digital Media programs. The digital media students and faculty work primarily on the first floor of the building at fixed workstations but need to transfer extremely large media files among various workspaces. The rest of the Fine Arts faculty can teach on any of the three floors in the building and need to access the network from wherever they may be teaching. Students will also need connectivity to the campus network and the Internet from any point in the building.

Instructions: Draft a memo (with supporting diagrams, if necessary) that details how to deploy network connectivity in the 25 classrooms, 12 faculty offices, and the common areas of the building. Justify the network topology you select, explain your choice of transmission media, and indicate the device(s) needed to connect the computers to the existing campus network.

Instructions: Answer the multiple-choice and true–false questions below for more practice with key terms and concepts from this chapter.

Multiple Choice

1. Which of the following is *not* an advantage of installing a client/server network in a college?
   a. Increased scalability
   b. Decentralization of network security protection
   c. Sharing of files and data
   d. Sharing of peripherals

2. Which is *not* a reason why client server networks are usually installed in large businesses?
   a. Peripherals can't be shared on peer-to-peer networks.
   b. Dedicated servers make large networks more efficient.
   c. Client/server networks are more scalable than peer-to-peer networks.
   d. Client/server networks feature centralized security.

3. When networks are deployed at two college campuses 30 miles apart, the networks would be classified as a
   a. WAN.   c. PAN.
   b. MAN.   d. LAN.

4. Which of the following is *not* necessary in every client/server network?
   a. Network adapters
   b. Database server
   c. Transmission media
   d. NOS software

5. To provide for sharing of an Internet connection, which server would a corporate network include?
   a. Database
   b. Authentication
   c. Communications
   d. Application

6. Which type of network topology favors equal access among nodes?
   a. Star   c. Ring
   b. Ethernet   d. Bus

7. Fiber-optic cable most likely would be used in a corporate network when
   a. cost is more important than speed.
   b. electrical or magnetic interference is not present.
   c. short cable runs are required.
   d. speed is more important than cost.

8. NOS software is
   a. needed on all computers in a client/server networks.
   b. needed only on the servers in a client/server network.
   c. needed only on client computers in a client/server network.
   d. needed only when configuring a network in a ring topology.

9. On client server networks, switches
   a. transfer data between two networks.
   b. route date between two collision domains on a single network.
   c. move data efficiently from node to node on the network.
   d. necessary only in networks using the ring topology.

10. Providing adequate security on a corporate network involves all of these issues, except
    a. authentication.
    b. packet screening.
    c. deploying a bastion host.
    d. installing NOS blocking software.

True–False

_____ 1. Bridges are used to route data between two or more network collision domains.

_____ 2. Two different types of network topologies can be deployed on the same network.

_____ 3. Twisted pair cable is never susceptible to magnetic interference.

_____ 4. Client/server networks are less scalable than peer-to-peer networks.

_____ 5. A communication server is used to control access on a client/server network.

1. A Truly Wireless Campus

Most schools have wireless networks now, but these are mainly for the convenience of the students. School employees are often still tied down to desktop computers with wired connections. The primary reason for this is cost as desktop computers are cheaper than notebooks (for the same amount of computing power), and computers that stay in one place put don't require as much maintenance and repair. Assuming your school can afford to begin transitioning to providing all employees with notebook computers (or other wireless computing devices), draft a plan that identifies the following:

a. Which two departments should be converted to wireless first?

b. What benefits will the employees in these departments gain from wireless connectivity?

c. How will wireless devices allow these employees to better serve or interact with the students?

d. What guidelines should the school establish for use of the computers when they are off campus?

e. What precautions should the school take to help recover the computers in the event they are lost or stolen?

2. Faster Networking for the Multimedia Department

Currently, the multimedia department at your school provides twenty Mac desktop computers in a wired Ethernet network for students to use to develop their multimedia projects. The lab uses one switch to connect all the computers, and the cabling is Cat 6 cable. The students are complaining about data transfers taking a long time on the network. In this chapter, we mentioned 10 Gigabit networks, which are used to provide extremely fast wired throughput. Research 10 Gigabit network equipment. Write a proposal to explain how to convert the Mac network to a 10 Gigabit network. Make sure to fully explain what equipment and cabling will be required and how much each component of the new network will cost.

3. Establishing a Business Network

You and three of your friends have a brilliant idea for a new line of clothing to be marketed to college students. All four of you attend colleges in different states. You want to set up a secure network for swapping your designs and other business ideas while you develop the business. Ultimately, you might establish a manufacturing facility/sales office in each town where you all currently go to college. Therefore, you will eventually need networks in your businesses in four varied geographic locations. Research ISPs that operate in multiple states and find one that you think can support your business networking needs. Consider using VPNs for increased security. How much will it cost you to establish connectivity in a secure environment for four point-to-point connections so that you and your business partners can communicate in the planning stages of your venture? When you establish the offices, how much will it cost to connect four networks (in different states) with twenty nodes at each network? What speed of data lines will you need to use between the offices?

1. Network Topology in the Workplace

You are interning at a small manufacturing company that is currently building a new manufacturing facility. All of the main manufacturing machines are computer-controlled and need to be connected to the client/server network in the administrative offices. Equal access for nodes on the factory floor is not an issue as the machinery will communicate infrequently with the network. The machinery generates a lot of electrical interference and wireless signals do not travel well on the factory floor due to the presence of metal beams. Consider the following:

a. What type of topology would you recommend for the factory network? Why?
b. What type of cabling would be appropriate to use in the factory portion of the network? Why?
c. What type of navigation device(s) would be required to enable the factory network to communicate with the administrative office network?

2. Transitioning to a Client/Server Network

The owner of the company for which you work announces that the company will be hiring another 50 workers over the next six months. Currently, your peer-to-peer network is adequately handling the needs of the 10 employees who now work at the company. However, you know that adding 50 more employees to the network would overload it.

a. Write a memo explaining why a switch to a client/server network would be appropriate. Be sure to explain which topology you think would be best to install.
b. In the memo, estimate the costs of constructing a 60-person client/server network, including the costs of one server, cabling, desktop computers for the 50 new employees, and switches. Use resources such as dell.com and hp.com to design the network and price its components.

3. Authentication on a Client/Server Network

Authentication with logon ids and passwords is only secure if the logon ids are difficult to deduce and the passwords are secure. The company you work for establishes all logon ids as the first initial of the given name and the full surname of the employees (i.e., John Smith would have the logon id jsmith). Passwords can be as few as four letters or numbers and never have to be changed. You know from your coursework at school that these are inadequate security procedures. Research password security on the Internet and draft a memo for upper management that addresses the following:

a. Suggest a new scheme for creating logon ids that would be difficult for a hacker to ascertain.
b. What length of passwords would you recommend? What combination of letters, numbers, and other symbols should they include?
c. How often would you recommend that employees be required to change their passwords? Would employees ever be allowed to repeat previous passwords?

Instructions: Albert Einstein used *Gedankenexperiments*, or critical thinking questions, to develop his theory of relativity. Some ideas are best understood by experimenting with them in our own minds. The following critical thinking questions are designed to demand your full attention but require only a comfortable chair—no technology.

1. **Biomentric Access on Campus**

   Biometric security devices are still expensive. But there are usually parts of any organization that need to be more secure than others, and you can often justify the cost of these devices for certain areas. Consider the following organizations and prepare a paper discussing in which areas of the business they could most benefit from installing biometric security devices:

   a. Financial institution (bank)
   b. Public university that conducts scientific research
   c. Pharmaceutical company

2. **Monitoring Computer Usage in the Workplace**

   Software tools for monitoring computer usage are readily available on the Internet, often for free (such as Best Free Keylogger). In most jurisdictions, it is legal for employers to install monitoring software on computer equipment they provide to employees. It is usually illegal for employees to install monitoring software on computers owned by their employers for purposes of monitoring computer usage of co-workers or bosses. The Ethics in IT feature "Who's Watching the Watchers" earlier in this chapter described the story of a man who was fired for installing monitoring software on his boss's computer even though he proved the boss was goofing off most of the time. Do you think this double standard is fair? What circumstances do you think would justify an employee monitoring other employers or their boss's computer usage? Whose approval should be sought before employees embarked on computer usage monitoring? Should whistleblowers have the right to conduct computer usage monitoring? Please fully explain your answers.

3. **Acceptable-Use Internet Policies**

   Most schools have drafted acceptable-use policies for computers and Internet access to inform students and employees of the approved uses of college computing assets. Consider these areas of a potential college policy:

   a. Should employees be allowed to use their computers and Internet access for personal tasks (such as checking non–college-related e-mail, accessing Facebook, or playing games)? If so, how much time per day is reasonable for employees to spend on personal tasks?
   b. Should student computer and Internet usage be monitored to ensure compliance with the personal use policies? Should the college inform students that they are being monitored? What should the penalties be for violating these policies?
   c. Many colleges block access to Web sites that enable students to participate in potentially illegal activities such as downloading music, gambling, or viewing pornography. Should colleges have the right to block students' access to these Web sites when they are on campus? Why or why not?

4. **Wireless Network Layout**

   You are working for a local outlet of a national sandwich franchise (such as Subway). Now that most customers have portable devices with wireless access, they have come to expect connectivity while they eat. Management has asked you to survey customers to determine their needs. Draft a survey for your boss that helps determine the following:

   a. Should access be free? If access is not free, how much would customers pay?
   b. What types of applications would the customers access while in the shop?
   c. How important is WiFi access to their dining experience?

Wireless Coverage on Campus

Problem

As wireless devices become more prevalent, increased demands for wireless access will be placed on networks. Although many schools already deploy adequate wireless access, there is room for improvement of coverage in some areas.

Task

As part of a task force studying proposed technology improvements at your school, you and your classmates have been requested to investigate the efficiency of the wireless coverage at your school. Before presenting your findings to the task force, your group needs to fine-tune its recommendations.

Process

Divide the class into small teams.

1. Explore the areas of your campus where students congregate to socialize or engage in research. Determine if these areas are covered by wireless Internet access and the speed (802.11g or 802.11n) at which connections are offered. This may require interviewing your school's network manager. You can also test the throughput with your notebook computer. First, install free connection speed monitoring software such as Net Meter or BitMeter 2 (both available at **download.cnet.com**). Next, test the upload and download speeds for areas of your school covered by wireless technology (such as the library) by connecting to the Internet in various locations. Make sure you connect in several different parts of the campus as speeds many vary significantly from location to location.

2. Present your findings to your class. Lead a discussion with the other students and solicit feedback as to their experiences with wireless connectivity on the campus. In which areas of the campus do you feel wireless technology should be improved? Are there parts of the campus that are not covered by wireless technology that you feel should feature it? What other technologies should be deployed that would benefit student learning?

3. Prepare a report for the task force that includes your suggestions for improvements and upgrades to the wireless network on your campus. If possible, address options for wireless connectivity when students are off campus for field trips, seminars, and so on.

Conclusion

Being tied down to a wired computer terminal just doesn't cut it in the 21st century. Although wireless technology can be difficult and expensive to deploy in some instances (such as in old campus buildings), today's students will continue to demand the portable, high-speed connections that they need to function effectively. Someday we'll probably wonder why we even bothered with wired connections at all!

In this exercise, you will research and then role-play a complicated ethical situation. The role you play might or might not match your own personal beliefs; in either case, your research and use of logic will enable you to represent the view assigned. An arbitrator will watch and comment on both sides of the arguments, and together the team will agree on an ethical solution.

Topic: Piggybacking on Wireless Networks

Piggybacking occurs when people use a wireless network without the permission of the owner. Although piggybacking is illegal in many jurisdictions, it is often hard to detect. Piggybacking often happens inadvertently when people trying to connect to their own home network accidentally connect to their neighbor's wireless network. With the proliferation of wireless networks, many businesses have set up networks for their customers. However, because of the close proximity of many businesses to each other in areas such as shopping centers, the potential for inadvertent (or intentional) piggybacking of wireless networks exists. Also, sharing wireless connections between two entities (whether they be two households or two businesses) may violate the terms of service of the Internet Service Provider. And although wireless networks can be secured, it is often easier on the customers to leave them completely open, which can encourage piggybacking.

Research Areas to Consider

- Detecting wireless piggybacking
- Piggybacking laws (legality of piggybacking)
- Securing wireless networks

Process

Divide the class into teams.

1. Research the areas cited above and devise a scenario in which the owner of a coffee shop at a shopping center has accused the proprietor of the sandwich shop next door of encouraging the sandwich shop's patrons to piggyback on the coffee shop's wireless network.

2. Team members should write a summary that provides background information for their character—for example: coffee shop owner, sandwich shop owner, and mall manager (arbitrator)—and details their character's behaviors to set the stage for the role-playing event. Then, team members should create an outline to use during the role-playing event.

3. Team members should arrange a mutually convenient time to meet for the exchange, either using the collaboration feature of MyITLab, the discussion board feature of Blackboard, or meeting in person.

4. Team members should present their case to the class, or submit a PowerPoint presentation for review by the rest of the class, along with the summary and resolution they developed.

Conclusion

As technology becomes ever more prevalent and integrated into our lives, more and more ethical dilemmas will present themselves. Being able to understand and evaluate both sides of the argument, while responding in a personally or socially ethical manner, will be an important skill.

chapter

thirteen
behind the scenes:
how the internet works

multimedia resources

Active Helpdesk

- Understanding IP Addresses, Domain Names, and Protocols **(p. 615)**
- Keeping E-Mail Secure **(p. 628)**

Sound Bytes

- Creating Web Pages with HTML **(p. 622)**

Companion Website

The Companion Website includes a variety of additional materials to help you review and learn more about the topics in this chapter. Go to: *pearsonhighered.com/techinaction*

how cool is *this?*

Do you have several e-mail accounts that need checking, such as your school e-mail account, which has directives from your instructor, and your personal e-mail account, which receives **messages from friends** and family? Do you have accounts on multiple social networking sites, such as Facebook and MySpace? Are half of your friends using AOL Instant Messenger while the other half uses Yahoo! Instant Messenger? Keeping up with your **online social life** can be challenging.

Digsby is a free tool that consolidates all of your online communications into a single application. You just enter all the login information for your social networking, e-mail, and IM accounts into the Digsby setup screen. Then, whenever you run **Digsby**, it logs into all your accounts and checks for updates. You can easily see all of your friends who are online, regardless of the IM service they use. You can also easily view the status of your **Facebook page** and see all activity at a glance. Clicking on any activity shown, such as a new e-mail received, takes you to a browser window for the relevant application so you can take appropriate action.

Digsby makes managing your digital life **a snap** no matter how many different applications you need to use!

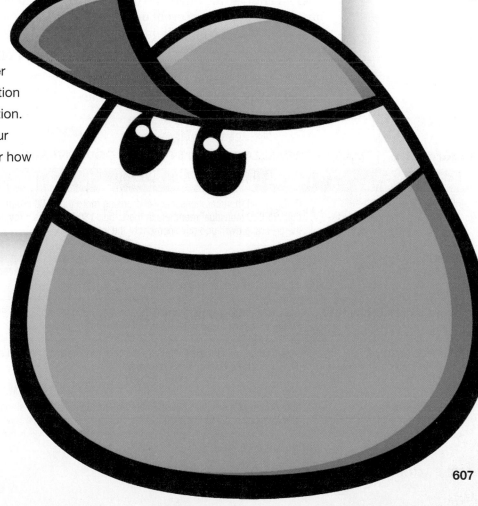

The Management of the Internet

The Internet is the largest network that you use. To keep a massive network like the Internet functioning at peak efficiency, it must be governed and regulated. However, no single entity is in charge of the Internet. In addition, new uses are created every day by a variety of individuals and companies.

Who owns the Internet? Even though the U.S. government funded the development of the technologies that spawned the Internet, no one really owns it. The particular local networks that constitute the Internet are all owned by different entities, including individuals, universities, government agencies, and private companies. Government entities such as the National Science Foundation (NSF) and the National Aeronautics and Space Administration (NASA), as well as many large, privately held companies, own pieces of the communications infrastructure (the high-speed data lines that transport data between networks) that makes the Internet work.

Does anyone manage the Internet? Because the individual networks that participate in the Internet are owned by several different entities, the Internet would cease to function without some sort of organization. Therefore, several nonprofit organizations and user groups, each with a specialized purpose, are responsible for its management. Figure 13.1 shows the major organizations that play a role in the governance and development of the Internet.

Many of the functions handled by these nonprofit groups were previously handled by U.S. government contractors because the Internet developed out of a defense project. However, because the Internet now serves the global community, not just the United States, assigning responsibilities to organizations with global membership is helping to speed the Internet's internationalization. Through close collaboration among the organizations listed in Figure 13.1 (and a few others such as the Internet Network Information Center and the Internet Research Task Force), the Internet's vast collection of users and networks is managed.

Who pays for the Internet? You do! The National Science Foundation (NSF), which is a U.S. government–funded agency, still pays for a large portion of the Internet's infrastructure and funds research and development for new technologies. The primary source of NSF funding is your tax dollars. Originally, U.S. taxpayers footed the entire bill for the Internet, but as the Internet grew and organizations were formed to manage it, businesses, universities, and other countries began paying for Internet infrastructure and development. And, of course, the fees you pay to your ISP for Internet access also contribute to defraying the costs of the Internet.

Internet Networking

The Internet's response to our requests for information seems almost magical at times. By simply entering a URL in your browser

Figure 13.1 | MAJOR ORGANIZATIONS IN INTERNET GOVERNANCE AND DEVELOPMENT

Organization	Purpose	Web Address
Internet Society (ISOC)	Professional membership society comprising more than 100 organizations and more than 28,000 individual members in more than 180 countries. Provides leadership for the orderly growth and development of the Internet.	isoc.org
Internet Engineering Task Force (IETF)	A subgroup of ISOC made up of individuals and organizations that research new technologies for the Internet that will improve its capabilities or keep the infrastructure functioning smoothly.	ietf.org
Internet Architecture Board (IAB)	Technical advisory group to the ISOC and a committee of the IETF. Provides direction for the maintenance and development of the protocols that are used on the Internet.	iab.org
Internet Corporation for Assigned Names and Numbers (ICANN)	Organization responsible for management of the Internet's domain name system (DNS) and the allocation of IP addresses.	icann.org
World Wide Web Consortium (W3C)	Consortium of more than 330 member organizations that sets standards and develops protocols for the Web.	w3.org

or going to a search engine and entering a search topic, you can summon up information that is stored on servers around the world. However, there is no magic involved, just a series of communication transactions that enable the Internet to function as a global network. In this section, we explore the various networks that make up the Internet, explain how to connect to them, and examine the workings of Internet data communications.

Connecting to the Internet

How are computers connected to the Internet? A "network of networks," the Internet is similar to the highway system in the United States. The top level of the highway system consists of interstate highways such as I-95, which runs up and down the East Coast; I-80, which runs from the Northeast to the West Coast; and I-5, which runs north and south along the West Coast. These are the fastest and largest roadways. Regional highways connect to the interstate highways, and local roads connect to the regional highways.

As shown in Figure 13.2, the main paths of the Internet, along which data travels the fastest, are known collectively as the **Internet backbone**. Analogous to the interstate highway system, the Internet backbone is a collection of large national and international networks, most of which are owned by commercial, educational, or government organizations (such as NASA). These backbone providers, which are required to connect to other backbone providers, have the fastest high-speed connections. At the time this was written, the large U.S. companies that provided backbone connectivity included Verizon Business, AT&T, Sprint, and Qwest.

How do the ISPs that form the Internet backbone communicate? Backbone ISPs initially connected with T lines. A **T line** carried digital data over twisted-pair wires. T-1 lines, which were the first to be used, transmit data at a throughput rate of 1.544 Mbps. T-3 lines, which were developed later, transmit data at 45 Mbps. Today, a backbone is typically a high-speed fiber-optic line, designated as an **optical carrier (OC) line**. OC lines come in a variety of speeds, as shown in Figure 13.3. Although most large ISPs connect to the Internet

with OC-192 lines, AT&T has begun to use OC-768 connections in its Internet backbone network.

The bandwidth of the connections between ISPs and end users depends on the amount of data traffic required. Whereas your home might connect to the Internet with DSL, cable, or even fiber-optic lines, the volume of Internet traffic at your college probably requires it to use at least T-3 lines or even an OC line to move data to the school's ISP. Large companies usually must connect to their ISPs using high-throughput OC lines.

How are the ISPs connected to each other? The points of connection between ISPs were once known as *network access points (NAPs)*. Network access points were designed to move large amounts of

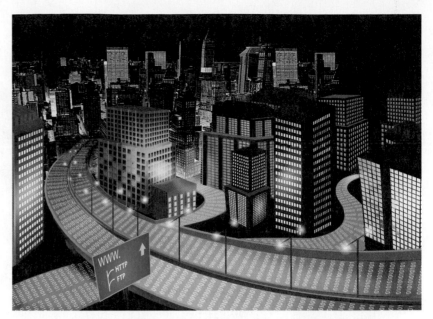

Figure 13.2

When you connect to the Internet at home, work, or school, you most likely connect through intermediate or local ISPs. Just as regional and local highways connect to the interstate highways, local and regional ISPs connect to the Internet backbone. The 1s and 0s on the road here represent data flow on the Internet.

Figure 13.3	SPEED AND CONFIGURATION OF OC LINES
OC-1	0.052 Gbps
OC-3	0.155 Gbps
OC-12	0.622 Gbps
OC-24	1.244 Gbps
OC-48	2.488 Gbps
OC-96	4.976 Gbps
OC-192	9.953 Gbps
OC-768	39.813 Gbps

Point of presence (POP)

Your teacher's home computer

High-speed connection

Networking devices

Dial-up connection

Your neighbor's computer

High-speed connection

Your computer

Your ISP

Figure 13.4

Home users connect to their ISPs through a single point of presence that can handle many simultaneous connections.

data quickly between networks. They allowed the early Internet, which began as a government-funded academic experiment, to grow into the modern Internet of many commercial companies working together—the Internet that we all know and use today. Now, private-sector companies make up the Internet system, and the data-exchange mechanism is known as an **Internet exchange point (IXP)**. A typical IXP is made up of one or more network switches to which ISPs connect. As you'll recall from Chapter 7, **switches** are devices that send data on a specific route through a network. By connecting directly to each other through IXPs, networks can reduce their costs and improve the speed and efficiency with which data is exchanged.

How do individuals connect to an ISP? Whether they dial up through a conventional modem or connect through high-speed access (such as cable or fiber), individual Internet users enter an ISP through a **point of presence (POP)**, which is a bank of modems, servers, routers, and switches (shown in Figure 13.4) through which many users can connect to an ISP simultaneously. ISPs maintain multiple POPs throughout the geographic area they serve.

The Network Model of the Internet

What type of network model does the Internet use? The majority of Internet communications follows the **client/server model** of network communications, which we defined in earlier chapters as one in which client computers request

services and other computers, known as *servers*, provide those services to the clients. In the case of the Internet, the clients are devices such as computers, netbooks, and smartphones that use browsers (or other interfaces) to request services such as Web pages. Various types of servers from which clients can request services are deployed (installed) on the networks that make up the Internet:

- **Web server**: Computer that runs specialized operating systems, enabling it to host (provide Web space for) Web pages and other information and provide requested Web pages to clients.

- **Commerce server**: Computer that hosts software that enables users to purchase goods and services over the Web. These servers generally use special security protocols to protect sensitive information (such as credit card numbers) from being intercepted.

- **File server**: Computer that is deployed to provide remote storage space or to act as a storehouse for files that users can download. Google Docs, Flickr, and Delicious offer online storage services for productivity documents, pictures, and Web pages, respectively.

Do all Internet connections take place in a client/server mode? Certain services on the Internet operate in a peer-to-peer (P2P) mode, as depicted in Figure 13.5. For example, BitTorrent (**bittorrent.com**) is a popular file-sharing service through which Internet users can exchange files. BitTorrent and other file-sharing services require the user's computer to act as both a client and a server. When requesting files from another user, the computer behaves like a client. It switches to

Tracker

Seeds | Seeds | Seeds | Seeds | Seeds | Seeds | Seeds | Seeds
37% of file | 100% of file | 18% of file | 65% of file | 13% of file | 100% of file | 49% of file | 33% of file

Swarm

Your computer

Figure 13.5
File-sharing services in action.

server mode when it provides a file stored on its system to another computer. The following steps are illustrated in Figure 13.5:

1. Your computer, acting as a client, runs the BitTorrent software (which you downloaded from BitTorrent's Web site). Using this software, you request access to a particular file. Your computer transmits this request to a BitTorrent tracking server (tracker).

2. The BitTorrent tracker makes your computer aware of other users running BitTorrent software who have pieces of the file (called *seeds*).

3. Your computer determines that a group of users (called a *swarm*) has seeds for the file you need. Acting as a client, your computer requests the file from the computers in the swarm.

4. Computers in the swarm, acting as servers, then transmit pieces of the file to your computer. At the same time, the tracker might identify your computer as having a file another computer needs and assigns your computer to a swarm. Your computer would then act as a server when delivering that file to the computer that requested it.

Data Transmission and Protocols

Just like any other network, the Internet follows standard protocols to send information between computers. A **computer protocol** is a set of rules for exchanging electronic information. If the Internet is the information superhighway, then protocols are the rules of the road.

Why were Internet protocols developed? To accomplish the early goals of the Internet, protocols needed to be written and agreed upon by users. Each protocol had to be an **open system**, meaning its design would be made public for access by any interested party. This was in direct opposition to the **proprietary system** (private system) model that was the norm at the time.

As we mentioned in earlier chapters, when common communication protocols (rules) are followed, networks can communicate even if they have different topologies, transmission media, or operating systems. The idea of an open system protocol is that anyone can use it on his or her computer system and be able to communicate with any other computer using the same protocol. The biggest Internet tasks—communicating, collaborating, creating content, seeking information, and shopping—are all executed the same way on any system that is following accepted Internet protocols.

Were there problems developing an open system Internet protocol? Agreeing on common standards was relatively easy. The tough part was developing a new method of communication because the technology available in the 1960s—circuit switching—was inefficient for computer communication. Circuit switching has been used since the early days of the telephone for establishing communication. In **circuit switching**, a dedicated connection is formed between two points (such as two people on telephones), and the connection remains active for the duration of the transmission. This method of communication is extremely important when communications must be received in the order in which they are sent (again, like telephone conversations).

When applied to computers, however, circuit switching is inefficient. Computers process communication in bursts. As a computer processor performs the operations necessary to complete a task, it transmits data in a group (or burst). The processor then begins working on its next task and ceases to communicate with output devices or other networks until it is ready to transmit data in the next burst. Circuit switching is inefficient for computers because the circuit either would have to remain open (and therefore unavailable to any other system) with long periods of inactivity or would have to be reestablished for each burst.

Packet Switching

If they can't use circuit switching, what do computers use to communicate? Packet switching is the communications methodology that makes computer communication efficient. Packet switching doesn't require a dedicated communications circuit to be maintained. With packet switching, data is broken into smaller chunks (each

one called a **packet** or a **data packet**) that are sent over various routes at the same time. When the packets reach their destination, they are reassembled by the receiving computer. This technology resulted from one of the original goals of creating the Internet: If Internet nodes are disabled or destroyed (such as through an act of warfare or terrorism), the data can travel an alternate route to its destination.

What information does a packet contain? Packet contents vary, depending on the protocol being followed. At a minimum, all packets must contain (1) an address to which the packet is being sent; (2) the address from where the packet originates; (3) reassembling instructions, if the original data was split between packets; and (4) the data that is being transmitted.

Sending a packet is like sending a letter. Assume you are sending a large amount of information in written format from your home in Philadelphia to your aunt in San Diego. The information is too large to fit in one small envelope, so you mail three different envelopes to your aunt. Each envelope includes your aunt's address, a return address (your address), and the information being sent inside it. The pages of the letters in each envelope are numbered so that your aunt will know in which order to read them.

Each envelope may not find its way to San Diego by the same route. However, even if the letters are routed through different post offices, they will all eventually arrive in your aunt's mailbox. Your aunt will then reassemble the message (put the pages of the letters in order) and read it. The process of sending a message through the Internet works in much the same way. This process is illustrated in Figure 13.6, which traces an e-mail message sent from a computer in Philadelphia to a computer in San Diego.

Why do packets take different routes, and how do they decide which route to use? The routers that connect ISPs with each other monitor traffic and decide on the most efficient route for packets to take to their destination. The router works in the same way as a police officer does during a traffic jam. When

> **"Packet switching is the communications methodology that makes computer communication efficient."**

E-mail to your aunt broken into packets by your computer

Packet 1

Packet 2

Packet 3

Your computer in Philadelphia

Your ISP in PA

ISP in MN

INTERNET

ISP in NC

ISP in NJ

ISP in OR

E-mail to your aunt reconstructed by her computer

Packet 1

Packet 2

Packet 3

Your aunt's computer in San Diego

Your aunt's ISP in CA

ISP in TX

ISP in FL

Figure 13.6

Each packet can follow its own route to its final destination. Sequential numbering of packets ensures they are reassembled in the correct order at their destination.

routes are clogged with traffic, police officers are deployed in areas of congestion, directing drivers to alternate routes to their destinations.

TCP/IP

What protocol does the Internet use for transmitting data? Although many protocols are available on the Internet, the main suite of protocols used is **TCP/IP**. The suite is named after the original two protocols that were developed for the Internet: the **Transmission Control Protocol (TCP)** and the **Internet Protocol (IP)**. Although most people think that the TCP/IP suite consists of only two protocols, it actually comprises many interrelated protocols (covered later in this chapter), the most important of which are listed in Figure 13.7.

Which particular protocol actually sends the information? The Internet Protocol (IP) is responsible for sending the information from one computer to another.

The IP is like a postal worker who takes a letter (a packet of information) that was mailed (created by the sending computer) and sends it on to another post office (router), which in turn routes it to the addressee (the receiving computer). The postal worker never knows whether the recipient actually receives the letter. The only thing the postal worker knows is that the letter was handed off to an appropriate post office that will assist in completing the delivery of the letter.

IP Addresses and Domain Names

Each computer, server, or device (such as a router) connected to the Internet is required to have a unique identification number. However, because humans are better at remembering and working with words than with numbers, the numeric IP addresses were given more "human," word-based addresses.

Figure 13.7 | TCP/IP PROTOCOL SUITE—MAIN PROTOCOLS

Internet Protocol (IP)	Sends data between computers on the Internet.
Transmission control protocol (TCP)	Prepares data for transmission and provides for error checking and resending of lost data.
User datagram protocol (UDP)	Prepares data for transmission; lacks resending capabilities.
File transfer protocol (FTP)	Enables files to be downloaded to a computer or uploaded to other computers.
Telnet	Enables user to log in to a remote computer and work on it as if sitting in front of it.
HyperText Transfer Protocol (HTTP) and Secure HTTP (S-HTTP)	Transfers HyperText Markup Language (HTML) data from servers to browsers. S-HTTP is an encrypted protocol for secure transmissions.
Simple mail transfer protocol (SMTP)	Used for transmission of e-mail messages across the Internet.

IP Addresses

What is an IP address? You will recall from Chapter 3 that an **IP address** is a unique identification number that defines each computer, service, or other device that connects to the Internet. IP addresses fulfill the same function as street addresses. For example, to send a letter to Carlos Mendoza's house in Walla Walla, Washington, you have to know his address. Carlos might live at 123 Main Street, which is not a unique address (many towns have a Main Street); but 123 Main Street, Walla Walla, WA 99362 *is* unique.

The numeric zip code is the unique postal identification for a specific geographic area. Zip codes are regulated by the U.S. Postal Service. Similarly, IP addresses must be registered with the **Internet Corporation for Assigned Names and Numbers (ICANN)** to ensure they are unique and have not been assigned to other users. The ICANN is responsible for allocating IP addresses to network administrators, just as the U.S. Postal Service is responsible for assigning zip codes to geographic areas.

What does an IP address look like? A typical IP address is expressed as follows:

197.169.73.63

An IP address expressed this way is called a **dotted decimal number** (also known as a **dotted quad**). However, recall that computers work with binary numbers. The same IP address in binary form is as follows:

11000101.10101001.01001001.00111111

Each of the 4 numbers in a dotted decimal number is referred to as an **octet**. This is because each number would have 8 positions when shown in binary form. Because 32 positions are available for IP address values (4 octets with 8 positions each), IP addresses are considered 32-bit numbers. A position is filled either by a 1 or a 0, resulting in 256 (2^8) possible values for each octet. Values start at 0 (not 1); therefore, each octet can have a value from 0 to 255. The entire 32-bit address can represent 4,294,967,296 values (or 2^{32}), which are quite a few Internet addresses!

Will we ever run out of IP addresses? When the original IP addressing scheme, **Internet Protocol version 4 (IPv4)**, was created in the early 1980s, no one foresaw the explosive growth of the Internet in the 1990s. Four billion values for an address field seemed like enough to last forever. However, as the Internet grew, it quickly became apparent that we were going to run out of IP addresses.

Because the unique IP addressing system described earlier offers only a fixed number of IP addresses, a different addressing scheme known as **classless interdomain routing (CIDR)**, pronounced "cider," was developed. CIDR, or supernetting, allows a single IP address to represent several unique IP addresses by adding a **network prefix** (a slash and a number) to the end of the last octet. The network prefix identifies how many

BITS AND BYTES

What's Your IP Address?

Curious as to what your IP address is? Just go to a Web site such as What Is My IP (**whatismyip.com**) or IP Chicken (**ipchicken.com**). Figure 13.8 displays the output from What Is My IP, which shows the IP address your PC is currently using.

> **What Is My IP** - The fastest, easiest way to determine your IP address.
>
> What Is My IP Address - Service provided by WhatIsMyIP.com
>
> WIMI Forum
> Internet Speed Test
>
> **Your IP Address Is: 173.49.33.124**
>
> Google Custom Search [Search]

Figure 13.8

Some Web sites, such as WhatIsMyIP.com, determine your IP address for you.

of the possible 32 bits in a traditional IP address are to be used as the unique identifier, leaving the remaining bits to identify the specific host. For example, in the IP address 206.13.01.48/25, "/25" is the network prefix. It indicates that the first 25 bits are used as the unique network identifier; the remaining 7 bits identify the specific host site.

Are there other Internet addressing systems? Internet Protocol version 6 (IPv6) is an IP addressing scheme developed by the Internet Engineering Task Force (IETF) to make IP addresses longer, thereby providing more available IP addresses. IPv6 uses 8 groups of 16-bit numbers, referred to as **hexadecimal notation** (*hex* for short), which you learned about in the Technology in Focus piece titled "Under the Hood." An IPv6 address would have the following format:

`0000:0000:0000:0000:0000:0000:0000:0000`

Hex addressing provides a much larger field size, which will enable a much larger number of IP addresses (approximately 340 followed by 36 zeros). This should provide a virtually unlimited supply of IP addresses and will allow many different kinds of non-PC devices such as cell phones and home appliances to join the Internet more easily in the future. Companies and government agencies are starting to replace their networking equipment with equipment that can handle the IPv6 protocol.

How does my computer get an IP address? You learned in Chapter 7 that IP addresses are assigned either statically or dynamically. **Static addressing** means that the IP address for a computer never changes and is most likely assigned manually by a network administrator or ISP. **Dynamic addressing**, in which your computer is assigned an address from an available pool of IP addresses, is more common. A connection to an ISP could use either method. If your ISP uses static addressing, then you were assigned an IP address when you applied for your service and had to configure your computer manually to use that address. More often, though, an ISP assigns a computer a temporary (dynamic) IP address, as shown in Figure 13.9.

How exactly are dynamic addresses assigned? Dynamic addressing is normally handled by the **dynamic host configuration protocol (DHCP)**, which belongs to the TCP/IP

protocol suite. DHCP takes a pool of IP addresses and shares them with hosts on the network on an as-needed basis. ISPs don't need to maintain a pool of IP addresses for all of their subscribers because not everyone is logged on to the Internet at one time. Thus, when a user logs on to an ISP's server, the DHCP server assigns that user an IP address for the duration of the session. Similarly, when you log on to your computer at work in the morning, DHCP assigns an IP address to your computer.

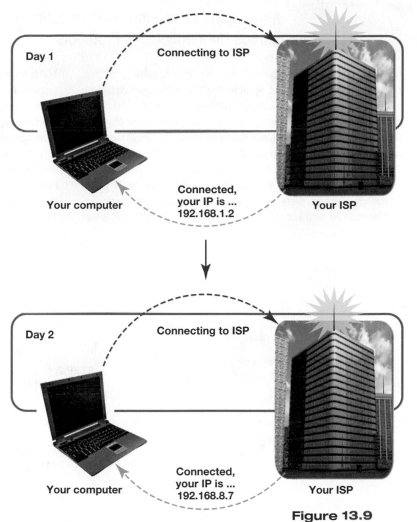

Day 1 — Connecting to ISP — Your computer — Connected, your IP is ... 192.168.1.2 — Your ISP

Day 2 — Connecting to ISP — Your computer — Connected, your IP is ... 192.168.8.7 — Your ISP

Figure 13.9
Dynamic IP addressing changes your IP address every time you connect to the Internet.

ACTIVE HELP-DESK

Understanding IP Addresses, Domain Names, and Protocols

In this Active Helpdesk call, you'll play the role of a helpdesk staffer, fielding calls about which data transmissions and protocols the Internet uses, and why IP addresses and domain names are important for Internet communications.

Making the Connection—Connection-Oriented Versus Connectionless Protocols

The Internet Protocol is responsible only for *sending* packets on their way. The packets are created by either the TCP or the **user datagram protocol (UDP)**. You don't decide whether to use TCP or UDP. The choice of protocol is made for you by the developers of the computer programs you are using or by the other protocols (such as those listed in Figure 13.7) that interact with your data packet.

As explained earlier, data transmission between computers is highly efficient if connections do not need to be established (as in circuit switching). However, there are benefits to maintaining a connection, such as reduced data loss. The difference between TCP and UDP is that

TCP is a connection-oriented protocol, whereas UDP is a connectionless protocol.

A **connection-oriented protocol** requires two computers to exchange control packets, thereby setting up the parameters of the data-exchange session, before sending packets that contain data. This process is referred to as **handshaking**. TCP uses a process called a **three-way handshake** to establish a connection, as shown in Figure 13.10a. Perhaps you need to report sales figures to your home office. You phone the sales manager and tell him or her that you are ready to report your figures. The sales manager then prepares to receive the information by

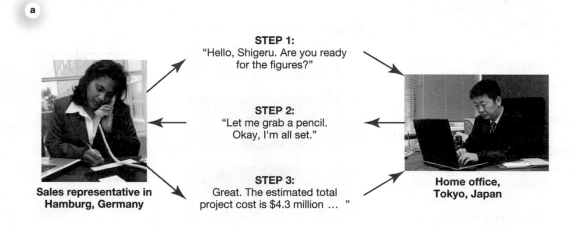

STEP 1:
"Hello, Shigeru. Are you ready for the figures?"

STEP 2:
"Let me grab a pencil. Okay, I'm all set."

STEP 3:
Great. The estimated total project cost is $4.3 million … "

Sales representative in Hamburg, Germany

Home office, Tokyo, Japan

STEP 1:
I want to send e-mail.

STEP 2:
Okay, I'm ready to receive.

STEP 3:
Here's the e-mail message for Aunt Sally.

Your computer

Your ISP's server

Figure 13.10

(a) Colleagues in Hamburg and Tokyo establish communication using a three-way handshake. (b) Here, two computers establish communication the same way.

These temporary IP addresses may or may not be the same from session to session.

What are the benefits of dynamic addressing? Although having a static address would seem to be convenient,

dynamic addressing provides a more secure environment by keeping hackers out of computer systems. Imagine how hard it would be for burglars to find your home if you changed your address every day!

getting a pencil and a piece of paper. By confirming that he or she is ready and by your beginning to report the figures, a three-way (three-step) hand-shaking process is completed.

Your computer does the same thing when it sends an e-mail through your ISP, as shown in Figure 13.10b. It establishes a connection to the ISP and announces it has e-mail to send. The ISP server responds that it is ready to receive the e-mail. Your computer then acknowledges the ready state of the server and begins to transmit the e-mail.

A **connectionless protocol** does not require any type of connection to be established or maintained between two computers that are exchanging information. Just like a letter that is mailed, the data packets are sent without notifying the receiving computer or receiving any acknowledgment that the data was received. UDP is the Internet's connectionless protocol.

Besides establishing a connection, TCP provides for reliable data transfer. Reliable data transfer means that the application that uses TCP can rely on this protocol to deliver all the data packets to the receiver free from errors and in the correct order. TCP achieves reliable data transfer by using acknowledgments and providing for the retransmission of data, as shown in Figure 13.11.

Assume that two systems, X and Y, have established a connection. When Y receives a data packet that it can read from X, it sends back a **positive acknowledgment (ACK)**. If X does not receive an ACK in an appropriate period of time, it resends the packet. If the packet is unreadable (damaged in transit), then Y sends a **negative acknowledgment (NAK)** to X, indicating the packet was not received in understandable form. X then retransmits that packet. Acknowledgments ensure that the receiver has received a complete set of data packets. If a packet is unable to get through after being resent several times, the user is generally presented with an error message indicating the communications were unsuccessful.

You may wonder why you wouldn't always want to use a protocol that provides for reliable data transfer. On the Internet, speed is often more important than accuracy. For certain applications (such as e-mail), it's critically important that your message be delivered completely and accurately. For streaming multimedia, it's not always important to have every frame delivered accurately because most streaming media formats provide for correction of errors caused by data loss. It is, however, extremely important for streaming media to be delivered at a high rate of speed. Otherwise, playback quality can be affected. Therefore, a protocol such as TCP, which uses handshakes and acknowledgments, would probably not be appropriate for transmitting a movie trailer over the Internet whereas the Real-time Transport Protocol (RTP) would be better.

Sending computer — **Receiving computer**

Packet 1

Packet 1 received and readable. ACK sent.

ACK for packet 1 received. Need to send next packet.

ACK 1

Packet 2

Packet 2 received and unreadable. NAK sent.

NAK for packet 2 received. Must resend packet 2.

NAK 2

Packet 2 resend

Packet 2 received and readable. ACK sent.

ACK 2 lost in transit

ACK for packet 2 never received. Must resend packet 2.

Packet 2 resend

Packet 2 already received. Resend ACK for packet 2.

Figure 13.11

Packet acknowledgment in action.

Domain Names

I've been on the Internet, so why have I never seen IP addresses?

Computers are fantastic at relating to IP addresses and other numbers. However, humans remember names better than they remember strings of numbers. (Would you rather call your friend 1476288 or Sanjay?) When the Web was being formed, a naming system was necessary so people could work with names instead of numbers. Hence, domain names were born.

As you learned in Chapter 3, a **domain name** is simply a name that takes the place of an IP address, making it easier for people to remember. You've most likely visited Yahoo! (**yahoo.com).** Yahoo.com is a domain name. The server where Yahoo!'s main Web site is deployed has an IP address (such as 69.147.125.65), but it's much easier for you to remember to tell your browser to go to **Yahoo.com** than it is to recall the ten-digit IP address.

How are domains organized?

Domains are organized by level. As you'll recall from Chapter 3, the portion of the domain name after the dot is the top-level domain (TLD). In the .com domain are popular sites such as Amazon (**amazon.com**), Google (**google.com**), and Microsoft (**microsoft.com**). The TLDs are standardized pools (such as .com and .org) that have been established by ICANN. (Refer back to Figure 3.23 in Chapter 3 for a list of the TLDs that are currently approved and in use.) Within each top-level domain are many second-level domains. A **second-level domain** needs to be unique within its own top-level domain but not necessarily unique to all top-level domains. For example, Mycoolsite.com and Mycoolsite.org could be registered as separate domain names.

Who controls domain name registration? ICANN assigns companies or organizations to manage domain name registration. Because names can't be duplicated within a top-level domain, one company is assigned to oversee each TLD and maintain a listing of all registered domains. VeriSign is the current ICANN-accredited domain name registrar for the .com and .net domains. VeriSign provides a database that lists all the registered .com and .net domains and their contact information. However, for simplicity you can look up any .com or .net domain at the Network Solutions Web site (**networksolutions.com**) to see if it is registered and who owns it. Country-specific domains such as .nz for New Zealand and .sg for Singapore are controlled by groups in those countries. You can find a complete list of country-code top-level domains on the Internet Assigned Numbers Authority Web site (**iana.org**).

DNS Servers

How does my computer know the IP address of another computer? Say you want to get to Yahoo.com. To do so, you type the URL—"yahoo.com"—into your browser's address box. However, the URL is not important to your computer; only the IP address of the computer hosting the Yahoo! site is. When you enter the URL in your browser, your computer must convert the URL to an IP address. To do this, your computer consults a database that is maintained on a **DNS (domain name system) server** that functions like a phone book for the Internet.

Your ISP's Web server has a default DNS server (one that is convenient to contact) that it goes to when it needs to translate a URL to an IP address (illustrated in Figure 13.12). It uses the following steps:

1. Your browser requests information from ABC.com.

2. Your ISP doesn't know the address of ABC.com, so it requests the address from its default DNS server.

3. The default DNS server doesn't know the IP address of ABC.com either, so it queries the root server of the .com domain.

BITS AND BYTES

How to Register a Domain Name

Would you like to create a Web site with your own domain name—for example, me.com? The process of creating your own Web site is straightforward, but finding a name that you like and that is available may be difficult.

The first thing you need to do is to create a list of domain names that are acceptable to you. If you are creating the Web site for business purposes, then you might want to keep search strategies in mind. With your list of acceptable domain names in hand, go to Whois.net (**whois.net**) to determine if your preferred name has already been taken. If the search results indicate that there is no match, then the name is available. If the name is already taken, try making small variations to that name.

After you find a name you like that's available, find an official Internet registrar (InterNIC has a link to the Accredited Registrar Directory). Registrars offer a variety of services for a range of prices, so compare prices among the registrars that offer the services you want. Once you provide the registrar with their required information, you've got yourself a Web domain ready for building your site.

STEP 1: Request from ABC.com.

STEP 2: Request IP address from DNS server.

STEP 3: Request IP address from root server.

Your computer

Your ISP's Web server

Your ISP's default DNS server

Root server for .com domain

STEP 6: Computer routes request to correct IP address.

STEP 5: DNS server stores IP address and passes it along.

STEP 4: Root server provides IP address.

4. The root server provides the default DNS server with the appropriate IP address of ABC.com.

5. The default DNS server stores the correct IP address for ABC.com for future reference and returns it to your ISP's Web server.

6. Your computer then routes its request to ABC.com and stores the IP address in cache for later use.

Your ISP or network administrator defines the default DNS server. If the default DNS server does not have an entry for the domain name you requested, then it queries another DNS server.

If all else fails, your ISP's Web server will contact one of the 13 root DNS servers maintained throughout the Internet. Each **root DNS server** knows the location of all the DNS servers that contain the master listings for an entire top-level domain. Your default DNS server receives the information from the master DNS server (say, for the .com domain). It then stores that information in its cache for future use and communicates the appropriate IP address to your computer.

Other Protocols: FTP and Telnet

The TCP/IP protocol suite contains numerous protocols, although some of them are used infrequently. Two of the more commonly used protocols on the Internet are the file transfer protocol and Telnet.

File Transfer Protocol

How does FTP work? The **file transfer protocol (FTP)** enables users to share files that reside on local computers with remote computers. If you're attempting to download files to your local computer using FTP, the FTP client application (most likely a Web browser) first establishes a TCP session with the remote computer. FTP provides for authentication and password protection, so you may be required to log in to an FTP site with a username and password.

Can you upload files with FTP? Most FTP sites allow you to upload files. To do so, you either need a browser that handles FTP transfers (current versions of Internet Explorer and Firefox do), or you need to obtain an FTP client application. Many FTP client programs are available as freeware or shareware. Searching on the term "FTP" on Download.com (**download. com**) will produce a list of programs from which to choose. FileZilla (**filezilla-project. org**) is an open source FTP program that is available free of charge.

Telnet

What is Telnet? Telnet is both a protocol for connecting to a remote computer and a TCP/IP service that runs on a remote computer to make it accessible to other computers. At colleges, students sometimes use Telnet to connect to mainframe computers or servers from their personal computers. The Telnet client application, which runs on your personal computer, connects to the Telnet server application, which runs on a

Figure 13.12
DNS servers in action.

remote computer, type "open" and the host name (or IP address) of the remote computer and follow the logon instructions. (These vary from system to system.)

HTTP, HTML, and Other Web Jargon

Although most people think that the Internet and the Web are the same thing, the World Wide Web (WWW or the Web) is actually a grouping of protocols and software that resides on the Internet. The Web provides an engaging interface for exchanging graphics, video, animations, and other multimedia over the Internet. One other aspect that distinguishes the Web from the Internet is the Web's use of special languages such as HTML (HyperText Markup Language) and protocols such as HTTP (HyperText Transfer Protocol), which facilitate communication between computers using different system and application software.

HTTP and SSL

Which Internet protocol does a browser use to send requests? The **HyperText Transfer Protocol (HTTP)** was created especially for the transfer of hypertext documents across the Internet. **Hypertext** documents are documents in which text is linked to other documents or media (such as video clips, pictures, and so on). Clicking a specific piece of text (called a *hyperlink*) that has been linked elsewhere takes you to the linked file.

When the browser sends a request, does it do anything to make the information secure? As you read in Chapter 3, some Web sites require extra layers of security to ensure that banking or

remote computer. Telnet enables you to take control of a remote computer (the server) with your computer (the client) and manipulate files and data on the server as if the server were your own computer.

How do you use Telnet? To establish a Telnet session, you need to know the domain name or IP address of the computer to be connected to using Telnet. In addition, logon information (ID and password) is generally required. With Windows, you also need to turn on the Telnet feature. To do so, click the Start button in the taskbar, select Control Panel, and then select Programs and Features. In the Programs and Features group, select the option to turn Windows features on or off. In the list of features, click Telnet Client and then click OK. After Telnet has been configured in Windows, click the Start button and enter "telnet" in the quick search box. You should see the window shown in Figure 13.13. Typing "?/" at the command prompt displays the available Telnet commands. To connect to

Figure 13.13

This Telnet command window shows available commands.

```
C:\Windows\system32\telnet.exe

Welcome to Microsoft Telnet Client

Escape Character is 'CTRL+]'

Microsoft Telnet> ?/

Commands may be abbreviated. Supported commands are:

c     - close             close current connection
d     - display           display operating parameters
o     - open hostname [port]  connect to hostname (default port 23).
q     - quit              exit telnet
set   - set               set options (type 'set ?' for a list)
sen   - send              send strings to server
st    - status            print status information
u     - unset             unset options (type 'unset ?' for a list)
?/h   - help              print help information
Microsoft Telnet> _
```

purchasing transactions can be done safely and without personal and financial information being mishandled. Commerce servers use security protocols to protect sensitive information from interception by hackers.

HyperText Transfer Protocol Secure (HTTPS) is actually a combination of the HTTP protocol and a network security protocol (usually SSL or TLS). HTTPS ensures data is sent securely over the Web. **Transport layer security (TLS)** and the **secure sockets layer (SSL)** are two protocols that provide data integrity and security for transmissions over the Internet. Online shopping sites frequently use HTTPS to safeguard credit card information. Online banking sites and other Web sites that require user authentication beyond just a simple user ID and password also use HTTPS.

HTML/XHTML

How are Web pages formatted? Web pages are text documents that are formatted using HTML or XHTML. Style sheets (described in more detail later in this chapter) provide developers an easier way to update and revise Web pages. Although XHTML is the development environment of choice for Web developers today, many people still refer to Web site formatting as "HTML tagging."

HTML and XHTML are not programming languages; rather, they are sets of rules for marking up blocks of text so that a browser knows how to display them. Blocks of text in HTML/XHTML documents are surrounded by pairs of **HTML tags** (such as <b> and </b>, which indicate bolding). HTML tags surround and define HTML content. Each pair of tags and the text between them are collectively referred to as an **element**. The elements are interpreted by the browser, and appropriate effects are applied to the text. The following is an element from an HTML/XHTML document:

```
<i>This should be
italicized.</i>
```

The browser would display this element as:

This should be italicized.

The first tag, <i>, tells the browser that the text following it should be italicized. The ending </i> tag indicates that the

browser should cease applying italics to the text. Note that multiple tags can be combined in a single element such as the following:

```
<b><i>This should be bolded and
italicized.</i></b>
```

The browser would display this element as

This should be bolded and italicized.

Obviously, the <b> tag indicates bolding. Tags for creating hyperlinks appear as follows:

```
<a href="http://www.
pearsonhighered.com">Pearson
Higher Education</a>
```

The code <a href="http://www. pearsonhighered.com"> defines the link's destination. The <a> tag is the anchor tag and creates a link to another resource on the Web (denoted by the href attribute), such as an HTML page, an image, or a sound. In this case, the link is to the **pearsonhighered. com** Web page. The text between the open and close of the anchor tag (Pearson Higher Education) is the link label. The link label is the text (or image) that is displayed on the Web page as clickable text for the hyperlink.

Can you see the HTML/XHTML coding of a Web page? HTML/ XHTML documents are merely text documents with tags applied to them. If you want to look at the HTML/XHTML coding behind your favorite Web page, just right-click anywhere on the page, select View Source from the shortcut menu, and the HTML/XHTML code for that page will be displayed, as shown in Figure 13.14. Alternatively, you

Figure 13.14

Viewing the source code of a Web site.

can select View Source in Internet Explorer (or View Page Source in Firefox) from the browser menu. For more information on how to build Web pages, see the Sound Byte "Creating Web Pages with HTML."

XML

How is XML different from HTML/ XHTML?   As you learned in Chapter 10, the eXtensible Markup Language (XML) describes the content in terms of what data is being described rather than how it is to be displayed. Instead of being locked into standard tags and formats for data, users can build their own markup languages to accommodate particular data formats and needs.

For example, three pieces of typical information that need to be captured for an e-commerce transaction are a credit card number, a price, and a zip code. In HTML/ XHTML, the paragraph tags (<p> and </p>) are used to define text and numeric elements. Almost any text or graphic can fall between these tags and be treated as a paragraph. Therefore, in our example, the HTML/ XHTML code would appear as follows:

```
<p>1234567890123456</p>
(credit card number)
<p>12.95</p> (price)
<p>19422</p> (zip code)
```

The browser will interpret the data contained within the <p> and </p> tags as separate paragraphs. However, the paragraph tags tell us nothing about the data contained within them. Without the labels (which are not part of the HTML/XHTML code), we may not realize what data was contained within. In addition, tags don't provide any methodology for data validation. Credit card numbers are usually 16 numbers long, but any length of data may be inserted between <p> and </p> tags. How would we know if the credit card number was a valid length? The answer lies in creating tags that are specific to the task at hand and that actually describe the data contained within them. Here's how our data might look in XML:

```
<credit_card_number>
1234567890123456
</credit_card_number>
<price>12.95</price>
<zip_code>19422</zip_code>
```

We have created the tags we need for data capture. Our XML specification provides a tag called "credit card number" that is used exclusively for credit card data.

How has XML influenced other Web page developments?   XML has spawned quite a few custom packages for specific communities. For example, Mathematical Markup Language (MathML) is an XML-based markup language that is used to describe mathematical symbols and formulas so that they can be presented in a familiar way in Web documents. Wireless Markup Language (WML) uses XML to output Web resources on mobile devices; MusicXML is used to create and publish musical scores online; and GraphML is an XML-based format for creating graphs. These are just a few of the many examples that illustrate the goal of XML—information exchange standards that can be easily constructed and customized to serve a growing variety of online applications.

The Common Gateway Interface

Can you use HTML/XHTML to make a Web page interactive?   Because HTML/XHTML was originally designed to link text documents, HTML/XHTML by itself can't do all the amazing things we expect modern Web pages to do. As we mentioned earlier, HTML and XHTML are not programming languages; rather, they are sets of tags that determine how text is displayed and where elements are placed. Fortunately, the limitations of HTML/XHTML were recognized early, and the common gateway interface (CGI) was developed.

Most browser requests merely result in a file such as the eBay home page (**eBay.com**) being displayed in your browser. Displaying a file is fine if you're just going to be reading text. However, to make a Web site interactive, you may need to run a program to perform a certain action (such as gathering a name and address and adding them to a database). The **common gateway interface (CGI)** provides a methodology by which your browser can request that a program file be executed (run) instead of just being delivered to the browser. This enables functionality beyond the simple display of information.

CGI files can be created in almost any programming language, and the programs created are often referred to as **CGI scripts**. Common languages that are used to create CGI scripts are Perl, C, and C++. Because programming languages are extremely powerful, almost any task can be accomplished by writing a CGI script. You have probably encountered CGI scripts on Web pages without realizing it. Have you ever left an entry in a guest book on a Web page? Have you used a search engine to create a customized results page based on keywords you entered? Have you filled out a form in which you asked to be added to a mailing list? All of these tasks are commonly done using CGI scripts.

How are CGI programs executed? On most Web servers, a directory called **cgi-bin** is created by the network administrator who configures the Web server. All CGI scripts are placed into this directory. The Web server knows that all files in this directory are not just to be read and sent but also need to be run. Because this type of program runs on the Web server rather than inside your browser, it is referred to as a **server-side program**.

For instance, a button on a Web site may say "Click Here to Join Mailing List" (see step 1 in Figure 13.15). Clicking the button

may call a script file (perhaps called "mailinglist.pl") from the cgi-bin directory on the Web server hosting the site (step 2). This file generates a form that is sent to your browser. The form includes fields for a name and e-mail address and a button that says "Submit" (step 3). After the user fills in the fields and clicks the Submit button, the mailinglist.pl program sends the information back to the server. The server then records the information in a database (step 4).

Dynamic HTML

Can Web pages be made more interactive without accessing Web servers? Dynamic HTML (DHTML) is a combination of technologies—HTML/XHTML, cascading style sheets (explained later in this chapter), and JavaScript—that is used to create lively and interactive Web sites. Recall that the Web is based on a client/server network. Once a Web server processes a Web page and sends the page to the computer that requested it (the client), the receiving computer cannot get any new data from the server unless a new request is made. If interactivity is required on a Web page, this exchange of data between the client and server can make the interactivity inefficient and slow. DHTML technologies allow a Web page to change after it has been loaded. Change generally occurs in response

Figure 13.15

Information flow when a CGI program is run.

STEP 1: You want to join XYZ's mailing list. You click a button on their Web site labeled "Click Here to Join Mailing List."

STEP 2: Clicking the button tells the XYZ.com server to execute a CGI program (called mailinglist.pl) located in the cgi-bin directory on the server.

STEP 3: The server executes the CGI program mailinglist.pl, which generates a form that is sent to your browser.

Your computer

XYZ.com server

STEP 4: You enter your mailing list information and click the "Submit" button on the mailing list form. This sends your information back to the server. The server saves your information into its database.

to such user actions as clicking a mouse or mousing over objects on a page. DHTML brings special effects to otherwise static Web pages without requiring users to download and install plug-ins or other special software.

AJAX is the acronym for a newer group of technologies that facilitates the creation of Web applications. These technologies can update information on the page without requiring the user to do a page refresh or leave the page. AJAX does not actually require the use of JavaScript or XML (even though they are in the name) but can use a variety of Web programming techniques and languages. JavaScript and XML are frequently used by AJAX Web developers.

What is JavaScript? JavaScript is the most commonly used scripting language for creating DHTML effects. It was developed through the joint efforts of Netscape and Sun Microsystems, two software development companies. JavaScript is often confused with the Java programming language because of the similarity in their names. However, though they share some common elements, the two languages function quite differently.

Pure HTML/XHTML documents don't respond to user input. With JavaScript, though, HTML/XHTML documents can be made responsive to mouse clicks and typing. For example, JavaScript is often used to validate the information you input in a Web form (for example, to make sure you filled in all required fields).

When JavaScript code is embedded in an HTML/XHMTL document, it is downloaded to the browser with the HTML/XHTML page. All actions dictated by the embedded JavaScript commands are executed on the client computer (the one with the browser). Without JavaScript and other scripting languages, Web pages would be lifeless.

How can you easily change the formatting of HTML/XHTML elements? In addition to the HTML/XHTML formatting tags described earlier, some tags describe areas of a Web page. This helps with layout. For example, the tag <h1>

declares an area as a header. Similarly, <p> says, "This is a paragraph," and <table> says, "This is a table." In addition to tags defining certain areas as headers, paragraphs, or tables, Web developers needed additional tags to indicate how each header, paragraph, or table would be formatted and displayed. Although this system worked for a while, as more and more tags and attributes were created it became increasingly difficult to manage the differences between content and presentation layout.

To solve this problem, cascading style sheets were created. A **cascading style sheet (CSS)** is a list of statements (also known as *rules*) that defines in one single location how to display HTML/XHTML elements. Style rules enable a Web developer to define a style for each HTML/XHTML element and apply it to multiple elements on as many Web pages as needed. Essentially, a template is created upon which the formatting for many Web pages within a site will be based.

Thus, when a global change is necessary, the developer only needs to change the style on the style sheet (template); all the elements in the Web document are then updated automatically (see Figure 13.16).

For example, a Web page has an <H1> heading tag, and all <H1> tags in the Web page are formatted with a white background and an orange border. Before CSS, if you wanted to change the border color from orange to yellow, you had to change the background color of every <H1> tag. With CSS, the change from orange to yellow only needs to happen once on the style sheet; all the <H1> tags on the Web pages then update to yellow without individual changes.

Where does the cascading come in? In Web documents, there are different layers of styles: external, embedded, and inline. Therefore, it's possible that different rules can be created for the same type of element. In other words, in an external style sheet, there might be a rule that defines the background color for all paragraphs as blue.

Figure 13.16

Cascading style sheets allow for the creation of formatting templates. Just as all the pages of this book have a similar look and feel, one style sheet can control the formatting of many Web pages.

Somewhere else, in an embedded style sheet, a rule for background color for paragraphs might be white; and in an inline style sheet, the background color might be light pink. Eventually, all these style sheets must be merged to form one style sheet for the document. This creates conflicts among rules. Therefore, rules are assigned weights so that when the rules are collected and merged, the rule or style with a higher weight overrides the rule or style with a lower weight. This hierarchy of competing styles creates a "cascade" of styles ranked according to their assigned weights.

How are the individual components of a Web page organized? Just as cascading style sheets organize and combine the attributes of objects on a Web page, DHTML uses the **document object model (DOM)** to organize the objects and page elements. The document object model defines every item on a Web page—including graphics, tables, and headers—as an object. Then with DOM, similar to CSS, Web developers can easily change the look and feel of these objects.

Client-Side Applications

Aside from CGI scripts, are there other ways to make a Web site interactive? Sometimes running programs on the server is not optimal. Server-side program execution can require many communication sessions between the client and the server to achieve the goal. Often it is more efficient to run programs on your computer (the client). Therefore, client-side programs were created. A **client-side program** is a computer program that runs on the client computer and requires no interaction with a Web server. Client-side programs are fast and efficient because they run on your desktop and don't depend on data going back and forth to the Web server. Two main types of client-side methods exist. The first involves embedding programming language code directly within the HTML or XHTML code of a Web page using an **HTML/XHTML embedded scripting language**. The most popular embedded language is JavaScript, which is used extensively in dynamic HTML files.

The second type of client-side program is an **applet**, a small application that resides on a server. When requested, a compiled version of the program is downloaded to the client computer and run there. The Java language is the most common language used to create applets for use in browsers. The applets can be requested from the server when a Web page is loaded; they will run once they're downloaded to the client computer.

Although the user can experience some delay in functionality while waiting for the Java applet to download to the client, once the applet arrives, it can execute all its functions without further communication with the server. Games are often sent to your browser as applets. As an example, in Figure 13.17 your browser makes contact with a game

Figure 13.17

Deployment of a Java applet on a computer.

STEP 1: Request from browser for game.

STEP 2: Java applet code sent to your computer.

Your computer

Computer executes Java applet code and game displays.

ArcadePod.com server

Keeping track of where you have been on the Internet can be quite a challenge. Think about how many Web sites you visited today or when you were researching that paper for your history class last week. Can you remember all the sites you visited? Probably not—most of us don't have total recall.

Fortunately, tools built into browser software help us remember the sites we visit. For example, in Internet Explorer and Firefox, the history feature tracks all the sites visited over a period of time using the same browser on the same computer. If you have a Google account and use the Google Toolbar (an add-on for the Internet Explorer and Firefox browsers), the Google Web History feature tracks your entire browsing history regardless of what computer you may be using (as long as you are logged into your Google account and use the toolbar). But how private is your browsing history?

Most individuals in our society value privacy, which simply stated is the right to be left alone and unobserved to do as you please. But having your browsing habits recorded by the software you are using is tantamount to having someone looking over your shoulder and watching exactly what you are doing. Did you browse to a site today that you wouldn't want your parents, teacher, or boss to know about? If you haven't cleared the history file in your browser, anyone could easily call up the history in your browser and find out (see Figure 13.18)!

Google Web History is even more of a conundrum. Your entire browsing history is potentially contained in your Google file for all computers that you use (at home, school, and work). If you are browsing the Web at the local coffee shop and have not taken measures to secure your data transmissions on your notebook, any hacker could potentially intercept and gain access to your entire browsing history. This could reveal to a hacker places where you have financial resources (such as banks) and help direct them to Web sites where they can attempt to access your accounts. Many people would feel that their privacy was severely violated if their entire Web browsing history were seen by a stranger even if that person didn't use that information in a malicious way.

So where does convenience stop and privacy start? This is one of the thorny ethical dilemmas that we face in today's wired world. Having a browser history is extremely convenient when you can't remember the name of a cool site you visited last week. But having a list of all the sites you visited could be downright embarrassing if your boss looked through them and found out you were surfing the "jobs available" section of a competitor's Web site. Do you really want the next person to use the computer in the lab at school to know what you were shopping for on the Internet?

Although users can erase browser histories and Google Web History, this is not automatic and requires user intervention. The current versions of the popular browsers contain features called InPrivate Browsing (Internet Explorer) and Private Browsing (Firefox) that allow you to surf the Web without the browser retaining your history. But again, you must invoke these features to take advantage of them. Are you going to remember to do so every time you need to keep your browsing private? Fortunately, Firefox allows you to make Private Browsing the default for all your browsing sessions.

Should the makers of browser software and add-on tools be required to remind users periodically to purge their browsing history? Should the surfing tools that enhance privacy be automatically invoked by default so people won't forget to use them? Where does convenience end and privacy begin? What do you think?

Figure 13.18
Nothing embarrassing in this Firefox Web history. But what's lurking in your browser's history?

on the game site ArcadePod.com (**arcadepod.com**) and makes your request to play a game (step 1). The Web server returns the Java applet (step 2) that contains all the code to run the game on your computer. Your computer executes the applet code, and the game runs on your computer.

Communications over the Internet

A new communications revolution was started when Internet use began to explode in the mid-1990s. The volume of Internet e-mail is growing exponentially every month.

Unfortunately, it is estimated that 97 percent of it is spam. Instant messaging is a major method of communication, and the popularity of Voice over Internet Protocol is also on the rise. In the following sections, we explore all of these communications media in more detail and show you how to keep your information exchanges efficient and secure.

E-Mail

Who invented e-mail? In 1971, Ray Tomlinson, a computer engineer who worked on the development of the ARPANET (the precursor to the Internet) for the U.S. government, created e-mail. E-mail grew from a simple program that Tomlinson wrote to enable computer users to leave text messages for each other on a single machine. The logical extension of this was sending text messages between machines on the Internet. Tomlinson created the convention of using the @ sign to distinguish between the mailbox name and the destination computer. E-mail became the most popular application on ARPANET; by 1973, it accounted for 75 percent of all data traffic.

How does e-mail travel the Internet? Just like other kinds of data that flow along the Internet, e-mail has its own protocol. The **simple mail transfer protocol (SMTP)** is responsible for sending e-mail along the Internet to its destination. As in most other Internet applications, e-mail is a client/server application. To send an e-mail message, you will need some form of e-mail software to compose the document as well as to include an attachment such as a spreadsheet or photograph. Popular client-based e-mail software (software that needs to be installed on your computer) includes Microsoft Outlook and Mozilla Thunderbird, as well as Web-based e-mail software such as the increasingly popular Yahoo!, Hotmail, and Gmail.

As you read in Chapter 3, client-based software is installed on your computer, and all of its functions are supported and run from your computer. Web-based software is launched from a Web site; the programs and features are stored on the Web and are accessible anywhere you have access to an Internet connection. No matter which type of client software you use, on the way to its destination your mail will pass through **e-mail**

servers—specialized computers whose sole function is to store, process, and send e-mail.

Where are e-mail servers located? If your ISP provides you with an e-mail account, it runs an e-mail server that uses SMTP. For example, as shown in Figure 13.19, say you are sending an e-mail message to your friend Cheyenne. Cheyenne uses Verizon.net as her ISP. Therefore, your e-mail to her is addressed to Cheyenne@verizon.net.

When you send the e-mail message, your ISP's Web e-mail server receives it. The e-mail server reads the domain name (**verizon.net**) and communicates with a DNS server to determine the location of juno.com. Once the address is located, the e-mail message is forwarded to verizon.net through the Internet and arrives at a mail server maintained by Cheyenne's ISP. The e-mail is then stored on Cheyenne's ISP's e-mail server. The next time Cheyenne logs on to her ISP and checks her mail, she will receive your message.

If e-mail was designed for text messages, why are we able to send files as attachments? SMTP was designed to handle text messages. When the need arose to send files by e-mail (in the early 1970s), a program had to be created to convert binary files to text. The text that represented the file was appended to the end of the e-mail message. When the e-mail arrived at its destination, the recipient had to run another program to translate the text back into a binary file. Uuencode and uudecode were the two most popular programs used for encoding and decoding binary files.

STEP 1: You send an e-mail message to your friend Cheyenne.

STEP 2: Your ISP's e-mail server consults the DNS server for Cheyenne's domain address.

Your computer

Your ISP's e-mail server (SMTP)

DNS server

STEP 3: The DNS server provides the domain IP address.

INTERNET

STEP 4: The e-mail server forwards your e-mail through the Internet to Cheyenne's ISP's Web server.

Cheyenne's ISP's e-mail server (SMTP)

STEP 5: The next time Cheyenne checks her e-mail, she gets your e-mail.

Cheyenne's computer

Figure 13.19

A sample route an e-mail takes on the Internet.

This was fine in the early days of the Internet when most users were computer scientists. However, when the Internet started to become popular (in the early 1990s), it became apparent that a simpler methodology was needed for sending and receiving files. The **multipurpose Internet mail extensions (MIME)** specification was introduced in 1991 to simplify attachments to e-mail messages. All e-mail client software now uses this protocol to attach files.

E-mail is still sent as text, but the e-mail client using the MIME protocol now handles the encoding and decoding for the users. For instance, in Yahoo! mail, on the Attach Files screen you merely browse to the file you want to attach (located somewhere on a storage device), select the file, and click the Attach Files button. The Yahoo! e-mail client transparently encodes and decodes the file for transmission and receipt.

E-Mail Security: Encryption and Specialized Software

If e-mail is sent in regular text, can other people read my mail? E-mail is highly susceptible to being read by

unintended parties because it's sent in plain text. Additionally, copies of your e-mail messages may exist (temporarily or permanently) on numerous servers as the messages make their way through the Internet. To protect your sensitive e-mail messages, encryption practices are used.

How do you encrypt e-mail? **Encryption** refers to the process of coding your e-mail so that only the person with the key to the code (the intended recipient) can decode (or decipher) and read the message. Secret codes for messages can be traced almost to the dawn of written language. The military and government espionage agencies are big users of codes and ciphers. The trick is making the coding system easy enough to use that everyone who needs to communicate with you can do so.

There are two basic types of encryption: private key and public key. In **private-key encryption**, only the two parties involved in

ACTIVE HELP-DESK

Keeping E-Mail Secure

In this Active Helpdesk call, you'll play the role of a helpdesk staffer, fielding calls about how e-mail works and how messages are kept secure.

sending the message have the code. This could be a simple shift code where letters of the alphabet are shifted to a new position (see Figure 13.20). For example, in a two-position right-shift code, the letter *a* becomes *c*, *b* becomes *d*, and so on. Alternatively, it could be a more complex substitution code ($a = h$, $b = r$, $c = g$, etc.). The main problem with private-key encryption is key security. If someone steals a copy of the code or is savvy about decoding, the code is broken.

In **public-key encryption**, two keys, known as a **key pair**, are created. You use one key for coding and the other for decoding. The key for coding is generally distributed as a **public key**. You can place this key on your Web site, for instance. Anyone wishing to send you a message can then download your public key and code the message using your public key.

When you receive the message, you use your **private key** to decode it. You are the only one who ever possesses the private key, and therefore it is highly secure. The keys are generated in such a way that they can work only with each other. The private key is generated first. The public key is then generated using a complex mathematical formula, often using values from the private key. The computations are so complex that they are considered unbreakable. Both keys are necessary to decode a message. If one key is lost, the other key cannot be used by itself.

What type of encryption is used on the Internet? Public-key encryption is the most commonly used encryption on the Internet. Tried-and-true public-key packages such as **Pretty Good Privacy (PGP)** are available for download at sites such as Download.com (**download.com**), and you can usually use them free of charge (although there are now commercial versions of PGP). After obtaining the PGP software, you can generate key pairs to

A = C	N = P
B = D	O = Q
C = E	P = R
D = F	Q = S
E = G	R = T
F = H	S = U
G = I	T = V
H = J	U = W
I = K	V = X
J = L	W = Y
K = M	X = Z
L = N	Y = A
M = O	Z = B

The word **C O M P U T E R** using the two-position code at the left now becomes:

E Q O R W V G T

This is difficult to interpret without the code key at the left.

Figure 13.20

Writing the word "COMPUTER" using a two-position right-shift encryption code.

provide a private key for you and a public key for the rest of the world.

What does a key look like? A key is a binary number. Keys vary in length, depending on how secure they need to be. A 10-bit key has 10 positions and might look like this:

1001101011

Longer keys are more secure because they have more values that are possible. A 10-bit key provides 1,024 different possible values, whereas a 40-bit key allows for 1,099,511,627,776 possible values. The key and the message are run through a complex algorithm in the encryption program (such as PGP) that converts the message into unrecognizable code. Each key turns the message into a different code.

BITS AND BYTES

Random Numbers: The Lifeblood of Encryption

E-mail encryption, SSL encryption, and just about anything we do to achieve privacy on the Internet requires random numbers. Encryption is accomplished using random number sequences, which are sequences of numbers in which no patterns can be recognized. Even for an e-commerce transaction (say, buying a book from Amazon.com) that uses SSL encryption to encode your credit card number, as many as 368 bits of random data might be needed. Only 128 bits are needed for the encryption key, but other random data is needed to create authentication codes and to prevent replay attacks. Replay attacks occur when hackers attempt to copy packets traveling across the Internet and extract data (such as encryption codes) from them. The hackers then can replay (reuse) the data to gain access to networks or transactions.

So where do all these random numbers come from? Generating true random sequences is more difficult than it sounds. However, in 1996, Landon Noll and two colleagues came up with a system called *LavaRnd* that used Lava Lite lamps (**lavalamp.com**) to generate random numbers. The lamps have since been replaced with another random source: a webcam with the lens cap still on. The webcam emits "thermal noise," which is then digitized and run through a mathematical algorithm that generates the number set and strips out any sections that are predictable. This service is open source, unpatented, and license free, so anyone can set up a server and generate much-needed random numbers. For more information, check out the LavaRnd site (**lavarnd.org**).

The Internet and the ways we use it are constantly evolving. In the 1990s, most home users connected to the Internet with a dial-up modem. Fiber-optic technology, once available only for corporate and urban America, today reaches many homes in suburban and rural areas and provides lightning-fast Internet connections. But this wired technology does not address the growing demand for wireless connectivity that is accessible everywhere. Web 2.0 tools—such as social networking sites like Facebook and MySpace, blogs, wikis, and video sharing sites like YouTube—are changing the way individuals and businesses use the Internet. Let's look at a few emerging trends in both of these areas.

WiMAX—Spreading the Signal Far and Wide

Because of the rise in portable computing devices, people want Internet access wherever they go. A wireless alternative to standard WiFi connections is WiMAX (short for worldwide interoperability for microwave access). Instead of the 300 feet of connectivity that WiFi offers, WiMAX has a range of as far as 31 miles, and its transmission speed can run up to 72 Mbps, making it much faster than current cable or DSL connections. The WiMAX Forum, a nonprofit group consisting mainly of WiMAX providers and component suppliers, reports there are more than 550 WiMAX networks deployed in 147 countries, and now providers such as Clear are deploying WiMAX networks in large cities throughout the United States. Clear offers mobile access over a large area, freeing you from needing to find a hot spot to connect. Your next provider of Internet services may well be a company that offers WiMAX wireless connectivity.

Crowdsourcing—Harnessing the Power of Social Networks

Starting and running a small business involves a fair amount of risk, especially when running a merchandising business. Deciding what products to buy and resell to customers is tricky. Will your customers purchase the products you think are so wonderful? Will they buy them quickly enough so that you can free up your cash to purchase more inventory? What quantities should you stock? If you're an entrepreneur, you usually have to make these decisions yourself. Wouldn't it be better to let your customers tell you what to sell?

Many businesses harness the power of their customers (and potential customers) by using the Internet to take advantage of a new technique known as **crowdsourcing**. When you crowdsource, you take a task that an employee or a contractor usually performs and instead outsource that task to a large group of people, usually via the Internet. In this way, you can have many individuals work on a task to take advantage of aggregated brainpower. Or you can aggregate and analyze the results of feedback from the crowdsourcers to make informed business decisions. Two companies that exemplify the crowdsourcing model of customer-driven merchandise buying are **Threadless.com** and **ModCloth.com**.

Threadless is a T-shirt company, but what makes Threadless stand out from the hundreds of other T-shirt companies on the Web is that they invite artists and designers to submit designs for T-shirts as part of an ongoing contest. Threadless posts submitted designs on the site and then lets anyone who visits the site vote on the best designs. The designs with the most votes get made into shirts and offered for sale (see Figure 13.21), and the designers of shirts that get printed win a

Figure 13.21

Threadless shirts such as A Simple Plan (based on the classic game Space Invaders) were voted on by customers before being offered for sale (crowdsourcing).

Is a private key really secure?

Because of the complexity of the algorithms used to generate key pairs, it is impossible to deduce the private key from the public key. However, that doesn't mean your coded message can't be cracked. As you learned in Chapter 12, a brute force attack occurs when hackers try every possible key combination to decode a message. This type of attack can enable hackers to deduce the key and decode the message.

What is considered a safe key?

In the early 1990s, 40-bit keys were thought to be totally resistant to brute force attacks and were the norm for encryption. However, in 1995, a French programmer used a unique algorithm of his own and 120 workstations simultaneously to attempt to break a 40-bit key. He succeeded in just eight days. Since then, 128-bit keys have become the standard. Even using supercomputers, no one has yet cracked a 128-bit key. It is believed that even with the most powerful computers in use today, it would take hundreds of billions of years to crack a 128-bit key.

Figure 13.22
Customers vote and comment on products that **ModCloth.com** is thinking about stocking.

cash prize of $2,500. Because potential customers have already indicated their interest in a particular design by voting on it, Threadless can be fairly confident that the designs they print will sell briskly.

ModCloth is a company founded in 2002 by two high-school students who were just 17 years old! They started selling only vintage clothing but then expanded to offer vintage-inspired designs by Indie designers. When ordering clothing from designers, there is usually a minimum order quantity that often exceeds 100 pieces. Although the buyers for ModCloth feel they have a good eye for what their customers like, it is still risky for a small business to order large quantities of items because they may take a long time to sell.

ModCloth started its Be the Buyer program to involve customers in the buying process. They post clothing they are considering buying on the ModCloth site, and then customers vote to either "Pick It" (stock the item) or "Skip It," as shown in Figure 13.22. Customers can post comments

about the items, which range from humorous to constructive. ModCloth also provides links so that voters can easily share items with their friends on social networks like Facebook and Twitter. Constructive ideas from potential customers can be sent back to designers who might make suggested alterations to items before ModCloth orders them. When ModCloth orders a popular item, customers who indicated they liked it can be contacted via e-mail to stimulate sales.

So don't let all those customers that have friended you on your company's Facebook page sit idle. Put them to work helping you make your business more profitable! And thanks to WiMAX, you soon should be able to communicate with your customers from wherever you happen to be standing.

Look for these and other Internet-related trends coming soon to computers near you.

What is an easy way for me to try encrypted e-mail? Many e-mail services offer built-in encryption, and they mostly market toward businesses. However, Hushmail (**hushmail.com**) and Comodo SecureEmail (**comodo.com**) offer free versions of their secure e-mail to individuals. You can sign up on their Web sites and experiment with sending encrypted e-mail. And you don't need to abandon your current e-mail accounts—just use your secure account when you require secure communications.

How do businesses protect e-mail? Encryption doesn't solve the other problems associated with e-mail. Messages leave a trail as they travel over the Internet, and copies of messages can exist on servers for long periods of time. In addition, immediate reading of sensitive documents is often essential, but encryption software doesn't provide a means for confirming that your messages have been delivered. To combat these issues, companies including Securus Systems Ltd. (**safemessage.com**) have developed secure data transmission software that works outside of the conventional SMTP mail servers. Let's look at Securus Systems' product, SafeMessage.

How is SafeMessage software used? Parties who wish to send or receive secure messages install the SafeMessage software. When messages are to be sent, a secure point-to-point connection is established between the sender's and the recipient's e-mail boxes. Instead of SMTP, proprietary protocols (protocols developed and owned by specific companies) with encryption are used to send the messages. Additional options are provided such as delivery confirmation, message shredding (destruction of messages on command), and the ability to have messages erase themselves after a set period of time. Although this type of software is not free, it is catching on in those sections of the business community where fear of industrial espionage is high.

Instant Messaging

What do you need to run instant messaging? As we explained in Chapter 3, instant messaging is the act of communicating over the Internet with one or more people in real time. It differs from e-mail in that conversations are able to

happen at the same time rather than lagging by minutes or hours. Instant messaging requires the use of a client program that connects to an instant messaging service. AOL Instant Messenger (AIM), ICQ, Yahoo! Messenger, and Windows Live Messenger are the top four instant messaging services in use today. No matter which one you choose, you need to have the appropriate client software installed on your computer.

How does instant messaging work? The client software running on your computer makes a connection with the chat server using your Internet connection, as shown in Figure 13.23. Once contact is established, you can log in to the server with your name and password. (You can sign up for a free account the first time you connect.) The client software provides the server with connection information (such as the IP address) for your computer. The server then consults the list of contacts ("Buddies" or friends) that you have previously established in your account and checks to see if any of your contacts are online (step 1). If any are, the server sends a message back to your client providing the necessary connection information (the IP addresses) for your friends who are online (step 2). You can now click your friends' names to establish a chat session with them (step 3).

Figure 13.23

How an instant messaging program works.

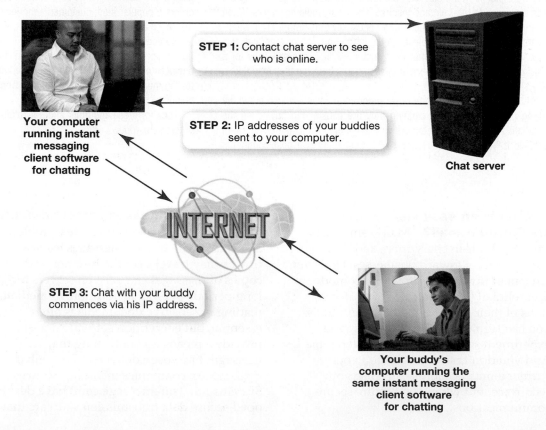

STEP 1: Contact chat server to see who is online.

Your computer running instant messaging client software for chatting

STEP 2: IP addresses of your buddies sent to your computer.

Chat server

INTERNET

STEP 3: Chat with your buddy commences via his IP address.

Your buddy's computer running the same instant messaging client software for chatting

Because both your computer and your friend's computer have the connection information (the IP addresses) for each other, the server isn't involved in the chat session. Chatting takes place directly between the two computers over the Internet.

Is sending an instant message secure?   Most instant messaging services do not use a high level of encryption for their messages—if they bother to use encryption at all. In addition to viruses, worms, and hacking threats, instant messaging systems are vulnerable to eavesdropping, in which someone using a packet sniffer "listens in" on IM conversations. Although several measures are under way to increase the security of this method of real-time communication, major vulnerabilities still exist. And employers can install monitoring software to record instant message sessions. Therefore, it is not a good idea to send sensitive information using instant messaging because it is susceptible to interception and possible misuse by hackers. Also, your company may be monitoring and logging instant message sessions.

Voice over Internet Protocol (VoIP)

What is Voice over Internet Protocol?
Voice over Internet Protocol (VoIP) turns a standard Internet connection into a way to make free long-distance phone calls. If you have friends and relatives that live a long-distance phone call away from you, then you need to know more about VoIP.

What's so good about VoIP?   From a user's perspective, the true advantage is that the service is cheaper than conventional phone service or, in some instances, is free. Even some cell phones are VoIP-enabled and can make calls through available wireless networks (although this usually still counts as used minutes for the month).

How does VoIP work?   From a user's perspective, there is little difference between VoIP and traditional phone service (see Figure 13.24), although the technology behind the wires and devices is a bit different. As explained in Chapter 3, VoIP is a method of taking analog voice signals that normally travel telephone wires and turning them into digital data that can be transmitted over the Internet. Like e-mail, VoIP uses packet switching as the method of transferring data. Unlike circuit switching (the method used with traditional phone calls), when a VoIP call is made, the transmission lines are only used when the two computers are communicating, thus allowing the computers to accept and process other information. Because digital data is far more efficient than analog data with respect to size, transmission speed, and compression capabilities,

Figure 13.24 | CONVENTIONAL AND VoIP CALLING COMPARED

Conventional Telephone Call	VoIP Telephone Call
1. Pick up the phone and wait for a dial tone to signal that you are connected to the local office of your telephone carrier.	1. Pick up the phone, which sends a signal to the computer or telephone adapter. The computer sends a dial tone, indicating that you have a connection to the Internet.
2. Dial the number of your friend's phone.	2. Dial the number of your friend's phone. The tones are converted into digital data.
3. The call is routed through the switch at your local carrier, passing through several switches along the way.	3. As long as the phone number is in a valid format, your VoIP company will translate the phone number into an IP address and then connects to the receiving device.
4. The phone at the other end rings, and your friend answers the call.	4. The signal "asks" the receiving device to ring, and your friend answers the call.
5. When the call is answered, a circuit is opened.	5. When your friend picks up the phone, each computer knows to expect packets of data from the other computer.
6. As you talk, the circuit remains open. No other data can be transmitted over the phone line during this time. A busy signal occurs if someone else tries to call.	6. As you talk, the packets of data are sent over the same Internet infrastructure as e-mail or a Web page. The digital data is translated into analog audio signals so that you and your friend can understand each other.
7. When you hang up, the circuit is closed, enabling another call to come in.	7. When you hang up, the session is terminated.

VoIP's long-term advantage is that it will be able to handle more phone calls at the same time. Although today's traditional phone calls have increased efficiency and reduced costs since they were first invented, there is considerable room for improvement compared to how digital data (such as e-mail) is transmitted.

How are VoIP security issues being handled? Because VoIP technology is similar to that of e-mail, VoIP is vulnerable to some of the same threats. However, the use of encryption methodologies, updated antivirus software, firewalls, and antispam tools helps cut down on VoIP's security vulnerabilities.

Using the Internet to Deliver Computer Services

Businesses are taking advantage of the Internet in some fairly obvious ways, such as the explosion in e-commerce over the last decade. In addition, businesses are using the Internet in ways that are transparent (invisible) to the end user and that result in considerable cost savings and increases in business efficiencies.

What is cloud computing? The Internet is often represented in diagrams as a picture of a cloud. **Cloud computing** refers to using the Internet to deliver business services online that were previously delivered locally by company-owned IT departments. You have probably used cloud

computing services yourself because many Web 2.0 applications (such as blogs, wikis, and social networks) and Web-based e-mail (such as Yahoo! or Gmail) are provided to you via cloud computing.

Why would a company need cloud computing? Amazon.com needs the computing power of many computers (servers) to manage the millions of products the company offers and handle the tens of thousands of orders it receives and delivers each day. Amazon has made a significant investment in computer hardware, software, and human programming talent to build a comprehensive e-commerce system to acquire, sell, and deliver products. If you were going to start a business that required a sophisticated inventory system such as the one Amazon uses to manage its stock, you would need a rather large pile of cash to purchase the equipment, software, and labor needed to develop your own product tracking system.

Certain companies, like Amazon, that have already made the investment in their systems have now started to offer services via cloud computing to other companies. Under the Amazon Elastic Compute Cloud (Amazon EC2), Amazon offers other companies (for a fee, of course) the capability to use its proven systems and technology to host computer applications that those other companies require. This means that companies can have Amazon set up and maintain servers for them that can be accessed via the Internet. The companies pay Amazon only for the storage and processing capacity that they use.

Figure 13.25

Jamglue uses Amazon.com's cloud computing services to process music mixes for its users.

Imagine that you wanted to start a company to sell shoes online. Instead of hiring an entire IT department and investing tens of thousands of dollars in software and hardware, you could lease server space from Amazon's computing services. Your computing systems would then be deployed on hardware and software maintained by Amazon, and your computer services would be delivered in the "cloud" (via the Internet). It would be much more cost effective for your company to use Amazon's proven systems and technology because Amazon can add servers to its network to meet your computing needs for a fraction of the cost of building your own system. You still would need experienced IT talent to customize the delivery of services for your employees and customers and to connect your employees' computers to Amazon's servers. However, you would need significantly fewer people than you would need to build and maintain your own complex system.

What types of businesses can benefit the most from cloud computing? Businesses that need to process large amounts of data every once in a while can significantly reduce costs by using cloud computing. Instead of investing in large amounts of equipment and software that it will use only infrequently, a company can rent as much computing power as it needs at specific times. Businesses that tend to be busy during certain months or seasons of the year are also good candidates. For example, a company that makes fireworks might want to acquire more computing power during the months that lead up to the Fourth of July to handle a large increase in orders pertaining to that holiday. The fireworks company could then scale back its processing capacity on July 5. Furthermore, a start-up business that might not have the capability to raise large amounts of capital can often save significant amounts of money by paying for just the computing power it needs, instead of installing a large data processing center early on.

One example of a company that relies on cloud computing is Jamglue (**jamglue.com**). Jamglue is a Web site that allows users to upload music or sound tracks and then mix them with other tracks that have been uploaded or mixed by other users (see Figure 13.25). Processing the mixes requires a lot of computing power, and Jamglue uses Amazon EC2 services to process user data.

> **"Security is one of the main concerns related to using cloud computing services."**

Is it safe to rely on other companies to process sensitive data? Security is one of the main concerns related to using cloud computing services. Running your own IT department requires careful consideration of how to protect and safeguard data. When you turn over processing to a third party, it's important to carefully investigate the security and backup capabilities of the cloud computing service provider to determine if their procedures meet your requirement for data security.

Security measures for all forms of communication technologies are constantly being evaluated. It is important for all users of Internet technologies to understand that threats to our security and privacy are real but controllable with the proper precautions.

1. Who owns, manages, and pays for the Internet?

Management of the Internet is carried out by several nonprofit organizations and user groups such as the Internet Society (ISOC), the Internet Engineering Task Force (IETF), the Internet Architecture Board (IAB), the Internet Corporation for Assigned Names and Numbers (ICANN), and the World Wide Web Consortium (W3C). Each group has different responsibilities and tasks. Currently, the U.S. government (and subsequently the U.S. taxpayer) funds a majority of the Internet's costs.

2. How do the Internet's networking components interact?

Individual computers or networks connect to the Internet using Internet service providers (ISPs). These providers vary in size and work like the physical highway system. The largest paths, along which data travels the most efficiently and quickly, make up the Internet backbone. Homes and all but the largest businesses connect to the Internet through these regional or local connections, which then connect to the Internet through the entities that make up the Internet backbone. The largest businesses, educational centers, and some government agencies such as NASA make up the Internet backbone.

3. What data transmissions and protocols does the Internet use?

Data is transmitted along the Internet using packet switching. Data is broken up into discrete units known as *packets*, which can take independent routes to the destination before being reassembled. Although many protocols are available on the Internet, the main suite of protocols used to move information over the Internet is TCP/IP. The suite is named after the original two protocols that were developed for the Internet: the Transmission Control Protocol (TCP) and the Internet Protocol (IP). Whereas TCP is responsible for preparing data for transmission, IP actually sends data between computers on the Internet.

4. Why are IP addresses and domain names important for Internet communications?

An IP address is a unique number assigned to all computers connected to the Internet. The IP address is necessary so that packets of data can be sent to a particular location (computer) on the Internet. A domain name is merely a name that stands for a certain IP address and makes it easier for people to remember it. For example, MyWebPage.com is a domain name and is much easier to remember than the IP address 124.53.111.14. DNS servers act as the phone books of the Internet. They enable your computer to find out the IP address of a domain by looking up its corresponding domain name (which you typed into your browser).

5. What are FTP and Telnet, and how do you use them?

The file transfer protocol (FTP) enables users to share files that reside on local computers with remote computers. Current versions of browsers enable you to connect to FTP sites on the Internet to facilitate downloading or uploading files to and from FTP sites. Telnet is both a protocol for connecting to a remote computer and a TCP/IP service that runs on a remote computer to make it accessible to other computers. Telnet enables you to take control of a remote computer (the server) with your computer (the client) and manipulate files and data on the server as if you were sitting in front of that server.

6. What are HTML/XHTML and XML used for?

The HyperText Markup Language (HTML) is a set of rules for marking up blocks of text so that a browser knows how to display them. Most Web pages are generated with at least some HTML code. Blocks of text in HTML documents are surrounded by a pair of tags (such as <b> and </b> to indicate bolding). These tags and the text between them are referred to as *elements*. By examining the elements, your browser determines how to display them on your computer screen. Because HTML was not designed for information exchange, eXtensible Markup Language (XML) was created. Instead of locking users into standard tags and formats for data, XML enables users to create their own markup languages to accommodate particular data formats and needs. XML is used extensively in e-commerce for exchanging data between corporations.

7. How do e-mail, instant messaging, and Voice over Internet Protocol work, and how is information using these technologies kept secure?

Simple mail transfer protocol (SMTP) is the protocol responsible for sending e-mail over the Internet. As is true of most other Internet applications, e-mail is a client/server application. E-mail passes through e-mail servers whose functions are to store, process, and send e-mail to its ultimate destination. ISPs and portals such as Yahoo! maintain e-mail servers to provide e-mail functionality to their customers. Your ISP's e-mail server uses DNS servers to locate the IP addresses for the recipients of the e-mail you send. Encryption software, such as Pretty Good Privacy (PGP), is used to code messages so that they can be decoded only by the authorized recipients.

8. How do businesses use the Internet to reduce computing costs?

Many businesses are taking advantage of cloud computing to reduce costs. *Cloud computing* refers to business services provided online by other companies and delivered to a customer through the Internet. These services were formerly delivered locally by company-owned IT departments. A company might use Amazon.com's cloud computing servers, for example, to store their data instead of purchasing and installing their own servers. Cloud computing initiatives, while cost effective, generate data security concerns because a third party is managing sensitive data.

key terms

Word Bank

- affective computing
- AJAX
- applet
- circuit switching
- DNS server
- FTP
- HTML tags
- HTTP
- ICANN
- Internet backbone
- IP address
- OC line
- packet switching
- PGP
- point of presence
- public-key encryption
- SMTP
- SSL
- TCP/IP

Instructions: Fill in the blanks using the words from the Word Bank above.

As a network administrator, Patricia knows that she can count on the organization (1) _____ to ensure that she has an appropriate range of IP addresses for her work site. Her high-speed connection to her company's ISP was vital to providing the connectivity her employees need to get their jobs done. Recently, the company moved up from a DSL connection to a(n) (2) _____ because of the high volume of Internet traffic it was generating. Patricia hopes the government will continue to fund projects to continue research to improve the Internet (3) _____, the main highway to the Internet, and other vital technologies.

But Patricia has indulged in enough daydreaming. It is time to ensure that the Internet connection to the bank of modems, or (4) _____, provided by the ISP her company is using is fully functional before the majority of the employees arrive for work. Because Patricia's company sends a tremendous amount of e-mail, old-fashioned (5) _____ technology would never have sufficed for sending messages. Fortunately, the Internet employs (6) _____ to enable messages to be sent over widely varying routes. Of course, she knows that the main suite of protocols that controls Internet data traffic is called (7) _____.

After ensuring that all is functional, Patricia begins to assist the Web development team with Web page creation. To provide robust interaction with company databases, (8) _____ is being used to code Web pages for the corporate Web site instead of HTML, which requires developers to use a standard set of (9) _____. Unsure of her instructions, she e-mails the director of Web development for clarification, knowing that the (10) _____ protocol will ensure that the e-mail is delivered to the director at the company's office in the United Kingdom. Requiring secure communications, she encrypts the e-mail using a(n) (11) _____ algorithm, knowing that the director can retrieve Patricia's key from her personal Web site.

After reading the director's response to her e-mail, she quickly writes a Java (12) _____ to produce an interactive form to collect customer information. Using the (13) _____ protocol, Patricia posts her Web page to the corporate site. Of course, users will view the Web page using the (14) _____ protocol. Because the Web page contains potentially sensitive information, Patricia makes sure to use the (15) _____ protocol to provide added security for the data.

becoming computer literate

While attending college, you are working at Shoe Station, a small retailer of children's and women's footwear. The owner has charged your supervisor with establishing a Web presence for the company by developing a company Web site and establishing online communications with international suppliers. Your supervisor has asked you to help draft a memo to the CEO that sets forth the technologies the company should deploy to create an Internet presence.

Instructions: Draft a memo for your boss that details the benefits of connecting the company to the Internet. Make sure to suggest which types of Internet connections will be appropriate and which type of ISP will be needed. Use as many of the keywords from the chapter as you can, and ensure that the report will be understandable by managers who may be unfamiliar with computers or the Internet.

Instructions: Answer the multiple-choice and true–false questions below for more practice with key terms and concepts from this chapter.

Multiple Choice

1. Which is a common protocol used on the Internet?
- a. DNS
- b. IP
- c. XHTML
- d. PGP

2. Data is sent over the Internet using
- a. circuit switching.
- b. protocol switching.
- c. DNS switching.
- d. packet switching.

3. A numeric IP address is usually represented by an alphanumeric
- a. URL.
- b. SMTP.
- c. routing address.
- d. DNS address.

4. IP addresses that are assigned by an ISP and do not change over long periods of time are
- a. called *static*.
- b. more secure.
- c. called *dynamic*.
- d. volatile.

5. Which is the primary Internet protocol used for viewing Web pages?
- a. JavaScript
- b. Telnet
- c. HTTP
- d. TCP/IP

6. What makes interactivity on the Web possible?
- a. HTML
- b. CGI
- c. FTP
- d. XML

7. Individuals connect to the Internet using
- a. points of presence.
- b. network access points
- c. Internet exchange points.
- d. Web servers.

8. Encryption of Internet e-mail
- a. requires the use of specially designed client software.
- b. is built into the SMTP protocol.
- c. is built into most Web-based e-mail.
- d. is prohibited by the Department of Homeland Security.

9. For what is PGP used?
- a. Creating a secure connection between client and server
- b. Loading Web pages into a browser
- c. Encrypting e-mail messages
- d. Uploading files to the Internet

10. Which is a key component of cloud computing?
- a. Increase in IT employee headcount
- b. Decreased computing start-up costs
- c. Delivery of offline computing services
- d. Difficulty in increasing computing capacity

True–False

_____ 1. The costs associated with running the Internet are paid primarily through ISPs collecting fees from customers and from funding by U.S. government agencies.

_____ 2. VoIP uses packet switching technology.

_____ 3. A computer needs the XML address to locate a Web page accurately.

_____ 4. The main suite of protocols used on the Internet is TCP/FTP.

_____ 5. Instant messages are generally secure because most instant-messaging software provides for encryption of messages.

1. **Creating a Web Site**

   As president of your school's Phi Beta Lambda (PBL) club, you would like to build a mailing list for your quarterly newsletter. You also would like to ensure that the newsletter is available on the college's Web site. When you visit the college Web developer, she asks you the following questions:

   a. What data will you require all online subscribers to provide?
   b. What optional data would you like subscribers to provide?
   c. Will an e-mail address be provided to potential subscribers if they wish to make inquiries? If so, who will be reviewing and responding to these e-mails? How quickly will you be answering these e-mails?

2. **Creating a Wiki Site: Issue 1**

   Your sociology instructor has asked your group to design a wiki site about preventing identity theft. The site will include textual and graphic information about identity theft as well as an interactive quiz. The wiki will be open for anyone to edit (just like Wikipedia), and it is hoped that other students will contribute to the site. The following issues need to be addressed:

   a. Which wiki hosting service will you use to host the site? Why do you think this is appropriate?
   b. What name would you choose for the site? What URL would you choose for the site?
   c. How would you publicize the site so that other students at your school can find it?
   d. Who will be responsible for monitoring and editing the site? What types of content would you remove from the site?

3. **Creating a Wiki Site: Issue 2**

   You have been asked to assist your psychology professor in creating a wiki for her students. The wiki will be used by the students to develop an online study guide for the Introduction to Psychology class. Investigate the following two options and explain which option you will recommend and why:

   a. Most schools provide course management software (CMS) such as Blackboard or Moodle to facilitate communication between faculty and students. Most CMS systems have the ability to host wikis. What CMS software does your school use? Is the wiki feature available? How much storage space is provided for wiki pages? Can the wiki be rolled over to the next semester so future classes can work on it?
   b. Many sites host wikis free of charge, including PBworks (**pbworks.com),** Wikidot (**wikidot.com**), and Wikispaces (**wikispaces.com**). Investigate at least two free wiki services and compare their features. Include the following items and any other features that would be useful to your professor:
      • Limitations on number of users that can participate in a single wiki
      • Amount of disk storage space
      • Restrictions on file uploads, including file size and number of files
      • Membership restrictions (e.g., can the wiki be private or editable only by members?)
      • Notification features (e.g., can members be notified of updates by e-mail or RSS feed?)

4. **Securing Your E-mail Communications**

   You have a brilliant idea for a new business and will begin developing it with several friends next semester. To help ensure no one steals your idea before you launch the business, you decide that encrypting your e-mail communications related to the business would be a good idea. Investigate the free secure e-mail products Hushmail (**hushmail.com**), S-Mail secure email (**s-mail.com**), and Comodo SecureEmail (**comodo.com**). Prepare a report for your friends that compares the features of these e-mail products and justifies the decision to use the e-mail package you chose.

1. Web Site Privacy Issues

Your employer, a distributor of high-end stereo equipment, recently discovered that an employee was using his Facebook account to post disparaging remarks about the company president. The employee was fired and has now lodged a wrongful discharge lawsuit against your employer. You don't feel comfortable with the way this employee was treated, and you are wondering if your employer's firing of the employee was legal. Investigate the following and prepare a narrative for your instructor:

a. Is the state in which you go to school an "employment-at-will" state? If so, generally an employee can be fired for almost any reason at any time as long as the firing does not violate another employment law (such as the Civil Rights Act). Should an employer have the right to fire a person for expressing an opinion about his or her boss or company on a social networking site?

b. Have employers been successful in terminating employees for making disparaging comments on social networking sites, wikis, and blogs? Research the case of Ellen Simonetti, whose firing over her blog posts is one of the most famous cases in this area. In your opinion, was Ms. Simonetti treated fairly? What kind of policy should an employer have to warn employees about the potential consequences of their actions on social networking sites?

c. If you were running a small business and you found out that one of your employees was disparaging you or the business on a public Web site, what would you do about it?

2. Creating an Online Presence for a Business

You work at a local coffee shop that offers live music on the weekends. Your boss has asked you to help the coffee shop enhance its Web presence to better connect with customers. The shop currently has a Web site but does not have pages on any social networking sites. Consider the following:

a. On which social networking sites would you create a page for the coffee shop? Why?

b. What types of information would you post on the social network pages for the coffee shop? What strategies would you use to make customers aware of the coffee shop's social networking sites?

c. What information would you solicit from customers who joined the coffee shop's social networking sites? How could you use the customers to help develop new products or services for the business?

3. "Googling"

At your company, someone was just fired because sensitive information related to a company product was associated with the person's name on the Internet. Discretion being the better part of valor, you decide to do a search for your name on the Web using a search engine such as Google (**google.com**) just to see what is out there. Prepare a report on what you found. Your report should answer the following questions:

a. Did you find any accurate information about yourself (such as your home page URL or résumé)? Did you find any erroneous information that you need to correct?

b. Did you find Web sites or information about other people with the same name as you? Could any of that information be damaging to your reputation if someone thought the other person was you? If so, provide examples.

c. Is there information that you found about yourself or others that you think should never be available on the Internet? Provide examples and an explanation of why you feel certain information should not be available.

d. Is there any information on social networking sites, such as MySpace (**myspace.com**) or Facebook (**facebook.com**), that could be damaging to you if an employer or school administrator were to see it?

Instructions: Albert Einstein used *Gedankenexperiments*, or critical thinking questions, to develop his theory of relativity. Some ideas are best understood by experimenting with them in our own minds. The following critical thinking questions are designed to demand your full attention but require only a comfortable chair—no technology.

1. Domain Names

Domain names often spark fierce controversy between competing companies. Legal wrangling over the rights to attractive names such as Buynow.com and Lowprices.com can generate large fees for attorneys. Meanwhile, some famous individuals such as Julia Roberts have had to fight for the right to own domains based on their own names.

a. Should everyone be entitled to a Web site in a certain domain (say, .com) that contains their own name? How would you handle disputes by people who have the exact same name (say, two people named John Smith)?

b. Cybersquatting is registering a domain name (say, Coke.net) just for the purpose of selling it to the organization that may benefit from it the most (in this case, the Coca-Cola Company). Is cybersquatting ethical? Why or why not? Is cybersquatting legal in the United States?

c. Typosquatting is related to cybersquatting. People often register domain names that they think are common misspellings of well known Web sites (such as gooogle.com or googgle.com). They then place Web pages at these addresses with clickable advertisements on them so they can potentially earn revenue when people mistype URLs into their browsers. Is typosquatting legal in the United States? Is typosquatting ethical? Why or why not?

2. Illegal File Sharing Among Students

The College Opportunity and Affordability Act, passed by Congress in 2008, almost included a provision requiring colleges to monitor and punish students who were illegally swapping or downloading copyrighted material such as music or movies.

a. As a condition to receiving federal funding, should colleges be required to prevent students from illegally downloading or sharing material? Why or why not?

b. What measures has your school taken to prevent the illegal downloading of media? Are these measures effective? What other actions would you recommend your school take?

3. Encryption of E-mail

a. Do you currently encrypt your personal e-mail? Why or why not? If you are sending business-related e-mail, do you think you should use encrypted e-mail? Explain your answers.

b. Do you think your school should provide encrypted e-mail for student use? If a problem arises, such as a student accusing another student of sexual harassment, do you think the software used for encryption should have code that enables school administrators able to break the encryption? Explain your answers.

c. Should all U.S. government agencies be required to use encrypted e-mail? What agencies should be required to use encrypted e-mail? Are there agencies that would never need to use encrypted e-mail? Explain your answers.

thirteen teen team time

Creating a Business Web Presence

Problem

In today's fast-paced business environment, establishing a Web presence for a new business is critical. Having a Web site that is designed around the needs of customers is essential if a business is to compete in the 21st century. In this Team Time, you'll research Web hosting options and providers for a start-up company.

Task

Your group has just received a request from a friend who is starting a new apparel company called Trendz. It will sell clothing designed by young, urban artists and will target active young adults who are skateboarders and snowboarders. Your friend wants to sell the clothing over the Internet and needs your group's advice as to where to deploy a Web site and what features to offer.

Process

Break the class into small teams of three or four students. Each team should prepare a report as follows:

1. Determine an appropriate domain name for the Trendz Web site. Make sure that the Web address you propose is available by using a Whois service such as **whois.net.**

2. Select a company that can cost effectively register the domain name you have chosen and host the Web site. Investigate companies such as Network Solutions, 1and1.com, Go Daddy, Tucows, and Yahoo!. You might also want to consider free hosting solutions from Google or Microsoft Office Live.

3. Investigate options such as PayPal, Google Checkout, Authorize.net, or Cyber Source and determine a provider for collecting payments from customers. Make sure to consider fixed monthly fees charged as well as per transaction fees.

4. Determine what shopping cart software will be necessary to manage customer orders. Volusion, Fortune 3, CS-Cart, and Early Impact are examples of companies that offer possible solutions.

5. Develop a PowerPoint presentation to summarize your findings and present your proposed solution to the class.

Conclusion

E-commerce Web sites are relatively easy to deploy using the vast array of tools available on the Internet today. Substantial growth of new small businesses is expected in the United States over the next several decades. Therefore, you may soon be in a position where you will need to set up an e-commerce solution for friends, family, or an employer.

In this exercise, you will research and then role-play a complicated ethical situation. The role you play may or may not match your own personal beliefs, but your research and use of logic will enable you to represent whichever view is assigned. An arbitrator will watch and comment on both sides of the arguments, and together the team will agree on an ethical solution.

Topic: Privacy at School

Many Americans consider privacy to be a fundamental and unalienable right even though privacy is not specifically spelled out as a right in the U.S. Constitution or the Bill of Rights. Parents seem especially concerned about protecting their children's privacy rights. With the widespread use of technology, infringing on personal privacy rights has become easier, even if it is often done innocently or inadvertently.

School administrators are quickly learning that they need to craft policies that set appropriate boundaries and guidelines for monitoring students. Should school districts be allowed to monitor students? Should school districts be required to inform students and parents of any monitoring takes place?

Research Areas to Consider

• Lower Merion school district in Pennsylvania uses webcams to monitors students in their homes.

• School district in California uses RFID chips to take attendance.

• The Family Educational Rights and Privacy Act (FERPA)

Process

Divide the class into teams.

1. Research the areas cited above and devise a scenario in which a school district has been monitoring students without their knowledge and has potentially violated their privacy.

2. Team members should write a summary that provides background information for their character—for example: student or parent, school official, and arbitrator—and details their character's behaviors to set the stage for the role-playing event. Then, team members should create an outline to use during the role-playing event.

3. Team members should arrange a mutually convenient time to meet for the exchange, either using the chat room feature of MyITLab, the discussion board feature of Blackboard, or meeting in person.

4. Team members should present their case to the class, or submit a PowerPoint presentation for review by the rest of the class, along with the summary and resolution they developed.

Conclusion

As technology becomes ever more prevalent and integrated into our lives, more and more ethical dilemmas will present themselves. Being able to understand and evaluate both sides of the argument, while responding in a personally or socially ethical manner, will be an important skill.

3D sound card An expansion card that enables a computer to produce sounds that are omnidirectional or three dimensional.

802.11 standard A wireless standard established in 1997 by the Institute of Electrical and Electronics Engineers; also known as WiFi (short for Wireless Fidelity), it enables wireless network devices to work seamlessly with other networks and devices.

A

access card reader A device that reads information from a magnetic strip on the back of a credit card–like access card (such as a student ID card); card readers are easily programmed by adding authorized ID card numbers, Social Security numbers, and so on.

access method A program or hardware mechanism that controls which computer is allowed to use the transmission media in a network at a certain time.

access time The time it takes a storage device to locate its stored data.

accounting software An application program that helps business owners manage their finances more efficiently by providing tools for tracking accounting transactions such as sales, accounts receivable, inventory purchases, and accounts payable.

ActionScript A programming language included in Flash; similar to JavaScript in its keywords, operators, and classes.

Active Server Pages (ASP) A scripting environment in which users combine HyperText Markup Language (HTML), scripts, and reusable Microsoft ActiveX server components to create dynamically generated Web pages.

active topology A network topology in which each node on the network is responsible for retransmitting the token, or the data, to other nodes.

Adobe Flash A software product for developing Web-based multimedia.

adware A program that downloads on your computer when you install a freeware program, game, or utility. Generally, adware enables sponsored advertisements to appear in a section of your browser window or as a pop-up ad box.

affective computing A type of computing that relates to emotion or deliberately tries to influence emotion.

aggregator A software program that goes out and grabs the latest update of Web material (usually podcasts) according to your specifications.

aircard A device that enables users to have wireless Internet access with mobile devices such as PDAs and notebooks.

AJAX A collection of technologies that allows the creation of Web applications that can update information on a page without requiring the user to do a page refresh or leave the page.

algorithm A set of specific, sequential steps that describe in natural language exactly what a computer program must do to complete its task.

all-in-one computer A desktop system unit that houses the computer's processor, memory, and monitor in a single unit.

all-in-one printer See *multifunction printer*.

alphabetic check Confirms that only textual characters are entered in a database field.

analog Waves that illustrate the loudness of a sound or the brightness of the colors in an image at a given moment in time.

analog-to-digital converter chip Converts analog signals into digital signals.

antivirus software Software that is specifically designed to detect viruses and protect a computer and files from harm.

applet A small program designed to be run from within another application. Java applets are often run on your computer by your browser through the Java Virtual Machine (an application built into current browsers).

application programming interface (API) A block of code in the operating system that software applications need to interact with.

application server A server that acts as a repository for application software.

application software The set of programs on a computer that helps a user carry out tasks such as word processing, sending e-mail, balancing a budget, creating

presentations, editing photos, taking an online course, and playing games.

artificial intelligence (AI) The science that attempts to produce computers that display the same type of reasoning and intelligence that humans do.

aspect ratio The width-to-height proportion of a monitor.

assembly language A language that enables programmers to write their programs using a set of short, English-like commands that speak directly to the central processing unit (CPU) and give the programmer very direct control of hardware resources.

audio editing software Programs that perform basic editing tasks on audio files such as cutting dead air space from the beginning or end of a song or cutting a portion from the middle.

authentication The process of identifying a computer user, based on a login or username and password. The computer system determines whether the computer user is authorized and what level of access is to be granted on the network.

authentication server A server that keeps track of who is logging on to the network and which services on the network are available to each user.

B

backdoor program A program that enables a hacker to take complete control of a computer without the legitimate user's knowledge or permission.

backup A backup is a copy of computer files that you can use to replace the originals if they are lost or damaged.

Backup and Restore utility A Windows utility (found in the Control Panel) that allows the user to create a duplicate copy of all the data on a hard drive (or just the folders and files the user specifies) and copy it to another storage device, such as a DVD or external hard drive.

backward compatibility The accommodation of current devices being able to use previously issued software standards in addition to the current standards.

bandwidth (data transfer rate) The maximum speed at which data can be transmitted between two nodes on a network; usually measured in megabits per second (Mbps). See also *data transfer rate*.

base class The original object class from which other classes derive.

base transceiver station A large communications tower with antennas, amplifiers, and receivers/transmitters.

basic input/output system (BIOS) A program that manages the data between a computer's operating system and all the input and output devices attached to the computer; also responsible for loading the operating system (OS) from its permanent location on the hard drive to random access memory (RAM).

bastion host A heavily secured server located on a special perimeter network between a company's secure internal network and its firewall.

batch processing The process of accumulating transaction data until a certain point is reached, then processing those transactions all at once.

BD-ROM disc BD-ROM is defined as BluRay Disc Read Only Memory. BD-ROM is an optical disc storage media format for high-definition video and data storage.

benchmark A measurement used in comparing software and hardware performance. Benchmarks are created using software applications that are specifically designed to push the limits of computer performance.

binary decision A decision point that can be answered in one of only two ways: *yes* (true) or *no* (false).

binary digit (bit) A digit that corresponds to the on and off states of a computer's switches. A bit contains a value of either 0 or 1.

binary language The language computers use to process data into information, consisting of only the values 0 and 1.

binary large object (BLOB) In databases, a type of object that holds extremely large chunks of data in binary form; this data is usually video clips, pictures, or audio clips.

biometric authentication device A device that uses some unique characteristic of human biology to identify authorized users.

bit depth The number of bits a video card uses to store data about each pixel on the monitor.

black-hat hacker A hacker who uses his knowledge to destroy information or for illegal gain.

bloatware The pre-installed software (often trial versions) on a new computer.

BLOB See *binary large object*.

blog See *Web log*.

Blu-ray disc A method of optical storage for digital data, developed for storing high-definition media. It has the largest storage capacity of all optical storage options.

Bluetooth technology A type of wireless technology that uses radio waves to transmit data over short distances (approximately 30 feet for Bluetooth 1 and 60 feet for Bluetooth 2). Often used to connect peripherals such as printers and keyboards to computers or headsets to cell phones.

bomb software Software that destroys data on a computing device if someone continually tries to access information by guessing the password.

bookmark A feature in some browsers that places a marker of a Web site's Uniform Resource Locator (URL) in an easily retrievable list. (Bookmarks are called Favorites in Microsoft Internet Explorer.)

Boolean operator A word used to refine logical searches. For Internet searches, the words AND, NOT, and OR describe the relationships between keywords in the search.

boot process The process for loading the operating system (OS) into random access memory (RAM) when the computer is turned on.

boot-sector virus A virus that replicates itself into the master boot record of a flash drive or hard drive.

botnet A large group of software applications (called *robots* or *bots*) that runs without user intervention on a large number of computers.

breadcrumb list A list that shows the hierarchy of previously viewed Web pages within the Web site that you are currently visiting. Shown at the top of some Web pages, it aids Web site navigation.

bridge A network device that is used to send data between two different local area networks (LANs) or two segments of the same LAN.

brightness A measure of the greatest amount of light showing when a monitor is displaying pure white; measured as candelas per square meter (cd/m²) or *nits*.

broadband A high-speed Internet connection such as cable, satellite, or digital subscriber line (DSL).

browser See *Web browser*.

browsing (1) The process of viewing database records. (2) The process of "surfing" the Web.

brute force attack An attack delivered by specialized hacking software that tries many combinations of letters, numbers, and pieces of a user ID in an attempt to discover a user password.

bus (linear bus) topology A system of networking connections in which all devices are connected to a central cable called the *bus* (or backbone).

business-to-business (B2B) E-commerce transactions between businesses.

business-to-consumer (B2C) E-commerce transactions between businesses and consumers.

byte Eight binary digits (bits).

C

C The predecessor language of C++; developed originally for system programmers by Brian Kernighan and Dennis Ritchie of AT&T Bell Laboratories in 1978. It provides higher-level programming language features (such as if statements and for loops) but still allows programmers to manipulate the system memory and central processing unit (CPU) registers directly.

C# A programming language released by Microsoft to compete with Java. Pronounced *see sharp*.

C++ The successor language to C. Developed by Bjarne Stroustrup, C++ uses all of the same symbols and keywords as C but extends the language with additional keywords, better security, and more support for the reuse of existing code through object-oriented design.

cable A type of broadband Internet connection that uses a television's cable service provider to connect to the Internet.

cache memory Small blocks of memory, located directly on and next to the central processing unit (CPU) chip, that act as holding places for recently or frequently used instructions or data that the CPU accesses the most. When these instructions or data are stored in cache memory, the CPU can more quickly retrieve them than if it had to access the instructions or data from random access memory (RAM).

cascading style sheets (CSS) A list of statements (also known as rules) that define in one single location how HTML/XHTML elements are to be displayed.

Cat 6 cable A UTP cable type that provides more than 1 GB of throughput.

cellular phone (cell phone) A telephone that operates over a wireless network. Cell phones can also offer Internet access, text messaging, personal information management (PIM) features, and more.

central processing unit (CPU or processor) The part of the system unit of a computer that is responsible for data processing (the "brains" of the computer); it is the largest and most important chip in the computer. The CPU controls all the functions performed by the computer's other components and processes all the commands issued to it by software instructions.

centralized A type of network design in which users are not responsible for creating their own data backups or providing security for their computers; instead, those tasks are handled by a centralized server, software, and a system administrator.

CGI script A computer program that conforms to the Common Gateway Interface (CGI) specification, which provides a method for sending data between end users (browser users) and Web servers.

cgi-bin A directory where Common Gateway Interface (CGI) scripts are normally placed.

chat room An area on the Web where people come together to communicate online. The conversations are in real time and are visible to everyone in the chat room.

circuit switching A method of communication in which a dedicated connection is formed between two points (such as two people on telephones) and the connection remains active for the duration of the transmission.

class A collection of descriptive variables and active functions that together define a set of common properties. Actual examples of the class are known as *objects*.

classless interdomain routing (CIDR) Pronounced "cider," this is an addressing scheme that allows a single IP address to represent several unique IP addresses by adding a network prefix (a slash and a number) to the end of the last octet; also known as *supernetting*.

clickstream data Information captured about each click that users make as they navigate a Web site.

client A computer that requests information from a server in a client/server network (such as your computer when you are connected to the Internet).

client/server model A way of describing typical network functions. Client computers (such as your desktop PC) request services, and servers provide ("serve up") those services to the clients.

client/server network A network, consisting of client and server computers, in which the clients make requests of the server and the server returns the response.

client/server network (server-based network) A type of network that uses servers to deliver services to computers that are requesting them (clients).

client-side program A computer program that runs on the client computer and requires no interaction with a Web server.

clock speed The steady and constant pace at which a computer goes through machine cycles, measured in hertz (Hz).

cloud computing The process of using the Internet to deliver business, entertainment, or other services that were previously delivered by conventional means.

coaxial cable A single copper wire surrounded by layers of plastic insulation and sheathing; used mainly in cable television and cable Internet service.

codec A rule, implemented in either software or hardware, which squeezes a given amount of audio and video information into less space.

code editing The step in which programmers actually type code into the computer.

coding The process of translating an algorithm into a programming language.

cold boot The process of starting a computer from a powered-down or off state.

command-driven interface Interface between user and computer in which the user enters commands to communicate with the computer system.

comment (remark) A plain English notation inserted into program code for documentation. The comment is not ever seen by the compiler.

commerce server A computer that hosts software that enables consumers to purchase goods and services over the Web. These servers generally use special security protocols to protect sensitive information (such as credit card numbers) from being intercepted.

Common Gateway Interface (CGI) Provides a methodology by which a browser can request that a program file be executed (or run) instead of just being delivered to the browser.

communications server A server that handles all communications between the network and other networks, including managing Internet connectivity.

compact disc (CD) A method of optical storage for digital data; originally developed for storing digital audio.

compilation The process by which code is converted into machine language, or the language the central processing unit (CPU) can understand.

compiler The program that understands both the syntax of the programming language and the exact structure of the central processing unit (CPU) and its machine language. It can "read" the source code and translate the source code directly into machine language.

completeness check A process that ensures that all database fields defined as "required" have data entered into them.

computational field (computed field) A numeric field in a database that is filled as the result of a computation.

computer A data-processing device that gathers, processes, outputs, and stores data and information.

computer forensics The application of computer systems and techniques to gather potential legal evidence; a law enforcement specialty used to fight high-tech crime.

computer literate Being familiar enough with computers that you understand their capabilities and limitations and know how to use them.

computer protocol A set of rules for accomplishing electronic information exchange. If the Internet is the information superhighway, then protocols are the driving rules.

computer-aided design (CAD) A 3D modeling program used to create automated designs, technical drawings, and model visualizations.

connectionless protocol A protocol that a host computer can use to send data over the network without establishing a direct connection with any specific recipient computer.

connection-oriented protocol A protocol that requires two computers to exchange control packets, which set up the parameters of the data exchange session, before sending packets that contain data.

connectivity port A port that enables the computer (or other device) to be connected to other devices or systems such as networks, modems, and the Internet.

consistency check The process of comparing the value of data in a database field against established parameters to determine whether the value is reasonable.

consumer-to-consumer (C2C) E-commerce transactions between consumers through online sites such as eBay.com.

contrast ratio A measure of the difference in light intensity between the brightest white and the darkest black colors that a monitor can produce. If the contrast ratio is too low, colors tend to fade when the brightness is adjusted to a high or low setting.

control structure The general term used for keywords in a programming language that allow the programmer to control, or redirect, the flow of the program based on a decision.

cookie A small text file that some Web sites automatically store on a client computer's hard drive when a user visits the site.

copyleft A simplified licensing scheme that enables copyright holders to grant certain rights to a work while retaining other rights.

core A complete processing section from a CPU, embedded into one physical chip.

course management software A program that provides traditional classroom tools, such as calendars and grade books, over the Internet, as well as areas for students to exchange ideas and information in chat rooms, discussion forums, and e-mail.

CPU usage The percentage of time a central processing unit (CPU) is working.

crowdsourcing The process of taking a task that an employee or a contractor usually performs (such as product design) and instead outsourcing that task to a large group of people, usually via the Internet.

CSMA/CD A method of data collision detection in which a node connected to the network listens (that is, has carrier sense) to determine that no other nodes are currently transmitting data signals; short for Carrier Sense Multiple Access with Collision Detection.

cursor control key A set of controls on standard keyboards that moves the *cursor* (the flashing symbol on the monitor that indicates where the next character will be inserted); also known as an *arrow key*.

custom installation The process of installing only those features of a software program that a user wants on the hard drive.

customer relationship management (CRM) software A business program used for storing sales and client contact information in one central database.

cybercrime Any criminal action perpetrated primarily through the use of a computer.

cybercriminal An individual who uses computers, networks, and the Internet to perpetrate crime.

cyberloafing Doing anything with a computer that is unrelated to a job (such as playing video games), while one is supposed to be working. Also called *cyberslacking*.

D

data Numbers, words, pictures, or sounds that represent facts, figures, or ideas.

data centralization Having all data in one central location (usually a database). Data centralization helps ensure data integrity by requiring data to be updated only in one place if the data changes.

data collision When two computers send data at the same time and the sets of data collide somewhere in the media.

data dictionary (database schema) A file that defines the name, data type, and length of each field in the database.

data file File that contains stored data.

data-flow diagram A design that traces all data in an information system from the point at which data enters the system to its final destination (storage or output).

data inconsistency Any difference in data in lists caused when data exists in multiple lists and not all lists are updated when a piece of data changes.

data integrity The process of ensuring that data contained in a database is accurate and reliable.

data mart Small slices of a data warehouse.

data plan A connectivity plan or text messaging plan in which data charges are separate from cell phone calling charges and are provided at rates different from those for voice calls.

data redundancy When the same data exists in more than one place in a database.

data staging A three-step process: extracting data from source databases, transforming (reformatting) the data, and storing the data in a data warehouse.

data transfer rate (bandwidth) The maximum speed at which data can be transmitted between two nodes on a network; usually measured in megabits per second (Mbps).

data type (field type) An attribute of a data field that determines what type of data can be stored in the database field or memory location.

data warehouse A large-scale electronic repository of data that contains and organizes in one place all the data related to an organization.

database A collection of related data that can be easily stored, sorted, organized, and queried.

database administrator (database designer) An individual trained in the design, construction, and maintenance of databases.

database designer See *database administrator.*

database management system (DBMS) A type of specially designed application software (such as Oracle or Microsoft Access) that interacts with the user, other applications, and the database to capture and analyze data.

database query An inquiry the user poses to a database to extract a meaningful subset of data.

database server A server that provides client computers with access to information stored in a database.

database software An electronic filing system best used for larger and more complicated groups of data that require more than one table and the ability to group, sort, and retrieve data and generate reports.

date field A field in a database that holds date data such as birthdays, due dates, and so on.

debugger A tool that helps programmers step through a program as it runs to locate errors.

debugging The process of repeatedly running a program to find errors and to make sure the program behaves in the way it should.

decentralized A type of network in which users are responsible for creating their own data backups and for providing security for their computers.

decision point A point at which a computer program must choose from a set of different actions based on the value of its current inputs.

decision support system (DSS) A system designed to help managers develop solutions for specific problems.

dedicated server A server used to fulfill one specific function (such as handling e-mail).

default value The value a database will use for a field unless the user enters another value.

denial of service (DoS) attack An attack that occurs when legitimate users are denied access to a computer system because a hacker is repeatedly making requests of that computer system that tie up its resources and deny legitimate users access.

derivative work Intellectual property that is based on an original work but is modified in some way.

derived class A class created based on a previously existing class (i.e., a base class). Derived classes inherit all of the member variables and methods of the base class from which they are derived.

desktop As its name implies, the computer's desktop puts at your fingertips all of the elements necessary for a productive work session and that are typically found on or near the top of a traditional desk, such as files and folders.

desktop computer A computer that is intended for use at a single location. A desktop computer consists of a case that houses the main components of the computer, plus peripheral devices.

desktop publishing (DTP) software Programs for incorporating and arranging graphics and text to produce creative documents.

detail report A report generated with data from a database that shows the individual transactions that occurred during a certain time period.

device driver Software that facilitates the communication between a device and the operating system.

Device Manager A feature in the Windows operating system that lets individuals view and change the properties of all hardware devices attached to the computer.

dial-up connection A connection to the Internet using a standard telephone line.

dial-up modem A device that converts (modulates) the digital signals the computer understands to analog signals that can travel over phone lines. The computer on the other end also must have a modem to translate (demodulate) the received analog signal back to a digital signal that the receiving computer can understand.

digital divide The discrepancy between those who have access to the opportunities and knowledge computers and the Internet offer and those who do not.

digital home A home that has a computer(s) and other digital devices that are all connected to a home network.

digital signal processor A specialized chip that processes digital information and transmits signals very quickly.

digital subscriber line (DSL) A type of connection that uses telephone lines to connect to the Internet and that allows both phone and data transmissions to share the same line.

digital video disc (DVD) A method of optical storage for digital data that has greater storage capacity than compact discs.

digital video editing software A program for editing digital video.

digital video interface (DVI) Video interface technology that newer LCD monitors, as well as other multimedia devices such as televisions, DVD players, and projectors, use to connect to a PC.

directory A hierarchical structure that include files, folders, and drives used to create a more organized and efficient computer.

Disk Cleanup A Windows utility that removes unnecessary files from the hard drive.

disk defragmenter A utility that regroups related pieces of files on the hard drive, enabling faster retrieval of the data.

distributed denial of service (DDoS) attack An automated attack that is launched from more than one zombie computer at the same time.

Document Object Model (DOM) A means to organize objects and page elements in a Web page. DOM defines every item on a Web page, such as graphics, tables, and headers, as an object.

documentation A description of the development and technical details of a computer program, including how the code works and how the user interacts with the program.

domain name A part of a Uniform Resource Locator (URL). Domain names consist of two parts: the site's host and a suffix that indicates the type of organization. (Example: popsci.com)

Domain Name System (DNS) server A server that contains location information for domains on the Internet and functions like a phone book for the Internet.

dotted decimal number (dotted quad) One of the numbers in an Internet Protocol (IP) address.

drawing software (illustration software) Programs for creating or editing two-dimensional line-based drawings.

drive bay A special shelf inside a computer that is designed to hold storage devices.

drive-by download The use of malicious software to attack your computer by downloading harmful programs onto your computer, without your knowledge, while you are surfing a Web site.

DVD-RAM One of three competing technologies for rewritable DVDs.

DVD-ROM DVD format in which data can only be read and not written.

DVD-R/RW One of two recognized DVD formats that enable you to read, record (R), and rewrite (RW) data on the disc.

DVD+R/RW One of two recognized DVD formats that enables you to both read, record (R), and rewrite (RW) data on the disc.

dynamic addressing The process of assigning Internet Protocol (IP) addresses when users log on using their Internet service provider (ISP). The computer is assigned an address from an available pool of IP addresses.

dynamic decision making A mechanism that allows a Web page to decide how to display itself, based on the choices the reader makes as he or she looks at the page.

Dynamic Host Configuration Protocol (DHCP) The protocol that handles dynamic addressing. Part of the Transmission Control Protocol/Internet Protocol (TCP/IP) protocol suite, DHCP takes a pool of IP addresses and shares them with hosts on the network on an as-needed basis.

Dynamic HyperText Markup Language (DHTML or dynamic HTML) A combination of Web development technologies including HTML, cascading style sheets, and a scripting language that are used to add interactivity to a Web site after the Web site has been loaded onto the client computer.

dynamic RAM (DRAM) The most basic type of random access memory (RAM); used in older systems or in systems for which cost is an important factor. DRAM offers access times on the order of 60 nanoseconds.

E

e-commerce (electric commerce) The process of conducting business online for purposes ranging from fund-raising to advertising to selling products.

e-mail (electronic mail) Internet-based communication in which senders and recipients correspond.

e-mail client A software program that runs on a computer and is used to send and receive e-mail through the ISP's server.

e-mail server A server that processes and delivers incoming and outgoing e-mail.

e-mail virus A virus transmitted by e-mail that often uses the address book in the victim's e-mail system to distribute itself.

editor A tool that helps programmers as they enter code, highlighting keywords and alerting the programmers to typos.

element The tags and the text between the tags in HyperText Markup Language (HTML).

embedded computer A specially designed computer chip that resides inside another device, such as a car. These self-contained computer devices have their own programming and typically neither receive input from users nor interact with other systems.

encryption The process of encoding data (ciphering) so that only the person with a corresponding decryption key (the intended recipient) can decode (or decipher) and read the message.

encryption virus A malicious program that searches for common data files and compresses them into a file using a complex encryption key, thereby rendering the files unusable.

entertainment software Programs designed to provide users with entertainment. Computer games make up the vast majority of entertainment software.

Entertainment Software Rating Board (ESRB) A self-regulatory body established in 1994 by the Entertainment Software Association that rates computer and video games according to the age appropriateness of content.

ergonomics How a user sets up his or her computer and other equipment to minimize risk of injury or discomfort.

error handling In programming, the instructions that a program runs if the input data is incorrect or another error is encountered.

Error-Checking A Windows utility that checks for lost files and fragments as well as physical errors on a hard drive.

Ethernet network A network that uses the Ethernet protocol as the means (or standard) by which the nodes on the network communicate.

Ethernet port A port that is slightly larger than a standard phone jack and transfers data at speeds of up to 10,000 Mbps; used to connect a computer to a DSL or cable modem or a network.

event The result of an action, such as a keystroke, mouse click, or signal to the printer, in the respective device (keyboard, mouse, or printer) to which the operating system responds.

exception report A report that shows conditions that are unusual or that need attention by users of a system.

executable program The binary sequence (code) that instructs the central processing unit (CPU) to perform certain calculations.

expansion card (adapter card) A circuit board with specific functions that augment the computer's basic functions and provide connections to other devices; examples include the sound card and the video card.

expert system A system designed to replicate the decision-making processes of human experts to solve specific problems.

export The process of putting data into an electronic file in a format that another application can understand.

Extensible HyperText Markup Language (XHTML) A standard established by the World Wide Web Consortium (W3C) that combines elements from both Extensible Markup Language (XML) and

HyperText Markup Language (HTML). XHTML has much more stringent rules than HTML does regarding tagging.

Extensible Markup Language (XML) A language that enables designers to define their own tags, making it much easier to transfer data between Web sites and Web servers.

extension (file type) In a file name, the three letters that follow the user-supplied file name after the dot (.); the extension identifies what kind of family of files the file belongs to, or which application should be used to read the file.

external data source Any source not owned by the company that owns a decision support system, such as customer demographic data purchased from third parties.

external hard drive An internal hard drive that is enclosed in a protective case to make it portable; the drive is connected to the computer with a data transfer cable and is often used to back up data.

external SATA See *eSata*.

extranet The portion of a company's intranet that is used to share business information with business partners such as vendors, suppliers, and customers.

F

Favorites A feature in Microsoft Internet Explorer that places a marker of a Web site's Uniform Resource Locator (URL) in an easily retrievable list in the browser's toolbar. (Called Bookmarks in some browsers.)

fiber-optic cable A cable that transmits data at close to the speed of light along glass or plastic fibers.

Fiber-Optic Service (FiOS) Internet access that is enabled by transmitting data at the speed of light through glass or plastic fibers.

field A field where a category of information in a database is stored. Fields are displayed in columns.

field constraint Any property that must be satisfied for an entry to be accepted into the database field.

field name An identifying name assigned to each field in a database.

field size The maximum number of characters (or numbers) that a field in a database can contain.

fifth-generation language (5GL) A computer language that uses natural language processing or expert systems to make the programming experience better matched to human thinking processes.

file A collection of related pieces of information stored together for easy reference; in database terminology, a file or *table* is a group of related records.

file allocation table (FAT) An index of all sector numbers that the hard drive stores in a table to keep track of which sectors hold which files.

file compression utility A program that takes out redundancies in a file to reduce the file size.

file management The process by which humans or computer software provide organizational structure to a computer's contents.

file name The first part of the label applied to a file; it is generally the name a user assigns to the file when saving it.

file path The exact location of a file, starting with the drive in which the file is located, and including all folders, subfolders (if any), the file name, and the extension. (Example: C:\Users\username\Documents\Illustrations\EBronte.jpg)

file server A computer deployed to provide remote storage space or to act as a repository for files that users can access.

File Transfer Protocol (FTP) A protocol used to upload and download files from one computer to another over the Internet.

financial planning software Programs for managing finances, such as Intuit's Quicken and Microsoft Money, which include electronic checkbook registers and automatic bill payment tools.

firewall A software program or hardware device designed to prevent unauthorized access to computers or networks.

FireWire 400 (IEEE 1394) An interface port that transfers data at 400 Mbps.

FireWire 800 One of the fastest ports available, moving data at 800 Mbps.

firmware System software that controls hardware devices.

first-generation language (1GL) The actual machine language of a central processing unit (CPU); the sequence of bits—1s and 0s—that the CPU understands.

flash drive A drive that plugs into a universal serial bus (USB) port on a computer and stores data digitally. Also called *USB drive*, *jump drive*, or *thumb drive*.

flash memory Portable, nonvolatile memory.

flash memory card A form of portable storage; this removable memory card is often used in digital cameras, portable media players, and personal digital assistants (PDAs).

flat-panel monitor A type of monitor that is lighter and more energy-efficient than a CRT monitor; often used with portable computers such as notebooks.

flowchart A visual representation of the patterns an algorithm comprises.

folder A collection of files stored on a computer.

For Keyword in Visual Basic used with the Next keyword to implement a loop.

foreign key The primary key of another database table that is included for purposes of establishing relationships with another table.

fourth-generation language (4GL) A sophisticated level of programming language such as a report generator or database query language.

frame A container designed to hold multiple data packets.

freeware Any copyrighted software that can be used for free.

front side bus (FSB) See *local bus*.

full installation The process of installing all the files and programs from the distribution CD to the computer's hard drive.

fuzzy logic A type of logic that allows the interjection of experiential learning into an equation by considering probabilities.

G

gadget A mini-application that runs on the desktop, offering easy access to a frequently used tool such as weather or a calendar item.

gateway See *wireless router*.

gigabit Ethernet The most commonly used wired Ethernet standard deployed in devices designed for home networks which provides bandwidth of up to 1 Gbps.

gigabyte (GB) About a billion bytes.

gigahertz (GHz) One billion hertz.

Global Positioning System (GPS) A system of 21 satellites (plus 3 working spares), built and operated by the U.S. military, that constantly orbit the earth. They provide information to GPS-capable devices to pinpoint locations on the earth.

graphical user interface (GUI) Unlike the command- and menu-driven interfaces used in earlier software, GUIs display graphics and use the point-and-click technology of the mouse and cursor, making them much more user-friendly.

graphics processing unit (GPU) A specialized logic chip that is dedicated to quickly displaying and calculating visual data such as shadows, textures, and luminosity.

H

hacker Anyone who unlawfully breaks into a computer system (whether an individual computer or a network).

handshaking The process of two computers exchanging control packets that set up the parameters of a data exchange.

hard drive A device that holds all permanently stored programs and data; can be located inside the system unit or attached to the system unit via a USB port.

hardware Any part of the computer you can physically touch.

head crash Impact of read/write head against magnetic platter of the hard drive; often results in data loss.

hexadecimal notation A number system that uses 16 digits to represent numbers; also called a *base 16 number system*.

hibernate A power-management mode that saves the current state of the current system to the computer's hard drive.

high-definition multimedia interface (HDMI) A compact audio–video interface standard that carries both high-definition video and uncompressed digital audio.

hoax An e-mail message or Web site that contains information that is untrue, and is published with the purpose of deceiving others.

home area network (HAN) A network located in a home that is used to connect all of its digital devices.

home network server A device designed to store media, share media across the network, and back up files on computers connected to a home network.

home page The main or opening page of a Web site.

host The portion of a domain name that identifies who maintains a given Web site. For example, *berkeley.edu* is the domain name for the University of California at Berkeley, which maintains that site.

HTML tag The bracketed information that surrounds elements of a Web page in order to convey information about them and define how their content is to be displayed.

HTML/XHTML embedded scripting language A client-side method of embedding programming language code directly within the HTML/XHTML code of a Web page.

hybrid topology A topology comprised of several topologies and combined into one network.

hyperlink A type of specially coded text that, when clicked, enables a user to jump from one location, or Web page, to another within a Web site or to another Web site altogether.

hyperlink field A field in a database that stores hyperlinks to Web pages.

hypertext Text that is linked to other documents or media (such as video clips or pictures).

HyperText Markup Language (HTML) A set of rules for marking up blocks of text so that a Web browser knows how to display them. It uses a series of tags that defines the display of text on a Web page.

HyperText Transfer Protocol (HTTP) The protocol that allows files to be transferred from a Web server so that you can see them on your computer by using a browser.

HyperText Transfer Protocol Secure (HTTPS) A combination of the HTTP protocol and a network security protocol (usually SSL or TLS) that ensure data is sent securely over the Web.

hyperthreading A technology that permits quicker processing of information by enabling a new set of instructions to start executing before the previous set has finished.

I

icon A picture on a computer display that represents an object such as a software application or a file or folder.

identity theft The process by which someone uses personal information about someone else (such as the victim's name, address, and Social Security number) to assume the victim's identity for the purpose of defrauding others.

if else In the programming language C++, keywords for a binary decision within an algorithm.

image backup A copy of an entire computer system, created for restoration purposes.

image editing software (photo editing software) Programs for editing photographs and other images.

impact printer A printer that has tiny hammer-like keys that strike the paper through an inked ribbon, thus making a mark on the paper. The most common impact printer is the dot-matrix printer.

incremental backup A type of backup that only backs up files that have changed since the last time those files were backed up.

information Data that has been organized or presented in a meaningful fashion.

information system A system that includes data, people, procedures, hardware, and software and that is used to gather and analyze information.

information technology (IT) The set of techniques used in processing and retrieving information.

inheritance The ability of a new class of objects to pick up all of the data and methods of an existing class automatically and then extend and customize those to fit its own specific needs.

initial value A beginning point in a loop.

inkjet printer A nonimpact printer that sprays tiny drops of ink onto paper.

inoculation A process used by antivirus software; compares old and current qualities of files to detect viral activity.

input device A hardware device used to enter, or input, data (text, images, and sounds) and instructions (user responses and commands) into a computer. Some input devices are keyboards and mice.

input form A form that provides a view of the data fields to be filled in a database, with appropriate labels to assist database users in populating the database.

instant messaging (IM) A program that enables users to communicate online in real time with others who are also online.

integrated development environment (IDE) A development tool that helps programmers write, compile, and test their programs.

integrated help Documentation for a software product that is built directly into the software.

integrated software application A single software program that incorporates the most commonly used tools of many productivity software programs.

internal hard drive A hard drive that is installed inside the system unit.

Internet A network of networks that is the largest network in the world, connecting millions of computers from more than one hundred countries.

Internet backbone The main pathway of high-speed communications lines over which all Internet traffic flows.

Internet cache A section of your hard drive that stores information that you may need again for surfing (such as IP addresses and frequently accessed Web pages).

Internet Corporation for Assigned Names and Numbers (ICANN) The organization responsible for allocating IP addresses to network administrators to ensure they are unique and have not been assigned to other users.

Internet exchange point A device that allows different Internet service providers to exchange information between networks.

Internet Explorer (IE) A popular graphical browser from Microsoft Corporation for displaying different Web sites, or locations, on the Web; it can display pictures (graphics) in addition to text, as well as other forms of multimedia such as sound and video.

Internet Protocol (IP) A protocol for sending data between computers on the Internet.

Internet Protocol address (IP address) The means by which all computers connected to the Internet identify each other. It consists of a unique set of four numbers separated by dots such as 123.45.178.91.

Internet Protocol version 4 (IPv4) The original IP addressing scheme.

Internet Protocol version 6 (IPv6) A proposed IP addressing scheme that makes IP addresses longer, thereby providing more available IP addresses. It uses eight groups of 16-bit numbers.

Internet Relay Chat (IRC) A means of synchronous group communication used in discussion forums.

Internet tablet A very light, portable computing device without a keyboard.

interpreter A software program that translates source code into an intermediate form line by line. Each line is then executed as it is translated.

interrupt A signal that tells the operating system that it is in need of immediate attention.

interrupt handler A special numerical code that prioritizes requests from various devices. These requests then are placed in the interrupt table in the computer's primary memory.

intranet A private corporate network that is used exclusively by company employees to facilitate information sharing, database access, group scheduling, videoconferencing, and other employee and customer collaborations.

IP address See *Internet Protocol address.*

 J

jam signal A special signal sent to all network nodes, alerting them that a data collision has occurred.

Java A platform-independent programming language that Sun Microsystems introduced in the early 1990s. It quickly became popular because its object-oriented model enables Java programmers to benefit from its set of existing classes.

Java applet A small Java-based program.

Java Server Pages (JSP) An extension of the Java servlet technology with dynamic scripting capability.

JavaScript A scripting language often used to add interactivity to Web pages. JavaScript is not as fully featured as Java, but its syntax, keywords, data types, and operators are a subset of Java's.

join query A database query that links (or joins) two database tables using a common field in both tables and extracts the relevant data from each.

 K

kernel (supervisor program) The essential component of the operating system that is responsible for managing the processor and all other components of the computer system. Because it stays in random access memory (RAM) the entire time the computer is powered on, the kernel is called *memory resident.*

kernel memory The memory that the computer's operating system uses.

key pair A public and a private key used for coding and decoding encrypted messages.

keyboard A hardware device used to enter typed data and commands into a computer.

keystroke logger A type of spyware program that monitors keystrokes with the intent of stealing passwords, login IDs, or credit card information.

keyword (1) A specific word a user wishes to query (or look for) in an Internet search. (2) A specific word that has a predefined

kilobyte (KB) A unit of computer storage equal to approximately one thousand bytes.

knowledge-based system A support system that provides additional intelligence that supplements the user's own intellect and makes a decision support system (DSS) more effective.

L

large-scale networking (LSN) A program created by the U.S. government, the objective of which is to fund the research and development of cutting-edge networking technologies. Major goals of the program are the development of enhanced wireless technologies and increased network throughput.

laser printer A nonimpact printer known for quick and quiet production and high-quality printouts.

Last Known Good Configuration A Windows feature that starts the computer by using the registry information that was saved during the last shutdown.

latency The process that occurs after the read/write head of the hard drive locates the correct track, and then waits for the correct sector to spin to the read/write head.

legacy technology Comprises computing devices, software, or peripherals that use techniques, parts, and methods from an earlier time that are no longer popular.

library In Windows 7, a folder that is used to display files from different locations as if they were all saved in a single folder, regardless of where they are actually stored in the file hierarchy.

Linux An open source operating system based on UNIX. Because of the stable nature of this operating system, it is often used on Web servers.

liquid crystal display (LCD) The technology used in flat-panel computer monitors.

live bookmark A bookmark that delivers updates to you as soon as they become available, using Really Simple Syndication (RSS).

local area network (LAN) A network in which the nodes are located within a small geographic area.

logic bomb A computer virus that runs when a certain set of conditions is met, such as when specific dates are keyed off the computer's internal clock.

logical error A mistake in the design and planning of the algorithm itself rather than in the use of syntax in the coding.

logical port A virtual communications gateway or path that enables a computer to organize requests for information (such as Web page downloads and e-mail routing) from other networks or computers.

logical port blocking A condition in which a firewall is configured to ignore all incoming packets that request access to a certain port so that no unwanted requests will get through to the computer.

loop An algorithm that performs a repeating set of actions. A logical yes/no expression is evaluated. As long as the expression evaluates to TRUE (yes), the algorithm will perform the same set of actions and continue to loop around. When the answer to the question is FALSE (no), the algorithm breaks free of the looping structure and moves on to the next step.

M

Mac OS The first commercially available operating system to incorporate a graphical user interface (GUI) with user-friendly point-and-click technology.

machine language A set of instructions executed directly by the central processing unit (CPU).

macro A small program that groups a series of commands to run as a single command.

macro virus A virus that is distributed by hiding it inside a macro.

massive multiplayer online role-playing games (MMORPG) A gaming environment in which thousands of participants interact in a virtual game world by assuming roles of fictitious characters.

mainframe A large, expensive computer that supports hundreds or thousands of

users simultaneously and executes many different programs at the same time.

malware Software that is intended to render a system temporarily or permanently useless or to penetrate a computer system completely for purposes of information gathering. Examples include spyware, viruses, worms, and Trojan horses.

management information system (MIS) A system that provides timely and accurate information that enables managers to make critical business decisions.

many-to-many relationship A database relationship in which one record in a database table (A) can have many related records in another table (B), and any record in table B can have many related records in table A.

mapping program Software that provides street maps and written directions to locations.

master boot record (MBR) A small program that runs whenever a computer boots up.

media access control (MAC) address A physical address, similar to a serial number on an appliance, that is assigned to each network adapter; it is made up of six 2-digit characters such as 01:40:87:44:79:A5.

megabyte (MB) A unit of computer storage equal to approximately 1 million bytes.

megahertz (MHz) A measure of processing speed equal to 1 million hertz.

memo field A text field in a database that is used to hold long pieces of text.

memory module (memory card) A small circuit board that holds a series of random access memory (RAM) chips.

menu A list of commands that displays on the screen.

menu-driven interface A user interface in which the user chooses a command from menus displayed on the screen.

metadata Data that describes other data.

metasearch engine A metasearch engine, such as Dogpile, searches other search engines rather than individual Web sites.

method (behavior) An action associated with a class of objects.

metropolitan area network (MAN) A wide area network (WAN) that links users in a specific geographic area (such as within a city or county).

microbrowser Software that makes it possible to access the Internet from a PDA/smartphone.

microphone (mic) A device that allows you to capture sound waves, such as those created by your voice, and transfer them to digital format on your computer.

Microsoft Disk Operating System (MS-DOS) A single-user, single-task operating system created by Microsoft. MS-DOS was the first widely installed operating system in personal computers.

mobile switching center A central location that receives cell phone requests for service from a base station.

model management system A type of software that assists in building management models in decision support systems (DSSs).

modem A communication device that works to translate digital data into an analog signal and back again.

modem card An expansion card that provides the computer with a connection to the Internet via conventional phone lines.

modem port A port that uses a traditional telephone signal to connect a computer to the Internet.

monitor (display screen) A common output device that displays text, graphics, and video as soft copies (copies that can be seen only on screen).

Moore's Law A prediction, named after Gordon Moore, the cofounder of Intel; states that the number of transistors on a CPU chip will double every two years.

motherboard A special circuit board in the system unit that contains the central processing unit (CPU), the memory (RAM) chips, and the slots available for expansion cards; all of the other boards (video cards, sound cards, and so on) connect to it to receive power and to communicate.

mouse A hardware device used to enter user responses and commands into a computer.

multidimensional database A database that stores data in multiple dimensions and is organized in a cube format.

multimedia Anything that involves one or more forms of media plus text.

multimedia message service (MMS) An extension of short message service (SMS) that enables messages that include text, sound, images, and video clips to be sent from a cell phone or PDA to other phones or e-mail addresses.

multimedia software Programs that include image, video, and audio editing software, animation software, and other specialty software required to produce computer games, animations, and movies.

multipartite virus Literally meaning "multipart" virus; a type of computer virus that attempts to infect both the boot sector and executable files at the same time.

multiplayer online game An online game in which play occurs among hundreds or thousands of other players over the Internet in a persistent or ever-on game environment. In some games, players can interact with other players through trading, chatting, or playing cooperative or combative mini-games.

Multiple Input Multiple Output (MIMO) A design in newer routers that provides for faster wireless data transmission by utilizing more than one antenna to transmit and receive data.

multipurpose Internet mail extensions (MIME) A specification that was introduced in 1991 to simplify attachments to e-mail messages. All e-mail client software now uses this protocol for attaching files.

multitask The ability of an operating system to perform more than one process at a time.

multiuser operating system (network operating system) An operating system (OS) that enables more than one user to access the computer system at one time by efficiently juggling all the requests from multiple users.

N

nanoscience The study of molecules and nanostructures whose size ranges from 1 to 100 nanometers (one billionth of a meter).

nanotechnology The science of using nanostructures to build devices on an extremely small scale.

natural language processing (NLP) system A system that enables users to communicate with computer systems using a natural spoken or written language as opposed to using computer programming languages.

negative acknowledgment (NAK) What computer Y sends to computer X if a packet is unreadable, indicating the packet was not received in understandable form.

netbook A computing device that runs a full-featured operating system but weighs two pounds or less.

netiquette The general rules of etiquette for Internet chat rooms and other online communication.

network A group of two or more computers (or nodes) that are configured to share information and resources such as printers, files, and databases.

network adapter A device that enables the computer (or peripheral) to communicate with the network using a common data communication language, or protocol.

network address translation (NAT) A process that firewalls use to assign internal Internet Protocol (IP) addresses on a network.

network administrator Someone who has training in computer and peripheral maintenance and repair, network design, and the installation of network software; installs new equipment, configures computers for users, repairs equipment, and assigns network access to users.

network architecture The design of a computer network; includes both physical and logical design.

network-attached storage (NAS) device A specialized computing device designed to store and manage network data.

network interface card (NIC) An expansion card that enables a computer to connect other computers or to a cable modem to facilitate a high-speed Internet connection.

network navigation device A device on a network such as a router, hub, and switch that moves data signals around the network.

network operating system (NOS) Software that handles requests for information, Internet access, and the use of peripherals for the rest of the network nodes.

network prefix The part of a network address under the CIDR IP addressing scheme. It consists of a slash and a number added to the end of the last octet in an IP address.

network topology The layout and structure of the network.

network-ready device A device (such as a printer or external hard drive) that can be attached directly to a network instead of needing to attach to a computer on the network.

newsgroup A method of communication, similar to a discussion group or forum, in which people create threads, or conversations. In a thread, a newsgroup member will post messages and read and reply to messages from other members of the newsgroup.

Next In the Visual Basic programming language, the keyword used to implement a loop.

node A device connected to a network such as a computer, a peripheral (such as a printer), or a communications device (such as a modem).

nonimpact printer A printer that sprays ink or uses laser beams to make marks on the paper. The most common nonimpact printers are inkjet and laser printers.

nonvolatile storage Permanent storage, as in read-only memory (ROM).

normalization The process of recording data only once in a database to reduce data redundancy.

notebook computer A small, compact portable computer.

numeric check A data validation routine that confirms that only numbers are entered in a database field.

numeric field A field in a database that stores numbers.

object A variable in a program that is an example of a class. Each object in a specific class is constructed from similar data and methods.

object field A field in a database that holds objects such as pictures, video clips, or entire documents.

object-oriented analysis An approach to software design that differs from the traditional "top-down" design. In object-oriented (OO) analysis, programmers first identify all of the classes (collections of data and methods) that are required to describe completely the problem the program is trying to solve.

object-oriented database A database that stores data in objects, not in tables.

object query language (OQL) A query language that is used to extract information from an object-oriented database.

octet Eight bits. For example, each of the four numbers in the dotted decimal notation of an Internet Protocol (IP) address is represented by an octet.

office support system (OSS) A system (such as Microsoft Office) designed to assist employees in accomplishing their day-to-day tasks and to improve communications.

offshore The process of sending jobs formerly performed in the U.S. to other countries.

one-to-many relationship A database relationship in which one record in a data table can have many related records in another data table.

one-to-one relationship A database relationship in which one record in a data table has only one related record in another data table.

online mapping service An alternative to more traditional mapping software programs; easily accessible with any Internet connection and updated more frequently than offline services. Examples include MapQuest, Yahoo! Maps, Google Maps, and Google Earth.

online transaction processing (OLTP) The immediate processing of user requests or transactions.

open source software Program code made publicly available for free; it can be copied, distributed, or changed without the stringent copyright protections of proprietary software products.

open system A system whose designs are public, enabling access by any interested party.

operating system (OS) The system software that controls the way in which a computer system functions, including the

management of hardware, peripherals, and software.

operator Any of the coding symbols that represent the fundamental actions of a computer language.

optical carrier line See *OC (optical carrier) line*.

optical drive A hardware device that uses lasers or light to read from, and maybe even write to, CDs, DVDs, or Blu-ray discs.

optical media Portable storage devices, such as CDs, DVDs, and Blu-ray discs, that use a laser to read and write data.

optical mouse A mouse that uses an internal sensor or laser to control the mouse's movement. The sensor sends signals to the computer, telling it where to move the pointer on the screen.

organic light-emitting diode (OLED) display A display that uses organic compounds to produce light when exposed to an electric current. Unlike LCDs, OLEDs do not require a backlight to function and therefore draw less power and have a much thinner display, sometimes as thin as 3 mm.

output device A device that sends processed data and information out of a computer in the form of text, pictures (graphics), sounds (audio), or video.

P2P network See *peer-to-peer network*.

P2P sharing See *peer-to-peer sharing*.

packet (data packet) A small segment of data that is bundled for sending over transmission media. Each packet contains the address of the computer or peripheral device to which it is being sent.

packet filtering A feature found in firewalls that filters out unwanted data packets sent to specific logical ports.

packet screening A process that involves examining incoming data packets to ensure they originated from, or are authorized by, valid users on the internal network.

packet sniffer A program that looks at (sniffs) each data packet as it travels on the Internet.

packet switching A communications methodology in which data is broken into small chunks (called packets) and sent over various routes at the same time. When the packets reach their destination, they are reassembled by the receiving computer.

paging The process of swapping data or instructions that have been placed in the swap file for later use back into active random access memory (RAM). The contents of the hard drive's swap file then become less active data or instructions.

Pascal The only modern computer language that was specifically designed as a teaching language; it is seldom taught now at the college level.

passive topology When data merely travels the entire length of the communications medium and is received by all network devices.

path (subdirectory) The information after the slash indicates a particular file or path (or subdirectory) within the Web site.

path separator The backslash mark (\) used by Microsoft Windows and DOS in file names. Mac files use a colon (:), and UNIX and Linux use the forward slash (/) as the path separator.

patient simulator A computer-controlled mannequin that simulates human body functions and reactions. Patient simulators are used in training doctors, nurses, and emergency services personnel by simulating dangerous situations that would put live patients at risk.

peer-to-peer (P2P) network A network in which each node connected to the network can communicate directly with every other node on the network.

peer-to-peer (P2P) sharing The process of users transferring files between computers.

peripheral device A device such as a monitor, printer, or keyboard that connects to the system unit through ports.

personal area network (PAN) A network used to connect wireless devices (such as Bluetooth-enabled devices) in close proximity to each other.

personal firewall A firewall specifically designed for home networks.

personal information manager (PIM) software Programs such as Microsoft

Outlook or Lotus Organizer that strive to replace the various management tools found on a traditional desk such as a calendar, address book, notepad, and to-do lists.

pharming Planting malicious code on a computer that alters the browser's ability to find Web addresses and directs users to bogus Web sites.

phishing The process of sending e-mail messages to lure Internet users into revealing personal information such as credit card or Social Security numbers or other sensitive information that could lead to identity theft.

PHP (Hypertext Preprocessor) A scripting language used to produce dynamic Web pages.

physical memory The amount of random access memory (RAM) that is installed in a computer.

piggybacking The process of connecting to a wireless network without the permission of the owner of the network.

pixel A single point that creates the images on a computer monitor. Pixels are illuminated by an electron beam that passes rapidly back and forth across the back of the screen so that the pixels appear to glow continuously.

platform The combination of a computer's operating system and processor. The two most common platform types are the PC and the Apple Macintosh.

platter A thin, round, metallic storage plate stacked onto the hard drive spindle.

player See *plug-in*.

plotter A large printer that uses a computer-controlled pen to produce oversize pictures that require precise continuous lines to be drawn, such as maps and architectural plans.

Plug and Play (PnP) The technology that enables the operating system, once it is booted up, to recognize automatically any new peripherals and configure them to work with the system.

plug-in (player) A small software program that "plugs in" to a Web browser to enable a specific function—for example, to view and hear certain multimedia files on the Web.

podcast A clip of audio or video content that is broadcast over the Internet using compressed audio or video files in formats such as MP3.

point of presence (POP) A bank of modems through which many users can connect to an Internet service provider (ISP) simultaneously.

polymorphic virus A virus that changes its virus signature (the binary pattern that makes the virus identifiable) every time it infects a new file. This makes it more difficult for antivirus programs to detect the virus.

port An interface through which external devices are connected to the computer.

portability The capability to move a completed solution easily from one type of computer to another.

portable media player (PMP) A small portable device (such as an iPod) that enables you to carry your MP3s or other media files around with you.

positive acknowledgment (ACK) What computer Y sends when it receives a data packet that it can read from computer X.

possessed object Any object that a user carries to identify him- or herself and that grants the user access to a computer system or computer facility.

power supply A power supply regulates the wall voltage to the voltages required by computer chips; it is housed inside the system unit.

power-on self-test (POST) The first job the basic input/output system (BIOS) performs, ensuring that essential peripheral devices are attached and operational. This process consists of a test on the video card and video memory, a BIOS identification process (during which the BIOS version, manufacturer, and data are displayed on the monitor), and a memory test to ensure memory chips are working properly.

preemptive multitasking When the operating system processes the task assigned a higher priority before processing a task that has been assigned a lower priority.

presentation software An application program for creating dynamic slide shows such as Microsoft PowerPoint or Apple Keynote.

pretexting The act of creating an invented scenario (the pretext) to convince someone to divulge information.

Pretty Good Privacy (PGP) A popular public-key encryption package.

primary key (key field) The unique field that each database record in a table must have.

print queue A software holding area for printing jobs.

print server A server that manages all client-requested printing jobs for all printers on the network.

printer A common output device that creates tangible or hard copies of text and graphics.

private key One-half of a pair of binary files that is needed to decrypt an encrypted message. The private key is kept only by the individual who created the key pair and is never distributed to anyone else. The private key is used to decrypt messages created with the corresponding public key.

private-key encryption A procedure in which only the two parties involved in sending a message have the code. This could be a simple shift code where letters of the alphabet are shifted to a new position.

problem statement A clear description of which tasks the computer program must accomplish and how the program will execute these tasks and respond to unusual situations. It is the starting point of programming work.

processing Manipulating or organizing data into information.

productivity software Programs that enable a user to perform various tasks generally required in home, school, and business. Examples include word processing, spreadsheet, presentation, personal information management (PIM), and database programs.

program A series of instructions to be followed by a computer to accomplish a task.

program development life cycle (PDLC) A number of stages, from conception to final deployment, which a programming project follows.

program file A file that is used in the running of software programs and does not store data.

programming The process of translating a task into a series of commands a computer will use to perform that task.

programming language A kind of "code" for the set of instructions the central processing unit (CPU) knows how to perform.

projector A device that can project images from your computer onto a wall or viewing screen.

project management software An application program, such as Microsoft Project, that helps project managers generate charts and tables used to manage aspects of a project.

protocol (1) A set of rules for exchanging data and communication. (2) The first part of the Uniform Resource Locator (URL) indicating the set of rules used to retrieve the specified document. The protocol is generally followed by a colon; two forward slashes; *www* (indicating World Wide Web); and then the domain name.

prototype A small model of a computer program, often built at the beginning of a large project.

proprietary software Custom software application that is owned and controlled by the company that created it.

proprietary system A software product whose code is not generally available (is kept private) and that is generally developed and marketed by a single company.

proxy server Acts as a go-between for computers on the internal network and the external network (the Internet).

pseudocode A text-based approach to documenting an algorithm.

public domain The status of software (or other created works) that are not protected by copyright.

public key One-half of a pair of binary files that is needed to decrypt an encrypted message. After creating the keys, the user distributes the public key to anyone he wishes to send him encrypted messages. A message encrypted with a public key can be unencrypted only using the corresponding private key.

public-key encryption A procedure in which the key for coding is generally distributed as a public key that may be placed on a Web site. Anyone wishing to send a message codes it using the public key. The

recipient decodes the message with a private key.

quarantining The placement (by antivirus software) of a computer virus in a secure area on the hard drive so that it won't spread infection to other files.

query The process of requesting information from a database.

query language A language used to retrieve and display records. A query language consists of its own vocabulary and sentence structure, used to frame the requests.

QWERTY keyboard A keyboard that gets its name from the first six letters on the top-left row of alphabetic keys on the keyboard.

radio frequency identification tag (RFID tag) A tag that looks like a sticker or label, is attached to a batch of merchandise, and contains a microchip that holds a unique sequence of numbers used to identify the product to which it is attached.

random access memory (RAM) The computer's temporary storage space or short-term memory. It is located in a set of chips on the system unit's motherboard, and its capacity is measured in megabytes or gigabytes.

range check A type of data validation used in databases to ensure that a value entered falls within a specified range (such as requiring a person's age to fall in a range of between 1 and 120).

rapid application development (RAD) A method of system development in which developers create a prototype first, generating system documents as they use and remodel the product.

read/write head The mechanism that retrieves (reads) and records (writes) the magnetic data to and from a data disk. They move from the outer edge of the spinning platters to the center, up to 50 times per second.

read-only memory (ROM) A set of memory chips, located on the motherboard, which stores data and instructions that cannot be changed or erased; it holds all the instructions the computer needs to start up.

real-time operating system (RTOS) A program with a specific purpose that must guarantee certain response times for particular computing tasks, or else the machine's application is useless. Real-time operating systems are found in many types of robotic equipment.

real-time processing The process of updating a database (or information system) immediately as changes are made.

Really Simple Syndication (RSS) technology An XML-based format that allows frequent updates of content on the World Wide Web.

record A collection of related fields in a database.

Recycle Bin A folder on a Windows desktop in which deleted files from the hard drive are held until permanently purged from the system.

referential integrity For each value in the foreign key of one table, there is a corresponding value in the primary key of the related table.

register A special memory storage area built into the central processing unit (CPU).

registry A portion of the hard drive containing all the different configurations (settings) used by the Windows operating system (OS) as well as by other applications.

relation A database table that contains related data.

relational algebra The use of English-like expressions that have variables and operations, much like algebraic equations.

relational database A database that organizes data in table format by logically grouping similar data into relations (or tables) that contain related data.

relationship In relational databases, the link between tables that defines how the data are related.

resolution The clearness or sharpness of an image, which is controlled by the number of pixels displayed on the screen.

response time The measurement (in milliseconds) of the time it takes for a pixel to change color; the lower the response time,

the smoother moving images will appear on the monitor.

reusability The ability to reuse existing classes of objects from other projects, enabling programmers to produce new code quickly.

ribbon A group of icons collected for easy access.

ring (loop) topology A network configuration in which the computers and peripherals are laid out in a configuration resembling a circle. Data flows around the circle from device to device in one direction only.

root directory The top level of the filing structure in a computer system. In Windows computers, the root directory of the hard drive is represented as C:\.

root DNS server A group of servers maintained throughout the Internet to which ISP Web servers connect to locate the master listings for an entire top-level domain.

router A device that routes packets of data between two or more networks.

runtime error An error in the problem logic that is only caught when the program executes.

S

Safe mode A special diagnostic mode designed for troubleshooting errors that occur during the boot process.

sampling rate The number of times per second a signal is measured and converted to a digital value. Sampling rates are measured in kilobits per second.

satellite Internet A way to connect to the Internet using a small satellite dish, which is placed outside the home and is connected to a computer with coaxial cable. The satellite company then sends the data to a satellite orbiting the Earth. The satellite, in turn, sends the data back to the satellite dish and to the computer.

scalability The ability to easily add more users to a network without affecting the performance of the other network nodes (computers or peripherals).

script A list of commands (mini-programs or macros) that can be executed on a computer without user interaction.

script kiddy An amateur hacker who lacks sophisticated computer skills. These individuals are typically teenagers, who don't create programs used to hack into computer systems but instead use tools created by skilled hackers that enable unskilled novices to wreak the same havoc as professional hackers.

scripting language A simple programming language that is limited to performing a specific set of specialized tasks.

scrollbar On the desktop, the bar that appears at the side or bottom of the window and controls which part of the information is displayed on the screen.

search engine A set of programs that searches the Web for specific words (or keywords) you wish to query (or look for) and then returns a list of the Web sites on which those keywords are found.

second-generation language (2GL) Also known as an assembly language. Second-generation languages deal directly with system hardware but provide acronyms that are easier for human programmers to work with.

second-level domain A domain that falls within top-level domains of the Internet. Each second-level domain needs to be unique within that particular domain but not necessarily unique to all top-level domains.

sector A section of a hard drive platter, wedge-shaped from the center of the platter to the edge.

Secure Sockets Layer (SSL) A protocol that provides for the encryption of data transmitted using the Internet. The current versions of all major Web browsers support SSL.

seek time The time it takes for the hard drive's read/write heads to move over the surface of the disk, between tracks, to the correct track.

select query A query that displays a subset of data from a table based on the criteria the user specifies.

Serial Advanced Technology Attachment (Serial ATA) A type of hard drive that uses much thinner cables, and can transfer data more quickly, than IDE drives.

server A computer that provides resources to other computers on a network.

server-side program A program that is run on a Web server as opposed to inside a Web browser.

service set identifier (SSID) A network name that wireless routers use to identify themselves.

shareware Software that enables users to "test" the software by running it for a limited time free of charge.

shielded twisted pair (STP) cable Twisted pair cable that contains a layer of foil shielding to reduce interference.

short message service (SMS) Technology that enables short text messages (up to 160 characters) to be sent over mobile networks.

simple mail transfer protocol (SMTP) A protocol for sending e-mail along the Internet to its destination.

simulation software Software, often used for training purposes, which allows the user to experience or control an event as if it is reality.

sleep mode A low-power mode for electronic devices such as computers that saves electric power consumption and saves your computer settings where you left off. When the computer is "woken up," you can resume working more quickly than when cold booting the computer.

smartphone A device that combines the functionality of a cell phone, a PMP, and a PDA into one unit.

social bookmark (tag) A keyword or term that Internet users assign to a Web resource such as a Web page, digital image, or video.

social engineering Any technique that uses social skills to generate human interaction for the purpose of enticing individuals to reveal sensitive information.

social networking A means by which people use the Internet to communicate and share information among their immediate friends, and meet and connect with others through common interests, experiences, and friends.

software The set of computer programs or instructions that tells the computer what to do and enables it to perform different tasks.

Software as a Service (SaaS) Software that is delivered on demand over the Internet.

software license An agreement between the user and the software developer that must be accepted before installing the software on a computer.

software piracy Violating a software license agreement by copying an application onto more computers than the license agreement permits.

software suite A collection of software programs that have been bundled together as a package.

software update (service pack) A downloadable software module that repairs errors identified in commercial program code.

solid state drive (SSD) A drive that uses the same kind of memory that flash drives use, but can reach data in only a tenth of the time a flash drive requires.

sort (index) The process of organizing a database into a particular order.

sound card An expansion card that attaches to the motherboard inside the system unit and that enables the computer to produce sounds by providing a connection for the speakers and microphone.

source code The instructions programmers write in a higher-level language.

spam Unwanted or junk e-mail.

spam filter An option you can select in your e-mail account that places known or suspected spam messages into a folder other than your inbox.

speaker An output device for sound.

speech-recognition software (voice-recognition software) Software that translates spoken words into typed text.

spider A program that constantly collects information on the Web, following links in Web sites and reading Web pages. Spiders get their name because they crawl over the Web using multiple "legs" to visit many sites simultaneously.

spooler A program that helps coordinate all print jobs being sent to the printer at the same time.

spreadsheet software An application program such as Microsoft Excel or Lotus 1-2-3 that enables a user to do calculations and numerical analyses easily.

spyware An unwanted piggyback program that downloads with the software you want to install from the Internet and then runs in the background of your system.

star topology An active topology (meaning that data is retransmitted) in which the nodes connect to a central communications device called a *switch*. The switch receives a signal from the sending node and retransmits it to the node that should receive it.

statement A sentence in programming code.

static addressing A means of assigning an Internet Protocol (IP) address that never changes and is most likely assigned manually by a network administrator.

stealth virus A virus that temporarily erases its code from the files where it resides and hides in the active memory of the computer.

streaming audio Technology that enables audio files to be fed to a browser continuously. This lets users avoid having to download an entire file before listening.

streaming video Technology that enables video files to be fed to a browser continuously. This lets users avoid having to download the entire file before viewing.

structured (analytical) data Data that can be identified and classified as discrete bits of information (such as a name or phone number). Unstructured data includes nontraditional data such as audio clips (including MP3 files), video clips, and pictures that must be viewed in their entirety rather than in discrete segments.

structured query language (SQL) The most popular database query language today.

stylus A pen-shaped device used to tap or write on touch-sensitive screens.

subject directory A structured outline of Web sites organized by topics and subtopics.

summary report A report that summarizes data in some fashion (such as a total of the day's concession sales at an amusement park). Also known as a *summary data report*.

supercomputer A specially designed computer that can perform complex calculations extremely rapidly; used in situations in which complex models requiring intensive mathematical calculations are needed (such as weather forecasting or atomic energy research).

surge protector A device that protects computers and other electronic devices from power surges.

surround sound A type of audio processing that makes the listener experience sound as if it were coming from all directions.

surround-sound speakers Speaker systems set up in such a way that they surround an entire area (and the people in it) with sound.

S-video (super video) A type of technology used to transmit video signals; used on newer LCD monitors, as well as other multimedia devices such as televisions, DVD players, and projectors.

swap file (page file) A temporary storage area on the hard drive where the operating system "swaps out" or moves the data or instructions from random access memory (RAM) that have not recently been used. This process takes place when more RAM space is needed.

switch A device for transmitting data on a network. A switch makes decisions, based on the media access control (MAC) address of the data, as to where the data is to be sent.

syncing (or synchronizing) The process of updating data on portable devices (such as a cell phone or iPod) and computer so that they contain the same data.

syntax An agreed-upon set of rules defining how a programming language must be structured.

syntax error An error that violates the strict, precise set of rules that defines a programming language.

system development life cycle (SDLC) An organized process (or set of steps) for developing an information processing system.

system evaluation The process of looking at a computer's subsystems, what they do, and how they perform to determine whether the computer system has the right hardware components to do what the user ultimately wants it to do.

system file Any of the main files of an operating system.

system requirements The set of minimum storage, memory capacity, and processing standards recommended by the software manufacturer to ensure proper operation of a software application.

System Restore A utility in Windows that restores system settings to a specific previous date when everything was working properly.

system restore point In Windows, a snapshot of your entire system's settings used for restoring your system to a prior point in time.

system software The set of programs that enables a computer's hardware devices and application software to work together; it includes the operating system and utility programs.

system unit The metal or plastic case that holds all the physical parts of the computer together, including the computer's processor (its brains), its memory, and the many circuit boards that help the computer function.

T

T line A high-speed fiber-optic communications line that is designed to provide much higher throughput than conventional voice (telephone) and data (DSL or cable) lines.

table In database terminology, a group of related records. Also called a *file*.

Tablet PC A notebook computer designed specifically to work with handwriting recognition technology.

Task Manager utility A Windows utility that shows programs currently running and permits you to exit nonresponsive programs when you click End Task.

Task Scheduler utility A Windows utility that enables you to schedule tasks to run automatically at predetermined times with no interaction necessary on your part.

taskbar In later versions of Windows operating systems, a feature that displays open and favorite applications for easy access.

tax preparation software An application program, such as Intuit's TurboTax or H&R Block's TaxCut, for preparing state and federal taxes. Each program offers a complete set of tax forms and instructions as well as expert advice on how to complete each form.

TCP/IP The main suite of protocols used on the Internet.

telephony The use of equipment to provide voice communications over a distance.

Telnet A network protocol used primarily on the Internet for connecting to a remote computer to make it accessible to other computers.

template A form included in many productivity applications that provides the basic structure for a particular kind of document, spreadsheet, or presentation.

terabyte 1,099,511,627,776 bytes or 2^{40} bytes.

terminator A device that absorbs a signal so that it is not reflected back onto parts of the network that have already received it.

test condition A check to see whether a loop is completed.

testing plan In the problem statement, a plan that lists specific input numbers that the program would typically expect the user to enter. It then lists the precise output values that a perfect program would return for those input values.

text field A database field that can hold any combination of alphanumeric data (letters or numbers) and is most often used to hold text.

thermal printer A printer that works either by melting wax-based ink onto ordinary paper (in a process called *thermal wax transfer printing*) or by burning dots onto specially coated paper (in a process called *direct thermal printing*).

third-generation language (3GL, or high-level language) A computer language that uses symbols and commands to help programmers tell the computer what to do.

thrashing A condition of excessive paging in which the operating system becomes sluggish.

three-way handshake A process used by the Transmission Control Protocol (TCP) to establish a connection.

throughput The actual speed of data transfer that is achieved. It is usually less than the data transfer rate and is measured in megabits per second (Mbps).

time bomb A virus that is triggered by the passage of time or on a certain date.

time-variant data Data that doesn't all pertain to one period in time—for example, data in a data warehouse.

token method The access method that ring networks use to avoid data collisions.

toolbar A group of icons collected for easy access.

top-down design A systematic approach in which a programming problem is broken down into a series of high-level tasks.

top-level domain (TLD) The suffix, often of three letters, in the domain name (such as .com or .edu) that indicates the kind of organization the host is.

touch screen A type of monitor (or display in a notebook or PDA) that accepts input from a user touching the screen.

touchpad A small, touch-sensitive screen at the base of a notebook keyboard. To use the touchpad, you simply move your finger across the pad to direct the cursor.

track A concentric circle that serves as a storage area on a hard drive platter.

trackball mouse A mouse with a rollerball on top instead of on the bottom. Because you move the trackball with your fingers, it doesn't require much wrist motion, so it's considered healthier for your wrists than a traditional mouse.

trackpoint device A small, joystick-like nub that enables you to move the cursor with the tip of your finger.

transaction processing system (TPS) A system used to keep track of everyday business activities (such as sales of products).

transceiver In a wireless network, a device that translates the electronic data that needs to be sent along the network into radio waves and then broadcasts these radio waves to other network nodes.

Transmission Control Protocol (TCP) A protocol that prepares data for transmission and provides for error checking and resending lost data.

transmission media The radio waves or cable that transport data on a network.

Transport Layer Security (TLS) A protocol that provides data integrity and security for transmissions over the Internet.

Trojan horse A computer program that appears to be something useful or desirable (such as a game or a screen saver), but at the same time does something malicious in the background without the user's knowledge.

twisted pair cable Cables made of copper wires that are twisted around each other and are surrounded by a plastic jacket (such as traditional home phone wire).

U

ubiquitous computing The condition in which computing is so woven into the fabric of everyday life that it becomes indistinguishable from it.

Uniform Resource Locator (URL) A Web site's unique address; an example is microsoft.com.

uninterruptible power supply (UPS) A device designed to power a computer from large batteries for a brief period during a loss of electrical power.

universal serial bus (USB) port A port that can connect a wide variety of peripheral devices to the computer, including keyboards, printers, mice, smartphones, PDAs, flash drives, and digital cameras.

UNIX An operating system originally conceived in 1969 by Ken Thompson and Dennis Ritchie of AT&T's Bell Labs. In 1974, the UNIX code was rewritten in the standard programming language C. Today there are various commercial versions of UNIX.

unshielded twisted pair (UTP) cable The most popular transmission media option for Ethernet networks. UTP cable is composed of four pairs of wires that are twisted around each other to reduce electrical interference.

unstructured data Nontraditional database data such as audio clips (including MP3 files), video clips, pictures, and extremely large documents. Data of this type is known as a *binary large object* (BLOB) because it is actually encoded in binary form.

urban legend A hoax that becomes so well known that it is accepted by society as true even though it is false. Also known as an *urban myth*.

USB 2.0 port An external bus that supports a data throughput of 480 Mbps; these buses are backward compatible with buses using the original universal serial bus (USB) standard.

User Datagram Protocol (UDP) A protocol that prepares data for transmission but that has no resending capabilities.

user interface Part of the operating system that enables individuals to interact with the computer.

utility program A small program that performs many of the general housekeeping tasks for the computer, such as system maintenance and file compression.

V

validation The process of ensuring that data entered into a database is correct (or at least reasonable) and complete.

validation rule A rule that is set up in a database to alert the user to possible wrong entries.

variable A name or symbol that stands for a value.

variable declaration A line of programming code that alerts the operating system that the program needs to allocate storage space in random access memory (RAM) for the variable.

VBScript A subset of Visual Basic; also used to introduce interactivity to Web pages.

vertical market software Software that is developed for and customized to a specific industry's needs (such as a wood inventory system for a sawmill) as opposed to software that is useful across a range of industries (such as word processing software).

video blog See *video log*.

video card (video adapter) An expansion card that is installed inside a system unit to translate binary data (the 1s and 0s the computer uses) into the images viewed on the monitor.

video graphics array (VGA) port A port to which a CRT monitor connects.

video log (vlog or **video blog)** A personal online journal that uses video as the primary content in addition to text, images, and audio.

video memory RAM that is included as part of a video card.

viewing angle Measured in degrees, this tells how far you can move to the side of (or above or below) the monitor before the image quality degrades to unacceptable levels.

virtual memory The space on the hard drive where the operating system stores data if there isn't enough random access memory (RAM) to hold all of the programs you're currently trying to run.

virtual private network (VPN) A network that uses public communication pathways (usually the Internet) to provide branch offices or employees who are not at the office with secure access to the company network. VPNs maintain privacy by using secure data communication protocols.

virtual reality program Software that turns an artificial environment into a realistic experience.

virus A computer program that attaches itself to another computer program (known as the host program) and attempts to spread itself to other computers when files are exchanged.

virus signature A portion of the virus code that is unique to a particular computer virus and makes it identifiable by antivirus software.

Visual Basic (VB) A programming language used to build a wide range of Windows applications quickly.

visual programming A technique for automatically writing code when the programmer says the layout is complete. It helps programmers produce a final application much more quickly.

VoIP (Voice over Internet Protocol).

volatile storage Temporary storage, such as in random access memory (RAM). When the power is off, the data in volatile storage is cleared out.

W

warm boot The process of restarting the system while it's powered on.

Web 2.0 Tools and Web-based services that emphasize online collaboration and sharing among users.

Web browser (browser) Software installed on a computer system that allows individuals to locate, view, and navigate the Web.

Web page authoring software Programs you can use to design interactive Web pages without knowing any HyperText Markup Language (HTML) code.

Web server A computer running a specialized operating system that enables it to host Web pages (and other information) and provide requested Web pages to clients.

Web service A program used by a Web site to make information available to other Web sites.

Web site A location on the Web.

Web-based application software A program that is hosted on a Web site and does not require installation on the computer.

webcam A small camera that sits on top of a computer monitor (connected to the computer by a cable) or is built into a notebook computer and is usually used to transfer live video.

webcast The broadcast of audio or video content over the Internet. Unlike a podcast, a webcast is not updated automatically.

white-hat hacker A hacker who breaks into systems just for the challenge of it (and who doesn't wish to steal or wreak havoc on the systems). Such hackers tout themselves as experts who are performing a needed service for society by helping companies realize the vulnerabilities that exist in their systems.

whole-house surge protector A surge protector that is installed on (or near) the breaker panel of a home and protects all electronic devices in the home from power surges.

wide area network (WAN) A network made up of local area networks (LANs) connected over long distances.

widget A mini-application developed for the Macintosh platform.

WiFi (Wireless Fidelity) The 802.11 standard for wireless data transmissions established by the Institute of Electrical and Electronics Engineers (IEEE).

wiki A type of Web site that allows anyone visiting the site to change its content by adding, removing, or editing the content.

window In a graphical user interface, a rectangular box that contains programs displayed on the screen.

Windows An operating system by Microsoft that incorporates a user-friendly, graphical interface.

Windows 7 Microsoft operating system that builds upon the security and user interface upgrades that the Windows Vista release provided, and gives users with touch-screen monitors the ability to use touch commands to scroll, resize windows, pan, and zoom.

Windows Explorer The main tool for finding, viewing, and managing the contents of your computer by showing the location and contents of every drive, folder, and file.

wireless access point (WAP) A device similar to a switch in an Ethernet network. It takes the place of a wireless network adapter and helps relay data between network nodes.

Wireless Application Protocol (WAP) The standard that dictates how handheld devices will access information on the Internet.

wireless Internet service provider (wireless ISP) An ISP that provides service to wireless devices such as PDA/smartphones.

Wireless Markup Language (WML) A format for writing content viewed on a cellular phone or personal digital assistant (PDA) that is text-based and contains no graphics.

wireless media Communications media that do not use cables but instead rely on radio waves to communicate.

wireless network interface card (wireless NIC) A card installed in a system that connects with wireless access points on the network.

wireless range extender A device that amplifies your wireless signal to get it out to parts of your home that are experiencing poor connectivity.

wizard A step-by-step guide that walks you through the necessary steps to complete a complicated task.

word processing software Programs used to create and edit written documents such as papers, letters, and résumés.

World Wide Web (WWW or Web) The part of the Internet used the most. What distinguishes the Web from the rest of the Internet are (1) its use of common communication protocols (such as Transmission Control Protocol/Internet Protocol, or TCP/IP) and special languages (such as the HyperText Markup Language, or HTML) that enable different computers to talk to each other and display information in compatible formats; and (2) its use of special links (called hyperlinks) that enable users to jump from one place to another in the Web.

worm A program that attempts to travel between systems through network connections to spread infections. Worms can run independently of host file execution and are active in spreading themselves.

Z

zombie A computer that is controlled by a hacker who uses it to launch attacks on other computer systems.

Index

Credits

Cover photo	Dieter Matthes\AGE Fotostock America, Inc.

Chapter 1

Figure 1.1	The Dell logo is a trademark of Dell Inc.
Figure 1.1b2	Logitech Inc.
Figure 1.1b3	Belkin International, Inc.
Figure 1.2	www.CartoonStock.com
Figure 1.3a	The Dell logo is a trademark of Dell Inc.
Figure 1.3b	PRNewsFoto/D-Link Systems\ D-Link Systems, Inc.
Figure 1.3c	Handout/MCT\Newscom
Figure 1.3d	Motorola\Motorola PCS/CSG
Figure 1.3e	Belkin International, Inc.
Figure 1.3e-1	ExpressCard - PCMCIA
Figure 1.3g	Apple Computer, Inc.
Figure 1.4a	Simon Krzic\Shutterstock
Figure 1.4b	Mclek\Shutterstock
Figure 1.4c	Richard Peterson\Shutterstock
Figure 1.4d	Dmitriy Shironosov\Shutterstock
Figure 1.4e	Saleeee\Shutterstock
Figure 1.4f	yuyangc\Shutterstock
Figure 1.4g	Dimitrije Paunovic\Shutterstock
Figure 1.5a	Editorial Image; LLC\Alamy Images
Figure 1.5b	United Parcel Service - DO NOT USE!!
Figure 1.5c	Mary Kate Denny\PhotoEdit Inc.
Figure 1.7	Peter Schaaf
Figure 1.8a	Camille Utterback, "Untitled 5", from the "External Measures" series. Photo by Peter Harris, © 2007
Figure 1.8b	Camille Utterback, "Untitled 5", from the "External Measures" series. Image courtesy of the artist.
Figure 1.8c	Camille Utterback, "Untitled 5", from the "External Measures" series. Image courtesy of the artist.
Figure 1.11a	Apple Computer, Inc.
Figure 1.11b	Moeskau Photography

Figure 1.12	Polhemus/Fast Scan
Figure 1.12b	Paul Ekman Group, LLC.
Figure 1.13	© Digital Art/CORBIS All Rights Reserved
Figure 1.13a	Paul Ekman Group, LLC.
Figure 1.14	Tom Pantages
Figure 1.16a	Stocktrek Images/Getty Images
Figure 1.16b	Lefteris Pitarakis\AP Wide World Photos
Figure 1.17	© Schlegelmilch/CORBIS All Rights Reserved
Figure 1.19a	Ed Pfueller/Columbia Daily Tribune/AP Photo
Figure 1.19b	Photo courtesy of METI © METI
Figure 1.20a	© 2008 Intuitive Surgical, Inc.
Figure 1.20b	© 2008 Intuitive Surgical, Inc.
Figure 1.21	Courtesy of Dr. Peter Fromherz/Max Planck Insitute of Biochemistry
Figure 1.22a	Shawn K Kelly PhD
Figure 1.22b	Shawn K Kelly PhD
Figure 1.23	Reuters/Eriko Sugita\Landov Media
Figure 1.23a	Steve Bloom Images\Alamy Images
Figure 1.23b	NOAA\Public Domain
Figure 1.25	Media from the Discovery Channel's Pompeii: The Last Day, courtesy of Crew Creative, Ltd.
Figure 1.26a	Interactive Sports Technologies
Figure 1.26b	Interactive Sports Technologies
Figure 1.27	Mazur Group
Figure 1.28	AP Wide World Photos
Figure 1.30a	SparkFun Electronics
Figure 1.30b	© (Photographer)/CORBIS All Rights Reserved
Figure 1.31	Gerald Herbert\AP Wide World Photos

TECHNOLOGY IN FOCUS: The History of the PC

Chapter opener a	SuperStock\Jupiter Images
Chapter opener b	Courtesy of Apple Computer, Inc.

Chapter 2

Figure 2.34h	Samsung Electronics America, Inc.
Figure 2.34i	Silicon Power Computer and Communicatons
Figure 2.35a	David A. Tietz
Figure 2.35b	Hewlett Packard HP 1
Figure 2.36	Phil Burton\Alamy Images
Figure 2.37	David A. Tietz
Figure 2.38	Editorial Image, LLC\Alamy Images Royalty Free
Figure 2.38a	Tim Arbaev\Shutterstock
Figure 2.38b	Szymon Apanowicz\Shutterstock
Figure 2.40	Syd M Johnson\The Image Works
Figure 2.42a	Artur Synenko\Shutterstock
Figure 2.43	Look Twice\Alamy Images
Figure 2.46	ROBYN BECK/AFP/Getty Images\Newscom
Figure 2.47	Courtesy of Sony Electronics Inc.
Figure 2.48	Tom Theobald\Alamy Images

Chapter 3

Chapter opener	Lukiyanova Natalia/frenta\Shutterstock
Figure 3.1	Apple Computer, Inc.
Figure 3.10a	jeny\Shutterstock
Figure 3.10b	Supri Suharjoto\Shutterstock
Figure 3.10c	AVAVA\Shutterstock
Figure 3.10R1	Monkey Business Images \Shutterstock
Figure 3.10R2	Jaimie Duplass\Shutterstock
Figure 3.15	Daniel Heghton\Alamy Images
Figure 3.16	Newscom
Figure 3.18a	Cecilia Lim H M\Shutterstock
Figure 3.18b	Tatiana Popova\Shutterstock
Figure 3.33	Courtesy of www.istockphoto.com
Figure 3.34a	Sierra Wireless, Inc.
Figure 3.34b	Sierra Wireless, Inc.
Figure 3.35a	William Casey\Shutterstock
Figure 3.35b	Tomasz Sz.\Shutterstock

TECHNOLOGY IN FOCUS: Ethics

Chapter opener	sjlocke\iStockphoto.com
Figure 2	© Anton Seleznev/Courtesy of www.istockphoto.com
Figure 5	Cartoon Stock
Figure 11	Michael D Brown\Shutterstock

Chapter 4

Chapter opener	Brent Walker\Shutterstock
Figure 4.10b	Avanquest North America Inc.
Figure 4.10d	Corel
Figure 4.20	PhotoEdit Inc.
Figure 4.26a	Second Life is a trademark of Linden Research, Inc. Certain materials have been reproduced with the permission of Linden Research, Inc.
Figure 4.26b	Second Life is a trademark of Linden Research, Inc. Certain materials have been reproduced with the permission of Linden Research, Inc.
Figure 4.26c	Second Life is a trademark of Linden Research, Inc. Certain materials have been reproduced with the permission of Linden Research, Inc.

Chapter 5

Chapter opener	siloto\Shutterstock
Figure 5.7c	B. O'Kane\Alamy Images
Figure 5.9	fuseproject

TECHNOLOGY IN FOCUS: Computing Alternatives

Figure 5.UN1	Marilyn Conway/Photographer's Choice/Getty Images

Chapter 6

Chapter 7

TECHNOLOGY IN FOCUS: Under the Hood

Chapter 8

Chapter 9

TECHNOLOGY IN FOCUS: Careers in IT

Figure 2a	Clive Streeter © Dorling Kindersley, Courtesy of The Science Museum, London
Figure 5b	Jenn Mackenzie\Shutterstock
Figure 5c	Stephen Coburn\Shutterstock
Figure 5d	wavebreakmedia ltd\Shutterstock
Figure 5a	photobank.ch \Shutterstock
Figure 5e	© Mark A. Johnson/CORBIS All Rights Reserved
Figure 9a	Supri Suharjoto\Shutterstock
Figure 9b	zimmylws\Shutterstock
Figure 9c	Andresr\Shutterstock
Figure 11	Arthur Kwiatkowski\ iStockphoto.com

Chapter 10

Figure 10.3	PHOTOTAKE Inc.\Alamy Images
Figure 10.19	Daft_Lion_Studio\iStockphoto.com
Figure 10.21	© CORBIS All Rights Reserved
Figure 10.28	Stichting Blender
Figure 10.29	Luis Guillermo Restrepo Rivas

Chapter 11

Chapter opener	John Schwegel/Alamy
Figure 11.4a	Sean Prior\Shutterstock
Figure 11.4b	Tan Klan Khoon\Shutterstock
Figure 11.4c	AVAVA\Shutterstock
Figure 11.4d	Monkey Business Images\Shutterstock

Figure 11.32a	AVAVA\Shutterstock
Figure 11.32b	Jace Tan\Shutterstock
Figure 11.33	Michael Jung\Shutterstock
Figure 11.33b	Sean Prior\Shutterstock
Figure 11.33c	Sean Prior\Shutterstock
Figure 11.33d	Raisa Kanareva\Shutterstock
Figure 11.34a	Dash\Shutterstock
Figure 11.34b	Monjey Business Images\Shutterstock
Figure 11.34c	Craig Hill\Shutterstock
Figure 11.34d	Fillip Fuxa\Shutterstock

Chapter 12

Chapter opener	HomeStudio\Shutterstock

Chapter 13

Chapter opener	dotSyntax, LLC
Figure 13.10a	Rob Marmion\Shutterstock
Figure 13.10b	Tan Kian Khoon\Shutterstock
Figure 13.21	© Brendan McDermid/epa/CORBIS All Rights Reserved
Figure 13.23	Thomas Peter Voss\Shutterstock
Figure UN.1	Bernhard Richter\Shutterstock
Figure UN.2	Simone van den Berg\Shutterstock
Figure UN.3	ampyang\Shutterstock
Figure UN.4	Adl\Shutterstock
Figure UN.5	Lisa F. Young\Shutterstock

SINGLE PC LICENSE AGREEMENT AND LIMITED WARRANTY

PLAYING ACTIVE HELPDESKS IN WINDOWS VISTA AND WINDOWS 7:
In order to play the Active Helpdesks in Windows Vista and Windows 7, you will need to disable Protected Mode in Internet Explorer. To do so, please follow these instructions:

1. **Open Internet Explorer**
2. **Click Tools**
3. **Select Internet Options**
4. **Select the Security Tab**
5. **Uncheck the "Enable Protected Mode" box**
6. **Restart Internet Explorer**